RELIGIONS OF
THE WORLD

THE CENTURY PHILOSOPHY SERIES

Justus Buchler *and* Sterling P. Lamprecht, *Editors*

RELIGIONS OF THE WORLD

Selected Readings

JAMES W. DYE
Northern Illinois University

WILLIAM H. FORTHMAN
San Fernando State College

New York

APPLETON CENTURY CROFTS
Division of Meredith Publishing Company

Preface

One hardly needs to argue for the importance of the comparative study of religions at a time when the peoples of the world, by virtue of technological advances and political conflicts, have come to realize more than ever before the virtue, indeed, the necessity, of understanding one another. Given the unique importance of religion within the structure of human culture, both as an expression of important ideals and as a concrete historical force influencing the decisions of individuals and of entire states, no mutual understanding would be very complete unless it involved some fairly adequate grasp of the beliefs, practices, and attitudes peculiar to divergent religious orientations. It is our conviction that such understanding can best be attained through the perusal of the literature which a given religious community has produced and in which it has given verbal form to the characteristic features of its spiritual heritage. Even if one were to undertake to become a convert to other religions so as to experience their distinctive values at first hand, as the famous Hindu religious leader, Ramakrishna Paramahamsa, attempted to do, one would still find it necessary to turn to their writings in order to genuinely comprehend, and perhaps even to completely appreciate, the devotional practices which one had newly adopted.

It is the purpose of this volume to provide a unified source containing several significant documents belonging to each of the major religions. It is to be hoped that this accumulation of representative religious literature into one volume will prove helpful both to the student wishing to uncover some of the basic principles of the various religions and to the teacher in need of a collection of important religious writing to serve either as the primary source for teaching the identifying features of each religion or as illustrative material to accompany his lectures on the character and history of the leading religions. Of course, in the pursuit of such a goal, it is always necessary to make some compromises among the various desirable features which may recommend themselves as good means for the achievement of the proposed aim. The editors have found the composition of this volume to be no exception to this general rule, and since compromises have been made, it seems desirable to afford some remarks by way of explaining the principles which have been employed in the production of this particular collection.

No prior acquaintance on the part of the reader with the materials represented in this volume has been presupposed. Since this is the case, one of our primary concerns has been to present selections whose length is such as to afford the reader a genuine basis for understanding the viewpoints propounded within those selections, without the necessity of added research in the original sources. Of course, our intent is not to discourage further reading of the primary sources—quite the contrary—, but it would seem preferable for such reading to be based upon a genuine interest in the sort of thinking which the anthology has presented, rather than upon the desire to understand a viewpoint which the anthology, due to the brevity of its selections, has inadequately represented. We have, therefore, reprinted entire articles, chapters, monographs, or sections whenever possible. It is hoped that this procedure will not only further more adequate comprehension of the content of the individual selections, but will also give the reader a somewhat better idea of the style and spirit of those works than would be possible if they had been mutilated by an excessively heavy editorial hand. The obvious disadvantage of this policy is that the coverage of the literature will be much less representative of the entire spectrum of authors and viewpoints than would be the case if smaller selections had been made for a book of equal length. There are undoubtedly many figures of considerable importance who have not been represented within the pages of this volume; and moreover, some of the figures who are omitted might well be of greater importance than some of those included. The western reader will probably be more keenly aware of this fact in reading the sections on Christianity and Judaism, due to his greater knowledge of the wealth of material available from these religious traditions and the relative poverty of the material contained within these covers. Nevertheless the lesser of the two evils, given that the final volume must be of manageable length, seems clearly to lie in the direction which will afford the reader some genuine understanding of typical religious emphases rather than merely a vague idea of the great diversity of such emphases. Furthermore, in the cases where the reader is more aware of the extreme selectivity of our material, it must be the case that he is *already* more familiar with the literature of that particular religious tradition, since it is that knowledge which forms the basis of his critical judgment.

Despite our concern with the adequacy of the individual selections, we have not ignored the problem of adequately representing each religion as a whole. Although the total number of selections may be somewhat restricted due to the implementation of the foregoing policy, those selections have been carefully chosen for their usefulness in representing the religious orientation involved. It is to be noticed that our aim has been to represent "religious orientations," and not especially theologies. Any religion is much more than the theologies which it fosters, since those are only the more intellectual and philosophical products of a culture which involves many more facets. We have attempted to give at least token expression to a variety of those facets by reprinting some of the writings of poets, mystics, and practical men alongside the works of some of the major theologians. It is our opinion that these essays contribute greatly to an appreciation of the spirit of any given religious tradition and that such appreciation would inevitably remain incomplete were one's reading restricted to the theologians. We have also attempted to take account of the temporal span of the individual religions by supplying works from the major periods of their development, always including some modern or contemporary literature in addition to the more classic writings. It is to be hoped that this procedure will afford some sense of the historical continuity of a religious tradition and some sense of its continuing vitality, which might not be imparted by an exclusive emphasis upon the classic literature. In short, our ideal has been to portray, in the bold strokes of a limited number of selections, the major features of each religious communion, both with respect to its historical development and to the variety of expression which it has fostered.

One important procedural difference has arisen in the implementation of this ideal. It is the opinion of the editors that no body of written work gives a more adequate insight into the significant features of a religious orientation than those documents which, by nearly universal assent, have been accepted as revelatory or especially sacred. Even when liberalizing movements within a given religion have repudiated the authority of the sacred scriptures, they generally continue to adhere to basic cultural ideals and practices whose primacy is clearly visible in the scriptural tradition. Consequently, we have ordinarily reprinted generous portions of the scriptures, as would be desirable and appropriate, given their importance as expressions of, and often as creators of, the spiritual climate of the various religious communions. However, we have reprinted none of the scriptures of Judaism or Christianity. Assuming that the majority of the readers of this volume would be within one or the other of these religious traditions, and that they could be expected to have some fair degree of familiarity with biblical literature, it has seemed more desirable to devote the available space to a wider representation of the non-scriptural literature in these two cases. Moreover, the Bible is readily available in a variety of inexpensive editions, and the reader who desires to read it should have little trouble in obtaining a copy. This omission of selections from the Bible is entirely due to these two reasons, and not to any modification in our view that perusal of the scriptures is extremely important for understanding a religion. On the contrary, Judaism and Christianity are perhaps even more unintelligible than usual to one who is not familiar with their scriptures, since they have been more historically conscious than the eastern religions and have emphasized the importance of scripture more than other religions, with the exception of Islam. In recognition of this importance, we have supplied brief Bible-reading guides in the sections devoted to these two religions, so that the reader may have some assistance in his investigation of these sources should he desire to do so, as we strongly recommend even for those who believe they already have a fair idea of what the Bible is all about, although they may never have read it systematically.

We have not thought it advisable to provide extensive commentaries on the selections, and have attempted to limit our contributions to brief introduction to each major religion and still shorter introductions to each selection. Readers who are quite unfamiliar with the religions might wish that we had provided more explanatory material, but we could do that only at the cost of further curtailing our coverage of the primary sources, which is, after all, the major purpose of the volume. There are several readily available publications which provide descriptive and explanatory accounts of the major religions, and since any reasonable amount of commentary which we might include would still fall far short of rivaling the coverage of these publications, it has seemed best to restrict our comments to the necessary minimum. We have provided very brief bibliographies at the end of each major division, in order that the reader will have some information regarding reliable sources for obtaining additional information, should he so desire.

J.W.D.
W.H.F.

Contents

Preface   *v*

Part I.   **HINDUISM**   *1*

1.   Rig Veda   9
2.   Upanishads   18
3.   Bhagavad-Gita   36
4.   Yoga Aphorisms—Patanjali   65
5.   Self-Knowledge—Shankara   74
6.   Bhagavata Purana   80
7.   Farewell—Mohandas Ghandi   91

Part II.   **BUDDHISM**   *95*

8.   Selections from the Pali Sermons   105
9.   Dhammapada   128
10.   The Bodhisattva   144
11.   The Pure Land   146
12.   The Heart Sutra   150
13.   Twenty Verses on the Mahāyanā—Nāgārjuna   152
14.   Thirty Verses on the Mind-Only Doctrine—Vasubandhu   154
15.   Treatise on the Golden Lion—Fa-Tsang   159
16.   On Believing in Mind—Seng T'san   164
17.   Treatise on the Essentials of the Transmission of Mind—Huang Po   169
18.   Practice of Dhyana—Soyen Shaku   174

Part III.   **CHINESE RELIGION**   *181*

19.   The Analects—Confucius   188
20.   Kaou Tsze—Mencius   207

ix

21.   Concerning Heaven—Hsun Tzu   216

22.   The Great Learning   223

23.   The Doctrine of the Mean   231

24.   Lao Tzu   246

25.   Chuang Tzu   269

26.   Universal Love—Mo Tzu   285

27.   The Classic of Filial Piety   289

28.   A Treatise on Jen—Chu Hsi   297

29.   Inquiry on the Great Learning—Wang Yang-Ming   300

30.   The Spirit of Chinese Philosophy—Fung Yu-Lan   307

Part IV.   JUDAISM   317

31.   The Manual of Discipline   323

32.   Creation as Moral Allegory—Philo Judaeus   340

33.   The Attributes of God—Joseph Albo   346

34.   The Hasidim on God and Man   354

35.   On the Founding of a Jewish Nation—Theodore Herzl   361

36.   I and Thou—Martin Buber   369

37.   The Universal Aspect of Jewish Religion—
           Mordecai M. Kaplan   387

Part V.   CHRISTIANITY   397

38.   The Martyrdom of St. Polycarp, Bishop of Smyrna   403

39.   On Pagan Literature—Basil of Caesarea   410

40.   On the Trinity—Gregory of Nyssa   420

41.   On His Conversion—St. Augustine   430

42.   Man's Ultimate Happiness—Thomas Aquinas   437

43.   The Freedom of a Christian—Martin Luther   448

44.   On the Christian Life—John Calvin   464

45.   Social Christianity and Personal Religion—
            Walter Rauschenbusch   474

46.   The Courage to Be—Paul Tillich   487

Part VI.   *ISLAM*   *503*

47.   The Koran   509

48.   On Prayer—Avicenna   544

49.   On the Incoherence of the Incoherence—Averroes   554

50.   On Love and Living—Jalāl Al-Dīn Rūmī   567

51.   The Physical, Moral, and Spiritual States of Man—
            Mirza Ghulam Ahmad   578

52.   The Religious Spirit of Islam—Amīr Alī   588

53.   The Sūfī Message—Inayat Khan   607

54.   Is Religion Possible?—Mohammed Iqbal   620

55.   The Relation of Islam to Christianity—Alfred Guillaume   632

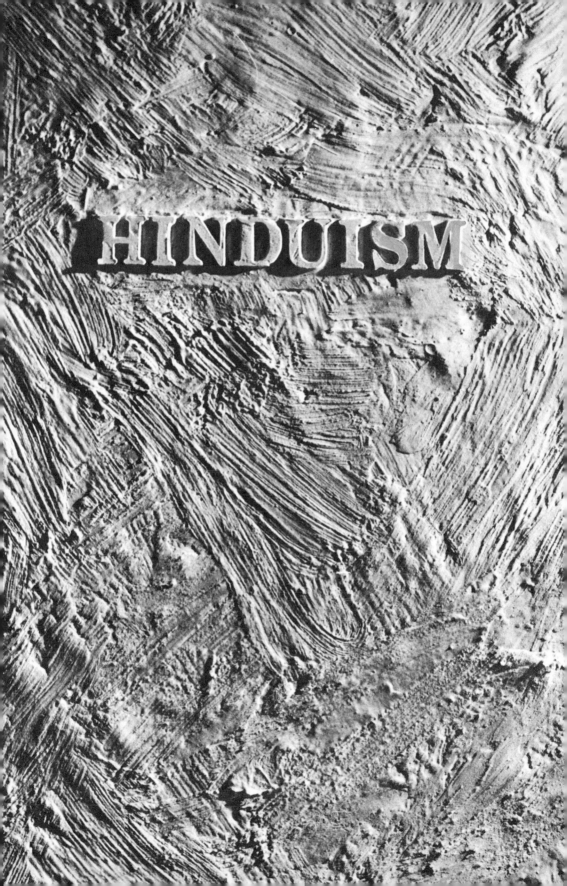

HINDUISM

PART I

Hinduism, the oldest, most eclectic, and most tolerant of the major religions, has never ceased growing, sprouting new cults and doctrines, while conserving most of the old. As a consequence, more than any other religion, it has something to offer to almost every kind and condition of man—elaborate ceremonies for the ritualist, an immense pantheon for the devotee, innumerable narratives for the lover of myth, a broad variety of metaphysical and theological theories for the speculative, a large selection of spiritual training techniques for the pragmatic, and a range of religious attitudes from intense emotionalism to profound detachment, from scrupulous social conformity to a radical rejection of conventions. Considered in the abstract, the many strands that enter into the fabric of Hinduism seem discordant, but no individual practices all the rites or subscribes to all the doctrines that can be found in this treasure house of religion. Rather, as in a cafeteria, each takes that which by tradition or inclination he finds attractive and peacefully ignores the rest.

Hinduism has no founder and no definite beginning, but the invasion of the Indus valley sometime before 1500 B.C. by Aryans from the Northwest led to the creation of the basic Hindu scriptures, the Vedas. The Indus Valley had been the home of one of the world's oldest civilizations centered on the twin cities at Mohenjo-Daro and Harappa, which had probably been built in the Fourth Millennium B.C. and occupied for perhaps 1500 years before being abandoned for an unknown reason. Possibly derived from Mesopotamia, this Indus Valley civilization displayed a high level of technology and social organization, while some of its material remains suggest that its religious conceptions and practices contributed significantly to the amalgam that is Hinduism. Images of a proto-Shiva, a Mother Goddess, phallic symbols, familiar signs such as the swastika, and evidence of the attachment of religious significance to such animals as the elephant and the buffalo have been found. Many of the non-Aryan elements in Hinduism have been speculatively attributed to this civilization by scholars, but the evidence is too sparse to establish most of these claims. The Aryans carried into India a pantheon of gods similar to those found in other Indo-European traditions such as in Iran, Greece, and Rome, the custom of a fire sacrifice, and the religious use of an exhilarating beverage called "soma." The religion introduced by these invaders and its development in India to

3

about 500 B.C. is reflected in the collection of Sanskrit hymns, incantations, ritual texts, ceremonial instructions, symbolic interpretations of ritual, and philosophical speculations called "the Vedas." Acknowledgment of the supreme religious authority of the Vedas is the criterion of orthodox Hinduism. Although some later scriptures are more frequently read, they derive their authority from the Vedas which are held to be divine in origin. From the standpoint of religious thought, the most interesting of the Vedas are the earliest and the latest portions, the *Rig Veda* and the Upanishads. The *Rig Veda* shows the beginnings of religio-philosophical reflection in a culture for the most part not very different from the one depicted by Homer. The Upanishads, on the other hand, are the pivotal scriptures of Hinduism. In them two of the most powerful of human conceptions, that of *moksha* or spiritual liberation and that of *Brahman*, the Absolute, received their first comparatively clear statements, and the introverted, world-transcending ideal that has been so prominent in India since, was established.

Overlapping the period of composition of the Upanishads was the rise of the great heterodox Indian faith, Buddhism, and its smaller companion Jainism. Although the teachings of the Upanishads and early Buddhism have much in common, the later histories of the two great Indian faiths call for separate treatments. Consequently, Buddhism is discussed in its own section of this book.

In Hinduism the Vedas alone are classified as direct divine revelations, but several other types of Sanskrit literature have been highly influential as containing sacred history and traditions or the teachings of great sages and commentators. The theoretical relationship of these books to the Vedas is similar to that between the *Talmud* and the *Torah* in Judaism.

The Vedangas, Dharma Sastras, and Nibandhas are comparatively minor forms of scripture. The Vedangas are treatises dealing with ritual codes and such other topics as grammar, astronomy, military science, poetry, and music. The Dharma Sastras, of which the *Laws of Manu* is the most famous, specify the traditional rules governing individual and social behavior. They have conferred upon ancient customs, such as the segregation of the caste system, a sanctity that has helped make Indian social habits possibly the most stable in the world. The Nibandhas codify Vedic laws and give elaborate instructions on the details of ritual. These three classes of books were studied primarily by scholars. When relevant to practical behavior or popular thought, their contents were normally communicated to the general population through illustrations and injunctions in the much more popular Epics and Puranas.

The Epics, the *Ramayana* and the *Mahabharata*, have been the most influential books in popular Hinduism for the last 1500 years. Hindus have heard the stories and maxims of these great poems from childhood as Greeks were once exposed to Homer. They knit together a mass of ancient tradition, legends of gods and sages, prudential maxims, dramatic action, and spiritual discourse. The sacrificial cult of the Vedas and the monistic metaphysics of the

Upanishads are subordinate in the Epics to the theistic devotion characteristic of later Hinduism centered upon the two great *avataras* or incarnations of Vishnu, Rama and Krishna. Many fold gods and goddesses were assured of their place in the national pantheon through their roles in the Epics. The date of completion of the present version of both books can only be guessed at, but many scholars think it must have been somewhere between 300 B.C. and A.D. 100.

The *Ramayana*, ascribed to the poet Valmiki, tells of the love, the tribulations, the struggles, the sorrows, and the deaths of the wise and good Prince Rama and his beautiful wife Sita. Rama is presented as the prototype of a brave and just ruler, while Sita is the ideal wife. The name "Rama" has become a common name for God in India and the story of the *Ramayana* has been told and retold by poets working in the many Indian languages.

Less poetic than the *Ramayana*, twice its length (over 180,000 verses), the *Mahabharata*, whose theme is a great and tragic dynastic war, is more an anthology than a single work of art. The central narrative is interrupted by fables, allegories, and religious, political, and moral discourses. Two religio-philosophic treatises, the *Mokshadharma* and the *Bhagavad-Gita* are included whole. The latter, containing the spiritual teaching of Sri Krishna, has often been declared to be an epitome of Hinduism and given such titles as "the New Testament of India."

An important branch of the religious literature of Hinduism is constituted by the sutras or aphoristic treatises setting forth the six orthodox *darsanas* or philosophical viewpoints. Like that of medieval Europe, Indian philosophy has usually been of a religious character. Its schools were traditionally divided into the orthodox which, whatever their positive doctrines, accepted the Vedas as an authoritative revelation and the unorthodox, notably Buddhism, Jainism, and Carvaka Materialism, which did not make this acknowledgment. Six orthodox schools achieved such pre-eminence that they are simply called "the orthodox schools." Indian philosophy was developed in discussions between teachers and their pupils, rather than by solitary thinkers working out their views on paper. The purport of such discussions was recorded in short summary statements or aphorisms which were gradually qualified, developed, and arranged by successive generations of investigators. Only a limited record exists of the contributions of the individual members of most Indian philosophical schools. The names attached to most of the sutras are simply those of the final compilers of the text. Consequently the systems cannot be accurately dated, for even if the date of the compiler of the classic formulation is known, the principal doctrines themselves may have been in existence for hundreds of years before the final codification. Because of their extreme economy, the texts require explication if their full import is to be grasped. Traditionally they were studied with a teacher who supplied such an explication, and around the major sutras there has grown up a body of written commentaries. The six orthodox systems of philosophy came to be coupled into three pairs, each containing a system which was primarily a metaphysical view and a system primarily a methodology. The *Vaiseshika* atomism and the *Nyaya* logic formed one pair. The *Sankhya* dualism of spirit and matter and the *Yoga* technique of spiritual training formed another. Vedanta, the metaphysical explication of the Upanishads, and the *Mimamsa* methodology of scriptural interpretation formed a third set. The system of Vedanta developed three major variants. The non-dualistic school led by Shankara (Eighth Century A.D.) taught that Brahman is the sole real being. The qualified non-dualistic school led by Ramanuja (Eleventh Century A.D.) argued that while Brahman is the only independent reality, it is qualified by two forms, that of selves and that of matter. The dualistic school led by Madhva (Thirteenth Century A.D.) held that God, individual selves, and material objects are absolutely distinct, although the latter two are completely dependent upon God. Among the methodological systems the most important from a religious viewpoint is Yoga, the principal tenets of which are summarized in Patanjali's *Yoga Aphorisms*. Among the metaphysical systems, that of non-dualistic Vedanta has been much the most popular and is the view of most educated devout Hindus today.

The Puranas constitute the largest part of the Sanskrit scriptures and one that has had great influence upon the general population. Written in verse less literary than the Epics, they provide a popular encyclopedia of Hinduism containing surprisingly detailed accounts of the mythical history of our cosmic epoch, including the genealogies and biographies of the gods, sages, saints, heroes, and rulers of prehistoric times. They also offer popular versions of the various schools of philosophy, summaries of caste rules, descriptions of the places of pilgrimage, discussions of temples and images, vows and austerities, and short excursions into astrology, medicine, augury, the fine arts, grammar, and much else. But particularly they describe the exploits of the *avataras*, the incarnations of God, and foster devotion to these great spiritual figures. Recounted to large audiences, they supplied religious instruction to the non-literate and were the channel by which many abstruse doctrines reached the masses.

The tradition is that there are eighteen major and eighteen minor Puranas, but actually there are many more. Although the surviving Puranas were probably written over a period of more than 1000 years, roughly from the beginning of our epoch to A.D. 1000, all of them are ascribed to Vyasa, who is also supposed to have written the *Mahabharata*. The most popular of the Puranas is the *Bhagavata Purana* which contains the life and teachings of Sri Krishna.

A popular group of sectarian scriptures are the Tantras or Agamas. Some of these are devoted to the worship of Shiva, some to Vishnu, a few to Ganesha, the elephant god, and Surya, the sun god, but most are dedicated to the worship of Shakti, the feminine consort of Shiva; and Shaktism is usually intended when the Tantras are mentioned. The Tantras are metrical works, probably compiled in the Sixth to Eighth Centuries A.D., and are generally divided into four sections. One section deals with meditative practices, one with philosophical doctrines, one with ritualistic worship or *puja,* and one with conduct. Great emphasis is put upon elaborate symbolic rituals, employing sacred phrases and movements, which are believed to arouse hidden stores of energy in the worshipper. In philosophy the Tantras taught that man is a microcosmic version of the universe, that all things contain a hidden divine power ("Shakti" means power or energy), that every god has his consort or shakti and that the god attains his highest power in his union with her. In the Tantric development the mother goddess, under many different names, emerged to a place of equality and often superiority to the male divinities.

Western scholars often assert that the religious innovations in India during the Post-Buddhist period, the innovations reflected in the teachings of the Epics, the Vedantic and Yogic treatises, the Puranas and the Tantras, are so extensive as to constitute a different religion from that of the Vedic period. The religion of the Aryans down to about 400 B.C. is sometimes called "Brahmanism" or "Vedism," while "Hinduism" is reserved for Indian religion after that date. Certainly during the last 2000 years popular devotion has centered on the *avataras* or divine incarnations, who may represent non-Aryan gods emerging into the literary record. The *Bhagavad-Gita* and the *Bhagavata Purana* have been more read than the *Rig-Veda* or the *Upanishads.* The public temples with their divine images, Tantric worship, and periodic festivals have replaced the Vedic altars. The three Great Gods of modern Hinduism are not Indra, Varuna, and Agni, but Vishnu, Shiva, and Shakti (for there is no popular cult of Brahma, the official creator god). Hindus, on the other hand, are apt to point to Vedic anticipations of these developments, to argue for early dates for the secondary scriptures, to point out the survival of numerous ancient traditions such as the teacher-student relationship, the caste system, and the veneration of the cow, to cite the unchallenged authority of the Vedas, and to observe that Hinduism is not a religion of rigid dogmas. While the Divine Spirit may be worshipped under new names with new ceremonies and celebrated in new scriptures, they argue, the essential quest of the Vedic period continues. In their eyes Hinduism may be compared to a great river whose identity survives despite the influx of many tributary streams. A religion, they hold, can remain both creative and tolerant of diversity without losing its identity; otherwise only fossilized faiths could endure.

The Golden Age of Hindu culture was the Gupta dynasty of the Fourth and Fifth Centuries A.D. In the Sixth Century the Huns repeatedly broke into Northern India, and while the Pallavas and Cholas maintained order in the South for another 500 years, Indian civilization entered a long decline. The Muslim invaders that came in successive waves from the Eleventh Century on were unassimilable, and in the face of political repression the leaders of Hinduism became increasingly conservative, particularly in social customs. From the Eleventh to the Eighteenth Century, the chief development in Hinduism was the spread of a fervent devotionalism (*bhakti*), first in the South and then in the North. This movement produced some philosophers such as Ramanuja and Madhva, great devotees such as Ramananda, Kabir, and Chaitanya, and a large mass of devotional poetry in the vernacular languages, but in general it was a period of low creativity.

By the beginning of the Nineteenth Century Hinduism was at a low ebb. Still a great force in the lives of the faithful, it lacked intellectual and spiritual leadership able to meet creatively the challenges presented by the culture of the European conquerors. During the Nineteenth Century Hinduism began to produce leadership worthy of its task. Ram Mohun Roy (1772–1833) fought for the internal reform of Hinduism and its customs. The great Sri Ramakrishna (1836–1886) extended the traditional Hindu tolerance to all religions, both in word and practice, and inspired a remarkable band of disciples. His most dynamic follower, Swami Vivekananda (1863–1902), carried the message of Vedanta to Europe and America, founded in India a new order of monks devoted equally to social service and spiritual development, and inspired in many young Indians a passionate desire to elevate India and Hinduism from their low state. In the Twentieth Century three of India's spiritual leaders have attracted world-wide interest. Through his own yogic experience, the gifted intellectual Sri Aurobindo Ghose (1872–1950) developed a new interpretation of Vedanta based on the ideal of transforming rather than transcending the world. Sri Ramana Maharishi (1879–1950) taught no special doctrines but challenged millions by the power of his presence and his simple question "Who are you?" The man who has done most to reform Hinduism and teach its high ideals to the world, however, was the lawyer, politician, and social reformer whom many, both in India and abroad, regard as the greatest religious figure of the Twentieth Century, Mahatma Gandhi (1869–1948). India today is undergoing tremendous and needed social changes, and it bodes well for the future of Hinduism that many of its leaders are active in promoting these changes.

SUGGESTIONS FOR FURTHER READING

Dasgupta, Surendranath, A History of Indian Philosophy, 5 vols., Cambridge, Cambridge University Press, 1922–1955.

Eliade, Mircea, Yoga: Immortality and Freedom, Willard R. Trask, trans., New York, Pantheon, 1958.

Fischer, Louis, Gandhi: His Life and Message for the World, New York, New American Library, 1950.

Morgan, K. W., ed., The Religion of the Hindus, New York, Ronald, 1953.

Nikhilananda, Swami, trans., The Gospel of Sri Ramakrishna, New York, Ramakrishna-Vivekananda Center, 1942.

Radhakrishnan, Sarvepalli and Moore, Charles A., A Source Book of Indian Philosophy, Princeton, New Jersey, Princeton University Press, 1957.

Zimmer, Heinrich, Philosophies of India, ed. by Joseph Campbell, New York, Meridian Books, Inc., 1957.

RIG VEDA

The Vedas are divided into four classes: the Mantras (which are sometimes simply called "the Vedas") containing hymns and sacrificial formulae, the Brahmanas or Priestly Treatises which supply ritual injunctions and explanations, the Aranyakas or Forest Treatises which offer symbolic interpretations of the rituals, and the Upanishads or Secret Teachings which affirm that salvation comes through mystical knowledge. The Brahmanas and Aranyakas are of restricted ideological interest and are seldom read today. The Mantras are gathered into four overlapping collections, most of the hymns being contained in the Rig Veda. This collection of 1017 metrical hymns in ten books is often said to contain the earliest surviving works of Indo-European literature. There is no reliable way to fix the date of their composition, but 2500 to 2000 B.C. is a popular estimate for the earliest hymns. Internal references to astronomical and meteorological phenomena have led some students to argue for a place of composition in North Asia. It is likely that the collection has existed in almost its present form since 1000 B.C.

Most of the hymns in the Rig Veda are expressions of praise and supplication directed to deities who appear to have originated as personified natural powers such as wind, fire, sky, sun, and rain. The hymns were used in a complicated sacrificial ritual by professional priests to please and win the support of the supernatural powers. Pre-eminent among the Vedic gods is Indra, the god of rain, who made human life possible by killing a great demon and releasing moisture, heat, and light from its belly. Other gods important in the hymns are Varuna, the sky god who established the cosmic order, Mitra, the god of light, Agni, the god of fire and sacrifice, and Soma, the god of the sacred fermented drink.

The Vedic hymns are usually polytheistic, recognizing an

Hymns from the Rigveda, I, 1. Agni, pp. 72–73; II, 12, Indra, pp. 48–50; V, 84. Earth, pp. 66–67; VII, 61. Mitra and Varuna, pp. 25–26; VIII, 48. Soma, pp. 79–81; X, 117, In Praise of Charity, pp. 91–93; X, 129, Creation, pp. 19–20. A. A. MacDonnell, trans. (London: Oxford University Press, 1922) Reprinted from Hymns from the Rigveda, trans. by A. A. MacDonnell by permission of the Executors of the estate of Sir William Max-Müller.

indefinite number of specialist gods, but sometimes one god is credited with all virtue and power. As such attributions seem to be due more to special veneration than to a denial of the other gods, scholars classify them as evidence of henotheism or worship of a single god rather than true monotheism. In a few hymns, however, an undescribed being, the All-maker, the Lord of Creatures, the Lord of the Holy Word, or an unamed One neither being nor non-being, is conceived as before the gods or as referred to by all the names of the gods. Although this tendency remained vague and tentative, it has been interpreted as an indication of the gradual emergence of monotheism or mystical monism.

HYMNS FROM THE RIG VEDA

Agni

I, 1.   *Metre: Gāyatrī.*

1. Agni I praise, the household priest,
   God, minister of sacrifice,
   Invoker, best bestowing wealth.

2. Agni is worthy to be praised,
   By present as by seers of old:
   May he to us conduct the gods.

3. Through Agni may we riches gain,
   And day by day prosperity
   Replete with fame and manly sons.

4. The worship and the sacrifice,
   Guarded by thee on every side,
   Go straight, O Agni, to the gods.

5. May Agni, the invoker, wise
   And true, of most resplendent fame,
   The god, come hither with the gods.

6. Whatever good thou wilt bestow,
   O Agni, on the pious man,
   That gift comes true, O Angiras.

7. To thee, O Agni, day by day,
   O thou illuminer of gloom,
   With thought we, bearing homage, come:

8. To thee the lord of sacrifice,
   The radiant guardian of the Law,
   That growest in thine own abode.

9. So, like a father to his son,
   Be easy of approach to us;
   Agni, for weal abide with us.

Indra

II, 12.　　　　　　　　　　　　　　　　*Metre: Triṣṭubh.*

1. He who just born as chief god full of spirit
   Went far beyond the other gods in wisdom:
   Before whose majesty and mighty manhood
   The two worlds trembled: he, O men, is Indra.

2. Who made the widespread earth when quaking steadfast,
   Who set at rest the agitated mountains,
   Who measured out air's middle space more widely,
   Who gave the sky support: he, men, is Indra.

3. Who slew the serpent, freed the seven rivers,
   Who drove the cattle out from Vala's cavern,
   Who fire between two rocks has generated,
   A conqueror in fights: he, men, is Indra.

4. He who has made all earthly things unstable,
   Who humbled and dispersed the Dāsa colour,
   Who, as the player's stake the winning gambler,
   The foeman's fortune gains: he, men, is Indra.

5. Of whom, the terrible, they ask, "Where is he?"
   Of him, indeed, they also say, "He is not."
   The foemen's wealth, like players' stakes, he lessens.
   Believe in him: for he, O men, is Indra.

6. He furthers worshippers, both rich and needy,
   And priests that supplicate his aid and praise him.
   Who, fair-lipped, helps the man that presses Soma,
   That sets the stones at work: he, men, is Indra.

7. In whose control are horses and all chariots,
   In whose control are villages and cattle;
   He who has generated sun and morning,
   Who leads the waters: he, O men, is Indra.

8. Whom two contending armies vie in calling,
   On both sides foes, the farther and the nearer;
   Two fighters mounted on the self-same chariot
   Invoke him variously: he, men, is Indra.

9. Without whose aid men conquer not in battle,
   Whom fighting ever they invoke for succour,
   Who shows himself a match for every foeman,
   Who moves what is unmoved: he, men, is Indra.

10. Who with his arrow slays the unexpecting
    Unnumbered crew of gravely guilty sinners;
    Who yields not to the boasting foe in boldness,
    Who slays the demons: he, O men, is Indra.

11. He who detected in the fortieth autumn
    Śambara dwelling far among the mountains;
    Who slew the serpent that put forth his vigour,
    The demon as he lay: he, men, is Indra.

12. Who with his seven rays, the bull, the mighty,
    Let loose the seven streams to flow in torrents;
    Who, bolt in arm, spurned Rauhiṇa, the demon,
    On scaling heaven bent: he, men, is Indra.

13. Both Heaven and Earth, themselves, bow down before him:
    Before his might the very mountains tremble,
    Who, famed as Soma-drinker, armed with lightning,
    Is wielder of the bolt: he, men, is Indra.

14. Who with his aid helps him that presses Soma,
    That bakes and lauds and ever sacrifices;
    Whom swelling prayer, whom Soma pressings strengthen,
    And now this offering: he, O men, is Indra.

15. Who, fierce, on him that bakes and him that presses
    Bestowest booty: thou, indeed, art trusted.
    May we, for ever dear to thee, O Indra,
    Endowed with hero sons address the synod.

Earth

V, 84.   *Metre: Anuṣṭubh.*

1. Thou bearest truly, Pṛthivī,
   The burden of the mountains' weight;

With might, O thou of many streams,
Thou quickenest, potent one, the soil.

2. With flowers of speech our songs of praise
Resound to thee, far-spreading one,
Who sendest forth the swelling cloud,
O bright one, like propelling speed;

3. Who, steadfast, holdest with thy might,
The forest-trees upon the ground,
When, from the lightning of thy cloud,
The rain-floods of the sky pour down.

Mitra and Varuṇa

VII, 61.   Metre: *Triṣṭubh.*

1. The beauteous eye of Varuṇa and Mitra,
The Sun, now rises up, his light extending,
Who with his gaze looks down upon all creatures:
He ever notes the burning zeal of mortals.

2. This pious priest, heard far away, here utters
His hymn for you, O Varuṇa and Mitra:
Do ye, O sages, treat his prayers with favour,
And may his autumns be replete with wisdom.

3. From wide-spread earth, O Varuṇa and Mitra,
Ye bounteous gods, and from the lofty heaven,
Ye have disposed your wandering spies in dwellings
And plants, ye who with watchful eye protect us.

4. Praise thou the law of Varuṇa and Mitra:
Their force the two worlds keeps with might asunder.
The months of impious men shall pass by sonless;
May those on worship bent increase their homestead.

5. Ye both are wise, O mighty ones, for you two
These lauds are sung without deceit or magic.
Avenging spies pursue men's falsehoods closely:
There are no secrets that ye cannot fathom.

6. With reverence I will consecrate your offering;
With zeal I call you, Varuṇa and Mitra.
These novel thoughts to praise you are intended:
May these the prayers that I have offered please you.

7. For you, O gods, this service has been rendered
   At sacrifices, Varuṇa and Mitra.
   Across all dangers do ye safely take us.
   Ye gods protect us evermore with blessings.

Soma

VIII, 48.   *Metre: Triṣṭubh; 5 Jagatī.*

1. I have partaken wisely of the sweet food
   That stirs good thoughts, best banisher of trouble,
   The food round which all deities and mortals,
   Calling it honey-mead, collect together.

2. Thou shalt be Aditi when thou hast entered
   Within, appeaser of celestial anger.
   May'st thou, O drop, enjoying Indra's friendship,
   Like willing mare the car, to wealth advance us.

3. We have drunk Soma and become immortal;
   We have attained the light the gods discovered.
   What can hostility now do against us?
   And what, immortal god, the spite of mortals?

4. Be cheering to our heart when drunk, O Indu,
   Kindly, like father to his son, O Soma.
   Like friend for friend, far-famed one, wisely
   Prolong our years that we may live, O Soma.

5. These glorious, freedom-giving drops, when drunk by me,
   Have knit my joints together as do thongs a car.
   May these protect me now from fracturing a limb.
   And may they ever keep me from disease remote.

6. Like fire produced by friction, make me brilliant;
   Do thou illumine us and make us richer;
   For then I seem in thy carouse, O Soma,
   Enriched. Now enter us for real welfare.

7. Of this thy juice pressed out with mind devoted,
   We would partake as of paternal riches.
   Prolong the years of life for us, King Soma,
   As Sūrya lengthens out the days of spring-time.

8. King Soma, gracious be to us for welfare:
   We are thy devotees; of that be mindful.

O Indu, might and anger rise against us:
Hand us not over to our foeman's mercies.

9. Thou, as the guardian of our body, Soma,
Surveying men, in every limb hast settled.
If we perchance infringed, O god, thy statutes,
As our good friend for greater wealth be gracious.

10. I would accompany the friend, the wholesome,
Who, Lord of Bays, imbibed, would never hurt me.
I come to Indra to prolong our life-time,
That we may relish Soma placed within us.

11. Away have fled those ailments and diseases;
The powers of darkness have been all affrighted.
With mighty strength in us has Soma mounted:
We have arrived where men prolong existence.

12. The drop drunk deeply in our hearts, O Fathers,
Us mortals that immortal god has entered.
That Soma we would worship with oblation;
We would be in his mercy and good graces.

13. Uniting with the Fathers thou, O Soma,
Hast over Heaven and Earth thyself extended.
So, Indu, we would serve thee with oblation:
Thus we would be the lords of ample riches.

14. Do ye, protecting gods, speak in our favour,
Let neither sleep nor idle talk subdue us;
May we, for evermore, beloved of Soma,
Endowed with hero sons, address the synod.

15. Thou, Soma, givest strength to us on all sides.
Light-finder, watching men, within us enter.
Do thou, O Indu, with thine aids accordant,
Behind for ever and before protect us.

In Praise of Charity

X, 117.   *Metre: Triṣṭubh; 1-2 Jagatī.*

1. The gods inflict not hunger as a means to kill:
Death frequently befalls even satiated men.
The charitable giver's wealth melts not away;
The niggard never finds a man to pity him.

2. Who, of abundant food possessed, makes hard his heart
   Towards a needy and decrepit suppliant
   Whom once he courted, come to pray to him for bread:
   A man like this as well finds none to pity him.

3. He is the liberal man who helps the beggar
   That, craving food, emaciated wanders,
   And coming to his aid, when asked to succour,
   Immediately makes him a friend hereafter.

4. He is no friend who gives not of his substance
   To his devoted, intimate companion:
   This friend should turn from him—here is no haven—
   And seek a stranger elsewhere as a helper.

5. The wealthier man should give unto the needy,
   Considering the course of life hereafter;
   For riches are like chariot wheels revolving:
   Now to one man they come, now to another.

6. The foolish man from food has no advantage;
   In truth I say: it is but his undoing;
   No friend he ever fosters, no companion:
   He eats alone, and he alone is guilty.

7. The plough that cleaves the soil produces nurture;
   He that bestirs his feet completes his journey.
   The speaking Brahmin earns more than the silent;
   A friend who gives is better than the niggard.

8. The one-foot strides more swiftly than the biped;
   The biped goes beyond him who has three feet.
   The quadruped comes at the call of bipeds,
   And watches near where groups of five are gathered.

9. Two hands though equal make not what is equal;
   No sister cows yield milk in equal measure;
   Unequal is the strength even of twin children;
   The gifts of even kinsmen are unequal.

Creation

X, 129.   Metre: Triṣṭubh.

1. Non-being then existed not nor being:
   There was no air, nor sky that is beyond it.

What was concealed? Wherein? In whose protection?
And was there deep unfathomable water?

2. Death then existed not nor life immortal;
Of neither night nor day was any token.
By its inherent force the One breathed windless:
No other thing than that beyond existed.

3. Darkness there was at first by darkness hidden;
Without distinctive marks, this all was water.
That which, becoming, by the void was covered,
That One by force of heat came into being.

4. Desire entered the One in the beginning:
It was the earliest seed, of thought the product.
The sages searching in their hearts with wisdom,
Found out the bond of being in non-being.

5. Their ray extended light across the darkness:
But was the One above or was it under?
Creative force was there, and fertile power:
Below was energy, above was impulse.

6. Who knows for certain? Who shall here declare it?
Whence was it born, and whence came this creation?
The gods were born after this world's creation:
Then who can know from whence it has arisen?

7. None knoweth whence creation has arisen;
And whether he has or has not produced it:
He who surveys it in the highest heaven,
He only knows, or haply he may know not.

UPANISHADS

The Upanishads are a continuation of the Vedic tradition. Most of the theological conceptions of the earlier scriptures can be found in them, but they perceive the evil of human life from a different perspective and provide a new vision of the goal of religion. Unsystematic, anecdotal, and rich with a variety of religious teachings, the Upanishads yet exhibit a recurrent gospel. This Upanishadic view assumes, as does most later Indian thought, the doctrine of reincarnation, the law of karma, and the round of samsara. Following death, according to the doctrine of reincarnation, a person will be reborn into another life either human or non-human. The law of karma asserts that the nature of this rebirth will be determined by the balance of good and evil acts in the individual's past. The conception of samsara is that the series of rebirths will continue indefinitely. The Upanishads teach that liberation from this weary round of lives can be achieved through a life of morality, asceticism, devotion, study, and meditation under the guidance of an illumined teacher and culminating in an ineffable and blissful experience in which the seer finds that his inmost self, the ātman, is identical with the unchanging divine reality of the universe, Brahman, and thus confirms for himself the truth of the celebrated Upanishadic formula "That art Thou."

While the traditional ennumeration lists 108 Upanishads, only the thirteen most philosophical are commonly discussed. The period of composition by unknown authors is often estimated as 800 B.C. to 300 B.C., but the central Upanishadic teaching was clearly contained in the early Upanishads. Four Upanishads, Isa, Kena, Katha, and Mundaka, are here given in full in Professor Radhakrishnan's translation.

Īṣa Upaniṣad, Kena Upaniṣad, Katha Upaniṣad, Mundaka Upaniṣad, S. Radhakrishnan, trans. (London: Allen & Unwin, Ltd., 1953), pp. 565–648, 669–692. Reprinted from *The Principal Upaniṣads* by S. Radhakrishnan, by permission of Allen & Unwin, Ltd.

ÍŚA UPANIŚAD

1. (Know that) all this, whatever moves in this moving world, is enveloped by God. Therefore find your enjoyment in renunciation; do not covet what belongs to others.

2. Always performing works here one should wish to live a hundred years. If you live thus as a man, there is no way other than this by which karman (or deed) does not adhere to you.

3. Demoniac, verily, are those worlds enveloped in blinding darkness, and to them go after death, those people who are the slayers of the self.

4. (The spirit) is unmoving, one, swifter than the mind. The senses do not reach It as It is ever ahead of them. Though Itself standing still It outstrips those who run. In It the all-pervading air supports the activities of beings.

5. It moves and It moves not; It is far and It is near; It is within all this and It is also outside all this.

6. And he who sees all beings in his own self and his own self in all beings, he does not feel any revulsion by reason of such a view.

7. When, to one who knows, all beings have, verily, become one with his own self, then what delusion and what sorrow can be to him who has seen the oneness?

8. He has filled all; He is radiant, bodiless, invulnerable, devoid of sinews, pure, untouched by evil. He, the seer, thinker, all-pervading, self-existent has duly distributed through endless years the objects according to their natures.

9. Into blinding darkness enter those who worship ignorance and those who delight in knowledge enter into still greater darkness, as it were.

10. Distinct, indeed, they say, is the result of knowledge and distinct, they say, is the result of ignorance. Thus have we heard from those wise who have explained to us these.

11. Knowledge and ignorance, he who knows the two together crosses death through ignorance and attains life eternal through knowledge.

12. Into blinding darkness enter those who worship the unmanifest and into still greater darkness, as it were, those who delight in the manifest.

13. Distinct, indeed, they say, is what results from the manifest, and distinct, they say, is what results from the unmanifest. Thus have we heard from those wise who have explained to us these.

14. He who understands the manifest and the unmanifest both together, crosses death through the unmanifest and attains life eternal through the manifest.

15. The face of truth is covered with a golden disc. Unveil it, O Pūṣan, so that I who love the truth may see it.

16. O Pūṣan, the sole seer, O controller, O Sun, offspring of *Prajāpati*,

spread forth your rays and gather up your radiant light that I may behold you of loveliest form. Whosoever is that person (yonder) that also am I.

17. May this life enter into the immortal breath; then may this body end in ashes. O Intelligence, remember, remember what has been done. Remember, O Intelligence, what has been done, Remember.

18. O Agni, lead us, along the auspicious path to prosperity, O God, who knowest all our deeds. Take away from us deceitful sins. We shall offer many prayers unto thee.

KENA UPANIṢAD

Section 1

1. By whom willed and directed does the mind light on its objects? By whom commanded does life the first, move? At whose will do (people) utter this speech? And what god is it that prompts the eye and the ear?

2. Because it is that which is the ear of the ear, the mind of the mind, the speech, indeed of the speech, the breath of the breath, the eye of the eye, the wise, giving up (wrong notions of their self-sufficiency) and departing from this world, become immortal.

3. There the eye goes not, speech goes not, nor the mind; we know not, we understand not how one can teach this.

4. Other, indeed, is it than the known; and also it is above the unknown. Thus have we heard from the ancients who have explained it to us.

5. That which is not expressed through speech but that by which speech is expressed; that, verily, know thou, is *Brahman*, not what (people) here adore.

6. That which is not thought by the mind but by which, they say, the mind is thought (thinks); that, verily, know thou, is *Brahman* and not what (people) here adore.

7. That which is not seen by the eye but by which the eyes are seen (see); that, verily, know thou, is *Brahman* and not what (people) here adore.

8. That which is not heard by the ear but by which the ears are heard (hear); that, verily, know thou, is *Brahman* and not what (people) here adore.

9. That which is not breathed by life, but by which life breathes; that verily, know thou, is *Brahman* and not what (people) here adore.

Section 2

1. If you think that you have understood *Brahman* well, you know it but slightly, whether it refers to you (the individual self) or to the gods. So then is it to be investigated by you (the pupil) (even though) I think it is known.

2. I do not think that I know it well; nor do I think that I do not know

it. He who among us knows it, knows it and he, too, does not know that he does not know.

3. To whomsoever it is not known, to him it is known: to whomsoever it is known, he does not know. It is not understood by those who understand it; it is understood by those who do not understand it.

4. When it is known through every state of cognition, it is rightly known, for (by such knowledge) one attains life eternal. Through one's own self one gains power and through wisdom one gains immortality.

5. If here (a person) knows it, then there is truth, and if here he knows it not, there is great loss. Hence, seeing or (seeking) (the Real) in all beings, wise men become immortal on departing from this world.

Section 3

1. *Brahman*, it is said, conquered (once) for the gods, and the gods gloried in that conquest of *Brahman*. They thought, ours, indeed, is this victory and ours, indeed, is this greatness.

2. (Brahman) indeed knew this (conceit of theirs). He appeared before them. They did not know what spirit it was.

3. They said to Agni, "O Jāta-vedas, find this out, what this spirit is." "Yes" (said he).

4. He hastened towards it and it said to him, "Who art thou?" (Agni) replied, "I am Agni indeed, I am Jāta-vedas."

5. He again asked, "What power is there in thee?" Agni replied, "I can burn everything whatever there is on earth."

6. (He) placed (a blade of) grass before him saying, "Burn this." He went towards it with all speed but could not burn it. He returned thence and said. "I have not been able to find out what this spirit is."

7. Then they said to Vāyu (Air), "O Vāyu, find this out—What this spirit is." "Yes" (said he).

8. He hastened towards it, and it said to him, "Who art thou?" Vāyu replied, "I am Vāyu indeed, I am Mātariśvan."

9. (He asked Vāyu) "What power is there in thee?" (Vāyu) replied, "I can blow off everything whatever there is on earth."

10. He placed before him (a blade of) grass saying, "Blow off." Vāyu went towards it with all speed but could not blow it off. He returned thence and said, "I have not been able to find out what this spirit is."

11. Then they said to Indra, "O Maghavan, find this out what this spirit is." "Yes" (said he). He hastened towards it (but) it disappeared from before him.

12. When in the same region of the sky, he (Indra) came across a lady, most beautiful, Umā, the daughter of Himavat, and said to her. "What is this spirit?"

Section 4

1. She replied, "This is *Brahman*, to be sure, and in the victory of *Brahman*, indeed, do you glory thus." Then only did he (Indra) know that it was *Brahman*.

2. Therefore, these gods, Agni, Vāyu and Indra, surpass greatly other gods, for they, it was that touched *Brahman* closest, for they, indeed, for the first time knew (it was) *Brahman*.

3. Therefore, Indra surpasses greatly, as it were, other gods. He, indeed, has come into close contact with *Brahman*. He, indeed, for the first time knew that (it was) *Brahman*.

4. Of this *Brahman*, there is this teaching: this is as it were, like the lightning which flashes forth or the winking of the eye. This teaching is concerning the gods.

5. Now the teaching concerning the self.—It is this toward which the mind appears to move; by the same (mind, one) remembers constantly; volition also likewise.

6. *Brahman*, the object of all desire, that, verily, is what is called the dearest of all. It is to be meditated upon as such (*tadvanam*). Whoever knows it thus, him, all beings seek.

7. (The pupil) "Sir, teach (me) the secret (Upaniṣad)." (The teacher): "The secret has been taught to thee; we have taught thee the secret relating to *Brahman*."

8. Austerities, self-control and work are its support; the Vedās are all its units; truth is its abode.

9. Whoever knows this, he, indeed, overcoming sin, in the end, is firmly established in the Supreme world of heaven; yes, he is firmly established.

KAṬHA UPANIṢAD

Chapter I, Section 1

1. Desirous (of the fruit of the Viśvajit sacrifice) Vājaśravasa, they say, gave away all that he possessed. He had a son by name Naciketas.

2. As the gifts were being taken to the priests, faith entered him, although but a (mere) boy; he thought.

3. Their water drunk, their grass eaten, their milk milked, their strength spent, joyless, verily, are those worlds, to which he, who presents such (cows) goes.

4. He said to his father, "O Sire, to whom wilt thou give me?" For a second and a third time (he repeated) (when the father) said to him, "Unto Death shall I give thee."

5. Naciketas, "Of many (sons or disciples) I go as the first; of many,

I go as the middling. What duty towards Yama [Lord of Death] that (my father has to accomplish) today, does he accomplish through me?"

6. "Consider how it was with the forefathers; behold how it is with the later (men); a mortal ripens like corn, and like corn is born again."

7. As a very fire a Brāhmana guest enters into houses and (the people) do him this peace-offering; bring water, O Son of the Sun!

8. Hope and expectation, friendship and joy, sacrifices and good works, sons, cattle and all are taken away from a person of little understanding in whose house a Brāhmana remains unfed.

9. [Yama said:] "Since thou, a venerable guest, has stayed in my house without food for three nights, I make obeisance to thee, O Brāhmana. May it be well with me. Therefore, in return, choose thou three gifts."

10. That Gautama (my father) with allayed anxiety, with anger gone, may be gracious to me, O Death, and recognizing me, greet me, when set free by you and this, I choose as the first gift of the three.

11. (Yama said): "As of old will he, recognising thee (thy father) Auddālaki, the son of Aruna, through my favour will he sleep peacefully through nights, his anger gone, seeing thee released from the jaws of death."

12. (Naciketas said): "In the world of heaven there is no fear whatever; thou art not there, nor does one fear old age. Crossing over both hunger and thirst, leaving sorrow behind, one rejoices in the world of heaven."

13. Thou knowest, O Death, that fire (sacrifice which is) the aid to heaven. Describe it to me, full of faith, how the dwellers in heaven gain immortality. This I choose, as my second boon.

14. (Yama said): "Knowing well as I do, that fire (which is) the aid to heaven, I shall describe it to thee—learn it of me, O Naciketas. Know that fire to be the means of attaining the boundless world, as the support (of the universe) and as abiding in the secret place (of the heart)."

15. (Yama) described to him that fire (sacrifice which is) the beginning of the world (as also) what kind of bricks (are to be used in building the sacrificial altar), how many and in what manner. And he (Naciketas) repeated all that just as it had been told; then, pleased with him, Death spoke again.

16. The great soul (Yama) extremely delighted, said to him (Naciketas). I give thee here today another boon. By thine own name will this fire become (known). Take also this many-shaped chain.

17. He who has lit the Nāciketa fire thrice, associating with the three, performs the three acts, crosses over birth and death. Knowing the son of Brahmā, the omniscient, resplendent and adorable and realising him, one obtains this everlasting peace.

18. The wise man who has sacrificed thrice to Naciketas and who knows this three, and so knowing, performs meditation on fire throwing off first the bonds of death and overcoming sorrow, rejoices in the world of heaven.

19. This is thy fire (sacrifice) O Naciketas, which leading to heaven, which thou hast chosen for thy second boon. This fire (sacrifice) people will call by thy name only. Choose now, O Naciketas, the third boon.

20. There is this doubt in regard to a man who has departed, some (holding) that he is and some that he is not. I would be instructed by thee in this knowledge. Of the boons, this is the third boon.

21. (Yama said): "Even the gods of old had doubt on this point. It is not, indeed, easy to understand; (so) subtle is this truth. Choose another boon, O Naciketas. Do not press me. Release me from this."

22. (Naciketas said:) "Even the gods had doubt, indeed, as to this, and thou, O Death, sayest that it is not easy to understand. (Instruct me) for another teacher of it, like thee, is not to be got. No other boon is comparable to this at all."

23. (Yama said:) "Choose sons and grandsons that shall live a hundred years, cattle in plenty, elephants, gold and horses. Choose vast expanses of land and life for thyself as many years as thou wilt."

24. If thou deemest (any) boon like unto this, choose (that) as also wealth and long life. O Naciketas, prosper then on this vast earth. I will make thee the enjoyer of thy desires.

25. Whatever desires are hard to attain in this world of mortals, ask for all those desires at thy will. Here are noble maidens with chariots and musical instruments: the like of them cannot be won by men. Be served by these whom I give to thee. O Naciketas, (pray) ask not about death.

26. (Naciketas said:) Transient (are these) and they wear out, O Yama, the vigour of all the senses of men. All life (a full life), moreover, is brief. Thine be the chariots, thine the dance and song.

27. Man is not to be contented with wealth. Shall we enjoy wealth when we have seen thee? Shall we live as long as thou art in power? That alone is (still) the boon chosen by me.

28. Having aproached the undecaying immortality, what decaying mortal on this earth below who (now) knows (and meditates on) the pleasures of beauty and love, will delight in an over-long life?

29. Tell us that about which they doubt, O Death, what there is in the great passing-on. This boon which penetrates the mystery, no other than that does Naciketas choose.

Section 2

1. (Yama said): "Different is the good, and different, indeed, is the pleasant. These two, with different purposes, bind a man. Of these two, it is well for him who takes hold of the good; but he who chooses the pleasant, fails of his aim."

2. Both the good and the pleasant approach a man. The wise man, pon-

dering over them, discriminates. The wise chooses the good in preference to the pleasant. The simple-minded, for the sake of worldly well-being, prefers the pleasant.

3. (But) thou, O Naciketas, hast rejected (after) examining, the desires that are pleasant and seem to be pleasing. Thou hast not taken to the way of wealth, where many mortals sink (to ruin).

4. Widely apart and leading to divergent ends are these, ignorance and what is known as wisdom. I know (thee) Naciketas, to be eager for wisdom for (even) many desires did not distract thee.

5. Abiding in the midst of ignorance, wise in their own esteem, thinking themselves to be learned, fools treading a tortuous path go about like blind men led by one who is himself blind.

6. What lies beyond shines not to the simple-minded, careless, (who is) deluded by the glamour of wealth. Thinking "this world exists, there is no other," he falls again and again into my power.

7. He who cannot even be heard of by many, whom many, even hearing, do not know, wondrous is he who can teach (Him) and skilful is he who finds (Him) and wondrous is he who knows, even when instructed by the wise.

8. Taught by an inferior man He cannot be truly understood, as He is thought of in many ways. Unless taught by one who knows Him as himself, there is no going thither for it is inconceivable, being subtler than the subtle.

9. Not by reasoning is this apprehension attainable, but dearest, taught by another, is it well understood. Thou hast obtained it, holding fast to truth. May we find, Naciketas, an inquirer like thee.

10. I know that wealth is impermanent. Not through the transient things is that abiding (one) reached; yet by me is laid the Nāciketa fire and by impermanent means have I reached the everlasting.

11. (Having seen) the fulfilment of (all) desire, the support of the world, the endless fruit of rites, the other shore where there is no fear, the greatness of fame, the far-stretching, the foundation, O wise Naciketas, thou hast steadfastly let (them) go.

12. Realising through self-contemplation that primal God, difficult to be seen, deeply hidden, set in the cave (of the heart), dwelling in the deep, the wise man leaves behind both joy and sorrow.

13. Hearing this and comprehending (it), a mortal, extracting the essence and reaching the subtle, rejoices, having attained the source of joy. I know that such an abode is wide open unto Naciketas.

14. (Naciketas asks:) "Tell me that which thou seest beyond right and wrong, beyond what is done or not done, beyond past and future."

15. (Yama says:) "That word which all the Vedas declare, which all the austerities proclaim, desiring which (people) live the life of a religious student, that word, to thee, I shall tell in brief. That is *Aum*."

16. This syllable is, verily, the everlasting spirit. This syllable, indeed, is the highest end; knowing this very syllable, whatever anyone desires will, indeed, be his.

17. This support is the best (of all). This support is the highest; knowing this support, one becomes great in the world of Brahmā.

18. The knowing self is never born; nor does he die at any time. He sprang from nothing and nothing sprang from him. He is unborn, eternal, abiding and primeval. He is not slain when the body is slain.

19. If the slayer thinks that he slays or if the slain think that he is slain, both of them do not understand. He neither slays nor is he slain.

20. Smaller than the small, greater than the great, the self is set in the heart of every creature. The unstriving man beholds Him, freed from sorrow. Through tranquillity of the mind and the senses (he sees) the greatness of the self.

21. Sitting, he moves far; lying he goes everywhere. Who, save myself, is fit to know that god who rejoices and rejoices not?

22. Knowing the self who is the bodiless among bodies, the stable among the unstable, the great, the all-pervading, the wise man does not grieve.

23. This self cannot be attained by instruction, nor by intellectual power, nor even through much hearing. He is to be attained only by the one whom the (self) chooses. To such a one the self reveals his own nature.

24. Not he who has not desisted from evil ways, not he who is not tranquil, not he who has not a concentrated mind, not even he whose mind is not composed can reach this (self) through right knowledge.

25. He for whom priesthood and nobility both are as food and death is as a sauce, who really knows where he is?

Section 3

1. There are two selves that drink the fruit of Karma in the world of good deeds. Both are lodged in the secret place (of the heart), the chief seat of the Supreme. The knowers of *Brahman* speak of them as shade and light as also (the householders) who maintain the five sacrificial fires and those too who perform the triple Nāciketas fire.

2. That bridge for those who sacrifice, and which is the highest imperishable *Brahman* for those who wish to cross over to the farther fearless shore, that Nāciketa fire, may we master.

3. Know the Self as the lord of the chariot and the body as, verily, the chariot, know the intellect as the charioteer and the mind as, verily, the reins.

4. The senses, they say, are the horses; the objects of sense the paths (they range over); (the self) associated with the body, the senses and the mind —wise men declare—is the enjoyer.

5. He who has no understanding, whose mind is always unrestrained, his senses are out of control, as wicked horses are for a charioteer.

6. He, however, who has understanding, whose mind is always re-strained, his senses are under control, as good horses are for a charioteer.

7. He, however, who has no understanding, who has no control over his mind (and is) ever impure, reaches not that goal but comes back into mundane life.

8. He, however, who has understanding, who has control over his mind and (is) ever pure, reaches that goal from which he is not born again.

9. He who has the understanding for the driver of the chariot and con-trols the rein of his mind, he reaches the end of the journey, that supreme abode of the all-pervading.

10. Beyond the senses are the objects (of the senses) and beyond the objects is the mind; beyond the mind is the understanding and beyond the understanding is the great self.

11. Beyond the great self is the unmanifest; beyond the unmanifest is the spirit. Beyond the spirit there is nothing. That is the end (of the journey); that is the final goal.

12. The Self, though hidden in all beings, does not shine forth but can be seen by those subtle seers, through their sharp and subtle intelligence.

13. The wise man should restrain speech in mind; the latter he should restrain in the understanding self. The understanding he should restrain in the great self. That he should restrain in the tranquil self.

14. Arise, awake, having attained thy boons, understand (them). Sharp as the edge of a razor and hard to cross, difficult to tread is that path (so) sages declare.

15. (The Self) without sound, without touch and without form, un-decaying, is likewise, without taste, eternal, without smell, without beginning, without end, beyond the great, abiding, by discerning that, one is freed from the face of death.

16. This ancient story of Nāciketas, told by Death, telling and hearing (it), a wise man grows great in the world of Brahmā.

17. Whoso shall cause to be recited this supreme secret before an assem-bly of Brāhmanas or devoutly at the time of the ceremonies for the dead, this will prepare (for him) everlasting life, this will prepare everlasting life.

Chapter II, Section 1

1. The Self is not to be sought through the senses. The Self-caused pierced the openings (of the senses) outward; therefore one looks outward and not within oneself. Some wise man, however, seeking life eternal, with his eyes turned inward, saw the self.

2. The small-minded go after outward pleasures. They walk into the snare of widespread death. The wise, however, recognising life eternal do not seek the stable among things which are unstable here.

3. That by which (one perceives) form, taste, smell, sounds and touches

of love, by that alone one perceives. What is there that remains (unknown to it)? This, verily, is that.

4. That by which one perceives both dream states and waking states, having known (that as) the great, omnipresent Self, the wise man does not grieve.

5. He who knows this Self, the experiencer as the living spirit close at hand as the lord of the past and the future—one does not shrink away from Him. This, verily, is that.

6. He who was born of old from austerity, was born of old from the waters, who stands, having entered the secret place (of the heart) and looked forth through beings. This, verily, is that.

7. She who arises with life, *Aditi*, the soul of the gods, who stands, having entered the secret place (of the heart), who was born with the beings. This, verily, is that.

8. Agni, the all-knower, hidden in the fire-sticks, like the embryo well borne by pregnant women, should be daily adored by the watchful men with oblations. This, verily, is that.

9. Whence the sun rises and where it goes to rest; in it are all gods founded and no one ever goes beyond that. This verily, is that.

10. Whatever is here, that (is) there. Whatever is there, that, too, is here. Whoever perceives anything like manyness here goes from death to death.

11. By mind alone is this to be obtained. There is nothing of variety here. Whoever perceives anything like variety here, goes from death to death.

12. The person of the size of a thumb resides in the middle of the body. After knowing him who is the lord of the past and the future, one does not shrink (from Him). This, verily, is that.

13. The person of the size of a thumb resides in the middle of the body, like a flame without smoke. He is the lord of the past and the future. He is the same today and the same tomorrow. This, verily, is that.

14. As water rained upon a height flows down in various ways among the hills; so he who views things as varied runs after them (distractedly).

15. As pure water poured forth into pure becomes the very same, so the self, O Gautama, of the seer who has understanding becomes (one with the Supreme).

Section 2

1. (There is) a city of eleven gates (belonging to) the unborn, un-crooked intelligence. By ruling it one does not grieve and being freed is freed indeed. This, verily, is that.

2. He is the swan (sun) in the sky, the pervader in the space (between earth and heaven), the priest at the altar, the guest in the sacrificial jar (house). He dwells in men, in gods, in the right and in the sky. He is (all

that is) born of water, sprung from the earth, born of right, born of mountain. He is the true and the great.

3. He leads the out-breath upward, he casts inwards the in-breath, the dwarf who is seated in the middle, all the gods adore.

4. When the embodied self that dwells within the body slips off and is released from the body, what is there that remains? This, verily, is that.

5. Not by any outbreath or inbreath does any mortal whatever live. But by another do they live on which these (lifebreaths) both depend.

6. Look (here). I shall explain to you the mystery of *Brahman*, the eternal, and also how the soul fares, after reaching death, O Gautama.

7. Some souls enter into a womb for embodiment; others enter stationary objects according to their deeds and according to their thoughts.

8. That person who is awake in those that sleep, shaping desire after desire, that, indeed, is the pure. That is *Brahman*, that, indeed, is called the immortal. In it all the worlds rest and no one ever goes beyond it. This, verily, is that.

9. As fire which is one, entering this world becomes varied in shape according to the object (it burns), so also the one Self within all beings becomes varied according to whatever (it enters) and also exists outside (them all).

10. As air which is one, entering this world becomes varied in shape according to the object (it enters), so also the one Self within all beings becomes varied according to whatever (it enters) and also exists outside (them all).

11. Just as the sun, the eye of the whole world, is not defiled by the external faults seen by the eye, even so, the One within all beings is not tainted by the sorrow of the world, as He is outside (the world).

12. The one, controller (of all), the inner self of all things, who makes his one form manifold, to the wise who perceive him as abiding in the soul, to them is eternal bliss—to no others.

13. The one eternal amid the transient, the conscious amid the conscious, the one amid many, who grants their desires, to the wise who perceive Him as abiding in the soul, to them is eternal peace and to no others.

14. This is that and thus they recognise, the ineffable Supreme bliss. How then may I come to know this? Does it shine (of itself) or does it shine (in reflection)?

15. The sun shines not there, nor the moon and the stars, these lightnings shine not, where then could this fire be? Everything shines only after that shining light. His shining illumines all this world.

Section 3

1. With the root above and the branches below (stands) this ancient fig tree. That (indeed) is the pure; that is *Brahman*. That, indeed, is called

immortal. In it all the worlds rest and no one ever goes beyond it. This, verily, is that.

2. The whole world, whatever here exists, springs from and moves in life. (It is) the great fear (like) the upraised thunderbolt. They that know that become immortal.

3. Through fear of him, fire burns; through fear (of him) the sun gives heat; through fear both Indra (the lord of the gods) and wind and Death, the fifth, speed on their way.

4. If one is able to perceive (Him) before the body falls away (one would be freed from misery); (if not) he becomes fit for embodiment in the created worlds.

5. As in a mirror, so (is it seen) in the soul, as in a dream, so in the world of the manes, as (an object) is seen in water, so in the world of the gandharvas; as shade and light in the world of Brahmā.

6. Knowing the separate nature of the senses, which spring separately (from the various subtle elements) and (knowing also) that their rising and setting (are separate), the wise man does not grieve.

7. Beyond the senses is the mind; above the mind is its essence (intelligence); beyond the intelligence is the great self; beyond the great (self) is the unmanifest.

8. Beyond the unmanifest is the person, all-pervading and without any mark whatever. By knowing whom, a man is liberated and goes to life eternal.

9. Not within the field of vision stands this form. No one soever sees Him with the eye. By heart, by thought, by mind apprehended, they who know Him become immortal.

10. When the five (senses) knowledges together with the mind cease (from their normal activities) and the intellect itself does not stir, that, they say, is the highest state.

11. This, they consider to be Yoga, the steady control of the senses. Then one becomes undistracted for Yoga comes and goes.

12. Not by speech, not by mind, not by sight can he be apprehended. How can he be comprehended except by him who says, "He is"?

13. He should be apprehended only as existent and then in his real nature—in both ways. When He is apprehended as existent, his real nature becomes clear (later on).

14. When all desires that dwell within the human heart are cast away, then a mortal becomes immortal and (even) here he attaineth to *Brahman*.

15. When all the knots that fetter here the heart are cut asunder, then a mortal becomes immortal. Thus far is the teaching.

16. A hundred and one are the arteries of the heart; one of them leads up to the crown of the head. Going upward through that, one becomes immortal; the others serve for going in various other directions.

17. The person of the size of a thumb, the inner self, abides always in

the hearts of men. Him one should draw out with firmness, from the body, as (one may do) the wind from the reed. Him one should know as the pure, the immortal, yea, Him one should know as the pure, the immortal.

18. Then Nāciketas, having gained this knowledge declared by Death and the whole rule of Yoga, attained *Brahman* and became freed from passion and from death. And so may any other who knows this in regard to the self.

MUṆḌAKA UPANIṢAD

Chapter I, Section 1

1. Brahmā arose as the first among the gods, the maker of the universe, the protector of the world. He taught the knowledge of *Brahman*, the foundation of all knowledges, to Atharvan, his eldest son.

2. That knowledge of *Brahman*, which Brahmā taught to Atharvan, and Atharvan in olden times told Aṅgiras. He (in his turn) taught it to Satayavāha, son of Bhāradvāja and the son of Bhāradvāja to Aṅgiras—both the higher and lower (knowledge).

3. Śaunaka, the great householder, duly approached Aṅgiras and asked, through what being known, Venerable Sir, does all this become known?

4. To him he said, two kinds of knowledge are to be known, as, indeed, the knowers of *Brahman* declare—the higher as well as the lower.

5. Of these, the lower is the Ṛg *Veda*, the *Yajur Veda*, the *Sāma Veda*, the *Atharva Veda*. Phonetics, Ritual, Grammar, Etymology, Metrics and Astrology. And the higher is that by which the Undecaying is apprehended.

6. That which is ungraspable, without family, without caste, without sight or hearing, without hands or feet, eternal, all-pervading, omnipresent, exceedingly subtle, that is the Undecaying which the wise perceive as the source of beings.

7. As a spider sends forth and draws in (its thread), as herbs grow on the earth, as the hair (grows) on the head and the body of a living person, so from the Imperishable arises here the universe.

8. By contemplative power *Brahman* expands. From that food is produced. From food, life (thence) mind, (thence) the reals (the five elements); (thence) the worlds; (thence the rituals) in the rituals, immortality.

9. He who is all-knowing and all-wise, whose austerity consists of knowledge, from him are born this Brahmā (*Hiraṇya-garbha*), name-shape and food.

Section 2

1. This is that truth. The works which the sages saw in the hymns are variously spread forth in the three vedas. Perform them constantly, ye lovers of truth. This is your path to the world of good deeds.

2. When the flame (which) moves after the fire has been kindled, then one should throw with faith his oblations between the two portions of melted butter.

3. He whose agnihotra sacrifice is not followed by the sacrifice of the new moon and of the full moon, by the four months' sacrifice, by the ritual (performed in the harvest season) is without guests, without oblations, without the ceremony to all the gods or gives offerings contrary to rule, (such conduct) destroys his worlds till the seventh.

4. The seven moving tongues of fire are the black, the terrific, the swift as mind, the very red, the very smoky-coloured, the spark blazing, the all-shaped goddess.

5. Whosoever performs works, makes offerings when these (tongues) are shining and at the proper time, these (offerings) in the form of the rays of the sun lead him to that (world) where the one lord of the gods abides.

6. The radiant offerings invite him with the words, "come, come," and carry the sacrificer by the rays of the sun, honouring him and saluting him with pleasing words: "This is your holy world of Brahmā won through good deeds."

7. Unsteady, verily, are these boats of the eighteen sacrificial forms, which are said to be inferior karma. The deluded who delight in this as leading to good, fall again into old age and death.

8. Abiding in the midst of ignorance, wise in their own esteem, thinking themselves to be learned, fools, afflicted with troubles, go about like blind men led by one who is himself blind.

9. The immature, living manifoldly in ignorance, think "we have accomplished our aim." Since those who perform rituals do not understand (the truth) because of attachment, therefore they sink down, wretched, when their worlds (i.e. the fruits of their merits) are exhausted.

10. These deluded men, regarding sacrifices and works of merits as most important, do not know any other good. Having enjoyed in the high place of heaven won by good deeds, they enter again this world or a still lower one.

11. But those who practise austerity and faith in the forest, the tranquil knowers who live the life of a mendicant, depart freed from sin, through the door of the sun to where dwells the immortal, imperishable person.

12. Having scrutinised the worlds won by works, let a Brāhmaṇa arrive at non-attachment. The (world) that is not made is not (won) by what is done. For the sake of this knowledge, let him only approach, with sacrificial fuel in hand, a teacher who is learned in the scriptures and established in Brahman.

13. Unto him who has approached in due form, whose mind is tranquil and who has attained peace, let the knowing (teacher) teach in its very truth that knowledge about Brahman by which one knows the Imperishable person, the true.

Chapter II, Section 1

1. This is the truth. As from a blazing fire, sparks of like form issue forth by the thousands, even so, O beloved, many kinds of beings issue forth from the immutable and they return thither too.

2. Divine and formless is the person. He is without and within, unborn, without breath and without mind, pure and higher than the highest immutable.

3. From him are born life, mind, all the sense-organs (also) ether, air, light, water and earth, the supporter of all.

4. Fire is His head, His eyes are the sun and the moon, the regions of space are His ears, His speech the revealed Vedas; air is His life and His heart the world. Out of His feet the earth (is born); indeed He is the self of all beings.

5. From him (proceeds) fire whose fuel is the sun; from the moon, the rain; herbs on the earth, (nourished by them) the male fire pours seed in the female, thus are creatures produced from the person.

6. From him are born the *ṛc* (verses), the *sāman* (chants), the *yajus* (formulas), the rites of initiation, all the sacrifices, ceremonies and sacrificial gifts, the year too, and the sacrificer, and the worlds where the moon purifies and where the sun (shines).

7. From him also the gods are born in manifold ways, the celestials, men, cattle, birds, the in-breath and the out-breath, rice and barley, austerity, faith, truth, chastity and the law.

8. From him come forth the seven life-breaths, the seven flames, their fuel, the seven oblations, these seven worlds in which move the life-breaths, seven and seven which dwell in the secret place (of the heart).

9. From him, all the seas and the mountains, from him flow rivers of every kind; from him are all herbs and their juice too; by which, together with the elements, the inner soul is upheld.

10. The person himself is all this, work, austerity and Brahmā beyond death. He who knows that which is set in the secret place (of the heart), he, here on earth, O beloved, cuts asunder the knot of ignorance.

Section 2

1. Manifest, well-fixed, moving, verily, in the secret place (of the heart) such is the great support. In it is centred all this which moves, breathes and winks. Know that as being, as non-being, as the supreme object to be desired, as the highest beyond the reach of man's understanding.

2. What is luminous, what is subtler than the subtle, in which are centred all the worlds and those that dwell in them, that is the imperishable *Brahman*. That is life, that is speech and mind. That is true, that is immortal, O beloved, that is to be known, know (that).

3. Taking as the bow the great weapons of the Upaniṣads, one should place in it the arrow sharpened by meditation. Drawing it with a mind engaged in the contemplation of that (*Brahman*), O beloved, know that Imperishable *Brahman* as the target.

4. The syllable *aum* is the bow: one's self, indeed, is the arrow. *Brahman* is spoken of as the target of that. It is to be hit without making a mistake. Thus one becomes united with it as the arrow (becomes one with the target).

5. He in whom the sky, the earth and the interspace are woven as also the mind along with all the vital breaths, know him alone as the one self. Dismiss other utterances. This is the bridge to immortality.

6. Where the arteries of the body are brought together like the spokes in the centre of a wheel, within it (this self, moves about) becoming manifold. Meditate on *aum* as the self. May you be successful in crossing over to the farther shore of darkness.

7. He who is all-knowing, all-wise, whose is this greatness on the earth, in the divine city of Brahmā, in the ether (of the heart) is that self-established.

8. He consists of mind and is the leader of life and body and is seated in food (*i.e.*, the body) controlling the heart. The wise perceive clearly by the knowledge (of *Brahman*) the blissful immortal which shines forth.

9. The knot of the heart is cut, all doubts are dispelled and his deeds terminate, when He is seen—the higher and the lower.

10. In the highest golden sheath is *Brahman* without stain, without parts; Pure is it, the light of lights. That is what the knowers of self know.

11. The sun shines not there, nor the moon and stars, these lightnings shine not, where then could this fire be? Everything shines only after that shining light. His shining illumines all this world.

12. *Brahman*, verily, is this immortal. In front is *Brahman*, behind is *Brahman*, to the right and to the left. It spreads forth below and above. *Brahman*, indeed, is this universe. It is the greatest.

Chapter III, Section 1

1. Two birds, companions (who are) always united, cling to the self-same tree. Of these two, the one eats the sweet fruit and the other looks on without eating.

2. On the self-same tree, a person immersed (in the sorrows of the world) is deluded and grieves on account of his helplessness. When he sees the other, the Lord who is worshipped and his greatness, he becomes freed from sorrow.

3. When a seer sees the creator of golden hue, the Lord, the Person, the source of Brahmā, then being a knower, shaking off good and evil and free from stain, he attains supreme equality with the lord.

4. Truly it is life that shines forth in all beings. Knowing him, the wise

man does not talk of anything else. Sporting in the self, delighting in the self, performing works, such a one is the greatest of the knowers of *Brahman.*

5. This self within the body, of the nature of light and pure, is attainable by truth, by austerity, by right knowledge, by the constant (practice) of chastity. Him, the ascetics with their imperfections done away, behold.

6. Truth alone conquers, not untruth. By truth is laid out the path leading to the gods by which the sages who have their desires fulfilled travel to where is that supreme abode of truth.

7. Vast, divine, of unthinkable form, subtler than the subtle. It shines forth, farther than the far, yet here near at hand, set down in the secret place (of the heart) (as such) even here it is seen by the intelligent.

8. He is not grasped by the eye nor even by speech nor by other sense-organs, nor by austerity nor by work, but when one's (intellectual) nature is purified by the light of knowledge then alone he, by meditation, sees Him who is without parts.

9. The subtle self is to be known by thought in which the senses in five different forms have centred. The whole of men's thought is pervaded by the senses. When it (thought) is purified, the self shines forth.

10. Whatever world a man of purified nature thinks of in his mind and whatever desires he desires, all these worlds and all these desires he attains. Therefore, let him who desires prosperity worship the knower of the self.

Section 2

1. He knows that supreme abode of *Brahman,* wherein founded, the world shines brightly. The wise men, who, free from desires, worship the Person, pass beyond the seed (of rebirth).

2. He who entertains desires, thinking of them, is born (again) here and there on account of his desires. But of him who has his desire fully satisfied, who is a perfected soul, all his desires vanish even here (on earth).

3. This self cannot be attained by instruction nor by intellectual power nor even through much hearing. He is to be attained by the one whom (the self) chooses. To such a one the self reveals his own nature.

4. This self cannot be attained by one without strength nor through heedlessness nor through austerity without an aim. But he who strives by these means, if he is a knower, this self of his enters the abode of *Brahman.*

5. Having attained Him, the seers (who are) satisfied with their knowledge (who are) perfected souls, free from passion, tranquil, having attained the omnipresent (self) on all sides, those wise, with concentrated minds, enter into the All itself.

6. The ascetics who have ascertained well the meaning of the Vedānta knowledge, who have purified their natures through the path of renunciation, they (dwelling) in the worlds of Brahmā, at the end of time, being one with the immortal, are all liberated.

7. Gone are the fifteen parts to their (respective) supports (the elements) and all the gods (the sense-organs) into their corresponding deities. One's deeds and the self, consisting of understanding, all become one in the Supreme Immutable Being.

8. Just as the flowing rivers disappear in the ocean casting off name and shape, even so the knower, freed from name and shape, attains to the divine person, higher than the high.

9. He, verily, who knows the Supreme *Brahman* becomes *Brahman* himself. In his family, no one who does not know *Brahman*, will be born. He crosses over sorrow. He crosses over sins. Liberated from the knots of the secret place (of the heart), he becomes immortal.

10. This very (doctrine) is declared in the verse. Those who perform the rites, who are learned in scriptures, who are well-established in *Brahman*, who offer of themselves oblations to the sole seer (a form of fire) with faith, to them alone one may declare this knowledge of *Brahman* (to them alone), by whom the rite (of carrying fire) on the head has been performed, according to rule.

11. This is the truth. The seer Aṅgiras declared it before. Let none who has not performed the rite read this. Salutation to the great seers. Salutation to the great seers.

3

BHAGAVAD-GITA

The Bhagavad-Gita *is the ·best known and best loved of Indian books. It is part of the enormous epic poem the* Mahabharata, *which describes the rivalry of two families of royal cousins, the Pandavas and the Kauravas. At the beginning of the* Gita *the good Pandava brothers are about to join battle with the wicked Kauravas who have usurped their kingdom. Arjuna, the Pandava hero, has Sri Krishna, an incarnation of the god Vishnu, as his unarmed charioteer. Surveying the battlelines and seeing the en-*

The Bhagavad Gita, Chs. 2–12, Swami Nikhilananda, trans. (New York: Ramakrishna-Vivekananda Center, 1944), pp. 14–146. Reprinted from *The Bhagavad Gita,* trans. by Swami Nikhilananda, by his permission.

emy ranks filled with his friends and relatives, Arjuna throws down his bow and declares that he would rather be killed than to slay so many kinsmen. The Gita records the dialogue in which Sri Krishna explains why Arjuna should follow his dharma *or vocation as a warrior. Sri Krishna does not confine himself to the immediate context but explains the nature of action, the goal of human life, the various yogas whereby man can realize union with the God-head, and reveals the vision of his Divine Form to Arjuna. At the end of the Gita Arjuna is prepared to undertake the battle as his duty.*

The Bhagavad-Gita is eclectic, including doctrines developed in several earlier schools. If this has led philosophers to charge it with inconsistency, it has also increased its popularity as a devotional manual for it contains, as a consequence, teachings appropriate for and appealing to a very wide audience. In it can be found the non-dualist metaphysics of the Upanishads, the Sankhya dualism of spirit and matter, and the religious dualism of a devotional theism. The Gita teaches that union with the Divine may be gained by the yoga of devotion and the yoga of selfless action as well as by the Upanishadic yoga of knowledge. It teaches the necessity of renunciation but emphasizes that the performance of one's worldly duties in the proper spirit will bring salvation. The Gita's synthesis of these diverse doctrines would be endorsed by most modern Hindus.

As with most Hindu scriptures, scholars have difficulty in estimating the date of composition for the Bhagavad-Gita. However, most would acknowledge that it was probably written some time between 500 B.C. and A.D. 100. Traditionally the Gita along with the rest of the Mahabharata has been credited to the poet Vyasa to whom all the Puranas and the editing of the Vedas are also attributed. Chapters II through XII of its eighteen chapters are here given in Swami Nikhilananda's translation.

THE WAY OF ULTIMATE REALITY

1. SANJAYA SAID: To Arjuna, who was thus overwhelmed with pity, and whose troubled eyes were filled with tears, Madhusudana spoke these words:

2. THE LORD SAID: In this crisis, O Arjuna, whence comes such lowness of spirit, unbecoming to an Āryan, dishonourable, and an obstacle to the attaining of heaven?

3. Do not yield to unmanliness, O son of Prithā. It does not become you. Shake off this base faint-heartedness and arise, O scorcher of enemies!

4. ARJUNA SAID: But how, O Destroyer of Madhu, O Slayer of enemies, can I fight with arrows on the battle-field against Bhishma and Drona, who are worthy of my worship?

5. It would be better, indeed, to live on alms in this world rather than to

slay these high-souled teachers. But if I kill them, even here I shall enjoy wealth and desires stained with their blood.

6. We do not know which would be the better for us: that we should conquer them or they should conquer us. Arrayed against us stand the very sons of Dhrītarāshtra, after slaying whom we should not wish to live.

7. Overpowered in the very essence of my being by this evil of commiseration, my mind confused about dharma, I supplicate You: tell me in sooth which is the better. I am Your disciple. Instruct me, who have taken refuge in You.

8. Indeed, I see naught to destroy the grief that is drying up my very senses—even the attainment of unrivalled and flourishing dominion on earth and lordship over the gods in heaven.

9. SANJAYA SAID: Having spoken thus to Hrishikeśa, Arjuna, scorcher of foes, said to Him, "I will not fight," and fell silent.

10. O Dhrītarāshtra, to him grieving in the midst of the two armies Hrishikeśa, smiling, spoke these words:

11. THE LORD SAID: You have been mourning for those who should not be mourned for; yet you speak words of wisdom. Neither for the living nor for the dead do the wise grieve.

12. Never was there a time when I did not exist, nor you, nor these kings of men. Never will there be a time hereafter when any of us shall cease to be.

13. Even as the embodied Self passes, in this body, through the stages of childhood, youth, and old age, so does It pass into another body. Calm souls are not bewildered by this.

14. Notions of heat and cold, of pain and pleasure, arise, O son of Kunti, only from contact of the senses with their objects. They come and go; they are impermanent. Endure them, O Bhārata.

15. That calm man who remains unchanged in pain and pleasure, whom these cannot disturb, alone is able, O greatest of men, to attain immortality.

16. The unreal never is. The Real never ceases to be. The conclusion about these two is truly perceived by the seers of Truth.

17. That by which all this is pervaded know to be imperishable. None can cause the destruction of that which is immutable.

18. Only the bodies, of which this eternal, imperishable, incomprehensible Self is the indweller, are said to have an end. Fight, therefore, O Bhārata.

19. He who looks on the Self as the slayer, and he who looks on the Self as the slain—neither of these apprehends aright. The Self slays not nor is slain.

20. It is never born, nor does It ever die, nor, having once been, does It again cease to be. Unborn, eternal, permanent, and primeval, It is not slain when the body is slain.

21. He who knows the Self to be indestructible, eternal, unborn, and immutable—how can that man, O son of Prithā, slay or cause another to slay?

22. Even as a person casts off worn-out clothes and puts on others that are new, so the embodied Self casts off worn-out bodies and enters into others that are new.

23. Weapons cut It not; fire burns It not; water wets It not; the wind does not wither It.

24. This Self cannot be cut nor burnt nor wetted nor withered. Eternal, all-pervading, unchanging, immovable, the Self is the same for ever.

25. This Self is said to be unmanifest, incomprehensible, and unchangeable. Therefore, knowing It to be so, you should not grieve.

26. But if you think the Self repeatedly comes into being and dies, even then, O mighty one, you should not grieve for It.

27. For to that which is born, death is certain, and to that which is dead, birth is certain. Therefore you should not grieve over the unavoidable.

28. All beings are unmanifest in their beginning, O Bhārata, manifest in their middle state, and unmanifest again in their end. Why, then, lament for them?

29. Some look on the Self as a wonder; some speak of It as a wonder; some hear of It as a wonder; still others, though hearing, do not understand It at all.

30. The Self, which dwells in all bodies, can never be slain, O Bhārata. Wherefore you should not mourn for any creature.

31. Considering, also, your own dharma, you should not waver; for to a kshatriya nothing is better than a righteous war.

32. Happy indeed are the kshatriyas, O Pārtha, to whom comes such a war, offering itself unsought, opening the gate to heaven.

33. But if you refuse to wage this righteous war, then, renouncing your own dharma and honour, you will certainly incur sin.

34. People, too, will recount for ever your infamy. And to a man who has been honoured, dishonour is worse than death.

35. The great warriors will think you have withdrawn from the battle through fear; and you will go down in the esteem of those who have thought much of you.

36. Your enemies will speak many a word that should not be uttered, scorning your prowess. Could anything be more bitter than that?

37. If you are killed in the battle, you will go to heaven; if you win, you will enjoy the earth. Therefore arise, O son of Kunti, resolved to fight.

38. Regarding alike pleasure and pain, gain and loss, success and defeat, prepare yourself for battle. Thus you will incur no sin.

39. What has been declared to you is the wisdom of Ultimate Reality. Now listen to the wisdom of yoga, armed with which, O son of Prithā, you will break through the bonds of karma.

40. In this no effort is ever lost and no harm is ever done. Even very little of this dharma saves a man from the Great Fear.

41. In this, O scion of Kuru, there is only one resolute and unwavering

thought; but the thoughts of the irresolute are many-branched and unending.

42–44. O Pārtha, no resolute and unwavering thought is formed in the minds of those who are deeply attached to pleasure and power; who allow their discrimination to be stolen away by the flowery words of the unwise; who permit their souls to be ridden with desires; who regard the attainment of heaven as the highest goal; and who take great delight in quoting the panegyric texts of the Vedas and declare that besides these there is nothing. These texts promise rebirths as the reward of their action and lay down specific rites for the attainment of pleasure and power.

45. The Vedas deal with the three gunas. Be free, O Arjuna, from the three gunas. Be free from the pairs of opposites. Be always established in sattva. Do not try to acquire what you lack or preserve what you have. Be established in the Self.

46. To the enlightened Brāhmin all the Vedas are of as much use as a pond when there is everywhere a flood.

47. To work, alone, you are entitled, never to its fruit. Neither let your motive be the fruit of action, nor let your attachment be to non-action.

48. Being established in yoga, O Dhananjaya, perform your actions, casting off attachment and remaining even-minded both in success and in failure. This evenness is called yoga.

49. Far inferior, indeed, is mere action, O Dhananjaya, to action performed with evenness of mind. Seek refuge in this evenness. Wretched are they who work for results.

50. Endued with evenness of mind, one casts off, in this very life, both good deeds and evil deeds. Therefore strive for yoga. Yoga is skill in action.

51. The wise, of even mind, renounce the fruit of action. Freed from the fetters of birth, they attain the state that is beyond all evil.

52. When your mind has crossed the slough of delusion, you will achieve indifference regarding things already heard and things yet to be heard.

53. When your mind—now perplexed by what you have heard—will stand firm and steady in the Self, then you will have attained yoga.

54. ARJUNA SAID: What, O Keśava, is the description of the man of steady wisdom merged in samādhi? How does the man of steady wisdom speak, how sit, how move?

55. THE LORD SAID: O Pārtha, when a man completely casts off all the desires of the mind, his Self finding satisfaction in Itself alone, then he is called a man of steady wisdom.

56. He who is not perturbed by adversity, who does not long for happiness, who is free from attachment, fear, and wrath, is called a muni of steady wisdom.

57. He who is not attached to anything, who neither rejoices nor is vexed when he obtains good or evil—his wisdom is firmly fixed.

58. When he completely withdraws the senses from their objects, as a tortoise draws in its limbs, then his wisdom is firmly fixed.

59. The objects of the senses fall away from a man practising abstinence, but not the taste for them. But even the taste falls away when the Supreme is seen.

60. The turbulent senses, O son of Kunti, violently carry off the mind even of a wise man striving for perfection.

61. The yogi restrains them all and remains intent on Me. His wisdom is steady whose senses are under control.

62–63. When a man dwells on objects, he feels an attachment for them. Attachment gives rise to desire, and desire breeds anger.

From anger comes delusion; from delusion, the failure of memory; from the failure of memory, the ruin of discrimination; and from the ruin of discrimination the man perishes.

64. The man of self-control, moving among objects with his senses under restraint, and free from attachment and hate, attains serenity of mind.

65. In that serenity there is an end of all sorrow; for the intelligence of the man of serene mind soon becomes steady.

66. The man whose mind is not under his control has no Self-knowledge and no contemplation either. Without contemplation he can have no peace; and without peace, how can he have happiness?

67. For even one of the roving senses, if the mind yields to it, carries away discrimination as a gale carries away a ship on the waters.

68. Therefore, O mighty Arjuna his wisdom is steady whose senses are completely restrained from their objects.

69. In that which is night to all beings, the man of self-control is awake; and where all beings are awake, there is night for the muni who sees.

70. Not the desirer of desires attains peace, but he into whom all desires enter as the waters enter into the ocean, which is full to the brim and grounded in stillness.

71. That man who lives completely free from desires, without longing, devoid of the sense of "I" and "mine," attains peace.

72. This is the Brāhmic state, O son of Pritha. Attaining it, one is no longer deluded. Being established therein even in the hour of death, one attains final liberation in Brahman.

Thus in the Bhagavad Gītā, the Essence of the Upanishads, the Science of Brahman, the Scripture of Yoga, the Dialogue between Sri Krishna and Arjuna, ends the Second Chapter, entitled:

THE WAY OF ULTIMATE REALITY

THE WAY OF ACTION

1. ARJUNA SAID: If You hold, O Janārdana, that knowledge is superior to action, why, then, O Keśava, do You engage me in this terrible action?

2. With these apparently contradictory words You seem to confuse my

understanding. Therefore tell me definitely that one thing by which I shall reach the Highest Goal.

3. THE LORD SAID: Even of yore, O sinless one, a twofold devotion was taught by Me to the world: devotion to knowledge for the contemplative and devotion to work for the active.

4. Not by merely abstaining from action does a man reach the state of actionlessness, nor by mere renunciation does he arrive at perfection.

5. Verily, no one can remain even for an instant without doing work. For, driven by the gunas born of Prakriti, everyone is made to act, in spite of himself.

6. He who restrains his organs of action, but continues to dwell in his mind on the objects of the senses, deludes himself and is called a hypocrite.

7. But he who restrains his senses with his mind and directs his organs of action to work, with no feeling of attachment—he, O Arjuna, is indeed superior.

8. Do your allotted action; for action is superior to inaction. And even the bare maintenance of your body will not be possible if you remain inactive.

9. The world becomes bound by action unless it be done for the sake of Sacrifice. Therefore, O son of Kunti, give up attachment and do your work for the sake of the Lord.

10. The Prajāpati, in the beginning, created men together with sacrifice, and said: "By this shall you multiply. Let this be the Cow of Plenty and yield unto you the milk of your desires.

11–12. "With sacrifice shall you nourish the gods; and may the gods nourish you. Thus nourishing one another, you will obtain the Highest Good.

"The gods, nourished by sacrifice, will bestow on you the enjoyments you desire." He is verily a thief who enjoys the things that they give without offering to them anything in return.

13. Good men, who eat the remnant of the sacrifice, are freed from all sins; but wicked men, who cook food only for themselves, verily eat sin.

14–15. From food all creatures are born; from rain food is produced; from sacrifice comes rain; sacrifice is born of action. Know that action arises from the Vedas, and the Vedas from the Imperishable. Therefore the all-pervading Vedas ever rest in sacrifice.

16. Thus was the wheel set in motion; and he who does not follow it, but takes delight in the senses and lives in sin, O Pārtha, lives in vain.

17. But verily, the man who rejoices in the Self and is satisfied with the Self and is content in the Self alone—he has nothing for which he should work.

18. He has no object to gain by what he does in this world, nor any to lose by what he leaves undone; nor is there anyone, among all beings, on whom he need depend for any object.

19. Therefore always do without attachment the work you have to do; for a man who does his work without attachment attains the Supreme.

20. Verily, by action alone men like Janaka attained perfection. Further, you should perform work with a view to guiding people along the right path.

21. Whatever a great man does, that others follow; whatever he sets up as a standard, that the world follows.

22. I have, O Pārtha, no duty; there is nothing in the three worlds that I have not gained and nothing that I have to gain. Yet I continue to work.

23. For should I not ever engage, unwearied, in action, O Pārtha, men would in every way follow in My wake.

24. If I should cease to work, these worlds would perish: I should cause the mixture of castes and destroy all these creatures.

25. As the ignorant act, attached to their work, O Bhārata, so should an enlightened man act, but without attachment, in order that he may set people on the right path.

26. Let no enlightened man unsettle the understanding of the ignorant, who are attached to action. He should engage them in action, himself performing it with devotion.

27. All work is performed by the gunas of Prakriti. But he whose mind is deluded by egotism thinks, "I am the doer."

28. But, O mighty Arjuna, he who knows the truth about the gunas and action, and what is distinct from them, holds himself unattached, perceiving that it is the gunas that are occupied with the gunas.

29. Those who are deluded by the gunas of Prakriti attach themselves to the actions that those gunas prompt. Nevertheless let no man who knows the whole unsettle the minds of the dull-witted, who know only a part.

30. Surrendering all action to Me, with mind intent on the Self, freeing yourself from longing and selfishness, fight—unperturbed by grief.

31. Those who, full of faith, ever follow this teaching of Mine and do not carp at Me—they too are released from their works.

32. But those who carp at My teaching and practise it not—know that such senseless men, blind to all wisdom, are doomed to destruction.

33. Even the man of knowledge acts in accordance with his own nature. All beings follow their nature; what can restraint do?

34. The love and hatred that the senses feel for their objects are inevitable. But let no one come under their sway; for they are one's enemies.

35. Better is one's own dharma, though imperfectly performed, than the dharma of another well performed. Better is death in the doing of one's own dharma: the dharma of another is fraught with peril.

36. ARJUNA SAID: But under what compulsion does a man commit sin, O Vārshneya, in spite of himself and driven, as it were, by force?

37. THE LORD SAID: It is desire, it is wrath, which springs from rajas. Know that this is our enemy here, all-devouring and the cause of all sin.

38. As fire is concealed by smoke, as a mirror by dust, as an unborn babe by the womb, so is Knowledge concealed by ignorance.

39. Enveloped is Knowledge, O son of Kunti, by the insatiable fire of desire, which is the constant foe of the wise.

40. The senses, the mind, and the understanding are said to be its seat; through these it veils Knowledge and deludes the embodied soul.

41. Therefore, O lord of the Bhāratas, control your senses at the outset and slay this foul destroyer of Knowledge and realization.

42–43. The senses are superior, they say; superior to the senses is the mind; superior to the mind is the understanding; superior to the understanding is the Self. Therefore know the Self, who is superior to the understanding, control the self by the Self, and destroy, O mighty Arjuna, the enemy, who comes in the guise of desire and is hard to overcome.

Thus in the Bhagavad Gītā, the Essence of the Upanishads, the Science of Brahman, the Scripture of Yoga, the Dialogue between Sri Krishna and Arjuna, ends the Third Chapter, entitled:

THE WAY OF ACTION

THE WAY OF KNOWLEDGE

1. THE LORD SAID: This eternal yoga I taught to Vivasvat; Vivasvat taught it to Manu; and Manu taught it to Ikshvāku.

2. Thus handed down from one to another, it became known to the royal sages. But through long lapse of time, O destroyer of foes, this yoga has been lost to the world.

3. The same ancient yoga I have told you today; for you are My devotee and friend, and it is a supreme secret.

4. ARJUNA SAID: Later was Your birth, and earlier the birth of Vivasvat. How, then, am I to understand that You taught him in the beginning?

5. THE LORD SAID: Many a birth have I passed through, O Arjuna, and so have you. I know them all, but you know them not, O scorcher of foes.

6. Though I am unborn and eternal by nature, and though I am the Lord of all beings, yet, subjugating My Prakriti, I accept birth through My own māya.

7. Whenever there is a decline of dharma, O Bhārata, and a rise of adharma, I incarnate Myself.

8. For the protection of the good, for the destruction of the wicked, and for the establishment of dharma, I am born in every age.

9. Whoso knows, in the true light, My divine birth and action will not be born again when he leaves his body; he will attain Me, O Arjuna.

10. Freed from passion, fear, and anger, absorbed in Me, taking refuge in Me, and purified by the fire of knowledge, many have become one with My Being.

11. In whatsoever way men approach Me, even so do I reward them; for it is My path, O Pārtha, that men follow in all things.

12. Those who desire success in their works worship the gods here; for quickly, in this world of man, comes success from works.

13. The four castes were created by Me according to the division of gunas and karma. Though I am their Creator, yet know that I neither act nor change.

14. Action does not defile Me; nor do I long for its fruit. He who knows Me thus is not bound by his action.

15. Men of old who sought liberation knew this and did their work. Therefore do your work as the ancients did in former times.

16. Even the wise are perplexed as to what is action and what is inaction. Therefore I will tell you what action is, that you may know and be freed from evil.

17. For verily, one has to understand what action really is, and likewise what forbidden action is, and also what inaction is. Hard to understand is the way of action.

18. He who sees inaction in action, and action in inaction, he is wise among men, he is a yogi, and he has performed all action.

19. He whose undertakings are all free from desires and self-will, and whose works are consumed in the fire of Knowledge—he, by the wise, is called a sage.

20. Giving up attachment to the fruit of action, ever content, and dependent on none, though engaged in work, he does no work at all.

21. Free from desire, with body and mind controlled, and surrendering all possessions, he incurs no sin through mere bodily activity.

22. Satisfied with what comes to him without any effort on his part, rising above the pairs of opposites; free from envy, and even-minded in success and failure, though acting, he is not bound.

23. The works of a man whose attachment is gone, who is free, and whose mind is established in Knowledge, melt away entirely, being done as for a yajna.

24. To him Brahman is the offering and Brahman is the oblation, and it is Brahman who offers the oblation in the fire of Brahman. Brahman alone is attained by him who thus sees Brahman in action.

25. Some yogis offer oblations to the devas alone, while others in the fire of Brahman offer the self by the self.

26. Some offer oblations of hearing and the other senses in the fires of restraint; and some offer sound and other sensations in the fires of their senses.

27. Some, again, offer all the actions of the senses and the functions of the prāna as oblations in the fire of self-control, kindled by knowledge.

28. Some, likewise, offer as oblations their wealth, austerity, and yoga; while others, of disciplined minds and severe vows, offer their scriptural study and knowledge.

29. Some, again, constantly practising the regulation of prāna, offer the oblation of prāna into apāna, and apāna into prāna, or stop the passage of both

prāna and apāna. Yet others, restricting their food, offer their prānas in the prānas.

30-31. All these know what sacrifice means, and by sacrifice are their sins consumed. Eating of the amrita, the remnant of a sacrifice, they go to the Eternal Brahman. This world is not for him who makes no sacrifice, O best of the Kurus, much less the other.

32. Thus many kinds of sacrifice are strewn through the pages of the Vedas; know them all to be born of action, and you will be free.

33. The Knowledge Sacrifice is superior to all material sacrifices, O scorcher of foes; for all works, without exception, culminate in Knowledge.

34. Learn it by prostration, by inquiry, and by service. The wise, who have seen the Truth, will teach you that Knowledge.

35. When you have known it, O Pāndava, you will not again fall into delusion; and through it you will see all beings in your Self and also in Me.

36. Even if you are the most sinful of sinners, yet by the raft of Knowledge alone will you be borne over all sin.

37. As a fire, well kindled, reduces wood to ashes, so, O Arjuna, does the fire of Knowledge reduce all works to ashes.

38. Verily, there exists no purifier on earth equal to Knowledge. A man who becomes perfect in yoga finds it within himself in course of time.

39. He who is full of faith and zeal and has subdued his senses obtains Knowledge; having obtained Knowledge, he soon attains the Supreme Peace.

40. But the man who is ignorant and without faith and always doubting goes to ruin. Not this world nor the world beyond nor happiness is for the doubting soul.

41. Works do not bind the man, O Dhananjaya, who relinquishes action through yoga, whose doubts are destroyed by Knowledge, and who is self-possessed.

42. Therefore with the sword of Knowledge cut asunder this doubt about the Self, born of ignorance and residing in your heart, and devote yourself to yoga. Arise, O Bhārata!

Thus in the Bhagavad Gītā, the Essence of the Upanishads, the Science of Brahman, the Scripture of Yoga, the Dialogue between Sri Krishna and Arjuna, ends the Fourth Chapter, entitled:

THE WAY OF KNOWLEDGE

THE WAY OF RENUNCIATION

1. ARJUNA SAID: You praise, O Krishna, the renunciation of works, and also yoga. Tell me for certain which of these two is the better.

2. THE LORD SAID: Both renunciation and yoga lead to the Highest Good; but of the two, performance of action is superior to renunciation of action.

3. He who neither hates nor desires may be known as constantly practising renunciation; for, free from the pairs of opposites, O mighty Arjuna, he is easily freed from bondage.

4. It is children, and not the wise, that speak of the path of knowledge and the path of action as distinct. He who is firmly set on one reaches the end of both.

5. The state reached by men of renunciation is reached by men of action too. He who sees that the way of renunciation and the way of action are one—he truly sees.

6. But renunciation of action, O mighty Arjuna, is hard to attain without performance of action; the sage, purified by devotion to action, quickly reaches Brahman.

7. He who is devoted to yoga and is pure in mind, who has conquered his body and subdued his senses, who has realized his Self as the Self of all beings—he is undefiled though he acts.

8–9. "I do nothing at all," thinks the yogi, the knower of Truth; for in seeing, hearing, touching, smelling, and tasting; in walking, breathing, and sleeping;

In speaking, emitting, and seizing; in opening and closing the eyes, he is assured that it is only the senses busied with their objects.

10. He who works without attachment, resigning his actions to Brahman, is untainted by sin, as a lotus-leaf by water.

11. Only with the body, the mind, the understanding, and the senses do the yogis act, without attachment, for the purification of the heart.

12. A selfless man who has renounced the fruit of his action attains peace, born of steadfastness. But the man who is not selfless and who is led by desire is attached to the fruit and therefore bound.

13. The embodied soul who has subdued his senses, having renounced all actions with a discerning mind, dwells happily in the city of nine gates, neither working nor causing work to be done.

14. Neither agency nor objects does the Supreme Spirit create for the world, nor does It bring about union with the fruit of action. It is Nature that does all this.

15. Nor does the all-pervading Spirit take on the sin or the merit of any. Knowledge is veiled in ignorance, and thereby mortals are deluded.

16. But for those in whom this ignorance is destroyed by the Knowledge of the Self, that Knowledge, like the sun, reveals the Supreme.

17. Fixing their minds in Him, at one with Him, abiding in Him, realizing Him alone as the Supreme Goal, they reach a state from which there is no return, their sins having been destroyed by their Knowledge.

18. The wise see the same in all—whether it be a brāhmin endowed with learning and humility, or a cow or an elephant or a dog or an outcaste.

19. Those whose minds are thus set on sameness have even here over-

come birth. Brahman is untainted and is the same in all; therefore in Brahman they rest.

20. He who knows Brahman and is established in It, he who is un-deluded and is steady of mind—he neither rejoices when experiencing what is pleasant nor is distressed when experiencing what is unpleasant.

21. His heart being unattached to outer objects, he finds the joy that is in the Self; his heart being devoted to the contemplation of Brahman, he en-joys undying bliss.

22. For the enjoyments that arise from contact with objects are only sources of pain. They have a beginning and an end, O son of Kunti, and the wise find no delight in them.

23. He who is able to withstand the force of lust and anger even here before he quits the body—he is a yogi, he is a happy man.

24. The yogi who is happy within, who rejoices within, and who is illumined within attains freedom in Brahman, himself becoming one with Brahman.

25. With sins destroyed, doubts dispelled, senses controlled, and devot-ing themselves to the welfare of all beings, the sages attain freedom in Brah-man.

26. Those who are free from lust and anger, who have subdued their minds and realized the Self—those sannyāsis, both here and hereafter, attain freedom in Brahman.

27–28. Shutting out all external objects; fixing the gaze of his eyes be-tween his brows; equalizing the outward and inward breaths moving in his nostrils; controlling his senses, mind, and understanding; being ever bent on liberation; ridding himself of desire, fear, and anger—such a man of contem-plation is indeed always free.

29. And having known Me, who am the Dispenser of all sacrifices and austerities, the Great Lord of all worlds, the Friend of all beings, he attains Peace.

Thus in the Bhagavad Gītā, the Essence of the Upanishads, the Science of Brahman, the Scripture of Yoga, the Dialogue between Sri Krishna and Arjuna, ends the Fifth Chapter entitled:

THE WAY OF RENUNCIATION

THE WAY OF MEDITATION

1. THE LORD SAID: He who does the work he ought to do and does not seek its fruit—he is a sannyāsi and he is a yogi: not he who does no work and maintains no sacred fire.

2. Know that what they call renunciation is the same as yoga, O Pān-dava; for no one who has not renounced his desire can ever become a yogi.

3. For a sage who wants to attain yoga, action is said to be the means; but when he has attained yoga, serenity is said to be the means.

4. When a man has no attachment to the objects of the senses or to works, and when he has wholly renounced his will, he is said to have attained yoga.

5. Let a man be lifted up by his own self; let him not lower himself; for he himself is his friend, and he himself is his enemy.

6. To him who has conquered himself by himself, his own self is a friend, but to him who has not conquered himself, his own self is hostile, like an external enemy.

7. He who has conquered himself and is serene in mind is constantly absorbed in the Supreme Self, alike in heat and cold, pleasure and pain, and honour and dishonour.

8. He is said to be a steadfast yogi whose heart, through knowledge and realization, is filled with satisfaction, who, having conquered his senses, never vacillates, and to whom a clod, a stone, and gold are the same.

9. He who has equal regard for well-wishers, friends, and foes; for those who are related or indifferent to him; for the impartial and the malicious; and even for the righteous and the sinful—he stands supreme.

10. A yogi should always try to concentrate his mind, retiring into solitude and living alone, having subdued his mind and body and got rid of his desires and possessions.

11–12. In a clean spot having fixed his seat—a firm seat, neither too high nor too low—and having spread over it kuśagrass, and then a deer skin, and then a cloth,

And sitting there, he should practise yoga for the purification of the self, restraining the activities of his mind and senses, and bringing his thoughts to a point.

13. He should sit firm, holding his body, neck, and head erect and still, and gaze steadily at the tip of his nose, without looking around.

14. Completely serene and fearless, steadfast in the vow of a brahmachari, disciplined in mind, and ever thinking on Me, he should sit in yoga, regarding Me as his Supreme Goal.

15. Keeping himself ever steadfast in this manner, the yogi of subdued mind attains the Peace abiding in Me—the Peace that culminates in Nirvāna.

16. Yoga is not for him who eats too much nor for him who eats too little. It is not for him, O Arjuna, who sleeps too much nor for him who sleeps too little.

17. For him who is temperate in his food and recreation, temperate in his exertion at work, temperate in sleep and waking, yoga puts an end to all sorrows.

18. When the well-controlled mind rests in the Self alone, free from longing for objects, then is one said to have attained yoga.

19. "As a lamp in a windless place does not flicker"—that is the figure used for the disciplined mind of a yogi practising concentration on the Self.

20–23. That in which the mind, restrained by the practice of concentration, rests quiescent; that in which, seeing the Self through the self, one rejoices in one's own Self;

That in which one knows the boundless joy beyond the reach of the senses and grasped only by the understanding; that in which being established, one never departs from Reality;

That on gaining which one thinks there is no greater gain, and wherein established one is not moved even by the heaviest of sorrows—

Let that be known as yoga, which is severance from the contact of pain. It is to be practised with perseverance and with an undaunted mind.

24–25. Renouncing entirely all the desires born of the will, drawing back by strength of mind the senses from every direction, let a man little by little attain tranquillity with the help of the buddhi armed with fortitude. Once the mind is established in the Self, he should think of nothing else.

26. Let him withdraw the fickle and unquiet mind from whatever causes it to wander away, and restore it to the control of the Self alone.

27. Supreme Bliss comes to the yogi whose mind is completely tranquil and whose passions are quieted, who is free from stain and who has become one with Brahman.

28. Thus making his self ever steadfast, the yogi, freed from sins, easily enjoys the touch of Brahman, which is exceeding bliss.

29. With the heart concentrated by yoga, viewing all things with equal regard, he beholds himself in all beings and all beings in himself.

30. He who sees Me everywhere and sees everything in Me, to him I am never lost, nor is he ever lost to Me.

31. He who, having been established in oneness, worships Me dwelling in all beings—that yogi, in whatever way he leads his life, lives in Me.

32. Him I hold to be the supreme yogi, O Arjuna, who looks on the pleasure and pain of all beings as he looks on them in himself.

33. ARJUNA SAID: This yoga, which You, O Madhusudana, have declared to be characterized by evenness—I do not see how it can long endure, because of the restlessness of the mind.

34. For the mind, O Krishna, is restless, turbulent, powerful, and obstinate. To control it is as hard, it seems to me, as to control the wind.

35. THE LORD SAID: Doubtless, O mighty Arjuna, the mind is restless and hard to control; but by practice and by detachment, O son of Kunti, it can be restrained.

36. Yoga is hard to attain, I think, by a man who cannot control himself; but it can be attained by him who has controlled himself and who strives by right means.

37. ARJUNA SAID: A man who is endowed with faith, but not with

steadfastness, and whose mind has wandered away from yoga—what end does he gain, O Krishna, having failed to obtain perfection in yoga?

38. Fallen from both, unsupported, and bewildered in the way leading to Brahman, does he not, O mighty Krishna, perish like a riven cloud?

39. You should completely dispel, O Krishna, this doubt of mine; for no one but You can destroy such a doubt.

40. THE LORD SAID: O Pārtha, there is no destruction for him either in this world or the next; no evil, My son, befalls a man who does good.

41. The man who has fallen away from yoga goes to the worlds of the righteous. Having lived there for unnumbered years, he is reborn in the home of the pure and the prosperous.

42. Or he is born in a family of yogis rich in wisdom. Verily, such a birth is hard to gain in this world.

43. There he comes in touch with the knowledge acquired in his former body, O son of the Kurus, and strives still further for perfection.

44. By that former practice alone he is led on in spite of himself. Even he who merely wishes to know of yoga rises superior to the performer of Vedic rites.

45. A yogi, striving diligently, is purified of all sins, and, becoming perfect through many births, reaches the Supreme Goal.

46. The yogi is greater than men of austerities, greater than men of knowledge, greater than men of action. Therefore become a yogi, O Arjuna.

47. And of all yogis, the one who worships Me with faith, his inmost self abiding in Me—him do I hold to be the most closely united with Me in yoga.

Thus in the Bhagavad Gītā, the Essence of the Upanishads, the Science of Brahman, the Scripture of Yoga, the Dialogue between Sri Krishna and Arjuna, ends the Sixth Chapter, entitled:

THE WAY OF MEDITATION

THE WAY OF REALIZATION

1. THE LORD SAID: Hear, O Pārtha, how, with your mind attached to Me, and taking refuge in Me, and practising yoga, you will without any doubt know Me in full.

2. I shall teach you in full both knowledge and experience, which being known, nothing more remains here for you to know.

3. Among thousands of men, one, here and there, strives for perfection; and of those who strive and succeed, one, perchance, knows Me in truth.

4. Earth, water, fire, air, ether, mind, understanding, and ego: such is the eightfold division of My nature.

5. This is My lower nature. But, different from it, know, O mighty

Arjuna, My higher nature—the Indwelling Spirit by which the universe is sustained.

6. Know that these two form the womb of all beings. I am the origin of the entire universe and also its dissolution.

7. There exists nothing whatever higher than I am, O Dhananjaya. All is strung on Me as a row of gems on a thread.

8. I am the savour of waters, O son of Kunti, the radiance of the sun and moon; I am the syllable Om in all the Vedas, the sound in ether, the manliness in man.

9. I am the sweet fragrance in earth and the brightness in fire. In all beings I am the life, and I am the austerity in ascetics.

10. Know Me, O son of Prithā, to be the Eternal Seed of all things that exist; I am the intelligence of the intelligent and the daring of the brave.

11. I am the strength of the strong, free from longing and attachment. I am, O lord of the Bhāratas, the desire in all beings that is not contrary to dharma.

12. And whatever things there be—of the nature of sattva, rajas, and tamas—know they are all from Me alone. I am not, however, in them; they are in Me.

13. Deluded by these threefold gunas constituting Nature, this whole world fails to recognize Me, who am above the gunas and immutable.

14. Verily, this divine māyā of Mine, consisting of the gunas, is hard to overcome. But those who take refuge in Me alone, shall cross over this māyā.

15. Evil-doers and the deluded and the vilest among men, deprived of knowledge by māyā and following the way of the asuras, do not worship Me.

16. Four types of virtuous men worship Me, O Arjuna: the man in distress, the man seeking knowledge, the man seeking enjoyment, and, O best of the Bhāratas, the man endowed with wisdom.

17. Of these, the wise man, ever steadfast and devoted to the One alone, is the best. For supremely dear am I to the man of wisdom, and he is dear to Me.

18. Noble indeed are they all; but the man endowed with wisdom I deem to be My very Self. For, steadfast in mind, he remains fixed in Me alone as the Supreme Goal.

19. At the end of many births the man of wisdom worships Me, realizing that Vāsudeva is all. Rare indeed is such a high-souled person.

20. But those whose discrimination has been led astray by various desires resort to other deities, following diverse rituals, constrained by their own natures.

21. Whatever may be the form a devotee seeks to worship with faith —in that form alone I make his faith unwavering.

22. Possessed of that faith, he worships that form and from it attains his desires, which are, in reality, granted by Me alone.

23. But finite is the result gained by these men of small minds. Those

who worship the deities go to the deities; those who worship Me come to Me.

24. Not knowing My supreme Nature, immutable and transcendent, foolish men think that I, the Unmanifest, am endowed with a manifest form.

25. Veiled by My māyā born of the gunas, I am not revealed to all. This deluded world knows Me not as the unborn and eternal.

26. I, O Arjuna, know the beings that are of the past, that are of the present, and that are to come; but Me no one knows.

27. All beings, from their very birth, O Bhārata, are deluded by the spell of the pairs of opposites arising from desire and aversion.

28. But the men of virtuous deeds, whose sin is ended, are free from the delusion of the pairs and worship Me with firm resolve.

29. Those who take refuge in Me to gain release from old age and death —they will come to know Brahman, they will come to know all about the individual soul, and all about action as well.

30. Those who know Me as the One that underlies all the elements, as the One that underlies all the gods, and as the One that sustains all the sacrifices, will, with steadfast mind, know Me even in the hour of death.

Thus in the Bhagavad Gītā, the Essence of the Upanishads, the Science of Brahman, the Scripture of Yoga, the Dialogue between Sri Krishna and Arjuna, ends the Seventh Chapter, entitled:

THE WAY OF REALIZATION

THE WAY TO THE IMPERISHABLE BRAHMAN

1–2. ARJUNA SAID: What is Brahman? What is the individual soul? And what is action, O Supreme Person? What is it that is said to underlie all the elements?

And what is it that is said to underlie all the gods? And who, O Madhusudana, sustains all the sacrifices, here in the body? And in what way? And how, again, are You to be known at the time of death by those who have practised self-control?

3. THE LORD SAID: Brahman is the Imperishable, the Supreme. Dwelling in each body, Brahman is called the individual soul. The offering of the oblation, which brings into existence all beings and supports them, is called action.

4. That which underlies all the elements is the perishable entity; and that which underlies all the gods is the Purusha, the Cosmic Spirit. And He who sustains all the sacrifices is Myself, here in the body, O best of men.

5. And whoso, at the time of death, leaves his body remembering Me alone and goes forth—he attains My being; concerning this there is no doubt.

6. For whatever object a man thinks of at the final moment, when he leaves his body—that alone does he attain, O son of Kunti, being ever absorbed in the thought thereof.

7. Therefore, at all times, constantly remember Me and fight. With your mind and understanding absorbed in Me, you will surely come to Me.

8. Engaged in the yoga of constant practice and not allowing the mind to wander away to anything else, he who meditates on the supreme, resplendent Purusha reaches Him, O son of Prithā.

9–10. He who, at the time of passing away, steady in mind, filled with love, and armed with the strength of yoga, well fixes his prāna between his brows and meditates on the omniscient and primal Being, the Ruler, the Dispenser of all, who is subtler than an atom, whose form is beyond comprehension, and who, like the glorious sun, is beyond all darkness—he who thus meditates reaches the resplendent Supreme Person.

11. I will now briefly describe to you that state which those who know the Vedas call the Imperishable, and into which enter the sannyāsis, self-controlled and freed from attachment, and in desire for which seekers lead the life of continence.

12–13. He who closes all the doors of the senses, confines the mind within the heart, draws the prāna into the head, and engages in the practice of yoga, uttering Om, the single syllable denoting Brahman, and meditates on Me—he who so departs, leaving the body, attains the Supreme Goal.

14. I am easy of access to that ever steadfast yogi who, O Pārtha, constantly meditates on Me and gives no thought to anything else.

15. Having come to Me, these high-souled men are no more subject to rebirth, which is transitory and the abode of pain; for they have reached the highest perfection.

16. The dwellers in all the worlds, from the realm of Brahmā downward, are subject to rebirth, O Arjuna; but for those who reach Me, O son of Kunti, there is no further return to embodiment.

17. Those who know that the day of Brahmā lasts a thousand aeons, and that the night of Brahmā lasts a thousand aeons again, are indeed the people who know day and night.

18. At the approach of the day all manifested objects come forth from the unmanifested, and at the approach of the night they merge again into that which is called the unmanifested.

19. The same multitude of beings, coming forth again and again, merge, in spite of themselves, O Pārtha, at the approach of the night, and remanifest themselves at the approach of the day.

20. But beyond this unmanifested there is yet another Unmanifested Eternal Being, who does not perish when all beings perish.

21. This Unmanifested is called the Imperishable; It is said to be the Ultimate Goal, from which those who reach It never come back. That is My Supreme Abode.

22. That Supreme Person, in whom all beings abide and by whom the entire universe is pervaded, can be attained, O Pārtha, by whole-souled devotion directed to Him alone.

23. Now I will tell you, O greatest of the Bhāratas, the time in which the yogis depart never to return, and also the time in which they depart to return.

24. Fire, light, day-time, the bright half of the moon, and the six months of the northward passage of the sun—taking this path, the knowers of Brahman go to Brahman.

25. Smoke, night, the dark half of the moon, and the six months of the southward passage of the sun—taking this path, the yogi reaches the lunar path and thence returns.

26. These two paths—the bright and the dark—are deemed to be the world's eternal paths. Following the one, a man does not come back, and following the other, he is reborn.

27. No yogi who understands these two paths is ever deluded. Therefore, O Arjuna, at all times be steadfast in yoga.

28. The yogi who knows this transcends all the rewards laid down for the study of the Vedas, for sacrifices, for austerities, for making gifts: he reaches the Supreme, Primal Abode.

Thus in the Bhagavad Gītā, the Essence of the Upanishads, the Science of Brahman, the Scripture of Yoga, the Dialogue between Sri Krishna and Arjuna, ends the Eighth Chapter entitled:

THE WAY TO THE IMPERISHABLE BRAHMAN

THE WAY OF THE SOVEREIGN WISDOM AND SOVEREIGN MYSTERY

1. THE LORD SAID: To you, O Arjuna, who do not carp, I will propound this, the greatest mystery of knowledge combined with realization, by understanding which you will be released from evil.

2. It is the sovereign science, the sovereign mystery, and the supreme purifier. It is perceived by direct experience, it accords with dharma, it is easy to practise, and it is imperishable.

3. Men without faith in this dharma do not attain Me, O dreaded Arjuna, but return to the path of the world fraught with death.

4. By Me, in My unmanifested form, are all things in this universe pervaded. All beings exist in Me, but I do not exist in them.

5. And yet the beings do not dwell in Me—behold, that is My divine mystery. My Spirit, which is the support of all beings and the source of all things, does not dwell in them.

6. As the mighty wind blowing everywhere ever rests in the ākāśa, know that in the same manner all beings rest in Me.

7. At the end of a cycle all beings, O son of Kunti, enter into My Prakriti, and at the beginning of a cycle I generate them again.

8. Controlling My own Prakriti, I send forth, again and again, all this multitude of beings, helpless under the sway of māyā.

9. And these acts, O Dhananjaya, do not bind Me; for I remain unattached to them, as one unconcerned.

10. Prakriti, under My guidance, gives birth to all things, moving and unmoving; and because of this, O son of Kunti, the world revolves.

11. Fools disregard Me when I assume a human form; for they are unaware of My higher nature as the Supreme Lord of all beings.

12. Being of the deceitful nature of fiends and demons, they cherish vain hopes, perform vain actions, pursue vain knowledge, and are devoid of judgement.

13. But the great-souled men, O Pārtha, who are endowed with the divine nature, worship Me with undisturbed minds, knowing that I am immutable and the origin of all beings.

14. Ever glorifying Me, always striving with self-control, remaining firm in their vows, bowing before Me, they worship Me with love and unwavering steadiness.

15. Others, again, offer the oblation of knowledge, and worship Me either as one with them or as distinct from them; and still others in various ways worship Me, whose form is the whole universe.

16. I am the sacrifice, I am the worship, I am the oblation to the manes, and I am cereal. I am the hymn, I am the melted butter, I am the fire, and I am the offering.

17. I am the father of this universe, the mother, the sustainer, and the grandsire. I am the knowable, the purifier, and the syllable Om. I am also the Rik, the Sāman, and the Yajus.

18. I am the goal and the support; the lord and the witness; the abode, the refuge, and the friend. I am the origin and the dissolution; the ground, the storehouse, and the imperishable seed.

19. I give heat; I hold back and send forth rain. I am immortality, O Arjuna, and also death. I am being and also non-being.

20. Those who know the three Vedas and drink the soma-juice and are purified from sin worship Me with sacrifices and pray for passage to heaven. They reach the holy world of Indra and enjoy in heaven the celestial pleasures of the gods.

21. Having enjoyed the vast heavenly world, they come back to the world of mortals when their merit is exhausted. Thus abiding by the injunctions of the three Vedas and desiring desires, they are subject to death and rebirth.

22. Those persons who worship Me, meditating on their identity with Me and ever devoted to Me—to them I carry what they lack and for them I preserve what they already have.

23. Even those devotees who, endowed with faith, worship other gods, worship Me alone, O son of Kunti, though in a wrong way.

24. For I alone am the Enjoyer and the Lord of all sacrifices. But these men do not know Me in reality; hence they fall.

25. Those who worship the gods go to the gods, those who worship the manes go to the manes, those who worship the spirits go to the spirits, and those who worship Me come to Me.

26. Whosoever offers Me, with devotion, a leaf, a flower, a fruit, or water—that I accept, the pious offering of the pure in heart.

27. Whatever you do, whatever you eat, whatever you offer in sacrifice, whatever you give away, and whatever you practise in the form of austerities, O son of Kunti—do it as an offering to Me.

28. Thus shall you be free from the bondage of actions, which bear good or evil results. With your mind firmly set on the yoga of renunciation, you shall become free and come to Me.

29. I am the same toward all beings; to Me there is none hateful or dear. But those who worship Me with devotion—they are in Me, and I too am in them.

30. Even the most sinful man, if he worships Me with unswerving devotion, must be regarded as righteous; for he has formed the right resolution.

31. He soon becomes righteous and attains eternal peace. Proclaim it boldly, O son of Kunti, that My devotee never perishes.

32. For those who take refuge in Me, O Pārtha, though they be of sinful birth—women, vaiśyas, and śudras—even they attain the Supreme Goal.

33. How much more, then, if they be holy brāhmins or royal seers devoted to God! Having come into this transitory, joyless world, worship Me.

34. Fix your mind on Me, be devoted to Me, sacrifice to Me, bow down to Me. Having thus disciplined yourself, and regarding Me as the Supreme Goal, you will come to Me.

Thus in the Bhagavad Gītā, the Essence of the Upanishads, the Science of Brahman, the Scripture of Yoga, the Dialogue between Sri Krishna and Arjuna, ends the Ninth Chapter, entitled:

THE WAY OF SOVEREIGN WISDOM AND SOVEREIGN MYSTERY

THE DIVINE MANIFESTATIONS

1. THE LORD SAID: Once more, O mighty Arjuna, listen to My supreme word, which I, from a desire for your welfare, will impart to you, to your great delight.

2. Neither the hosts of gods nor the great sages know My origin; for, in all respects, I am the source of the gods and the sages.

3. He who knows that I am unborn and without a beginning, and also that I am the Supreme Lord of the worlds—he, undeluded among mortals, is freed from all sins.

4-5. Intelligence, knowledge, non-delusion, forbearance, truth, self-control and calmness, pleasure and pain, birth and death, fear and fearlessness;

Non-injury, equanimity, contentment, austerity, charity, fame and obloquy—these different attributes of beings arise from Me alone.

6. The seven great sages and the four Manus of ancient times, endowed with My power, were born of My mind; and from them have sprung all the creatures in the world.

7. He who knows in truth this glory and power of Mine acquires unshakable devotion; of this there is no doubt.

8. I am the origin of all; from Me all things evolve. The wise know this and worship Me with all their heart.

9. With their thought fixed on Me, with their life absorbed in Me, enlightening one another about Me, and always conversing about Me, they derive satisfaction and delight.

10. On those who are ever devoted to Me and worship Me with love, I bestow the yoga of understanding, by which they come to Me.

11. Solely out of compassion for them, I, dwelling in their hearts, dispel with the shining lamp of wisdom the darkness born of ignorance.

12–13. ARJUNA SAID: You are the Supreme Brahman, the Supreme Abode, the Supreme Holiness. All the sages have declared You to be the eternal, self-luminous Person, the first of the gods, unborn and all-pervading; likewise have the divine sages Nārada, Asita, Devala, and Vyāsa proclaimed. So, too, have You said unto me.

14. I hold as true all that You have said to me, O Keśava. Verily, neither the gods nor the demons, O Lord, know Your manifestations.

15. You alone know Yourself through Yourself, O Supreme Person, O Creator of all beings, O Lord of all beings, O God of gods, O Ruler of the world.

16. You should indeed tell me, in full, of Your divine powers, whereby You pervade all the worlds and abide in them.

17. How may I know You, O Yogi, by constant meditation? In what various things, O Lord, are You to be contemplated by me?

18. Tell me once more, in detail, O Janārdana, of Your yoga-powers and glories; for I am never filled with hearing Your ambrosial words.

19. THE LORD SAID: I shall tell you now of My divine attributes, O best of the Kurus—only of those that are preeminent; for there is no limit to My extent.

20. I am the Self, O Guḍākeśa, seated in the hearts of all creatures. I am the beginning, the middle, and the end of all beings.

21. Of the Ādityas I am Vishnu; of lights I am the radiant sun. I am Marichi of the Maruts, and among the orbs of night I am the moon.

22. Of the Vedas I am the Sāman; of the gods I am Indra. Of the senses I am the mind, and in living beings I am intelligence.

23. Of the Rudras I am Śiva; of the Yakshas and Rākshasas I am Kuvera. Of the Vasus I am fire, and of mountains I am Meru.

24. Of priests, O Pārtha, know Me to be the chief, Brihaspati. Of generals I am Skanda; of reservoirs of water I am the ocean.

25. Of the great rishis I am Bhrigu, and of words I am the monosyllable "Om." Of sacrifices I am the sacrifice of japa; of immovable things I am the Himālaya.

26. Of all trees I am the aśvattha, and of the devarshis I am Nārada. Of the Gandharvas I am Chitraratha, and of the perfected ones I am the sage Kapila.

27. Of horses know Me to be Uchchaissravas, born of the amrita; of lordly elephants I am Airāvata, and of men I am the monarch.

28. Of weapons I am the thunderbolt; of cows I am Kāmadhuk. I am Kandarpa, the cause of offspring, and of serpents I am Vāsuki.

29. Of the Nāgas I am Ananta; of the dwellers in water I am Varuna. Of the Pitris I am Aryamā, and of those that practise self-control I am Yama.

30. Of the Daityas I am Prahlāda, and of measurers I am Time. Of beasts I am the lion, and of birds I am Garuda.

31. Of purifiers I am the wind; of warriors I am Rāma. Of fishes I am the shark, and of rivers I am the Ganges.

32. Of created things I am the beginning and the end and also the middle, O Arjuna. Of all sciences I am the Science of the Self, and in disputation I am reason.

33. Of letters I am the letter A, and of compound words I am the Dvanda. I Myself am inexhaustible Time, and I am the Dispenser facing everywhere.

34. I am all-seizing Death. I am the prosperity of those who are to be prosperous, and of female powers I am Glory, Fortune, Speech, Memory, Intelligence, Constancy, and Forbearance.

35. Of the Sāman hymns I am the Brihat-Sāman, and of metres I am the Gāyatri. Of months I am Mārgaśirsha, and of seasons I am the flowery spring.

36. I am the gambling of cheats; I am the vigour of the strong. I am victory; I am effort; I am the quality of sattva in the good.

37. Of the Yādavas I am Vāsudeva, and of the Pāndavas I am Arjuna. Of the sages I am Vyāsa, and of seers I am Uśanas the seer.

38. I am the rod of those that chastise and the statesmanship of those that conquer. Of secret things I am silence, and of the wise I am the wisdom.

39. And that which is the seed of all beings—that am I, O Arjuna. There is no being, whether moving or unmoving, that can exist without Me.

40. There is no end of My divine manifestations, O dreaded Arjuna. This is but a partial statement by Me of the multiplicity of My attributes.

41. Whatever glorious or beautiful or mighty being exists anywhere, know that it has sprung from but a spark of My splendour.

42. But what need is there of your acquiring this detailed knowledge, O Arjuna? With a single fragment of Myself I stand supporting the whole universe.

Thus in the Bhagavad Gītā, the Essence of the Upanishads, the Science of Brahman, the Scripture of Yoga, the Dialogue between Sri Krishna and Arjuna, ends the Tenth Chapter, entitled:

THE DIVINE MANIFESTATIONS

THE VISION OF THE UNIVERSAL FORM

1. ARJUNA SAID: Out of compassion for me You have spoken words of ultimate profundity concerning the Self, and they have dispelled my delusion.

2. I have learnt from You at length, O lotus-eyed Krishna, of the origin and dissolution of beings, and also of Your inexhaustible greatness.

3. As You have declared Yourself to be, O Supreme Lord—even so it is. Yet do I desire to see Your Iśvara-form, O Supreme Purusha.

4. If, O Lord, You think me able to behold it, then, O Master of yogis, reveal to me Your immutable Self.

5. THE LORD SAID: Behold My forms, O Pārtha, by the hundreds and the thousands—manifold and divine, various in shape and hue.

6. Behold the Ādityas and the Vasus and the Rudras and the twin Aświns and the Maruts; behold, O Bhārata, many wonders that no one has ever seen before.

7. Behold here today, O Gudākeśa, the whole universe, of the moving and the unmoving, and whatever else you desire to see, all concentrated in My body.

8. But with these eyes of yours you cannot see Me. I give you a divine eye; behold now My sovereign yoga-power.

9. SANJAYA SAID: Having spoken thus, O King, Hari, the great Lord of Yoga, revealed to Arjuna His supreme form as Iśvara:

10–11. With many faces and eyes, presenting many wondrous sights, bedecked with many celestial ornaments, armed with many divine uplifted weapons; wearing celestial garlands and vestments, anointed with divine perfumes, all-wonderful, resplendent, boundless, and with faces on all sides.

12. If the radiance of a thousand suns were to burst forth at once in the sky, that would be like the splendour of the Mighty One.

13. There, in the person of the God of gods, Arjuna beheld the whole universe, with its manifold divisions, all gathered together in one.

14. Then, overcome with wonder, his hair standing on end, Arjuna bowed his head to the Lord, joined his palms in salutation, and thus addressed Him:

15. ARJUNA SAID: In Thy body, O Lord, I behold all the gods and all

the diverse hosts of beings—the Lord Brahmā, seated on the lotus, and all the rishis and the celestial serpents.

16. I behold Thee with myriads of arms and bellies, with myriads of faces and eyes; I behold Thee, infinite in form, on every side, but I see not Thy end nor Thy middle nor Thy beginning, O Lord of the universe, O Universal Form!

17. I behold Thee on all sides glowing like a mass of radiance, with Thy diadem and mace and discus, blazing everywhere like burning fire and the burning sun, hard to look at, and passing all measure.

18. Thou art the Imperishable, the Supreme Being to be realized; Thou art the Supreme Support of the universe; Thou art the undying Guardian of the Eternal Dharma; Thou art, in my belief, the Primal Being.

19. I behold Thee as one without beginning, middle, or end; with infinite arms and immeasurable strength; with the sun and moon as Thine eyes; with Thy face shining like a blazing fire; and burning with Thy radiance the whole universe.

20. By Thee alone are filled all the space between heaven and earth, and all the quarters of the sky. O Mighty One, the three worlds behold Thy marvellous and appalling form and tremble with fear.

21. Into Thee enter these hosts of gods, and some in fear extol Thee with folded hands. And bands of Rishis and Siddhas exclaim, "May there be peace!" and praise Thee with splendid hymns.

22. The Rudras, Ādityas, Vasus, and Sādhyas; the Viśwas, Aświns, Maruts, and Ushmapās; and the hosts of Grandharvas, Yakshas, Asuras, and Siddhas—all behold Thee and are amazed.

23. Beholding Thy great form, O Mighty Lord, with myriads of mouths and eyes, with myriads of arms and thighs and feet, with myriads of bellies, and with myriads of terrible tusks—the worlds are affrighted, and so am I.

24. When I look upon Thy blazing form reaching to the skies and shining in many colours, when I see Thee with Thy mouths opened wide and Thy great eyes glowing bright, my inmost soul trembles in fear, and I find neither courage nor peace, O Vishnu!

25. When I behold Thy mouths, striking terror with their tusks, like Time's all-consuming fire, I am disoriented and find no peace. Be gracious, O Lord of the gods, O Abode of the universe!

26–27. All these sons of Dhritarāshtra, together with the hosts of monarchs, and Bhishma, Drona, and Karna, and the warrior chiefs of our side as well, enter precipitately Thy tusked and terrible mouths, frightful to behold. Some are seen caught between Thy teeth, their heads crushed to powder.

28. As the many torrents of the rivers rush toward the ocean, so do the heroes of the mortal world rush into Thy fiercely flaming mouths.

29. As moths rush swiftly into a blazing fire to perish there, even so do these creatures swiftly rush into Thy mouths to their own destruction.

30. Thou lickest Thy lips, devouring all the worlds on every side with Thy flaming mouths. Thy fiery rays fill the whole universe with their radiance and scorch it, O Vishnu!

31. Tell me who Thou art that wearest this frightful form. Salutations to Thee, O God Supreme! Have mercy. I desire to know Thee, who art the Primal One; for I do not understand Thy purpose.

32. THE LORD SAID: I am mighty, world-destroying Time, now engaged here in slaying these men. Even without you, all these warriors standing arrayed in the opposing armies shall not live.

33. Therefore stand up and win glory; conquer your enemies and enjoy an opulent kingdom. By Me and none other have they already been slain; be an instrument only, O Arjuna.

34. Kill Drona and Bhishma and Jayadratha and Karna, and the other great warriors as well, who have already been killed by Me. Be not distressed by fear. Fight, and you shall conquer your foes in the battle.

35. SANJAYA SAID: Having heard these words of Krishna, Arjuna trembled, folded his hands in adoration, and bowed down. Overwhelmed with fear, he saluted Krishna and then addressed Him again, with faltering voice.

36. ARJUNA SAID: It is right, O Hrishikeśa, that the world rejoices and delights in glorifying Thee; the Rākshasas flee on all sides in terror, and the hosts of Siddhas all bow to Thee in adoration.

37. And why should they not bow down to Thee, O Mighty Being, greater than all, since Thou art the Primal Cause even of Brahmā? O Infinite One, Lord of gods, Abode of the universe, Thou art the Imperishable, Being and non-being, and that which is the Supreme.

38. Thou art the first of gods, the ancient Soul; Thou art the supreme Resting-place of the universe; Thou art the Knower and That which is to be known and the Ultimate Goal. And by Thee is the world pervaded, O Thou of infinite form.

39. Thou art Wind and Death and Fire and Moon and the Lord of Water. Thou art Prajāpati and the Great-grandsire. Salutations, salutations to Thee a thousand times, and again and yet again salutations, saultations to Thee!

40. Salutations to Thee before, salutations to Thee behind, salutations to Thee on every side, O All! Infinite in might and immeasurable in strength, Thou pervadest all and therefore Thou art all.

41-42. Whatever I have rashly said from inadvertence or love, addressing Thee as "O Krishna," "O Yādava," or "O Friend," regarding Thee merely as a friend, unaware of Thy greatness; and in whatever other ways I may have shown disrespect to Thee while playing or resting, while sitting or eating, while alone, O Eternal Lord, or in the presence of others—all that I implore Thee, O Immeasurable, to forgive.

43. Thou art the Father of the world—of all that move and all that do not move. Thou art the object of its worship, its most venerable Teacher.

There is no one equal to Thee; how then, in the three worlds, could there be another superior to Thee, O Thou of incomparable might?

44. Therefore I bow down and prostrate my body before Thee, the adorable Lord, and seek Thy grace. Bear with me, O Lord, as a father with a son, as a friend with a friend, as a lover with his beloved.

45–46. I rejoice that I have seen what was never seen before; but my mind is also troubled with fear. Show me that other form of Thine. Be gracious, O Lord of gods, O Abode of the universe. I would see Thee as before, with Thy crown and Thy mace and the discus in Thy hand. Assume again Thy four-armed shapes, O Thou of a thousand arms and of endless shapes.

47. THE LORD SAID: By My grace, through My own yoga-power, O Arjuna, I have shown you this supreme form, resplendent, universal, infinite, and primeval, which none but you has ever seen.

48. Neither by the study of the Vedas and sacrifices, nor by gifts, nor by rituals, nor by severe penances, is this form of Mine to be seen in the world of men by anyone but you, O chief of the Kurus.

49. Be not afraid, be not bewildered, on seeing this terrific form of Mine. Free from fear and glad at heart, behold again My other form.

50. SANJAYA SAID: Having thus addressed Arjuna, Vāsudeva revealed to him His own form. The Great One assumed a graceful shape again and comforted the terrified Pāndava.

51. ARJUNA SAID: Looking at this gentle form of Yours, O Janārdana, I now feel composed in mind; I am myself again.

52. THE LORD SAID: It is very hard to see this form of Mine, which you have seen. Even the gods are ever eager to see this form.

53. Neither by the Vedas, nor by penances, nor by alms-giving, nor yet by sacrifice, am I to be seen in the form in which you have now beheld Me.

54. But by devotion to Me alone may I be known in this form, O Arjuna, realized truly, and entered into, O dreaded prince.

55. He who does My work and looks on Me as the Supreme Goal, who is devoted to Me, who is without attachment and without hatred for any creature—he comes to Me, O Pāndava.

Thus in the Bhagavad Gītā, the Essence of the Upanishads, the Science of Brahman, the Scripture of Yoga, the Dialogue between Sri Krishna and Arjuna, ends the Eleventh Chapter, entitled:

THE VISION OF THE UNIVERSAL FORM

THE WAY OF DIVINE LOVE

1. ARJUNA SAID: Those devotees who, ever steadfast, worship You after this fashion, and those others who worship the Imperishable and Unmanifest —which of these have greater knowledge of yoga?

2. THE LORD SAID: Those who have fixed their minds on Me, and

who, ever steadfast and endowed with supreme faith, worship Me—them do I hold to be perfect in yoga.

3–4. And those who have completely controlled their senses and are of even mind under all conditions and thus worship the Imperishable, the Ineffable, the Unmanifest, the Omnipresent, the Incomprehensible, the Immutable, the Unchanging, the Eternal—they, devoted to the welfare of all beings, attain Me alone, and none else.

5. The task of those whose minds are set on the Unmanifest is more difficult; for the ideal of the Unmanifest is hard to attain for those who are embodied.

6–7. But those who consecrate all their actions to Me, regarding Me as the Supreme Goal, and who worship Me, meditating on Me with single-minded concentration—to them, whose minds are thus absorbed in Me, verily I become ere long, O Pārtha, the Saviour from the death-fraught ocean of the world.

8. Fix your mind on Me alone, rest your thoughts on Me alone, and in Me alone you will live hereafter. Of this there is no doubt.

9. If you are unable to fix your mind steadily on Me, O Dhananjaya, then seek to reach Me by the yoga of constant practice.

10. If you are incapable of constant practice, then devote yourself to My service. For even by rendering service to Me you will attain perfection.

11. If you are unable to do even this, then be self-controlled, surrender the fruit of all action, and take refuge in Me.

12. Knowledge is better than practice, and meditation is better than knowledge. Renunciation of the fruit of action is better than meditation; peace immediately follows such renunciation.

13–14. He who never hates any being and is friendly and compassionate to all, who is free from the feelings of "I" and "mine" and even-minded in pain and pleasure, who is forbearing, ever content, and steady in contemplation, who is self-controlled and possessed of firm conviction, and who has consecrated his mind and understanding to Me—dear to Me is the one who is thus devoted to Me.

15. He by whom the world is not afflicted and whom the world cannot afflict, he who is free from joy and anger, fear and anxiety—he is dear to Me.

16. He who is free from dependence, who is pure and prompt, unconcerned and untroubled, and who has renounced all undertakings—dear to Me is the man who is thus devoted to Me.

17. He who rejoices not and hates not, who grieves not and desires not, who has renounced both good and evil and is full of devotion—he is dear to Me.

18–19. He who is alike to foe and friend, unaltered in honour and dishonour; who is the same in cold and heat, in pleasure and pain; who is free from attachment, who is unchanged by praise and blame; who is silent, content with whatever he has, homeless, firm of mind, and full of devotion—that man is dear to Me.

20. Exceedingly dear to Me are they who regard Me as the Supreme Goal and, endowed with faith and devotion, follow this Immortal Dharma.

Thus in the Bhagavad Gītā, the Essence of the Upanishads, the Science of Brahman, the Scripture of Yoga, the Dialogue between Sri Krishna and Arjuna, ends the Twelfth Chapter, entitled:

THE WAY OF DIVINE LOVE

4

YOGA APHORISMS
Patanjali

Patanjali's Sutras or Aphorisms constitute the classic Indian text on Yoga. The severe condensation of the aphoristic form provides a sentence outline of the subject rather than a full exposition. Traditionally the text was studied with a competent teacher who furnished such an explication, but for those lacking such instruction there are classic commentaries such as Vyasa's Yoga-bhasya and a number of modern books devoted to the interpretation of Patanjali's Aphorisms.

Yoga, according to Patanjali, is the methodical training whereby one learns to control his thoughts through moral discipline and spiritual exercises. Its principal goal is called "Kaivalya," a term which has been translated as "independence," "freedom," and "isolation." It names a state in which the spirit is no longer identified with thoughts, emotions, and desires, a blissful and poised condition comparable to the Upanishadic moksha. Yoga practice also produces, according to Patanjali, remarkable powers such as supernormal knowledge, extraordinary strength, and magical capacities.

The psychological training technique summarized by Patanjali is sometimes called "Raja" (or "royal") Yoga to distinguish it

From the book *Practical Yoga* by Ernest E. Wood. Copyright, 1948, by E. P. Dutton & Co., Inc. Reprinted by permission of the publishers, pp. 231–245.

from other spiritual paths, such as those taught in the Bhagavad-Gita, *which are also called "yogas." Patanjali is usually said to have lived in the Third or Second Century B.C., although some scholars think he may have been as late as the Fifth Century A.D. The complete work is given here in Professor Ernest Wood's translation.*

SECTION I, ON CONTEMPLATION

1. Now, instruction in yoga.
2. Yoga is the control of the ideas in the mind.
3. Then there is the dwelling of the Looker in his own proper nature.
4. Otherwise there is identification with the ideas.
5. The ideas are of five kinds, painful and pleasant.
6. Right knowledge, wrong knowledge, fancy, sleep and memories.
7. Right knowledges are perceptions, inferences and testimonies.
8. Wrong knowledge is false knowledge, fixed in a form not according to the thing.
9. Fancy is settling upon word-knowledge, there being no such thing.
10. Sleep is the idea based upon the conception of absence.
11. Memory is the non-loss of objects in knowledge.
12. Control of them is by practice and uncoloredness.
13. In this matter, practice is the effort towards steadiness.
14. It becomes firmly grounded when attended to devotedly without interruption for a long time.
15. Uncoloredness is the consciousness of power of one who is free from thirst for objects seen or heard about.
16. It is higher when there is no thirst for the Qualities of Nature, on account of knowledge about the real man.
17. It (*i.e.,* Contemplation) is cognitive when accompanied by forms of inspection, investigation, delight or sense of power.
18. The other (Contemplation), with only habit-molds for its residue, follows upon practice on the mental image of stoppage.
19. There is the thought of existence in the case of the bodiless beings and those who are absorbed in Nature.
20. In the case of others, it is preceded by faith, vigor, memory, Contemplation and understanding.
21. It (*i.e.,* the non-cognitive Contemplation) is near for those whose impetus is intense.
22. Even in this a distinction of mild, medium and highest measure (may be seen).
23. Or, it (*i.e.,* the non-cognitive Contemplation) comes from Attentiveness to God.
24. God is a particular soul, unaffected by containers of Sources of Trouble, works and (their) fruition.

25. In Him is the unexcelled source of all knowledge.

26. He was the teacher also of the ancients, because He is not limited by time.

27. His indicator is the sacred word.

28. (There should be) repetition of it, with thought upon its meaning.

29. From this there is understanding of the individual consciousness, also an absence of obstacles.

30. Disease, dullness, indecision, carelessness, sloth, worldliness, mistaken views, losing the way and instability—these splurgings of the mind are obstacles.

31. Co-existing with these splurgings are distress, despair, nervousness and disordered inbreathing and outbreathing.

32. For the purpose of preventing these, there should be practice of the one truth.

33. From the habitual mood of friendliness, sympathy, gladness and disregard respectively towards those who are happy, suffering, good and bad, comes purity of mind.

34. Or, (the obstacles can be reduced) by throwing out and holding of the breath.

35. Another thing: The rise of oncoming sensitivity causes mental steadiness.

36. Also: (The rise of the) peaceful inner light (causes mental steadiness).

37. Again: The mind regarding those free from Desire (will be steady).

38. Or: Dwelling upon knowledge of dream and sleep (conduces to steadiness).

39. Another way: From Meditation upon whatever you are specially interested in (comes mental steadiness).

40. Its mastery extends from the smallest to the greatest (things).

41. Correct imagery is the reception of anything that is within the classes of knower, knowing or known, when the ideas have declined—like the action of a flawless gem.

42. In that case, when there is a mixture of thoughts about word, meaning and knowledge, it is the correct imagery called inspectional.

43. When memory is cleared away (and the mind) shines forth as the object alone, as though devoid of its own nature, it is non-inspectional.

44. In the same way the investigational and the non-investigational, which have the subtle as their objects, are also explained.

45. And that objectiveness of the subtle ends only at that which is beyond definition.

46. These (four) are only the Contemplation with seed.

47. When there is full skill in the non-investigational Contemplation, there is the very pellucidity of the supreme self.

48. In that the cognition is full of truth.

49. Its objects are different from those of testamentary and inferential cognition, because its business is with particulars.

50. The habit-mold arising from that overcomes (all) other habit-molds.

51. When there is control of that also, the seedless Contemplation arrives, because there is now the control of all.

SECTION II, DESCRIPTION OF THE PRACTICE

1. Yoga in active life consists of Body-conditioning, Self-study and Attentiveness to God.

2. It has the purposes of promoting Contemplation and causing reduction of the Sources of Trouble.

3. The Sources of Trouble are Ignorance, Self-personality, Desire, Aversion and Possessiveness.

4. Ignorance is the field for all the others, whether they be (at any given time) dormant, slight, obstructed or vigorous.

5. Ignorance is regarding the non-eternal, impure, painful and not-self as the eternal, pure, pleasant and self.

6. Self-personality is the unification, as it were, of the Looker and the instrument of looking.

7. Desire is a follower of pleasure.

8. Aversion is a follower of pain.

9. Possessiveness, which is firmly established even in the learned, carries on by its own relish.

10. These (Sources of Trouble), when subtle, are removable by the generation of their contraries.

11. Their forms (in expression) are removable by Meditation.

12. The karma-container has its root in the Sources of Trouble and is experienced in seen and unseen births.

13. The root being there, it ripens into life-condition, length of life and experience.

14. These fructify in joy and grief, caused by virtue and vice.

15. Everything is painful to the discriminating person, because of transformation, worry, and habit-mold, and because of obstruction by the formations in the Qualities of Nature.

16. Pain which has not yet come is avoidable.

17. The cause of that avoidable (pain) is the conjunction of the Looker with the things seen.

18. The visible (world) consists of things produced and the senses, conducts itself as luminous, moving or fixed, and exists for the sake of experience and fulfillment.

19. The Qualities of Nature have divisions—the specialized, the general, the ideal and the undefinable.

20. The Looker is consciousness only, which, though pure, sees mental images.

21. The essential nature of the seen is for his sake.

22. Although destroyed for him who has finished his purpose, it is not destroyed, because of the community of others.

23. It is conjunction that causes the acceptance for oneself of the powers of ownership and being owned.

24. Of this, Ignorance is the cause.

25. When that is absent, conjunction is absent: that abandonment is independence for the Looker.

26. The means to the abandonment is unwavering Discrimination-knowledge.

27. His wisdom in the last stage is sevenfold.

28. The light of wisdom goes up to the Discrimination-knowledge when there is destruction of impurity through the performance of the limbs of yoga.

29. There are eight limbs, which are Abstinences, Observances, Seat, Breath-control, Withdrawal, Concentration, Meditation and Contemplation.

30. Of these (eight), the Abstinences are non-injury, non-lying, non-theft, non-sensuality and non-greed.

31. Abstinence is a great vow for all occasions and not exempted by life-condition, place, time or circumstances.

32. The Observances are Cleanliness, Contentment, Body-conditioning, Self-study and Attentiveness to God.

33. When there is annoyance by bad thoughts, let there be reflection to the contrary.

34. Reflection to the contrary is: "The bad thought of injury, et cetera, whether done, caused to be done, or approved, whether preceded by greed, anger or infatuation, whether mild, medium or strong, results in endless pain and error."

35. When non-injury is accomplished, there will be abandonment of animosity in his presence.

36. When non-lying is accomplished, the results of actions become sub-servient to him.

37. When non-theft is accomplished, all jewels approach him.

38. When non-sensuality is accomplished, vigor is obtained.

39. When non-greed is accomplished, there arises perception of the method of births.

40. From (external) cleanliness arises protectiveness of the body and detachment from others.

41. And then, when there is Mind-cleanliness, come (in order) high-mindedness, attentiveness (or one-pointedness), mastery of the senses, and fitness for vision of the self.

42. From Contentment comes the obtaining of the highest form of pleasure.

43. From Body-conditioning, with the decline of impurity, come the powers of the body and the senses.

44. From Self-study arises contact with the desired divinity.

45. From Attentiveness to God comes the power of contemplation.

46. Sitting is to be steady and pleasurable.

47. (This is done) by loosening of effort and thinking on the Endless.

48. Thence there is no disturbance from the pairs of opposites.

49. When that exists, regulation of breath is the next consideration. It is control of the manner of movement of inbreathing and outbreathing.

50. The condition of the breath as outgoing, incoming or standing still, is regulated as to place, time and number, and becomes lengthy and fine.

51. A fourth (condition arises) which casts aside the business of external and internal (breathing).

52. In consequence, the covering of the light is diminished.

53. And there is fitness of the mind for Concentration.

54. There is withdrawal of the senses, when they are detached from their own proper business and are imitating, as it were, the nature of the mind.

55. From that comes complete obedience of the senses.

SECTION III, ON PSYCHIC POWERS

1. Concentration is the binding of the mind to one place.

2. Meditation is continued mental effort there.

3. Contemplation is the same when there is the shining of the mere object alone, as if devoid of one's own form.

4. The three, in oneness, are Mind-poise.

5. From mastery of it (i.e., Mind-poise) comes intuition.

6. Its application is to grounds.

7. The three are more within than the preceding ones.

8. Even that is an outer limb with reference to the seedless.

9. The control-mood is the association of the mind with the control-moment, when there is the decline of the habit-mold of mind-spreading and the rise of that of control.

10. By habit-mold there arises a peaceful flow of it.

11. When there is the rise of one-pointedness and the decline of all-interestedness, there is the contemplative condition of the mind.

12. Further than that, when the subsided and arisen mental images are similar, there is the one-pointedness condition of the mind.

13. Similarly are described the transformations, properties, characteristics and states of objects and senses.

14. The object is the preserver of the characters, whether subsided, risen or still to be named.

15. The change due to succession is the cause of the change of transformations.

16. By Mind-poise upon the triple transformation comes knowledge of past and future.

17. There is confusion of word, object and mental image, because of super-imposition upon one another. By Mind-poise upon the distinction (between them) comes understanding of the sounds made by all creatures.

18. From bringing into consciousness the habit-molds, results knowledge of previous life-conditions.

19. (From bringing into consciousness) the mental images (in the minds of others) arises knowledge of other minds.

20. From Mind-poise on the form of the body, when there is a stoppage of the visibility of it, light and the eye being disconnected, comes the "internal state."

21. Karma is (of two kinds), with commencement and without commencement; by Mind-poise on these, or from omens, there is knowledge of the latter end (*i.e.*, death).

22. (From Mind-poise) on friendliness, etc. arise (various kinds of) strength.

23. (From Mind-poise) upon (various kinds of) strengths arise the strength of an elephant, etc.

24. By putting forth advanced sight comes knowledge of the minutely small, the concealed and the distant.

25. From Mind-poise on the sun comes knowledge of the inhabited regions.

26. On the moon, knowledge of the array of stars.

27. On the pole-star, knowledge of their motions.

28. On the center at the navel, knowledge of the arrangement of the body.

29. On the pit of the throat, the cessation of hunger and thirst.

30. On the "tortoise-tube," steadiness.

31. On the light in the head, seeing of the adepts.

32. Or, from intuition (knowledge) of all things.

33. In the heart, understanding of the mind.

34. Although the pure mind and the real man are absolutely incognate, experience does not present the idea of their difference, because it exists for the sake of another. From Mind-poise with himself as object comes knowledge of the real man.

35. From this arise insight, higher hearing, touch, sight, taste and smell.

36. These powers in the spreading mind are injurious to Contemplation.

37. The mind can enter another's body when there is a loosening of the causes of bondage and also knowledge of the procedure.

38. From control of the "upward air" comes freedom from contact with water, mud, thorns and similar things, and the power to rise up.

39. From control of the "equalizing air" comes brightness.

40. From Mind-poise upon the connection between the ear and the ether arises higher hearing.

41. From Mind-poise upon the connection between the body and the ether and from (Mind-poise upon) the attainment of the lightness of cotton, arises traveling in the ether.

42. In external, not fanciful, form it is "the great disembodiment"; from that there is diminution of the covering of the light.

43. Control of the forms of matter (i.e., elements) arises from Mind-poise on their solid state, character, finer forms, connections and utility or function.

44. From that come into existence minuteness etc. and excellence of the body, and absence of resistance from their (i.e., the elements') qualities.

45. Excellence of the body consists of correct form, beauty, strength and very firm well-knitness.

46. Control of the senses comes from Mind-poise on their function, character, individuality, connections, and utility.

47. From that comes quickness as of the mind, sensing without organs and control of substances.

48. In the case of him who has reached as far as the knowledge of the otherness of the pure mind and the real man, there is mastery in all states of existence, and knowership with regard to all.

49. When the seeds of bondage have been destroyed by his being un-colored even by that (i.e., the pure mind), there will be Independence.

50. If there is an invitation from the deities presiding over some place, it must be no cause for proud concurrence, for there may (thus) be renewed contact with what is not wanted.

51. From Mind-poise on moments and their succession arises the knowledge produced by Discrimination.

52. From this comes perception (as to which is which) of two equals which are not marked off as different by their classes, specific characters or positions.

53. And, the intuitional, which is knowledge produced by Discrimination, has all things for its objects, and all times for its objects, but is without succession.

54. When there is equality of purity of the pure mind and the real man, there is Independence.

SECTION IV, ON INDEPENDENCE

1. The psychic powers are produced at birth, and by drugs, incantations, asceticism and Contemplation.

2. Transformation into another condition of life is by the inflow of Nature.

3. The instrumental cause is not the director of Nature, but from it comes the removal of obstacles, as in the case of the cultivator of a field.

4. The artificial minds arise only from the self-personality.

5. One mind is the director of the several, in their divided business.

6. In this case (a mind) produced by Meditation is without a receptacle (for karmas).

7. The karma of a yogī is neither white nor black. Of others it is of three kinds.

8. From those, there is the manifestation only of those latencies which are suitable for ripening.

9. Even when they (i.e., the latencies) are obstructed by life-condition, place and time, they are still within, because habit-molds are similar to memories.

10. And they are beginningless, as the wish to live is eternal.

11. Because it (the latent) is held together by cause, effect, receptacle and object, it is absent when these are absent.

12. What has gone and what is to come exist in their own forms, because of the differences of the paths (or modes) of their characters.

13. They are manifest and subtle, and have the nature of the Qualities.

14. Things are real, because of unity within the transformations.

15. From the difference of minds in regarding the same object (we infer) the different ways of the two (that is, mind and the world).

16. And if an object depending on one mind were (at some time) not cognized by it, would it then exist?

17. An object can be known or unknown to the mind, because of its requiring to be colored by it.

18. The ideas in the mind are always known to its owner, the real man, because he is without transformations.

19. It (the mind) is not self illuminate, on account of its perceptibility.

20. Further, there is no knowledge of both at one time.

21. In perceptibility (of the mind) by another mind, there would be excess of cognition, and confusion of memories.

22. Consciousness knows its own higher mind—though it does not move in connection (with anything)—by the arising of its image.

23. The mind being colored by (both) the Looker and the seen, has everything within its scope.

24. Also, the mind, with all its innumerable latencies, exists for the sake of another, for it works by combination (with the real man).

25. On the part of him who sees the distinction (between mind and real man), there is a turning away from thoughts about the nature of self.

26. Then the mind is deep in Discrimination and mainly pointed to Independence.

27. At intervals there are other thoughts, arising from the habit-molds.

28. The abandoning of those is like that of the Sources of Trouble, as already described.

29. In the case of one having no interest of any kind even in intellection, on account of Discrimination-knowledge, there is the Contemplation called "cloud of rectitude."

30. From that follows the retirement of Sources of Trouble and karmas.

31. Then, in the case of him who is free from all coverings and impurities, what-is-to-be-known becomes small, on account of the infinity of (his) knowledge.

32. And from that comes the end of the succession of transformations of the Qualities, which have finished their work.

33. Succession, which is the counter-correlative of a moment, is to be given up at the end of the last transformation.

34. Independence is the counter-product when the Qualities of Nature are devoid of purpose for the real man, or, the power of consciousness stands firm in its own nature.

5

SELF-KNOWLEDGE
Shankara

      Most educated Hindus view Shankara as both the greatest of Indian philosophers and the most profound interpreter of the Upanishads and the Bhagavad-Gita. *The non-dualistic* (advaita) *Vedanta he defended has long been the prevailing Indian metaphysical position. According to it all plurality is an appearance superimposed by ignorance upon the single reality, Brahman. The ordinary distinctions between individuals, between a subject and his objects, and between man and God have a relative validity; they are not classed with delusory judgments based on dreams or hallucinations, but neither are they believed to represent correctly the absolute reality. Shankara defended his position with dialectical reasoning and by an appeal to the authority of the Vedas. He*

     Sankaracharya Ātmabodha, Swami Nikhilananda, trans. (New York: Ramakrishna-Vivekananda Center, 1946), pp. 117–171. Reprinted from *Self-Knowledge (Ātmabodha)* trans. by Swami Nikhilananda, by his permission.

also clarified the path by which a spiritual aspirant under the guidance of a competent teacher can come to a first-hand realization of the Upanishadic teachings that "This self is Brahman," "All of this is Brahman," and "Brahman is consciousness."

Shankara was probably born in the Eighth Century in South India. He is reputed to have been an intellectual prodigy who entered monastic life at an early age and soon became a famous teacher. He wrote voluminously, both philosophical treatises and devotional hymns, debated with other philosophers, traveled throughout India, and founded several monasteries before his death which is said to have occurred at the age of thirty-two in the Himalayas.

Shankara did not originate the non-dualistic interpretation of the Upanishads, although he was its greatest champion. He presented his views in detail in his commentaries on the Upanishads, the Bhagavad-Gita *and, especially, on the* Brahma-Sutras, *the basic text of the Vedanta school. "Atmabodha" means "Self-knowledge" and the book of this title is a short, comparatively simple introduction to Shankara's thought. It is here given complete in Swami Nikhilananda's translation.*

1. I am composing the *Ātmabodha*, or *Self-Knowledge*, to serve the needs of those who have been purified through the practice of austerities, and who are peaceful in heart, free from cravings, and desirous of Liberation.

2. As fire is the direct cause of cooking, so Knowledge, and not any other form of discipline, is the direct cause of Liberation; for Liberation cannot be attained without Knowledge.

3. Action cannot destroy ignorance, for it is not in conflict with ignorance. Knowledge alone destroys ignorance, as light destroys dense darkness.

4. It is only because of ignorance that the Self appears to be finite. When ignorance is destroyed, the Self, which does not admit of any multiplicity whatsoever, truly reveals Itself by Itself, like the sun when the cloud is removed.

5. Through repeated practice, Knowledge purifies the embodied soul stained by ignorance, and then itself disappears, as the powder of the kataka-nut disappears after it has cleansed muddy water.

6. The world, filled with attachments and aversions, and the rest, is like a dream: it appears to be real as long as one is ignorant, but becomes unreal when one is awake.

7. The world appears to be real as long as the non-dual Brahman, which is the basis of all, is not known. It is like the illusion of silver in an oyster-shell.

8. All the various forms exist in the imagination of the perceiver, the substratum being the eternal and all-pervading Vishnu, whose nature is Existence and Intelligence. Names and forms are like bangles and bracelets, and Vishnu is like gold.

9. As the all-pervading ākāśa appears to be diverse on account of its association with various upādhis, which are different from each other, and becomes one on the destruction of the upādhis, so also the omnipresent Lord appears to be diverse on account of His association with various upādhis and becomes one on the destruction of these upādhis.

10. Owing to Its association with various upādhis, such ideas as caste, colour, and position are superimposed on Atman, as flavour, colour, and so forth, on water.

11. The gross body, the medium through which the Soul experiences pleasure and plain, is determined by past action and formed out of the five great subtle elements, which become gross when one half portion of one subtle element becomes united with one eighth of each of the other four.

12. The subtle body, the instrument of the Soul's experience, consists of the five prānas, the ten organs, the manas, and the buddhi—all formed from the rudimentary elements before their subdivision and combination with one another.

13. Avidyā, or nescience, indescribable and beginningless, is called the cause, which is an upādhi superimposed on Ātman. Know for certain that Ātman is other than the three upādhis.

14. On account of union with the five sheaths, the pure Atman appears to be like them, as is the case with a crystal, which appears to be endowed with such colours as blue or red when in contact with a blue or red cloth.

15. One should, through discrimination, separate the pure and inmost Self from the sheaths by which It is covered, as one separates the rice-kernel from the covering husk by striking it with a pestle.

16. Though all-pervading, Ātman does not shine in everything; It is manifest only in the buddhi, like a reflection in clear water or in a stainless mirror.

17. Realize Ātman to be distinct from the body, sense-organs, mind, buddhi, and non-differentiated Prakriti, but the Witness of their functions, comparable to a king.

18. As the moon appears to be moving when the clouds move in the sky, so also, to the non-discriminating, Atman appears to be active when in reality the senses are active.

19. The body, senses, mind, and buddhi engage in their respective activities with the help of Consciousness, which is inherent in Atman, just as men work with the help of the light that is inherent in the sun.

20. Fools, through non-discrimination, superimpose on the stainless Atman, which is Existence and Consciousness Absolute, the characteristics and functions of the body and the senses, just as people attribute such traits as blueness and concavity to the sky.

21. As the movement that belongs to water is attributed, through ignorance, to the moon reflected in it, so also agency, enjoyment, and other limitations, which belong to the mind, are falsely attributed to Ātman.

22. Attachment, desire, pleasure, pain, and the rest, are perceived to exist as long as the buddhi, or mind, functions. They are not perceived in deep sleep, when the mind ceases to exist. Therefore they belong to the mind alone and not to Ātman.

23. The nature of Ātman is Eternity, Purity, Reality, Consciousness, and Bliss, just as luminosity is the nature of the sun, coolness of water, and heat of fire.

24. Such a notion as "I know" is produced by the union, due to non-discrimination, of a modification of the mind with two aspects of Ātman, namely, Existence and Consciousness.

25. Ātman never undergoes change, and the buddhi is never endowed with consciousness. But man believes Ātman to be identical with the buddhi and falls under such delusions as that he is the seer and the knower.

26. The Soul regarding Itself as a jiva is overcome by fear, just like the man who regards a rope as a snake. The Soul regains fearlessness by realizing that It is not a jiva but the Supreme Soul.

27. The mind, the sense-organs, and so on, are illumined by Ātman alone, as a jar or pot by a lamp. But these material objects cannot illumine their own Self.

28. As a lighted lamp does not need another lamp to manifest its light, so Ātman, being Consciousness itself, does not need another instrument of consciousness to illumine Itself.

29. By negating all the upādhis through the help of the scriptural statement "It is not this, It is not this," realize the oneness of the individual soul and the Supreme Soul by means of the great Vedic aphorisms.

30. The body and so on, created by avidyā and of the nature of an object, are perishable, like bubbles. Realize through discrimination that you are the stainless Brahman, completely different from them.

31. I am free from changes such as birth, thinness, senility, and death; for I am other than the body. I am unattached to the objects of the senses, such as sound and taste; for I am without sense-organs.

32. I am free from sorrow, attachment, malice, and fear; for I am other than the mind. "He is without breath and without mind, pure, higher than the high, and imperishable."

33. "From It are born breath, mind, and all organs of sense, ether, air, light, water, and earth, which is the support of all."

34. I am without attributes and action, eternal and pure, free from stain and desire, changeless and formless, and always free.

35. I fill all things, inside and out, like the ether. Changeless and the same in all, I am pure, unattached, stainless, and immutable.

36. I am verily that Supreme Brahman, which is eternal, stainless, and free; which is One, indivisible, and non-dual; and which is of the nature of Bliss, Truth, Knowledge, and Infinity.

37. The impression of "I am Brahman," thus created by uninterupted

reflection, destroys ignorance and its distractions, as rasāyana medicine destroys diseases.

38. Sitting in a solitary place, freeing the mind from desires, and controlling the senses, meditate with unswerving attention on the Infinite Ātman, which is One without a second.

39. The wise one should intelligently merge the entire objective world in Ātman alone and constantly think of that Ātman as the stainless sky.

40. He who has attained the Supreme Goal discards all such objects as name and form, and dwells as the embodiment of Infinite Consciousness and Bliss.

41. The Supreme Self, on account of Its being of the nature of exceeding Bliss, does not admit of the distinction of the knower, knowledge, and the object of knowledge. It alone shines.

42. By constant meditation (comparable to the rubbing of the firewood) is kindled the flame of Knowledge, which completely burns up the fuel of ignorance.

43. As the sun appears after the destruction of darkness by dawn, so Ātman appears after the destruction of ignorance by Knowledge.

44. Though Ātman is an ever present reality, yet because of ignorance It is unrealized. On the destruction of ignorance, Atman is realized. It is like the case of the ornament on one's neck.

45. Brahman appears to be a jiva through ignorance, as the stump of a tree appears to be a man. This jivahood is destroyed when the real nature of the jiva is realized.

46. The Knowledge produced by the realization of the true nature of Reality destroys immediately the ignorance characterized by the notions of "I" and "mine," as the sun the mistake regarding one's direction.

47. The yogi endowed with complete enlightenment sees, through the eye of Knowledge, the entire universe in his own Self and regards everything as the Self and nothing else.

48. The tangible universe is verily Ātman; nothing whatsoever exists that is other than Atman. As pots and jars are verily clay and cannot be anything but clay, so, to the enlightened, all that is perceived is the Self.

49. A jivanmukta, endowed with Self-Knowledge, gives up the traits of his previous upādhis. Because of his realization that he is of the nature of Existence-Knowledge-Bliss Absolute, he verily becomes Brahman, like the cockroach becoming a bhramara insect.

50. A yogi who is a jivanmukta, after crossing the ocean of delusion and killing the monsters of passion and aversion, becomes united with Peace and dwells in the Bliss derived from the realization of the Self alone.

51. Relinquishing attachment to illusory external happiness, the Self-abiding jivanmukta, satisfied with the Bliss derived from Atman, shines inwardly, like a lamp placed inside a jar.

52. Though associated with upādhis, he, the contemplative one, is undefiled by their traits, like the sky, and he remains unaltered under all conditions, like a dumb person. He moves about unattached, like the wind.

53. On the destruction of the upādhis, he, the contemplative one, is totally absorbed in Vishnu, the All-pervading Spirit, like water in water, space in space, and light in light.

54. Realize that to be Brahman the attainment of which leaves nothing more to be attained, the blessedness of which leaves no other bliss to be desired, and the knowledge of which leaves nothing more to be known.

55. Realize that to be Brahman which, when seen, leaves nothing more to be seen, having become which one is not born again into the world of becoming, and which, when known, leaves nothing else to be known.

56. Realize that to be Brahman which is Existence-Knowledge-Bliss Absolute, which is non-dual and infinite, eternal and One, and which fills all the quarters—all that is above and below and all that exists between.

57. Realize that to be Brahman which is non-dual, indivisible, One, and blissful, and which is indicated by Vedānta as the irreducible substratum after the negation of all tangible objects.

58. Deities like Brahmā and Indra taste only a particle of the unlimited Bliss of Brahman and enjoy, in proportion, their shares of that particle.

59. All objects are pervaded by Brahman, all actions are possible because of Brahman; therefore Brahman permeates everything, as butter permeates milk.

60. Realize that to be Brahman which is neither subtle nor gross; neither short nor long; without birth and change; without form, qualities, or colour.

61. Realize that to be Brahman by the light of which luminous orbs like the sun and moon are illumined, but which cannot be illumined by their light, and by which everything is illumined.

62. The Supreme Brahman pervades the entire universe outwardly and inwardly and shines of Itself, like the fire that permeates a red-hot iron ball both inwardly and outwardly and shines of itself.

63. Brahman is other than the universe. There exists nothing that is not Brahman. If any object other than Brahman appears to exist, it is unreal, like a mirage.

64. All that is perceived, all that is heard, is Brahman, and nothing else. Attaining the Knowledge of Reality, one sees the universe as the non-dual Brahman, Existence-Knowledge-Bliss Absolute.

65. Though Ātman is Reality and Consciousness, and ever present everywhere, yet It is perceived by the eye of Wisdom alone. But one whose vision is obscured by ignorance does not see the radiant Ātman, as the blind do not see the resplendent sun.

66. The jiva free from impurities, being well heated in the fire of Knowledge kindled by hearing and so on, shines of himself, like gold.

67. Ātman, which is the Sun of Knowledge, arises in the firmament of the heart and destroys the darkness. The Pervader of all and the Sustainer of all, It illumines all and also Itself.

68. He who, renouncing all activities, worships in the sacred and stainless shrine of Ātman, which is independent of time, place, and distance; which is present everywhere; which is the destroyer of heat and cold, and the other opposites; and which is the giver of eternal happiness, becomes all-knowing and all-pervading and attains, hereafter, Immortality.

6

BHAGAVATA PURANA

The most influential of the Puranas, the Bhagavata Purana or Purana of the Lord, was probably written in the Eighth or Ninth Century A.D. The most important of its twelve books are the tenth and eleventh devoted to the life and teachings of Sri Krishna. The tenth book was considered somewhat shocking in Victorian England as it describes the blissful love of Krishna experienced by the Gopi maidens of Brindaban. In India, however, love between the sexes is regarded as one suitable symbol of the love between man and God. Other human affections, such as the love between mother and son, the veneration of a student for his teacher, the mutual affection of mature friends, and the respect of a subject for his ruler, are also considered appropriate symbols of the divine-human relationship and the devotee is free to adopt the attitude he finds most helpful. The eleventh book contains an outstanding compendium of advice on morality and the spiritual life attributed to Sri Krishna. Three chapters from this book, one discussing devotion, one on caste and the stages of life, and one on monasticism, are here reprinted from Swami Madhavananda's translation.

Bhagavata Purana, Book XI, Swami Madhavananda, trans. (Calcutta: Advaita Ashrama, 1956), Ch. IX, pp. 126–140; Ch. XII, pp. 167–184; Ch. XIII, pp. 185–200. Reprinted from *The Last Message of Shri Krishna* trans. by Swami Madhavananda, by permission.

THE GLORY OF DEVOTION; DIRECTIONS ON MEDITATION

UDDHAVA SAID:

1. O Krishna, the teachers of Brahman speak of various means of attaining well-being. Are all of them equally important, or only one is the foremost of them?

2. Thou too hast described the path of devotion to the Lord, which is independent (of other means),—by which the mind getting rid of attachment to everything merges in Thee.

THE LORD SAID:

3. These words of Mine known as the Vedas, which had been destroyed by Time at the dissolution of the universe, I first revealed to Brahmâ. In them is set forth that religion which inclines the mind to wisdom.

4. He declared it unto his eldest son, Manu, from whom the seven Patriarchs and sages, Bhrigu and the rest, got it.

5-6. From those fathers it passed on to their sons—the Devas, Asuras, Guhyakas, men, Siddhas, Gandharvas, Vidyâdharas, Châranas, Kindevas, Kinnaras, Nâgas, Râkshasas, Kimpurushas, and others. Various are their natures, being the outcome of Sattva, Rajas, and Tamas:

7. By which beings are differentiated as well as their minds. And according to their natures their interpretation (of the Vedas) is various.

8. Thus, owing to the difference of natures, people differ in their ideas; while some differ owing to instructions handed down to them through a succession of teachers, and others even go against the Vedas.

9. O best of men, people deluded by My Mâyâ describe various things as means to the highest good, according to their occupation and taste.

10. As means to the goal some mention duty; others fame, self-gratification, truth, control of the senses, and control of the mind; yet others mention splendour, gifts, food; and some, again sacrifice, austerity, charity, vows, or moral rules, universal and particular.

11. The results attained by these means, being the outcome of work, have a beginning and an end, produce misery, and end in infatuation. They give but transient joy and are attended with grief.

12. My friend, how can one attached to sense-objects have that bliss which a man, with his mind given up to Me and indifferent to all objects, derives from Me, their (Blissful) Self?

13. To the man who craves for nothing, who has subdued his senses and mind, who is even-minded to all, and is satisfied with Me, all the quarters are full of bliss.

14. Neither the position of Brahmâ nor that of Indra, neither suzerainty nor the rulership of the nether regions, neither powers that come through Yoga nor liberation—the man who has surrendered his mind unto Me desires nothing else but Me.

15. Neither Brahmâ, nor Shiva, nor Balarâma, nor Lakshmi, nor My own form is so very dear to Me as you.

16. With a view to purify Myself by the dust of his feet, I always follow the sage who cares for nothing, is calm, bears enmity to none, and is even-minded.

17. High-souled sages—penniless, devoted to Me, and unsmitten by desires, calm and compassionate to all creatures—derive that bliss of Mine which they only know who care for no gain, and not others.

18. Even a devotee of Mine who not being a master of his senses is troubled by sense-objects, is generally not overcome by them, owing to his powerful devotion.

19. As fire kindled into a blaze burns the faggots to ashes, so, O Uddhava, devotion to Me totally destroys all sins.

20. O Uddhava, neither Yoga, nor knowledge, nor piety, nor study, nor austerity, nor renunciation captivates Me so much as a heightened devotion to Me.

21. I, the dear Self of the pious, am attainable by devotion alone, which is the outcome of faith. The devotion to Me purges even outcasts of their congenital impurity.

22. Piety joined to truthfulness and compassion or learning coupled with austerity, never wholly purifies a mind which is devoid of devotion to Me.

23. How can the mind be purified without devotion characterised by a softening of the heart, the hair standing on end and tears of joy flowing out of the eyes?

24. A devotee of Mine whose speech is broken by sobs, whose heart melts and who, without any idea of shame, sometimes weeps profusely, or laughs, or sings aloud, or dances, purifies the whole universe.

25. As gold smelted by fire gives up its dross and gets back its real state, so the mind by means of a systematic devotion to Me winnows off its desire for work and attains to Me.

26. The more this mind is cleansed by listening to and reciting the sacred tales about Me, the more it sees the subtle Reality, like eyes through an application of collyrium.

27. The mind of a man who thinks of sense-objects is attached to them, but the mind of one who remembers Me is merged in Me alone.

28. Therefore giving up the dwelling on unreal things, which are no better than dreams or fancies, concentrate the mind, clarified by devotion to Me, on Me.

29. The man of self-control should avoid from a safe distance the company of women as well as of those who associate with the latter, sit in a secluded and congenial place, and ever alert think of Me.

30. No other association causes so much misery and bondage as that of women and those that associate with them.

UDDHAVA SAID:

31. O lotus-eyed Krishna, please tell me how and in what aspect, personal or impersonal, a seeker after liberation should meditate on Thee.

THE LORD SAID:

32–33. Sitting on an even seat at ease with the body erect, placing the hands on the lap and with the eye directed towards the tip of the nose, one should purify the passage of Prâna by means of inhalation, retention, and exhalation of the breath, and should also practise slowly in the inverse order, with the senses under control.

34. Raising the syllable Om to the heart by means of Prânâyâma, one should add to it the vowel. The Om is like the continuous peal of a bell, and extending in a thin line like a thread in a lotus stalk.

35. Thus one should practise the Prânâyâma coupled with Om, ten times, thrice daily. Within a month one will then control the Prâna.

36. Within the body there is the lotus of the heart, with its stalk above and point below, and with eight petals and a pericarp.

37. One should meditate on this as inverted with the flower upwards and opened, and in the pericarp should think of the sun, moon, and fire, one within the other. In the fire, again, one should reflect on the following form of Mine which is good for meditation:

38. Symmetrical, serene, of a benign face, with four long and beautiful arms, with a well-formed and beautiful neck, beautiful cheeks, and a graceful smile:

39. With shining alligator-shaped pendants in the well-matched ears, with a golden cloth, dark-complexioned like a cloud and with the peculiar marks known as Shrivatsa and Lakshmi on the chest:

40. Adorned with conch, disc, mace, lotus, and a garland of wild flowers, with the feet adorned with ringing anklets, and the chest resplendent with the gem Kaustubha:

41. Decked with a shining crown, bracelets, and a waist-band, beautiful in every feature, appealing, with the face and eyes beaming with graciousness, and exquisitely tender.

42. One should meditate on this form, concentrating the mind on all the features. The man of self-control should withdraw the organs from the sense-objects with the help of the mind, and with the intellect as guide, direct the mind to My whole body.

43. Then one should concentrate that mind—distributed all over My body—on one part, and think of the smiling countenance alone and nothing else.

44. Drawing the mind which is concentrated on that, one should fix it on the Supreme Cause. Then leaving that too, one should rest on Me and think of nothing whatsoever.

45. With one's mind thus absorbed, one sees Me alone in oneself and sees oneself united to Me, the Self of all—like light united to light.

46. A Yogi who thus concentrates his mind through intense meditation will soon blow out the delusion about objects, finite knowledge, and action.

CASTES AND ORDERS OF LIFE

UDDHAVA SAID:

1-2. Thou hast already spoken of religion which makes for devotion to Thee, and is meant for all human beings, with or without the observances of caste and order of life; please tell me, O Lotus-eyed One, how by practising that religion for himself a man may attain to devotion to Thee.

3-4. The supreme and blissful religion which Thou, O Mighty-armed Lord, O Mâdhava, didst once expound—so it is said—to Brahmâ in Thy Swan-form, has now, O Queller of foes, almost ceased to be in the mortal world, owing to the great passage of time, even though it was once inculcated.

5. O Achyuta, there is no other teacher, originator, or defender of religion on earth than Thou, no, not even in the court of Brahmâ, where the sciences are present in visible forms.

6. O Slayer of Madhu, when Thou, the Originator, Defender, and Expounder of it, wilt leave the earth, religion too will die. Who, O Lord, will, then explain it?

7. Therefore, O Lord, who knowest all religions, please describe to me which of us is fit for that religion which makes for devotion to Thee, and how he is to practise it.

SHUKA SAID:

8. Thus asked by his own foremost servant, the Lord Hari was pleased and described the time-honoured religions for the good of men.

THE LORD SAID:

9. This question of yours, O Uddhava, is righteous, for it will promote the highest good of men who observe the duties of caste and order of life. Learn that religion of Me.

10. In the beginning, in the Krita or Satya Yuga, men had but one caste which was known as Hamsa. People attained the consummation of their desires from their very birth, and hence the age was called Krita ("achieved").

11. In that primeval age, Om was the Veda, and I was religion in the form of a bull. The people of that age, who were pure and given to contemplation, used to reflect on Me, the Pure One.

12. At the beginning of the Tretâ Yuga, O noble soul, the science of the Veda appeared from My heart, through the agency of the Prâna. Out of that I became the sacrifice with its threefold adjunct.

13. From the Virât sprang the Brâhmana, Kshatriya, Vaishya, and

Shudra, from the mouth, arms, thighs, and feet respectively. They were distinguished by their specialised duties.

14. The householder's life sprang from My thighs, the student life from My heart, the life of retirement into the woods from My chest, and monasticism was on My head.

15. The tendencies of the different castes and orders of life among men were according to the place of the origin: Inferior positions produced inferior tendencies and superior positions superior ones.

16. Control of mind and the senses, contemplation, cleanliness, contentment, forbearance, straightforwardness, devotion to Me, compassion, and truthfulness—these are the tendencies of the Brâhmana.

17. An indomitable spirit, strength, patience, valour, fortitude, liberality, enterprise, steadiness, devotion to Brâhmanas, and lordship—these are the tendencies of a Kshatriya.

18. Faith in God, charity, humility, service unto the Brâhmanas, and an insatiety from the amassing of wealth—these are the tendencies of the Vaishya.

19. Attending on the Brâhmanas, the cows, and the gods with sincerity, and being contented with what he gets therefrom—these are the tendencies of the Shudra.

20. Uncleanliness, falsehood, theft, atheism, barren disputation, lust, anger, and greed—these are the tendencies of a fifth class beyond the pale of the other four.

21. Non-injury, truthfulness, freedom from theft, lust, anger and greed, and an effort to do what is agreeable and beneficial to all creatures—this is the common duty of all castes.

22. Receiving in order the second birth known as the sacred thread ceremony, a Dvija (twice-born) should live in the house of the teacher with self-control, and summoned by him, should study the Vedas.

23. He should wear a girdle, deer-skin, rosary of Rudrâksha beads, and the holy thread, and carry a staff, water-pot and some Kusha grass. He should wear matted locks, must not wash his teeth and clothes, and never use a painted seat.

24. He should observe silence while bathing, eating, offering oblations to the fire, repeating his Mantra, and answering the calls of nature. He must not pare his nails, nor cut his hair in any part of the body.

25. He should observe strict Brahmacharya (continence) and never make any conscious lapses. If he is accidentally impure, he should have a plunge-bath in water, and after making Prânâyama, repeat the Gayatri.

26. Of mornings and evenings, after attending to cleanliness, he should silently repeat his Mantra with a concentrated mind, and offer his worship to the fire, the sun, the teacher, cows, Brâhmanas, superiors, old people, and the gods.

27. He should know the teacher to be My own self, and never disregard or look down upon him as a man, for the teacher represents all the gods.

28. In the morning and evening, he should bring the doles of food, or whatever else he may have received, to his teacher, and eat what he orders him to, with moderation.

29. He should always worship the teacher, serving him as a menial, by following, resting, sitting, and being near with folded palms.

30. Behaving thus he should live in the house of the teacher, shunning comforts, and maintaining absolute chastity, till his study is complete.

31. If he wishes to get to the Brahmaloka, where the Vedas reside, he should, while observing continence, surrender his body unto the teacher as a tribute for the study.

32. Being sinless and possessed of the strength that comes of studying the Vedas, he should worship Me, the Supreme Being, in the fire, the teacher, his own self, and in all beings, in a spirit of identity.

33. Persons other than householders should forbear to look at, touch, converse, and cut jokes, etc., with women, and avoid seeing animals pair.

34-35. Cleanliness; the sipping of water preparatory to certain functions; performance of the services due in the morning, noon, and evening; straightforwardness; the visiting of holy places; repetition of the Mantra; avoidance of things not to be touched or eaten, and of persons not to be accosted; looking upon all beings as Myself; and control of mind, speech, and body;—these, O Uddhava, are the observances meant for all the orders of life.

36. The Brâhmana who thus practises Brahmacharya becomes as a blazing fire, and if he is unselfish, by this intense asceticism his desires are burnt out, and he attains devotion to Me.

37. Then, after having properly studied the Vedas, if the student wishes to enter the householder's life, he should make the teacher some reverential present, and with his permission perform the usual ablution.

38. The qualified Dvija may enter the householder's life, the hermit's life in the woods, or the monastic life; or, with his mind intent on Me, he may proceed from one order of life to the next; but never otherwise.

39. A person wishing to lead a householder's life should marry an unblemished girl of the same caste, who must be younger in age; and if he wishes to marry any other, he should do so after the above marriage, and even then, in the succeeding order.

40. The performance of sacrifices, study, and the making of gifts are the duties of the twice-born. The acceptance of gifts, teaching, and the helping of others to perform sacrifices are the occupations of the Brâhmana.

41. A Brâhmana who regards the acceptance of gifts as destructive of austerity, spirit of independence, and fame, should live by either of the other two means, or if he considers them harmful, live upon the grains left ungathered in the fields.

42. The body of a Brâhmana is certainly not meant for the satisfaction of petty ends. It is for rigorous austerity here, and endless happiness hereafter.

43. A Brâhmana content to live upon grains left in the fields and in

front of shops, and observing the great taintless duty, while he lives at home, with his mind given up to Me and not over-attached, attains Peace.

44. Those that rescue a Brâhmana devoted to Me from his misfortune, I will quickly deliver from dangers, as a boat picks up a drowning man from the sea.

45. A king (specially) should deliver all his subjects from misfortunes like a father, and as the leader of elephants rescues the elephants in his herd, he should, preserving his balance, deliver himself by his own efforts.

46. Such a king shakes off all his sins on earth, and ascending the heaven in an aerial car resplendent like the sun, enjoys in the company of Indra, the king of gods.

47. A helpless Brâhmana should get over his trouble by setting up as a merchant, selling only things allowable. If he is still overtaken by misfortune, he should have recourse to the sword, but never resort to dog-like servility.

48. A king in adversity should take up the occupation of a Vaishya, or live by hunting, or even as a Brâhmana; but never take to dog-like servility.

49. A Vaishya in trouble should lead the life of a Shudra, and a Shudra adopt the weaving of mats etc., which is the occupation of the Kârus. Once free from the adversity, none should desire to maintain himself by a despicable profession.

50. By means of study of the Vedas, the utterance of Svadhâ, and Svâhâ, little food-offerings and distribution of food etc., a householder should, according to his means, daily worship the Rishis, the manes, the gods, the lower animals, and men respectively, considering them as forms of Mine.

51. By means of wealth that comes of itself, or is acquired legitimately, he should judiciously perform the above sacrifices, without taxing his dependants.

52. He should not get attached to his family, and, even though he is a householder, should not forget God. The wise man should consider the unseen enjoyments of future life just as perishable as the visible enjoyments of this life.

53. The association with one's sons, wife, relatives, and friends is like the chance meeting of travellers. They depart with the end of each body, as dreams are inextricably bound to sleep.

54. One who reflecting thus lives at home without attachment and egoism, like a guest, is not fettered by the home, and is free.

55. A devotee, worshipping Me through his household duties, may lead a householder's life, may retire into the forest, or, if he has progeny, may embrace monasticism.

56. But he who is attached to his house, is afflicted by the desire for sons and wealth, and is henpecked—is foolish, and being beguiled, he comes under the bondage of "I and mine."

57. "Alas, my parents are old; my wife has got young children; and how can she in her helpless state live, with these poor children, without me?"

58. Thus does this foolish man, with his heart distracted by thoughts of home, continue to think of them without satisfaction. Then he dies and enters into abysmal darkness.

FOREST LIFE AND MONASTICISM

THE LORD SAID:

1. When a man wishes to retire into the woods, he should put his wife in the care of his sons, or go with her, and live peacefully in the woods the third quarter of his span of life.

2. He should live on purifying wild tubers, roots, and fruits, and wear a bark, or a cloth, or a garment of straw, or leaves, or a deer-skin.

3. He should allow the hair on his head and body as well as his beard to grow, and not remove the dirt on his person; he should not wash his teeth, should plunge in water thrice a day, and lie on the ground.

4. In the summer he should subject himself to the five fires, in the rainy season expose himself to showers, and in the winter remain immersed up to his neck in water. Thus should he practise austerity.

5. He should eat food cooked over a fire, or ripening naturally in the process of time, powdering it with a pestle or stone, or even making his teeth serve the purpose.

6. Aware of the efficacy of place and time, he should himself collect all his means of subsistence, and not eat things procured at some past time.

7. The hermit living in the woods should perform his observances of the season with oblations prepared from grains that grow in the woods and not with animal sacrifice as prescribed in the Vedas.

8. On the recluse the expounders of the Vedas also enjoin the daily tending of the sacrificial fires (Agnihotra), the observances in connection with the new moon and the full moon (Darsha and Purnamâsa), as well as that of Châturmâsya—as in the household life.

9. The recluse, with arteries and veins prominent all over his body on account of this practice of austerity, worships Me, the embodiment of austerity, and attains to Me from the sphere of the Rishis.

10. Who is a greater fool than he who applies this great austerity practised with such hardship and calculated to confer liberation, to the fulfilment of petty desires?

11. When the hermit is unable to observe those rules, being overtaken by a shaking of the limbs consequent on old age, he should mentally put the sacrificial fires within him, and with his mind intent on Me, enter into fire.

12. When he is perfectly sick of the spheres that are the outcome of work, seeing that they are attended with misery, he should discard the fires, and from that stage embrace the monastic life.

13. Sacrificing unto Me according to scriptural injunctions and giving

his all to the officiating priests, he should mentally put the sacrificial fires in his own self, and renounce without caring for anything.

14. To a Brâhmana who is about to renounce, the gods, thinking that he may verily transcend them and attain to Brahman, offer obstructions in the form of the wife and other relations.

15. If the monk retains a second piece of cloth, it should be only as much as covers the loin-cloth. And except in times of danger, he should not have anything that he has already discarded, other than his staff and his begging bowl.

16. He should place his foot on the ground after looking well, should drink water filtered through a cloth, should speak words that have the stamp of truth on them, and act as his reason dictates.

17. Silence, inaction, and control of the Prânas are the restraints of speech, body, and mind respectively. One who has not these, My friend, never becomes a Sannyâsin by simply carrying some staves.

18. A Sannyâsin should beg his food from the four castes, excepting the culpable. He should visit not more than seven houses, must not think of the food beforehand, and must be satisfied with as much as is obtained.

19. Going to a tank outside the village, and bathing there, he should purify the food he has collected, and offering portions to the deities and all creatures, silently eat the remnant, without saving anything.

20. He should roam over this earth alone, without attachment, and with his senses under control. All his pastimes should be in the Self, as well as all his pleasures; he should be of a steady mind and look evenly upon everything.

21. Taking shelter in a secluded and congenial spot, and with his mind purified by rapt devotion to Me, the sage should meditate on the One Self as identified with Me.

22. He should reflect on the bondage and liberation of the Self, through the pursuit of knowledge. Bondage consists in the outgoing of the senses, and liberation in their control.

23. Therefore the sage, controlling the senses, should roam, looking upon everything as Myself. Deriving great bliss from the Self, he should turn away from petty desires.

24. Going to towns, villages, cowherds settlements, and assemblies of pilgrims for the purpose of begging his food, he should wander over the earth abounding in holy countries, rivers, mountains, forests, and hermitages.

25. He should beg his food mostly from the hermitages of people who have retired into the forest, for by partaking of their food consisting of grains picked up from the fields, he soon becomes purified in mind, and freed from delusion, attains perfection.

26. The visible world he should not consider as a reality, for it perishes. With his mind unattached to this world and the next, he should desist from activities tending to enjoyments in them.

27. This world, and this body with the mind, speech, and Prânas, are all a delusive superimposition on the Self—reasoning thus he should take his stand on the Self, and giving the former up, should not more think of them.

28. He who, averse to the objective world, is devoted to knowledge, or not caring even for liberation, is devoted to Me, should move about, regardless of the orders of life with their respective insignia; he should be above the ties of formality.

29. Though wise, he should play as a child; though expert, he should move about like an idiot; though erudite, he should talk like a lunatic; and though well versed in the scriptures, he should live as if he were a cow.

30. He should not be fond of upholding the ritualistic portion of the Vedas, nor be a heretic, nor be given to barren argument; in disputes arising out of empty discussions, he should take neither side.

31. The sage should not be vexed by people nor vex them himself. He should put up with vilifications and never insult anybody. For the sake of the body he should bear enmity to none, as beasts do.

32. The One Supreme Self alone dwells in the bodies of all beings and in one's own body, as the moon is reflected in so many vessels of water. And all bodies are of the same nature.

33. Possessed of steadiness, he should not be sorry when he gets no food, nor be delighted when he gets it, for both these are controlled by destiny.

34. He should strive to procure his food, for continuity of life is desirable. Through it one can reflect on Truth, knowing which one becomes free.

35. The sage should eat food, good or bad, which comes of itself, and use clothes and bedding just as he obtains them.

36. The man of realisation should observe cleanliness, wash his mouth, and bathe, and go through all other observances, but not because of scriptural injunctions, as I, the Lord, do everything of My free will.

37. He has no perception of differences, and if he ever had any, it has been removed by his realisation of Me. Till the dissolution of his body he sometimes has a semblance of it, and after that he is one with Me.

38. A man who has got sick of works that produce only pain, and is possessed of self-control, but has not inquired into the religion that leads to Me, should go to a sage as to a Master.

39. Until he has realised Brahman, he should serve the Teacher like Me, with care and devotion, having faith in him and never carping at him.

40–41. But one who has not mastered his passions, whose intellect—the guide to his sense-organs—is wild, and who is devoid of discrimination and renunciation—such a man taking up the monk's triple staff for the sake of subsistence, is a destroyer of religion, and cheats the gods, cheats himself, and Me who reside in his self. With his impurities unconsumed, he is deprived of both this life and the life to come.

42. The duties of a monk are control of the mind and non-injury, those of a forest-dwelling hermit are austerity and discrimination; those of a house-

holder are preservation of the lives of animals and performance of sacrifices; while the duty of a Brahmachâri is service unto the Teacher.

43. Continence, with the option of deviating from it at prescribed times, the performance of his duties, purity, contentment, and kindness to animals are also duties for a householder. Worship of Me is a duty for all.

44. He who thus worships Me constantly and exclusively, through the performance of his duties, knowing My presence in all beings, soon attains to a steadfast devotion to Me.

45. O Uddhava, through his undying devotion he comes to Me, the great Lord of all beings, the originator and destroyer of all, their cause, the Brahman.

46. Having his mind thus purified by the performance of his duties, and knowing My Divinity, he becomes endowed with knowledge and realisation and soon attains to Me.

47. All this duty, consisting of specific rites, of those belonging to the castes and orders of life, if attended with devotion to Me, becomes supreme and conducive to liberation.

48. So I have told you, My friend, what you asked Me about, viz how a person attending to his duties becomes a devotee and attains to Me the Supreme Being.

7

FAREWELL
Mohandas Gandhi

Mohandas Karamchand Gandhi (1869–1948), usually called "Mahatma" or "Great Spirit," demonstrated to the world the creative vitality still to be found in Hinduism. Raised in a prosperous Gujarat Vaishnavite family, Gandhi studied law in London, then practiced briefly in India before business took him to South Africa. Beaten and ejected from a train for insisting that his first-class ticket be honored, Gandhi remained in South Africa to help the

M. K. Gandhi, "Farewell," (Ahmedabad, India: Navajivan Press, 1957), vol. II, pp. 588–593. Reprinted from *The Story of My Experiments with Truth*, by M. K. Gandhi, by permission of the Navajivan Trust.

oppressed Indian community secure justice. In the twenty years he devoted to that struggle, Gandhi developed a religious social philosophy as well as practical methods whereby the oppressed, by refusing to acquiesce in injustice despite coercion, could non-violently exert a strong force for reform. After considerable success in South Africa, Gandhi returned to India in 1915 and soon became the leader of the movement for home rule. Living a celibate life, wearing the clothes of a peasant, eating a sparse vegetarian diet, serving untouchables, promoting the creation of a cottage textile industry, and teaching the theory and methods of non-violent non-cooperation, Gandhi combined the dedication and austerity of the traditional sannyasin or monk with large-scale programs to deal with the political, economic, and social problems of his own day. By his example and the power of his loving and truthful spirit he aroused in millions a willingness to undergo pain, hardship, and personal loss in the service of social ideals. He thus helped prepare India for independence as well as hastening the day when the British would surrender their colonial rule. In the communal warfare following the partition of India, Gandhi struggled to stop the violence and to bring the rival governments to agreement until an extremist's bullet ended his life.

Gandhi acknowledged many influences upon his thought. Kropotkin, Tolstoy, Thoreau, Ruskin, and the Sermon on the Mount were some, but the Indian ancestry of his ideals of ahimsa or non-violence, satyagraha or truth force, and karma yoga or selfless work as a path to God, are evident. Through his life and work millions have been introduced to the ideals of the Bhagavad-Gita as well as to the realization that those ideals can be an effective force for social reform. The following selection is the last chapter of his autobiography The Story of My Experiments with Truth.

But the time has now come to bring these chapters to a close.

My life from this point onward has been so public, that there is hardly anything about it, that the people do not know. Moreover since 1921 I have worked in such close association with the Congress leaders, that I can hardly describe any episode in my life since then without referring to my relations with them. For though Shraddhanandji, the Deshabandhu, Hakim Saheb and Lalaji are no more with us today, we have the good luck to have a host of other veteran Congress leaders still living and working in our midst. The history of the Congress, since the great changes in it that I have described above, is still in the making. And my principal experiments during the past seven years have all been made through the Congress. A reference to my relations with the leaders would therefore be unavoidable, if I set about describing my experiments further. And this I may not do, at any rate for the present, if only from a sense of propriety. Lastly my conclusions from my current experiments can hardly as yet be regarded as decisive. It therefore seems to me to be my plain duty to close this narrative here. In fact my pen instinctively refuses to proceed further.

It is not without a wrench that I have to take leave of the reader. I set a high value on my experiments. I do not know whether I have been able to do justice to them. I can only say that I have spared no pains to give a faithful narrative. To describe truth, as it has appeared to me, and in the exact manner in which I have arrived at it, has been my ceaseless effort. The exercise has given me ineffable mental peace, because it has been my fond hope, that it might bring faith in Truth and Ahimsa to waverers.

My uniform experience has convinced me, that there is no other God than Truth. And if every page of these chapters does not proclaim to the reader, that the only means for the realisation of Truth is Ahimsa, I shall deem all my pains in writing these chapters to have been in vain. And, even though my efforts in this behalf may prove fruitless, let the readers know that the vehicle, not the great principle, is at fault. After all, however sincere my strivings after Ahimsa may have been, they have still been imperfect and inadequate. The little fleeting glimpses, therefore, that I have been able to have of Truth can hardly convey an idea of the indescribable lustre of Truth, a million times more intense than that of the sun we daily see with our eyes. In fact what I have caught is only the faintest glimmer of that mighty effulgence. But this much I can say with assurance, as a result of all my experiments, that a perfect vision of Truth can only follow a complete realisation of Ahimsa.

To see the universal and all-pervading Spirit of Truth face to face one must be able to love the meanest of creation as oneself. And a man who aspires after that cannot afford to keep out of any field of life. That is why my devotion to Truth has drawn me into the field of politics; and I can say without the slightest hesitation, and yet in all humility, that those, who say that religion has nothing to do with politics, do not know what religion means.

Identification with everything that lives is impossible without self-purification; without self-purification the observance of the law of Ahimsa must remain an empty dream; God can never be realised by one who is not pure of heart. Self-purification therefore must mean purification in all the walks of life. And purification being highly infectious, purification of oneself necessarily leads to the purification of one's surroundings.

But the path of self-purification is hard and steep. To attain to perfect purity one has to become absolutely passion-free in thought, speech and action; to rise above the opposing currents of love and hatred, attachment and repulsion. I know, that I have not in me as yet that triple purity, in spite of constant ceaseless striving for it. That is why the world's praise fails to move me, indeed it very often stings me. To conquer the subtle passions seems to me to be harder far than the physical conquest of the world by the force of arms. Ever since my return to India I have had experiences of the dormant passions lying hidden within me. The knowledge of them has made me feel humiliated but not defeated. The experiences and experiments have sustained me, and given me great joy. But I know that I have still before me a difficult path to traverse. I must reduce myself to zero. So long as one does not of his own free will put himself last among his fellow creatures, there is no salvation for him. Ahimsa is the farthest limit of humility.

In bidding farewell to the reader, for the time being at any rate, I ask him to join with me in prayer to the God of Truth, that He may grant me the boon of Ahimsa in mind, word and deed.

BUDDHISM

PART II

According to the traditional account, the main lines of which scholars have no reason to reject, Buddhism sprang from the teaching and personality of a single remarkable man. Siddhartha Gautama is said to have been the son of the ruler of the small hill state of the Shakyas on the border of present day Nepal. He was married and the father of a son, but at the age of twenty-nine he became disenchanted with worldly life and abandoned his family for the career of a homeless ascetic. After six years of intense physical and psychological discipline, including disappointing experiences as a student of two Brahmin teachers, he is said to have achieved enlightenment while meditating beneath a pipal tree at a place now called "Buddhagaya." The title "Buddha" or "Enlightened One" is used by his followers to refer to Gautama after this experience. Two other common titles are "Shakyamuni" or "Sage of the Shakyas" and "Tathagata," a term by which the illumined Gautama referred to himself, which is sometimes rendered as "One who has gone thus far." For the next forty-five years Gautama preached his "Middle Way" of salvation in Northcentral India and gathered a band of yellow-garbed, mendicant, celibate followers. He is said to have died of a digestive disorder as an old man of eighty about the year 483 B.C.

Gautama's followers continued his mission. His order of monks and nuns spread widely in Northern India during the two centuries following his death, while lay devotees increased even faster. Although no written scriptures preserving the words of the Master were to appear for several centuries, oral collections of his teachings developed. Half-way through the order's second century, disagreement between the monks, ostensibly over points of discipline but probably over doctrines also, became so heated that the Buddhists split into a liberal and a conservative sect. By then the early practice of spending the eight dry months in traveling and preaching had largely been abandoned and most monks had settled into permanent monasteries.

During the late Fourth Century B.C., Chandragupta Maurya built an empire in Northern India by ejecting the Macedonian garrisons left by Alexander the Great and conquering the other Indian states. His capital was in the rich kingdom of Magadha in South Behar, the center of Buddhist activity. Chandragupta's grandson, the great Ashoka Maurya who ruled from about 268 to 233 B.C., completed the creation of the first Indian empire, bringing all the subcontinent except the southern tip under a single rule. After the bloody capture of what is today Orissa, however, Ashoka declared regret for the suffering he had caused and announced that he had become a follower of the Buddha. Through edicts which have survived as the earliest intelligible writing in India because they were engraved upon rocks and pillars, Ashoka exhorted his subjects to abjure violence, to love righteousness, to obey parents and teachers, to feel pity for all creatures, to honor members of all religious sects, and thus insure themselves of a heavenly rebirth. He also praised himself, "the Beloved of the Gods," for having planted medicinal herbs and shade trees, dug wells and ponds, ordered just treatment of all, and for abandoning hunting, meat-eating, and expensive pleasures in favor of gifts to brahmins and ascetics and interviews with his subjects. In fact, Ashoka seems to have been an unusually benevolent and competent emperor, while his support for Buddhism has sometimes earned him the title of "the Second Founder." He built monasteries; erected stupas; sponsored a council, according to tradition, in an effort to reform the order and eliminate heretical doctrines; and sent teams of Buddhist missionaries to those parts of India in which the Middle Way was not popular, to the lands surrounding India, and as far afield as Syria, Egypt, Cyrene, and Greece. The most successful foreign mission was that to Ceylon, said to have been led by a monk who was Ashoka's son. Ceylon became and has remained the most conservative of the Buddhist lands and played an important role in preserving the scriptures.

After Ashoka, Buddhism became one of the major faiths of Asia. Although Hinduism was never entirely eclipsed, the period from 200 B.C. to A.D. 200 is often referred to as the Buddhist centuries in India. As it attracted more adherents, Buddhism divided into more sects. The conservative school of the original schism split into eight sects of which only one, Theravada ("Teaching of the Elders"), is still alive. This conservative form of Buddhism is today the dominant faith of Ceylon, Burma, Thailand, Cambodia and Laos. The original liberal school, which apparently defended the interests of the lay Buddhists, split into ten sects, none of which has survived. However, between 100 B.C. and A.D. 100, in a way historians have not yet clarified, a major new movement of thought emerged in Indian Buddhism which embodied many features of the earlier liberal schools. Adherents of this movement eventually named it the "Mahayana" ("Great Way") and contrasted it with other Buddhist schools which they sometimes condescendingly classified as "Hinayana" ("Lesser Way"). Mahayana Buddhism has a complex history, developing many sects of which more than a dozen are still flourishing. Various forms of Mahayana Buddhism are popular today in Japan, Tibet, Mongolia, Korea, and Viet-Nam, and once were influential in India, China, and Central Asia.

Almost all the surviving historically credible information about the Buddha and his teaching is contained in the Theravada scriptures, called the "Pali Canon" after the language in which it is written. Pali is derived from Sanskrit, and the differences between the two languages are not great. The

Sanskrit "Dharma" and "Nirvana," for example, become in Pali "Dhamma" and "Nibbana." About four times the length of the Christian Bible, the Pali Canon is divided into three *Pitakas* or baskets, possibly named for the receptacles for storing the dried palm leaves on which the scriptures were originally written. The "Discipline-Basket" contains five books detailing the rules and practices of the monastic order and the circumstances under which the Buddha allegedly gave the rules. The large "Sermon-Basket" is the portion of the canon of principal interest to those concerned with Buddhist thought. Its five books contain, for the most part, discourses attributed to Gautama, but also sermons by his disciples, Buddhist poetry, and collected sayings. The "Further Teach-ings-Basket" contains seven technical and arid treatises largely designed as a guide to the proper analysis of experience. A method of phenomenal reduction is taught that helps the spiritual aspirant to gain detachment from allegedly fictitious entities, such as an enduring self.

The content of the Pali Canon is acknowledged as scripture by all Buddhists. To Theravadins it is the only scripture, although some other Pali works, such as Buddhaghosa's commentaries and *The Questions of King Menander,* are also treated with reverence. The various Mahayana schools, on the other hand, possess an enormous quantity of other scriptures, many of which are held in greater esteem and are more studied than the materials found in the Pali scriptures. Conservative Theravadins hold that everything attributed to Gautama in the Pali Canon was actually uttered by him and that no other source contains his authentic teaching. His disciples gathered, the tradition runs, shortly after Buddha's death to rehearse his words and establish the scriptural version. Scholars agree, however, that not only is the third basket the result of several centuries of monastic development, but that portions of the first two baskets are also late. The Pali Canon was transmitted orally until the First Century B.C., when the Singhalese finally wrote it down, but oral transmission of sacred texts can be surprisingly accurate as the considerable agreement between the surviving Sanskrit versions and the Pali Canon show. Although several scholars have undertaken to establish that the original gospel of Buddhism was markedly different from that presented in the Pali scriptures, their work has not won wide acceptance. The picture of the Buddha and his teaching given in the Pali Canon, pruned of its more obvious exaggerations and legends, appears as a plausible representation to many Buddhist scholars.

In religions with historic founders, the personality as well as the doctrine of the founder is a major influence. What manner of man was Gautama? If the account of the Pali Canon is literally accurate, he was a superman—wiser, more virtuous, more devoted, and more loving than any other man; not only head and shoulders, but chest and waist above his contemporaries. The Mahayana scriptures, on the other hand, usually represent him not as a superman but as a supergod. Allowing for the effects of his followers' reverence and discounting the legendary elements in the Pali scriptures, what does the bare history of his life and teaching suggest about him? First, that he was a man of great self-confidence and inner strength, able to abandon family and home in a religious quest, able to propound a new doctrine based on his own experience, able to convert intelligent men to it by outdoor evangelism, and able to serve as an effective leader of a new religious organization. Second, his teachings show a man of unusually powerful intellect, much more skeptical and analytic than is common among religious men. The Buddha is an important figure in the history of philosophy as well as in that of religion. Third, he was an outstanding teacher, methodical, patient, able to adapt to the capacity of his audience, and always prepared to provide rational grounds for his views. More than any other great faith, Buddhism has sought to attract adherents by reasoned argument, and the Buddha provides an outstanding example of this approach. Fourth, his teachings as well as his example reveal Gautama as the most ascetic of the great religious founders. He called his path "the Middle Way" because he held it to be a mean between the extremes of self-mortification and self-indulgence, but the life extolled in the Pali Canon is that of a homeless, possessionless, celibate monk, sleeping little, eating lightly and then only in the forenoon, and striving to transcend all passions, while following a rigorous course of mental and spiritual training. Contrasted with the extreme asceticism that some contemporaries of the Buddha practiced, and which the scriptures say Gautama, before his enlightenment, tried himself, the life of a Buddhist monk or nun might seem a middle course. Most of mankind, though, would judge it to be profoundly ascetic. Early Buddhism was a religion focussed on a severe monasticism; the life of the householder was considered distinctly inferior. Fifth, to an extent unusual in a hard-headed man, the Buddha was tender-hearted and sympathetic. It has been asserted that men normally renounce the world driven by their own sorrows, but that Gautama left it driven by a desire to find a solution to other men's sorrows. Whatever his initial motive, after finding his path, Gautama spent the rest of his life actively carrying it to other men. The deep devotion he awakened in his followers suggests that the scriptural stories of his great interest and affection for his fellow men are based on fact. The teachings of early Buddhism highly value compassion toward men and animals and include directions for spiritual exercises designed to increase loving kindness and joyous sympathy. It is understandable that to his followers the Buddha has become known as "The Compassionate One." Each of these five traits in a developed form is somewhat unusual; their combination is rare indeed. It is safe to conclude that Gautama was one of the more remarkable men in history.

In his teaching the Buddha clearly revealed his Indian heritage. It has been seriously argued that the doctrine of early Buddhism is essentially the same as that of Brahmanism, the teaching of the Upanishads. Although an exaggeration, this calls attention to the continuation in Buddhism of such central Hindu beliefs as the doctrine of reincarnation, the law of karma, the belief in the wheel of *samsara* or the cycle of birth, death, and rebirth, and the faith in the possibility of liberation from this cycle by means of study, asceticism, and yogic meditative exercises. Pali Buddhism most notably diverges from Brahmanism in the rational, public, and systematic nature of its teaching, in its metaphysical interpretation of man, existence, and *moksha,* in its traditional form of worship, and in its universalistic and rationalistic rather than traditional attitude on moral and social issues.

Pali Buddhism is the oldest form of an exoteric, rationalized, and systematized way of liberation. The Upanishads, which are older, were originally esoteric; their persuasiveness rested almost completely upon the spiritual authority of the sages whose words they recorded; and they lacked systematic organization and development of their doctrines. Something of the magical attitude of the period of the Vedic incantations still attached to them; to have the secret formulation is to have power, consequently the deepest teachings must be kept from the majority unfitted by birth and training to possess them. As unargued revelations, they could be accepted or rejected; but they could not be rationally sifted and evaluated point by point. Pali Buddhism, on the other hand, was open to the public. The Buddha was a teacher skilled in suiting his discourse to the interests and understanding of his audience, but it was his boast that he concealed nothing from inquirers. The Pali scriptures present many arguments designed to secure assent upon rational grounds, and the doctrine has been highly systematized in a scholastic manner with many distinctions and numbered lists. The contrast is not complete; the Upanishads were not totally lacking in reasoned support, while it is doubtful that many critical men have been convinced by the arguments of the Pali Canon unless they had faith that the authors were men of deep and genuine spiritual experience. Still, in its classical order and rational attitude, Pali Buddhism represented something new in Indian religion.

The major metaphysical innovation of Theravada Buddhism was its attack upon the concept of substance. Aimed primarily at the belief that there is some enduring ego-entity in a human being, the doctrine is known as *Anatta* or no-self in Pali. However the same kind of analysis is also applied to every phenomenon, physical or mental. All things are said to be compounded out of momentary entities called *dharmas* which are comparable to what recent western philosophy has called "sense-data." What is ignorantly taken to be a permanent substance, such as a human personality, is actually, according to this view, a process, a stream of momentary *dharmas;* consequently every phenomenon is impermanent, constantly changing, and imperfect. Only Nirvana is uncompounded, and therefore unchanging and perfect. Although Nirvana plays in Theravada Buddhism a role in many ways similar to *Atman* and *Brahman* in the Upanishads, the Pali texts do not make metaphysical affirmations about Nirvana. It is simply the ineffable goal, the state of enlightenment, contrasted with the unsubstantial, changing, and imperfect phenomena which are all we now know.

Theravada Buddhism contains a fair amount of religious ritual. Like all

Buddhists, Theravadins repeat the formula known as the "Three Jewels": "I take refuge in the Buddha, I take refuge in the Doctrine, I take refuge in the Order." In Theravada countries there are many stupas and temples containing images of the Blessed One to which the devout come to make offerings and to pray. The more philosophical monks justify such practices as subjectively beneficial, but deprecate the belief that a transaction of some kind is taking place between the Buddha and his devotees. Salvation and self-improvement come as a result of a man's own efforts, Theravada Buddhism teaches, not as a gift of a transcendent being.

Expositions of Theravada Buddhism sometimes stress so strongly the Four Noble Truths, the Noble Eightfold Path, Nirvana, the Three Characteristics of Being, and the cultivation of Mindfulness and Concentration, that it is overlooked that most devout Theravada Buddhists are not monks or nuns but laymen, and that Buddhism is an intensely moral faith as well as a way to liberation. Most Theravadins have no expectation of attaining Nirvana in this life, indeed most would think this impossible outside the monastic life; and few monks expect to achieve final success in their present life, but they do desire and expect a favorable heavenly rebirth as a result of meritorious karma or action in this life. A strong moral earnestness pervades the Pali scriptures, and right action is not conceived primarily as fulfilling the particular obligations of one's caste and place in life but as kindness, truthfulness, usefulness, and purity. The welfare of all sentient beings becomes a central criterion of moral behavior, and a rational, universal moral code is substituted for traditional pre-reflective morality.

During the first five centuries A.D., while Theravadins were faithfully preserving the rationalistic doctrines and monastic life taught in the Pali scriptures, the new movement of Mahayana Buddhism, promising universal salvation and offering a wide variety of cults, philosophies, and spiritual practices, rose to dominance in India. Mahayanists have traditionally claimed that their basic doctrines were secretly taught by the Buddha to his more advanced followers and then hidden for 500 years until rediscovered by the Mahayana founders. Scholars do not take this claim seriously, but they do point out seeds of the Mahayana development in early Buddhism. The Buddhist stress upon compassion and helpfulness, for example, is seen as the germ of the Mahayana ideal of the Bodhisattva ("being of wisdom"). Bodhisattvas are beings who have attained the brink of Nirvana but then refused to cross it in order to remain in samsara and help others. Many Mahayanists, viewing the Theravada goal of personal deliverance as selfish, have vowed that they will not themselves enter Nirvana until all suffering is extinguished. It is but a short extension of this notion to hold that there are already great spiritual beings, freed from passions and limitations, wholly dedicated to the service of struggling beings. These great Bodhisattvas, such as Avalokitesvara (Kwan-Yin in China), are venerated in ritual and petitioned by those in need.

Deep reverence for the Tathagata, which had been present in Buddhism from its beginning and expressed in the first jewel ("I take refuge in the Buddha"), developed into full-fledged worship. Rather than concede that Gautama had passed into an impersonal deliverance, the Mahayanists urged that he had not been a man at all, but rather the manifestation on earth of the supreme spiritual being. The Buddha, it was explained, has three kinds of bodies. The *Dharmakaya* or Body of the Law is the Absolute, the World Soul, the Mahayana Buddhist equivalent of *Brahman*. From this body emanated many *Sambhogakayas* or Bodies of Bliss which can be compared with personal gods such as Vishnu, each of which reigns in his own heaven. The most popular of these heavenly Buddhas was Amitabha (Amida in Japan), the ruler of the heaven of the West. These heavenly Buddhas, in turn, sometimes appeared in an earthly emanation in the *Nirmanakaya* or Body of Transformation. Gautama had been one such appearance, but others had preceded him and at least one, Maitreya, will appear in the future as a kind of Buddhist messiah. The introduction of the great Bodhisattvas and Heavenly Buddhas gave the Mahayanists a Buddhist pantheon, which in the end came to include more than 500 figures. These gracious supernatural beings were available to the worshipper, anxious to help all who called upon them. A new way of salvation for those unable or uninclined to follow the strenuous path of self-purification through asceticism and meditation, a path of faith, was also developed. It was taught that the great Amitabha had vowed that he would not enter Buddhahood unless everyone who was innocent of slandering the true religion and of the five heinous sins and had called upon his name should upon death be reborn in his Paradise. To this day millions of Mahayanists, particularly in Japan, are devoutly reciting the name of Amitabha in the confident faith that following death they will, by virtue of his vow, be reborn in the Pure Land.

Mahayana Buddhism produced a number of philosophical schools as well as devotional cults. Their central concern was the nature of the Absolute, the Unconditioned, the Ultimate Being about which the Gautama of the Pali scriptures had remained silent. The Mahayanists found it difficult to speak intelligibly of the Unconditioned, but like intellectual mystics elsewhere, they attempted it. The earliest class of works in this genre is that of the *Prajna-paramita* (Perfection of Wisdom) Sutras. These contain little in the way of argument, being largely hymns of praise to the Absolute, which is called "Emptiness" (*Sunyata*). The most celebrated of the Mahayana philosophers was Nagarjuna, founder of the *Madhyamika* (Middle Doctrine) School. In a subtle and difficult dialectic, which has been interpreted as an effort to undermine every positive metaphysical position, Nagarjuna held that only Emptiness truly exists. Vasubandhu, one of the two leading figures of the *Yogacara* (Way of Yoga) School, argued for the idealistic view that to exist is to be perceived (except in the case of the Absolute). The most important Mahayana philosophies were developed in India between 100 and 500 A.D., but toward the end of this period they were imported into China where they stimulated an interest in mystical metaphysics. The most important Chinese contribution to Buddhist philosophy was the development of the doctrine of the *Avatamsaka Sutra* into the school known as "Hua-yen" in China and "Kegon" in Japan. This school is a form of objective idealism which teaches that every element in the world interpenetrates every other so that the entire universe is present in each particle of dust.

In addition to the Mahayana philosophical schools, China also imported the Mahayana devotional schools. The Pure Land cult became very popular in China and Japan. Members of the various sects into which it split have produced a large body of devotional poetry and prose. Today these sects are the largest Buddhist groups in Japan. After A.D. 500, forms of Tantric Buddhism developed in India, parallel with the rising Hindu Tantric sects. This Buddhist Tantra, which arose as the intellectual vigor of Buddhism in India was declining, drew freely upon the materials of the Prajnaparamita sutras, the Madhyamikas, the Yogacaras, and the devotional schools and developed its own large literature of hymns, incantations, accounts of mythological beings, and treatises upon the power of the sacred formulae. It spread to Tibet, where it became dominant, as well as to China and Japan. Under the name *Shingon* (True Word), it is a popular form of Buddhism in Japan today.

The most characteristic and influential form of Far Eastern Buddhism, however, is the one that owes the least to an Indian inspiration. Ch'an Buddhism, better known by its Japanese name of "Zen," exhibits a blending of Chinese, particularly Taoist, attitudes and values with Buddhism. The Zen distrust of metaphysical speculation, its severe monastic discipline, and its stress upon "self-power" resemble Theravada Buddhism; its implicit sense of the unity of all existence, its poetic imagination, and its conventional pieties are typical of the Mahayana, while its practicality, love of nature and of art, and its humor are characteristically Chinese. Still a major factor in the spiritual life of Japan, Zen has exerted a growing influence upon western thought in the last three decades, largely through the work of Dr. D. T. Suzuki.

SUGGESTIONS FOR FURTHER READING

Blyth, R. H., *Zen in English Literature and Oriental Classics,* Tokyo, Hokuseido Press, 1942.

Carus, Paul, *The Gospel of the Buddha,* Chicago, Open Court, 1897.

Conze, Edward, ed., *Buddhist Texts Through the Ages,* New York, Philosophical Library, 1954.

Conze, Edward, *Buddhist Thought in India, Three Phases of Buddhist Philosophy,* London, G. Allen, 1962.

Pratt, J. B., *The Pilgrimage of Buddhism,* New York, Macmillan, 1928.

Suzuki, D. T., *Essays in Zen Buddhism,* 3 vols., London, Luzac, 1927, 1933, 1934.

Thomas, E. J., *The History of Buddhist Thought* (2nd ed.), New York, Barnes & Noble, 1951.

SELECTIONS FROM THE PALI SERMONS

In their original form the Pali scriptures are very repetitive, a heritage of their centuries of oral transmission. In the selections which follow, all of which are from the second or Sermon-Basket, the translators have abridged the originals.

The most famous statement of the Buddhist Dharma or doctrine, one accepted by all schools, is that of the Four Noble Truths or Principles realized by Gautama at his enlightenment and taught in his first sermon. In the form of a physician's diagnosis and prescription, the Four Principles assert the painfulness or imperfection of existence, attribute it to craving, view its cessation as following from the cessation of craving, and prescribe the Noble Eightfold Way as the path to this double cessation.

The Chain of Causation or Dependent Origination occurs in several slightly different forms in the Pali Canon. It is an effort to explain both the origin and the cessation of pain.

In "All Signs of an Ego are Absent" a short and canonical form of the arguments against any substantial and enduring self are given. A more complete and more famous example of this argument is found in the book entitled The Questions of King Menander.

Something of the emotional depth of Buddhism's sense of the misery of normal existence and the urgency of the spiritual life is seen in the Fire-Sermon. Its account of liberation or Nirvana is characteristic of Theravada Buddhism in describing it merely as the absence of passion and the end of rebirth. Nirvana is ineffable and can only be characterized by saying what it is not. This custom led some early western interpreters to assert that Nirvana is sheer annihilation, but the scriptures say rather that it is the annihilation of ignorance and pain. One source of confusion is that "Nirvana" is used ambiguously in the early scriptures for the state attained at liberation and for the death of an enlightened man. Later the term

"Sermon at Benares," as "The First Sermon," from Samyutta, V, 420, E. J. Thomas, trans. (London: Kegan Paul, Trench, Trubner, Co. Ltd., 1935), pp. 29–33. Reprinted from Early Buddhist Scriptures by E. J. Thomas, by permission of Routledge & Kegan Paul Ltd.

*"Pari-nirvana" was introduced for the death of a person who has
reached Nirvana.*

*Although a philosophic religion, Theravada Buddhism val-
ues philosophy only to the extent that it is an aid in the pursuit of
Nirvana and the moral life. The pragmatic rejection of speculation
on issues which have no relevance for behavior in "Questions
Which Tend Not to Edification" represents a break with the ex-
uberant metaphysical tradition of Indian thought.*

*The Ascetic's Training provides a thumb-nail sketch of the
motives, the moral restrictions, the spiritual exercises, and the possible accomplishments of the monk's life. One of the most important practices in the spiritual life of a monk is that of Mindfulness,
a practice which has undergone a remarkable revival in Burma in
this century. "The Four Stations of Mindfulness" is the classic
text on how one can progressively become aware of what is happening within oneself.*

In The Buddha's Last Words *the spirit of self-reliance in
the religious quest, so prominent in Theravda Buddhism, received
its classic statement.*

THE FIRST SERMON

Thus have I heard: at one time the Lord dwelt at Benares at Isipatana in the
Deer Park. There the Lord addressed the five monks:—

"These two extremes, monks, are not to be practised by one who has
gone forth from the world. What are the two? That conjoined with the passions and luxury, low, vulgar, common, ignoble, and useless, and that conjoined with self-torture, painful, ignoble, and useless. Avoiding these two
extremes the Tathāgata has gained the enlightenment of the Middle Path,
which produces insight and knowledge, and tends to calm, to higher knowledge, enlightenment, Nirvāna.

"And what, monks, is the Middle Path, of which the Tathāgata has
gained enlightenment, which produces insight and knowledge, and tends to
calm, to higher knowledge, enlightenment, Nirvāna? This is the noble Eightfold Way, namely right view, right intention, right speech, right action, right
livelihood, right effort, right mindfulness, right concentration. This, monks, is
the Middle Path, of which the Tathāgata has gained enlightenment, which
produces insight and knowledge, and tends to calm, to higher knowledge, enlightenment, Nirvāna.

"(1) Now this, monks, is the noble truth of pain: birth is painful, old
age is painful, sickness is painful, death is painful, sorrow, lamentation, dejec-
tion, and despair are painful. Contact with unpleasant things is painful, not
getting what one wishes is painful. In short the five groups of grasping are
painful.

"(2) Now this, monks, is the noble truth of the cause of pain: the
craving, which tends to rebirth, combined with pleasure and lust, finding

pleasure here and there, namely the craving for passion, the craving for existence, the craving for non-existence.

"(3) Now this, monks, is the noble truth of the cessation of pain, the cessation without a remainder of craving, the abandonment, forsaking, release, non-attachment.

"(4) Now this, monks, is the noble truth of the way that leads to the cessation of pain: this is the noble Eightfold Way, namely, right views, right intention, right speech, right action, right livelihood, right effort, right mindfulness, right concentration.

" 'This is the noble truth of pain': Thus, monks, among doctrines unheard before, in me sight and knowledge arose, wisdom arose, knowledge arose, light arose.

" 'This noble truth of pain must be comprehended.' Thus, monks, among doctrines unheard before, in me sight and knowledge arose, wisdom arose, knowledge arose, light arose.

" 'It has been comprehended.' Thus, monks among doctrines unheard before, in me sight and knowledge arose, wisdom arose, knowledge arose, light arose. (Repeated for the second truth, with the statement that the cause of pain must be abandoned and has been abandoned, for the third truth that the cessation of pain must be realized and has been realized, and for the fourth that the Way must be practised and has been practised.)

"As long as in these four noble truths my due knowledge and insight with the three sections and twelve divisions was not well purified, even so long, monks, in the world with its gods, Māra, Brahmā, its beings with ascetics, brahmins, gods, and men, I had not attained the highest complete enlightenment. This I recognized.

"And when, monks in these four noble truths my due knowledge and insight with its three sections and twelve divisions was well purified, then monks . . . I had attained the highest complete enlightenment. This I recognized. Knowledge arose in me, insight arose that the release of my mind is unshakable: this is my last existence; now there is no rebirth."

Thus spoke the Lord, and the five monks expressed delight and approval at the Lord's utterance. And while this exposition was being uttered there arose in the elder Koṇḍañña the pure and spotless eye of the Doctrine that whatever was liable to origination was all liable to cessation.

Thus when the Wheel of the Doctrine was set turning by the Lord, the earth-dwelling gods raised a shout: "This supreme Wheel of the Doctrine has been set going by the Lord at Benares at Isipatana in the Deer Park, a Wheel which has not been set going by any ascetic, brahmin, god, Māra, Brahmā, or by anyone in the world." The gods of the heaven of the four Great Kings hearing the shout of the earth-dwelling gods raised a shout. . . . The gods of the heaven of the Thirty-three hearing the shout of the gods of the four Great Kings . . . the Yāma gods . . . the Tusita gods . . . the Nimmānarati gods . . . the Paranimmitavasavattin gods . . . the gods of the Brahma-world raised a shout: "This supreme Wheel of the Doctrine has been set going by the Lord at Benares at Isipatana in the Deer Park, a Wheel which has not been set going by any ascetic, brahmin, god, Māra, Brahmā, or by anyone in the world."

Thus at that very time, at that moment, at that second, a shout went up as far as the Brahma-world, and this ten-thousandfold world system shook, shuddered, and trembled, and a boundless great light appeared in the world surpassing the divine majesty of the gods.

So the Lord uttered this fervent utterance: "Verily Koṇḍañña has attained the knowledge; verily Koṇḍañña has attained the knowledge." Thus Aññāta-Koṇḍañña became the name of the elder Koṇḍañña, "Koṇḍañña who has attained the knowledge."

THE CHAIN OF CAUSATION

Before my enlightenment, monks, when I was unenlightened and still a bodhisatta, I thought: "Into wretchedness, alas, has this world fallen, it is born, grows old, dies, passes away, and is reborn. But from this pain it knows no escape, from old age and death. When indeed from this pain shall an escape be known, from old age and death?"

Then, monks, I thought, "Now when what exists do old age and death exist, and what is the cause of old age and death?" And as I duly reflected, there came the comprehension of full knowledge: it is when there is rebirth that there is old age and death. Old age and death have rebirth as cause.

Then, monks, I thought, "Now when what exists does rebirth exist, and what is the cause of rebirth?" And as I duly reflected there came the comprehension of full knowledge: it is when there is becoming (or desire to be) that there is rebirth, rebirth has desire to be as cause.

(In the same way desire to be is said to be caused by grasping, grasping by craving, craving by feeling, feeling by contact or stimulation of any of the senses, contact by the six sense-organs, the six sense-organs by mind-and-body, mind-and-body by consciousness, consciousness by the aggregates, and the aggregates by ignorance.)

Thus with ignorance as cause there are the aggregates, with the aggregates as cause there is consciousness (etc. down to) with rebirth as cause there is old age and death. Even so is the origin of this whole mass of pain.

The origin, the origin: thus as I duly reflected on these things unheard before, vision arose, knowledge arose, full knowledge arose, understanding arose, light arose.

Then, monks, I thought, "Now when what does not exist do old age and death not exist, and with the cessation of what do old age and death cease?"

"The Chain of Causation," (Samyutta, ii, 10) Edward J. Thomas, trans. (London: Kegan Paul, Trench, Trubner, and Co. Ltd. 1935), pp. 119–121. Reprinted from *Early Buddhist Scriptures* by Edward J. Thomas by permission of Routledge & Kegan Paul, Ltd.

Then as I duly reflected there came the comprehension of full knowledge: when there is no rebirth there is no old age and death, and with the cessation of rebirth there is the cessation of old age and death.

Then, monks, I thought: "Now when what does not exist does rebirth not exist, and with the cessation of what does rebirth cease?" Then as I duly reflected there came the comprehension of full knowledge: when there is no desire to be there is no rebirth, and with the cessation of the desire to be there is cessation of rebirth.

(Then with the cessation of grasping follows the cessation of the desire to be, with the cessation of craving the cessation of grasping, with the cessation of feeling the cessation of craving, with the cessation of contact the cessation of feeling, with the cessation of the six sense-organs the cessation of contact, with the cessation of mind-and-body the cessation of the six sense-organs, with the cessation of consciousness the cessation of mind-and-body, with the cessation of the aggregates the cessation of consciousness, and with the cessation of ignorance the cessation of the aggregates.)

Thus with the cessation of ignorance there is the cessation of the aggregates, with the cessation of the aggregates the cessation of consciousness, with the cessation of consciousness the cessation of mind-and-body, with the cessation of mind-and-body the cessation of the six sense-organs, with the cessation of the six sense-organs the cessation of contact, with the cessation of contact the cessation of feeling, with the cessation of feeling the cessation of craving, with the cessation of craving the cessation of grasping, with the cessation of grasping the cessation of the desire to be, with the cessation of the desire to be the cessation of rebirth, with the cessation of rebirth the cessation of old age and death. Even so is the cessation of this whole mass of pain.

Cessation, cessation: thus as I duly reflected on these things unheard before, vision arose, knowledge arose, full knowledge arose, understanding arose, light arose.

ALL SIGNS OF AN EGO ARE ABSENT

Then The Blessed One addressed the band of five priests:—

"Form, O priests, is not an Ego. For if now, O priests, this form were an Ego, then would not this form tend towards destruction, and it would be possible to say of form, 'Let my form be this way; let not my form be that way!' But inasmuch, O priests, as form is not an Ego, therefore does form tend towards destruction, and it is not possible to say of form, 'Let my form be this way; let not my form be that way!'

"Sensation . . . perception . . . the predispositions . . . consciousness, is not an Ego. For if now, O priests, this consciousness were an Ego,

"All Signs of an Ego are Absent," from *Mahā-Vagga*, i, 6, 28, Henry Clarke Warren, trans. (Cambridge, Massachusetts: Harvard University Press, 1896), pp. 146–148. Reprinted from *Buddhism in Translations* by Henry Clarke Warren.

then would not this consciousness tend towards destruction, and it would be possible to say of consciousness, 'Let my consciousness be this way; let not my consciousness be that way!' But inasmuch, O priests, as consciousness is not an Ego, therefore does consciousness tend towards destruction, and it is not possible to say of consciousness, 'Let my consciousness be this way; let not my consciousness be that way!'

"What think you, O priests? Is form permanent, or transitory?"

"It is transitory, Reverend Sir."

"And that which is transitory—is it evil, or is it good?"

"It is evil, Reverend Sir."

"And that which is transitory, evil, and liable to change—is it possible to say of it: 'This is mine; this am I; this is my Ego'?"

"Nay, verily, Reverend Sir."

"Is sensation . . . perception . . . the predispositions . . . consciousness, permanent, or transitory?"

"It is transitory, Reverend Sir."

"And that which is transitory—is it evil, or is it good?"

"It is evil, Reverend Sir."

"And that which is transitory, evil, and liable to change—is it possible to say of it: 'This is mine; this am I; this is my Ego'?"

"Nay, verily, Reverend Sir."

"Accordingly, O priests, as respects all form whatsoever, past, future, or present, be it subjective or existing outside, gross or subtile, mean or exalted, far or near, the correct view in the light of the highest knowledge is as follows: 'This is not mine; this am I not; this is not my Ego.'

"As respects all sensation whatsoever . . . as respects all perception whatsoever . . . as respects all predispositions whatsoever . . . as respects all consciousness whatsoever, past, future, or present, be it subjective or existing outside, gross or subtile, mean or exalted, far or near, the correct view in the light of the highest knowledge is as follows: 'This is not mine; this am I not; this is not my Ego.'

"Perceiving this, O priests, the learned and noble disciple conceives an aversion for form, conceives an aversion for sensation, conceives an aversion for perception, conceives an aversion for the predispositions, conceives an aversion for consciousness. And in conceiving this aversion he becomes divested of passion, and by the absence of passion he becomes free, and when he is free he becomes aware that he is free; and he knows that rebirth is exhausted, that he has lived the holy life, that he has done what it behooved him to do, and that he is no more for this world."

Thus spake The Blessed One, and the delighted band of five priests applauded the speech of The Blessed One. Now while this exposition was being delivered, the minds of the five priests became free from attachment and delivered from the depravities.

Now at that time there were six saints in the world.

THE FIRE-SERMON

Then The Blessed One, having dwelt in Uruvelā as long as he wished, proceeded on his wanderings in the direction of Gayā Head, accompanied by a great congregation of priests, a thousand in number, who had all of them aforetime been monks with matted hair. And there in Gayā, on Gayā Head, The Blessed One dwelt, together with the thousand priests.

And there The Blessed One addressed the priests:—

"All things, O priests, are on fire. And what, O priests, are all these things which are on fire?

"The eye, O priests, is on fire; forms are on fire; eye-consciousness is on fire; impressions received by the eye are on fire; and whatever sensation, pleasant, unpleasant, or indifferent, originates in dependence on impressions received by the eye, that also is on fire.

"And with what are these on fire?

"With the fire of passion, say I, with the fire of hatred, with the fire of infatuation; with birth, old age, death, sorrow, lamentation, misery, grief, and despair are they on fire.

"The ear is on fire; sounds are on fire; . . . the nose is on fire; odors are on fire; . . . the tongue is on fire; tastes are on fire; . . . the body is on fire; things tangible are on fire; . . . the mind is on fire; ideas are on fire; . . . mind-consciousness is on fire; impressions received by the mind are on fire; and whatever sensation, pleasant, unpleasant, or indifferent, originates in dependence on impressions received by the mind, that also is on fire.

"And with what are these on fire?

"With the fire of passion, say I, with the fire of hatred, with the fire of infatuation; with birth, old age, death, sorrow, lamentation, misery, grief, and despair are they on fire.

"Perceiving this, O priests, the learned and noble disciple conceives an aversion for the eye, conceives an aversion for forms, conceives an aversion for eye-consciousness, conceives an aversion for the impressions received by the eye; and whatever sensation, pleasant, unpleasant, or indifferent, originates in dependence on impressions received by the eye, for that also he conceives an aversion. Conceives an aversion for the ear, conceives an aversion for sounds, . . . conceives an aversion for the nose, conceives an aversion for odors, . . . conceives an aversion for the tongue, conceives an aversion for tastes, . . . conceives an aversion for the body, conceives an aversion for things tangible, . . . conceives an aversion for the mind, conceives an aversion for ideas, conceives an aversion for mind-consciousness, conceives an aversion for the impressions received by the mind; and whatever sensation,

"The Fire Sermon," from the *Mahā-Vagga*, i, 21, 1, Henry Clarke Warren, trans. (Cambridge, Massachusetts: Harvard University Press, 1896), pp. 351–353. Reprinted from *Buddhism in Translations* by Henry Clarke Warren.

pleasant, unpleasant, or indifferent, originates in dependence on impressions received by the mind, for this also he conceives an aversion. And in conceiving this aversion, he becomes divested of passion, and by the absence of passion he becomes free, and when he is free he becomes aware that he is free; and he knows that rebirth is exhausted, that he has lived the holy life, that he has done what it behooved him to do, and that he is no more for this world."

Now while this exposition was being delivered, the minds of the thousand priests became free from attachment and delivered from the depravities.

QUESTIONS WHICH TEND NOT TO EDIFICATION

Thus have I heard.

On a certain occasion The Blessed One was dwelling at Sāvatthi in Jetavana monastery in Anāthapindika's Park. Now it happened to the venerable Māluṅkyāputta, being in seclusion and plunged in meditation, that a consideration presented itself to his mind, as follows:—

"These theories which The Blessed One has left unelucidated, has set aside and rejected,—that the world is eternal, that the world is not eternal, that the world is finite, that the world is infinite, that the soul and the body are identical, that the soul is one thing and the body another, that the saint exists after death, that the saint does not exist after death, that the saint both exists and does not exist after death, that the saint neither exists nor does not exist after death,—these The Blessed One does not elucidate to me. And the fact that The Blessed One does not elucidate them to me does not please me nor suit me. Therefore I will draw near to The Blessed One and inquire of him concerning this matter. If The Blessed One will elucidate to me, either that the world is eternal, or that the world is not eternal, or that the world is finite, or that the world is infinite, or that the soul and the body are identical, or that the soul is one thing and the body another, or that the saint exists after death, or that the saint does not exist after death, or that the saint both exists and does not exist after death, or that the saint neither exists nor does not exist after death, in that case will I lead the religious life under The Blessed One. If The Blessed One will not elucidate to me, either that the world is eternal, or that the world is not eternal, . . . or that the saint neither exists nor does not exist after death, in that case will I abandon religious training and return to the lower life of a layman."

Then the venerable Māluṅkyāputta arose at eventide from his seclusion, and drew near to where The Blessed One was; and having drawn near and greeted The Blessed One, he sat down respectfully at one side. And seated respectfully at one side, the venerable Māluṅkyāputta spoke to The Blessed One as follows:—

"Questions which Tend Not to Edification," from the *Majjhima-Nikāya,* constituting *Sutta 63;* Henry Clarke Warren, trans. (Cambridge, Massachusetts: Harvard University Press, 1896), pp. 117–122. Reprinted from *Buddhism in Translations* by Henry Clarke Warren.

"Reverend Sir, it happened to me, as I was now in seclusion and plunged in meditation, that a consideration presented itself to my mind, as follows: 'These theories which The Blessed One has left unelucidated, has set aside and rejected,—that the world is eternal, that the world is not eternal, . . . that the saint neither exists nor does not exist after death,—these The Blessed One does not elucidate to me. And the fact that The Blessed One does not elucidate them to me does not please me nor suit me. I will draw near to The Blessed One and inquire of him concerning this matter. If The Blessed One will elucidate to me, either that the world is eternal, or that the world is not eternal, . . . or that the saint neither exists nor does not exist after death, in that case will I lead the religious life under The Blessed One. If The Blessed One will not elucidate to me, either that the world is eternal, or that the world is not eternal, . . . or that the saint neither exists nor does not exist after death, in that case will I abandon religious training and return to the lower life of a layman."

"If The Blessed One knows that the world is eternal, let The Blessed One elucidate to me that the world is eternal; if The Blessed One knows that the world is not eternal, let The Blessed One elucidate to me that the world is not eternal. If The Blessed One does not know either that the world is eternal or that the world is not eternal, the only upright thing for one who does not know, or who has not that insight, is to say, 'I do not know; I have not that insight.'

"If The Blessed One knows that the world is finite, . . .'

"If The Blessed One knows that the soul and the body are identical, . . .'

"If The Blessed One knows that the saint exists after death, . . .'

"If The Blessed One knows that the saint both exists and does not exist after death, let The Blessed One elucidate to me that the saint both exists and does not exist after death; if The Blessed One knows that the saint neither exists nor does not exist after death, let The Blessed One elucidate to me that the saint neither exists nor does not exist after death. If The Blessed One does not know either that the saint both exists and does not exist after death, or that the saint neither exists nor does not exist after death, the only upright thing for one who does not know, or who has not that insight, is to say, 'I do not know; I have not that insight.'"

"Pray, Māluṅkyāputta, did I ever say to you, 'Come, Māluṅkyāputta, lead the religious life under me, and I will elucidate to you either that the world is eternal, or that the world is not eternal, . . . or that the saint neither exists nor does not exist after death'?"

Nay, verily, Reverend Sir."

"Or did you ever say to me, 'Reverend Sir, I will lead the religious life under The Blessed One, on condition that The Blessed One elucidate to me either that the world is eternal, or that the world is not eternal, . . . or that the saint neither exists nor does not exist after death'?"

"Nay, verily, Reverend Sir."

"So you acknowledge, Māluṅkyāputa, that I have not said to you, 'Come, Māluṅkyāputta, lead the religious life under me and I will elucidate to you either that the world is eternal, or that the world is not eternal, . . . or that the saint neither exists nor does not exist after death;' and again that you have not said to me, 'Reverend Sir, I will lead the religious life under The Blessed One, on condition that The Blessed One elucidate to me either that the world is eternal, or that the world is not eternal, . . . or that the saint neither exists nor does not exist after death.' That being the case, vain man, whom are you so angrily denouncing?

"Māluṅkyāputta, any one who should say, 'I will not lead the religious life under The Blessed One until The Blessed One shall elucidate to me either that the world is eternal, or that the world is not eternal, . . . or that the saint neither exists nor does not exist after death;'—that person would die, Māluṅkyāputta, before The Tathāgata had ever elucidated this to him.

"It is as if, Māluṅkyāputta, a man had been wounded by an arrow thickly smeared with a poison, and his friends and companion, his relatives and kinsfolk, were to procure for him a physician or surgeon; and the sick man were to say, 'I will not have this arrow taken out until I have learnt whether the man who wounded me belonged to the warrior caste, or to the Brahman caste, or to the agricultural caste, or to the menial caste.'

"Or again he were to say, 'I will not have this arrow taken out until I have learnt the name of the man who wounded me, and to what clan he belongs.'

"Or again he were to say, 'I will not have this arrow taken out until I have learnt whether the man who wounded me was tall, or short, or of the middle height.'

"Or again he were to say, 'I will not have this arrow taken out until I have learnt whether the man who wounded me was black, or dusky, or of a yellow skin.'

"Or again he were to say, 'I will not have this arrow taken out until I have learnt whether the man who wounded me was from this or that village, or town, or city.'

"Or again he were to say, 'I will not have this arrow taken out until I have learnt whether the bow which wounded me was a cāpa, or a kodanda.'

"Or again he were to say, 'I will not have this arrow taken out until I have learnt whether the bow-string which wounded me was made from swallow-wort, or bamboo, or sinew, or maruva, or from milk-weed.'

"Or again he were to say, 'I will not have this arrow taken out until I have learnt whether the shaft which wounded me was a kaccha or a ropima.'

"Or again he were to say, 'I will not have this arrow taken out until I have learnt whether the shaft which wounded me was feathered from the wings of a vulture, or of a heron, or of a falcon, or of a peacock, or of a sithilahanu.'

"Or again he were to say, 'I will not have this arrow taken out until I have learnt whether the shaft which wounded me was wound round with the sinews of an ox, or of a buffalo, or of a ruru deer, or of a monkey.'

"Or again he were to say, 'I will not have this arrow taken out until I have learnt whether the arrow which wounded me was an ordinary arrow, or a claw-headed arrow, or a vekaṇḍa, or an iron arrow, or a calf-tooth arrow, or a karavīrapatta.' That man would die, Māluṅkyāputta, without ever having learnt this.

"In exactly the same way, Māluṅkyāputta, any one who should say, 'I will not lead the religious life under The Blessed One until The Blessed One shall elucidate to me either that the world is eternal, or that the world is not eternal, . . . or that the saint neither exists nor does not exist after death;'— that person would die, Māluṅkyāputta, before The Tathāgata had ever elucidated this to him.

"The religious life, Māluṅkyāputta, does not depend on the dogma that the world is eternal; nor does the religious life, Māluṅkyāputta, depend on the dogma that the world is not eternal. Whether the dogma obtain, Māluṅkyāputta, that the world is eternal, or that the world is not eternal, there still remain birth, old age, death, sorrow, lamentation, misery, grief, and despair, for the extinction of which in the present life I am prescribing.

"The religious life, Māluṅkyāputta, does not depend on the dogma that the world is finite; . . .

"The religious life, Māluṅkyāputta, does not depend on the dogma that the soul and the body are identical; . . .

"The religious life, Māluṅkyāputta, does not depend on the dogma that the saints exists after death; . . .

"The religious life, Māluṅkyāputta, does not depend on the dogma that the saint both exists and does not exist after death; nor does the religious life, Māluṅkyāputta, depend on the dogma that the saint neither exists nor does not exist after death. Whether the dogma obtain, Māluṅkyāputta, that the saint both exists and does not exist after death, or that the saint neither exists nor does not exist after death, there still remain birth, old age, death, sorrow, lamentation, misery, grief, and despair, for the extinction of which in the present life I am prescribing.

"Accordingly, Māluṅkyāputta, bear always in mind what it is that I have not elucidated, and what it is that I have elucidated. And what, Māluṅkyāputta, have I not elucidated? I have not elucidated, Māluṅkyāputta, that the world is eternal; I have not elucidated that the world is not eternal; I have not elucidated that the world is finite; I have not elucidated that the world is infinite; I have not elucidated that the soul and the body are identical; I have not elucidated that the soul is one thing and the body another; I have not elucidated that the saint exists after death; I have not elucidated that the saint does not exist after death; I have not elucidated that the saint both exists and does not exist after death; I have not elucidated that the saint neither exists nor does not exist after death. And why, Māluṅkyāputta, have I not elucidated this? Because, Māluṅkyāputta, this profits not, nor has to do with the fundamentals of religion, nor tends to aversion, absence of passion, cessation, quiescence, the supernatural faculties, supreme wisdom, and Nirvana; therefore have I not elucidated it.

"And what, Māluṅkyāputta, have I elucidated? Misery, Māluṅkyāputta, have I elucidated; the origin of misery have I elucidated; the cessation of misery have I elucidated; and the path leading to the cessation of misery have I elucidated. And why, Māluṅkyāputta, have I elucidated this? Because, Māluṅkyāputta, this does profit, has to do with the fundamentals of religion, and tends to aversion, absence of passion, cessation, quiescence, knowledge, supreme wisdom, and Nirvana; therefore have I elucidated it. Accordingly Māluṅkyāputta, bear always in mind what it is that I have not elucidated, and what it is that I have elucidated."

Thus spake The Blessed One; and, delighted, the venerable Māluṅkyāputta applauded the speech of The Blessed One.

THE ASCETIC'S TRAINING

Ajātasattu Visits Buddha

Thus have I heard: at one time the Lord dwelt at Rājagaha in the mango-grove of Jīvaka, who had been brought up by the prince, with a great assembly of monks, with twelve hundred and fifty monks. Now at that time the Magadha king Ajātasattu, son of the Videha woman, was keeping the Fast-day on the fifteenth day of the month Kattika when the moon was full, at the·time of the four-monthly sacrifice, surrounded by his royal ministers. He had gone to the top of the palace and was seated there. Then Ajātasattu on that Fast-day uttered this fervent utterance: "Pleasant indeed is the bright night, lovely indeed is the bright night, fair indeed is the bright night, pleasing indeed is the bright night, auspicious indeed is the bright night; to what ascetic or brahmin may we pay homage to-day, so that having paid homage to him our mind may find satisfaction?" (He refuses the suggestions of his ministers to visit the six teachers.)

Now at that time Jīvaka, who had been brought up by the prince, was seated silent near the king. So the king said to Jīvaka, "Now, friend Jīvaka, why are you silent?" "O king, this Lord, this arahat, the perfectly enlightened one, is dwelling in our mango-grove, with a great assembly of monks, with twelve hundred and fifty monks. And of the Lord Gotama the fair fame is spread abroad thus, 'The Lord, the arahat, the all-enlightened, endowed with knowledge and conduct, the Happy One, knower of the

"The Ascetic's Training," from the *Samannaphala-sutta, Digha* i, 47, E. J. Thomas, trans. (London: Kegan Paul, Trench, Trubner & Co. Ltd. 1935), pp. 54–69. Reprinted from *Early Buddhist Scriptures* by E. J. Thomas, by permission of Routledge & Kegan Paul, Ltd.

world, supreme charioteer of men to be tamed, teacher of gods and men, Buddha, the Lord.' Let the king pay homage to the Lord; surely if the king pays homage to the Lord his mind will find satisfaction." "Then, friend Jīvaka, make ready the riding elephants." "Even so, O king," Jīvaka replied to king Ajātasattu.

Jīvaka made ready as many as five hundred she-elephants and one royal riding elephant, and announced to the king, "O king, the elephants are ready, now is the time for what seems good to you." So the king placing his wives each on an elephant mounted the royal elephant, and with a procession of torches left Rājagaha with a great royal retinue and set out for the mango-grove of Jīvaka. Then when the king drew near to the mango-grove fear arose in him and consternation, and his hair rose. So the king, afraid, agitated, and with his hair rising said to Jīvaka, "Surely, friend Jīvaka, you are not deceiving me, surely you are not deluding me, surely you are not betraying me to an enemy? How now is it that in this assembly of as many as twelve hundred and fifty monks there is not even a sound of sneezing or coughing or a shout?" "Fear not, O king; I am not deceiving or deluding you or betraying you to an enemy. Advance, O king, advance, O king, those are the lights burning in the pavilion."

So the king going on the elephant as far as was possible, then dismounted and went on foot to the door of the pavilion. On arriving he said to Jīvaka, "Where, friend Jīvaka, is the Lord?" "That, O king, is the Lord. That, O king, is the Lord near the middle pillar, seated facing the assembly of monks, who are facing him." So the king approached the Lord and stood on one side. As he stood at one side he looked at the assembly of monks, each of them silent like a pure lake, and uttered a fervent utterance: "With this calm might prince Udāyibhadda be endowed, with which the assembly of monks is now endowed." "Have you fared, O king, according to your desire?" "Dear to me, Lord, is prince Udāyibhadda. With this calm might prince Udāyibhadda be endowed, with which the assembly of monks is now endowed."

Ajātasattu's Question

So king Ajātasattu having saluted the Lord, bowed with clasped hands to the assembly, and sat on one side. Sitting on one side the king said to the Lord, "Lord, I should like to ask the Lord about a certain matter, if the Lord gives me the opportunity to have an explanation." "Ask, O king, what you wish."

"Now, just as, Lord, there are these many kinds of crafts, such as elephant-drivers, horse-drivers, charioteers, archers, standard-bearers, camp-officers, camp-caterers, lofty nobles, kings' sons, princes, military scouts (like) great trained elephants, heroes, soldiers in leather, slaves' sons, cooks, barbers, bath-attendants, scullions, garland-makers, washermen, weavers, basket-makers, potters, calculators, accountants, or any other of the many kinds of crafts like these, they in this actual life enjoy the visible fruit of their craft; by means of it they make themselves happy and prosperous, they make their parents, their wives and children, their friends and companions, happy and prosperous; and for ascetics and brahmins they establish the highest kind of sacrifices, which are worthy of heaven, produce happiness, and tend to heaven. Now, Lord, is it possible to show in this actual life a visible fruit of the life of an ascetic?"

"Do you admit, O king that you have asked this question of other ascetics and brahmins?"(The king admits that he has, and gives an account of the replies of the six rival teachers. Buddha after pointing out two advantages in merely leaving the world, shows the advantages of doing so when there is a Buddha, by describing the Buddhist ascetic's career through his training in morality, concentration, and full knowledge.)

The Disciple's Conversion

"In this case, O king, a Tathāgata arises in the world, an arahat, an all-enlightened Buddha, endowed with knowledge and conduct, a Happy One, a knower of the world, a supreme charioteer of men to be tamed, a teacher of gods and men, a Buddha, a Lord. He of himself by higher knowledge having comprehended and realized this world with its gods, Māra, Brahmā, its beings with ascetics and brahmins, gods and men, preaches. He teaches the Doctrine good in the beginning, good in the middle, good in the end, in the spirit and the letter, and proclaims a perfectly complete and pure religious life.

"A householder or a householder's son or someone reborn in a certain family hears that Doctrine. Having heard it he acquires faith in the Tathāgata. Endowed with the faith he has acquired he thus reflects: 'Encumbered is a household life, a place of dust; going forth from home is in the open air. It is not easy for one who dwells in a house to practise a perfectly complete and pure religious life polished as a pearl. What if I remove my hair and beard, put on yellow robes, and go forth from a house to a houseless life.' Later he gives up his small or great wealth, gives up a small or large circle of relatives, and removing his hair and beard puts on yellow robes, and goes forth from a house to a houseless life.

Morality

"Having thus gone forth he dwells restrained with the restraint of the precepts, accomplished in the practice of right behaviour, seeing the danger of even minute faults, he adopts the rules of training and becomes trained in them, exercising good action in body and speech, getting a livelihood by pure means, (1) being accomplished in morality, (2) having the door of his senses guarded, (3) being endowed with mindfulness and self-possession, and (4) being content.

(1) THE MORAL RULES.

"And how, O king, is a monk accomplished in morality?

"Herein a monk abandons the killing of living things and refrains from killing; laying aside the use of a stick or a knife he dwells modest, full of kindliness, and compassionate for the welfare of all living things. This is his behaviour in morality.

"Abandoning the taking of what is not given he refrains from taking what is not given; he takes and expects only what is given, he dwells purely and without stealing.

"Abandoning incontinence he practises continence and lives apart, avoiding the village practice of sex intercourse.

"Abandoning falsehood he refrains from falsehood; he speaks truth, he is truthful, trustworthy, and reliable, not deceiving people.

"Abandoning slanderous speech he refrains from slanderous speech; what he has heard from one place he does not tell in another to cause dissension. He is even a healer of dissensions and a producer of union, delighting and rejoicing in concord, eager for concord, and an utterer of speech that produces concord.

"Abandoning harsh speech he refrains from harsh speech; the speech that is harmless, pleasant to the ear, kind, reaching the heart, urbane, amiable, and attractive to the multitude, that kind of speech does he utter.

"Abandoning frivolous speech he refrains from frivolous speech; he speaks of the good, the real, the profitable, of the doctrine and the discipline; he is an utterer of speech worth hoarding, with timely reasons and purpose and meaning.

"He refrains from injuring seeds and plants.

"He eats only within one meal time, abstaining from food at night and avoiding untimely food.

"He refrains from seeing dancing, singing, music, and shows.

"He refrains from the use of garlands, scents, unguents, and objects of adornment; from a high or large bed; from accepting gold and silver; from accepting raw grain and raw meat.

"He refrains from accepting women, girls, male and female slaves, goats and rams, fowls and pigs, elephants, oxen, horses, mares, and farm-lands.

"He refrains from going on messages and errands; from buying and selling; from cheating in weighing, false metal, and measuring; from practices of cheating, trickery, deception, and fraud; from cutting, killing, binding, robbery, pillage, and violence. . . .

(2) GUARDING OF THE SENSES.

"And how, O king, does the monk have the door of his senses guarded? In this case a monk, when with his eyes he sees objects, does not occupy himself with their characteristics or minor features. Whatever bad or evil thoughts might flow into him on account of his not being restrained in the use of the organ of sight, towards all that he exercises restraint, he guards his organ of sight, and applies restraint. When with his sense of hearing . . . smelling . . . taste . . . touch . . . when with his mind he perceives internal impressions, he does not occupy himself with their characteristics or minor features. . . . Endowed with this noble restraint of the senses he experiences internally unimpaired happiness. Thus, O king, a monk has the door of his senses guarded.

(3) MINDFULNESS AND SELF-POSSESSION.

"And how, O king, is a monk endowed with mindfulness and self-possession? In this case a monk is self-possessed in advancing or withdrawing, in looking forward or looking round, in bending, or stretching his limbs, in wearing his inner and outer robes and bowl, in eating, drinking, masticating, and tasting, in answering the calls of nature, in walking, standing, sitting, sleeping, waking, speaking, and keeping silence. Thus, O king, is a monk endowed with mindfulness and self-possession.

(4) ACQUIRING CONTENTMENT.

"And how, O king, is a monk content? In this case a monk is content with a robe to protect his body and alms to keep him alive. Wherever he goes he takes them with him. . . . Thus, O king, is a monk content.

Getting Rid of the Five Hindrances

"Endowed with this noble group of moral rules, with this noble restraint of the senses, with this noble mindfulness and self-possession, and with this noble contentment he resorts to a secluded lodging, a forest, the root of a tree, a hill, a grotto, a mountain cave, a cemetery, a jungle, or a heap of straw in the open air. After his meal when he has returned from collecting alms he sits down cross-legged and upright, setting mindfulness before him.

"(1) Dispelling longing for the world he abides with his mind free from longing, and purifies his mind from longing.

"(2) Dispelling malice he abides with his mind free from malice, having compassion for all living things, and purifies his mind from malice.

"(3) Dispelling sloth and torpor he dwells free from sloth and torpor, with clear sight, mindful and self-possessed, and purifies his mind from sloth and torpor.

"(4) Dispelling distraction and agitation he dwells without excitement, with mind internally calmed, and purifies his mind from distraction and agitation.

"(5) Dispelling doubt he dwells free from doubt, without uncertainty about good thoughts, and purifies his mind from doubt. . . .

"Thus, O king, like one getting rid of a debt, sickness, prison, slavery, or a path in a wilderness, a monk gets rid of these five hindrances and contemplates himself. . . .

Concentration: The Four Trances

"(1) When these five hindrances are dispelled and he contemplates himself, exultation arises, as he exults joy arises, as his mind feels joy his body becomes serene, as his body becomes serene he feels pleasure, when he feels pleasure his mind is concentrated. Free from sensual desires, free from evil thoughts he attains and abides in the first trance of joy and pleasure, which is accompanied with reasoning and investigation and arises from seclusion. He suffuses, pervades, fills, and permeates his body with the pleasure and joy arising from seclusion, and there is nothing at all in his body untouched by the pleasure and joy arising from seclusion.

"(2) Again the monk with the ceasing of reasoning and investigation, in a state of internal serenity, with his mind fixed on one point, attains and abides in the second trance of joy and pleasure arising from concentration, and free from reasoning and investigation. He suffuses, pervades, fills, and permeates his body with the pleasure and joy arising from concentration, and there is nothing at all in his body untouched by the pleasure and joy arising from concentration.

"(3) Again the monk with indifference towards joy abides with equanimity, mindful and self-possessed, and with his body experiences the pleasure that the noble ones call, 'dwelling with equanimity, mindful, and happy,' and attains and abides in the third trance. He suffuses, pervades, fills, and permeates his body with pleasure without joy, and there is nothing at all in his body untouched by this pleasure without joy.

"(4) Again the monk, with the dispelling of pleasure and pain, and even before the disappearance of elation and depression attains and abides in the fourth trance which is without pain and pleasure and with the purity of equanimity and mindfulness. He sits permeating his body with mind purified and cleansed, and there is nothing at all in his body untouched by his mind purified and cleansed.

Full Knowledge: Meditation on the Body

"With his mind thus concentrated, purified, and cleansed, without lust, free from the depravities, supple, ready to act, firm, and impassible, he turns and directs his mind to knowledge and insight. He thus understands: 'This is my body, having shape, formed of the four elements, produced by a mother and father, a collection of milk and gruel, subject to rubbing, pounding, breaking, and dissolution; and this is my consciousness, on this (body) it rests, to this it is bound. . . .'

"With his mind thus concentrated . . . he turns and directs his mind to the production of a mind-formed body; with his (material) body he produces another body, having shape, mind-formed, possessing all its limbs and not lacking any faculty.

The Four Psychic Powers

"With his mind thus concentrated . . . he turns and directs his mind to different kinds of psychic power. . . .

The Divine Ear

"With his mind thus concentrated . . . he turns and directs his mind to divine hearing. With purified divine hearing, far surpassing human hearing, he hears the two kinds of sounds, the divine and the human, and both distant and near.

Mind-Reading

"With his mind thus concentrated . . . he turns and directs his mind to acquiring a knowledge of minds. By grasping the minds of other beings and individuals he understands that of a mind affected by passion that it is affected by passion, of one free from passion that it is free from passion. . . .

Knowledge of Former Existences

"With his mind thus concentrated . . . he turns and directs his mind to the the knowledge of his former existences. He remembers various kinds of his former existence, such as one birth, two, three, four, five, ten, twenty, thirty, forty, fifty, a hundred, a thousand, a hundred thousand births, many cycles of evolution of the universe, of dissolution, and of evolution and dissolution. 'In that one I had such a name, clan, caste, such sustenance, experiencing such pleasure and pain, and having such an end of life. Passing away thence I was reborn in such a place. There too I had such a name, clan . . . and such an end of life. Passing away thence I was reborn here.' Thus he remembers various kinds of his former existence with their modes and details.

Divine Vision

"With his mind thus concentrated . . . he turns and directs his mind to the passing away and rebirth of beings. With his divine vision, purified and superhuman, he sees beings passing away and being reborn again, low and high, of good and bad colour, in happy or miserable existences, according to their karma. He understands that those beings who are given to evil conduct in deed, word, and thought, who are revilers of the noble ones, who are of false views, who acquire the karma of their false views, at the dissolution of the body after death have been reborn in a miserable existence in hell. But those beings who are given to good conduct in deed, word, and thought, who are not revilers of the noble ones, who are of right views, who acquire the karma of their right views, at the dissolution of the body after death have been reborn in a happy existence in the world of heaven. . . .

Knowledge of the Truths and Destruction of the Āsavas

"With his mind thus concentrated, purified, and cleansed, without lust, free from the depravities, subtle, ready to act, firm, and impassible, he turns and directs his mind to the knowledge of the destruction of the āsavas. He duly understands, 'this is pain'; he duly understands, 'this is the cause of pain'; he duly understands, 'this is the cessation of pain'; he duly understands, 'this is the path that leads to the cessation of pain'; he duly understands, 'these are the āsavas'; he duly understands, 'this is the cause of the āsavas'; he duly understands, 'this is the path that leads to the destruction of the āsavas.' As he thus knows and thus perceives, his mind is released from the āsava of sensual desire, from the āsava of desire for existence, from the āsava of ignorance. In the released is the knowledge of his release: ignorance is destroyed, the religious life had been led, done is what was to be done, there is nothing further for this world."

Ajātasattu's Repentance

At these words king Ajātasattu said to the Lord: "Wonderful, Lord, wonderful, Lord. Just as if, Lord, one were to set up what had been bent down or uncover what had been hid, or show the way to one gone astray, or bring an oil-lamp into the dark so that those with eyes might see forms, even so had the Doctrine been explained by the Lord in many ways. I go, Lord, to the Lord as a refuge, I go to the Doctrine and to the Assembly of monks. May the Lord receive me as a layman from this day forth while life lasts, who have gone for refuge. My misdeed overcame me, who was so foolish, so infatuated, so wicked, that for the sake of lordship I deprived my righteous father, the righteous king, of life. Lord, may the Lord accept (the confession of) my misdeed as misdeed for restraint in the future."

"Verily, O king, your misdeed overcame you, who were so foolish, so infatuated, so wicked that you deprived your righteous father, the righteous king, of life. And in that you, O king, seeing the misdeed as misdeed, make amends according as is right, that do we accept of you. For it is increase, O king, in the discipline of the noble disciple, who seeing his misdeed as misdeed makes amends according as is right and exercises restraint in the future."

At these words the Magadha king Ajātasattu, son of the Videha woman, said, "Well now, Lord, we go; we have much to do and many duties." "As it seems good to you, O king." So the king having expressed delight and approval rose from his seat, saluted the Lord, and passing round him to the right went away.

Then the Lord, soon after the king had gone, addressed the monks: "Uprooted, monks, is the king, damaged, monks, is the king. If, monks, the king had not deprived his righteous father, the righteous king, of life, in this very session the pure and spotless eye of the Doctrine would have arisen." Thus spoke the Lord, and the monks expressed delight and approval of the Lord's utterance.

THE FOUR STATIONS OF MINDFULNESS

This is the road with one goal for the purification of beings, for passing beyond grief and lamentation, for the ending of pain and misery, for the attaining of truth, for the realizing of Nirvāna, namely the four Stations of Mindfulness. What are the four?

1. Herein a monk abides reflecting on the body, zealous, self-possessed and mindful, dispelling longing for the world;
2. he abides reflecting on sensations . . .
3. he abides reflecting on mind . . .
4. he abides reflecting on thoughts, zealous, self-possessed, and mindful, dispelling longing for the world.

Reflection on the Body

And how does a monk abide reflecting on the body? Herein a monk having gone to the forest or the root of a tree or an empty place sits down cross-legged and upright, setting mindfulness before him. Mindful he breathes out, mindful he breathes in; emitting a long breath he understands that he is emitting a long breath, or drawing a long breath he understands that he is drawing a long breath; emitting a short breath he understands that he is emitting a short breath, or drawing a short breath he understands that he is drawing a short breath. He repeats: "Conscious of my whole body I will breathe out, conscious of my whole body I will breathe in, calming the elements of my body I will breathe out, calming the elements of my body I will breathe in. . . ."

Thus he abides reflecting on the body (1) inwardly, (2) outwardly, (3) inwardly and outwardly, reflecting on it as liable to origination or as liable to decay or as liable to origination and decay. His mindfulness becomes established with the thought that the body exists, so far as required for knowledge and remembrance. He abides independent, and grasps at nothing in the world. Even so a monk abides reflecting on the body.

Again a monk when walking understands, "I walk," or when standing, "I stand," or when sitting, "I am seated," or when lying down, "I am lying down." In whatever way his body is directed he understands it to be such.

"The Four Stations of Mindfulness," from the *Satipatthana-sutta, Majjhima,* i, 55, E. J. Thomas, trans. (London: Kegan Paul, Trench, Trubner & Co., Ltd., 1935) pp. 73–78. Reprinted from *Early Buddhist Scriptures* by E. J. Thomas, by permission of Routledge & Kegan Paul, Ltd.

Again a monk is self-possessed in advancing or withdrawing, in looking forward or looking round, in bending or stretching his limbs, in wearing his inner and outer robes and bowl, in eating, drinking, masticating, and tasting, in answering the calls of nature, in walking, standing, sitting, sleeping, waking, speaking, and keeping silence. . . . Even so a monk abides reflecting on the body. . . .

(Here follow reflections on the body as composed of the thirty-two parts, hair, nails, teeth, skin, etc., then on the body as composed of the four elements, and lastly on the several stages of the decay of a corpse.)

Reflection on Sensations

And how does a monk abide reflecting on sensations? Herein a monk feeling a pleasant sensation understands that he is feeling a pleasant sensation. Feeling a painful sensation . . . a neutral sensation . . . a pleasant sensual sensation . . . a pleasant non-sensual sensation . . . a painful sensual sensation . . . a painful non-sensual sensation . . . a neutral sensual or non-sensual sensation, he understands that he is feeling such sensation. . . . His mindfulness becomes established with the thought that there is sensation so far as required for knowledge and remembrance. He abides independent, and grasps at nothing in the world. Even so does a monk abide reflecting on sensations.

Reflection on Mind

And how does a monk abide reflecting on mind? Herein a monk, when his mind is affected by passion, understands that it is affected by passion, when it is free from passion . . . when it is affected by hatred or not, affected by delusion or not, when it is composed or distracted, in the world of form or in the world of passion, in the world of form or beyond, concentrated or not concentrated, released or not released. . . .

Even so does a monk abide reflecting on the mind.

Reflection on Thoughts

And how does a monk abide reflecting on thoughts? Herein a monk abides reflecting on thoughts as the five hindrances. When an impulse of passion is present in himself he understands that he has an impulse of passion. When no impulse of passion is present in himself he understands that he has no impulse of passion. He understands how there is the arising of an impulse that has not (previously) arisen, how there is the dispelling of an impulse that has arisen, and how there is the non-arising in the future of an impulse that has been dispelled. (In the same way he reflects on the other hindrances: malice, sloth and torpor, distraction and agitation, doubt.)

Again a monk abides reflecting on thoughts as the five groups of grasping (khandha). . . . He reflects: the body, its origin, its passing away; sensation . . . perception . . . the mental elements . . . consciousness, its origin, its passing away. . . . Even so does a monk abide reflecting on thoughts as the five groups of grasping.

Again a monk abides reflecting on thoughts as the six inner and outer bases of cognition (*āyatana*). . . . He understands the eye and he understands visible objects; he understands that on account of them both a fetter arises, how there is the arising of a fetter that had not previously arisen, how there is the dispelling of a fetter that has arisen, and how there is the non-arising in the future of a fetter that has been dispelled. (The other bases are reflected on in the same way: the ear and sounds, the nose and smells, the tongue and tastes, the body and tangibles, the mind and thoughts.)

Again a monk abides reflecting on thoughts as the seven parts of enlightenment. . . . Herein a monk, when mindfulness is present in himself, understands that he has mindfulness in himself; or if it is not present he understands that he does not have it. He understands how there is the arising of mindfulness that has not (previously) arisen, and how there is the practising and perfecting of the mindfulness that has arisen. (The other six parts, investigation of the Doctrine, energy, joy, repose, concentration, and equanimity are reflected on in the same way.)

Again a monk reflects on thoughts as the four Noble Truths. . . . He duly understands, "this is pain"; he duly understands, "this is the cessation of pain"; he duly understands, "this is the path leading to the cessation of pain. . . ." Even so a monk abides reflecting on thoughts as the four Noble Truths.

Now whoever should thus practise these four stations of mindfulness for seven years, he may expect one or other of two fruits: either complete knowledge in this present life or, if there is a remainder tending to rebirth, the state of one who does not return to this world; or let alone seven years, he who should thus practise them for six years, five, four, three, two, one—or let alone one year, he who should thus practise them for seven months may expect one or other of two fruits: either complete knowledge in this present life or the state of one who does not return to this world—or let alone seven months, he who should practise them for six months, five, four, three, two, one, or half a month—or let alone half a month, he who should practise them for seven days may expect one or other of two fruits, either complete knowledge in this present life or, if there is a remainder tending to rebirth, the state of one who does not return to this world.

THE BUDDHA'S LAST WORDS

'So long as the monks shall persevere in kindly acts, words and thoughts towards their fellow both in public and in private—so long as they shall share

"The Buddha's Last Words," from the *Mahā Pari-Nibbāna Sutta Dīgha Nikāya*, xvi, G. F. Allen, trans. (London: Allen & Unwin, 1959), pp. 154–156. Reprinted from *The Buddha's Philosophy* by G. F. Allen, by permission of George Allen & Unwin, Ltd.

impartially with their modest companions all that they receive in accordance
with the recognized discipline of the Sangha, even down to the contents of the
food bowl—so long as they shall live among the worthy in the practice, both
in public and private, of those qualities that bring freedom and are praised by
the wise; that are pure (of desire); and that are conducive to concentration—
so long as the monks shall live among the worthy, cherishing, both in public
and private, that infallible intuition that results in the utter cessation of the
sorrow of him who acts according to it—so long may you be expected not to
decline but to prosper.'

'It is through not understanding and grasping the four aryan Truths,
monks, that we have had to continue so long, to wander so long, in this weary
path of rebirths, both you and I!

'And what are these four?—The aryan Truth as to sorrow; the aryan
Truth as to the origin of sorrow; the aryan Truth as to the elimination of sorrow; and the aryan Truth as to the way of eliminate sorrow. But when these
aryan Truths are grasped and understood the desire for more life ceases, that
which results in rebirth is destroyed and there then is an end of sorrow!'

To Ānanda: 'I have taught the Dhamma without making any distinction between exoteric and esoteric doctrine; for in respect of the norm, Ānanda,
the *Tathāgata* has no such thing as the closed fist of those teachers who hold
back certain things . . .

'Be islands unto yourselves, Ānanda! Be a refuge to yourselves; do not
take to yourselves any other refuge. See Truth as an island, see Truth as a
refuge. Do not seek refuge in anyone but yourselves.

'And how, Ānanda, is a *bhikkhu* to be an island unto himself, a refuge
to himself, taking to himself no other refuge, seeing Truth as an island, seeing
as a refuge Truth, not seeking refuge in anyone but himself?

'Thus, monks: as to the body, a *bhikkhu* continues so to regard the body
that he remains alert, mindful, and self-possessed, having conquered desire-
attachment for the things of the world. (And similarly:) as to sensations . . .
as to states of mind . . . as to mental conceptions, a *bhikkhu* continues so to
regard each that he remains alert, mindful, and self-possessed, having conquered desire-attachment for the things of the world.

'And whoever, Ānanda, now or after I am dead, shall be an island unto
themselves and a refuge to themselves, shall take to themselves no other refuge, but seeing Truth as an island, seeing as a refuge Truth, shall not seek
refuge in anyone but themselves—it is they, Ānanda, among my disciples, who
shall reach the Further Shore! *But they must make the effort themselves.'*

'Have done, Ānanda! do not weep, do not distress yourself! Have I not
often told you that it is in the very nature of things that we must eventually
be parted from all that is near and dear to us? For how, Ānanda, can it be
otherwise? Since everything born, evolved, and organized contains within itself

the germs of disintegration, how can it be otherwise than that a being should pass away? No other condition is possible!

'For long you, Ānanda, have been very near to me by acts of devotion, faithful and affectionate, ever loyal beyond all reckoning. For long you, Ānanda, have been very near to me by words of devotion, faithful and affectionate, ever loyal beyond all reckoning. For long you, Ānanda, have been very near to me by thoughts of devotion, faithful and affectionate, ever loyal beyond all reckoning. You have done splendidly, Ānanda! Only persevere in your efforts and you too shall soon be free from all hindrances' (to liberation).

'Maybe, Ānanda, some of you will have the idea: "The word of the teacher is no more, and now we are without a leader!" But, Ānanda, you must not think of it like this. The Dhamma, and the *Vinaya* directions for the Saṅgha, which I have expounded and established for you, they, after I am gone, shall be your Teacher.'

'After I am gone, Ānanda, let the Saṅgha, if it think fit, abolish the lesser and minor rules of discipline.'

Finally, the Buddha exhorted the monks, saying: 'This I tell you, disciples —"All conditioned things disintegrate. Strive without ceasing to attain your liberation!"'

9

DHAMMAPADA

The Dhammapada or "Path of Truth" is an outstanding collection of the Buddha's moral teachings. An anthology organized under topical heads, it reproduces maxims and poems spoken on various occasions and thus overlaps the chronological accounts of the sermons. It was probably formed by the time of Ashoka, possibly by "reciters" who traveled in India repeating the teachings of the Blessed One. The book has long been one of the most popular

Dhammapada, Chs. I–XVIII. F. Max-Müller, trans. (London: Oxford Press, 1898) v. 10, pp. 3–63. Reprinted from *Sacred Books of the East*, ed. by F. Max-Müller.

of Buddhist texts. Eighteen of its twenty-six short chapters are here reprinted in Professor Max-Müller's translation.

THE TWIN-VERSES

1. All that we are is the result of what we have thought: it is founded on our thoughts, it is made up of our thoughts. If a man speaks or acts with an evil thought, pain follows him, as the wheel follows the foot of the ox that draws the carriage.

2. All that we are is the result of what we have thought: it is founded on our thoughts, it is made up of our thoughts. If a man speaks or acts with a pure thought, happiness follows him, like a shadow that never leaves him.

3. 'He abused me, he beat me, he defeated me, he robbed me,'—in those who harbour such thoughts hatred will never cease.

4. 'He abused me, he beat me, he defeated me, he robbed me,'—in those who do not harbour such thoughts hatred will cease.

5. For hatred does not cease by hatred at any time: hatred ceases by love, this is an old rule.

6. The world does not know that we must all come to an end here;—but those who know it, their quarrels cease at once.

7. He who lives looking for pleasures only, his senses uncontrolled, immoderate in his food, idle, and weak, Mâra (the tempter) will certainly overthrow him, as the wind throws down a weak tree.

8. He who lives without looking for pleasures, his senses well controlled, moderate in his food, faithful and strong, him Mâra will certainly not overthrow, any more than the wind throws down a rocky mountain.

9. He who wishes to put on the yellow dress without having cleansed himself from sin, who disregards also temperance and truth, is unworthy of the yellow dress.

10. But he who has cleansed himself from sin, is well grounded in all virtues, and endowed also with temperance and truth, he is indeed worthy of the yellow dress.

11. They who imagine truth in untruth, and see untruth in truth, never arrive at truth, but follow vain desires.

12. They who know truth in truth, and untruth in untruth, arrive at truth, and follow true desires.

13. As rain breaks through an ill-thatched house, passion will break through an unreflecting mind.

14. As rain does not break through a well-thatched house, passion will not break through a well-reflecting mind.

15. The evil-doer mourns in this world, and he mourns in the next; he mourns in both. He mourns and suffers when he sees the evil (result) of his own work.

16. The virtuous man delights in this world, and he delights in the next; he delights in both. He delights and rejoices, when he sees the purity of his own work.

17. The evil-doer suffers in this world, and he suffers in the next; he suffers in both. He suffers when he thinks of the evil he has done; he suffers more when going on the evil path.

18. The virtuous man is happy in this world, and he is happy in the next; he is happy in both. He is happy when he thinks of the good he has done; he is still more happy when going on the good path.

19. The thoughless man, even if he can recite a large portion (of the law), but is not a doer of it, has no share in the priesthood, but is like a cow-herd counting the cows of others.

20. The follower of the law, even if he can recite only a small portion (of the law), but, having forsaken passion and hatred and foolishness, possesses true knowledge and serenity of mind, he, caring for nothing in this world or that to come, has indeed a share in the priesthood.

ON EARNESTNESS

21. Earnestness is the path of immortality (Nirvâna), thoughtlessness the path of death. Those who are in earnest do not die, those who are thoughtless are as if dead already.

22. Having understood this clearly, those who are advanced in earnestness delight in earnestness, and rejoice in the knowledge of the Ariyas (the elect).

23. These wise people, meditative, steady, always possessed of strong powers, attain to Nirvâna, the highest happiness.

24. If an earnest person has roused himself, if he is not forgetful, if his deeds are pure, if he acts with consideration, if he restrains himself, and lives according to law,—then his glory will increase.

25. By rousing himself, by earnestness, by restraint and control, the wise man may make for himself an island which no flood can overwhelm.

26. Fools follow after vanity, men of evil wisdom. The wise man keeps earnestness as his best jewel.

27. Follow not after vanity, nor after the enjoyment of love and lust! He who is earnest and meditative, obtains ample joy.

28. When the learned man drives away vanity by earnestness, he, the wise, climbing the terraced heights of wisdom, looks down upon the fools, free from sorrow he looks upon the sorrowing crowd, as one that stands on a mountain looks down upon them that stand upon the plain.

29. Earnest among the thoughtless, awake among the sleepers, the wise man advances like a racer, leaving behind the hack.

30. By earnestness did Maghavan (Indra) rise to the lordship of the gods. People praise earnestness; thoughtlessness is always blamed.

31. A Bhikshu (mendicant) who delights in earnestness, who looks with fear on thoughtlessness, moves about like fire, burning all his fetters, small or large.

32. A Bhikshu (mendicant who delights in reflection, who looks with fear on thoughtlessness, cannot fall away (from his perfect state)—he is close upon Nirvâna.

THOUGHT

33. As a fletcher makes straight his arrow, a wise man makes straight his trembling and unsteady thought, which is difficult to guard, difficult to hold back.

34. As a fish taken from his watery home and thrown on the dry ground, our thought trembles all over in order to escape the dominion of Mâra (the tempter).

35. It is good to tame the mind, which is difficult to hold in and flighty, rushing wherever it listeth; a tamed mind brings happiness.

36. Let the wise man guard his thoughts, for they are difficult to perceive, very artful, and they rush wherever they list: thoughts well guarded bring happiness.

37. Those who bridle their mind which travels far, moves about alone, is without a body, and hides in the chamber (of the heart), will be free from the bonds of Mâra (the tempter).

38. If a man's faith is unsteady, if he does not know the true law, if his peace of mind is troubled, his knowledge will never be perfect.

39. If a man's thoughts are not dissipated, if his mind is not perplexed, if he has ceased to think of good or evil, then there is no fear for him while he is watchful.

40. Knowing that this body is (fragile) like a jar, and making his thought firm like a fortress, one should attack Mâra (the tempter) with the weapon of knowledge, one should watch him when conquered, and should never rest.

41. Before long, alas! this body will lie on the earth, despised, without understanding, like a useless log.

42. Whatever a hater may do to a hater, or an enemy to an enemy, a wrongly-directed mind will do him greater mischief.

43. Not a mother, not a father will do so much, nor any other relatives; a well-directed mind will do us greater service.

FLOWERS

44. Who shall overcome this earth, and the world of Yama (the lord of the departed), and the world of the gods? Who shall find out the plainly shown path of virtue, as a clever man finds the (right) flower?

45. The disciple will overcome the earth, and the world of Yama, and the world of the gods. The disciple will find out the plainly shown path of virtue, as a clever man finds the (right) flower.

46. He who knows that this body is like froth, and has learnt that it is as unsubstantial as a mirage, will break the flower-pointed arrow of Mâra, and never see the king of death.

47. Death carries off a man who is gathering flowers, and whose mind is distracted, as a flood carries off a sleeping village.

48. Death subdues a man who is gathering flowers, and whose mind is distracted, before he is satiated in his pleasures.

49. As the bee collects nectar and departs without injuring the flower, or its colour or scent, so let a sage dwell in his village.

50. Not the perversities of others, not their sins of commission or omission, but his own misdeeds and negligences should a sage take notice of.

51. Like a beautiful flower, full of colour, but without scent, are the fine but fruitless words of him who does not act accordingly.

52. But, like a beautiful flower, full of colour and full of scent, are the fine and fruitful words of him who acts accordingly.

53. As many kinds of wreaths can be made from a heap of flowers, so many good things may be achieved by a mortal when once he is born.

54. The scent of flowers does not travel against the wind, nor (that of) sandal-wood, or (of) Tagara and Mallikâ flowers; but the odour of good people travels even against the wind; a good man pervades every place.

55. Sandal-wood or Tagara, a lotus-flower, or a Vassiki, among these sorts of perfumes, the perfume of virtue is unsurpassed.

56. Mean is the scent that comes from Tagara and sandal-wood;—the perfume of those who possess virtue rises up to the gods as the highest.

57. Of the people who possess these virtues, who live without thoughtlessness, and who are emancipated through true knowledge, Mâra, the tempter, never finds the way.

58, 59. As on a heap of rubbish cast upon the highway the lily will grow full of sweet perfume and delight, thus among those who are mere rubbish the disciple of the truly enlightened Buddha shines forth by his knowledge above the blinded worldling.

THE FOOL

60. Long is the night to him who is awake; long is a mile to him who is tired; long is life to the foolish who do not know the true law.

61. If a traveller does not meet with one who is his better, or his equal, let him firmly keep to his solitary journey; there is no companionship with a fool.

62. 'These sons belong to me, and this wealth belongs to me,' with such

thoughts a fool is tormented. He himself does not belong to himself; how much less sons and wealth?

63. The fool who knows his foolishness, is wise at least so far. But a fool who thinks himself wise, he is called a fool indeed.

64. If a fool be associated with a wise man even all his life, he will perceive the truth as little as a spoon perceives the taste of soup.

65. If an intelligent man be associated for one minute only with a wise man, he will soon perceive the truth, as the tongue perceives the taste of soup.

66. Fools of poor understanding have themselves for their greatest enemies, for they do evil deeds which bear bitter fruits.

67. That deed is not well done of which a man must repent, and the reward of which he receives crying and with a tearful face.

68. No, that deed is well done of which a man does not repent, and the reward of which he receives gladly and cheerfully.

69. As long as the evil deed done does not bear fruit, the fool thinks it is like honey; but when it ripens, then the fool suffers grief.

70. Let a fool month after month eat his food (like an ascetic) with the tip of a blade of Kusa grass, yet is he not worth the sixteenth particle of those who have well weighed the law.

71. An evil deed, like newly-drawn milk, does not turn (suddenly); smouldering, like fire covered by ashes, it follows the fool.

72. And when the evil deed, after it has become known, turns to sorrow for the fool, then it destroys his bright lot, nay, it cleaves his head.

73. Let the fool wish for a false reputation, for precedence among the Bhikshus, for lordship in the convents, for worship among other people!

74. 'May both the layman and he who has left the world think that this is done by me; may they be subject to me in everything which is to be done or is not to be done,' thus is the mind of the fool, and his desire and pride increase.

75. 'One is the road that leads to wealth, another the road that leads to Nirvâna;' if the Bhikshu, the disciple of Buddha, has learnt this, he will not yearn for honour, he will strive after separation from the world.

THE WISE MAN (PANDITA)

76. If you see a man who shows you what is to be avoided, who administers reproofs, and is intelligent, follow that wise man as you would one who tells of hidden treasures; it will be better, not worse, for him who follows him.

77. Let him admonish, let him teach, let him forbid what is improper!—he will be beloved of the good, by the bad he will be hated.

78. Do not have evil-doers for friends, do not have low people for friends: have virtuous people for friends, have for friends the best of men.

79. He who drinks in the law lives happily with a serene mind: the sage rejoices always in the law, as preached by the elect (Ariyas).

80. Well-makers lead the water (wherever they like); fletchers bend the arrow; carpenters bend a log of wood; wise people fashion themselves.

81. As a solid rock is not shaken by the wind, wise people falter not amidst blame and praise.

82. Wise people, after they have listened to the laws, become serene, like a deep, smooth, and still lake.

83. Good men indeed walk (warily) under all circumstances; good men speak not out of a desire for sensual gratification; whether touched by happiness or sorrow wise people never appear elated or depressed.

84. If, whether for his own sake, or for the sake of others, a man wishes neither for a son, nor for wealth, nor for lordship, and if he does not wish for his own success by unfair means, then he is good, wise, and virtuous.

85. Few are there among men who arrive at the other shore (become Arhats); the other people here run up and down the shore.

86. But those who, when the law has been well preached to them, follow the law, will pass over the dominion of death, however difficult to cross.

87, 88. A wise man should leave the dark state (of ordinary life), and follow the bright state (of the Bhikshu). After going from his home to a homeless state, he should in his retirement look for enjoyment where enjoyment seemed difficult. Leaving all pleasures behind, and calling nothing his own, the wise man should purge himself from all the troubles of the mind.

89. Those whose mind is well grounded in the (seven) elements of knowledge, who without clinging to anything, rejoice in freedom from attachment, whose appetites have been conquered, and who are full of light, they are free (even) in this world.

THE VENERABLE (ARHAT)

90. There is no suffering for him who has finished his journey, and abandoned grief, who has freed himself on all sides, and thrown off all fetters.

91. They exert themselves with their thoughts well-collected, they do not tarry in their abode; like swans who have left their lake, they leave their house and home.

92. Men who have no riches, who live on recognised food, who have perceived void and unconditioned freedom (Nirvâna), their path is difficult to understand, like that of birds in the air.

93. He whose appetites are stilled, who is not absorbed in enjoyment, who has perceived void and unconditioned freedom (Nirvâna), his path is difficult to understand, like that of birds in the air.

94. The gods even envy him whose senses, like horses well broken in by the driver, have been subdued, who is free from pride, and free from appetites;

95. Such a one who does his duty is tolerant like the earth, or like a threshold; he is like a lake without mud; no new births are in store for him.

96. His thought is quiet, quiet are his word and deed, when he has obtained freedom by true knowledge, when he has thus become a quiet man.

97. The man who is free from credulity, but knows the uncreated, who has cut all ties, removed all temptations, renounced all desires, he is the greatest of men.

98. In a hamlet or in a forest, on sea or on dry land, wherever venerable persons (Arahanta) dwell, that place is delightful.

99. Forests are delightful; where the world finds no delight, there the passionless will find delight, for they look not for pleasures.

THE THOUSANDS

100. Even though a speech be a thousand (of words), but made up of senseless words, one word of sense is better, which if a man hears, he becomes quiet.

101. Even though a Gâthâ (poem) be a thousand (of words), but made up of senseless words, one word of a Gâthâ is better, which if a man hears, he becomes quiet.

102. Though a man recite a hundred Gâthâs made up of senseless words, one word of the law is better, which if a man hears, he becomes quiet.

103. If one man conquer in battle a thousand times a thousand men, and if another conquer himself, he is the greatest of conquerors.

104, 105. One's own self conquered is better than all other people; not even a god, a Gandharva, not Mâra with Brahman could change into defeat the victory of a man who has vanquished himself, and always lives under restraint.

106. If a man for a hundred years sacrifice month by month with a thousand, and if he but for one moment pay homage to a man whose soul is grounded (in true knowledge), better is that homage than a sacrifice for a hundred years.

107. If a man for a hundred years worship Agni (fire) in the forest, and if he but for one moment pay homage to a man whose soul is grounded (in true knowledge), better is that homage than sacrifice for a hundred years.

108. Whatever a man sacrifice in this world as an offering or as an oblation for a whole year in order to gain merit, the whole of it is not worth a quarter (a farthing); reverence shown to the righteous is better.

109. He who always greets and constantly reveres the aged, four things will increase to him, viz. life, beauty, happiness, power.

110. But he who lives a hundred years, vicious and unrestrained, a life of one day is better if a man is virtuous and reflecting.

111. And he who lives a hundred years, ignorant and unrestrained, a life of one day is better if a man is wise and reflecting.

112. And he who lives a hundred years, idle and weak, a life of one day is better if a man has attained firm strength.

113. And he who lives a hundred years, not seeing beginning and end, a life of one day is better if a man sees beginning and end.

114. And he who lives a hundred years, not seeing the immortal place, a life of one day is better if a man sees the immortal place.

115. And he who lives a hundred years, not seeing the highest law, a life of one day is better if a man sees the highest law.

EVIL

116. A man should hasten toward the good, and should keep his thought away from evil; if a man does what is good slothfully, his mind delights in evil.

117. If a man commits a sin, let him not do it again; let him not delight in sin: the accumulation of evil is painful.

118. If a man does what is good, let him do it again; let him delight in it: the accumulation of good is delightful.

119. Even an evil-doer sees happiness so long as his evil deed does not ripen; but when his evil deed ripens, then does the evil-doer see evil.

120. Even a good man sees evil days so long as his good deed does not ripen; but when his good deed ripens, then does the good man see good things.

121. Let no man think lightly of evil, saying in his heart, It will not come nigh unto me. Even by the falling of water-drops a water-pot is filled; the fool becomes full of evil, even if he gather it little by little.

122. Let no man think lightly of good, saying in his heart, It will not come nigh unto me. Even by the falling of water-drops a water-pot is filled; the wise man becomes full of good, even if he gather it little by little.

123. Let a man avoid evil deeds, as a merchant, if he has few companions and carries much wealth, avoids a dangerous road; as a man who loves life avoids poison.

124. He who has no wound on his hand, may touch poison with his hand; poison does not affect one who has no wound; nor is there evil for one who does not commit evil.

125. If a man offend a harmless, pure, and innocent person, the evil falls back upon that fool, like light dust thrown up against the wind.

126. Some people are born again; evil-doers go to hell; righteous people go to heaven; those who are free from all worldly desires attain Nirvâna.

127. Not in the sky, not in the midst of the sea, not if we enter into the clefts of the mountains, is there known a spot in the whole world where a man might be freed from an evil deed.

128. Not in the sky, not in the midst of the sea, not if we enter into

the clefts of the mountains, is there known a spot in the whole world where death could not overcome (the mortal).

PUNISHMENT

129. All men tremble at punishment, all men fear death; remember that you are like unto them, and do not kill, nor cause slaughter.

130. All men tremble at punishment, all men love life; remember that thou art like unto them, and do not kill, nor cause slaughter.

131. He who, seeking his own happiness, punishes or kills beings who also long for happiness, will not find happiness after death.

132. He who seeking his own happiness does not punish or kill beings who also long for happiness, will find happiness after death.

133. Do not speak harshly to anybody; those who are spoken to will answer thee in the same way. Angry speech is painful, blows for blows will touch thee.

134. If, like a shattered metal plate (gong), thou utter nothing, then thou hast reached Nirvâna; anger is not known to thee.

135. As a cowherd with his staff drives his cows into the stable, so do Age and Death drive the life of men.

136. A fool does not know when he commits his evil deeds: but the wicked man burns by his own deeds, as if burnt by fire.

137. He who inflicts pain on innocent and harmless persons, will soon come to one of these ten states:

138. He will have cruel suffering, loss, injury of the body, heavy affliction, or loss of mind,

139. Or a misfortune coming from the king, or a fearful accusation, or loss of relations, or destruction of treasures,

140. Or lightning-fire will burn his houses; and when his body is destroyed, the fool will go to hell.

141. Not nakedness, not platted hair, not dirt, not fasting, or lying on the earth, not rubbing with dust, not sitting motionless, can purify a mortal who has not overcome desires.

142. He who, though dressed in fine apparel, exercises tranquillity, is quiet, subdued, restrained, chaste, and has ceased to find fault with all other beings, he indeed is a Brâhmaṇa, an ascetic (sramaṇa), a friar (bhikshu).

143. Is there in this world any man so restrained by shame that he does not provoke reproof, as a noble horse the whip?

144. Like a noble horse when touched by the whip, be ye strenuous and eager, and by faith, by virtue, by energy, by meditation, by discernment of the law you will overcome this great pain, perfect in knowledge and in behaviour, and never forgetful.

145. Well-makers lead the water (wherever they like); fletchers bend the arrow; carpenters bend a log of wood; good people fashion themselves.

OLD AGE

146. How is there laughter, how is there joy, as this world is always burning? Do you not seek a light, ye who are surrounded by darkness?

147. Look at this dressed-up lump, covered with wounds, joined together, sickly, full of many schemes, but which has no strength, no hold!

148. This body is wasted, full of sickness, and frail; this heap of corruption breaks to pieces, life indeed ends in death.

149. After one has looked at those grey bones, thrown away like gourds in the autumn, what pleasure is there (left in life)!

150. After a stronghold has been made of the bones, it is covered with flesh and blood, and there dwell in it old age and death, pride and deceit.

151. The brilliant chariots of kings are destroyed, the body also approaches destruction, but the virtue of good people never approaches destruction,—thus do the good say to the good.

152. A man who has learnt little, grows old like an ox; his flesh grows, but his knowledge does not grow.

153, 154. Looking for the maker of this tabernacle, I have run through a course of many births, not finding him; and painful is birth again and again. But now, maker of the tabernacle, thou hast been seen; thou shalt not make up this tabernacle again. All thy rafters are broken, thy ridge-pole is sundered; the mind, approaching the Eternal (visankhâra, nirvâna), has attained to the extinction of all desires.

155. Men who have not observed proper discipline, and have not gained wealth in their youth, perish like old herons in a lake without fish.

156. Men who have not observed proper discipline, and have not gained wealth in their youth, lie, like broken bows, sighing after the past.

SELF

157. If a man hold himself dear, let him watch himself carefully; during one at least out of the three watches a wise man should be watchful.

158. Let each man direct himself first to what is proper, then let him teach others; thus a wise man will not suffer.

159. If a man make himself as he teaches others to be, then, being himself well subdued, he may subdue (others); for one's own self is difficult to subdue.

160. Self is the lord of self, who else could be the lord? With self well subdued, a man finds a lord such as few can find.

161. The evil done by oneself, self-begotten, self-bred, crushes the foolish, as a diamond breaks even a precious stone.

162. He whose wickedness is very great brings himself down to that

state where his enemy wishes him to be, as a creeper does with the tree which it surrounds.

163. Bad deeds, and deeds hurtful to ourselves, are easy to do; what is beneficial and good, that is very difficult to do.

164. The foolish man who scorns the rule of the venerable (Arahat), of the elect (Ariya), of the virtuous, and follows a false doctrine, he bears fruit to his own destruction, like the fruits of the Katthaka reed.

165. By oneself the evil is done, by oneself one suffers; by oneself evil is left undone, by oneself one is purified. The pure and the impure (stand and fall) by themselves, no one can purify another.

166. Let no one forget his own duty for the sake of another's, however great; let a man, after he has discerned his own duty, be always attentive to his duty.

THE WORLD

167. Do not follow the evil law! Do not live on in thoughtfulness! Do not follow false doctrine! Be not a friend of the world.

168. Rouse thyself! do not be idle! Follow the law of virtue! The virtuous rests in bliss in this world and in the next.

169. Follow the law of virtue; do not follow that of sin. The virtuous rests in bliss in this world and in the next.

170. Look upon the world as you would on a bubble, look upon it as you would on a mirage: the king of death does not see him who thus looks down upon the world.

171. Come, look at this world, glittering like a royal chariot; the foolish are immersed in it, but the wise do not touch it.

172. He who formerly was reckless and afterwards became sober, brightens up this world, like the moon when freed from clouds.

173. He whose evil deeds are covered by good deeds, brightens up this world, like the moon when freed from clouds.

174. This world is dark, few only can see here; a few only go to heaven, like birds escaped from the net.

175. The swans go on the path of the sun, they go miraculously through the ether; the wise are led out of this world, when they have conquered Mâra and his train.

176. If a man has transgressed the one law, and speaks lies, and scoffs at another world, there is no evil he will not do.

177. The uncharitable do not go to the world of the gods; fools only do not praise liberality; a wise man rejoices in liberality, and through it becomes blessed in the other world.

178. Better than sovereignty over the earth, better than going to heaven, better than lordship over all worlds, is the reward of Sotâpatti, the first step in holiness.

THE BUDDHA (THE AWAKENED)

179. He whose conquest cannot be conquered again, into whose conquest no one in this world enters, by what track can you lead him, the Awakened, the Omniscient, the trackless?

180. He whom no desire with its snares and poisons can lead astray, by what track can you lead him, the Awakened, the Omniscient, the trackless?

181. Even the gods envy those who are awakened and not forgetful, who are given to meditation, who are wise, and who delight in the repose of retirement (from the world).

182. Difficult (to obtain) is the conception of men, difficult is the life of mortals, difficult is the hearing of the True Law, difficult is the birth of the Awakened (the attainment of Buddhahood).

183. Not to commit any sin, to do good, and to purify one's mind, that is the teaching of (all) the Awakened.

184. The Awakened call patience the highest penance, long-suffering the highest Nirvâna; for he is not an anchorite (pravragita) who strikes others, he is not an ascetic (sramana) who insults others.

185. Not to blame, not to strike, to live restrained under the law, to be moderate in eating, to sleep and sit alone, and to dwell on the highest thoughts,—this is the teaching of the Awakened.

186. There is no satisfying lusts, even by a shower of gold pieces; he who knows that lusts have a short taste and cause pain, he is wise;

187. Even in heavenly pleasures he finds no satisfaction, the disciple who is fully awakened delights only in the destruction of all desires.

188. Men, driven by fear, go to many a refuge, to mountains and forests, to groves and sacred trees.

189. But that is not a safe refuge, that is not the best refuge; a man is not delivered from all pains after having gone to that refuge.

190. He who takes refuge with Buddha, the Law, and the Church; he who, with clear understanding, sees the four holy truths:—

191. Viz. pain, the origin of pain, the destruction of pain, and the eightfold holy way that leads to the quieting of pain;—

192. That is the safe refuge, that is the best refuge; having gone to that refuge, a man is delivered from all pain.

193. A supernatural person (a Buddha) is not easily found, he is not born everywhere. Wherever such a sage is born, that race prospers.

194. Happy is the arising of the awakened, happy is the teaching of the True Law, happy is peace in the church, happy is the devotion of those who are at peace.

195, 196. He who pays homage to those who deserve homage, whether the awakened (Buddha) or their disciples, those who have overcome the host (of evils), and crossed the flood of sorrow, he who pays homage to such as have found deliverance and know no fear, his merit can never be measured by anybody.

HAPPINESS

197. We live happily indeed, not hating those who hate us! among men who hate us we dwell free from hatred!

198. We live happily indeed, free from ailments among the ailing! among men who are ailing let us dwell free from ailments!

199. We live happily indeed, free from greed among the greedy! among men who are greedy let us dwell free from greed!

200. We live happily indeed, though we call nothing our own! We shall be like the bright gods, feeding on happiness!

201. Victory breeds hatred, for the conquered is unhappy. He who has given up both victory and defeat, he, the contented, is happy.

202. There is no fire like passion; there is no losing throw like hatred; there is no pain like this body; there is no happiness higher than rest.

203. Hunger is the worst of diseases, the elements of the body the greatest evil; if one knows this truly, that is Nirvâna, the highest happiness.

204. Health is the greatest of gifts, contentedness the best riches; trust is the best of relationships, Nirvâna the highest happiness.

205. He who has tasted the sweetness of solitude and tranquillity, is free from fear and free from sin, while he tastes the sweetness of drinking in the law.

206. The sight of the elect (Arya) is good, to live with them is always happiness; if a man does not see fools, he will be truly happy.

207. He who walks in the company of fools suffers a long way; company with fools, as with an enemy, is always painful; company with the wise is pleasure, like meeting with kinsfolk.

208. Therefore, one ought to follow the wise, the intelligent, the learned, the much enduring, the dutiful, the elect; one ought to follow such a good and wise man, as the moon follows the path of the stars.

PLEASURE

209. He who gives himself to vanity, and does not give himself to meditation, forgetting the real aim (of life) and grasping at pleasure, will in time envy him who has exerted himself in meditation.

210. Let no man ever cling to what is pleasant, or to what is unpleasant. Not to see what is pleasant is pain, and it is pain to see what is unpleasant.

211. Let, therefore, no man love anything; loss of the beloved is evil. Those who love nothing, and hate nothing, have no fetters.

212. From pleasure comes grief, from pleasure comes fear; he who is free from pleasure knows neither grief nor fear.

213. From affection comes grief, from affection comes fear; he who is free from affection knows neither grief nor fear.

214. From lust comes grief, from lust comes fear; he who is free from lust knows neither grief nor fear.

215. From love comes grief, from love comes fear; he who is free from love knows neither grief nor fear.

216. From greed comes grief, from greed comes fear; he who is free from greed knows neither grief nor fear.

217. He who possesses virtue and intelligence, who is just, speaks the truth, and does what is his own business, him the world will hold dear.

218. He in whom a desire for the Ineffable (Nirvâna) has sprung up, who in his mind is satisfied, and whose thoughts are not bewildered by love, he is called ûrdhvamsrotas (carried upwards by the stream).

219. Kinsmen, friends, and lovers salute a man who has been long away, and returns safe from afar.

220. In like manner his good works receive him who has done good, and has gone from this world to the other;—as kinsmen receive a friend on his return.

ANGER

221. Let a man leave anger, let him forsake pride, let him overcome all bondage! No sufferings befall the man who is not attached to name and form, and who calls nothing his own.

222. He who holds back rising anger like a rolling chariot, him I call a real driver; other people are but holding the reins.

223. Let a man overcome anger by love, let him overcome evil by good; let him overcome the greedy by liberality, the liar by truth!

224. Speak the truth, do not yield to anger; give, if thou art asked for little; by these three steps thou wilt go near the gods.

225. The sages who injure nobody, and who always control their body, they will go to the unchangeable place (Nirvâna), where, if they have gone, they will suffer no more.

226. Those who are ever watchful, who study day and night, and who strive after Nirvana, their passions will come to an end.

227. This is an old saying, O Atula, this is not as if of to-day: 'They blame him who sits silent, they blame him who speaks much, they also blame him who says little; there is no one on earth who is not blamed.'

228. There never was, there never will be, nor is there now, a man who is always blamed, or a man who is always praised.

229, 230. But he whom those who discriminate praise continually day after day, as without blemish, wise, rich in knowledge and virtue, who would dare to blame him, like a coin made of gold from the Gambû river? Even the gods praise him, he is praised even by Brahman.

231. Beware of bodily anger, and control thy body! Leave the sins of the body, and with thy body practise virtue!

232. Beware of the anger of the tongue, and control thy tongue! Leave the sins of the tongue, and practise virtue with thy tongue!

233. Beware of the anger of the mind, and control thy mind! Leave the sins of the mind, and practise virtue with thy mind!

234. The wise who control their body, who control their tongue, the wise who control their mind, are indeed well controlled.

IMPURITY

235. Thou art now like a sear leaf, the messengers of death (Yama) have come near to thee; thou standest at the door of thy departure, and thou hast no provision for thy journey.

236. Make thyself an island, work hard, be wise! When thy impurities are blown away, and thou art free from guilt, thou wilt enter into the heavenly world of the elect (Ariya).

237. Thy life has come to an end, thou art come near to death (Yama), there is no resting-place for thee on the road, and thou hast no provision for thy journey.

238. Make thyself an island, work hard, be wise! When thy impurities are blown away, and thou art free from guilt, thou wilt not enter again into birth and decay.

239. Let a wise man blow off the impurities of himself, as a smith blows off the impurities of silver, one by one, little by little, and from time to time.

240. As the impurity which springs from the iron, when it springs from it, destroys it; thus do a transgressor's own works lead him to the evil path.

241. The taint of prayers is non-repetition; the taint of houses, non-repair; the taint of complexion is sloth; the taint of a watchman, thoughtlessness.

242. Bad conduct is the taint of woman, niggardliness the taint of a benefactor; tainted are all evil ways, in this world and in the next.

243. But there is a taint worse than all taints—ignorance is the greatest taint. O mendicants! throw off that taint, and become taintless!

244. Life is easy for a man who is without shame: a crow hero, a mischief-maker, an insulting, bold, and wretched fellow.

245. But life is hard to live for a modest man, who always looks for what is pure, who is disinterested, quiet, spotless, and intelligent.

246. He who destroys life, who speaks untruth, who in the world takes what is not given him, who goes to another man's wife; and the man who gives himself to drinking intoxicating liquors, he, even in this world, digs up his own root.

247. O man, know this, that the unrestrained are in a bad state; take care that greediness and vice do not bring thee to grief for a long time!

248. The world gives according to their faith or according to their pleasure: if a man frets about the food and the drink given to others, he will find no rest either by day or by night.

249. He in whom that feeling is destroyed, and taken out with the very root, finds rest by day and by night.

250. There is no fire like passion, there is no shark like hatred, there is no snare like folly, there is no torrent like greed.

251. The fault of others is easily perceived, but that of one's self is difficult to perceive; a man winnows his neighbor's faults like chaff, but his own fault he hides, as a cheat hides the bad die from the player.

252. If a man looks after the faults of others, and is always inclined to be offended, his own passions will grow, and he is far from the destruction of passions.

253. There is no path through the air, a man is not a Samana outwardly. The world delights in vanity, the Tathāgatas (the Buddhas) are free from vanity.

254. There is no path through the air, a man is not a Samana outwardly. No creatures are eternal; but the awakened (Buddah) are never shaken.

10

THE BODHISATTVA

If one single doctrinal disagreement had to be singled out as the most important difference between Theravada and Mahayana Buddhism, a good choice would be the Mahayana affirmation and the Theravada denial of the Bodhisattva ideal. The term "Bodhisattva" was not unknown in Pali Buddhism. Many popular tales in that tradition relate how the figure that would later become Guatama displayed unprecedented self-sacrifice and compassion in a series of lives. This Buddha-to-be was called a "Bodhisattva." His

"The Bodhisattva's Infinite Compassion," from *Vajradhvaja Sutra* (Edward Conze, trans. (Oxford, England: Bruno Cassirer, Ltd. 1954), pp. 131–132. Reprinted from *Buddhist Texts through the Ages* by Edward Conze, by permission of Bruno Cassirer, Publishers, Ltd.

*actions were motivated entirely by love and wisdom, not at all by
ignorance and craving. The Mahayana innovation consisted in
asserting that this ideal of selfless service through life after life as
long as need remained was a higher ideal than liberation while
others remained in fetters and that it was a suitable ideal for all
men. To the Bodhisattva, pain is bad wherever it exists and he is
free of the sense of personal separation which makes most of us
regard our pain as important and other men's as negligible. There
is a large Mahayana literature about the "skilful means" which
Bodhisattvas are supposed to adopt to forward the spiritual lives of
suffering beings. A Bodhisattva will not wander solitary as a rhi-
noceros like the disciples of the Theravada school, but will appear
to men in a form and manner designed to attract and help them.
The Theravadins hold the doctrine to be pernicious in leading
men to expect help from outside forces rather than from their own
disciplined effort.*

THE BODHISATTVA'S INFINITE COMPASSION

A Bodhisattva resolves: I take upon myself the burden of all suffering,
I am resolved to do so, I will endure it. I do not turn or run away, do not
tremble, am not terrified, nor afraid, do not turn back or despond.

And why? At all costs I must bear the burdens of all beings, In that I
do not follow my own inclinations. I have made the vow to save all beings.
All beings I must set free. The whole world of living beings I must rescue,
from the terrors of birth, of old age, of sickness, of death and rebirth, of all
kinds of moral offence, of all states of woe, of the whole cycle of birth-and-
death, of the jungle of false views, of the loss of wholesome dharmas, of the
concomitants of ignorance,—from all these terrors I must rescue all beings.
. . . I walk so that the kingdom of unsurpassed cognition is built up for all
beings. My endeavours do not merely aim at my own deliverance. For with
the help of the boat of the thought of all-knowledge, I must rescue all these
beings from the stream of Samsara, which is so difficult to cross, I must pull
them back from the great precipice, I must free them from all calamities, I
must ferry them across the stream of Samsara. I myself must grapple with the
whole mass of suffering of all beings. To the limit of my endurance I will
experience in all the states of woe, found in any world system, all the abodes
of suffering. And I must not cheat all beings out of my store of merit. I am
resolved to abide in each single state of woe for numberless aeons; and so I
will help all beings to freedom, in all the states of woe that may be found in
any world system whatsoever.

And why? Because it is surely better that I alone should be in pain
than that all these beings should fall into the states of woe. There I must
give myself away as a pawn through which the whole world is redeemed
from the terrors of the hells, of animal birth, of the world of Yama, and with

this my own body I must experience, for the sake of all beings, the whole mass of all painful feelings. And on behalf of all beings I give surety for all beings, and in doing so I speak truthfully, am trustworthy, and do not go back on my word. I must not abandon all beings.

And why? There has arisen in me the will to win all-knowledge, with all beings for its object, that is to say, for the purpose of setting free the entire world of beings. And I have not set out for the supreme enlightenment from a desire for delights, not because I hope to experience the delights of the five sense-qualities, or because I wish to indulge in the pleasures of the senses. And I do not pursue the course of a Bodhisattva in order to achieve the array of delights that can be found in the various worlds of sense-desire.

And why? Truly no delights are all these delights of the world. All this indulging in the pleasures of the senses belongs to the sphere of Mara.

11

THE PURE LAND

It has been observed that while the immensity of the universe as conceived by modern astronomy was a shock to western religious cosmologies, it was no more than expected by Mahayana Buddhism. The universe was conceived by Mahayanists to contain an innumerable number of world systems, each of which had its own Buddha and hence each of which was a Buddha-field. Buddha-fields could either be impure, containing evils, like the one in which we now live, or they could be "Pure Lands," ideal worlds inhabited by spiritualized beings who blissfully contemplate the reigning Buddha and listen to his teachings until they too attain Buddhahood. Although there are an indefinite number of Pure Lands, popular interest was centered upon the wonderful Western Paradise of Amitabha.

The Mahayana philosophies did not dispute the existence of the Pure Lands of the Buddhism of faith, but gave a psychological or symbolic interpretation of them. The Avatamsaka Sutra, for example, taught that all the Buddha-lands rise from the mind,

"The Pure Land," *Sukhavativyuha*, Edward Conze, trans. (Oxford, England: Bruno Cassirer, Ltd., 1954), pp. 202–206. Reprinted from *Buddhist Texts through the Ages* by Edward Conze, by permission of Bruno Cassirer, Publishers, Ltd.

*and the great Pure Lands are the mental creations of great spiritual
beings. A paradox close to the heart of Mahayana philosophizing
is that ultimately all the worlds are but one world, that this present world is actually the Pure Land and that salvation consists in
recognizing this. To the average peasant, on the other hand, the
jewel trees were no doubt conceived as very solid and distinct, and
the Mahayana philosophers, for the most part, saw no reason to
try to shake this belief. It was deemed to have a relative truth
and to be a step toward a more profound truth.*

15. This world Sukhavati, Ananda, which is the world system of the
Lord Amitabha, is rich and prosperous, comfortable, fertile, delightful and
crowded with many Gods and men. And in this world system, Ananda, there
are no hells, no animals, no ghosts, no Asuras and none of the inauspicious
places of rebirth. And in this our world no jewels make their appearance like
those which exist in the world system Sukhavati.

16. And that world system Sukhavati, Ananda, emits many fragrant
odours, it is rich in a great variety of flowers and fruits, adorned with jewel
trees, which are frequented by flocks of various birds with sweet voices, which
the Tathagata's miraculous power has conjured up. And these jewel trees,
Ananda, have various colours, many colours, many hundreds of thousands of
colours. They are variously composed of the seven precious things, in varying
combinations, i.e. of gold, silver, beryl, crystal, coral, red pearls or emerald.
Such jewel trees, and clusters of banana trees and rows of palm trees, all
made of precious things, grow everywhere in this Buddha-field. On all sides
it is surrounded with golden nets, and all round covered with lotus flowers
made of all the precious things. Some of the lotus flowers are half a mile in
circumference, others up to ten miles. And from each jewel lotus issue thirty-
six hundred thousand kotis of rays. And at the end of each ray there issue
thirty-six hundred thousand kotis of Buddhas, with golden-coloured bodies,
who bear the thirty-two marks of the superman, and who, in all the ten
directions, go into countless world systems, and there demonstrate Dharma.

17. And further, Ananda, in this Buddha-field there are nowhere any
mountains,—black mountains, jewel mountains, Sumerus, kings of mountains,
circular mountains and great circular mountains. But the Buddha-field is
everywhere even, delightful like the palm of the hand, and in all its parts the
ground contains a great variety of jewels and gems. . . .

18. And many kinds of rivers flow along in this world system Sukhavati.
There are great rivers there, one mile broad, and up to fifty miles broad and
twelve miles deep. And all these rivers flow along calmly, their water is
fragrant with manifold agreeable odours, in them there are bunches of flowers to which various jewels adhere, and they resound with various sweet
sounds. And the sound which issues from these great rivers is as pleasant as
that of a musical instrument, which consists of hundreds of thousands of
kotis of parts, and which, skilfully played, emits a heavenly music. It is deep,

commanding, distinct, clear, pleasant to the ear, touching the heart, delightful, sweet, pleasant, and one never tires of hearing it, it always agrees with one and one likes to hear it, like the words 'Impermanent, peaceful, calm, and not-self'. Such is the sound that reaches the ears of those beings.

And, Ananda, both the banks of those great rivers are lined with variously scented jewel trees, and from them bunches of flowers, leaves and branches of all kinds hang down. And if those beings wish to indulge in sports full of heavenly delights on those river-banks, then, after they have stepped into the water, the water in each case rises as high as they wish it to, —up to the ankles, or the knees, or the hips, or their sides, or their ears. And heavenly delights arise. Again, if beings wish the water to be cold, for them it becomes cold; if they wish it to be hot, for them it becomes hot; if they wish it to be hot and cold, for them it becomes hot and cold, to suit their pleasure. And those rivers flow along, full of water scented with the finest odours, and covered with beautiful flowers, resounding with the sounds of many birds, easy to ford, free from mud, and with golden sand at the bottom. And all the wishes those beings may think of, they all will be fulfilled, as long as they are rightful.

And as to the pleasant sound which issues from the water (of these rivers), that reaches all the parts of this Buddha-field. And everyone hears the pleasant sound he wishes to hear, i.e. he hears of the Buddha, the Dharma, the Samgha, of the (six) perfections, the (ten) stages, the powers, the grounds of self-confidence, of the special dharmas of a Buddha, of the analytical knowledges, of emptiness, the signless, and the wishless, of the uneffected, the unborn, of non-production, non-existence, non-cessation, of calm, quietude and peace, of the great friendliness, the great compassion, the great sympathetic joy, the great evenmindedness, of the patient acceptance of things which fail to be produced, and of the acquisition of the stage where one is consecrated (as a Tathagata). And, hearing this, one gains the exalted zest and joyfulness, which is associated with detachment, dispassion, calm, cessation, Dharma, and brings about the state of mind which leads to the accomplishment of enlightenment. And nowhere in this world-system Sukhavati does one hear of anything unwholesome, nowhere of the hindrances, nowhere of the states of punishment, the states of woe and the bad destinies, nowhere of suffering. Even of feelings which are neither pleasant nor unpleasant one does not hear here, how much less of suffering! And that, Ananda, is the reason why this world-system is called the 'Happy Land' (Sukhavati). But all this describes it only in brief, not in detail. One aeon might well reach its end while one proclaims the reasons for happiness in the world-system Sukhavati, and still one could not come to the end of (the enumeration of) the reasons for happiness.

19. Moreover, Ananda, all the beings who have been reborn in this world-system Sukhavati, who are reborn in it, or who will be reborn in it,

they will be exactly like the Paranirmitavasavartin Gods: of the same colour, strength, vigour, height and breadth, dominion, store of merit and keenness of super-knowledges; they enjoy the same dresses, ornaments, parks, palaces and pointed towers, the same kind of forms, sounds, smells, tastes and touchables, just the same kinds of enjoyments. And the beings in the world-system Su-khavati do not eat gross food, like soup or raw sugar; but whatever food they may wish for, that they perceive as eaten, and they become gratified in body and mind, without there being any further need to throw the food into the body. And if, after their bodies are gratified, they wish for certain perfumes, then the whole of that Buddha-field becomes scented with just that kind of heavenly perfumes. But if someone does not wish to smell that perfume, then the perception of it does not reach him. In the same way, whatever they may wish for, comes to them, be it musical instruments, banners, flags, etc.; or cloaks of different colours, or ornaments of various kinds. If they wish for a palace of a certain colour, distinguishing marks, construction, height and width, made of various precious things, adorned with hundreds of thousands of pinnacles, while inside it various heavenly woven materials are spread out, and it is full of couches strewn with beautiful cushions,—then just such a palace appears before them. In those delightful palaces, surrounded and hon-oured by seven times seven thousand Apsaras, they dwell, play, enjoy and disport themselves.

21. . . . And the beings who are touched by the winds, which are per-vaded with various perfumes, are filled with a happiness as great as that of a monk who has achieved the cessation of suffering.

22. And in this Buddha-field one has no conception at all of fire, sun, moon, planets, constellations, stars or blinding darkness, and no conception even of day and night, except (where they are mentioned) in the sayings of the Tathagata. There is nowhere a notion of monks possessing private parks for retreats.

24. And all the beings who have been born, who are born, who will be born in this Buddha-field, they all are fixed on the right method of salvation, until they have won Nirvana. And why? Because there is here no place for and no conception of the two other groups, i.e. of those who are not fixed at all, and those who are fixed on wrong ways. For this reason also that world-system is called the 'Happy Land'. . . .

26. And further again, Ananda, in the ten directions, in each single di-rection, in Buddha-fields countless like the sands of the river Ganges, Buddhas and Lords countless like the sands of the river Ganges, glorify the name of the Lord Amitabha, the Tathagata, praise him, proclaim his fame, extol his virtue. And why? Because all beings are irreversible from the supreme enlight-enment if they hear the name of the Lord Amitabha, and, on hearing it, with one single thought only raise their hearts to him with a resolve connected with serene faith.

27. And if any beings, Ananda, again and again reverently attend to this Tathagata, if they will plant a large and immeasurable root of good, having raised their hearts to enlightenment, and if they vow to be reborn in that world system, then, when the hour of their death approaches, that Tathagata Amitabha, the Arhat, the fully Enlightened One, will stand before them, surrounded by hosts of monks. Then, having seen that Lord, and having died with hearts serene, they will be reborn in just that world-system Sukhavati. And if there are sons or daughters of good family, who may desire to see that Tathagata Amitabha in this very life, they should raise their hearts to the supreme enlightenment, they should direct their thought with extreme resoluteness and perseverance unto this Buddha-field and they should dedicate their store of merit to being reborn therein.

12

THE HEART SUTRA

The Prajnaparamita sutras, of which the Heart Sutra is a famous epitome, form a class of important and difficult Mahayana documents composed in India between 100 B.C. and A.D. 600. Their two main themes are the perfections of the Bodhisattva and the Emptiness of all things. The Sanskrit word translated as "Emptiness" or "Voidness" is "Sunya." This is a highly numinous term, a word used in Mahayana Buddhism to refer to something of the highest importance and sacredness though incomprehensible to the rational intellect. It connotes an absence of self as Nirvana connotes an absence of craving. But, like Nirvana, even though lacking all specifiable positive content, it is not a conception of pure absence but of what there is when everything describable and conceivable is gone. From the standpoint of the Absolute, all things are always empty, but a man knows this only when he is himself empty from the relative standpoint. Emptiness is non-duality; it is Suchness; it is the Ultimate Reality and the goal of

"The Heart Sutra," Edward Conze, trans. (London: Allen & Unwin, 1958), pp. 77–102. Reprinted from The Buddhist Wisdom Books, by Edward Conze, by permission of George Allen & Unwin, Ltd.

the spiritual quest, but from the ultimate viewpoint it is the only reality and consequently there is really no spiritual quest and no ignorance. Switching back and forth between the relative and Absolute standpoint, the Mahayana scriptures are paradoxical. They declare that Nirvana and Samsara are the same even while teaching how one can pass from Samsara into Nirvana by realizing that they are the same.

The reader who desires to penetrate into the meaning of the cryptic passages of the Heart Sutra *is advised to consult Dr. Conze's commentary.*

1. Homage to the Perfection of Wisdom, the Lovely, the Holy!

2. Avalokita, The Holy Lord and Bodhisattva, was moving in the deep course of the Wisdom which has gone beyond. He looked down from on high, He beheld but five heaps, and he saw that in their own-being they were empty.

3. Here, O Śāriputra, form is emptiness and the very emptiness is form; emptiness does not differ from form, form does not differ from emptiness; whatever is form, that is emptiness, whatever is emptiness, that is form, the same is true of feelings, perceptions, impulses and consciousness.

4. Here, O Śāriputra, all dharmas are marked with emptiness; they are not produced or stopped, not defiled or immaculate, not deficient or complete.

5. Therefore, O Śāriputra, in emptiness there is no form, nor feeling, nor perception, nor impulse, nor consciousness; No eye, ear, nose, tongue, body, mind; No forms, sounds, smells, tastes, touchables or objects of mind; No sight-organ element, and so forth, until we come to: No mind-consciousness element; There is no ignorance, no extinction of ignorance, and so forth, until we come to: there is no decay and death, no extinction of decay and death. There is no suffering, no origination, no stopping, no path. There is no cognition, no attainment and no non-attainment.

6. Therefore, O Śāriputra, it is because of his non attainmentness that a Bodhisattva, through having relied on the perfection of wisdom, dwells without thought-coverings. In the absence of thought-coverings he has not been made to tremble, he has overcome what can upset, and in the end he attains to Nirvana.

7. All those who appear as Buddhas in the three periods of time fully awake to the utmost, right and perfect enlightenment because they have relied on the perfection of wisdom.

8. Therefore one should know the prajñāpāramitā as the great spell, the spell of great knowledge, the utmost spell, the unequalled spell, allayer of all suffering, in truth—for what could go wrong? By the prajñāpāramitā has this spell been delivered. It runs like this: Gone, gone, gone beyond, gone altogether beyond, O what an awakening, all-hail!—This completes the Heart of perfect wisdom.

TWENTY VERSES ON THE MAHĀYANĀ
Nāgārjuna

To comprehend a philosophical position it is not only necessary to know its conclusions, but also to understand the reasoning whereby these conclusions are defended. The second requirement is often difficult in the study of an author within one's own tradition; it is harder with a thinker in a foreign tradition, and is usually impossible in a brief selection. In presenting three famous summary treatises by Mahayana philosophers, it is not expected that the arguments of these thinkers will be comprehensible from these summaries, only that some of their main conclusions and their style of thought will be exhibited.

Nagarjuna, who probably lived during the Second Century A.D. in South India, was a prolific writer of philosophical works. He was mythically credited with having discovered in a Himalayan cave the Prajnaparamita sutras containing the esoteric teachings of the Buddha, while he actually did more than any other thinker to crystallize Mahayana thought. Starting from the Pali view that the apparent objects of the world are actually composed of an ever-changing complex of momentary dharmas, he argued that these elements are themselves the product of the perceiving mind. Reality is consequently empty of the characteristics we attribute to it. In the area of relative truth our concepts can yield knowledge, but we can never conceptually grasp the transcendental truth. It is ineffable. To pass into Nirvana is, from the viewpoint of conceptual cognition, to pass into Emptiness. Nagarajuna also developed an acute dialectical method designed to undercut all positive metaphysical views by reductio ad absurdum arguments. He is a prime example of a thinker employing philosophical arguments primarily to reveal the limits of philosophical knowledge.

Nāgārjuna's Mahāyāna Vimsaka, Susumu Yamaguchi, trans. The Eastern Buddhist, IV, No. 2 (Kyoto, Japan, 1927), pp. 169–171. Reprinted by permission of Dr. Yamaguchi.

(Tsa) Adoration to Mañjśrī-kumāra-bhūtā.

(Gi) Adoration to the Three Treasures.

1. The Buddha who is undefiled and enlightened, elucidates well, being full of mercy, that which is not a word nor is to be expressed in words: therefore I adore the [Buddha's] power which is beyond thought.

2. From the absolute point of view there is no birth, here again is there no annihilation; the Buddha is like sky, so are beings; they are of one nature.

3. There is no birth on the other side, nor on this side; Nirvāna too in its self-nature exists not. Thus when surveyed by a knowledge which knows all things, empty are the created.

4. The self-nature of all things is regarded as like shadow; they are in substance pure, serene, non-dualistic and same as suchness.

5. [To think of] self or of no-self is not the truth; they are discriminated by the confused; pleasure and pain are relative; so are passions and emancipation from them.

6. Transmigration in the six paths of existence, the excellence and enjoyability of the heavenly world, or the great painfulness of the purgatories,—all these come from apprehending the external world [as reality].

7. One suffers very much when there is nothing pleasurable; even when there are things to enjoy, they pass away because they are impermanent; but it is so settled that goods indeed come from good deeds.

8. Things are produced by false discrimination where there is no origination, so, when the purgatories, etc., are manifested, the erroneous are burned like a forest fire.

9. Like unto things magic-created, so are the deeds of sentient beings who take the external world [for reality]. The [six] paths of existence are in substance magic-creations, and they exist conditionally.

10. As the painter painting a terrible monster is himself frightened thereby, so is the fool frightened with transmigration.

11. As a stupid child making a muddy pool is himself drowned in it, so are sentient beings drowned in the mire of false discrimination and unable to get out of it.

12. As they regard non-existence as existence they suffer the feeling of pain. In the external world as well as in thought they are bound by the poison of false discrimination.

13. Seeing that beings are weak, one with a heart of love and wisdom is to discipline oneself for perfect enlightenment in order to benefit them.

14. Again, if one with such [a heart] accumulates [spiritual] provisions, one attains, from the relative point of view, supreme enlightenment and is delivered from the bondage of false discrimination. Such an enlightened one is a friend of the world.

15. When a man perceives the true meaning [of reality] as it becomes, he understands that the paths of existence are empty, and cuts asunder [the chain of] the first, middle and last.

16. Thus regarded, samsāra and nirvāṇa have no real substance. Passions have not any substance. Such notions as the first, middle, and last are done away with when their self-nature is understood.

17. As perception takes place in a dream which when awakened disappears; so it is with sleeping in the darkness of ignorance: when awakened, transmigrations no more obtain.

18. When things created by magic are seen as such, they have no existence; such is the nature of all things.

19. They are all nothing but mind, they are established as phantoms; therefore a blissful or an evil existence is matured according to deeds good or evil.

20. When the mind-wheel ceases to exist all things indeed cease to exist; thus there is no ego in the nature of all things and therefore their nature is pure indeed.

21. When the ignorant wrapped in the darkness of ignorance conceive eternity or bliss in objects as they appear or as they are in themselves, they drift in the ocean of transmigration.

22. Where the great ocean of birth and death filled with waters of false discrimination, who could ever reach the other shore unless carried by the raft of the Mahāyāna?

23. When it is rightly understood that the world arises conditioned by ignorance, where could false discrimination obtain?

14

THIRTY VERSES ON THE MIND-ONLY DOCTRINE
Vasubandhu

The Absolute for Nagarjuna is Emptiness, for Vasubandhu and the Yogacarins it is Consciousness. Like the later western idealists, Vasubandhu begins from what is immediately given, mental representations, and then finds no need to posit any fur-

"The Thirty Verses on the Mind-Only Doctrine by Vasubandhu," Hsüan Tsang's version: Wing-tsit Chan, trans. (Princeton, New Jersey: Princeton University Press, 1927), pp. 333–337. Reprinted from *A Source Book in Indian Philosophy* by Radhakrishnan and Moore, by permission of Princeton University Press.

*ther entities except a kind of eternal storehouse from which ideas
and images can be drawn in an orderly fashion. This "repository
consciousness" is itself beyond all possibility of conception, although it is the source of all thoughts. Every phenomenal object
is the product of the flow of thought in it. When an individual
discovers this consciousness, he ceases to be an individual, as the
thoughts that constitute his individuality are then merged into
the totality of thought. This consciousness constitutes the true
reality of all things.*

*The Yogacara trend of thought began in the Second Cen-
tury A.D., but the developed doctrine is attributed to two brothers, Asanga and Vasubandhu, who lived in Northwest India in
the Fourth Century. The name "Yogacarin" means "practitioner
of Yoga," and although this school did recommend Yoga exercises
as a path to liberation, so did many others. The attachment of the
title to this school of Buddhist idealism is probably due to the
fact that it occurs in the title of Asanga's chief work.*

I. Because our ideation gives rise to the false ideas of the ego and
    dharmas (elements of existence),
  There are various revulsions of appearances.
  This ideation, depending on the mind, goes through certain trans-
    formations.
  These transformations are of three kinds.

II. They are the consciousness of "ripening in a different life,"
  The consciousness of intellection, and the consciousness of the dis-
    crimination of the objective world.
  First of all, *ālaya* (ideation-store) consciousness,
  Which brings into fruition all seeds [or effects of good and evil deeds].

III. [In its state of pure consciousness], it is not conscious of its clingings
    and impressions.
  In both its objective and subjective functions, it is always associated
    with touch,
  Volition, feeling, thought, and cognition.
  But it is always indifferent to its associations.

IV. It is not affected by the darkness of ignorance or by the memory [of
    the distinction of good and evil].
  The same is true in the case of touch, etc.
  It is always flowing like a torrent,
  And is abandoned in the state of the *arhat*.

V. The second transformation
  Is called the mind-consciousness,

Which, while it depends on the ideation-store consciousness, in turn
  conditions it.
Its nature and characteristic consists of intellection.

vi. It is always accompanied by the four evil desires,
  Namely, ignorance of the self, view of the self [as being real and
    permanent],
  Self-pride, and self-love,
  And by touch, etc. [volition, feeling, thought, and cognition].

vii. It is free from the memory [of the distinction of good and evil] but not
    from the darkness of ignorance.
  It follows its objects in their emergence and dependence.
  It is abandoned by the *arhat* when he arrives at the state of complete
    extinction of sensation and thought,
  And transcends this mundane world.

viii. Next comes the third transformation,
  Which consists of the last six categories of discrimination [the con-
    sciousness of touch, sight, hearing, smell, taste, and the sense-center
    consciousness].
  Its nature and characteristic consists of the discrimination of objects.
  It is neither good nor evil.

ix. Mental functions consist of general mental functions,
  Particular mental functions, good functions, evil functions,
  Minor evil functions, and indeterminate mental functions.
  They all impress the mind in three ways [of joy, of suffering, and of
    indifference].

x. General mental functions are touch, etc. [volition, feeling, thought,
    cognition].
  Particular mental functions are desire,
  Resolve, remembrance, concentration, and wisdom,
  Each depending on different conditions.

xi. Good mental functions are belief, sense of shame, bashfulness,
  The three roots of the absence of covetousness, etc. [the absence of
    hatred and the absence of attachment],
  Energy, repose of mind, vigilance,
  Equanimity, and non-injury.

xii. Evil mental functions are covetousness, hatred,
  Attachment, arrogance, doubt, and false view.

Minor evil mental functions are anger,
Enmity, concealment, affliction, envy, parsimony,

XIII. Deception, fraudulence, injury, pride,
Absence of the sense of shame, absence of bashfulness,
High-mindedness, low-mindedness,
Unbelief, indolence,

XIV. Idleness, forgetfulness,
Distraction, and non-discernment.
Indeterminate mental functions are repentance, drowsiness,
Reflection, and investigation, the former two composing a different
class from the latter.

XV. Based on the mind-consciousness
The five consciousnesses [of the senses] manifest themselves in con-
comitance with the objective world.
Sometimes the senses manifest themselves together, and sometimes
not,
Just as waves are dependent on the water.

XVI. The sense-center consciousness always arises and manifests itself,
Except when born in the realm of the absence of thought,
In the state of unconsciousness, in the two forms of concentration,
In sleep, and in that state where the spirit is depressed or absent.

XVII. Thus the various consciousnesses are but transformations.
That which discriminates and that which is discriminated
Are, because of this, both unreal.
For this reason, everything is mind only.

XVIII. As the result of various ideations which serve as seeds,
Different transformations take place.
The revulsion-energy of these ideations
Gives rise to all sorts of discrimination.

XIX. Due to the habit-energy of various *karmas*
The habit-energy of both the six organs and their objects is influenced.
As the previous "ripening in a different life" is completed,
Succeeding "ripenings in a different life" are produced.

XX. Because of false discriminations,
Various things are falsely discriminated.
What is grasped by such false discrimination
Has no self-nature whatsoever.

xxi. The self-nature which results from dependence on others
Is produced by the condition of discrimination.
The difference between the Absolute (perfect wisdom) and the dependent
Is that the former is eternally free from what is grasped by false discrimination.

xxii. Thus the Absolute and the dependent
Are neither the same nor different;
As in the case of impermanence and permanence,
The one can be seen only in the other.

xxiii. From the three aspects of entity,
The three aspects of non-entity are established.
Therefore the Enlightened One abstrusely preached
That all *dharmas* have no entity.

xxiv. The first is the non-entity of phenomenon.
The second is the non-entity of self-existence.
The last is the non-entity of the ultimate existence
Of the falsely discriminative ego and *dharmas* now to be eliminated.

xxv. The supreme truth of all *dharmas*
Is nothing other than the True Norm [suchness].
It is forever true to its nature,
Which is the true nature of mind-only.

xxvi. Inasmuch as consciousness in its unawakened state
Is not in the abode of the reality of mind-only,
The six sense-organs, their objects, and the seeds of evil desires
Cannot be controlled and extirpated.

xxvii. To hold something before oneself,
And to say that it is the reality of mind-only,
Is not the state of mind-only,
Because it is the result of grasping.

xxviii. But when [the objective world which is] the basis of conditioning as
well as the wisdom [which does the conditioning]
Are both eliminated,
The state of mind-only is realized,
Since the six sense-organs and their objects are no longer present.

xxix. Without any grasping and beyond thought
Is the supra-mundane wisdom [of *bodhisattva*hood].

Because of the abandonment of the habit-energy of various *karmas*
and the six sense-organs as well as their objects,
The revulsion from relative knowledge to perfect wisdom is attained.

xxx. This is the realm of passionlessness or purity,
Which is beyond description, is good, and is eternal,
Where one is in the state of emancipation, peace, and joy.
This is the law of the Great Buddha.

15

TREATISE ON THE GOLDEN LION
Fa-Tsang

The dominant school of Chinese Buddhist metaphysics was
the Hua-yen (Flowery Splendor) philosophy based upon the Sanskrit Avatamsaka Sutra which had not led to a specific Indian
school. Like the Yogacarins, the Hua-yen school regarded all
phenomena as manifestations of the one permanent and unchanging mind. The special feature of the school is its doctrine that all
things are so interpenetrated that each thing includes all the others. A favorite metaphor for the doctrine is that of Indra's net
which carries a bright jewel at each knot. Each of these perfect
jewels reflects all the others, so that to know one is to know all.
The monk Fa-tsang (A.D. 643–712) is said to have been an
assistant to the great Hsüan-tsang who had studied in India for
sixteen years and then became the great Chinese exponent of the
Yogacara. Fa-tsang is credited with some sixty philosophical works.
He enjoyed the support of the Empress of his day for whom he is
said to have invented the analogy of the Golden Lion in an effort
to make his abtruse doctrines more comprehensible.

Fa-tsang, "A Treatise on the Golden Lion," Wing-Tsit Chan, trans. (Princeton,
New Jersey: Princeton University Press, 1963), pp. 409–414. Reprinted from *A Source
Book in Chinese Philosophy* by Wing-Tsit Chan, by permission of Princeton University
Press.

1. CLARIFYING THE FACT THAT THINGS ARISE THROUGH CAUSATION

It means that gold has no nature of its own. As a result of the condition-ing of the skillful craftsman, the character of the lion consequently arises. This arising is purely due to causes. Therefore it is called arising through causation.

2. DISTINGUISHING MATTER AND EMPTINESS

It means that the character of the lion is unreal; there is only real gold. The lion is not existent, but the substance of the gold is not nonexistent. Therefore they are [separately] called matter and Emptiness. Furthermore, Emptiness has no character of its own; it shows itself by means of matter. This does not obstruct its illusory existence. Therefore they are [separately] called matter and Emptiness.

3. SIMPLY STATING THE THREE NATURES

The lion exists because of our feelings. This is called [the nature] aris-ing from vast imagination. The lion seems to exist. This is called [the nature of] dependence on others (gold and craftsman) [for production]. The nature of the gold does not change. This is therefore called [the nature of] Perfect Reality.

4. SHOWING THE NONEXISTENCE OF CHARACTERS

It means that as the gold takes in the lion in its totality, apart from the gold there is no character of the lion to be found. Therefore it is called the nonexistence of characters.

5. EXPLAINING NON-COMING-INTO-EXISTENCE

It means that at the moment when we see the lion come into existence, it is only gold that comes into existence. There is nothing apart from the gold. Although the lion comes into existence and goes out of existence, the sub-stance of the gold at bottom neither increases nor decreases. Therefore we say that [dharmas] do not come into existence [nor go out of existence].

6. DISCUSSING THE FIVE DOCTRINES

(1) Although the lion is a dharma produced through causation, and comes into and goes out of existence every moment, there is really no char-acter of the lion to be found. This is called the Small Vehicle (Hīnayāna) Doctrine of Ordinary Disciples [that is, the Hīnayāna schools].

(2) These dharmas produced through causation are each without self-nature. It is absolutely Emptiness. This is called the Initial Doctrine of the Great Vehicle (Mahāyāna) [that is, the Three-Treatise and Conscious-Only Schools].

(3) Although there is absolutely only Emptiness, this does not prevent the illusory dharmas from being clearly what they are. The two characters of coming into existence through causation and dependent existence coexist. This is called the Final Doctrine of the Great Vehicle [that is, the Zen School].

(4) These two characters eliminate each other and both perish, and [consequently] neither [the products of] our feelings nor false existence remain. Neither of them has any more power, and both Emptiness and existence perish. Names and descriptions will be completely discarded and the mind will be at rest and have no more attachment. This is called the Great Vehicle's Doctrine of Sudden Enlightenment [that is, the Hua-yen School].

(5) When the feelings have been eliminated and true substance revealed, all becomes an undifferentiated mass. Great function then arises in abundance, and whenever it does, there is surely Perfect Reality. All phenomena are in great profusion, and are interfused but not mixed (losing their own identity). The all is the one, for both are similar in being nonexistent in nature. And the one is the all, for [the relation between] cause and effect is perfectly clear. As the power [of the one] and the function [of the many] embraces each other, their expansion and contraction are free and at ease. This is called the Rounded (inclusive) Doctrine of the One [all-inclusive] Vehicle.

7. MASTERING THE TEN MYSTERIES (GATES)

(1) The gold and the lion exist simultaneously, all-perfect and complete in their possession. This is called the gate of simultaneous completion and mutual correspondence.

(2) If the eye of the lion completely takes in the lion, then the all (the whole lion) is purely the eye (the one). If the ear completely takes in the lion, then the all is purely the ear. If all the sense organs simultaneously take in [the lion] and all are complete in their possession, then each of them is at the same time mixed (involving others) and pure (being itself), thus constituting the perfect storehouse. This is called the gate of full possession of the attributes of purity and mixture by the various storehouses.

(3) The gold and the lion are mutually compatible in their formation, the one and the many not obstructing each other. In this situation the principle (the one or the gold) and facts (the many or the lion) are each different, but whether the one or the many, each remains in its own position. This is called the gate of mutual compatibility and difference between the one and the many.

(4) Since the various organs and each and every hair of the lion com-

pletely take in the lion by means of the gold, each and every one of them penetrates the whole. The eye of the lion is its ear, its ear is its nose, its nose is its tongue, and its tongue is its body. They each exist freely and easily, one not hindering or obstructing the other. This is called the gate of mutual identification of all dharmas existing freely and easily.

(5) If we look at the lion [as lion], there is only the lion and no gold. This means that the lion is manifest while the gold is hidden. If we look at the gold, there is only the gold and no lion. This means that the gold is manifest while the lion is hidden. If we look at them both, then both are manifest and both hidden. Being hidden, they are secret, and being manifest, they are evident. This is called the gate of the completion of the secret, the hidden, and the manifest.

(6) The gold and the lion may be hidden or manifest, one or many, definitely pure or definitely mixed, powerful or powerless, the one or the other. The principal and the companion mutually shine. Principle and fact appear together and are completely compatible with each other. They do not obstruct each other's peaceful existence, and thus the subtle and the minute are accomplished. This is called the gate of the compatibility and peaceful existence of the subtle and the minute.

(7) In each of the lion's eyes, ears, limbs, joints, and in each and every hair, there is the golden lion. All the lions embraced by all the single hairs simultaneously and instantaneously enter a single hair. Thus in each and every hair there are an infinite number of lions, and in addition all the single hairs, together with their infinite number of lions, in turn enter into a single hair. In this way the geometric progression is infinite, like the jewels of Celestial Lord Indra's net. This is called the gate of the realm of Indra's net.

(8) The lion is spoken of in order to show the meaning of ignorance while its golden substance is spoken of in order to make sufficiently clear the true nature. And principle and fact are discussed together as a description of the storehouse consciousness so that correct understanding may be created. This is called the gate of relying on facts in order to explain dharmas and create understanding.

(9) The lion is a dharma produced from causes, coming into existence and going out of existence at every moment. Each of these instants is divided into three periods, that is, past, present, and future, and each of these periods contains past, present, and future. Altogether there are three times three units, thus forming nine ages, and these, grouped together, become the total gate [to truth]. Although there are nine ages, each separate from the other, yet, since they are formed because of one another, they are harmoniously merged and mutually penetrated without obstacle and together constitute one instant of time. This is called the gate of different formation of separate dharmas in ten ages (the nine ages separately and all of them together).

(10) The gold and the lion may be hidden or manifest, and may be one or many. Neither has self-nature. They are [always] turning and trans-

forming in accordance with the mind. Whether spoken of as fact or principle, there is the way (the mind) by which they are formed and exist. This is called the gate of the excellent completion through the turning and transformation of the mind only.

8. PUTTING TOGETHER THE SIX CHARACTERS

The lion represents the character of universality. The five sense organs, being various and different, represent the character of specialty. The fact that they all arise from one single cause represents the character of similarity. The fact that its eyes, ears, and so forth do not exceed their bounds represents the character of difference. Since the combination of the various organs becomes the lion, this is the character of integration. And as each of the several organs remains in its own position, this is the character of disintegration.

9. ACHIEVING PERFECT WISDOM (BODHI)

"Bodhi" means in Chinese the Way or enlightenment. It means that when we look at the lion, we see right away that all dharmas produced through causes, even before disintegration, are from the very beginning quiescent and extinct. By being free from attachment or renunciation one will flow right along this way into the sea of perfect knowledge. Therefore it is called the Way. One understands right away that from time immemorial all afflictions resulting from passions originally have no reality. This is called enlightenment. The ultimate possession of the wisdom that knows all is called the achievement of perfect wisdom.

10. ENTERING NIRVĀNA

When we look at the lion and the gold, the two characters both perish and afflictions resulting from passions will no longer be produced. Although beauty and ugliness are displayed before the eye, the mind is as calm as the sea. Erroneous thoughts all cease, and there are no compulsions. One gets out of bondage and is free from hindrances, and forever cuts off the source of suffering. This is called entry into Nirvāna.

ON BELIEVING IN MIND
Seng T'san

"Zen" is the Japanese and "Ch'an" the Chinese version of
the Sanskrit term "Dhyana," which is usually rendered into English as "Meditation." While Zen has traditionally stressed meditation, so have many other Buddhist schools; what has made Zen
unique has been its success in opening in men a new apprehension
that is hard to describe, but has been called the intuitive perception of the infinite in the finite. The Zen realization or Satori involves a disappearance of the sense of duality, of separation between the self and the not-self, in everyday life and in relationship
to nature. Mystical experience often leads to a transcendence of
the sense of separate selfhood, but seldom with such an easy and
deep harmony with the natural and human world. In Zen the
mysticism of India and the love and respect for nature of Taoism
have combined to produce a mysticism more this-worldly than that
characteristic of any other religious school.

Seng T'san is an early figure in the history of Chinese Zen,
traditionally described as the Third Patriarch of the school. He is
said to have died in A.D. 606. The word here translated as "mind,"
"hsin," also denotes heart and spirit. The title of this celebrated
poem has sometimes been translated as "On Trusting in the
Heart" rather than "On Believing in Mind."

1. The Perfect Way knows no difficulties
   Except that it refuses to make preferences;
   Only when freed from hate and love,
   It reveals itself fully and without disguise;
   A tenth of an inch's difference,
   And heaven and earth are set apart;
   If you wish to see it before your own eyes,
   Have no fixed thoughts either for or against it.

Seng T'san, "On Believing in Mind," D. T. Suzuki, trans. (Kyoto, Japan: The
Eastern Buddhist Society, 1935), pp. 91–97. Reprinted from *Manual of Zen Buddhism*,
by D. T. Suzuki, by permission of Christmas Humphreys.

2. To set up what you like against what you dislike—
This is the disease of the mind:
When the deep meaning [of the Way] is not understood
Peace of mind is disturbed to no purpose.

3. [The Way is] perfect like unto vast space,
With nothing wanting, nothing superfluous:
It is indeed due to making choice
That its suchness is lost sight of.

4. Pursue not the outer entanglements,
Dwell not in the inner void;
Be serene in the oneness of things,
And [dualism] vanishes by itself.

5. When you strive to gain quiescence by stopping motion,
The quiescence thus gained is ever in motion;
As long as you tarry in the dualism,
How can you realise oneness?

6. And when oneness is not thoroughly understood,
In two ways loss is sustained:
The denying of reality is the asserting of it,
And the asserting of emptiness is the denying of it.

7. Wordiness and intellection—
The more with them the further astray we go;
Away therefore with wordiness and intellection,
And there is no place where we cannot pass freely.

8. When we return to the root, we gain the meaning;
When we pursue external objects, we lose the reason.
The moment we are enlightened within,
We go beyond the voidness of a world confronting us.

9. Transformations going on in an empty world which confronts us
Appear real all because of Ignorance:
Try not to seek after the true,
Only cease to cherish opinions.

10. Abide not with dualism,
Carefully avoid pursuing it;
As soon as you have right and wrong,
Confusion ensues, and Mind is lost.

11. The two exist because of the One,
    But hold not even to this One;
    When a mind is not disturbed,
    The ten thousand things offer no offence.

12. No offence offered, and no ten thousand things;
    No disturbance going, and no mind set up to work:
    The subject is quieted when the object ceases,
    The object ceases when the subject is quieted.

13. The object is an object for the subject,
    The subject is a subject for the object:
    Know that the relativity of the two
    Rests ultimately on one Emptiness.

14. In one Emptiness the two are not distinguished,
    And each contains in itself all the ten thousand things;
    When no discrimination is made between this and that,
    How can a one-sided and prejudiced view arise?

15. The Great Way is calm and large-hearted,
    For it nothing is easy, nothing is hard;
    Small views are irresolute,
    The more in haste the tardier they go.

16. Clinging is never kept within bounds,
    It is sure to go the wrong way;
    Quit it, and things follow their own courses,
    While the Essence neither departs nor abides.

17. Obey the nature of things, and you are in concord with the Way,
    Calm and easy and free from annoyance;
    But when your thoughts are tied, you turn away from the truth,
    They grow heavier and duller and are not at all sound.

18. When they are not sound, the spirit is troubled;
    What is the use of being partial and one-sided then?
    If you want to walk the course of the One Vehicle,
    Be not prejudiced against the six sense-objects.

19. When you are not prejudiced against the six sense-objects,
    You are then one with the Enlightenment;
    The wise are non-active,

While the ignorant bind themselves up;
While in the Dharma itself there is no individuation,
They ignorantly attach themselves to particular objects.
It is their own mind that creates illusions—
Is this not the greatest of all self-contradictions?

20. The ignorant cherish the idea of rest and unrest,
The enlightened have no likes and dislikes:
All forms of dualism
Are contrived by the ignorant themselves.
They are like unto visions and flowers in the air:
Why should we trouble ourselves to take hold of them?
Gain and loss, right and wrong—
Away with them once for all!

21. If an eye never falls asleep,
All dreams will by themselves cease:
If the Mind retains its absoluteness,
The ten thousand things are of one Suchness.

22. When the deep mystery of one Suchness is fathomed,
All of a sudden we forget the external entanglements;
When the ten thousand things are viewed in their oneness,
We return to the origin and remain where we ever have been.

23. Forget the wherefore of things,
And we attain to a state beyond analogy;
Movement stopped and there is no movement,
Rest set in motion and there is no rest;
When dualism does no more obtain,
Oneness itself abides not.

24. The ultimate end of things where they cannot go any further,
Is not bound by rules and measures:
In the Mind harmonious [with the Way] we have the principle of
    identity,
In which we find all strivings quieted;
Doubts and irresolutions are completely done away with,
And the right faith is straightened;
There is nothing left behind,
There is nothing retained,
All is void, lucid, and self-illuminating,
There is no exertion, no waste of energy—

This is where thinking never attains,
This is where the imagination fails to measure.

25. In the higher realm of true Suchness
There is neither "self" nor "other":
When direct identification is sought,
We can only say, "Not two."

26. In being "not two" all is the same,
All that is comprehended in it;
The wise in the ten quarters,
They all enter into this Absolute Reason.

27. This Absolute Reason is beyond quickening [time] and extending [space],
For it one instant is ten thousand years;
Whether we see it or not,
It is manifest everywhere in all the ten quarters.

28. Infinitely small things are as large as large things can be,
For here no external conditions obtain;
Infinitely large things are as small as small things can be,
For objective limits are here of no consideration.

29. What is is the same as what is not,
What is not is the same as what is:
Where this state of things fails to obtain,
Indeed, no tarrying there.

30. One in All,
All in One—
If only this is realised,
No more worry about your not being perfect!

31. Where Mind and each believing mind are not divided,
And undivided are each believing mind and Mind,
This is where words fail;
For it is not of the past, present, and future.

TREATISE ON THE ESSENTIALS OF THE TRANSMISSION OF MIND
Huang Po

> Huang Po is a mountain in China upon which a Zen master
> called in his lifetime "Hsi Yün" and "T'uan Chi," lived for many
> years in the Ninth Century. Posthumously the master has been
> known by the name of the mountain (Obaku in Japanese). As
> the founder of the flourishing Rinzai sect of Zen was his disciple,
> Huang Po is sometimes considered the father of this school.
>   His sermon is a forceful statement of the Zen position that
> enlightenment consists in an intuitive realization of one's own
> deepest nature which is also the deepest nature of everything. The
> term "mushin," which Professor Suzuki has left in Japanese, liter-
> ally means "no-mind" or "no-thought." It denotes a state in which
> there is no hankering after a self, a state in which anatta has been
> realized and accepted.

HUANG-PO'S SERMON, FROM "TREATISE ON THE ESSENTIALS OF THE TRANSMISSION OF MIND"

The master said to Pai-hsiu:

Buddhas and sentient beings both grow out of One Mind, and there is
no other reality than this Mind. It has been in existence since the beginningless past; it knows neither birth nor death; it is neither blue nor yellow; it has
neither shape nor form; it is beyond the category of being and non-being; it is
not to be measured by age, old or new; it is neither long nor short; it is neither
large nor small; for it transcends all limits, words, traces, and opposites. It
must be taken just as it is in itself; when an attempt is made on our part to

Huang-po, "Treatise on the Essentials of Transmission of Mind," D. T. Suzuki,
trans. (Kyoto, Japan: The Eastern Buddhist Society, 1935), pp. 132–140. Reprinted from
Manual of Zen Buddhism by D. T. Suzuki, by permission of Christmas Humphreys.

grasp it in our thoughts, it eludes. It is like space whose boundaries are altogether beyond measurement, no concepts are applicable here.

This One Mind only is the Buddha, who is not to be segregated from
sentient beings. Only because we seek it outwardly in a world of form, the
more we seek the further it moves away from us. To make Buddha seek after
himself, or to make Mind take hold of itself—this is an impossibility to the end
of eternity. We do not realise that as soon as our thoughts cease and all attempts at forming ideas are forgotten the Buddha reveals himself before us.

This Mind is no other than the Buddha, and Buddha is no other than
sentient being. When Mind assumes the form of a sentient being, it has suffered no decrease; when it becomes a Buddha, it has not added anything to itself. Even when we speak of the six virtues of perfection (*pāramitās*) and
other ten thousand meritorious deeds equal in number to the sands of the
Ganges, they are all in the being of Mind itself; they are not something that
can be added to it by means of discipline. When conditions are at work, it is
set up; when conditions cease to operate, it remains quiet. Those who have
no definite faith in this that Mind is Buddha and attempt an achievement
by means of a discipline attached to form, are giving themselves up to wrong
imagination; they deviate from the right path.

This Mind is no other than Buddha; there is no Buddha outside Mind,
nor is there any Mind outside Buddha. This Mind is pure and like space has
no specific forms [whereby it can be distinguished from other objects]. As
soon as you raise a thought and begin to form an idea of it, you ruin the
reality itself, because you then attach yourself to form. Since the beginningless
past, there is no Buddha who has ever had an attachment to form. If you seek
Buddhahood by practising the six virtues of perfection and other ten thousand
deeds of merit, this is grading [the attainment of Buddhahood]; but since the
beginningless past there is no Buddha whose attainment was so graded. When
you get an insight into the One Mind you find that there is no particular
reality [which you can call Mind]. This unattainability is no other than the
true Buddha himself.

Buddhas and sentient beings grow out of the One Mind and there are
no differences between them. It is like space where there are no complexities,
nor is it subject to destruction. It is like the great sun which illumines the
four worlds: when it rises, its light pervades all over the world, but space
itself gains thereby no illumination. When the sun sets, darkness reigns everywhere, but space itself does not share this darkness. Light and darkness drive
each other out and alternately prevail, but space itself is vast emptiness and
suffers no vicissitudes. The same may be said of the Mind that constitutes the
essence of Buddha as well as that of sentient being. When you take Buddha
for a form of purity, light, and emancipation and sentient beings for a form
of defilement, darkness, and transmigration, you will never have the occasion
however long [your striving may go on] for attaining enlightenment; for so
long as you adhere to this way of understanding, you are attached to form.

And in this One Mind there is not a form of particularity to lay your hand on.

That Mind is no other than Buddha is not understood by Buddhists of the present day; and because of their inability of seeing into the Mind as it is, they imagine a mind beside Mind itself and seek Buddha outwardly after a form. This way of disciplining is an error, is not the way of enlightenment.

It is better to make offerings to a spiritual man who is free from mind-attachment than to make offerings to all the Buddhas in the ten quarters. Why? Because to be free from mind-attachment means to be free from all forms of imagination.

Suchness as it expresses itself inwardly may be likened to wood or rock, it remains there unmoved, unshaken; while outwardly it is like space, nothing is obstructed or checked. Suchness, as it is free both from activity and passivity, knows no orientation, it has no form, there is in it neither gain nor loss. Those who are running [wildly] do not dare enter this path, for they are afraid of falling into an emptiness where there is no foothold to keep them supported. They beat a retreat as they face it. They are as a rule seekers of learning and intellectual understanding. Many are indeed such seekers, like hair, while those who see into the truth are as few as horns.

Mañjuśrī corresponds to li (reason or principle) and Samantabhadra to hsing (life or action). Li is the principle of true emptiness and non-obstruction, hsing is a life of detachment from form, and inexhaustible. Avalokitésvara corresponds to perfect love and Sthāmaprāpta to perfect wisdom. Vimalakīrti means "undefiled name;" undefiled is Essence and name is form. Essence and form are not two different things, hence the name Vimala-kīrti ("pure name"). All that is represented by each one of the great Bodhisattvas is present in each of us, for it is the contents of One Mind. All will be well when we are awakened to the truth.

Buddhists of the present day look outward, instead of inwardly into their own minds. They get themselves attached to forms and to the world—which is the violation of the truth.

To the sands of the Ganges the Buddha refers in this way: these sands are trodden and passed over by all the Buddhas, Bodhisattvas, Sakrendra, and other devas, but the sands are not thereby gladdened; they are again trodden by cattle, sheep, insects, and ants, but they are not thereby incensed; they may hide within themselves all kinds of treasures and scented substances, but they are not covetous; they may be soiled with all kinds of filth and ill-smelling material, but they do not loathe them. A mental attitude of this nature is that of one who has realised the state of mushin ("being free from mind-attachment"). When a mind is free from all form, it sees into [the fact] that there is no distinction between Buddhas and sentient beings; when once this state of mushin is attained it completes the Buddhist life. If Buddhists are unable to see into the truth of mushin without anything mediating, all their discipline of eons would not enable them to attain enlightenment. They would ever be in bondage with the notion of discipline and merit as cherished by followers of the Triple Vehicle, they would never achieve emancipation.

In the attainment of this state of mind (*mushin*), some are quicker than others. There are some who attain to a state of *mushin* all at once by just listening to a discourse on the Dharma, while there are others who attain to it only after going through all the grades of Bodhisattvaship such as the ten stages of faith, the ten stages of abiding, the ten stages of discipline, and the ten stages of turning-over. More or less time may be required in the attainment of *mushin*, but once attained it puts an end to all discipline, to all realisation; and yet there is really nothing attained. It is truth and not falsehood. Whether this *mushin* is attained in one thought or attained after going through the ten stages its practical working is the same and there is no question of the one being deeper or shallower than the other. Only the one has passed through long ages of hard discipline.

Committing evils or practising goodness—both are the outcome of attachment to form. When evils are committed on account of attachment to form, one has to suffer transmigration; when goodness is practised on account of attachment to form, one has to go through a life of hardships. It is better therefore to see all at once into the essence of the Dharma as you listen to it discoursed.

By the Dharma is meant Mind, for there is no Dharma apart from Mind. Mind is no other than the Dharma, for there is no Mind apart from the Dharma. This Mind in itself is no-mind (*mushin*), and there is no no-mind either. When no-mind is sought after by a mind, this is making it a particular object of thought. There is only testimony of silence, it goes beyond thinking. Therefore it is said that [the Dharma] cuts off the passage to words and puts an end to all form of mentation.

This Mind is the Source, the Buddha absolutely pure in its nature, and is present in every one of us. All sentient beings however mean and degraded are not in this particular respect different from Buddhas and Bodhisattvas—they are all of one substance. Only because of their imaginations and false discriminations, sentient beings work out their karma and reap its result, while, in their Buddha-essence itself, there is nothing corresponding to it; the Essence is empty and allows everything to pass through, it is quiet and at rest, it is illuminating, it is peaceful and productive of bliss. When you have within yourself a deep insight into this you immediately realise that all that you need is there in perfection, and in abundance, and nothing is at all wanting in you. You may have most earnestly and diligently disciplined yourself for the past three asamkhyeya kalpas and passed through all the stages of Bodhisattvahood; but when you come to have a realisation in one thought, it is no other than this that you are from the first the Buddha himself and no other. The realisation has not added anything to you over this truth. When you look back and survey all the disciplinary measures you have gone through, you only find that they have been no more than so many idle doings in a dream. Therefore, it is told by the Tathagata that he had nothing attained when he had enlightenment, and that if he had really something attained, Buddha Dīpankara would never have testified to it.

It is told again by the Tathagata that this Dharma is perfectly even and free from irregularities. By Dharma is meant Bodhi. That is, this pure Mind forming the source of all things is perfectly even in all sentient beings, in all the Buddha-lands, and also in all the other worlds together with mountains, oceans, etc., things with form and things without form. They are all even, and there are no marks of distinction between this object and that. This pure Mind, the Source of all things, is always perfect and illuminating and all-pervading. People are ignorant of this and take what they see or hear or think of or know for Mind itself; and their insight is then veiled and unable to penetrate into the substance itself which is clear and illuminating. When you realise *mushin* without anything intervening [that is, intuitively], the substance itself is revealed to you. It is like the sun revealing itself in the sky, its illumination penetrates the ten quarters and there is nothing that will interfere with its passage.

For this reason, when followers of Zen fail to go beyond a world of their senses and thoughts, all their doings and movements are of no significance. But when the senses and thoughts are annihilated, all the passages to the Mind are blocked and no entrance then becomes possible. The original Mind is to be recognised along with the working of the senses and thoughts, only it does not belong to them, nor is it independent of them. Do not build up your views on your senses and thoughts, do not carry on your understanding based on the senses and thoughts; but at the same time do not seek the Mind away from your senses and thoughts, do not grasp the Dharma by rejecting your senses and thoughts. When you are neither attached to nor detached from them, when you are neither abiding with nor clinging to them, then you enjoy your perfect unobstructed freedom, then you have your seat of enlightenment.

When people learn that what is transmitted from one Buddha to another is Mind itself, they imagine that there is a particular object known as a mind which they attempt to grasp or to realise; but this is seeking something outside Mind itself, or creating something which does not exist. In reality, Mind alone is. You cannot pursue it by setting up another mind; however long, through hundreds of thousands of kalpas, you are after it, no time will ever come to you when you can say that you have it. Only when you have an immediate awakening to the state of *mushin* you have your own Mind. It is like the strong man's seeking for his own gem hidden within his forehead: as long as he seeks it outside himself in the ten quarters, he will not come across it; but let the wise once point at it where it lies hidden, and the man instantly perceives his own gem as having been there from the very first.

That followers of Zen fail to recognise the Buddha is due to their not rightly recognising where their own Mind is. They seek it outwardly, set up all kinds of exercises which they hope to master by degrees, and work themselves out most diligently through ages. Yet they fail to reach enlightenment. No works compare with an immediate awakening to a state of *mushin* itself.

When you come to a most decided understanding to the effect that all things in their nature are without possessions, without attainments, without dependence, without an abiding place, without mutual conditioning, you will become free from cherishing imagination, which is to realise Bodhi. When Bodhi is realised your own Mind which is Buddha is realised. All the doings of long ages are then found to have been anything but real disciplining. When the strong man recovered his own gem on his own forehead, the recovery had nothing to do with all his efforts wasted in his outside research. So says the Buddha, "I have not had anything attained in my attainment of Enlightenment." Being anxious of our not believing this, he refers to the five eyes and the five statements. But it is truth, not falsehood, for it is the first true statement.

18

PRACTICE OF DHYANA
Soyen Shaku

Soyen Shaku was a disciple of the great Nineteenth Century Zen master and reformer Kosen, who had worked to foster Zen among laymen, secular education among Zen monks, and cherished the hope that knowledge of Zen would be transmitted to the western world. Soyen Shaku himself became a famous Zen teacher, the Abbot of Engaku-ji and Kencho-ji in Kamakura. In 1893 he became the first Zen priest to visit the West when he attended the World Parliament of Religions in Chicago, bringing with him as his translator a young lay disciple, D. T. Suzuki. Soyen Shaku returned again to America in 1905–1906 and during his stay delivered a number of lectures which Suzuki, who had remained in the United States, revised, translated, and published. With the permission of Soyen Shaku, Suzuki replaced some of the Buddhist expressions that were little understood in America in

Soyen Shaku, "Practice of Dhyana," D. T. Suzuki, trans. (LaSalle, Illinois: Open Court Publishing Company, 1906), pp. 146–159. Reprinted from *Sermons of a Buddhist Abbot* by Soyen Shaku.

*1906 with terms more conventional in the West. Consequently
the terminology is not always that native to Soyen Shaku, although otherwise the lecture is a faithful presentation of his views
as well as his style of preaching.*

Three things are usually considered necessary for the realization of the
Buddhist life: 1, *Sîla* (moral precepts), 2, *Dhyâna* (contemplation), 3,
Prajñâ (wisdom); and these are coöperative and mutually related.

To be a good Buddhist, first of all, a man must be ethical and regulate
his life according to the moral precepts, which were laid down by Buddha
and are universally applicable. Next, he must be philosophical, that is, he
must train his mind so as to be capable of practising introspection. The mechanical observance of the moral laws is not becoming to the dignity of a
rational, conscious being. Man must be master of himself, intellectually, morally, and spiritually. To be so, he must be able to examine his own states of
consciousness and direct his thoughts and desires to the end where lies the
rationale of existence. This habit of self-examination is attainable only
through the practice of dhyâna, contemplation. Lastly, he must be religious,
by which is meant that he should have an insight going deep into the indwelling reason of things, and this insight, according to Buddhism, is the
outcome of the mental training acquired by self-introspection. Prajñâ, which
is the most fundamental of all the psychic faculties possessed by man, lies
inactive and altogether unrecognized when the mind is busily engaged in receiving impressions and elaborating on them through the ordinary process
of understanding. It has no time to withdraw within itself and watch how
impulses are awakened, stimuli felt, thoughts matured, in short, how the
inner working goes on. It never knows what a precious stone it harbors within
its being, which, when discovered, will illuminate the inmost significance of
life and put an end to all vanities and vexations of spirit. The practice of
dhyâna, however, brings this latent faculty of consciousness to the surface
and makes a new man out of old, worn-out, and apparently unpromising stuff.

Therefore, the three requisites of the Buddhist life are helping one another like a tripod to stand together and to accomplish their common purpose.
The moral precepts cannot be intelligently and thoroughly followed unless a
man has gained a complete control of himself through contemplation and
self-introspection. But this dhyâna-practice will not be of much value, religiously considered, to his daily life unless it leads to the awakening of Prajñâ
(wisdom) and to the comprehension of the ultimate facts of life. Whatever
difference there may be in the different schools of Buddhism, those three
forms of discipline, as they are often called, are admitted by them all as most
essential for the realization of their ideal life. The importance of the moral
codes as formulated by Buddha will not be questioned even by followers of
non-Buddhist faiths, and as to the signification of spiritual insight, which
constitutes the essence of religious life, I have somewhere touched upon the

subject. In this short discourse I wish to say a few words concerning the practice of dhyâna.

Dhyâna is essentially Hindu or, rather broadly speaking, Oriental in its origin as well as in its significance. In this we can trace one of the many characteristics which lend a peculiarly charming color to Oriental culture. The Oriental mind ever strives after the One and is so idealistic in all its tendencies as sometimes altogether to ignore the external world. It shuts out all the impressions the senses may bring in from without, thus endeavoring to realize the aspiration after unity and eternality. It does not care so much for the subjugation of natural forces to its own will as for the deliverance of self from its illusory imprisonment. It does not antagonize the world in which it lives, but calmly contemplates it, reviewing its vagaries or vicissitudes, or whatever they may be termed. It dwelleth not in the manyness of things, but in their oneness, for its ultimate abode is in the region of the absolute and not in the phenomenal realm. A mind like this naturally takes more to contemplation than to the strenuous life; it thinks more and acts less; it appreciates instead of criticizing; it synthesizes instead of analyzing. The practice of dhyâna, therefore, was the most natural thing for the Oriental people.

The Western people were not altogether unfamiliar with dhyâna, as we can judge from the life of a mystic or a medieval Christian monk. But their so-called contemplation or meditation was not as systematic and did not necessarily form a part of their religious discipline. The Hebrews were too fanatically religious to allow themselves the time to reflect. The Greeks were rather scientific and intellectual, while the Romans were pre-eminently practical. The German mystics perhaps were more or less after the Hindu type in their general mental constitution, but they seem not to have made the practice of dhyâna a prominent feature of their doctrine. Be that as it may, there is no doubt that dhyâna is an Oriental production.

What is dhyâna, then? Dhyâna literally means, in Sanskrit, pacification, equilibration, or tranquillization, but as religious discipline it is rather self-examination or introspection. It is not necessarily to cogitate on the deep subjects of metaphysics, nor is it to contemplate on the virtues of a deity, or on the transitoriness of mundane life. To define its import in Buddhism, roughly and practically, it is the habit of withdrawing occasionally from the turbulence of worldliness and of devoting some time to a quiet inspection of one's own consciousness. When this habit is thoroughly established, a man can keep serenity of mind and cheerfulness of disposition even in the midst of his whirlwind-like course of daily life. Dhyâna is then a discipline in tranquillization. It aims at giving to a mind the time for deliberation and saving it from running wild; it directs the vain and vulgar to the path of earnestness and reality; it makes us feel interest in higher things which are above the senses; it discovers the presence in us of a spiritual faculty which bridges the chasm between the finite and the infinite; and it finally delivers us from the bondage and torture of ignorance, safely leading us to the other shore of Nirvâna.

Dhyâna is sometimes made a synonym for çamatha and samâdhi and samâpatti. Çamatha is tranquillity and practically the same as dhyâna, though the latter is much more frequently in use than the former. Samâpatti literally is "put together evenly" or "balanced," and means the equilibrium of consciousness in which takes place neither wakefulness nor apathy, but in which the mind is calmly concentrated on the thought under consideration. Samâdhi is a perfect absorption, voluntary or involuntary, of thought into the object of contemplation. A mind is sometimes said to be in a state of samâdhi when it identifies itself with the ultimate reason of existence and is only conscious of the unification. In this case, dhyâna is the method or process that brings us finally to samâdhi.

Now, the benefits arising from the exercise of dhyâna are more than one, and are not only practical but moral and spiritual. Nobody will deny the most practical advantage gained through presence of mind, moderation of temper, control of feelings, and mastery of oneself. A passion may be so violent at the time of its agitation that it will fairly consume itself to utter destruction, but a cool-headed man knows well how to give it the necessary psychological time of rest and deliberation and thus to save himself from plunging headlong into the Charybdis of emotion. And this cool-headedness, though in some measure due to heredity, is attainable through the exercise of dhyâna.

Intellectually, dhyâna will keep the head clear and transparent and, whenever necessary, make it concentrate itself on the subject at issue. Logical accuracy depends greatly on the dispassionateness of the arguing mind, and scientific investigation gains much from the steadiness of the observing eye. Whatever be a man's intellectual development, he has surely nothing to lose, but a great deal to gain, by training himself in the habit of tranquillization.

In these days of industrial and commercial civilization, the multitudes of people have very little time to devote themselves to spiritual culture. They are not altogether ignorant of the existence of things which are of permanent value, but their minds are so engrossed in details of everyday life that they find it extremely difficult to avoid their constant obtrusion. Even when they retire from their routine work at night, they are bent on something exciting which will tax their already over-stretched nervous system to the utmost. If they do not die prematurely, they become nervous wrecks. They seem not to know the blessings of relaxation. They seem to be unable to live within themselves and find there the source of eternal cheerfulness. Life is for them more or less a heavy burden and their task consists in the carrying of the burden. The gospel of dhyâna, therefore, must prove to them a heaven-sent boon when they conscientiously practise it.

Dhyâna is physiologically the accumulation of nervous energy; it is a sort of spiritual storage battery in which an enormous amount of latent force is sealed,—a force which will, whenever demand is made, manifest itself with tremendous potency. A mind trained in dhyâna will never waste its energy, causing its untimely exhaustion. It may appear at times, when superficially observed, dull, uninteresting, and dreamy, but it will work wonders when the occasion arises; while a mind ordinarily addicted to dissipation succumbs to the intensity of an impulse or a stimulus without much struggling, which ends in complete collapse, for it has no energy in reserve. Here, let me remark incidentally, can be seen one of the many characteristic differences between Orientalism and Occidentalism. In all departments of Oriental culture a strong emphasis is placed upon the necessity of preserving the latent nervous energy and of keeping the source of spiritual strength well fed and nourished. Young minds are trained to store up within and not to make any wasteful display of their prowess and knowledge and virtue. It is only shallow waters, they would say, that make a noisy, restless stream, while a deep whirlpool goes on silently. The Occidentals, as far as I can judge, seem to be fond of making a full display of their possessions with the frankness of a child; and they are prone to a strenuous and dissipating life which will soon drain all the nervous force at their command. They seem not to keep anything in reserve which they can make use of later on at their leisure. They are indeed candid and open-hearted—traits which sometimes seem wanting in the Orientals. But they certainly lack the unfathomableness of the latter, who never seem to be enthusiastic, clamorous, or irrepressible. The teaching of Lao-tze or that of the *Bhagavadgîta* was not surely intended for the Western nations. Of course, there are exceptions in the West as well as in the East. Generally speaking, however, the West is energetic, and the East mystical; for the latter's ideal is to be incomprehensible, immeasurable, and undemonstrative even as an absolute being itself. And the practice of dhyâna may be considered in a way one of the methods of realizing this ideal.

In the *Chandradîpa-samâdhi Sûtra,* the benefits of dhyâna-practice are enumerated as follows: (1) When a man practises dhyâna according to the regulation, all his senses become calm and serene, and, without knowing it on his part, he begins to enjoy the habit. (2) Lovingkindness will take possession of his heart, which, then freeing itself from sinfulness, looks upon all sentient beings as his brothers and sisters. (3) Such poisonous and harassing passions as anger, infatuation, avarice, etc., gradually retire from the field of consciousness. (4) Having a close watch over all the senses, dhyâna guards them against the intrusion of evils. (5) Being pure in heart and serene in disposition, the practiser of dhyâna feels no inordinate appetite in lower passions. (6) The mind being concentrated on higher thoughts, all sorts of temptation and attachment and egotism are kept away. (7) Though he well knows the emptiness of vanity, he does not fall into the snare of nihilism. (8) However entangling the nets of birth and death, he is well aware of the way to deliverance therefrom. (9) Having fathomed the deepest depths of the Dharma, he abides in the wisdom of Buddha. (10) As he is not disturbed by any temptation, he feels like an eagle that, having escaped from imprisonment, freely wings his flight through the air.

The practice of dhyâna is often confounded with a trance of self-hypnotism,—a grave error which I here propose to refute. The difference between the two is patent to every clear-sighted mind, for a trance is a pathological disturbance of consciousness, while dhyâna is a perfectly normal state of it. Trance is a kind of self-illusion which is entirely subjective and cannot be objectively verified, but dhyâna is a state of consciousness in which all mental powers are kept in equilibrium so that no one thought or faculty is made predominant over others. It is like the pacification of turbulent waters by pouring oil over them: no waves are roaring, no foams are boiling, no splashes are spattering, but a smooth, glossy mirror of immense dimension. And it is in this perfect mirror of consciousness that myriads of reflections, as it were, come and go without ever disturbing its serenity. In trances certain mental and physiological functions are unduly accelerated, while others are kept altogether in abeyance, the whole system of consciousness thus being thrown into disorder; and its outcome is the loss of equilibrium in the organism—which is very opposite to what is attained through the practice of dhyâna.

Again, some superficial critics think that Buddhist dhyâna is a sort of intense meditation on some highly abstracted thoughts, and that the concentration which works in the same way as self-hypnotism leads the mind to the state of a trance, called Nirvâna. This is a very grievous error committed by those who have never comprehended the essence of religious consciousness, for Buddhist dhyâna has nothing to do with abstraction or hynotization. What it proposes to accomplish is to make our consciousness realize the inner reason of the universe which abides in our minds. Dhyâna strives to make us acquainted with the most concrete and withal the most universal fact of life. It is the philosopher's business to deal with dry, lifeless, uninteresting generalizations. Buddhists are not concerned with things like that. They want to see the fact directly and not through the medium of philosophical abstractions. There may be a god who created heaven and earth, or there may not; we could be saved by simply believing in his goodness, or we could not; the destination of evil-doers may be hell and that of good men paradise, or this may be reversed: true Buddhists do not trouble themselves with such propositions as these. Let them well alone; Buddhists are not so idle and superficial as to waste their time in pondering over the questions which have no vital concern with our religious life. Buddhists through dhyâna endeavor to reach the bottom of things and there to grasp with their own hands the very life of the universe, which makes the sun rise in the morning, makes the bird cheerfully sing in the balmy spring breeze, and also makes the biped called man hunger for love, righteousness, liberty, truth, and goodness. In dhyâna, therefore, there is nothing abstract, nothing dry as a bone and cold as a corpse, but all animation, all activity, and eternal revelation.

Some Hindu philosophers, however, seem to have considered hallucinations and self-suggested states of mind as real and the attainment of them as the aim of dhyâna practice. Their conception of the eightfold dhyâna-heaven in which all sorts of angels are living is evidence of it. When the mythical beings in those regions practise dhyâna, they enter into different stages of samâdhi. They first come to think that they are lifted up in the air like a cloud; (2) they feel the presence of some indescribable luminosity; (3) they experience a supernatural joy; (4) their minds become so clarified and transparent as to reflect all the worlds like a very brilliant mirror; (5) they feel as if the soul has escaped bodily confinement and expanded itself to the immensity of space; (6) they now come back to a definite state of consciousness in which all mental functions are presented and the past and present and future reveal themselves; (7) they then have the feeling of absolute nothingness, in which not a ripple of mentation stirs; (8) lastly, they are not conscious of anything particular, nor have they lost consciousness, and here they are said to have reached the highest stage of samâdhi.

But according to Buddhism all these visionary phenomena as the outcome of dhyâna are rejected, for they have nothing to do with the realization of the religious life. In the *Sûrangâma Sûtra* fifty abnormal conditions of consciousness are mentioned against which the practiser of dhyâna has to guard himself, and among them we find those psychical aberrations mentioned above.

To conclude. Dhyâna, beside its being an indispensable religious discipline for attaining enlightenment, is one of the most efficient means of training oneself morally and physically. It is beyond question that dhyâna leads to the awakening of a hidden spiritual faculty possessed by all conscious beings and to the realization of one's spiritual significance in spite of the various material limitations. But, apart from this religious importance, dhyâna is singularly effective in the tranquillization of the mind, the purification of the heart, as well as in the relaxation of the nervous tension. A man will never realize, until he is thoroughly trained in dhyâna, how confused and entangled his thoughts are, how susceptible he is and how easily his mind is unbalanced, how soon his nervous force in reserve is exhausted and his entire system is given up to an utter breakdown, how fully his senses are occupied in seeking excitement and gratification, and finally how neglectful he has been in the promotion of higher and nobler interests of life and in the cultivation of refined thoughts and purer feelings. Dhyâna, therefore, whatever its religious merits, is not devoid of its practical utilities and even for this reason alone its exercise is universally to be recommended.

CHINESE RELIGION

PART III

Religion in China differs from religion in the West in many ways, but three characteristic features deserve special notice. The first is that the dominant faith of the educated class, Confucianism, has been so humanistic in emphasis that many Chinese scholars deny that it is a religion at all. The second is the common Chinese practice of "multiple belonging." Many Chinese freely and unselfconsciously follow several faiths. For example, Confucian traditions may be maintained in the home, Buddhist rites employed at the time of death, while a basically Taoist ideology is espoused. The third feature, arising from the same tolerance and eclecticism manifested in the second, is the large degree of interpenetration that has occurred in the Chinese faiths. This is most clearly seen in Neo-Confucianism which contains such an admixture of Taoist and Buddhist elements that it could be called "Neo-Taoist-Buddhist-Confucianism."

The phenomena of multiple belonging and ideological interpenetration complicate the task of the student of Chinese religion; but the claim that Confucianism is not a religion, a claim defended and also extended to Philosophical Taoism and Philosophical Buddhism by Professor Fung Yu-lan in the final selection in this section, presents a more fundamental challenge. The distinction between religion and philosophy that applies fairly well in Europe, where it was invented, does not apply as well in China. Philosophy as a cognitive discipline unconcerned with the fostering of morality, social harmony, and spirituality is little known in China. The name "philosophy" has there been principally applied to the more rationally coherent and subtle forms of moral and spiritual teachings, while "religion" has been reserved for foreign importations and the crude supernaturalisms popular among the uneducated. If a cultured Chinese were asked to identify the major spiritual mentors of his civilization, however, he would surely mention men such as Confucius, Mencius, Lao Tzu, Chuang Tzu, Huang Po, Chu Hsi, and Wang Yang-ming,*

* In China it is customary for the family name to precede the personal name. "Tzu" is a title meaning "master," which has been bestowed upon most of the ancient teachers. Famous Chinese usually have one or more honorific names; but the private name is used for each author represented here except Wang Yang-ming, whose private name is less commonly used.

figures comparable to Isaiah, Jeremiah, Jesus, St. Paul, St. Augustine, John Calvin, and George Fox, and he would as surely urge the western inquirer into the spiritual life of China to read their works in preference to the legends, magical formulae, and ritual texts that pass as "religious literature" in China. The dispute about the classification of Confucianism is primarily due to different connotations of the word "religion" in China and the West. Certainly the teachings of Confucius and his disciples belong in a book of this nature.

The history of Chinese religious thought can be roughly but conveniently divided into five major epochs: the Auguristic-Sacrificial, the Germinal, the Han Orthodoxy, the Buddhist Interlude, and the Neo-Confucian.

The earliest known phase of Chinese religion, which Arthur Waley has called the "Auguristic-Sacrificial," is similar to the pre-moral phase in western religious history. Archaeological excavations show that it was flourishing in North China by the Sixteenth Century B.C., and it continued as the dominant religious attitude for the next 1000 years. By means of augury and sacrifice men sought to communicate with the ancestors in Heaven. The ancestors were believed to have knowledge of the future, and by study of omens such as involuntary bodily sensations, the paths of birds, insects, and the stars, the patterns formed by cracking oracle bones and shells, falling sticks, and handheld divining instruments, men attempted to dispel some of their ignorance. As astrology has retained some influence in contemporary western society, divining is still popular with many Chinese.

The central feature of the ancient religious rituals, intended to insure the prosperity and health of the family and state, was the offering of burnt sacrifices of animals, grain, and liquor to the male ancestors upon special days. The remarkable family solidarity which has characterized Chinese culture was undoubtedly strengthened by this custom. Sacrifices were also offered to spirits of the soil, conceived in a manner similar to the baalim mentioned in the Old Testament. The ruler was the chief priest, and after the unification of China into a single empire, the most important official duty of the emperor, "the Son of Heaven," was to offer sacrifices. The magnificent white marble Altar of Heaven outside Peking was the final site of these rites. Although Confucianism was reticent in speaking of the supernatural, it was also conservative in defending the traditional rituals which continued until the overthrow of the empire in 1911. The title of the chief object of worship—"Heaven"—was richly ambiguous, sometimes referring to the sky, sometimes to fate, sometimes to nature, sometimes to the moral law, sometimes to the spirits collectively, and sometimes to the ruling spirit. Consequently archaic rituals could easily be interpreted in ways consonant with opposing metaphysical views.

Before Confucius (551–479 B.C.) Chinese religious thought was a collective product; no record exists of anyone publishing personal religious or philosophical views prior to the Fifth Century B.C. From Confucius to Han Fei Tzu, who died in 233 B.C., a series of able thinkers, deeply concerned with the social disorder of "the period of Warring States," produced the germinal works of Chinese intellectual history. The most influential religious thinkers of this period fall into three classes. Confucius, his two ablest ancient interpreters, Mencius and Hsün Tzu, and the unknown authors of the *Great Learning* and the *Doctrine of the Mean* provided the foundation of the orthodox Chinese tradition. The second class consists of the authors of the *Lao Tzu* and the *Chuang Tzu*, the basic Taoist scriptures. Taoism, the most successful native rival of Confucianism, taught a gospel in many respects antithetical to Confucianism but thereby provided a complement to the orthodox view that would ultimately serve to broaden and deepen orthodoxy. The third class consists of the single figure Mo Tzu, who founded and provided the ideology of the religious movement that was the chief rival to Confucianism from the Fifth to the Third Centuries B.C. Although Mohism disappeared as a religious movement during the Han dynasty (206 B.C.–A.D. 220), Mo Tzu's rational mode of argument, his doctrine of universal love, his hatred of aggression, his egalitarianism, his moral theism, and his utilitarianism have evoked a renewed interest in his work in the present century.

In 221 B.C. China was united into a single empire by the ruthless and able king of Ch'in, who adopted the title "First Emperor," built the Great Wall, ordered all non-utilitarian books burned, and executed or banished recalcitrant intellectuals. Surviving only fifteen years, the Ch'in dynasty began the pattern of imperial rule that has usually governed China since. Under its successor, the Han dynasty (206 B.C.–A.D. 220), China became a rich and relatively peaceful empire but the intellectual creativity of the pre-Ch'in period was replaced by an official scholarship that respected equally all the ancient classics. Venerating Confucius as their ideal prototype, these scholars attributed to him all the ideas they had themselves adopted. In this way an orthodox Confucianism developed containing many Taoist and Legalist doctrines, much numerology, divinatory lore, and naturalistic speculation, a ritual in honor of Confucius, and an enormous emphasis upon filial piety. The *Classic of Filial Piety,* which became very popular in the Han, illustrates the prudential, traditionalist, family-centered system of loyalties that had become second-nature to the Confucian.

Although knowledge of Buddhism was present before the Han dynasty and Buddhist missionaries were at work by the First Century A.D., it was only after the collapse of the Han from internal decay and barbarian invasions that the Indian faith spread widely in China. Mahayana Buddhism offered sophisticated cosmological, ontological, and anthropological doctrines, a lofty moral attitude, promises of posthumous happiness secured by faith or enlightenment gained by meditation, a developed religious art, a pantheon of gracious supernatural beings, elaborate ceremonies, a remarkable body of scriptures, and a tradition of monastic training. Spreading downward from the aristocrats to the peasants, Buddhism had converted most of China by the end of the Fifth Century. However, as China became Buddhist, the Buddhism it practiced became increasingly Chinese. New sects arose in which Chinese conceptions and attitudes modified those imported from India. The most radical of these new sects, usually known by its Japanese name—Zen, is typically Buddhist in its emphasis on meditation and monasticism but typically Taoist in its love of nature, paradox, poetry, painting, gardening, manual labor, and self-reliance. Several Chinese Buddhist works are included in the Buddhism section of this book. By the Ninth Century, partly because of imperial persecution but mostly because of a decline in intellectual and spiritual vitality, Buddhism had begun to wane. Increasingly the allegiance of the educated shifted to the rising Neo-Confucianism, and Chinese Buddhism began its long decline into a largely lower-class and superstition-ridden minority cult.

During the T'ang (A.D. 618–907) and Sung (960–1279) dynasties China attained a high level in technology, wealth, power, and artistic achievement. Intellectually it was not as creative a period as the germinative pre-Ch'in epoch, but it produced the philosophical and religious syntheses that would dominate Chinese reflection until the Twentieth Century. Buddhism had raised metaphysical questions to which traditional Confucianism had no answers. Freely drawing upon both Taoist and Buddhist concepts, Confucian scholars developed two prominent schools of Neo-Confucianist metaphysics which provided theoretic support to the traditional social morality and intellectual justification for a meditative and mystical religion. The more influential was the so-called "Rationalist School," culminating in Chu Hsi (1130–1200), which held that the principles of all things constitute a timeless Supreme Ultimate, while concrete objects are formed by a combination of principle and matter. During the Ming Dynasty (1368–1644) the more mystical "Idealist School" became dominant under the influence of Wang Yang-Ming (1472–1529). This school denied the existence of two realms and taught that through meditative investigation of one's own mind one could gain knowledge of the Supreme Ultimate, but that such knowledge is not completed until it results in right conduct.

At the death of Chu Hsi in 1200, Chinese civilization might have been favorably compared with any in the world, but the intervening period has been one of spectacular intellectual, technological, and social development in Europe, while China has passed through a period of comparatively low creativity. No philosophers or religious thinkers of the first rank have appeared in China in the last 400 years. Since the middle of the last century, while China has been reeling from military and economic collisions with technologically superior nations, some of her intellectuals have attempted to assimilate western developments and use them to revitalize the Chinese tradition. Professor Fung Yu-lan is an outstanding historian of Chinese thought, familiar with European philosophy, who, during the Second World War, offered a revision of Neo-Confucianism to meet the objections of modern critics. His work is a good example of one way in which contemporary Chinese thinkers have sought to make their intellectual heritage relevant to the needs of today.

SUGGESTIONS FOR FURTHER READING

Chan, Wing-tsit, *Religious Trends in Modern China*, New York, Columbia University Press, 1953.

Chan, Wing-tsit, trans. and ed., *A Source Book in Chinese Philosophy*, Princeton, New Jersey, Princeton University Press, 1963.

Creel, H. G., *Confucius, the Man and the Myth*, New York, John Day, 1949.

Fung Yu-lan, *A History of Chinese Philosophy*, Derk Bodde, trans., Princeton, New Jersey, Princeton University Press, 1952–1953.

Hughes, E. R., and Hughes, K., *Religion in China*, London, Hutchinson's University Library, 1950.

Needham, Joseph, *Science and Civilization in China*, vol. 2, *History of Scientific Thought*, Cambridge, Cambridge University Press, 1956.

Welch, Holmes, *The Parting of the Way: Lao Tzu and the Taoist Movement*, Boston, Beacon Press, 1957.

THE ANALECTS
Confucius

After the triumph of his school in the Han dynasty, Confucius (551–479 B.C.) came to be portrayed as a great statesman and a man of superhuman knowledge. The Analects, a collection of sayings attributed to him and his disciples and the most reliable source of information about them, gives a different picture. The Confucius of the Analects, living at a time of feudal anarchy and brutality, longed for political power in order to reform society through a return to the principles of government he credited to the semi-legendary founders of the Chou dynasty. He spent years vainly seeking some ruler who would follow his counsel. Meanwhile he supported himself precariously by teaching young men to be gentlemen and scholars. The influence of his ideas and his character upon these youths and through them and their successors upon subsequent generations of Chinese students has been enormous. The Confucian tradition contains strands derived from sources other than Confucius, but much of that which is most characteristic and most admirable in that tradition can be traced to the life and thought of "the First Teacher." Prominent among these contributions are Confucius's veneration of filial piety, tradition, and propriety, his moral earnestness, his praise of moderation, his ideal of the gentleman, his faith in the efficacy of moral character, his love of learning, his reticence about the supernatural, his confidence in the perfectibility of man through education and the establishment of a proper social order, his hatred of war, his esteem for the arts, his belief that society should be governed by educated and virtuous men, and his reverence for jen, human Goodness at its highest.

The date of the Analects is not known. Internal evidence leads scholars to judge that major portions may have been collected by disciples of the disciples of Confucius. The classic contains

Confucius, The Analects of Confucius, Books III to IX, Arthur Waley, trans. (London: Allen & Unwin, 1938), pp. 94–145. Reprinted from The Analects of Confucius trans. by Arthur Waley, by permission of George Allen & Unwin, Ltd.

twenty books, some of which were probably added generations after the original compilation and contain ideas distinct from and sometimes inconsistent with those attributed to Confucius in the early books. Arthur Waley has conjectured that Books III to IX, here reprinted in his translation, are the oldest stratum, and they provide a clear and consistent picture of Confucius and his teaching.

BOOK III

1. Master K'ung said of the head of the Chi family when he had eight teams of dancers performing in his courtyard, If this man can be endured, who cannot be endured!

2. The Three Families used the *Yung Song* during the removal of the sacrificial vessels. The Master said,

> By rulers and lords attended,
> The Son of Heaven, mysterious———

What possible application can such words have in the hall of the Three Families?

3. The Master said, A man who is not Good, what can he have to do with ritual? A man who is not Good, what can he have to do with music?

4. Lin Fang asked for some main principles in connexion with ritual. The Master said, A very big question. In ritual at large it is a safe rule always to be too sparing rather than too lavish; and in the particular case of mourning-rites, they should be dictated by grief rather than by fear.

5. The Master said, The barbarians of the East and North have retained their princes. They are not in such a state of decay as we in China.

6. The head of the Chi family was going to make the offerings on Mount T'ai. The Master said to Jan Ch'iu, Cannot you save him from this? Jan Ch'iu replied, I cannot. The Master said, Alas, we can hardly suppose Mount T'ai to be ignorant of matters that even Lin Fang enquires into!

7. The Master said, Gentlemen never compete. You will say that in archery they do so. But even then they bow and make way for one another when they are going up to the archery-ground, when they are coming down and at the subsequent drinking-bout. Thus even when competing, they still remain gentlemen.

8. Tzu-hsia asked, saying, What is the meaning of

> Oh the sweet smile dimpling,
> The lovely eyes so black and white!
> Plain silk that you would take for coloured stuff.

The Master said, The painting comes after the plain groundwork. Tzu-hsia said, Then ritual comes afterwards? The Master said, Shang it is who bears me up. At last I have someone with whom I can discuss the Songs!

9. The Master said, How can we talk about the ritual of the Hsia? The State of Ch'i supplies no adequate evidence. How can we talk about the ritual of Yin? The State of Sung supplies no adequate evidence. For there is a lack both of documents and of learned men. But for this lack we should be able to obtain evidence from these two States.

10. The Master said, At the Ancestral Sacrifice, as for all that comes after the libation, I had far rather not witness it!

11. Someone asked for an explanation of the Ancestral Sacrifice. The Master said, I do not know. Anyone who knew the explanation could deal with all things under Heaven as easily as I lay this here; and he laid his finger upon the palm of his hand.

12. Of the saying, 'The word "sacrifice" is like the word "present"; one should sacrifice to a spirit as though that spirit was present,' the Master said, If I am not present at the sacrifice, it is as though there were no sacrifice.

13. Wang-sun Chia asked about the meaning of the saying,

> Better pay court to the stove
> Than pay court to the Shrine.

The Master said, It is not true. He who has put himself in the wrong with Heaven has no means of expiation left.

14. The Master said, Chou could survey the two preceding dynasties. How great a wealth of culture! And we follow upon Chou.

15. When the Master entered the Grand Temple he asked questions about everything there. Someone said, Do not tell me that this son of a villager from Tsou is expert in matters of ritual. When he went to the Grand Temple, he had to ask about everything. The Master hearing of this said, Just so! such is the ritual.

16. The Master said, the saying

> In archery it is not the hide that counts,
> For some men have more strength than others,

is the way of the Ancients.

17. Tzu-kung wanted to do away with the presentation of a sacrificial sheep at the announcement of each new moon. The Master said, Ssu! You grudge sheep, but I grudge ritual.

18. The Master said, Were anyone to-day to serve his prince according to the full prescriptions of ritual, he would be thought a sycophant.

19. Duke Ting (died 495 B.C.) asked for a precept concerning a ruler's use of his ministers and a minister's service to his ruler. Master K'ung replied saying, A ruler in employing his ministers should be guided solely by the prescriptions of ritual. Ministers in serving their ruler, solely by devotion to his cause.

20. The Master said, The Ospreys! Pleasure not carried to the point of debauch; grief not carried to the point of self-injury.

21. Duke Ai asked Tsai Yü about the Holy Ground. Tsai Yü replied, The Hsia sovereigns marked theirs with a pine, the men of Yin used a cypress, the men of Chou used a chestnut-tree, saying, 'This will cause the common people to be in fear and trembling.' The Master hearing of it said, What is over and done with, one does not discuss. What has already taken its course, one does not criticize; what already belongs to the past, one does not censure.

22. The Master said, Kuan Chung was in reality a man of very narrow capacities. Someone said, Surely he displayed an example of frugality? The Master said, Kuan had three lots of wives, his State officers performed no double duties. How can he be cited as an example of frugality? That may be, the other said; but surely he had a great knowledge of ritual? The Master said, Only the ruler of a State may build a screen to mask his gate; but Kuan had such a screen. Only the ruler of a State, when meeting another such ruler, may use cup-mounds; but Kuan used one. If even Kuan is to be cited as an expert in ritual, who is not an expert in ritual?

23. When talking to the Grand Master of Lu about music, the Master said, Their music in so far as one can find out about it began with a strict unison. Soon the musicians were given more liberty; but the tone remained harmonious, brilliant, consistent, right on till the close.

24. The guardian of the frontier-mound at I asked to be presented to the Master, saying, No gentleman arriving at this frontier has ever yet failed to accord me an interview. The Master's followers presented him. On going out the man said, Sirs, you must not be disheartened by his failure. It is now a very long while since the Way prevailed in the world. I feel sure that Heaven intends to use your Master as a wooden bell.

25. The Master spoke of the Succession Dance as being perfect beauty and at the same time perfect goodness; but of the War Dance as being perfect beauty, but not perfect goodness.

26. The Master said, High office filled by men of narrow views, ritual performed without reverence, the forms of mourning observed without grief— these are things I cannot bear to see!

BOOK IV

1. The Master said, It is Goodness that gives to a neighbourhood its beauty. One who is free to choose, yet does not prefer to dwell among the Good —how can he be accorded the name of wise?

2. The Master said, Without Goodness a man

> Cannot for long endure adversity,
> Cannot for long enjoy prosperity.

The Good Man rests content with Goodness; he that is merely wise pursues Goodness in the belief that it pays to do so.

3, 4. Of the adage 'Only a Good Man knows how to like people, knows how to dislike them,' the Master said, He whose heart is in the smallest degree set upon Goodness will dislike no one.

5. Wealth and rank are what every man desires; but if they can only be retained to the detriment of the Way he professes, he must relinquish them. Poverty and obscurity are what every man detests; but if they can only be avoided to the detriment of the Way he professes, he must accept them. The gentleman who ever parts company with Goodness does not fulfil that name. Never for a moment does a gentleman quit the way of Goodness. He is never so harried but that he cleaves to this; never so tottering but that he cleaves to this.

6. The Master said, I for my part have never yet seen one who really cared for Goodness, nor one who really abhorred wickedness. One who really cared for Goodness would never let any other consideration come first. One who abhorred wickedness would be so constantly doing Good that wickedness would never have a chance to get at him. Has anyone ever managed to do Good with his whole might even as long as the space of a single day? I think not. Yet I for my part have never seen anyone give up such an attempt because he had not the *strength* to go on. It may well have happened, but I for my part have never seen it.

7. The Master said, Every man's faults belong to a set. If one looks out for faults it is only as a means of recognizing Goodness.

8. The Master said, In the morning, hear the Way; in the evening, die content!

9. The Master said, A Knight whose heart is set upon the Way, but who is ashamed of wearing shabby clothes and eating coarse food, is not worth calling into counsel.

10. The Master said, A gentleman in his dealings with the world has neither enmities nor affections; but wherever he sees Right he ranges himself beside it.

11. The Master said, Where gentlemen set their hearts upon moral force (*tê*), the commoners set theirs upon the soil. Where gentlemen think only of punishments, the commoners think only of exemptions.

12. The Master said, Those whose measures are dictated by mere expediency will arouse continual discontent.

13. The Master said, If it is really possible to govern countries by ritual and yielding, there is no more to be said. But if it is not really possible, of what use is ritual?

14. The Master said, He does not mind not being in office; all he minds about is whether he has qualities that entitle him to office. He does not mind failing to get recognition; he is too busy doing the things that entitle him to recognition.

15. The Master said, Shên! My Way has one (thread) that runs right through it. Master Tsêng said, Yes. When the Master had gone out, the disciples asked, saying What did he mean? Master Tsêng said, Our Master's Way is simply this: Loyalty, consideration.

16. The Master said, A gentleman takes as much trouble to discover what is right as lesser men take to discover what will pay.

17. The Master said, In the presence of a good man, think all the time how you may learn to equal him. In the presence of a bad man, turn your gaze within!

18. The Master said, In serving his father and mother a man may gently remonstrate with them. But if he sees that he has failed to change their opinion, he should resume an attitude of deference and not thwart them; may feel discouraged, but not resentful.

19. The Master said, While father and mother are alive, a good son does not wander far afield; or if he does so, goes only where he has said he was going.

20. The Master said, If for the whole three years of mourning a son manages to carry on the household exactly as in his father's day, then he is a good son indeed.

21. The Master said, It is always better for a man to know the age of his parents. In the one case such knowledge will be a comfort to him; in the other, it will fill him with a salutary dread.

22. The Master said, In old days a man kept a hold on his words, fearing the disgrace that would ensue should he himself fail to keep pace with them.

23. The Master said, Those who err on the side of strictness are few indeed!

24. The Master said, A gentleman covets the reputation of being slow in word but prompt in deed.

25. The Master said, Moral force (*tê*) never dwells in solitude; it will always bring neighbours.

26. Tzu-yu said, In the service of one's prince repeated scolding can only lead to loss of favour; in friendship, it can only lead to estrangement.

BOOK V

1. The Master said of Kung Yeh Ch'ang, Though he has suffered imprisonment, he is not an unfit person to choose as a husband; for it was not through any fault of his own. He married him to his daughter.

The Master said of Nan Jung, In a country ruled according to the Way, he would not be overlooked; in a country not ruled according to the Way, he would manage to avoid capital punishment or mutilation. He married him to his elder brother's daughter.

2. Of Tzu-chien he said, A gentleman indeed is such a one as he! If the land of Lu were indeed without gentlemen, how could he have learnt this?

3. Tzu-kung asked saying, What do you think of me? The Master said, You are a vessel. Tzu-kung said, What sort of vessel? The Master said, A sacrificial vase of jade!

4. Someone said, Jan Yung is Good, but he is a poor talker. The Master said, What need has he to be a good talker? Those who down others with

clap-trap are seldom popular. Whether he is Good, I do not know. But I see no need for him to be a good talker.

5. The Master gave Ch'i-tiao K'ai leave to take office, but he replied, 'I have not yet sufficiently perfected myself in the virtue of good faith.' The Master was delighted.

6. The Master said, The Way makes no progress. I shall get upon a raft and float out to sea. I am sure Yu would come with me. Tzu-lu on hearing of this was in high spirits. The Master said, That is Yu indeed! He sets far too much store by feats of physical daring. It seems as though I should never get hold of the right sort of people.

7. Mêng Wu Po asked whether Tzu-lu was Good. The Master said, I do not know. On his repeating the question the Master said, In a country of a thousand war-chariots Yu could be trusted to carry out the recruiting. But whether he is Good I do not know. 'What about Ch'iu?' The Master said, In a city of a thousand families or a baronial family with a hundred chariots he might do well as Warden. But whether he is Good, I do not know. 'What about Ch'ih?' The Master said, Girt with his sash, standing in his place at Court he might well be charged to converse with strangers and guests. But whether he is Good, I do not know.

8. The Master in discussing Tzu-kung said to him, Which do you yourself think is the better, you or Hui? He answered saying, I dare not so much as look at Hui. For Hui has but to hear one part in ten, in order to understand the whole ten. Whereas if I hear one part, I understand no more than two parts. The Master said, Not equal to him—you and I are not equal to him!

9. Tsai Yü used to sleep during the day. The Master said, Rotten wood cannot be carved, nor a wall of dried dung be trowelled. What use is there in my scolding him any more?

The Master said, There was a time when I merely listened attentively to what people said, and took for granted that they would carry out their words. Now I am obliged not only to give ear to what they say, but also to keep an eye on what they do. It was my dealings with Tsai Yü that brought about the change.

10. The Master said, I have never yet seen a man who was truly steadfast. Someone answered saying, 'Shên Ch'êng.' The Master said, Ch'êng! He is at the mercy of his desires. How can *he* be called steadfast?

11. Tzu-kung said, What I do not want others to do to me, I have no desire to do to others. The Master said, Oh Ssu! You have not quite got to that point yet.

12. Tzu-kung said, Our Master's views concerning culture and the outward insignia of goodness, we are permitted to hear; but about Man's nature and the ways of Heaven he will not tell us anything at all.

13. When Tzu-lu heard any precept and was still trying unsuccessfully to put it into practice, his one fear was that he might hear some fresh precept.

14. Tzu-kung asked saying, Why was K'ung Wên Tzu called Wên

('The Cultured')? The Master said, Because he was diligent and so fond of learning that he was not ashamed to pick up knowledge even from his inferiors.

15. Of Tzu-ch'an the Master said that in him were to be found four of the virtues that belong to the Way of the true gentleman. In his private conduct he was courteous, in serving his master he was punctilious, in providing for the needs of the people he gave them even more than their due; in exacting service from the people, he was just.

16. The Master said, Yen P'ing Chung is a good example of what one's intercourse with one's fellowmen should be. However long he has known anyone he always maintains the same scrupulous courtesy.

17. The Master said, Tsang Wên Chung kept a Ts'ai tortoise in a hall with the hill-pattern on its pillar tops and the duckweed pattern on its kingposts. Of what sort, pray, was his knowledge?

18. Tzu-chang asked saying, The Grand Minister Tzu-wên was appointed to this office on three separate occasions, but did not on any of these three occasions display the least sign of elation. Three times he was deposed; but never showed the least sign of disappointment. Each time, he duly informed his successor concerning the administration of State affairs during his tenure of office. What should you say of him? The Master said, He was certainly faithful to his prince's interests. Tzu-chang said, Would you not call him Good? The Master said, I am not sure. I see nothing in that to merit the title Good.

(Tzu-chang said) When Ts'ui Tzu assassinated the sovereign of Ch'i, Ch'ên Wên Tzu who held a fief of ten war chariots gave it up and went away. On arriving in another State, he said, 'I can see they are no better here than our minister Ts'ui Tzu'; and he went away. On arriving in the next country, he said, 'I can see they are no better here than our minister Ts'ui Tzu'; and went away. What should you say of him? The Master said, He was certainly scrupulous. Tzu-chang said, Would you not call him Good? The Master said, I am not sure. I see nothing in that to merit the title Good.

19. Chi Wên Tzu used to think thrice before acting. The Master hearing of it said, Twice is quite enough.

20. The Master said, Ning Wu Tzu 'so long as the Way prevailed in his country showed wisdom; but when the Way no longer prevailed, he showed his folly.' To such wisdom as his we may all attain; but not to such folly!

21. When the Master was in Ch'ên he said, Let us go back, let us go back! The little ones at home are headstrong and careless. They are perfecting themselves in all the showy insignia of culture without any idea how to use them.

22. The Master said, Po I and Shu Ch'i never bore old ills in mind and had but the faintest feelings of rancour.

23. The Master said, How can we call even Weishêng Kao upright? When someone asked him for vinegar he went and begged it from the people next door, and then gave it as though it were his own gift.

24. The Master said, Clever talk, a pretentious manner and a reverence that is only of the feet—Tso Ch'iu Ming was incapable of stooping to them, and I too could never stoop to them. Having to conceal one's indignation and keep on friendly terms with the people against whom one feels it—Tso Ch'iu Ming was incapable of stooping to such conduct, and I too am incapable of stooping to such conduct.

25. Once when Yen Hui and Tzu-lu were waiting upon him the Master said, Suppose each of you were to tell his wish. Tzu-lu said, I should like to have carriages and horses, clothes and fur rugs, share them with my friends and feel no annoyance if they were returned to me the worse for wear. Yen Hui said, I should like never to boast of my good qualities nor make a fuss about the trouble I take on behalf of others. Tzu-lu said, A thing I should like is to hear the Master's wish. The Master said, In dealing with the aged, to be of comfort to them; in dealing with friends, to be of good faith with them; in dealing with the young, to cherish them.

26. The Master said, In vain have I looked for a single man capable of seeing his own faults and bringing the charge home against himself.

27. The Master said, In an hamlet of ten houses you may be sure of finding someone quite as loyal and true to his word as I. But I doubt if you would find anyone with such a love of learning.

BOOK VI

1. The Master said, Now Yung, for example. I should not mind setting him with his face to the south. Jan Yung then asked about Tzu-sang Po-tzu. The Master said, He too would do. He is lax. Jan Yung said, I can understand that such a man might do as a ruler, provided he were scrupulous in his own conduct and lax only in his dealings with the people. But you would admit that a man who was lax in his own conduct as well as in government would be too lax. The Master said, What Yung says is quite true.

2. Duke Ai asked which of the disciples had a love of learning. Master K'ung answered him saying, There was Yen Hui. He had a great love of learning. He never vented his wrath upon the innocent nor let others suffer for his faults. Unfortunately the span of life allotted to him by Heaven was short, and he died. At present there are none or at any rate I have heard of none who are fond of learning.

3. When Kung-hsi Hua was sent on a mission to Ch'i, Master Jan asked that Hua's mother might be granted an allowance of grain. The Master said, Give her a cauldron full. Jan said that was not enough. The Master said, Give her a measure. Master Jan gave her five bundles. The Master said, When Ch'ih went to Ch'i he drove sleek horses and was wrapped in light furs. There is a saying, A gentleman helps out the necessitous; he does not make the rich richer still.

When Yüan Ssu was made a governor, he was given an allowance of nine hundred measures of grain, but declined it. The Master said, Surely you could find people who would be glad of it among your neighbours or in your village?

4. The Master said of Jan Yung, If the offspring of a brindled ox is ruddy-coated and has grown its horns, however much people might hesitate to use it, would the hills and streams really reject it?

5. The Master said, Hui is capable of occupying his whole mind for three months on end with no thought but that of Goodness. The others can do so, some for a day, some even for a month; but that is all.

6. Chi K'ang-tzu asked whether Tzu-lu was the right sort of person to put into office. The Master said, Yu is efficient. It goes without saying that he is capable of holding office. Chi K'ang-tzu said, How about Tzu-kung? Would he be the right sort of person to put into office? The Master said, He can turn his merits to account. It goes without saying, that he is capable of holding office. Chi K'ang-tzu said, How about Jan Ch'iu? Would he be the right sort of person to put into office? The Master said, He is versatile. It goes without saying that he is capable of holding office.

7. The Chi Family wanted to make Min Tzu-ch'ien governor of Pi. Min Tzu-ch'ien said, Invent a polite excuse for me. If that is not accepted and they try to get at me again, I shall certainly install myself on the far side of the Wên.

8. When Jan Kêng was ill, the Master went to enquire after him, and grasping his hand through the window said, It is all over with him! Heaven has so ordained it—— But that such a man should have such an illness! That such a man should have such an illness!

9. The Master said, Incomparable indeed was Hui! A handful of rice to eat, a gourdful of water to drink, living in a mean street—others would have found it unendurably depressing, but to Hui's cheerfulness it made no difference at all. Incomparable indeed was Hui!

10. Jan Ch'iu said, It is not that your Way does not commend itself to me, but that it demands powers I do not possess. The Master said, He whose strength gives out collapses during the course of the journey (the Way); but you deliberately draw the line.

11. The Master said to Tzu-hsia, 'You must practise the ju of gentlemen, not that of the common people.

12. When Tzu-yu was Warden of the castle of Wu, the Master said, Have you managed to get hold of the right sort of people there? Tzu-yu said, There is someone called T'an-t'ai Mieh-ming who 'walks on no by-paths.' He has not once come to my house except on public business.

13. The Master said, Mêng Chih-fan is no boaster. When his people were routed he was the last to flee; but when they neared the city-gate, he whipped up his horses, saying, It was not courage that kept me behind. My horses were slow.

14. The Master said, Without the eloquence of the priest T'o and the beauty of Prince Ch'ao of Sung it is hard nowadays to get through.

15. The Master said, Who expects to be able to go out of a house except by the door? How is it then that no one follows this Way of ours?

16. The Master said, When natural substance prevails over ornamentation, you get the boorishness of the rustic. When ornamentation prevails over natural substance, you get the pedantry of the scribe. Only when ornament and substance are duly blended do you get the true gentleman.

17. The Master said, Man's very life is honesty, in that without it he will be lucky indeed if he escapes with his life.

18. The Master said, To prefer it is better than only to know it. To delight in it is better than merely to prefer it.

19. The Master said, To men who have risen at all above the middling sort, one may talk of things higher yet. But to men who are at all below the middling sort it is useless to talk of things that are above them.

20. Fan Ch'ih asked about wisdom. The Master said, He who devotes himself to securing for his subjects what it is right they should have, who by respect for the Spirits keeps them at a distance, may be termed wise. He asked about Goodness. The Master said, Goodness cannot be obtained till what is difficult has been duly done. He who has done this may be called Good.

21. The Master said, The wise man delights in water, the Good man delights in mountains. For the wise move; but the Good stay still. The wise are happy; but the Good, secure.

22. A single change could bring Ch'i to the level of Lu; and a single change would bring Lu to the Way.

23. The Master said, A horn-gourd that is neither horn nor gourd! A pretty horn-gourd indeed, a pretty horn-gourd indeed.

24. Tsai Yü asked saying, I take it a Good Man, even if he were told that another Good Man were at the bottom of a well, would go to join him? The Master said, Why should you think so? 'A gentleman can be broken, but cannot be dented; may be deceived, but cannot be led astray.'

24 (Paraphrased). Tsai Yü, half playfully asked whether, since the Good always go to where other Good Men are, a Good Man would leap into a well on hearing that there was another Good Man at the bottom of it. Confucius, responding in the same playful spirit, quotes a maxim about the true gentleman, solely for the sake of the reference in it to *hsien,* which means 'throw down' into a pit or well, but also has the sense 'to pit,' 'to dent.'

25. The Master said, A gentleman who is widely versed in letters and at the same time knows how to submit his learning to the restraints of ritual is not likely, I think, to go far wrong.

26. When the Master went to see Nan-tzu, Tzu-lu was not pleased. Whereupon the Master made a solemn declaration concerning his visit, saying, Whatsoever I have done amiss, may Heaven avert it, may Heaven avert it!

27. The Master said, How transcendent is the moral power of the

Middle Use! That it is but rarely found among the common people is a fact long admitted.

28. Tzu-kung said, If a ruler not only conferred wide benefits upon the common people, but also compassed the salvation of the whole State, what would you say of him? Surely, you would call him Good? The Master said, It would no longer be a matter of 'Good.' He would without doubt be a Divine Sage. Even Yao and Shun could hardly criticize him. As for Goodness —you yourself desire rank and standing; then help others to get rank and standing. You want to turn your own merits to account; then help others to turn theirs to account—in fact, the ability to take one's own feelings as a guide —that is the sort of thing that lies in the direction of Goodness.

BOOK VII

1, 2, 3. The Master said, I have 'transmitted what was taught to me without making up anything of my own.' I have been faithful to and loved the Ancients. In these respects, I make bold to think, not even our old P'êng can have excelled me. The Master said, I have listened in silence and noted what was said, I have never grown tired of learning nor wearied of teaching others what I have learnt. These at least are merits which I can confidently claim. The Master said, The thought that 'I have left my moral power (*tê*) untended, my learning unperfected, that I have heard of righteous men, but been unable to go to them; have heard of evil men, but been unable to reform them'—it is these thoughts that disquiet me.

4. In his leisure hours the Master's manner was very free-and-easy, and his expression alert and cheerful.

5. The Master said, How utterly have things gone to the bad with me! It is long now indeed since I dreamed that I saw the Duke of Chou.

6. The Master said, Set your heart upon the Way, support yourself by its power, lean upon Goodness, seek distraction in the arts.

7. The Master said, From the very poorest upwards—beginning even with the man who could bring no better present than a bundle of dried flesh— none has ever come to me without receiving instruction.

8. The Master said, Only one who bursts with eagerness do I instruct; only one who bubbles with excitement, do I enlighten. If I hold up one corner and a man cannot come back to me with the other three, I do not continue the lesson.

9. If at a meal the Master found himself seated next to someone who was in mourning, he did not eat his fill. When he had wailed at a funeral, during the rest of the day he did not sing.

10. The Master said to Yen Hui, The maxim

> When wanted, then go;
> When set aside; then hide.

is one that you and I could certainly fulfil. Tzu-lu said, Supposing you had command of the Three Hosts, whom would you take to help you? The Master said, The man who was ready to 'beard a tiger or rush a river' without caring whether he lived or died—that sort of man I should not take. I should certainly take someone who approached difficulties with due caution and who preferred to succeed by strategy.

11. The Master said, If any means of escaping poverty presented itself that did not involve doing wrong, I would adopt it, even though my employment were only that of the gentleman who holds the whip. But so long as it is a question of illegitimate means, I shall continue to pursue the quests that I love.

12. The rites to which the Master gave the greatest attention were those connected with purification before sacrifice, with war and with sickness.

13. When he was in Ch'i the Master heard the Succession, and for three months did not know the taste of meat. He said, 'I did not picture to myself that any music existed which could reach such perfection as this.'

14. Jan Ch'iu said, Is our Master on the side of the Prince of Wei? Tzu-kung said, Yes, I must ask him about that. He went in and said, What sort of people were Po I and Shu Ch'i? The Master said, They were good men who lived in the days of old. Tzu-kung said, Did they repine? The Master said, They sought Goodness and got Goodness. Why should they repine? On coming out Tzu-kung said, Our Master is not on his side.

15. The Master said, He who seeks only coarse food to eat, water to drink and a bent arm for pillow, will without looking for it find happiness to boot. Any thought of accepting wealth and rank by means that I know to be wrong is as remote from me as the clouds that float above.

16. The Master said, Give me a few more years, so that I may have spent a whole fifty in study, and I believe that after all I should be fairly free from error.

17. The occasions upon which the Master used correct pronunciation were when reciting the *Songs* or the *Books* and when practising ritual acts. At all such times he used the correct pronunciation.

18. The 'Duke of Shê' asked Tzu-lu about Master K'ung (Confucius). Tzu-lu did not reply. The Master said, Why did you not say 'This is the character of the man: so intent upon enlightening the eager that he forgets his hunger, and so happy in doing so, that he forgets the bitterness of his lot and does not realize that old age is at hand. That is what he is.'

19. The Master said, I for my part am not one of those who have innate knowledge. I am simply one who loves the past and who is diligent in investigating it.

20. The Master never talked of prodigies, feats of strength, disorders or spirits.

21. The Master said, Even when walking in a party of no more than three I can always be certain of learning from those I am with. There will be

good qualities that I can select for imitation and bad ones that will teach me what requires correction in myself.

22. The Master said, Heaven begat the power (*tê*) that is in me. What have I to fear from such a one as Huan T'ui?

23. The Master said, My friends, I know you think that there is something I am keeping from you. There is nothing at all that I keep from you. I take no steps about which I do not consult you, my friends. Were it otherwise, I should not be Ch'iu.

24. The Master took four subjects for his teaching: culture, conduct of affairs, loyalty to superiors and the keeping of promises.

25. The Master said, A Divine Sage I cannot hope ever to meet; the most I can hope for is to meet a true gentleman. The Master said, A faultless man I cannot hope ever to meet; the most I can hope for is to meet a man of fixed principles. Yet where all around I see Nothing pretending to be Something, Emptiness pretending to be Fulness, Penury pretending to be Affluence, even a man of fixed principles will be none too easy to find.

26. The Master fished with a line but not with a net; when fowling he did not aim at a roosting bird.

27. The Master said, There may well be those who can do without knowledge; but I for my part am certainly not one of them. To hear much, pick out what is good and follow it, to see much and take due note of it, is the lower of the two kinds of knowledge.

28. At Hu village the people were difficult to talk to. But an uncapped boy presented himself for an interview. The disciples were in two minds about showing him in. But the Master said, In sanctioning his entry here I am sanctioning nothing he may do when he retires. We must not be too particular. If anyone purifies himself in order to come to us, let us accept this purification. We are not responsible for what he does when he goes away.

29. The Master said, Is Goodness indeed so far away? If we really wanted Goodness, we should find that it was at our very side.

30. The Minister of Crime in Ch'ên asked whether Duke Chao of Lu knew the rites. Master K'ung said, He knew the rites. When Master K'ung had withdrawn, the Minister motioned Wu-ma Ch'i to come forward and said, I have heard the saying 'A gentleman is never partial.' But it seems that some gentlemen are very partial indeed. His Highness married into the royal family of Wu who belong to the same clan as himself, calling her Wu Mêng Tzu. If his Highness knew the rites, who does not know the rites? Wu-ma Ch'i repeated this to the Master, who said, I am a fortunate man. If by any chance I make a mistake, people are certain to hear of it!

31. When in the Master's presence anyone sang a song that he liked, he did not join in at once, but asked for it to be repeated and then joined in.

32. The Master said, As far as taking trouble goes, I do not think I compare badly with other people. But as regards carrying out the duties of a gentleman in actual life, I have never yet had a chance to show what I could do.

33. The Master said, As to being a Divine Sage or even a Good Man, far be it from me to make any such claim. As for unwearying effort to learn and unflagging patience in teaching others, those are merits that I do not hesitate to claim. Kung-hsi Hua said, The trouble is that we disciples cannot learn!

34. When the Master was very ill, Tzu-lu asked leave to perform the Rite of Expiation. The Master said, Is there such a thing? Tzu-lu answered saying, There is. In one of the Dirges it says, 'We performed rites of expiation for you, calling upon the sky-spirits above and the earth-spirits below.' The Master said, My expiation began long ago!

35. The Master said, Just as lavishness leads easily to presumption, so does frugality to meanness. But meanness is a far less serious fault than presumption.

36. The Master said, A true gentleman is calm and at ease; the Small Man is fretful and ill at ease.

37. The Master's manner was affable yet firm, commanding but not harsh, polite but easy.

BOOK VIII

1. The Master said, Of T'ai Po it may indeed be said that he attained to the very highest pitch of moral power. No less than three times he renounced the sovereignty of all things under Heaven, without the people getting a chance to praise him for it.

2. The Master said, Courtesy not bounded by the prescriptions of ritual becomes tiresome. Caution not bounded by the prescriptions of ritual becomes timidity, daring becomes turbulence, inflexibility becomes harshness.

The Master said, When gentlemen deal generously with their own kin, the common people are incited to Goodness. When old dependents are not discarded, the common people will not be fickle.

3. When Master Tsêng was ill he summoned his disciples and said, Free my feet, free my hands. The *Song* says:

> In fear and trembling,
> With caution and care,
> As though on the brink of a chasm,
> As though treading thin ice.

But I feel now that whatever may betide I have got through safely, my little ones.

4. When Master Tsêng was ill, Mêng Ching Tzu came to see him. Master Tsêng spoke to him saying, When a bird is about to die its song touches the heart. When a man is about to die, his words are of note. There are three things that a gentleman, in following the Way, places above all the rest: from every attitude, every gesture that he employs he must remove all trace of vio-

lence or arrogance; every look that he composes in his face must betoken good faith; from every word that he utters, from every intonation, he must remove all trace of coarseness or impropriety. As to the ordering of ritual vessels and the like, there are those whose business it is to attend to such matters.

5. Master Tsêng said, Clever, yet not ashamed to consult those less clever than himself; widely gifted, yet not ashamed to consult those with few gifts; having, yet seeming not to have; full, yet seeming empty; offended against, yet never contesting—long ago I had a friend whose ways were such as this.

6. Master Tsêng said, The man to whom one could with equal confidence entrust an orphan not yet fully grown or the sovereignty of a whole State, whom the advent of no emergency however great could upset—would such a one be a true gentleman? He I think would be a true gentleman indeed.

7. Master Tsêng said, The true Knight of the Way must perforce be both broad-shouldered and stout of heart; his burden is heavy and he has far to go. For Goodness is the burden he has taken upon himself; and must we not grant that it is a heavy one to bear? Only with death does his journey end; then must we not grant that he has far to go?

8. The Master said, Let a man be first incited by the *Songs,* then given a firm footing by the study of ritual, and finally perfected by music.

9. The Master said, The common people can be made to follow it; they cannot be made to understand it.

10. The Master said, One who is by nature daring and is suffering from poverty will not long be law-abiding. Indeed, any men, save those that are truly Good, if their sufferings are very great, will be likely to rebel.

11. The Master said, If a man has gifts as wonderful as those of the Duke of Chou, yet is arrogant and mean, all the rest is of no account.

12. The Master said:

> One who will study for three years
> Without thought of reward
> Would be hard indeed to find.

13. The Master said, Be of unwavering good faith, love learning, if attacked be ready to die for the good Way. Do not enter a State that pursues dangerous courses, nor stay in one where the people have rebelled. When the Way prevails under Heaven, then show yourself; when it does not prevail, then hide. When the Way prevails in your own land, count it a disgrace to be needy and obscure; when the Way does not prevail in your land, then count it a disgrace to be rich and honoured.

14. The Master said, He who holds no rank in a State does not discuss its policies.

15. The Master said, When Chih the Chief Musician led the climax of the *Ospreys,* what a grand flood of sound filled one's ears!

16. The Master said, Impetuous, but tricky! Ingenuous, but dishonest!

Simple-minded, but capable of breaking promises! To such men I can give no recognition.

17. The Master said, Learn as if you were following someone whom you could not catch up, as though it were someone you were frightened of losing.

18. The Master said, Sublime were Shun and Yü! All that is under Heaven was theirs, yet they remained aloof from it.

19. The Master said, Greatest, as lord and ruler, was Yao. Sublime, indeed, was he. 'There is no greatness like the greatness of Heaven,' yet Yao could copy it. So boundless was it that the people could find no name for it; yet sublime were his achievements, dazzling the insignia of his culture!

20. Shun had five ministers and all that is under Heaven was well ruled. King Wu said, I have ten ministers. Master K'ung said, True indeed is the saying that 'the right material is hard to find'; for the turn of the T'ang and Yü dynasties was the time most famous for this. (As for King Wu), there was a woman among his ten, so that in reality there were only nine men. Yet of all that is under Heaven he held two parts in three, using them in submissive service to the dynasty of Yin. The moral power (*tê*) of Chou may, indeed, be called an absolutely perfect moral power!

21. The Master said, In Yü I can find no semblance of a flaw. Abstemious in his own food and drink, he displayed the utmost devotion in his offerings to spirits and divinities. Content with the plainest clothes for common wear, he saw to it that his sacrificial apron and ceremonial head-dress were of the utmost magnificence. His place of habitation was of the humblest, and all his energy went into draining and ditching. In him I can find no semblance of a flaw.

BOOK IX

1. The Master seldom spoke of profit or fate or Goodness.

2. A villager from Ta-hsiang said, Master K'ung is no doubt a very great man and vastly learned. But he does nothing to bear out this reputation. The Master, hearing of it, said to his disciples, What shall I take up? Shall I take up chariot-driving? Or shall it be archery? I think I will take up driving!

3. The Master said, The hemp-thread crown is prescribed by ritual. Nowadays people wear black silk, which is economical; and I follow the general practice. Obeisance below the daïs is prescribed by ritual. Nowadays people make obeisance after mounting the daïs. This is presumptuous, and though to do so is contrary to the general practice, I make a point of bowing while still down below.

4. There were four things that the Master wholly eschewed: he took nothing for granted, he was never over-positive, never obstinate, never egotistic.

5. When the Master was trapped in K'uang, he said, When King Wên

perished, did that mean that culture (*wên*) ceased to exist? If Heaven had really intended that such culture as his should disappear, a latter-day mortal would never have been able to link himself to it as I have done. And if Heaven does not intend to destroy such culture, what have I to fear from the people of K'uang?

6. The Grand Minister (of Wu?) asked Tzu-kung saying, Is your Master a Divine Sage? If so, how comes it that he has many practical accomplishments? Tzu-kung said, Heaven certainly intended him to become a Sage; it is also true that he has many accomplishments. When the Master heard of it he said, The Grand Minister is quite right about me. When I was young I was in humble circumstances; that is why I have many practical accomplishments in regard to simple, everyday matters. Does it befit a gentleman to have many accomplishments? No, he is in no need of them at all.

Lao says that the Master said, It is because I have not been given a chance that I have become so handy.

7. The Master said, Do I regard myself as a possessor of wisdom? Far from it. But if even a simple peasant comes in all sincerity and asks me a question, I am ready to thrash the matter out, with all its pros and cons, to the very end.

8. The Master said, The phoenix does not come; the river gives forth no chart. It is all over with me!

9. Whenever he was visited by anyone dressed in the robes of mourning or wearing ceremonial headdress, with gown and skirt, or a blind man, even if such a one were younger than himself, the Master on seeing him invariably rose to his feet, and if compelled to walk past him always quickened his step.

10. Yen Hui said with a deep sigh, The more I strain my gaze up towards it, the higher it soars. The deeper I bore down into it, the harder it becomes. I see it in front; but suddenly it is behind. Step by step the Master skilfully lures one on. He has broadened me with culture, restrained me with ritual. Even if I wanted to stop, I could not. Just when I feel that I have exhausted every resource, something seems to rise up, standing out sharp and clear. Yet though I long to pursue it, I can find no way of getting to it at all.

11. When the Master was very ill, Tzu-lu caused some of the disciples to get themselves up as official retainers. Coming to himself for a short while, the Master said, How like Yu, to go in for this sort of imposture! In pretending to have retainers when I have none, whom do I deceive? Do I deceive Heaven? Not only would I far rather die in the arms of you disciples than in the arms of retainers, but also as regards my funeral—even if I am not accorded a State Burial, it is not as though I were dying by the roadside.

12. Tzu-kung said, Suppose one had a lovely jewel, should one wrap it up, put it in a box and keep it, or try to get the best price one can for it? The Master said, Sell it! Most certainly sell it! I myself am one who is waiting for an offer.

13. The Master wanted to settle among the Nine Wild Tribes of the East. Someone said, I am afraid you would find it hard to put up with their lack of refinement. The Master said, Were a true gentleman to settle among them there would soon be no trouble about lack of refinement.

14. The Master said, It was only after my return from Wei to Lu that music was revised, Court pieces and Ancestral Recitations being at last properly discriminated.

15. The Master said, I can claim that at Court I have duly served the Duke and his officers; at home, my father and elder brother. As regards matters of mourning, I am conscious of no neglect, nor have I ever been overcome with wine. Concerning these things at any rate my mind is quite at rest.

16. Once when the Master was standing by a stream, he said, Could one but go on and on like this, never ceasing day or night!

17. The Master said, I have never yet seen anyone whose desire to build up his moral power was as strong as sexual desire.

18. The Master said, The case is like that of someone raising a mound. If he stops working, the fact that it perhaps needed only one more basketful makes no difference; I stay where I am. Whereas even if he has not got beyond levelling the ground, but is still at work, the fact that he has only tilted one basketful of earth makes no difference. I go to help him.

19. The Master said, It was Hui whom I could count on always to listen attentively to anything I said.

20. The Master said of Yen Hui, Alas, I saw him go forward, but had no chance to see whither this progress would have led him in the end.

21. The Master said, There are shoots whose lot it is to spring up but never to flower; others whose lot it is to flower, but never bear fruit.

22. The Master said, Respect the young. How do you know that they will not one day be all that you are now? But if a man has reached forty or fifty and nothing has been heard of him, then I grant there is no need to respect him.

23. The Master said, The words of the *Fa Yü* (Model Sayings) cannot fail to stir us; but what matters is that they should change our ways. The words of the *Hsüan Chü* cannot fail to commend themselves to us; but what matters is that we should carry them out. For those who approve but do not carry out, who are stirred, but do not change, I can do nothing at all.

24. The Master said, First and foremost, be faithful to your superiors, keep all promises, refuse the friendship of all who are not like you; and if you have made a mistake, do not be afraid of admitting the fact and amending your ways.

25. The Master said, You may rob the Three Armies of their commander-in-chief, but you cannot deprive the humblest peasant of his opinion.

26. The Master said, 'Wearing a shabby hemp-quilted gown, yet capable of standing unabashed with those who wore fox and badger.' That would apply quite well to Yu, would it not?

> Who harmed none, was foe to none,
> Did nothing that was not right.

Afterwards Tzu-lu (Yu) kept on continually chanting those lines to himself. The Master said, Come now, the wisdom contained in them is not worth treasuring to that extent!

27. The Master said, Only when the year grows cold do we see that the pine and cypress are the last to fade.

28. The Master said, he that is really Good can never be unhappy. He that is really wise can never be perplexed. He that is really brave is never afraid.

29. The Master said, There are some whom one can join in study but whom one cannot join in progress along the Way; others whom one can join in progress along the Way, but beside whom one cannot take one's stand; and others again beside whom one can take one's stand, but whom one cannot join in counsel.

30.
> The flowery branch of the wild cherry
> How swiftly it flies back!
> It is not that I do not love you;
> But your house is far away.

The Master said, He did not really love her. Had he done so, he would not have worried about the distance.

20

KAOU TSZE
Mencius

Mencius (371–289 B.C.?), the most influential of the ancient followers of Confucius, had a career strikingly similar to that of his master two centuries before. Reputed to have studied with disciples of Confucius' grandson, Mencius spoke of Confucius with reverence. He was, like Confucius, a teacher of young

Mencius, *The Works of Mencius*, James Legge, trans. (Oxford, England: Clarendon Press, 1895), pp. 394–421. Reprinted from *The Chinese Classics*, vol. 2, by James Legge.

*men, but his ambition was to become the prime minister of one
of the small Chinese states in order to institute sweeping reforms.
Although he appears to have been more prosperous than Confucius and to have been treated with considerable respect by some
rulers, his ambition to govern was never realized nor his schemes
of reform adopted. Many of the themes of the Analects were developed in his teachings, but original doctrines were also advanced. Confucius had lived before the period in which rival
schools of moral and political philosophy had developed in China,
but Mencius was aware of a number of competing prescriptions
for the ills of society and undertook to combat them both by argument and appeals to the practice of the legendary culture heroes.
His most famous thesis was that human nature is originally good;
every man possesses the feelings that form the root of moral character and is consequently a potential sage. The aim of education
and moral training should be to recover this good original nature.
The basis of successful government, he held, is morality. The wise
ruler will treat his subjects justly in all things. Mencius advocated,
more specifically, land redistribution, public schools, diversified
farming, and conservation of natural resources. While he supported the traditional hereditary aristocracy, he held that a bad
ruler could forfeit the Mandate of Heaven and consequently be
legitimately deposed by a revolution.*

*The book the Mencius is 35,000 characters long, a big book
by Chinese standards. It was probably compiled by the disciples
of Mencius, and appears to contain little if any material interpo-
lated in later times. Book six, part one, the most influential section,
is here given in full in the Legge translation.*

BOOK VI

Kaou Tsze. Part I

Chapter I: 1. The philosopher Kaou said, "Man's nature is like the *ke*
willow, and righteousness is like a cup or a bowl. The fashioning benevolence
and righteousness out of man's nature is like the making cups and bowls from
the *ke* willow."

2. Mencius replied, "Can you, leaving untouched the nature of the
willow, make with it cups and bowls? You must do violence and injury to the
willow, before you can make cups and bowls with it. If you must do violence
and injury to the willow in order to make cups and bowls with it, *on your
principles* you must in the same way do violence and injury to humanity in
order to fashion from it benevolence and righteousness! Your words, alas!
would certainly lead all men on to reckon benevolence and righteousness to
be calamities."

Chapter II. 1. The philosopher Kaou said, "Man's nature is like water whirling round *in a corner*. Open a passage for it to the east, and it will flow to the east; open a passage for it to the west, and it will flow to the west. Man's nature is indifferent to good and evil, just as the water is indifferent to the east and west."

2. Mencius replied, "Water indeed *will flow* indifferently to the east or west, but will it flow indifferently up or down? The tendency of man's nature to good is like the tendency of water to flow downwards. There are none but have this tendency to good, *just as* all water flows downwards.

3. "Now by striking water and causing it to leap up, you may make it go over your forehead, and, by damming and leading it, you may force it up a hill;—but are such movements according to the nature of water? It is the force applied which causes them. When men are made to do what is not good, their nature is dealt with in this way."

Chapter III. 1. The philosopher Kaou said, "Life is what is to be understood by nature."

2. Mencius asked him, "Do you say that by nature you mean life, just as you say that white is white?" "Yes, I do," was the reply. Mencius added, "Is the whiteness of a white feather like that of white snow, and the whiteness of white snow like that of a white gem?" *Kaou again* said "Yes."

3. "Very well," *pursued Mencius*. "Is the nature of a dog like the nature of an ox, and the nature of an ox like the nature of a man?"

Chapter IV. 1. The philosopher Kaou said, "*To enjoy* food and *delight in* colors is nature. Benevolence is internal and not external; righteousness is external and not internal."

2. Mencius asked him, "What is the ground of your saying that benevolence is internal and righteousness external?" He replied, "There is a man older than I, and I give honor to his age. It is not that there is *first* in me a principle of such reverence to age. It is just as when there is a white man, and I consider him white;—according as he is so externally to me. On this account, I pronounce *of righteousness* that it is external."

3. Mencius said, "There is no difference between our pronouncing of a white horse to be white and our pronouncing a white man to be white. But is there no difference between the regard with which we acknowledge the age of an old horse and that with which we acknowledge the age of an old man? And what is it which is called righteousness?—the fact of a man's being old? or the fact of our giving honor to his age?"

4. *Kaou* said, "There is my younger brother;—I love him. But the younger brother of a man of Ts'in I do not love; that is, the feeling is determined by myself, and therefore I say that benevolence is internal. *On the other hand,* I give honor to an old man of Ts'oo, and I also give honor to an old man of my own *people*: that is, the feeling is determined by the age, and therefore I say that righteousness is external."

5. *Mencius* answered him, "Our enjoyment of meat roasted by a man of Ts'in does not differ from our enjoyment of meat roasted by ourselves. Thus,

what you insist on takes place also in the case of such things, and will you say likewise that our enjoyment of a roast is external?"

Chapter V. 1. The disciple Măng Ke asked Kung-too, saying, "On what ground is it said that righteousnes is internal?"

2. Kung-too replied, "We *therein* act out our feeling of respect, and therefore it is said to be internal."

3. *The other objected,* "Suppose the case of a villager older than your elder brother by one year, to which of them would you show the *greater* respect?" "To my brother," was the reply. "But for which of them would you first pour out wine *at a feast?*" "For the villager." *Măng Ke argued,* "Now your feeling of reverence rests on the one, and *now* the honor due to age is rendered to the other;—this is certainly determined by what is without, and does not proceed from within."

4. Kung-too was unable to reply, and told the conversation to Mencius. Mencius said, *"You should ask him,* 'Which do you respect most,—your uncle, or your younger brother?' He will answer, 'My uncle.' Ask him *again,* 'If your younger brother be personating a dead ancestor, to which do you show the greater respect,—*to him or to your uncle?*' He will say, 'To my younger brother.' You can go on, 'But where is the respect due, as you said, to your uncle?' He will reply to this, *'I show the respect to my younger brother,* because of the position which he occupies,' and you can likewise say, 'So *my respect to the villager is* because of the position which he occupies. Ordinarily, my respect is rendered to my elder brother; for a brief season, *on occasion,* it is rendered to the villager.'"

5. *Măng* Ke heard this and observed, "When respect is due to my uncle, I respect him, and when respect is due to my younger brother, I respect him; —the thing is certainly determined by what is without, and does not proceed from within." Kung-too replied, "In winter we drink things hot, in summer we drink things cold; and so, *on your principle,* eating and drinking also depend on what is external!"

Chapter VI. 1. The disciple Kung-too said, "The philosopher Kaou says, '*Man's* nature is neither good nor bad.'"

2. "Some say, '*Man's* nature may be made to practice good, and it may be made to practice evil,' and accordingly, under Wăn and Woo, the people loved what was good, *while* under Yew and Le, they loved what was cruel."

3. "Some say, 'The nature of some is good, and the nature of others is bad.' Hence it was that under such a sovereign as Yaou there yet appeared Seang; that with such a father as Koo-sow there yet appeared Shun; and that with Chow for their sovereign, and the son of their elder brother besides, there were found K'e, the viscount of Wei, and the prince Pe-kan."

4. "And now you say, 'The nature is good.' Then are all those wrong?"

5. Mencius said, "From the feelings proper to it, it is constituted for the practice of what is good. This is what I mean in saying that *the nature* is good.

6. "If men do what is not good, the blame cannot be imputed to their natural powers."

7. "The feeling of commiseration belongs to all men; so does that of shame and dislike; and that of reverence and respect; and that of approving and disapproving. The feeling of commiseration *implies the principle of* benevolence; that of shame and dislike, the principle of righteousness; that of reverence and respect, the principle of propriety; and that of approving and disapproving, the principle of knowledge. Benevolence, righteousness, propriety, and knowledge are not infused into us from without. We are certainly furnished with them. *And a different view* is simply from want of reflection. Hence it is said: 'Seek and you will find them. Neglect and you will lose them.' Men differ from one another in regard to them;—some as much again as others, some five times as much, and some to an incalculable amount:—it is because they cannot carry out fully their *natural* powers.

8. "It is said in the 'Book of Poetry':

'Heaven, in producing mankind,
Gave them their *various* faculties and relations with *their specific* laws.
These are the invariable rules of nature for all to hold,
And *all* love this admirable virtue.'

Confucius said, 'The marker of this ode knew indeed the principle *of our nature!*' We may thus see that every faculty and relation must have its law, and since there are invariable rules for all to hold, they consequently love this admirable virtue."

Chapter VII. 1. Mencius said, "In good years the children of the people are most of them good, while in bad years the most of them abandon themselves to evil. It is not owing to their natural powers conferred by Heaven that they are thus different. The abandonment is owing to the circumstances through which they allow their minds to be ensnared and drowned *in evil.*

2. "There now is barley.—Let it be sown and covered up; the ground being the same, and the time of sowing likewise the same, it grows rapidly up, and when the full time is come, it is all found to be ripe. Although there may be inequalities *of produce,* that is owing to the *difference of the* soil, as rich or poor, to the *unequal* nourishment afforded by the rains and dews, and to the different ways in which man has performed his business *in reference to it.*

3. "Thus all things which are the same in kind are like to one another; —why should we doubt in regard to man, as if he were a solitary exception to this? The sage and we are the same in kind.

4. "In accordance with this the scholar Lung said, 'If a man make hempen sandals without knowing *the size of people's* feet, *yet* I know that he will not make *them like* baskets.' Sandals are all like one another, because all men's feet are like one another.

5. "*So* with the mouth and flavors;—all mouths have the same relishes.

Yih-ya *only* apprehended before me what my mouth relishes. Suppose that his mouth in its relish for flavors differed from that of other men, as is the case with dogs or horses which are not the same in kind with us, why should all men be found following Yih-ya in their relishes? In the matter of tastes the whole empire models itself after Yih-ya; that is, the mouths of all men are like one another.

6. "And so also it is with the ear. In the matter of sounds, the whole empire models itself after the music master K'wang; that is, the ears of all men are like one another.

7. "And so also it is with the eye. In the case of Tsze-too, there is no man but would recognize that he was beautiful. Any one who would not recognize the beauty of Tsze-too must have no eyes.

8. "Therefore I say,—*Men's* mouths agree in having the same relishes; their ears agree in enjoying the same sounds; their eyes agree in recognizing the same beauty:—shall their minds alone be without that which they similarly approve? What is it, then, of which they similarly approve? It is, I say, the principles *of our nature,* and the determinations of righteousness. The sages only apprehended before me that of which my mind approves along with other men. Therefore the principles of our nature and the determinations of righteousness are agreeable to my mind, just as the flesh of grass and grain-fed animals is agreeable to my mouth."

Chapter VIII. 1. Mencius said, "The trees of the New Mountain were once beautiful. Being situated, however, in the borders of a large state, they were hewn down with axes and bills;—and could they retain their beauty? Still through the activity of the vegetative life day and night, and the nourishing influence of the rain and dew, they were not without buds and sprouts springing forth, but then came the cattle and goats and browsed upon them. To these things is owing the bare and stripped appearance *of the mountain,* which when people see, they think it was never finely wooded. But is this the nature of the mountain?

2. "And so *also of* what properly belongs to man;—shall it be said that the mind *of any man* was without benevolence and righteousness? The way in which a man loses his proper goodness of mind is like the way in which the trees are denuded by axes and bills. Hewn down day after day, can it—*the mind*—retain its beauty? But there is a development of its life day and night, and in the *calm* air of the morning, just between night and day, the mind feels in a degree those desires and aversions which are proper to humanity, but the feeling is not strong, and it is fettered and destroyed by what takes place during the day. This fettering taking place again and again; the restorative influence of the night is not sufficient to preserve *the proper goodness of the mind;* and when this proves insufficient for that purpose, the nature becomes not much different from that of the irrational animals, which when people see, they think that it never had those powers *which I assert.* But does this condition represent the feelings proper to humanity?

3. "Therefore, if it receive its proper nourishment, there is nothing which will not grow. If it lose its proper nourishment, there is nothing which will not decay away.

4. "Confucius said, 'Hold it fast, and it remains with you. Let it go, and you lose it. Its outgoing and incoming cannot be defined as to time or place.' It is the mind of which this is said!"

Chapter IX. 1. Mencius said, "It is not to be wondered at that the king is not wise!

2. "Suppose the case of the most easily growing thing in the world;—if you let it have one day's genial heat, and then expose it for ten days to cold, it will not be able to grow. It is but seldom that I have an audience of the king, and when I retire, there come *all* those who act upon him like the cold. Though I succeed in bringing out some buds *of goodness*, of what avail is it!

3. "Now chess playing is but a small art, but without his whole mind being given, and his will bent to it, a man cannot succeed at it. Chess Ts'ew is the best chess player in all the kingdom. Suppose that he is teaching two men to play.—The one gives to the subject his whole mind and bends to it all his will, doing nothing but listening to Chess Ts'ew. The other, although *he seems to be* listening to him, has his whole mind running on a swan which he thinks is approaching, and wishes to bend his bow, adjust the string to the arrow, and shoot it. Although he is learning along with the other, he does not come up to him. Why?—because his intelligence is not equal? Not so."

Chapter X. 1. Mencius said, "I like fish and I also like bear's paws. If I cannot have the two together, I will let the fish go, and take the bear's paws. So, I like life, and I also like righteousness. If I cannot keep the two together, I will let life go and choose righteousness.

2. "I like life indeed, but there is that which I like more than life, and therefore, I will not seek to possess it by any improper ways. I dislike death indeed, but there is that which I dislike more than death, and therefore there are occasions when I will not avoid danger.

3. "If among the things which man likes there were nothing which he liked more than life, why should he not use every means by which he could preserve it? If among the things which man dislikes there were nothing which he disliked more than death, why should he not do everything by which he could avoid danger?

4. "There are cases when men by a certain course might preserve life, and they do not employ it; when by certain things they might avoid danger, and they will not do them.

5. "Therefore, men have that which they like more than life, and that which they dislike more than death. They are not men of distinguished talents and virtue only who have this mental nature. All men have it; what belongs to such men is simply that they do not lose it.

6. "Here are a small basket of rice and a platter of soup, and the case is one in which the getting them will preserve life, and the want of them will be

death;—if they are offered with an insulting voice, even a tramper will not receive them, or if you first tread upon them, even a beggar will not stoop to take them.

7. *"And yet* a man will accept of ten thousand chung, without any consideration of propriety or righteousness. What can the ten thousand chung add to him? *When he takes them,* is it not that he may obtain beautiful mansions, that he may secure the services of wives and concubines, or that the poor and needy of his acquaintance may be helped by him?

8. "In the former case *the offered bounty* was not received, though it would have saved from death, and now *the emolument* is taken for the sake of beautiful mansions. *The bounty* that would have preserved from death was not received, and *the emolument* is taken to get the service of wives and concubines. *The bounty* that would have saved from death was not received, and *the emolument* is taken that one's poor and needy acquaintance may be helped by him. Was it then not possible likewise to decline this? This is a case of what is called—'Losing the proper nature of one's mind.'"

Chapter XI. 1. Mencius said, "Benevolence is man's mind, and righteousness is man's path.

2. "How lamentable is it to neglect the path and not pursue it, to lose this mind and not know to seek it again!

3. "When men's fowls and dogs are lost, they know to seek for them again, but they lose their mind, and do not know to seek for it.

4. "The great end of learning is nothing else but to seek for the lost mind."

Chapter XII. 1. Mencius said, "Here is a *man whose* fourth finger is bent, and cannot be stretched out straight. It is not painful, nor does it incommode his business, and yet if there be any one who can make it straight, he will not think the way from Ts'in to Ts'oo far *to go to him;*—because his finger is not like the finger of other people.

2. "When a man's finger is not like those of other people, he knows to feel dissatisfied, but if his mind be not like that of other people, he does not know to feel dissatisfaction. This is called—'Ignorance of the relative *importance of things.'"*

Chapter XIII. Mencius said, "Anybody who wishes to cultivate the *t'ung* or the *tsze,* which may be grasped with both hands, *perhaps* with one, knows by what means to nourish them. In the case of their own persons, men do not know by what means to nourish them. Is it to be supposed that their regard of their own persons is inferior to their regard for a *t'ung* or a *tsze*? Their want of reflection is extreme."

Chapter XIV. 1. Mencius said, "There is no part of himself which a man does not love, and as he loves all, so he must nourish all. There is not an inch of skin which he does not love, and so there is not an inch of skin which he will not nourish. For examining whether *his way of nourishing* be good or not, what other rule is there but this, that he determine by *reflecting on* himself where it should be applied?

2. "Some parts of the body are noble, and some ignoble; some great, and some small. The great must not be injured for the small, nor the noble for the ignoble. He who nourishes the little belonging to him is a little man, and he who nourishes the great is a great man.

3. "Here is a plantation keeper, who neglect his *woo* and *kea*, and cultivates his sour wild date trees;—he is a poor plantation keeper.

4. "He who nourishes one of his fingers, neglecting his shoulders or his back, without knowing *that he is doing so*, is a man *who resembles* a hurried wolf.

5. "A man who *only* eats and drinks is counted mean by others;—because he nourishes what is little to the neglect of what is great.

6. "If a man, *fond of his* eating and drinking, were not to neglect *what is of more importance,* how should his mouth and belly be considered as no more than an inch of skin?"

Chapter XV. 1. The disciple Kung-too said, "All are equally men, not some are great men, and some are little men;—how is this?" Mencius replied, "Those who follow that part of themselves which is great are great men; those who follow that part which is little are little men."

2. Kung-too pursued, "All are equally men, but some follow that part of themselves which is great, and some follow that part which is little;—how is this?" Mencius answered, "The senses of hearing and seeing do not think, and are obscured by *external* things. When one thing comes into contact with another, as a matter of course it leads it away. To the mind belongs the office of thinking. By thinking, it gets *the right view of things;* by neglecting to think, it fails to do this. These—*the senses and the mind*—are what Heaven has given to us. Let a man first stand fast in *the supremacy of* the nobler part of his constitution, and the inferior part will not be able to take it from him. It is simply this which makes the great man."

Chapter XVI. 1. Mencius said, "There is a nobility of Heaven, and there is a nobility of man. Benevolence, righteousness, self-consecration, and fidelity, with unwearied joy in *these* virtues;—these constitute the nobility of Heaven. To be a *kung,* a *k'ing,* or a *ta-foo;*—this constitutes the nobility of man.

2. "The mean of antiquity cultivated their nobility of Heaven, and the nobility of man came to them in its train.

3. "The men of the present day cultivate their nobility of Heaven in order to seek for the nobility of man, and when they have obtained that, they throw away the other:—their delusion is extreme. The issue is simply this that they must lose *that nobility of man* as well."

Chapter XVII. 1. Mencius said, "To desire to be honored is the common mind of men. And all men have in themselves that which is *truly* honorable. Only they do not think of it.

2. "The honor which men confer is not good honor. Those whom Chaou the Great ennobles he can make mean *again.*

3. "It is said in the 'Book of Poetry,'

'He has filled us with his wine,
He has satiated us with his goodness.'

'*Satiated us with his goodness*,' that is, satiated us with benevolence and right-eousness, and he who is so, consequently, does not wish for the fat meat and fine millet of men. A good reputation and far-reaching praise fall to him, and he does not desire the elegant embroidered garments of men."

Chapter XVIII. 1. Mencius said, "Benevolence subdues its opposite just as water subdues fire. Those, however, who nowadays practice benevolence *do it* as if with one cup of water they could save a whole wagonload of fuel which was on fire, and when the flames were not extinguished, were to say that water cannot subdue fire. This conduct, moreover, greatly encourages those who are not benevolent.

2. "The final issue will simply be this—the loss *of that small amount of benevolence*."

Chapter XIX. Mencius said, "Of all seeds the best are the five kinds of grain, yet if they be not ripe, they are not equal to the *t'e* or the *pae*. So the value of benevolence depends entirely on its being brought to maturity."

Chapter XX. 1. Mencius said, "E, in teaching men to shoot, made it a rule to draw the bow to the full, and his pupils also did the same.

2. "A master workman, in teaching others, uses the compass and square, and his pupils do the same."

21

CONCERNING HEAVEN
Hsun Tzu

Hsün Tzu (ca. 300–237 B.C.) was the most eminent scholar of his generation and remained the most influential interpreter of the Confucian tradition until the end of the Han dynasty (A.D. 220). Like most Chinese scholars he aspired to political office and did hold several minor and ceremonial posts. As a logician, a meta-physician, and a political philosopher, however, he was one of the ablest thinkers in Chinese history. After the Han, the more ideal-

Hsün Tzu, *Hsüntze Works*, Homer Dubs, trans. (London: Arthur Probsthain, 1928), pp. 173–185. Reprinted from *Hsüntze Works*, by permission of Arthur Probsthain.

istic and democratic views of Mencius became the standard of
Confucian orthodoxy and the thought of Hsün Tzu was comparatively neglected until the present century, when some Chinese
intellectuals have praised his naturalistic interpretation of the
world and his unsentimental attitude toward political institutions.

Hsün Tzu rejected the optimistic view that man is innately
good. Man's original nature, he thought, is greedy, violent, dishonest, malicious, and self-seeking. Goodness is acquired only
through rigorous training by strong rulers, teachers, and laws. He
ridiculed the notion that natural occurrences were signs of Heav-
en's approval or disapproval. Nature operates with a mechanical
order and the welfare of the people depends entirely upon the
wisdom and strength of the government. Still, he favored the retention of traditional ritual for its social and emotional value. He
particularly exalted the study of the classics as a means of redi-
recting men's desires from material things to moral principles.
Distrusting the average man's intellectual and moral accomplishments, he emphasized the authority of the sages of the past and
of the hereditary ruler. He did not favor totalitarianism, but some
of his disciples, without departing too far from his political views,
became apologists for the totalitarian regime of Ch'in that gained
control of China in 221 B.C.

The book the Hsün Tzu is supposed to have been written
by Hsün Tzu himself, but some of it was probably written by his
disciples and the last chapters may have been added during the
Han period (206 B.C.–A.D. 220). Chapter seventeen, "On
Heaven," is given in full in Dubs's translation.

Heaven has a constant regularity of action. Yao was not necessary to
support its order, nor could Ch'ie destroy its order. Respond to it in governing a
country and success will result; follow it in misgovernment, and calamity will result. If the fundamentals for life are plentiful and are economically used, then
Heaven cannot impoverish the country; if the essentials of life are sufficient
and the activities of man in preparing them are well timed, then Heaven cannot afflict the country. If the right Way of Life (Tao) is cultivated and not
opposed, then Heaven cannot send misfortune; flood or drought cannot cause
a famine; extreme cold or heat cannot cause suffering; supernatural powers
cannot cause calamity. But if the fundamentals for life are neglected and used
extravagantly, then Heaven cannot cause the country to be rich; if the essentials of life are scarce and the activities of men in preparing them are inoppor-
tune, then Heaven cannot make that country prosperous. If a person rebels
against the right Way of life (Tao), and acts unseemly, then Heaven cannot
make him fortunate. Therefore even if flood or drought do not come, there will
be famine; even if cold or heat do not approach, there will be suffering; even
if supernatural powers do not act, there will be calamity. Observing the proper
time for action and a good government and prosperity are contemporaneous;

calamities and good government are not contemporaneous. One ought not to grumble at Heaven that things happen according to its Way (Tao). Hence to know the Way of Heaven is man's duty; he who does this is a great Sage. To produce without acting and to obtain without seeking, this is what is meant by the office of Heaven. Therefore although the Way of Heaven is deep, this man will not put deep thought on it; although it is great, he will not use his ability for its investigation; although it is mysterious, he will not scrutinize it —this is what is meant by refraining from contesting with Heaven. Heaven has its seasons, Earth has its wealth, Man has his government. The foregoing is what is meant by being able to form a triad with Heaven and Earth. To give up that wherewith one can form such a triad and to desire to know those with whom he forms a triad is to be led into error.

The fixed stars make their round; the sun and moon alternately shine; the four seasons come in succession; the Yin and Yang go through their great mutations; the wind and rain widely affect things; all things acquire their germinating principle, and are brought into existence; each gets its nourishing principle and develops to its completed state. We do not see the cause of these occurrences, but we do see their effects—this is what is meant by the influence of the spirits. The results of all these changes are known, but we do not know the invisible source—this is, what is meant by the work of Heaven. Only the Sage does not seek to know Heaven. When the office of Heaven has been established, and the work of Heaven has been perfected, the human body is prepared and the human spirit is born; love, hatred, joy, anger, sorrow, and pleasure are embodied—these are what are meant by the natural (T'ien) emotions. The ear, the eye, the nose, the mouth, the body, and the limbs, each receive stimuli and cannot be interchanged—these are what are meant by the natural (T'ien) senses. The heart is established in the central cavity to control the five senses—this is what is meant by the natural (T'ien) ruler.

To use what is not of one's kind to nourish one's kind—this is what is meant by the natural (T'ien) nourishing. To act according to one's station is what is called happiness; to act contrary to one's station is called calamity— this is what is meant by the natural (T'ien) government. To darken one's natural (T'ien) ruler, to confuse the natural (T'ien) senses, to throw away the natural (T'ien) nourishing, to act contrary to the natural (T'ien) govern- ment, to violate the natural (T'ien) emotions so as to destroy the work of Nature (T'ien)—this is what is called the great calamity. The Sage purifies his natural (T'ien) ruler, rectifies his natural (T'ien) senses, makes the nat- ural (T'ien) nourishment sufficient, obeys the natural (T'ien) government, nourishes his natural (T'ien) emotions, in order to develop to perfection his natural usefulness. When he acts thus, he knows what he can do and what he cannot do. Then heaven and earth fulfil their proper function, and he can employ the material world. When his actions are completely governed, the nourishment for the people is completely obtained, and in his life he injures none—this is what is meant by knowing Heaven (T'ien). For great skill consists in knowing how to do a thing without striving; and great wisdom consists in not needing to reflect about things. What is known about Heaven is that we see its phenomena have their regular sequences; what is known about Earth is that it is seen that it meets the conditions of life and can produce; what is known about the four seasons is that it is seen that they have a definite number, and can be used to serve humanity; what is known about the *Yin* and *Yang* is that it is seen that they interact and can be used in ruling a country. If the man who has a responsible post attends to what belongs to Nature (*T'ien*), the people of themselves will keep to the right Way of life (*Tao*).

Are good and bad government, prosperity and calamity, from Heaven (*T'ien*)? I reply: The sun, the moon, the heavenly bodies, the auspicious times, the astrological calculations of the calendar were the same in the time of Yu as in that of Ch'ie. In the time of Yu there was good government and prosperity; in the time of Ch'ie there was ill-government and calamity; prosperity and calamity do not come from Heaven.

Do they come from the seasons? I answer: The myriad plants spring up, flourish, and grow in spring and summer; they are nourished, the grain develops, is reaped and gathered in in the fall and winter. In this also the times of Yu and Ch'ie were the same. Yu had prosperity and Ch'ie had disaster; prosperity and disaster do not come from the seasons.

Do they come from the Earth? I answer: When a plant or a state obtains a place on the earth, it lives; when its place on the earth is lost, it dies; in this too Yu and Ch'ie were the same. Yu had prosperity, Ch'ie had misfortune. Prosperity and misfortune, good and bad government, are not from the Earth.

The ode says:—

> "Heaven made the high hill:
>   King T'ai brought it under cultivation;
> He began the work:
>   King Wen tranquillized it"

this is the answer to the problem.

Nature (*T'ien*) does not suspend the winter because men dislike cold; the Earth does not suspend its spaciousness because men dislike distances; the superior man does not suspend his good actions because of the railings of little-minded men.

Heaven (*T'ien*) has a constant way of action; Earth has a constant numerical size; the superior man has a constant decorous demeanour. The superior man talks of what is constant with him, but the little-minded man counts his accomplishments. The ode says:—

> "If a person acts according to the rules of proper conduct
> (*Li*) and justice (*Yi*),
>   And does not overpass their bounds,
>   Why should he be anxious about people's talk?"—

this expresses what I mean.

The King of Ts'u has a thousand chariots following him—this is not wisdom. The superior man eats pulse and drinks water—this is not foolishness. It is what is fitting to the circumstances.

If a person's will is cultivated, his virtuous acts are many, his knowledge and thoughts are clear, then his reputation will spring forth in the present, and be recorded with the worthies of ancient times. It springs forth from what is within one's power. Therefore the superior man is anxious about what is within his power, and does not seek for what is from Heaven. The little-minded man does not concern himself with what is within his power, and desires what comes from Heaven. The superior man is anxious about what is within his power, and does not seek for what comes from Heaven—this causes daily progress. The little-minded man does not concern himself with what is within his power and seeks for what comes from Heaven—this causes daily retrogression. Therefore the reason why the superior man progresses daily and the reason why the little-minded man retrogresses daily is the same. The reason for the difference between the superior man and the little-minded man consists in what we have just said.

When stars fall or the sacred tree groans, the people of the whole state are afraid. We ask, "Why is it?" I answer: There is no reason. This is due to a modification of Heaven and Earth, to the mutation of the *Yin* and *Yang*. These are rare events. We may marvel at them, but we should not fear them. For there is no age that has not experienced eclipses of the sun and moon, unseasonable rain or wind, or strange stars seen in groups. If the ruler is illustrious and the government tranquil, although these events should all come together in one age, it would do no harm. If the ruler is unintelligent and his government is bent on evil, although not one of these strange events should occur, their non-occurrence would be without avail to prevent his fall. Hence the falling of stars and the groaning of the sacred tree are from the modification of Heaven and Earth, the mutation of the *Yin* and *Yang*. These are rare events. We may marvel at them, but we should not fear them. When human ominous signs come, then we should be really afraid.

What is a human ominous sign? Using a poor plough and thereby injuring the grain; the losing of the effect of the fertilizer in hoeing and weeding; the losing of the allegiance of the people by a government bent on evil; when the fields are uncultivated and the harvest is bad; when the price of grain is high and the people are starving; when there are dead bodies on the roads—these are what I mean by human ominous signs. When the government is not wise; when appointments to office and degradations from office are not opportune; when the fundamental matters are not attended to—these are what I mean by human ominous signs. When the rules of proper conduct (*Li*) and justice (*Yi*) are not cultivated; when the inhabitants of the inner and outer apartments do not keep apart; when men and women are immoral; when parents and children distrust each other; when the ruler and ruled are at cross purposes and separate; when distress from robbers becomes common

—these are what I mean by human ominous signs. These ominous signs are born of disorder. When all three kinds of ominous signs come together, the country cannot be peaceful. To speak of things in this way, is to come very much nearer the truth; these misfortunes are the most grievous ones. It is said: The *History* does not speak of supernatural events. To set aside discussions and investigations which are not pressing, and not to engage in them—this is the right thing for princes and their vassals to do. The love of father and son, the proprieties separating husband and wife, should be daily cultivated like the cutting and polishing of a precious stone, and they will not be lost.

If people pray for rain and get rain, why is that? I answer: There is no reason for it. If people do not pray for rain, it will nevertheless rain. When people save the sun or moon from being eaten, or when they pray for rain in a drought, or when they decide an important affair only after divination—this is not because they think in this way they will get what they seek, but only to gloss over the matter. Hence the prince thinks it is glossing over the matter, but the people think it supernatural. He who thinks it is glossing over the matter is fortunate; he who thinks it is supernatural is unfortunate.

Of the things that are in heaven there are none brighter than the sun and moon; of the things that are on earth, there are none brighter than water and fire; of goods there are none brighter than pearls and jade; of the things that are human there are none brighter than the rules of proper conduct (*Li*) and justice (*Yi*). For if the sun and moon were not high, their brightness would not be great; if water and fire are not gathered together, their sheen would not be great; if pearls and jade were not gleaming on the outside, kings and nobles would not think them precious; when the observance of proper conduct (*Li*) and justice (*Yi*) are not added to the wealth of a country, its merit and fame do not shine. Hence the destiny of men is from Heaven; the destiny of a country is from observing the rules of proper conduct (*Li*). The prince who exalts the rules of proper conduct (*Li*) and gives office to the worthy can rule as king; he who makes law important and loves the people can rule as lord protector; he who loves his own profit and multiplies deceit is in dangerous circumstances; he who strives for power and seeks to overturn others, he whose ways are dark and bent on evil will be overthrown.

How can exalting Heaven and wishing for its gifts be as good as heaping up wealth and using it advantageously? How can obeying Heaven and praising it be as good as adapting oneself to the appointments of Heaven and using them? How can hoping for the proper time and waiting for it be as good as seizing the opportunity and acting? How can relying on things increasing of themselves be as good as putting forth one's energy and developing things? How can thinking of things and comparing them be as good as looking after things and not losing them? How can wishing that things may come to pass be as good as taking what one has and bringing things to pass? Therefore if a person neglects what men can do and seeks for what Heaven does, he fails to understand the nature of things.

The principles of proper conduct have remained unchanged through the time of all the Kings. They are sufficient to permeate the Way of life (*Tao*). One king fell and another rose; that which conformed to these principles permeated them all. When these principles permeate a government, there can be no misgovernment or disorder. He who does not know how to make them permeate his actions does not know how to alter his actions to suit changing conditions. When they permeate the whole of a person's conduct, he can never fail. Ill-government and calamity is born of their lack; good government comes from exhausting their minutiæ. For when that which the Way of life (*Tao*) stresses is the golden mean, it can be followed; when it is an extreme, it should not be done; when it is evil, a person is greatly misled. One who walks in the water tests its depth. If he does not test it rightly, then he is likely to fall into the water. The one who governs the people tests their virtue. If he does not test rightly there is likely to be disorder. What he tests by is the rules of proper conduct (*Li*). If there is no proper conduct (*Li*) the age is dark. When the age is dark there will be great disorder. For the right Way of life (*Tao*) is never unclear. Conduct relating to what is without and within the family circle is tested differently. Conduct which refers to these inner and outer circles has its uniform principles. Thus we can remove the causes which would make the people sink into trouble.

All things are one section of the Way (*Tao*); one thing is a section of all things; the stupid man sees only one section of one thing, and thinks that he knows the Way (*Tao*); but he has no such knowledge. Shentze has insight about what is behind but none about what is before. Laotze has insight about what is bent, but not about what is straight. Micius has insight about what is universal, but not about the individual. Sungtze has insight about the few, but not about the many. If one considers what is behind, but not what is before, then the common people cannot enter into the gate of progress. If one considers the bent but not the straight, then the noble and base are not distinguished. If one considers the universal, but not the particular, then the government cannot operate. If one considers the few but not the many, then the common people will not progress. The *History* says:—

> "Without any selfish likings,
>   Reverence the Way (*Tao*) of the Kings;
> Without any selfish dislikes
>   Reverence the path of the Kings"—

this expresses what I mean.

22

THE GREAT LEARNING

For the last seven centuries the Great Learning *has been regarded as an outline summary of the social and political teachings of the Confucian tradition. The great Neo-Confucianist Chu Hsi (A.D. 1130–1200) assumed that the first seven verses were the words of Confucius preserved by his disciple Tseng Tzu, while the rest of the book was Tseng's explanation of these verses as recorded by his disciples. Actually it is not known by whom or when the book was written. It is often ascribed to the Third Century B.C., and scholars have disagreed on the extent to which the author was influenced by Mencius and Hsün Tzu. The two main schools of Neo-Confucianism debated for centuries whether the book taught the investigation of things or the sincerity of the will as the first principle of the Confucian way. The book presents three ideals: to illustrate illustrious virtue, to renovate the people, and to rest in the highest excellence, along with eight steps toward these ideals: investigation of things, extension of knowledge, sincerity in thought, rectification of the heart, cultivation of the personal life, regulation of the family, ordering of the state, and making the whole kingdom peaceful and happy.*

The Great Learning *was originally Chapter Forty-two of the* Book of Rites, *but during the Sung dynasty (A.D. 960–1279) it came to be treated as a separate work. Chu Hsi rearranged the verses to strengthen his interpretation and added a brief commentary. This version has been the most influential and is here printed in Legge's translation.*

My master, the philosopher Ch'ǎng, says: "The Great Learning is a Book transmitted by the Confucian School, and forms the gate by which first learners enter into virtue. That we can now perceive the order in which the ancients pursued their learning is solely owing to the preservation of this work, the Analects and Mencius coming after it. Learners must commence their course with this, and then it may be hoped they will be kept from error."

The Great Learning, James Legge, trans. (Oxford, England: Clarendon Press, 1893), pp. 355–381. Reprinted from *The Chinese Classics*, vol. 1, by James Legge.

THE TEXT OF CONFUCIUS

1. What the Great Learning teaches, is—to illustrate illustrious virtue; to renovate the people; and to rest in the highest excellence.

2. The point where to rest being known, the object of pursuit is then determined; and, that being determined, a calm unperturbedness may be attained to. To that calmness there will succeed a tranquil repose. In that repose there may be careful deliberation, and that deliberation will be followed by the attainment *of the desired end.*

3. Things have their root and their branches. Affairs have their end and their beginning. To know what is first and what is last will lead near to what is taught *in the Great Learning.*

4. The ancients who wished to illustrate illustrious virtue throughout the kingdom, first ordered well their own states. Wishing to order well their states, they first regulated their families. Wishing to regulate their families, they first cultivated their persons. Wishing to cultivate their persons, they first rectified their hearts. Wishing to rectify their hearts, they first sought to be sincere in their thoughts. Wishing to be sincere in their thoughts, they first extended to the utmost their knowledge. Such extension of knowledge lay in the investigation of things.

5. Things being investigated, knowledge became complete. Their knowledge being complete, their thoughts were sincere. Their thoughts being sincere, their hearts were then rectified. Their hearts being rectified, their persons were cultivated. Their persons being cultivated, their families were regulated. Their families being regulated, their states were rightly governed. Their states being rightly governed, the whole kingdom was made tranquil and happy.

6. From the Son of Heaven down to the mass of the people, all must consider the cultivation of the person the root of *everything besides.*

7. It cannot be, when the root is neglected, that what should spring from it will be well ordered. It never has been the case that what was of great importance has been slightly cared for, and, at the same time, that what was of slight importance has been greatly cared for.

The preceding chapter of classical text is in the words of Confucius, handed down by the philosopher Tsăng. The ten chapters of explanation which follow contain the views of Tsăng, and were recorded by his disciples. In the old copies of the work, there appeared considerable confusion in these, from the disarrangement of the tablets. But now, availing myself of the decisions of the philosopher Ch'ăng, and having examined anew the classical text, I have arranged it in order, as follows:

COMMENTARY OF THE PHILOSOPHER TSĂNG

Chapter I. 1. In the Announcement to K'ang, it is said, "He was able to make his virtue illustrious."

2. In the Tâi Chiâ, it is said, "He contemplated and studied the illustrious decrees of Heaven."

3. In the Canon of the emperor (Yâo), it is said, "He was able to make illustrious his lofty virtue."

4. These *passages* all *show how those sovereigns* made themselves illustrious.

The above first chapter of commentary explains the illustration of illustrious virtue.

Chapter II. 1. On the bathing tub of T'ang, the following words were engraved: "If you can one day renovate yourself, do so from day to day. Yea, let there be daily renovation."

2. In the Announcement to K'ang, it is said, "To stir up the new people."

3. In the Book of Poetry, it is said, "Although Châu was an ancient state, the ordinance which lighted on it was new."

4. Therefore, the superior man in everything uses his utmost endeavors.

The above second chapter of commentary explains the renovating of the people.

Chapter III. 1. In the Book of Poetry, it is said, "The royal domain of a thousand li is where the people rest."

2. In the Book of Poetry, it is said, "The twittering yellow bird rests on a corner of the mound." The Master said, "When it rests, it knows where to rest. Is it possible that a man should not be equal to this bird?"

3. In the Book of Poetry, it is said, "Profound was King Wǎn. With how bright and unceasing a feeling of reverence did he regard his resting places!" As a sovereign, he rested in benevolence. As a minister, he rested in reverence. As a son, he rested in filial pity. As a father, he rested in kindness. In communication with his subjects, he rested in good faith.

4. In the Book of Poetry, it is said, "Look at that winding course of the Ch'î, with the green bamboos so luxuriant! Here is our elegant and accomplished prince! As we cut and then file; as we chisel and then grind: *so has he cultivated himself.* How grave is he and dignified! How majestic and distinguished! Our elegant and accomplished prince never can be forgotten." *That expression*—"As we cut and then file," indicates the work of learning. "As we chisel and then grind," indicates that of self-culture. "How grave is he and dignified!" indicates the feeling of cautious reverence. "How commanding and distinguished!" indicates an awe-inspiring deportment. "Our elegant and accomplished prince never can be forgotten," indicates how, when virtue is complete and excellence extreme, the people cannot forget them.

5. In the Book of Poetry, it is said, "Ah! the former kings are not forgotten." *Future* princes deem worthy what they deemed worthy, and love what

they loved. The common people delight in what delighted them, and are benefited by their beneficial arrangements. It is on this account that the former kings, after they have quit the world, are not forgotten.

The above third chapter of commentary explains resting in the highest excellence.

Chapter IV. The Master said, "In hearing litigations, I am like any other body. What is necessary to cause the people to have no litigations?" *So,* those who are devoid of principle find it impossible to carry out their speeches, and a great awe would be struck into men's minds;—this is called knowing the root.

The above fourth chapter of commentary explains the root and the issue.

Chapter V. 1. This is called knowing the root.
2. This is called the perfecting of knowledge.

The above fifth chapter of the commentary explained the meaning of "investigating things and carrying knowledge to the utmost extent," but it is now lost. I have ventured to take the views of the scholar Ch'ăng to supply it, as follows: The meaning of the expression, "The perfecting of knowledge depends on the investigation of things," is this:—If we wish to carry our knowledge to the utmost, we must investigate the principles of all things we come into contact with, for the intelligent mind of man is certainly formed to know, and there is not a single thing in which its principles do not inhere. But so long as all principles are not investigated, man's knowledge is incomplete. On this account, the Learning for Adults, at the outset of its lessons, instructs the learner, in regard to all things in the world, to proceed from what knowledge he has of their principles, and pursue his investigation of them, till he reaches the extreme point. After exerting himself in this way for a long time, he will suddenly find himself possessed of a wide and far-reaching penetration. Then, the qualities of all things, whether external or internal, the subtle or the coarse, will all be apprehended, and the mind, in its entire substance and its relation to things, will be perfectly intelligent. This is called the investigation of things. This is called the perfection of knowledge.

Chapter VI. 1. What is meant by "making the thoughts sincere," is the allowing no self-deception, as *when* we hate a bad smell, and as *when* we love what is beautiful. This is called self-enjoyment. Therefore, the superior man must be watchful over himself when he is alone.
2. There is no evil to which the mean man, dwelling retired, will not proceed, but when he sees a superior man, he instantly tries to disguise himself, concealing his evil, and displaying what is good. The other beholds him, as if he saw his heart and reins;—of what use *is his disguise?* This is an

instance of the saying—" What truly is within will be manifested without."
Therefore, the superior man must be watchful over himself when he is alone.

3. The disciple Tsăng said, "What ten eyes behold, what ten hands
point to, is to be regarded with reverence!"

4. Riches adorn a house, and virtue adorns the person. The mind is
expanded, and the body is at ease. Therefore, the superior man must make
his thoughts sincere.

The above sixth chapter of commentary explains the thoughts sincere.

Chapter VII. 1. What is meant by, "The cultivation of the person
depends on rectifying the mind," *may be thus illustrated:*—If a man be under
the influence of passion, he will be incorrect in his conduct. He will be the
same, if he is under the influence of terror, or under the influence of fond
regard, or under that of sorrow and distress.

2. When the mind is not present, we look and do not see; we hear and
do not understand; we eat and do not know the taste of what we eat.

3. This is what is meant by saying that the cultivation of the person
depends on the rectifying of the mind.

*The above seventh chapter of commentary explains rectifying the mind
and cultivating the person.*

Chapter VIII. 1. What is meant by "The regulation of one's family
depends on the cultivation of his person," is this:—Men are partial where they
feel affection and love; partial where they despise and dislike; partial where
they stand in awe and reverence; partial where they feel sorrow and compassion; partial where they are arrogant and rude. Thus it is that there are few
men in the world who love and at the same time know the bad qualities of
the object of their love, or who hate and yet know the excellences of *the object
of their hatred.*

2. Hence it is said, in the common adage, "A man does not know the
wickedness of his son; he does not know the richness of his growing corn."

3. This is what is meant by saying that if the person be not cultivated,
a man cannot regulate his family.

*The above eighth chapter of commentary explains cultivating the person
and regulating the family.*

Chapter IX. 1. What is meant by "In order rightly to govern the state,
it is necessary first to regulate the family," is this:—It is not possible for one
to teach others, while he cannot teach his own family. Therefore, the ruler,
without going beyond his family, completes the lessons for the state. There is
filial piety:—therewith the sovereign should be served. There is fraternal sub-

mission:—therewith elders and superiors should be served. There is kindness:
—therewith the multitude should be treated.

2. In the Announcement to K'ang, it is said, "*Act* as if you were watching over an infant." If (*a mother*) is really anxious about it, though she may
not hit *exactly the wants of her infant,* she will not be far from doing so.
There never has been *a girl* who learned to bring up a child, that she might
afterwards marry.

3. From the loving *example* of one family a whole state becomes loving,
and from its courtesies the whole state become courteous, while, from the
ambition and perverseness of the One man, the whole state may be led to
rebellious disorder;—such is the nature of the influence. This verifies the saying, "Affairs may be ruined by a single sentence; a kingdom may be settled by
its One man."

4. Yâo and Shun led on the kingdom with benevolence, and the people
followed them. Chieh and Châu led on the kingdom with violence, and the
people followed them. The orders which these issued were contrary to the
practices which they loved, and so the people did not follow them. On this
account, the ruler must himself be possessed of the *good* qualities, and then
he may require them in the people. He must not have *the bad qualities* in
himself, and then he may require that they shall not be in the people. Never
has there been a man, who, not having reference to his own character and
wishes in dealing with others, was able effectually to instruct them.

5. Thus we see how the government of the state depends on the regulation of the family.

6. In the Book of Poetry, it is said, "That peach tree, so delicate and
elegant! How luxuriant is its foliage! This girl is going to her husband's house.
She will rightly order her household." Let the household be rightly ordered,
and then the people of the state may be taught.

7. In the Book of Poetry, it is said, "They can discharge their duties to
their elder brothers. They can discharge their duties to their younger brothers." Let the ruler discharge his duties to his elder and younger brothers, and
then he may teach the people of the state.

8. In the Book of Poetry, it is said, "In his deportment there is nothing
wrong; he rectifies all the people of the state." Yes; when the ruler, as a father,
a son, and a brother, is a model, then the people imitate him.

9. This is what is meant by saying, "The government of his kingdom
depends on his regulation of the family."

*The above ninth chapter of commentary explains regulating the family
and governing the kingdom.*

Chapter X. 1. What is meant by "The making the whole kingdom
peaceful and happy depends on the government of his state," is this:—When
the sovereign behaves to his aged, as the aged should be behaved to, the people

become filial; when the sovereign behaves to his elders, as the elders should be behaved to, the people learn brotherly submission; when the sovereign treats compassionately the young and helpless, the people do the same. Thus the ruler has a principle with which, as with a measuring square, he may regulate his conduct.

2. What a man dislikes in his superiors, let him not display in the treatment of his inferiors; what he dislikes in inferiors, let him not display in the service of his superiors; what he hates in those who are before him, let him not therewith precede those who are behind him; what he hates in those who are behind him, let him not therewith follow those who are before him; what he hates to receive on the right, let him not bestow on the left; what he hates to receive on the left, let him not bestow on the right:—this is what is called "The principle with which, as with a measuring square, to regulate one's conduct."

3. In the Book of Poetry, it is said, "How much to be rejoiced in are these princes, the parents of the people!" When *a prince* loves what the people love, and hates what the people hate, then is he what is called the parent of the people.

4. In the Book of Poetry, it is said, "Lofty is that southern hill, with its rugged masses of rocks! Greatly distinguished are you, O *grand*-teacher Yin, the people all look up to you." Rulers of states may not neglect to be careful. If they deviate *to a mean selfishness*, they will be a disgrace in the kingdom.

5. In the Book of Poetry, it is said, "Before the sovereigns of the Yin *dynasty* had lost the *hearts of the* people, they could appear before God. Take warning from *the house of* Yin. The great decree is not easily preserved." This shows that, by gaining the people, the kingdom is gained, and, by losing the people, the kingdom is lost.

6. On this account, the ruler will first take pains about *his own* virtue. Possessing virtue will give him the people. Possessing the people will give him the territory. Possessing the territory will give him its wealth. Possessing the wealth, he will have resources for expenditure.

7. Virtue is the root; wealth is the result.

8. If he make the root his secondary object, and the result his primary, he will *only* wrangle with his people, and teach them rapine.

9. Hence, the accumulation of wealth is the way to scatter the people; and the letting it be scattered among them is the way to collect the people.

10. And hence, the ruler's words going forth contrary to right, will come back to him in the same way, and wealth, gotten by improper ways, will take its departure by the same.

11. In the Announcement to K'ang, it is said, "The decree indeed may not always rest on *us;*" that is, goodness obtains the decree, and the want of goodness loses it.

12. In the Book of Ch'û, it is said, "The kingdom of Ch'û does not consider that to be valuable. It values, *instead,* its good men."

13. *Duke Wăn's* uncle, Fan, said, "Our fugitive does not account that to be precious. What he considers precious is the affection due to his parent."

14. In the Declaration *of the duke of* Ch'in, it is said, "Let me have but one minister, plain and sincere, not *pretending to* other abilities, but with a simple, upright, mind; and possessed of generosity, *regarding* the talents of others as if he himself possessed them, and, where he finds accomplished and perspicacious men, loving them in his heart more than his mouth expresses, and really showing himself able to bear them *and employ them:*—such a minister will be able to preserve my sons and grandsons and black-haired people, and benefits likewise to the kingdom may well be looked for from him. But if *it be his character,* when he finds men of ability, to be jealous and hate them; and, when he finds accomplished and perspicacious men, to oppose them and not allow their advancement, showing himself really not able to bear them:—such a minister will not be able to protect my sons and grandsons and black-haired people; and may he not also be pronounced dangerous *to the state?"*

15. It is only the truly virtuous man who can send away such a man and banish him, driving him out among the barbarous tribes around, determined not to dwell along with him in the Middle Kingdom. This is in accordance with the saying, "It is only the truly virtuous man who can love or who can hate others."

16. To see men of worth and not be able to raise them to office; to raise them to office, but not to do so quickly:—this is disrespectful. To see bad men and not be able to remove them; to remove them, but not to do so to a distance:—this is weakness.

17. To love those whom men hate, and to hate those whom men love;—this is to outrage the natural feeling of men. Calamities cannot fail to come down on him who does so.

18. Thus *we see that* the sovereign has a great course *to pursue.* He must show entire self-devotion and sincerity to attain it, and by pride and extravagance he will fail of it.

19. There is a great course *also* for the production of wealth. Let the producers be many and the consumers few. Let there be activity in the production, and economy in the expenditure. Then the wealth will always be sufficient.

20. The virtuous *ruler,* by means of his wealth, makes himself more distinguished. The vicious ruler accumulates wealth, at the expense of his life.

21. Never has there been a case of the sovereign loving benevolence, and the people not loving righteousness. Never has there been a case where the people have loved righteousness, and the affairs of the sovereign have not been carried to completion. And never has there been a case where the wealth in such a state, collected in the treasuries and arsenals, did not continue in the sovereign's possession.

22. The officer Măng Hsien said, "He who keeps horses and a carriage does not look after fowls and pigs. The family which keeps its stores of ice

does not rear cattle or sheep. So, the house which possesses a hundred chariots should not keep a minister to look out for imposts that he may lay them on the people. Than to have such a minister, it were better for that house to have one who should rob it *of its revenues.*" This is in accordance with the saying: —"In a state, *pecuniary* gain is not to be considered to be prosperity, but its prosperity *will* be found in righteousness."

23. When he who presides over a state or a family makes his revenues his chief business, he must be under the influence of some small, mean man. He may consider this man to be good; but when such a person is employed in the administration of a state or family, calamities *from Heaven,* and injuries *from men,* will befall it together, and, though a good man may take his place, he will not be able to remedy the evil. This illustrates *again* the saying, "In a state, gain is not to be considered prosperity, but its prosperity will be found in righteousness."

The above tenth chapter of commentary explains the government of the state, and the making the kingdom peaceful and happy.

There are thus, in all, ten chapters of commentary, the first four of which discuss, in a general manner, the scope of the principal topic of the Work; while the other six go particularly into an exhibition of the work required in its subordinate branches. The fifth chapter contains the important subject of comprehending true excellence, and the sixth, what is the foundation of the attainment of true sincerity. Those two chapters demand the especial attention of the learner. Let not the reader despise them because of their simplicity.

23

THE DOCTRINE OF THE MEAN

The Doctrine of the Mean *contains two main strands of thought. The central section (Chapters II through XX, verse 16) develops the Confucian ideal of the superior man as one who follows the Mean, avoids rigid rules that neglect the context of action, properly observes the conventions in the five basic relationships between sovereign and minister, father and son, husband and wife,*

The Doctrine of the Mean, James Legge, trans. (Oxford, England: Clarendon Press, 1893), pp. 382–434. Reprinted from *The Chinese Classics,* vol. 1, by James Legge.

elder and younger brother, and friends, and practices the virtues of knowledge, magnanimity, and energy. The first chapter and the last twelve, on the other hand, praise a more mystical ideal, a sincerity so profound that it develops a man's nature to the full and makes him a collaborator in the transforming and nourishing functions of Heaven and Earth. This doctrine of the harmony of man and nature made the book popular with Buddhists and Taoists and facilitated the Neo-Confucian assimilation of cosmological and spiritual doctrines from these faiths in the Sung dynasty (A.D. 960–1279).

Although present as Chapter Twenty-eight in the Book of Rites, the Doctrine of the Mean has circulated for 2000 years as an independent work. The traditional view is that Tzu-ssu (492–431 B.C.), Confucius' grandson, wrote it, but some scholars think it may be a compilation from the work of two or more writers. Estimates of its date of composition range from the Fifth to the Third Century B.C. The mystical passages resemble chapters in the Mencius suggesting that the author may have been influenced by that work. Chu Hsi (A.D. 1130–1200) was instrumental in raising the book to great prominence. He divided the text into the present thirty-three chapters and wrote the standard commentary. The complete work with Chu Hsi's commentary is here given in Legge's translation.

My master, the philosopher Ch'ăng, says—"Being without inclination to either side is called CHUNG; *admitting of no change is called* YUNG. *By* CHUNG *is denoted the correct course to be pursued by all under heaven; by* YUNG *is denoted the fixed principle regulating all under heaven. This work contains the law of the mind, which was handed down from one to another, in the Confucian school, till Tsze-sze, fearing lest in the course of time errors should arise about it, committed it to writing, and delivered it to Mencius. The Book first speaks of one principle; it next spreads this out, and embraces all things; finally, it returns and gathers them all up under the one principle. Unroll it, and it fills the universe; roll it up, and it retires and lies hid in mysteriousness. The relish of it is inexhaustible. The whole of it is solid learning. When the skillful reader has explored it with delight till he has apprehended it, he may carry it into practice all his life, and will find that it cannot be exhausted."*

Chapter I. 1. What Heaven has conferred is called THE NATURE; an accordance with this nature is called THE PATH of *duty;* the regulation of this path is called INSTRUCTION.

2. The path may not be left for an instant. If it could be left, it would not be the path. On this account, the superior man does not wait till he sees things, to be cautious, nor till he hears things, to be apprehensive.

3. There is nothing more visible than what is secret, and nothing more manifest than what is minute. Therefore the superior man is watchful over himself, when he is alone.

4. While there are no stirrings of pleasure, anger, sorrow, or joy, the mind may be said to be in the state of EQUILIBRIUM. When those feelings have been stirred, and they act in their due degree, there ensues what may be called the state of HARMONY. This EQUILIBRIUM is the great root *from which grow all the human actings* in the world, and this HARMONY is the universal path *which they all should pursue.*

5. Let the states of equilibrium and harmony exist in perfection, and a happy order will prevail throughout heaven and earth, and all things will be nourished and flourish.

In the first chapter, which is given above, Tsze-sze states the views which had been handed down to him, as the basis of his discourse. First, it shows clearly how the path of duty is to be traced to its origins in Heaven, and is unchangeable, while the substance of it is provided in ourselves, and may not be departed from. Next, it speaks of the importance of preserving and nourishing this, and of exercising a watchful self-scrutiny with reference to it. Finally, it speaks of the meritorious achievements and transforming influence of sage and spiritual men in their highest extent. The wish of Tsze-sze was that hereby the learner should direct his thoughts inwards, and by searching in himself, there find these truths, so that he might put aside all outward temptations appealing to his selfishness, and fill up the measure of the goodness which is natural to him. This chapter is what the writer Yang called it,—"The sum of the whole work." In the ten chapters which follow, Tsze-sze quotes the words of the Master to complete the meaning of this.

Chapter II. 1. Chung-nî said, "The superior man *embodies* the course of the Mean; the mean man acts contrary to the course of the Mean.

2. "The superior man's embodying the course of the Mean is because he is a superior man, and so always maintains the Mean. The mean man's acting contrary to the course of the Mean is because he is a mean man, and has no caution."

Chapter III. The Master said, "Perfect is the virtue which is according to the Mean! Rare have they long been among the people, who could practice it!"

Chapter IV. 1. The Master said, "I know how it is that the path *of the Mean* is not walked in:—The knowing go beyond it, and the stupid do not come up to it. I know how it is that the path of the Mean is not understood:—The mean of talents and virtue go beyond it, and the worthless do not come up to it.

2. "There is nobody but eats and drinks. But they are few who can distinguish flavors."

Chapter V. The Master said, "Alas! How is the path of the Mean untrodden!"

Chapter VI. The Master said, "There was Shun:—He indeed was greatly wise! Shun loved to question *others,* and to study their words, though they might be shallow. He concealed what was bad *in them,* and displayed what was good. He took hold of their two extremes, *determined* the Mean, and employed it in *his government of* the people. It was by this that he was Shun!"

Chapter VII. The Master said, "Men all say, 'We are wise'; but being driven forward and taken in a net, a trap, or a pitfall, they know not how to escape. Men all say, 'We are wise'; but happening to choose the course of the Mean, they are not able to keep it for a round month."

Chapter VIII. The Master said, "This was the manner of Hûi:—he made choice of the Mean, and whenever he got hold of what was good, he clasped it firmly, as if wearing it on his breast, and did not lose it."

Chapter IX. The Master said, "The kingdom, its states, and its families, may be perfectly ruled; dignities and emoluments may be declined; naked weapons may be trampled under the feet;—but the course of the Mean cannot be attained to."

Chapter X. 1. Tsze-lû asked about energy.

2. The Master said, "Do you mean the energy of the South, the energy of the North, or the energy which you should cultivate yourself?

3. "To show forbearance and gentleness in teaching others; and not to revenge unreasonable conduct:—this is the energy of southern regions, and the good man makes it his study.

4. "To lie under arms; and meet death without regret:—this is the energy of northern regions, and the forceful make it their study.

5. "Therefore, the superior man cultivates *a friendly* harmony, without being weak.—How firm is he in his energy! He stands erect in the middle, without inclining to either side.—How firm is he in his energy! When good principles prevail in the government of his country, he does not change from what he was in retirement.—How firm is he in his energy! When bad principles prevail in the country, he maintains his course to death without changing.—How firm is he in his energy!"

Chapter XI. 1. The Master said, "To live in obscurity, and yet practice wonders, in order to be mentioned with honor in future ages:—this is what I do not do.

2. "The good man tries to proceed according to the right path, but when he has gone halfway, he abandons it:—I am not able *so* to stop.

3. "The superior man accords with the course of the Mean. Though he may be all unknown, unregarded by the world, he feels no regret.—It is only the sage who is able for this."

Chapter XII. 1. The way which the superior man pursues, reaches wide and far, and yet is secret.

2. Common men and women, however ignorant, may intermeddle with the knowledge of it; yet in its utmost reaches, there is that which even the sage does not know. Common men and women, however much below the ordinary standard of character, can carry it into practice; yet in its utmost reaches,

there is that which even the sage is not able to carry into practice. Great as heaven and earth are, men still find some things in them with which to be dissatisfied. Thus it is that, were the superior man to speak of his way in all its greatness, nothing in the world would be found able to embrace it, and were he to speak of it in its minuteness, nothing in the world would be found able to split it.

3. It is said in the Book of Poetry, "The hawk flies up to heaven; the fishes leap in the deep." This expresses how this *way* is seen above and below.

4. The way of the superior man may be found, in its simple elements, in the intercourse of common men and women; but in its utmost reaches, it shines brightly through heaven and earth.

The twelfth chapter above contains the words of Tsze-sze, and is designed to illustrate what is said in the first chapter, that "The path may not be left." In the eight chapters which follow, he quotes, in a miscellaneous way, the words of Confucius to illustrate it.

Chapter XIII. 1. The Master said, "The path is not far from man. When men try to pursue a course, which is far from the common indications of consciousness, this course cannot be considered THE PATH.

2. "In the Book of Poetry, it is said, 'In hewing an ax handle, in hewing an ax handle, the pattern is not far off.' We grasp one ax handle to hew the other; and yet, if we look askance from the one to the other, we may consider them as apart. Therefore, the superior man governs men, according to their nature, with what is proper to them, and as soon as they change *what is wrong*, he stops.

3. "When one cultivates to the utmost the principles of his nature, and exercises them on the principle of reciprocity, he is not far from the path. What you do not like when done to yourself, do not do to others.

4. "In the way of the superior man there are four things, to not one of which have I as yet attained.—To serve my father, as I would require my son to serve me: to this I have not attained; to serve my prince as I would require my minister to serve me: to this I have not attained; to serve my elder brother, as I would require my younger brother to serve me: to this I have not attained; to set the example in behaving to a friend, as I would require him to behave to me: to this I have not attained. Earnest in practicing the ordinary virtues, and careful in speaking about them, if, in his practice, he has anything defective, the superior man dares not but exert himself; and if, in his words, he has any excess, he dares not allow himself such license. Thus his words have respect to his actions, and his actions have respect to his words; is it not just an entire sincerity which marks the superior man?"

Chapter XIV. 1. The superior man does what is proper to the station in which he is; he does not desire to go beyond this.

2. In a position of wealth and honor, he does what is proper to a posi-

tion of wealth and honor. In a poor and low position, he does what is proper to a poor and low position. Situated among barbarous tribes, he does what is proper to a situation among barbarous tribes. In a position of sorrow and difficulty, he does what is proper to a position of sorrow and difficulty. The superior man can find himself in no situation in which he is not himself.

3. In a high situation, he does not treat with contempt his inferiors. In a low situation, he does not court the favor of his superiors. He rectifies himself, and seeks for nothing from others, so that he has no dissatisfactions. He does not murmur against Heaven, nor grumble against men.

4. Thus it is that the superior man is quiet and calm, waiting for the appointments *of Heaven,* while the mean man walks in dangerous paths, looking for lucky occurrences.

5. The Master said, "In archery we have something like the way of the superior man. When the archer misses the center of the target, he turns round and seeks for the cause of his failure in himself."

Chapter XV. 1. The way of the superior man may be compared to what takes place in traveling, when to go to a distance we must first traverse the space that is near, and in ascending a height, when we must begin from the lower ground.

2. It is said in the Book of Poetry, "Happy union with wife and children is like the music of lutes and harps. When there is concord among brethren, the harmony is delightful and enduring. *Thus* may you regulate your family, and enjoy the pleasure of your wife and children."

3. The Master said, "In such a state of things, parents have entire complacence!"

Chapter XVI. 1. The Master said, "How abundantly do spiritual beings display the powers that belong to them!

2. "We look for them, but do not see them; we listen to, but do not hear them; yet they enter into all things, and there is nothing without them.

3. "They cause all the people in the kingdom to fast and purify themselves, and array themselves in their richest dresses, in order to attend at their sacrifices. Then, like overflowing water, they seem to be over the heads, and on the right and left *of their worshipers.*

4. "It is said in the Book of Poetry, 'The approaches of the spirits, you cannot surmise;—and can you treat them with indifference?'

5. "Such is the manifestness of what is minute! Such is the impossibility of repressing the outgoings of sincerity!"

Chapter XVII. 1. The Master said, "How greatly filial was Shun! His virtue was that of a sage; his dignity was the throne; his riches were all within the four seas. He offered his sacrifices in his ancestral temple, and his descendants preserved the sacrifices to himself.

2. "Therefore having such great virtue, it could not but be that he should obtain the throne, that he should obtain those riches, that he should obtain his fame, that he should attain to his long life.

3. "Thus it is that Heaven, in the production of things, is sure to be bountiful to them, according to their qualities. Hence the tree that is flourishing, it nourishes, while that which is ready to fall, it overthrows.

4. "In the Book of Poetry, it is said, 'The admirable, amiable prince displayed conspicuously his excelling virtue, adjusting his people, and adjusting his officers. *Therefore,* he received from Heaven the emoluments of dignity. It protected him, assisted him, decreed him the throne; sending from Heaven these favors, *as it were* repeatedly.'

5. "*We may say* therefore that he who is greatly virtuous will be sure to receive the appointment of Heaven."

Chapter XVIII. 1. The Master said, "It is only King Wăn of whom it can be said that he had no cause for grief! His father was King Chî, and his son was King Wû. His father laid the foundations of his dignity, and his son transmitted it.

2. "King Wû continued the enterprise of King T'âi, King Chî, and King Wăn. He once buckled on his armor, and got possession of the kingdom. He did not lose the distinguished personal reputation which he had throughout the kingdom. His dignity was the royal throne. His riches were the possession of all within the four seas. He offered his sacrifices in his ancestral temple, and his descendants maintained the sacrifices to himself.

3. "It was in his old age that King Wû received the appointment *to the throne,* and the duke of Châu completed the virtuous course of Wăn and Wû. He carried up the title of king to T'âi and Chî, and sacrificed to all the former dukes above them with the royal ceremonies. And this rule he extended to the princes of the kingdom, the great officers, the scholars, and the common people. If the father were a great officer and the son a scholar, then the burial was that due to a great officer, and the sacrifice that due to a scholar. If the father were a scholar and the son a great officer, then the burial was that due to a scholar, and the sacrifice that due to a great officer. The one year's mourning was made to extend *only* to the great officers, but the three years' mourning extended to the Son of Heaven. In the mourning for a father or mother, he allowed no difference between the noble and the man."

Chapter XIX. 1. The Master said, "How far-extending was the filial piety of King Wû and the duke of Châu!

2. "Now filial piety is seen in the skillful carrying out of the wishes of our forefathers, and the skillful carrying forward of their undertakings.

3. "In spring and autumn, they repaired and beautified the temple halls of their fathers, set forth their ancestral vessels, displayed their various robes, and presented the offerings of the several seasons.

4. "By means of the ceremonies of the ancestral temple, they distinguished the royal kindred according to their order of descent. By ordering the parties present according to their rank, they distinguished the more noble and the less. By the arrangement of the services, they made a distinction of

talents and worth. In the ceremony of general pledging, the inferiors presented the cup to their superiors, and thus something was given the lowest to do. At the *concluding* feast, places were given according to the hair, and thus was made the distinction of years.

5. "They occupied the places of their forefathers, practiced their ceremonies, and performed their music. They reverenced those whom they honored, and loved those whom they regarded with affection. Thus they served the dead as they would have served them alive; they served the departed as they would have served them had they been continued among them.

6. "By the ceremonies of the sacrifices to Heaven and Earth they served God, and by the ceremonies of the ancestral temple they sacrificed to their ancestors. He who understands the ceremonies of the sacrifices to Heaven and Earth, and the meaning of the several sacrifices to ancestors, would find the government of a kingdom as easy as to look into his palm!"

Chapter XX. 1. The duke Ai asked about government.

2. The Master said, "The government of Wǎn and Wǔ is displayed in *the records,*—the tablets of wood and bamboo. Let there be the men and the government will flourish; but without the men, their government decays and ceases.

3. "With the *right* men the growth of government is rapid, just as vegetation is rapid in the earth; and, moreover, *their* government *might be called* an easily-growing rush.

4. "Therefore the administration of government lies in *getting proper* men. Such men are to be got by means of *the ruler's own* character. That character is to be cultivated by his treading in the ways *of duty.* And the treading those ways of duty is to be cultivated by the cherishing of benevolence.

5. "Benevolence is *the characteristic element of* humanity, and the great exercise of it is in loving relatives. Righteousness is *the accordance of actions with what is* right, and the great exercise of it is in honoring the worthy. The decreasing measures of the love due to relatives, and the steps in the honor due to the worthy, are produced by *the principle of* propriety.

6. "When those in inferior situations do not possess the confidence of their superiors, they cannot retain the government of the people.

7. "Hence the sovereign may not neglect the cultivation of his own character. Wishing to cultivate his character, he may not neglect to serve his parents. In order to serve his parents, he may not neglect to acquire a knowledge of men. In order to know men, he may not dispense with a knowledge of Heaven.

8. "The duties of universal obligation are five, and the virtues wherewith they are practiced are three. The duties are those between sovereign and minister, between father and son, between husband and wife, between elder brother and younger, and those belonging to the intercourse of friends. Those five are the duties of universal obligation. Knowledge, magnanimity, and en-

ergy, these three, are the virtues universally binding. And the means by which they carry *the duties* into practice is singleness.

9. "Some are born with the knowledge *of those duties;* some know them by study; and some acquire the knowledge after a painful feeling of their ignorance. But the knowledge being possessed, it comes to the same thing. Some practice them with a natural ease; some from a desire for their advantages; and some by strenuous effort. But the achievement being made, it comes to the same thing."

10. The Master said, "To be fond of learning is to be near to knowledge. To practice with vigor is to be near to magnanimity. To possess the feeling of shame is to be near to energy.

11. "He who knows these three things knows how to cultivate his own character. Knowing how to cultivate his own character, he knows how to govern other men. Knowing how to govern other men, he knows how to govern the kingdom with all its states and families.

12. "All who have the government of the kingdom with its states and families have nine standard rules to follow;—viz., the cultivation of their own characters; the honoring of men of virtue and talents; affection towards their relatives; respect towards the great ministers; kind and considerate treatment of the whole body of officers; dealing with the mass of the people as children; encouraging the resort of all classes of artisans; indulgent treatment of men from a distance; and the kindly cherishing of the princes of the states.

13. "By the ruler's cultivation of his own character, the duties of *universal obligation* are set forth. By honoring men of virtue and talents, he is preserved from errors of judgment. By showing affection to his relatives, there is no grumbling nor resentment among his uncles and brethren. By respecting the great ministers, he is kept from errors in the practice of government. By kind and considerate treatment of the whole body of officers, they are led to make the most grateful return for his courtesies. By dealing with the mass of the people as his children, they are led to exhort one another to what is good. By encouraging the resort of all classes of artisans, his resources for expenditure are rendered ample. By indulgent treatment of men from a distance, they are brought to resort to him from all quarters. And by kindly cherishing the princes of the states, the whole kingdom is brought to revere him.

14. "Self-adjustment and purification, with careful regulation of his dress, and the not making a movement contrary to the rules of propriety:—this is the way for a ruler to cultivate his person. Discarding slanderers, and keeping himself from *the seductions of* beauty; making light of riches, and giving honor to virtue:—this is the way for him to encourage men of worth and talents. Giving them places *of honor* and large emolument, and sharing with them in their likes and dislikes:—this is the way for him to encourage his relatives to love him. Giving them numerous officers to discharge their orders and commissions:—this is the way for him to encourage the great ministers. According to them a generous confidence, and making their emoluments

large:—this is the way to encourage the body of officers. Employing them only at the proper times, and making the imposts light:—this is the way to encourage the people. By daily examinations and monthly trials, and by making their rations in accordance with their labors:—this is the way to encourage the classes of artisans. To escort them on their departure and meet them on their coming; to commend the good among them, and show compassion to the incompetent:—this is the way to treat indulgently men from a distance. To restore families whose line of succession has been broken, and to revive states that have been extinguished; to reduce to order states that are in confusion, and support those which are in peril; to have fixed times for their own reception at court, and the reception of their envoys; to send them away after liberal treatment, and welcome their coming with small contributions:—this is the way to cherish the princes of the states.

15. "All who have the government of the kingdom with its states and families have the above nine standard rules. And the means by which they are carried into practise is singleness.

16. "In all things success depends on previous preparation, and without such previous preparation there is sure to be failure. If what is to be spoken be previously determined, there will be no stumbling. If affairs be previously determined, there will be no difficulty with them. If one's actions have been previously determined, there will be no sorrow in connection with them. If principles of conduct have been previously determined, the practice of them will be inexhaustible.

17. "When those in inferior situations do not obtain the confidence of the sovereign, they cannot succeed in governing the people. There is a way to obtain the confidence of the sovereign;—if one is not trusted by his friends, he will not get the confidence of his sovereign. There is a way to being trusted by one's friends;—if one is not obedient to his parents, he will not be true to friends. There is a way to being obedient to one's parents;—if one, on turning his thoughts in upon himself, finds a want of sincerity, he will not be obedient to his parents. There is a way to the attainment of sincerity in one's self;—if a man does not understand what is good, he will not attain sincerity in himself.

18. "Sincerity is the way of Heaven. The attainment of sincerity is the way of men. He who possesses sincerity is he who, without an effort, hits what is right, and apprehends, without the exercise of thought;—he is the sage who naturally and easily embodies the *right* way. He who attains to sincerity is he who chooses what is good, and firmly holds it fast.

19. "To this attainment there are requisite the extensive study of what is good, accurate inquiry about it, careful reflection on it, the clear discrimination of it, and the earnest practice of it.

20. "The superior man, while there is anything he has not studied, or while in what he has studied there is anything he cannot understand, will not intermit his labor. While there is anything he has not inquired about, or anything in what he has inquired about which he does not know, he will not

intermit his labor. While there is anything which he has not reflected on, or anything in what he has reflected on which he does not apprehend, he will not intermit his labor. While there is anything which he has not discriminated, or his discrimination is not clear, he will not intermit his labor. If there be anything which he has not practiced, or his practice fails in earnestness, he will not intermit his labor. If another man succeed by one effort, he will use a hundred efforts. If another man succeed by ten efforts, he will use a thousand.

21. "Let a man proceed in this way, and, though dull, he will surely become intelligent; though weak, he will surely become strong."

Chapter XXI. When we have intelligence resulting from sincerity, this condition is to be ascribed to nature; when we have sincerity resulting from intelligence, this condition is to be ascribed to instruction. But given the sincerity, and there shall be the intelligence; given the intelligence, and there shall be the sincerity.

The above is the twenty-first chapter. Tsze-sze takes up in it, and discourses the subjects of "the way of Heaven" and "the way of men," mentioned in the preceding chapter. The twelve chapters that follow are all from Tsze-sze, repeating and illustrating the meaning of this one.

Chapter XXII. It is only he who is possessed of the most complete sincerity that can exist under heaven, who can give its full development to his nature. Able to give its full development to his own nature, he can do the same to the nature of other men. Able to give its full development to the nature of other men, he can give their full development to the natures of animals and things. Able to give their full development to the natures of creatures and things, he can assist the transforming and nourishing powers of Heaven and Earth. Able to assist the transforming and nourishing powers of Heaven and Earth, he may with Heaven and Earth form a ternion.

Chapter XXIII. Next to the above is he who cultivates to the utmost the shoots of goodness in him. From those he can attain to the possession of sincerity. This sincerity becomes apparent. From being apparent, it becomes manifest. From being manifest, it becomes brilliant. Brilliant, it affects others. Affecting others, they are changed by it. Changed by it, they are transformed. It is only he who is possessed of the most complete sincerity that can exist under heaven, who can transform.

Chapter XXIV. It is characteristic of the most entire sincerity to be able to foreknow. When a nation or family is about to flourish, there are sure to be happy omens; and when it is about to perish, there are sure to be unlucky omens. *Such events are* seen in the milfoil and tortoise, and affect the movements of the four limbs. When calamity or happiness is about to come, the good shall certainly be foreknown by him, and the evil also. Therefore the individual possessed of the most complete sincerity is like a spirit.

Chapter XXV. 1. Sincerity is that whereby self-completion is effected, and *its* way is that by which man must direct himself.

2. Sincerity is the end and beginning of things; without sincerity there would be nothing. On this account, the superior man regards the attainment of sincerity as the most excellent thing.

3. The possessor of sincerity does not merely accomplish the self-completion of himself. With this quality he completes *other men and* things *also.* The completing himself *shows his* perfect virtue. The completing *other men and* things *shows his* knowledge. *Both these are* virtues belonging to the nature, and *this is* the way by which a union is effected of the external and internal. Therefore, whenever he—*the entirely sincere man*—employs them,—*that is, these virtues,—their action will be* right.

Chapter XXVI. 1. Hence to entire sincerity there belongs ceaselessness.

2. Not ceasing, it continues long. Continuing long, it evidences itself.

3. Evidencing itself, it reaches far. Reaching far, it becomes large and substantial. Large and substantial, it becomes high and brilliant.

4. Large and substantial;—this is how it contains *all* things. High and brilliant;—this is how it overspreads *all* things. Reaching far and continuing long;—this is how it perfects *all* things.

5. So large and substantial, *the individual possessing it* is the co-equal of Earth. So high and brilliant, it makes him the co-equal of Heaven. So far-reaching and long-continuing, it makes him infinite.

6. Such being its nature, without any display, it becomes manifested; without any movement, it produces changes; and without any effort, it accomplishes its ends.

7. The way of Heaven and Earth may be completely declared in one sentence.—They are without any doubleness, and so they produce things in a manner that is unfathomable.

8. The way of Heaven and Earth is large and substantial, high and brilliant, far-reaching and long-enduring.

9. The heaven now before us is only this bright shining spot; but when viewed in its inexhaustible extent, the sun, moon, stars, and constellations of the zodiac, are suspended in it, and all things are overspread by it. The earth before us is but a handful of soil; but when regarded in its breadth and thickness, it sustains mountains like the Hwâ and the Yo, without feeling their weight, and contains the rivers and seas, without their leaking away. The mountain now before us appears only a stone; but when contemplated in all the vastness of its size, we see how the grass and trees are produced on it, and birds and beasts dwell on it, and precious things which men treasure up are found on it. The water now before us appears but a ladleful; yet extending our view to its unfathomable depths, the largest tortoises, iguanas, iguanodons, dragons, fishes, and turtles, are produced in them, articles of value and sources of wealth abound in them.

10. It is said in the Book of Poetry, "The ordinances of Heaven, how profound are they and unceasing!" The meaning is, that it is thus that Heaven is Heaven. *And again,* "How illustrious was it, the singleness of the virtue of

King Wăn!" indicating that it was thus that King Wăn was what he was. Singleness likewise is unceasing.

Chapter XXVII. 1. How great is the path proper to the Sage!

2. Like overflowing water, it sends forth and nourishes all things, and rises up to the height of heaven.

3. All-complete is its greatness! It embraces the three hundred rules of ceremony, and the three thousand rules of demeanor.

4. It waits for the proper man, and then it is trodden.

5. Hence it is said, "Only by perfect virtue can the perfect path, in all its courses, be made a fact."

6. Therefore, the superior man honors his virtuous nature, and maintains constant inquiry and study, seeking to carry it out to its breadth and greatness, so as to omit none of the more exquisite and minute points which it embraces, and to raise it to its greatest height and brilliancy, so as to pursue the course of the Mean. He cherishes his old knowledge, and is continually acquiring new. He exerts an honest, generous earnestness, in the esteem and practice of all propriety.

7. Thus, when occupying a high situation he is not proud, and in a low situation he is not insubordinate. When the kingdom is well governed, he is sure by his words to rise; and when it is ill governed, he is sure by his silence to command forbearance to himself. Is not this what we find in the Book of Poetry,—"Intelligent is he and prudent, and so preserves his person?"

Chapter XXVIII. 1. The Master said, "Let a man who is ignorant be fond of using his own judgment; let a man without rank be fond of assuming a directing power to himself; let a man who is living in the present age go back to the ways of antiquity;—on the persons of all who act thus calamities will be sure to come.

2. To no one but the Son of Heaven does it belong to order ceremonies, to fix the measures, and to determine the written characters.

3. Now, over the kingdom, carriages have all wheels of the same size; all writing is with the same characters; and all conduct there has the same rules.

4. One may occupy the throne, but if he have not the proper virtue, he may not dare to make ceremonies or music. One may have the virtue, but if he do not occupy the throne, he may not presume to make ceremonies or music.

5. The Master said, "I may describe the ceremonies of the Hsiâ dynasty, but Chî cannot sufficiently attest my words. I have learned the ceremonies of the Yin dynasty, and in Sung they still continue. I have learned the ceremonies of Châu, which are now used, and I follow Châu."

Chapter XXIX. 1. He who attains to the sovereignty of the kingdom, having *those* three important things, shall be able to effect that there shall be few errors under his government.

2. However excellent may have been the regulations of those of former

times, they cannot be attested. Not being attested, they cannot command credence, and not being credited, the people would not follow them. However excellent might be the regulations made by one in an inferior situation, he is not in a position to be honored. Unhonored, he cannot command credence, and not being credited, the people would not follow his rules.

3. Therefore the institutions of the Ruler are rooted in his own character and conduct, and sufficient attestation of them is given by the masses of the people. He examines them *by comparison* with those of the three kings, and finds them without mistake. He sets them up before heaven and earth, and finds nothing in them contrary to their mode of operation. He presents himself with them before spiritual beings, and no doubts about them arise. He is prepared to wait for the rise of a sage a hundred ages after, and has no misgivings.

4. His presenting himself *with his institutions* before spiritual beings, without any doubts arising about them, shows that he knows Heaven. His being prepared, without any misgivings, to wait for the rise of a sage a hundred ages after, shows that he knows men.

5. Such being the case, the movements of such a ruler, *illustrating his institutions,* constitute an example to the world for ages. His acts are for ages a law to the kingdom. His words are for ages a lesson to the kingdom. Those who are far from him look longingly for him; and those who are near him are never wearied with him.

6. It is said in the Book of Poetry,—"Not disliked there, not tired of here, from day to day and night to night, will they perpetuate their praise." Never has there been a ruler, who did not realize this description, that obtained an early renown throughout the kingdom.

Chapter XXX. 1. Chung-nî handed down the doctrines of Yâo and Shun, as if they had been his ancestors, and elegantly displayed the regulations of Wăn and Wû, taking them as his model. Above, he harmonized with the times of heaven, and below, he was conformed to the water and land.

2. He may be compared to heaven and earth in their supporting and containing, their overshadowing and curtaining, all things. He may be compared to the four seasons in their alternating progress, and to the sun and moon in their successive shining.

3. All things are nourished together without their injuring one another. The courses *of the seasons, and of the sun and moon,* are pursued without any collision among them. The smaller energies are like river currents; the greater energies are seen in mighty transformations. It is this which makes heaven and earth so great.

Chapter XXXI. 1. It is only he, possessed of all sagely qualities that can exist under heaven, who shows himself quick in apprehension, clear in discernment, of far-reaching intelligence, and all-embracing knowledge, fitted to exercise rule; magnanimous, generous, benign, and mild, fitted to exercise forbearance; impulsive, energetic, firm, and enduring, fitted to maintain a firm hold; self-adjusted, grave, never swerving from the Mean, and correct, fitted to command reverence; accomplished, distinctive, concentrative, and searching, fitted to exercise discrimination.

2. All-embracing is he and vast, deep and active as a fountain, sending forth in their due season his virtues.

3. All-embracing and vast, he is like heaven. Deep and active as a fountain, he is like the abyss. He is seen, and the people all reverence him; he speaks, and the people all believe him; he acts, and the people all are pleased with him.

4. Therefore his fame overspreads the Middle Kingdom, and extends to all barbarous tribes. Wherever ships and carriages reach; wherever the strength of man penetrates; wherever the heavens overshadow and the earth sustains; wherever the sun and moon shine; wherever frosts and dews fall:—all who have blood and breath unfeignedly honor and love him. Hence it is said,— "He is the equal of Heaven."

Chapter XXXII. 1. It is only the individual possessed of the most entire sincerity that can exist under heaven, who can adjust the great invariable relations of mankind, establish the great fundamental virtues of humanity, and know the transforming and nurturing operations of Heaven and Earth;—shall this individual have any being or anything beyond himself on which he depends?

2. Call him man in his ideal, how earnest is he! Call him an abyss, how deep is he! Call him Heaven, how vast is he!

3. Who can know him, but he who is indeed quick in apprehension, clear in discernment, of far-reaching intelligence, and all-embracing knowledge, possessing all heavenly virtue?

Chapter XXXIII. 1. It is said in the Book of Poetry, "Over her embroidered robe she puts a plain, single garment," intimating a dislike to the display of the elegance of the former. Just so, it is the way of the superior man to prefer the concealment *of his virtue,* while it daily becomes more illustrious, and it is the way of the mean man to seek notoriety, while he daily goes more and more to ruin. It is characteristic of the superior man, appearing insipid, yet never to produce satiety; while showing a simple negligence, yet to have his accomplishments recognized; while seemingly plain, yet to be discriminating. He knows how what is distant lies in what is near. He knows where the wind proceeds from. He knows how what is minute becomes manifested. Such a one, we may be sure, will enter into virtue.

2. It is said in the Book of Poetry, "Although *the fish* sink and lie at the bottom, it is still quite clearly seen." Therefore the superior man examines his heart, that there may be nothing wrong there, and that he may have no cause for dissatisfaction with himself. That wherein the superior man cannot be equaled is simply this,—his *work* which other men cannot see.

3. It is said in the Book of Poetry, "Looked at in your apartment, be there free from shame as being exposed to the light of heaven." Therefore, the superior man, even when he is not moving, has *a feeling of* reverence, and while he speaks not, he has *the feeling of* truthfulness.

4. It is said in the Book of Poetry, "In silence is the offering presented, and *the spirit* approached to; there is not the slightest contention." Therefore the superior man does not use rewards, and the people are stimulated *to virtue*. He does not show anger, and the people are awed more than by hatchets and battleaxes.

5. It is said in the Book of Poetry, "What needs no display is virtue. All the princes imitate it." Therefore, the superior man being sincere and reverential, the whole world is conducted to a state of happy tranquillity.

6. It is said in the Book of Poetry, "I regard with pleasure your brilliant virtue, making no great display of itself in sounds and appearances." The Master said, "Among the appliances to transform the people, sounds and appearances are but trivial influences. It is said in another ode, 'His virtue is light as a hair.' Still, a hair will admit of comparison *as to its size*. 'The doings of the supreme Heaven have neither sound nor smell.'—That is perfect virtue."

The above is the thirty-third chapter. Tsze-sze having carried his descriptions to the extremest point in the preceding chapters, turns back in this, and examines the source of his subject; and then again from the work of the learner, free from all selfishness, and watchful over himself when he is alone, he carries out his description, till by easy steps he brings it to the consummation of the whole kingdom tranquilized by simple and sincere reverentialness. He further eulogizes its mysteriousness, till he speaks of it at last as without sound or smell. He here takes up the sum of his whole Work, and speaks of it in a compendious manner. Most deep and earnest was he in thus going again over his ground, admonishing and instructing men:—shall the learner not do his utmost in the study of the Work?

24

LAO TZU

The Lao Tzu or Tao Te Ching (Classic of the Way and its Power), the basic scripture of Taoism, has had more influence in China than any other single volume and is the Chinese book best known to the rest of the world. Only slightly more than 5000 characters in length, it has inspired hundreds of commentaries, dozens of translations, and a number of still unresolved scholarly controversies. According to a popular biography, it was written at the

*request of a gate-keeper on the Chinese border by a 160-year-old,
Sixth Century B.C. sage, Master Lao (Lao Tzu), who had been
custodian of the Imperial Archives and an advisor to the young
Confucius and was about to disappear into the West. Modern
scholars disagree concerning the extent to which this and other
legends about the author have a basis in fact, some judging them
wholly fabulous, others urging that they contain a germ of truth.
Scholars also disagree about the date of the book, most placing
it somewhere in the Sixth, Fifth, Fourth, or Third Centuries
B.C. Another controversy concerns the manner of its production,
whether written by a single author, though containing quotations
and interpolations, or compiled as an anthology of Taoist teaching
drawn from various sources. Commentators vary in their explica-
tions of the cryptic and vague passages which abound in the book
and in their overall interpretations of the relationship and relative
importance of the political, ethical, metaphysical, practical, mystical, occult, and poetic elements in the work.*

*"Tao" is the most important term in the Lao Tzu. The word
can refer to a physical track, a path or road, but it also denotes the
way in which something should be done. The Tao of Man, for
example, is the way in which a man should live. Every Chinese
philosophical school had its own version of the Tao, its own system
of ethical and political principles. The Lao Tzu is distinctive in its
claim to derive the Way of Man and the Way of Government from
the Way of Nature and this, in turn, from the ineffable Way that
antedates Heaven and Earth yet is immanent in all existence. This
conception of a mysterious "Unnameable Tao" cannot be equated
with that of a personal God but resembles such mystical concepts
as the Plotinian One and the Indian Brahman. The mysticism of
the Lao Tzu, however, is low-keyed, vague, and problematic. The
book focusses rather upon moral and political life, where it strenuously opposes the conventional propriety advocated by the Con-
fucians, the totalitarianism defended by the Legalists, and the
sensualism of the Hedonists. The ideals of the Lao Tzu are
simplicity, spontaneity, non-aggressiveness, harmony with nature,
quietness, desirelessness, and governmental passivity.*

*The Lao Tzu consists of eighty-one "chapters" or "poems"
arranged rather haphazardly. This translation by Professors Constant C. C. Chang and William Forthman rearranges the poems to
bring together those dealing with a single topic. It also omits twenty
poems of minor importance.*

LAO TZU (TAO-TE CHING)

[Part I: The Tao of Heaven]

There was a formless actuality
Before heaven and earth developed;

Lonely, isolated,
Independent, unchanging,
Revolving unfailingly,
Able to be mother of all things under heaven.
Not knowing its name
I call it "Tao."
Forced to name it,
I call it "Great."
To be Great is to pass on;
To pass on is to go far;
To go far is to return.
Therefore Tao is great;
Heaven is great;
Earth is great;
The king is also great.
In the realm
There are four great ones,
And the king is one of them.
Man follows the earth;
The earth follows heaven;
Heaven follows Tao;
Tao follows its own nature.   (Chapter 25 in the traditional order)

Tao is like an empty bowl
That yields without ever needing to be filled.
Deep as the ancestor of ten thousand things,
It breaks off sharpness,
Unwinds tangles,
Softens light,
Settles dust.
Yet it remains in dark profundity.
Whose son it is, I do not know.
It is like the creator's predecessor.   (4)

Everyone under heaven says that my Tao is so great that it seems unreal.
It seems unreal just because it is great.
If it seemed real,
It would have long been a small thing.
I have three treasures.
Take them and guard them!
The first is compassion;
The second is frugality;
The third is not trying to be the first under heaven.
By compassion one is able to be brave;

By frugality one is able to have an abundance;
By not trying to be the first under heaven one is able to be a leader.
If you were brave without compassion,
Had abundance without frugality,
Would lead without humility,
This would be fatal.
He who fights wins by compassion,
He who defends holds firm by compassion,
By compassion heaven helps and protects him.   (67)

The Tao that can be talked about is not the unchanging Tao.
The names that can be talked about are not the unchanging names.
We call the beginning of heaven and earth "Non-being";
We call the mother of the ten thousand things "Being."
Therefore to see the secret essences we must keep to Non-being;
By holding to Being we see only the surface of things,
These two came from the same source but have different names.
Both of them are called "mysterious,"
Or "mysterious and more mysterious,"
The gate whence came all secret essences.   (1)

What is looked at but not seen is called "invisible."
What is listened to but not heard is called "inaudible."
What is grasped for but not touched is called "intangible."
These three cannot be investigated,
Therefore they blend into one.
Its rising causes no light;
Its sinking, no darkness.
Endless, unnameable,
Returning again into nothing,
It is called "the form of the formless,"
"The image of nothingness."
It is called "the elusive."
Meet it, you do not see its front.
Follow it, you do not see its back.
He who holds to the Tao of old
In order to rule today's affairs
Can know the ancient origin
Which is called the essence of Tao.   (14)

The marks of great virtue
Follow only from Tao.
Tao is a thing elusive and evasive,
Evasive and elusive, yet within it are images.

Elusive and evasive, yet within it are objects.
Profound and dark, yet within it is the life-force.
The life-force is very potent.
There is reliability!
From ancient times until now
Its manifestations have never ceased,
Through which we may discern the origin of all things.
How do I know the nature of the origin of all things?
By this!   (21)

Returning is the motion of Tao.
Weakness is the usefulness of Tao.
Everything under heaven came from Being.
Being comes from Non-being.   (40)

Tao gave birth to the One:
The One gave birth to two;
The two gave birth to three;
The three gave birth to the ten thousand things.
The ten thousand things bear the feminine shade on their backs and clasp the
       masculine sun to their front,
And these blended principles produce their harmony.
Men most dislike being orphaned, lonely, and needy,
But kings and dukes call themselves by these names.
Truly things are sometimes increased by being diminished,
And sometimes diminished by being increased.
What other men have taught,
I also teach:
"The violent man will die a violent death."
I shall take this as my main teaching.   (42)

Tao gives them birth,
Virtue fosters them,
Matter forms them,
Circumstances complete them.
Therefore none of the ten thousand things can help reverencing Tao and exalt-
       ing Virtue.
Tao is reverenced, Virtue is exalted,
Not by order but by unchanging nature.
Therefore Tao gives them birth,
Virtue fosters them,
Makes them grow, develops them,
Completes and matures them,
Feeds and shelters them.

It gives them birth but does not claim them,
Helps them but is not dependent on them,
Is superior to them but does not dominate them.
This is the highest Virtue. (51)

The Great Tao is like overflowing water;
It can go to the left and to the right.
The ten thousand things depend upon it for their growth,
And it does not reject them.
Its task achieved, it claims no possession.
Clothing and nourishing the ten thousand things,
It seeks not to be their master.
As forever desireless,
It may be called "small."
As home of the ten thousand things, yet not their master,
It may be called "great."
Because it never seeks to be great itself,
Therefore it achieves greatness. (34)

[Part II: The Tao of the World]

Attain emptiness to the utmost,
Hold quietness firmly.
The ten thousand things develop simultaneously,
Yet in them I can see the process of returning.
Things, however flourishing,
Return each to their root.
To return to the root is called "quietude."
It is called "accepting fate."
Accepting fate is called "constancy."
To know constancy is called "enlightenment."
Not to know constancy
Leads to reckless actions which bring misfortune.
To know constancy is to be open.
To be open is to be impartial.
To be impartial is to be kingly.
To be kingly is to be in accord with heaven.
To be in accord with heaven is to be in accord with Tao,
To be in accord with Tao is to endure.
Though the body dies, it does not die. (16)

When people of the highest type hear of Tao,
Diligently they follow it.
When people of the mediocre type hear of Tao,

It seems to them as if existing and as if not existing.
When people of the lowest type hear of Tao,
They laugh loudly.
If they didn't laugh, it would not truly be Tao.
Therefore the maxim says:
"The Tao of brightness seems darkness,
The Tao of advance seems a retreat,
The Tao of smoothness seems rough."
High virtue seems low,
Sheer white seems tainted,
Abundant virtue seems insufficient,
Unshakeable virtue seems lax,
Pure substance seems faulty.
The greatest square has no corners,
The greatest vessel takes the longest to make,
The greatest music has the least noise,
The greatest image has no form.
Tao is hidden and has no name,
But only Tao's skill can support and fulfill.   (41)

The greatest perfection seems deficient,
But its usefulness never fails.
The greatest abundance seems empty,
But its usefulness will never be exhausted.
The greatest straightness seems crooked,
The greatest skill seems clumsy,
The greatest eloquence seems stuttering.
Activity overcomes cold,
But quietude overcomes heat.
Calmness and quietude are the norm under heaven.   (45)

Honest words are not beautiful,
Beautiful words are not honest.
The good man does not argue,
The arguer is not good.
The wise man is not learned,
The learned is not wise.
The sage does not hoard.
Since he acts for other men,
He is richer himself.
Since he gives to others,
He has much more himself.
The Tao of Heaven
Benefits but never harms.

The Tao of the sage
Accomplishes but never contends.   (81)

The Tao of Heaven,
Is it not like the stringing of a bow?
The upper is bent down, the lower is lifted,
The excess is diminished, the deficiency is compensated.
The Tao of Heaven is to diminish excess
And to compensate deficiencies.
The Tao of man is not so.
It diminishes the deficient
With offerings to those who have excess.
Who can offer an excess to everyone under heaven?
Only he who has Tao.
Therefore the sage acts but does not possess,
Accomplishes but claims no merit.
He does not desire to appear worthy.   (77)

When the government is dull,
People are pure.
When the government is efficient,
People are faulty.
"Bad fortune is what good fortune leans upon,
Good fortune is what conceals bad fortune."
Who can know the ultimate result?
There is no standard.
The standard would become deceptive.
The good would revert to the sinister.
Man has long since gone astray.
Therefore the sage is square but not cutting,
Sharp but not wounding,
Straight but not over-bearing,
Illumines but not by shining.   (58)

On tiptoes is not standing,
Overstriding is not walking,
Self assertion is not illuminating,
Self justification is not convincing,
Self boasting has no merit,
Self exalting is not to be a leader.
These, according to Tao,
May be called "the dregs and tumors of behavior,"
Which disgust all.
Therefore the man of Tao turns from them.   (24)

To take to the overflowing
Is not like stopping.
Grind it and whet it,
It will not keep an edge long.
Overflow the hall with gold and jade,
And it cannot be kept.
Wealth and rank with pride
Themselves leave ruin.
When your task is accomplished, retire.
This is the Tao of Heaven.   (9)

To yield is to be kept whole.
To be bent is to become straight.
To be a low spot is to be filled.
To be worn out is to be made new.
To be sparse is to gain.
To have plenty is to be confused.
Therefore the sage clasps unity
As the standard under Heaven.
He does not assert himself, therefore illumines.
He does not justify himself, therefore convinces.
He does not boast of himself, therefore has merit.
He does not pride himself, therefore leads.
As he does not contend,
No one under Heaven can contend with him.
Is it not true, what they said in ancient times,
"To yield is to be kept whole"?
Real wholeness comes from returning to it.   (22)

The skilled knight is not fierce;
The skilled fighter is not angry;
The skilled conqueror wins without battle;
The skilled employer of men takes the low place.
This is called "the virtue of not-contending,"
This is called "the power of employing others."
This is called "being mated to Heaven, to the most ancient."   (68)

The highest good is like water.
Water benefits the ten thousand things
But does not contend.
It dwells in places disdained by ordinary men,
Thereby it approaches Tao.
Earth is good to live on,
Depth is good for the mind,

Kindness is good in relationships,
Sincerity is good in speech,
Proper order is good in government,
Skill is good in business,
Timeliness is good in action.
Just for not contending,
These are above reproach.   (8)

Nothing under heaven is as soft and weak as water,
But those who can attack the hard and strong cannot defeat it.
Nothing can alter it.
That weakness overcomes strength
And softness overcomes hardness
Is known by everyone under heaven,
Yet none can practice it.
Therefore the sage said:
To accept the country's slander
Is to be master of the state;
To receive the country's misfortune,
Is to be king of the world.
True words seem contradictory.   (78)

Man at birth is soft and weak;
At death he is hard and strong.
The ten thousand things, grass, trees, alive are soft and supple;
In death they are withered and dry.
Therefore hardness and strength are the fellows of death;
Softness and weakness are the fellows of birth.
Therefore the strong army cannot win,
The strong tree will be felled.
The big and the strong will dwell below,
The soft and weak will dwell above.   (76)

The softest thing under heaven
Penetrates the hardest thing under heaven.
Insubstantial, it goes where there is no gap;
By this I know the benefit of non-doing.
Teaching without speaking,
The benefits of non-doing
Can scarcely be compared with anything else under heaven.   (43)

To be brave in daring is to be killed;
To be brave in not daring is to live.
Of these two, one profits, one harms.
It is what heaven hates,

Who can know the reason?
Therefore even the sage has difficulty here.
The Tao of Heaven is not to contend but to be skilled in winning,
Not to speak but yet to be skilled in replying,
Not to call but yet things come of themselves,
At leisure but yet skilled in planning.
Heaven's net is broad,
Loose-meshed, yet loses nothing.   (73)

Harmonizing a great complaint must lead to further complaints.
How can this be good?
Therefore the sage takes the debtor's position
And does not blame others.
The virtuous man makes trustworthy agreements,
The man without virtue makes vague agreements.
The Tao of Heaven has no partiality,
It always stands with the good man.   (79)

[Part III: The Tao of Man]

To know the male
But keep to the female
Is to be the ravine of the world.
To be the ravine of the world
Is to have the constant virtue which never deserts,
Is to return to infancy.
To know the white
But keep to the black
Is to be the standard for everything under heaven.
To be the standard for everything under heaven
Is to have the constant virtue which never errs,
Is to return to the Limitless
To know glory
But keep to obscurity
Is to be the valley of the world.
To be the valley of the world
Is to have the constant virtue, always sufficient,
Is to return to the Uncarved Block.
The Uncarved Block diffuses into tools.
If the sage uses it, he becomes the governor.
Therefore the greatest carver does not cut.   (28)

To know others is to be wise;
To know oneself is to be illumined.

To overcome others is to have force;
To overcome oneself is to be strong.
To be content is to be rich,
To act forcibly is to be strong willed,
But not to lose your place is to endure.
To die but not to be forgotten is to have long life.   (33)

If the things under heaven followed Tao
Racing horses would be turned back to fertilize the fields.
When things under heaven do not follow Tao
War horses are produced in the country.
There is no greater calamity than not to be content,
No greater fault than the desire for gain.
Therefore to be contented with contentment is to be always content.   (46)

Fame or self, which is dearer?
Self or gods, which is worth more?
Gaining or losing, which is more harmful?
Therefore to covet much necessitates great spending.
To hoard much necessitates losing heavily.
To be content is to avoid shame,
To know when to stop is to avoid danger.
This makes it possible to endure long.   (44)

The five colors blind man's eye;
The five sounds deafen man's ear;
The five flavors weary man's taste.
Horse-racing and hunting madden man's mind,
Goods hard to obtain impede his actions.
Therefore the sage cares for the belly, not for the eye.
Therefore he throws that away and takes this.   (12)

Banish learning and have no sorrows.
Between "yes" and "yeah"
How much difference is there?
Between "good" and "evil"
What difference is there?
What others fear we cannot help fearing;
So ignorance still goes on.
All men revel
As if enjoying a great feast,
As if mounting the terrace in spring.
I alone am quiet, not yet giving an omen,
Like an infant who has not yet smiled.

I am worn out as though homeless.
All men have more than enough,
But I alone am as if I had lost all.
O, I have a foolish man's mind,
Nebulous and confused.
Vulgar men are bright and shining;
I alone am dark.
Vulgar men are efficient;
I alone am dull,
Broad as the sea,
Drifting endlessly.
All men have some purpose;
I alone am stupid and rustic.
I alone differ from others
And value the food of the Mother.   (20)

In ancient times the skilled masters were subtle, abstruse, mysterious and
      penetrating,
Too profound to be understood.
Because they cannot be understood,
Therefore I must only try to describe them:
Hesitant, as if wading a river in winter,
Watchful, as if fearing all the neighbors,
Grave, as if a guest,
Self-effacing, like melting ice,
Simple, like an uncarved block,
Vacant, like a valley,
Confused, like murky water.
Who can stay with this murkiness
And be quiet while it slowly becomes clear?
Who can keep his calm long,
Till it moves and gradually grows?
To keep this Tao do not hope to be filled.
Just because you are unfilled,
Though worn out, you can become new again.   (15)

Rich in virtue, like an infant,
Noxious insects will not sting him;
Fierce beasts will not attack him;
Birds of prey will not seize him.
His bones are weak, his sinews soft, but his grip is firm.
Not yet knowing the union of male and female but with erect organ—
His life-force is at its height.
Screaming all day but without getting hoarse—

His harmony is at its perfection.
To know harmony is called "constancy."
To know constancy is called "enlightenment."
But to complicate life is called "an ill-omen";
To let the emotions follow impulse is called "violence."
Things reach their prime, then age.
They are contrary to Tao,
And what is contrary to Tao soon perishes.   (55)

"Favor and disgrace cause dismay.
Exalt self and equally you exalt great fears."
What does this mean: "Favor and disgrace cause dismay"?
Favor is undesirable,
For to receive it causes dismay,
And to lose it causes dismay.
This is the meaning of "Favor and disgrace cause dismay."
What does this mean: "Exalt self and equally you exalt great fears"?
The reason I have great fears is because I have a self.
When I have no self,
What have I to fear?
Therefore he who values the world as his self
May be entrusted with the world.
Therefore he who loves the world as his self,
May be entrusted with the world.   (13)

[Part IV: The Tao of Government]

Tao is the mysterious home of the ten thousand things,
The good man's treasure,
The bad man's protector.
Beautiful sayings can be passed on,
Noble conduct can be handed on,
So why abandon the man who is not good?
Therefore at the crowning of an emperor
And at the installation of the three Grand Ministers,
Rather than send a four horse chariot preceded by a jade disk,
It would be better to send this Tao.
For what reason did the ancients exalt this Tao?
Did they not say:
"Pursuing they shall catch; guilty, they shall be exempt"?
Therefore it is exalted under heaven.   (62)

Tao invariably does nothing,
Yet there is nothing that is not done.

If the lords and kings can follow this,
The ten thousand things will transform themselves.
If, transformed, they stir,
I would calm them with the nature of the nameless uncarved block.
The nameless uncarved block is desirelessness.
Be desireless and quiet,
Then the world will be at peace of itself.   (37)

Learning proceeds by daily adding,
Tao proceeds by daily losing
Losing and again losing
Till the state of non-doing is reached.
By non-doing, there is nothing that is not done.
Usually the world may be overcome without activity.
When activity is required,
It is not possible to overcome the world.   (48)

Do through non-doing,
Act without activity,
Taste the tasteless.
Great or slight, many or few,
Requite injury with virtue.
Dispose of the difficult while still easy,
Deal with the great while still small.
Everything difficult under heaven must grow from something easy.
Everything great under heaven must grow from something small.
Therefore the sage never deals with the great,
Hence he is able to achieve greatness.
To lightly promise
Leads to little honesty.
To take many things as easy
Leads to many difficulties.
Therefore the sage treats them as difficult,
Hence never has difficulties!   (63)

It is easy to hold what is stable,
It is easy to plan for what lacks omens,
It is easy to break what is brittle,
It is easy to scatter what is minute.
Deal with things before they arise,
Put the country in order before it is confused.
The tree large as a man's embrace grows from a tiny sprout,
The nine storey terrace rises from a clod of earth,
The thousand mile journey begins from the ground underfoot.

He who acts, fails;
He who grasps, loses.
The sage does not act, therefore he does not fail,
Does not grasp, therefore does not lose.
People's affairs often fail when almost accomplished.
Take care at the end as at the beginning,
Then there will be no failing affairs.
Therefore the sage desires to have no desires,
Does not value goods difficult to obtain,
Learns not to learn,
Corrects what common men have gotten wrong,
In order to help the ten thousand things back to their nature,
But without daring to act.   (64)

To desire to overcome the world
By means of action,
I see, cannot succeed.
The world is a holy vessel,
It cannot be successfully acted upon.
He who acts, fails.
He who grasps, loses.
For some things go first,
Some follow,
Some blow lightly,
Some blow hard,
Some are strong,
Some are weak;
Some break,
Some fall.
Therefore the sage discards excesses,
Discards luxuries,
Discards extremes.   (29)

Govern a state by the standard,
Employ an army with surprise,
Overcome the world by inactivity.
How do I know that it is so?
By this:
The more prohibitions under heaven,
The poorer the people.
The more sharp tools people have,
The more chaotic the state.
The more technical skills men have,
The more cunning things appear.

The more laws and regulations are promulgated,
The more robbers and thieves there are.
Therefore the sage says,
"If I practice non-doing then the people will transform themselves.
If I like quietude then the people will do right of themselves.
If I have no activity then the people will grow rich of themselves,
If I have no desires, then the people will return to the state of the uncarved
　　block of themselves." (57)

The people are hungry,
For their rulers eat too much tax-grain.
That is why the people are hungry.
The difficulty of ruling people
Comes from the activity of their rulers.
That is why they are difficult to rule.
The people take death lightly,
For their rulers take too much for their living.
That is why they take death lightly.
Because they have nothing to live for,
They are superior to those who exalt life. (75)

The people do not fear death,
Why threaten them with it?
Suppose people did always fear death,
That we could seize and kill those who do evil,
Who would dare to?
There is always an executioner for killing,
And to take the place of the executioner
Is called "Doing the hacking for the master carpenter."
In doing the hacking for the master carpenter
It is seldom that one's hand escapes injury. (74)

He who helps the king with Tao
Will not compel the World by armed force,
For such things easily rebound.
Thorns will grow where armies have been.
After a great war,
There must be a cruel year.
The good general achieves his purpose and just that.
He does not dominate further.
He achieves his purpose but does not glory in it,
Achieves his purpose but does not boast,
Achieves his purpose but does not pride himself,
Achieves his purpose but cannot help regretting it,

Achieves his purpose but does not like strength.
Things reach their prime, then age.
That is called "not Tao."
And what is contrary to Tao soon perishes.   (30)

Armies are not things of good omen;
Perhaps nature hates them.
Therefore the man of Tao avoids them.
When the gentleman is in civil life he favors the left,
But in war he favors the right.
Armies are not things of good omen,
Not the tool of a gentleman.
When their use is unavoidable
Quiet restraint is best.
Even in victory do not think them beautiful.
Who finds them beautiful
Delights in the killing of men.
To delight in the killing of men
Is to fail in the ambition to overcome the world.
The things of good omen favor the left.
The things of ill omen favor the right.
The assistant general stands on the left.
The supreme general stands on the right.
That is to say it is treated as a funeral rite.
The killing of many men is a matter for sorrow and weeping.
A victory should be treated as a funeral rite.   (31)

In Ancient times those skilled in Tao
Did not enlighten the people
But kept them ignorant.
People are difficult to rule
Because their knowledge is too great.
Therefore to rule the state by giving knowledge is to be the bandit of the state.
To rule the state without giving knowledge is to be the blessing of the state.
To know these two
Is to know the right standard.
To always know the right standard,
That is called "the mysterious virtue."
The mysterious virtue, profound and far reaching,
Returns with things
Until they arrive at the great harmony.   (65)

When everyone under Heaven knows beauty as beauty,
The idea of ugliness arises.

When all know good as good,
The idea of evil arises.
Thus being and non-being grow out of each other,
Difficult and easy complete each other,
Long and short measure each other,
High and low lean on each other,
Voice and accompaniment harmonize with each other,
Front and back follow each other.
Therefore the sage abides in the activity of non-doing,
Teaching without speaking.
The ten thousand things grow and he does not reject them.
He rears them but does not claim them,
Helps them but is not dependent on them,
Accomplishes, but claims no merit.
Because he claims no merit,
He is not displaced.   (2)

When the Great Tao declined,
Humaneness and justice came.
When knowledge and cleverness appeared,
Hypocrisy came.
When the six relationships became inharmonious,
Filial piety and parental care came.
When the state became confused,
Loyal ministers came.   (18)

Superior virtue is not concerned with virtue,
Therefore it has virtue.
Inferior virtue seeks not to lose virtue,
Therefore it has no virtue.
Superior virtue does nothing,
Yet there is nothing for it to do.
Inferior virtue acts,
But need for action remains.
Superior humaneness acts,
Yet there is nothing for it to do.
Superior justice acts,
But need for action remains.
Superior ritualism acts, but getting no response
Lays bare its arm and forces itself on people.
Therefore after Tao was lost, then came virtue;
After virtue was lost, then came humaneness;
After humaneness was lost, then came justice;
After justice was lost, then came ritual.

Ritual is the thinning out of loyalty and honesty
And the beginning of disorder.
Foreknowledge is the flowery appearance of Tao
And the origin of folly.
Therefore the great man dwells in its depth,
Not in its shallows,
Abides in its fruitfulness
Not in its flowery appearance.
Therefore he throws that away and takes this.   (38)

Banish sageness, discard knowledge,
And the people will profit a hundredfold;
Banish humaneness, discard justice,
And the people will again have filial piety and parental care.
Banish ingenuity, discard utility,
And brigands and thieves will disappear.
These three are used to decorate men's lack,
Therefore let them have what belongs:
Simplicity to look at, the uncarved block to carry,
Selflessness, few desires.   (19)

Exalt not the worthies,
So that the people shall not contend.
Prize not goods difficult to gain,
So that people shall not steal.
Display not desirable things,
So that people's hearts shall not be confused.
Therefore this is the sage's policy:
To empty their hearts,
Fill their bellies,
Weaken their will,
Strengthen their frames.
Always keep the people without knowledge and desire,
So that any knowing one will not dare to act.
Do what is non-doing,
Then there is nothing that is not governed.   (3)

If I had little knowledge
And followed the Great Tao,
Side paths would be the only thing I would fear.
The Great Tao is smooth,
But people prefer by-paths.
The royal court is in order,
But the fields are untilled,

The granaries are completely empty.
To wear embroidered cloth,
Carry sharp swords,
Be surfeited with food and drink,
Have excess wealth and goods,
That is called "the great robbery,"
But surely is not the Tao.   (53)

Let there be a small state with few people,
Though there be tools of tenfold or hundredfold utility they are not used,
Let the people value their lives and not migrate far.
Though there be boats and carriages, no cause to ride in them;
Though there be armor and weapons, no cause to display them.
Let people again knot ropes for reckoning,
Enjoy their food,
Be satisfied with their clothing,
Content with their homes,
Be happy in their customs.
Neighboring places overlook each other,
Their cocks' and dogs' sounds can be heard by each other,
But the people will grow old and die without visiting each other.   (80)

The sage has no fixed opinions,
But takes the people's mind as his own.
The good I call "good";
The bad I also call "good."
This is highest goodness.
The honest I believe;
The dishonest I also believe.
This is highest honesty.
The sage here under heaven is undiscriminating,
Then everyone under heaven has his mind made undiscerning.
The sage regards them all as children.   (49)

Everything under heaven had a beginning,
Which may be taken to be the mother of everything under heaven.
When we know the mother, then we may know her sons.
When we know her sons, we will again hold to the mother
And throughout life will be free of danger.
Stop up the apertures,
Close the doors,
And the whole life is without toil.
Open the apertures,
Be busy about affairs,
And the whole life is without redemption.

To see the small is called "enlightenment,"
To keep to the weak is called "strength."
Use the light,
Then return again to enlightenment;
Thus avoid danger to your life.
This is practicing constancy.   (52)

[Part V: The Tao of the Leader]

Of the best rulers people only know that they exist;
The next they love and praise;
The next they fear;
The next they revile.
When trust is lacking,
There is no trustworthiness.
Be quiet, treasure your words,
When the task is accomplished, the work done,
The people will all say, "It is the natural result."   (17)

When people do not fear your authority, great authority comes.
Do not disturb their residence,
Do not make them weary of life.
Just because you do not make them weary,
They will not turn from you.
Therefore the sage knows himself, but does not assert himself.
Esteems himself, but does not exalt himself.
Therefore he throws that away and takes this.   (72)

The reason the rivers and seas are able to be lords of the ravines
Lies in their skill at keeping below them.
Therefore they are able to be lords of the hundred ravines.
Therefore in order to be above people
One must speak as if lower than they.
In order to lead the people
One must put himself behind them.
Thus the sage stays above,
But is not heavy on the people.
Stays in front,
But does not harm the people.
Therefore the world is glad untiringly to support him.
As he does not contend,
No one under heaven can contend with him.   (66)

A big state should be like the low delta regions,
Concourse to the world,

Female to the world.
By quietude the female overcomes the male,
For quietude belongs to the low.
Therefore if a big state puts itself below a small state,
It wins the small state.
If a small state puts itself below a big state,
It wins the big state.
Therefore some put themselves low in order to win,
Some are low and thus win.
The big state wants to shelter others,
The small state wants to enter and serve others.
As the two both get what they want,
It is suitable for the big one to be lower.   (61)

Heaven is everlasting, earth enduring.
The reason heaven and earth can last and endure
Is that they do not live for themselves.
Hence they can be everlasting.
Therefore the sage puts himself behind, but is in front,
Puts himself aside, but still remains.
Is it not because he seeks no personal end
That his personal ends can be achieved?   (7)

Tao gave birth to the One;
The One gave birth to two;
The two gave birth to three;
The three gave birth to the ten thousand things.
The ten thousand things bear the feminine shade on their backs and clasp the
        masculine sun to their front,
And these blended principles produce their harmony.
Men most dislike being orphaned, lonely and needy,
But kings and dukes call themselves by these names.
Truly things are sometimes increased by being diminished
And sometimes diminished by being increased.
What other men have taught,
I also teach:
"The violent man will die a violent death."
I shall take this as my main teaching.   (42)

Nothing under heaven is as soft and weak as water,
But those who can attack the hard and strong cannot defeat it.
Nothing can alter it.
That weakness overcomes strength
And softness overcomes hardness

Is known by everyone under heaven,
Yet none can practice it.
Therefore the sage said:
To accept the country's slander
Is to be master of the state;
To receive the country's misfortune,
Is to be king of the world.
True words seem contradictory.   (78)

25

CHUANG TZU

  After the Lao Tzu, *the most influential Taoist book has been the* Chuang Tzu. *Most of the themes of the first have been developed and illustrated in the second, but the style and tone of the two books is quite different. The* Lao Tzu *is serious, solemn, even oracular in its epigrams, while the graceful prose of the* Chuang Tzu *is marked by fantasy, humor, and satire as well as subtle reasoning. The* Chuang Tzu *is even more irreverent than the* Lao Tzu *toward tradition, convention, and power. Less concerned with social remedies and more concerned with individual spirituality, the* Chuang Tzu *is a mystical book but one full of reverence for the unceasing process of transformation that is Nature. One of the acknowledged literary masterpieces of the Chou dynasty, its lack of a political program has made its position unacceptable to Chinese intellectuals, but its love of nature, spirit of detachment, and aesthetic orientation have been important influences upon Chinese culture. Chinese poetry, landscape painting, and Zen Buddhism reflect much of the spirit of the* Chuang Tzu.

  Little is known about the author Chuang Chou. According to the traditional account, he was a minor official in the Fourth Century B.C. who refused to become a prime minister because he loved freedom more than power. The Chuang Tzu *contains thirty-three chapters. Most scholars agree that the first seven are by the Master and that the rest are largely the work of his disciples or later writers, although they may contain passages by Chuang Chou. Chapters Two and Six are here reprinted from Lin Yutang's translation.*

From *The Wisdom of China and India,* edited by Lin Yutang, pp. 633–643, 657–666. Copyright 1942 by Random House, Inc. Reprinted by permission.

ON LEVELLING ALL THINGS

Tsech'i of Nankuo sat leaning on a low table. Gazing up to heaven, he sighed and looked as though he had lost his mind.

Yench'eng Tseyu, who was standing by him, exclaimed, "What are you thinking about that your body should become thus like dead wood, your mind like burnt-out cinders? Surely the man now leaning on the table is not he who was here just now."

"My friend," replied Tsech'i, "your question is apposite. Today I have lost my Self . . . Do you understand? . . . Perhaps you only know the music of man, and not that of Earth. Or even if you have heard the music of Earth, perhaps you have not heard the music of Heaven."

"Pray explain," said Tseyu.

"The breath of the universe," continued Tsech'i, "is called wind. At times, it is inactive. But when active, all crevices resound to its blast. Have you never listened to its deafening roar?

"Caves and dells of hill and forest, hollows in huge trees of many a span in girth—some are like nostrils, and some like mouths, and others like ears, beam-sockets, goblets, mortars, or like pools and poodles. And the wind goes rushing through them, like swirling torrents or singing arrows, bellowing, sousing, trilling, wailing, roaring, purling, whistling in front and echoing behind, now soft with the cool blow, now shrill with the whirlwind, until the tempest is past and silence reigns supreme. Have you never witnessed how the trees and objects shake and quake, and twist and twirl?"

"Well, then," enquired Tseyu, "since the music of Earth consists of hollows and apertures, and the music of man of pipes and flutes, of what consists the music of Heaven?"

"The effect of the wind upon these various apertures," replied Tsech'i, "is not uniform, but the sounds are produced according to their individual capacities. Who is it that agitates their breasts?

"Great wisdom is generous; petty wisdom is contentious. Great speech is impassioned, small speech cantankerous.

"For whether the soul is locked in sleep or whether in waking hours the body moves, we are striving and struggling with the immediate circumstances. Some are easy-going and leisurely, some are deep and cunning, and some are secretive. Now we are frightened over petty fears, now disheartened and dismayed over some great terror. Now the mind flies forth like an arrow from a cross-bow, to be the arbiter of right and wrong. Now it stays behind as if sworn to an oath, to hold on to what it has secured. Then, as under autumn and winter's blight, comes gradual decay, and submerged in its own occupations, it keeps on running its course, never to return. Finally, worn out and imprisoned, it is choked up like an old drain, and the failing mind shall not see light again.

"Joy and anger, sorrow and happiness, worries and regrets, indecision and fears, come upon us by turns, with everchanging moods, like music from the hollows, or like mushrooms from damp. Day and night they alternate within us, but we cannot tell whence they spring. Alas! Alas! Could we for a moment lay our finger upon their very Cause?

"But for these emotions I should not be. Yet but for me, there would be no one to feel them. So far we can go; but we do not know by whose order they come into play. It would seem there was a soul; but the clue to its existence is wanting. That it functions is credible enough, though we cannot see its form. Perhaps it has inner reality without outward form.

"Take the human body with all its hundred bones, nine external cavities and six internal organs, all complete. Which part of it should I love best? Do you not cherish all equally, or have you a preference? Do these organs serve as servants of some one else? Since servants cannot govern themselves, do they serve as master and servants by turn? Surely there is some soul which controls them all.

"But whether or not we ascertain what is the true nature of this soul, it matters but little to the soul itself. For once coming into this material shape, it runs its course until it is exhausted. To be harassed by the wear and tear of life, and to be driven along without possibility of arresting one's course,— is not this pitiful indeed? To labor without ceasing all life, and then, without living to enjoy the fruit, worn out with labor, to depart, one knows not whither,—is not this a just cause for grief?"

"Men say there is no death—of what avail? The body decomposes, and the mind goes with it. Is this not a great cause for sorrow? Can the world be so dull as not to see this? Or is it I alone who am dull, and others not so?"

Now if we are to be guided by our prejudices, who shall be without a guide? What need to make comparisons of right and wrong with others? And if one is to follow one's own judgments according to his prejudices, even the fools have them! But to form judgments of right and wrong without first having a mind at all is like saying, "I left for Yüeh today, and got there yesterday." Or, it is like assuming something which does not exist to exist. The (illusions of) assuming something which does not exist to exist could not be fathomed even by the divine Yü; how much less could we?

For speech is not mere blowing of breath. It is intended to say something, only what it is intended to say cannot yet be determined. Is there speech indeed, or is there not? Can we, or can we not, distinguish it from the chirping of young birds?

How can Tao be so obscured that there should be a distinction of true and false? How can speech be so obscured that there should be a distinction of right and wrong? Where can you go and find Tao not to exist? Where can you go and find that words cannot be proved? Tao is obscured by our inadequate understanding, and words are obscured by flowery expressions. Hence the affirmations and denials of the Confucian and Motsean schools, each denying what the other affirms and affirming what the other denies. Each denying what the other affirms and affirming what the other denies brings us only into confusion.

There is nothing which is not *this*; there is nothing which is not *that*. What cannot be seen by *that* (the other person) can be known by myself. Hence I say, *this* emanates from *that*; *that* also derives from this. This is the theory of the interdependence of *this* and *that* (relativity of standards).

Nevertheless, life arises from death, and *vice versa*. Possibility arises from impossibility, and *vice versa*. Affirmation is based upon denial, and *vice versa*. Which being the case, the true sage rejects all distinctions and takes his refuge in Heaven (Nature). For one may base it on *this*, yet *this* is also *that* and *that* is also *this*. *This* also has its 'right' and 'wrong', and *that* also has its 'right' and 'wrong.' Does then the distinction between *this* and *that* really exist or not? When *this* (subjective) and *that* (objective) are both without their correlates, that is the very 'Axis of Tao.' And when that Axis passes through the centre at which all Infinities converge, affirmations and denials alike blend into the infinite One. Hence it is said that there is nothing like using the Light.

To take a finger in illustration of a finger not being a finger is not so good as to take something which is not a finger to illustrate that a finger is not a finger. To take a horse in illustration of a horse not being a horse is not so good as to take something which is not a horse to illustrate that a horse is not a horse. So with the universe which is but a finger, but a horse. The possible is possible: the impossible is impossible. Tao operates, and the given results follow; things receive names and are said to be what they are. Why are they so? They are said to be so! Why are they not so? They are said to be not so! Things are so by themselves and have possibilities by themselves. There is nothing which is not so and there is nothing which may not become so.

Therefore take, for instance, a twig and a pillar, or the ugly person and the great beauty, and all the strange and monstrous transformations. These are all levelled together by Tao. Division is the same as creation; creation is the same as destruction. There is no such thing as creation or destruction, for these conditions are again levelled together into One.

Only the truly intelligent understand this principle of the levelling of all things into One. They discard the distinctions and take refuge in the common and ordinary things. The common and ordinary things serve certain functions and therefore retain the wholeness of nature. From this wholeness, one comprehends, and from comprehension, one comes near to the Tao. There it stops without knowing how it stops—this is Tao.

But to wear out one's intellect is an obstinate adherence to the individuality of things, not recognizing the fact that all things are One,—this is called "Three in the Morning." What is "Three in the Morning?" A keeper of monkeys said with regard to their rations of nuts that each monkey was to have three in the morning and four at night. At this the monkeys were very angry. Then the keeper said they might have four in the morning and three at night, with which arrangement they were all well pleased. The actual number of nuts remained the same, but there was a difference owing to (subjective evaluations of) likes and dislikes. It also derives from this (principle of subjectivity). Wherefore the true Sage brings all the contraries together and rests in the natural Balance of Heaven. This is called (the principle of following) two courses (at once).

The knowledge of the men of old had a limit. What was the limit? It extended back to a period when matter did not exist. That was the extreme point to which their knowledge reached. The second period was that of matter, but of matter unconditioned (undefined). The third epoch saw matter conditioned (defined), but judgements of true and false were still unknown. When these appeared, Tao began to decline. And with the decline of Tao, individual bias (subjectivity) arose.

Besides, did Tao really rise and decline? In the world of (apparent) rise and decline, the famous musician Chao Wen did play the string instrument; but in respect to the world without rise and decline, Chao Wen did not play the string instrument. When Chao Wen stopped playing the string instrument, Shih K'uang, (the music master) laid down his drum-stick (for keeping time), and Hueitse (the sophist) stopped arguing, they all understood the approach of Tao. These people are the best in their arts, and therefore known to posterity. They each loved his art, and wanted to excel in his own line. And because they loved their arts, they wanted to make them known to others. But they were trying to teach what (in its nature) could not be known. Consequently (Hueitse) ended in the obscure discussions of the "hard" and "white"; and Chao Wen's son tried to learn to play the string instrument all his life and failed. If this may be called success, then I, too, have succeeded. But if neither of them could be said to have succeeded, then neither I nor others have succeeded. Therefore the true Sage discards the light that dazzles and takes refuge in the common and ordinary. Through this comes understanding.

Suppose here is a statement. We do not know whether it belongs to one category or another. But if we put the different categories in one, then the differences of category cease to exist. However, I must explain. If there was a beginning, then there was a time before that beginning, and a time before the time which was before the time of that beginning. If there is existence, there must have been non-existence. And if there was a time when nothing existed, then there must have been a time when even nothing did not exist. All of a sudden, nothing came into existence. Could one then really say whether it belongs to the category of existence or of non-existence? Even the very words I have just now uttered,—I cannot say whether they say something or not.

There is nothing under the canopy of heaven greater than the tip of a bird's down in autumn, while the T'ai Mountain is small. Neither is there any longer life than that of a child cut off in infancy, while P'eng Tsu himself died young. The universe and I came into being together; I and everything therein are One.

If then all things are One, what room is there for speech? On the other hand, since I can say the word 'one' how can speech not exist? If it does exist, we have One and speech—two; and two and one—three from which point onwards even the best mathematicians will fail to reach (the ultimate); how much more then should ordinary people fail?

Hence, if from nothing you can proceed to something, and subsequently reach three, it follows that it would be still easier if you were to start from something. Since you cannot proceed, stop here.

Now Tao by its very nature can never be defined. Speech by its very nature cannot express the absolute. Hence arise the distinctions. Such distinctions are: "right" and "left," "relationship" and "duty," "division" and "discrimination," "emulation" and "contention." These are called the Eight Predicables.

Beyond the limits of the external world, the Sage knows that it exists, but does not talk about it. Within the limits of the external world, the Sage talks but does not make comments. With regard to the wisdom of the ancients, as embodied in the canon of *Spring and Autumn*, the Sage comments, but does not expound. And thus, among distinctions made, there are distinctions that cannot be made; among things expounded, there are things that cannot be expounded.

How can that be? The true Sage keeps his knowledge within him, while men in general set forth theirs in argument, in order to convince each other. And therefore it is said that one who argues does so because he cannot see certain points.

Now perfect Tao cannot be given a name. A perfect argument does not employ words. Perfect kindness does not concern itself with (individual acts of) kindness. Perfect integrity is not critical of others. Perfect courage does not push itself forward.

For the Tao which is manifest is not Tao. Speech which argues falls short of its aim. Kindness which has fixed objects loses its scope. Integrity which is obvious is not believed in. Courage which pushes itself forward never accomplishes anything. These five are, as it were, round (mellow) with a strong bias towards squareness (sharpness). Therefore that knowledge which stops at what it does not know, is the highest knowledge.

Who knows the argument which can be argued without words, and the Tao which does not declare itself as Tao? He who knows this may be said to enter the realm of the spirit. To be poured into without becoming full, and pour out without becoming empty, without knowing how this is brought about,—this is the art of "Concealing the Light."

Of old, the Emperor Yao said to Shun, "I would smite the Tsungs, and the Kueis, and the Hsü-aos. Since I have been on the throne, this has ever been on my mind. What do you think?"

"These three States," replied Shun, "lie in wild undeveloped regions. Why can you not shake off this idea? Once upon a time, ten suns came out together, and all things were illuminated thereby. How much greater should be the power of virtue which excels the suns?"

Yeh Ch'üeh asked Wang Yi, saying, "Do you know for certain that all things are the same?"

"How can I know?" answered Wang Yi.

"Do you know what you do not know?"

"How can I know?" replied Yeh Ch'üeh.

"But then does nobody know?"

"How can I know?" said Wang Yi. "Nevertheless, I will try to tell you. How can it be known that what I call knowing is not really not knowing and that what I call not knowing is not really knowing? Now I would ask you this, If a man sleeps in a damp place, he gets lumbago and dies. But how about an eel? And living up in a tree is precarious and trying to the nerves. But how about monkeys? Of the man, the eel, and the monkey, whose habitat is the right one, absolutely? Human beings feed on flesh, deer on grass, centipedes on little snakes, owls and crows on mice. Of these four, whose is the right taste, absolutely? Monkey mates with the dog-headed female ape, the buck with the doe, eels consort with fishes, while men admire Mao Ch'iang and Li Chi, at the sight of whom fishes plunge deep down in the water, birds soar high in the air, and deer hurry away. Yet who shall say which is the correct standard of beauty? In my opinion, the doctrines of humanity and justice and the paths of right and wrong are so confused that it is impossible to know their contentions."

"If you then," asked Yeh Ch'üeh, "do not know what is good and bad, is the Perfect Man equally without this knowledge?"

"The Perfect Man," answered Wang Yi, "is a spiritual being. Were the ocean itself scorched up, he would not feel hot. Were the great rivers frozen hard, he would not feel cold. Were the mountains to be cleft by thunder, and the great deep to be thrown up by storm, he would not tremble with fear. Thus, he would mount upon the clouds of heaven, and driving the sun and the moon before him, pass beyond the limits of this mundane existence. Death and life have no more victory over him. How much less should he concern himself with the distinctions of profit and loss?"

Chü Ch'iao addressed Ch'ang Wutse as follows: "I heard Confucius say, 'The true Sage pays no heed to worldly affairs. He neither seeks gain nor avoids injury. He asks nothing at the hands of man and does not adhere to rigid rules of conduct. Sometimes he says something without speaking and sometimes he speaks without saying anything. And so he roams beyond the limits of this mundane world. These,' commented Confucius, 'are futile fantasies.' But to me they are the embodiment of the most wonderful Tao. What is your opinion?"

"These are things that perplexed even the Yellow Emperor," replied Ch'ang Wutse. "How should Confucius know? You are going too far ahead. When you see a hen's egg, you already expect to hear a cock crow. When you see a sling, you are already expecting to have broiled pigeon. I will say a few words to you at random, and do you listen at random.

"How does the Sage seat himself by the sun and moon, and hold the universe in his grasp? He blends everything into one harmonious whole, rejecting the confusion of this and that. Rank and precedence, which the vulgar sedulously cultivate, the Sage stolidly ignores, amalgamating the disparities of ten thousand years into one pure mould. The universe itself, too, conserves and blends all in the same manner.

"How do I know that love of life is not a delusion after all? How do I know but that he who dreads death is not as a child who has lost his way and does not know his way home?

"The lady Li Chi was the daughter of the frontier officer of Ai. When the Duke of Chin first got her, she wept until the bosom of her dress was drenched with tears. But when she came to the royal residence, shared with the Duke his luxurious couch, and ate rich food, she repented of having wept. How then do I know but that the dead may repent of having previously clung to life?

"Those who dream of the banquet, wake to lamentation and sorrow. Those who dream of lamentation and sorrow wake to join the hunt. While they dream, they do not know that they are dreaming. Some will even interpret the very dream they are dreaming; and only when they awake do they know it was a dream. By and by comes the great awakening, and then we find out that this life is really a great dream. Fools think they are awake now, and flatter themselves they know—this one is a prince, and that one is a shepherd. What narrowness of mind! Confucius and you are both dreams; and I who say you are dreams—I am but a dream myself. This is a paradox. Tomorrow a Sage may arise to explain it; but that tomorrow will not be until ten thousand generations have gone by. Yet you may meet him around the corner.

"Granting that you and I argue. If you get the better of me, and not I of you, are you necessarily right and I wrong? Or if I get the better of you and not you of me, am I necessarily right and you wrong? Or are we both partly right and partly wrong? Or are we both wholly right and wholly wrong? You and I cannot know this, and consequently we all live in darkness.

"Whom shall I ask as arbiter between us? If I ask some one who takes your view, he will side with you. How can such a one arbitrate between us? If I ask some one who takes my view, he will side with me. How can such a one arbitrate between us? If I ask some one who differs from both of us, he will be equally unable to decide between us, since he differs from both of us. And if I ask some one who agrees with both of us, he will be equally unable to decide between us, since he agrees with both of us. Since then you and I and other men cannot decide, how can we depend upon another? The words of arguments are all relative; if we wish to reach the absolute, we must harmonize them by means of the unity of God, and follow their natural evolution, so that we may complete our allotted span of life.

"But what is it to harmonize them by means of the unity of God? It is this. The right may not be really right. What appears so may not be really so. Even if what is right is really right, wherein it differs from wrong cannot be made plain by argument. Even if what appears so is really so, wherein it differs from what is not so also cannot be made plain by argument.

"Take no heed of time nor of right and wrong. Passing into the realm of the Infinite, take your final rest therein."

The Penumbra said to the Umbra. "At one moment you move: at another you are at rest. At one moment you sit down: at another you get up. Why this instability of purpose?" "Perhaps I depend," replied the Umbra, "upon something which causes me to do as I do; and perhaps that something depends in turn upon something else which causes it to do as it does. Or perhaps my dependence is like (the unconscious movements) of a snake's scales or of a cicada's wings. How can I tell why I do one thing, or why I do not do another?"

Once upon a time, I, Chuang Chou, dreamt I was a butterfly, fluttering hither and thither, to all intents and purposes a butterfly. I was conscious only of my happiness as a butterfly, unaware that I was Chou. Soon I awaked, and there I was, veritably myself again. Now I do not know whether I was then a man dreaming I was a butterfly, or whether I am now a butterfly, dreaming I am a man. Between a man and a butterfly there is necessarily a distinction. The transition is called the transformation of material things.

THE GREAT SUPREME

He who knows what is of God and who knows what is of Man has reached indeed the height (of wisdom). One who knows what is of God patterns his living after God. One who knows what is of Man may still use his knowledge of the known to develop his knowledge of the unknown, living till the end of his days and not perishing young. This is the fullness of knowledge.

Herein, however, there is a flaw. Correct knowledge is dependent on objects, but the objects of knowledge are relative and uncertain (changing). How can one know that the natural is not really of man, and what is of man is not really natural? We must, moreover, have true men before we can have true knowledge.

But what is a true man? The true men of old did not override the weak, did not attain their ends by brute strength, and did not gather around them counsellors. Thus, failing they had no cause for regret; succeeding, no cause for self-satisfaction. And thus they could scale heights without trembling, enter water without becoming wet, and go through fire without feeling hot. That is the kind of knowledge which reaches to the depths of Tao. The true men of old slept without dreams, and waked up without worries. They ate with indifference to flavor, and drew deep breaths. For true men draw breath from their heels; the vulgar only from their throats. Out of the crooked, words are retched up like vomit. When man's attachments are deep, their divine endowments are shallow.

The true men of old did not know what it was to love life or to hate death. They did not rejoice in birth, nor strive to put off dissolution. Unconcerned they came and unconcerned they went. That was all. They did not forget whence it was they had sprung, neither did they seek to inquire their return thither. Cheerfully they accepted life, waiting patiently for their restoration (the end). This is what is called not to lead the heart astray from Tao, and not to supplement the natural by human means. Such a one may be called a true man.

Such men are free in mind and calm in demeanour, with high foreheads. Sometimes disconsolate like autumn, and sometimes warm like spring, their joys and sorrows are in direct touch with the four seasons, in harmony with all creation, and none know the limit thereof. And so it is that when the Sage wages war, he can destroy a kingdom and yet not lose the affection of the people; he spreads blessing upon all things, but it is not due to his (conscious) love of fellowmen. Therefore he who delights in understanding the material world is not a Sage. He who has personal attachments is not humane. He who calculates the time of his actions is not wise. He who does not know the interaction of benefit and harm is not a superior man. He who pursues fame at the risk of losing his self is not a scholar. He who loses his life and is not true to himself can never be a master of man. Thus Hu Puhsieh, Wu Kuang, Po Yi, Shu Ch'i, Chi Tse, Hsü Yü, Chi T'o, and Shent'u Ti, were the servants of rulers, and did the behests of others, not their own.

The true men of old appeared of towering stature and yet could not topple down. They behaved as though wanting in themselves, but without looking up to others. Naturally independent of mind, they were not severe. Living in unconstrained freedom, yet they did not try to show off. They appeared to smile as if pleased, and to move only in natural response to surroundings. Their serenity flowed from the store of goodness within. In social relationships, they kept to their inner character. Broad-minded, they appeared great; towering, they seemed beyond control. Continuously abiding, they seemed like doors kept shut; absent-minded, they seemed to forget speech. They saw in penal laws an outward form; in social ceremonies, certain means; in knowledge, tools of expediency; in morality, a guide. It was for this reason that for them penal laws meant a merciful administration; social ceremonies, a means to get along with the world; knowledge a help for doing what they could not avoid; and morality, a guide that they might walk along with others to reach a hill. And all men really thought that they were at pains to make their lives correct.

For what they cared for was ONE and what they did not care for was ONE also. That which they regarded as ONE was ONE, and that which they did not regard as ONE was ONE likewise. In that which was ONE, they were of God; in that which was not ONE, they were of man. And so between the human and the divine no conflict ensued. This was to be a true man.

Life and Death are a part of Destiny. Their sequence, like day and night, is of God, beyond the interference of man. These all lie in the inevitable nature of things. He simply looks upon God as his father; if he loves him with what is born of the body, shall he not love him also with that which is greater than the body? A man looks upon a ruler of men as one superior to himself; if he is willing to sacrifice his body (for his ruler), shall he not then offer his pure (spirit) also?

When the pond dries up and the fishes are left upon the dry ground, rather than leave them to moisten each other with their damp and spittle, it would be far better to let them forget themselves in their native rivers and lakes. And it would be better than praising Yao and blaming Chieh to forget both (the good and bad) and lose oneself in Tao.

The Great (universe) gives me this form, this toil in manhood, this repose in old age, this rest in death. And surely that which is such a kind arbiter of my life is the best arbiter of my death.

A boat may be hidden in a creek, or concealed in a bog, which is generally considered safe. But at midnight a strong man may come and carry it away on his back. Those dull of understanding do not perceive that however you conceal small things in large ones, there will always be a chance of losing them. But if you entrust that which belongs to the universe to the whole universe, from it there will be no escape. For this is the great law of things.

To have been cast in this human form is to us already a source of joy. How much greater joy beyond our conception to know that that which is now in human form may undergo countless transitions, with only the infinite to look forward to? Therefore it is that the Sage rejoices in that which can never be lost, but endures always. For if we emulate those who can accept graciously long age or short life and the vicissitudes of events, how much more that which informs all creation on which all changing phenomena depend?

For Tao has its inner reality and its evidences. It is devoid of action and of form. It may be transmitted, but cannot be received. It may be obtained, but cannot be seen. It is based in itself, rooted in itself. Before heaven and earth were, Tao existed by itself from all time. It gave the spirits and rulers their spiritual powers, and gave Heaven and Earth their birth. To Tao, the zenith is not high, nor the nadir low; no point in time is long ago, nor by the lapse of ages has it grown old.

Hsi Wei obtained Tao, and so set the universe in order. Fu Hsi obtained it, and was able to steal the secrets of eternal principles. The Great Bear obtained it, and has never erred from its course. The sun and moon obtained it, and have never ceased to revolve. K'an P'i obtained it, and made his abode in the K'unlun mountains. P'ing I obtained it, and rules over the streams. Chien Wu obtained it, and dwells on Mount T'ai. The Yellow Emperor obtained it, and soared upon the clouds to heaven. Chuan Hsü obtained it, and dwells in the Dark Palace. Yü Ch'iang obtained it, and established himself at the North Pole. The Western (Fairy) Queen Mother obtained it, and settled at Shao Kuang, since when and until when, no one knows. P'eng Tsu obtained it, and lived from the time of Shun until the time of the Five Princes. Fu Yüeh obtained it, and as the Minister of Wu Ting extended his rule to the whole empire. And now, charioted upon the Tungwei (one constellation) and drawn by the Chiwei (another constellation), he has taken his station among the stars of heaven.

Nanpo Tsek'uei said to Nü Yü (or Female Yü), "You are of a high age, and yet you have a child's complexion. How is this?"

Nü Yü replied, "I have learnt Tao."

"Could I get Tao by studying it?" asked the other.

"No! How can you?" said Nü Yü. "You are not the type of person. There was Puliang I. He had all the mental talents of a sage, but not Tao of the sage. Now I had Tao, though not those talents. But do you think I was able to teach him to become indeed a sage? Had it been so, then to teach Tao to one who has a sage's talents would be an easy matter. It was not so, for I had to wait patiently to reveal it to him. In three days, he could transcend this mundane world. Again I waited for seven days more, then he could transcend all material existence. After he could transcend all material existence, I waited for another nine days, after which he could transcend all life. After he could transcend all life, then he had the clear vision of the morning, and after that, was able to see the Solitary (One). After seeing the Solitary, he could abolish the distinctions of past and present. After abolishing the past and present, he was able to enter there where life and death are no more, where killing does not take away life, nor does giving birth add to it. He was ever in accord with the exigencies of his environment, accepting all and welcoming all, regarding everything as destroyed and everything as in completion. This is to be 'secure amidst confusion,' reaching security through chaos."

"Where did you learn this from?" asked Nanpo Tsek'uei.

"I learned it from the Son of Ink," replied Nü Yü, "and the Son of Ink learned it from the Grandson of Learning, the Grandson of Learning from Understanding, and Understanding from Insight, Insight learned it from Practice, Practice from Folk Song, and Folk Song from Silence, Silence from the Void, and the Void learned it from the Seeming Beginning."

Four men: Tsesze, Tseyü, Tseli, and Tselai, were conversing together, saying, "Whoever can make Not-being the head, Life the backbone, and Death the tail, and whoever realizes that death and life and being and non-being are of one body, that man shall be admitted to friendship with us." The four looked at each other and smiled, and completely understanding one another, became friends accordingly.

By-and-by, Tseyü fell ill, and Tsesze went to see him. "Verily the Creator is great!" said the sick man. "See how He has doubled me up." His back was so hunched that his viscera were at the top of his body. His cheeks were level with his navel, and his shoulders were higher than his neck. His neck bone pointed up towards the sky. The whole economy of his organism was deranged, but his mind was calm as ever. He dragged himself to a well, and said, "Alas, that God should have doubled me up like this!"

"Do you dislike it?" asked Tsesze.

"No, why should I?" replied Tseyü. "If my left arm should become a cock, I should be able to herald the dawn with it. If my right arm should become a sling, I should be able to shoot down a bird to broil with it. If my buttocks should become wheels, and my spirit become a horse, I should be able to ride in it—what need would I have of a chariot? I obtained life because it was my time, and I am now parting with it in accordance with Tao. Content with the coming of things in their time and living in accord with Tao, joy and sorrow touch me not. This is, according to the ancients, to be freed from bondage. Those who cannot be freed from bondage are so because they are bound by the trammels of material existence. But man has ever given away before God; why, then, should I dislike it?"

By-and-by, Tselai fell ill, and lay gasping for breath, while his family stood weeping around. Tseli went to see him, and cried to the wife and children: "Go away! You are impeding his dissolution." Then, leaning against the door, he said, "Verily, God is great! I wonder what He will make of you now, and whither He will send you. Do you think he will make you into a rat's liver or into an insect leg?"

"A son," answered Tselai, "must go whithersoever his parents bid him, East, West, North, or South. *Yin* and *Yang* are no other than a man's parents. If *Yin* and *Yang* bid me die quickly, and I demur, then the fault is mine, not theirs. The Great (universe) gives me this form, this toil in manhood, this repose in old age, this rest in death. Surely that which is such a kind arbiter of my life is the best arbiter of my death.

"Suppose that the boiling metal in a smelting-pot were to bubble up and say, 'Make of me a Moyeh! I think the master caster would reject that metal as uncanny. And if simply because I am cast into a human form, I were to say, 'Only a man! only a man!' I think the Creator too would reject me as uncanny. If I regard the universe as the smelting pot, and the Creator as the Master Caster, how should I worry wherever I am sent?" Then he sunk into a peaceful sleep and waked up very much alive.

Tsesang Hu, Mengtse Fan, and Tsech'in Chang, were conversing together, saying, "Who can live together as if they did not live together? Who can help each other as if they did not help each other? Who can mount to heaven, and roaming through the clouds, leap about to the Ultimate Infinite, oblivious of existence, for ever and ever without end?" The three looked at each other and smiled with a perfect understanding and became friends accordingly.

Shortly afterwards, Tsesang Hu died, whereupon Confucious sent Tsekung to attend the mourning. But Tsekung found that one of his friends was arranging the cocoon sheets and the other was playing string instruments and (both were) singing together as follows:

> "Oh! come back to us, Sang Hu,
> Oh! come back to us, Sang Hu,
> Thou hast already returned to thy true state,
> While we still remain here as men! Oh!"

Tsekung hurried in and said, "How can you sing in the presence of a corpse? Is this good manners?"

The two men looked at each other and laughed, saying, "What should this man know about the meaning of good manners indeed?" Tsekung went back and told Confucious, asking him, "What manner of men are these? Their object is to cultivate nothingness and that which lies beyond their corporeal frames. They can sit near a corpse and sing, unmoved. There is no name for such persons. What manner of men are they?"

"These men," replied Confucius, "play about beyond the material things; I play about within them. Consequently, our paths do not meet, and I was stupid to have sent you to mourn. They consider themselves as companions of the Creator, and play about within the One Spirit of the universe. They look upon life as a huge goiter or excrescence, and upon death as the breaking of a tumor. How could such people be concerned about the coming of life and death or their sequence? They borrow their forms from the different elements, and take temporary abode in the common forms, unconscious of their internal organs and oblivious of their senses of hearing and vision. They go through life backwards and forwards as in a circle without beginning or end, strolling forgetfully beyond the dust and dirt of mortality, and playing about with the affairs of inaction. How should such men bustle about the conventionalities of this world, for the people to look at?"

"But if such is the case," said Tsekung, "which world (the corporeal or the spiritual) would you follow?"

"I am one condemned by God," replied Confucius. "Nevertheless, I will share with you (what I know)."

"May I ask what is your method?" asked Tsekung.

"Fishes live their full life in water. Men live their full life in Tao," replied Confucius. "Those that live their full life in water thrive in ponds. Those that live their full life in Tao achieve realization of their nature in inaction. Hence the saying 'Fish lose themselves (are happy) in water; man loses himself (is happy) in Tao.'"

"May I ask," said Tsekung, "about (those) strange people?"

"(Those) strange people," replied Confucius, "are strange in the eyes of man, but normal in the eyes of God. Hence the saying that the meanest thing in heaven would be the best on earth; and the best on earth, the meanest in heaven."

Yen Huei said to Chungni (Confucius), "When Mengsun Ts'ai's mother died, he wept, but without snivelling; his heart was not grieved; he wore mourning but without sorrow. Yet although wanting in these three points, he is considered the best mourner in the State of Lu. Can there be really people with a hollow reputation? I am astonished."

"Mr. Mengsun," said Chungni, "has really mastered (the Tao). He has gone beyond the wise ones. There are still certain things he cannot quite give up, but he has already given up some things. Mr. Mengsun knows not whence we come in life nor whither we go in death. He knows not which to put first and which to put last. He is ready to be transformed into other things without caring into what he may be transformed—that is all. How could that which is changing say that it will not change, and how could that which regards itself as permanent realize that it is changing already? Even you and I are perhaps dreamers who have not yet awakened. Moreover, he knows his form is subject to change, but his mind remains the same. He believes not in real death, but regards it as moving into a new house. He weeps only when he sees others weep, as it comes to him naturally.

"Besides, we all talk of 'me.' How do you know what is this 'me' that we speak of? You dream you are a bird, and soar to heaven, or dream you are a fish, and dive into the ocean's depths. And you cannot tell whether the man now speaking is awake or in a dream.

"A man feels a pleasurable sensation before he smiles, and smiles before he thinks how he ought to smile. Resign yourself to the sequence of things, forgetting the changes of life, and you shall enter into the pure, the divine, the One."

Yi-erh-tse went to see Hsü Yu. The latter asked him, saying, "What have you learned from Yao?"

"He bade me," replied the former, "practice charity and do my duty, and distinguish clearly between right and wrong."

"Then what do you want here?" said Hsü Yu. "If Yao has already branded you with charity of heart and duty, and cut off your nose with right and wrong, what are you doing here in this free-and-easy, unfettered, take-what-comes neighborhood?"

"Nevertheless," replied Yi-erh-tse. "I should like to loiter on its confines."

"If a man has lost his eyes," retorted Hsü Yu, "it is impossible for him to join in the appreciation of beauty of face and complexion or to tell a blue sacrificial robe from a yellow one."

"Wu Chuang's (No-Decorum's) disregard of her beauty," answered Yi-erh-tse, "Chü Liang's disregard of his strength, the Yellow Emperor's abandonment of his wisdom,—all these came from a process of purging and purification. And how do you know but that the Creator would rid me of my brandings, and give me a new nose, and make me fit to become a disciple of yourself?"

"Ah!" replied Hsü Yu, "that cannot be known. But I will give you an outline. Ah! my Master, my Master! He trims down all created things, and does not account it justice. He causes all created things to thrive and does not account it kindness. Dating back further than the remotest antiquity, He does not account himself old. Covering heaven, supporting earth, and fashioning the various forms of things, He does not account himself skilled. It is He whom you should seek."

Yen Huei spoke to Chungni (Confucius), "I am getting on."

"How so?" asked the latter.

"I have got rid of charity and duty," replied the former.

"Very good," replied Chungni, "but not quite perfect."

Another day, Yen Huei met Chungni and said, "I am getting on."

"How so?"

"I have got rid of ceremonies and music," answered Yen Huei.

"Very good," said Chungni, "but not quite perfect."

Another day, Yen Huei again met Chungni and said, "I am getting on."

"How so?"

"I can forget myself while sitting," replied Yen Huei.

"What do you mean by that?" said Chungni, changing his countenance.

"I have freed myself from my body," answered Yen Huei. "I have discarded my reasoning powers. And by thus getting rid of my body and mind, I have become One with the Infinite. This is what I mean by forgetting myself while sitting."

"If you have become One," said Chungni, "there can be no room for bias. If you have lost yourself, there can no more hindrance. Perhaps you are really a wise one. I trust to be allowed to follow in your steps."

Tseyü and Tsesang were friends. Once when it had rained for ten days, Tseyü said, "Tsesang is probably ill." So he packed up some food and went to see him. Arriving at the door, he heard something between singing and weeping, accompanied with the sound of a string instrument, as follows: "O Father! O mother! Is this due to God? Is this due to man?" It was as if his voice was broken and his words faltered.

Whereupon Tseyü went in and asked, "Why are you singing in such manner?" "I was trying to think who could have brought me to this extreme," replied Tsesang, "but I could not guess it. My father and mother would hardly wish me to be poor. Heaven covers all equally. Earth supports all equally. How can they make me in particular so poor? I was seeking to find out who was responsible for this, but without success. Surely then I am brought to this extreme by *Destiny*."

26

UNIVERSAL LOVE
Mo Tzu

Mo Tzu (c. 479–381 B.C.), the founder of the religion that was Confucianism's chief rival during the Warring States period (403–222 B.C.), was markedly more rational in argument and more theistic in belief than either his Confucian or Taoist contemporaries. His condemnation of aggressive war, fatalism, luxuries, ceremonies, elaborate funerals, and music are argued upon purely utilitarian grounds. His teaching that the Will of Heaven was one of beneficent love applying equally to men of all classes and nations and requiring a universal love on the part of mankind would be acceptable to many western theists. In addition to preaching to rulers and writing, Mo Tzu organized a group of several hundred followers who lived a simple life of obedience, hard labor, and self-denial and eventually may have become a band of specialists in defensive warfare.

The book of Mo Tzu once had seventy-one chapters but eighteen have been lost. Six of the remaining chapters are believed to have been written by Mo Tzu's disciples. Chapter Fifteen, the most influential, is here given in Mei's translation.

Mo Tzu, "Universal Love," Yi-Pao Mei, trans. (London: Arthur Probsthain, 1929), pp. 81–86. Reprinted from *Ethical and Political Works of Motse*, by Yi-Pao Mei by permission of Arthur Probsthain.

MOTSE SAID: The purpose of the magnanimous is to be found in procuring benefits for the world and eliminating its calamities.

But what are the benefits of the world and what its calamities?

MOTSE SAID: Mutual attacks among states, mutual usurpation among houses, mutual injuries among individuals; the lack of grace and loyalty between ruler and ruled, the lack of affection and filial piety between father and son, the lack of harmony between elder and younger brothers—these are the major calamities in the world.

But whence did these calamities arise, out of mutual love?

MOTSE SAID: They arise out of want of mutual love. At present feudal lords have learned only to love their own states and not those of others. Therefore they do not scruple about attacking other states. The heads of houses have learned only to love their own houses and not those of others. Therefore they do not scruple about usurping other houses. And individuals have learned only to love themselves and not others. Therefore they do not scruple about injuring others. When feudal lords do not love one another there will be war on the fields. When heads of houses do not love one another they will usurp one another's power. When individuals do not love one another they will injure one another. When ruler and ruled do not love one another they will not be gracious and loyal. When father and son do not love each other they will not be affectionate and filial. When elder and younger brothers do not love each other they will not be harmonious. When nobody in the world loves any other, naturally the strong will overpower the weak, the many will oppress the few, the wealthy will mock the poor, the honoured will disdain the humble, the cunning will deceive the simple. Therefore all the calamities, strifes, complaints, and hatred in the world have arisen out of want of mutual love. Therefore the benevolent disapproved of this want.

Now that there is disapproval, how can we have the condition altered?

Motse said it is to be altered by the way of universal love and mutual aid.

But what is the way of universal love and mutual aid?

MOTSE SAID: It is to regard the state of others as one's own, the houses of others as one's own, the persons of others as one's self. When feudal lords love one another there will be no more war; when heads of houses love one another there will be no more mutual usurpation; when individuals love one another there will be no more mutual injury. When ruler and ruled love each other they will be gracious and loyal; when father and son love each other they will be affectionate and filial; when elder and younger brothers love each other they will be harmonious. When all the people in the world love one another, then the strong will not overpower the weak, the many will not oppress the few, the wealthy will not mock the poor, the honoured will not disdain the humble, and the cunning will not deceive the simple. And it is all due to mutual love that calamities, strifes, complaints, and hatred are prevented from arising. Therefore the benevolent exalt it.

But the gentlemen of the world would say: "So far so good. It is of course very excellent when love becomes universal. But it is only a difficult and distant ideal."

MOTSE SAID: This is simply because the gentlemen of the world do not recognize what is to the benefit of the world, or understand what is its calamity. Now, to besiege a city, to fight in the fields, or to achieve a name at the cost of death—these are what men find difficult. Yet when the superior encourages them, the multitude can do them. Besides, universal love and mutual aid is quite different from these. Whoever loves others is loved by others; whoever benefits others is benefited by others; whoever hates others is hated by others; whoever injures others is injured by others. Then, what difficulty is there with it (universal love)? Only, the ruler fails to embody it in his government and the ordinary man in his conduct.

Formerly, Lord Wen of the state of Chin (about 630 B.C.) liked the uncouth uniform of the soldier. And so all his ministers and officers wore sheepskin jackets, carried their swords in leather girdles, and put on silk-spun hats. Thus attired, they attended the Lord when they went in and paced the court when they stayed out. What was the reason for this? It was that what the ruler encourages the ruled will carry out. And Lord Ling of the state of Ch'u (about 535 B.C.) liked slender waists. And so all his ministers and officers limited themselves to a single meal (a day). They tied their belts after exhaling, and could not stand up without leaning against the wall. Within a year the court looked grim and dark. What was the reason for this? It was that what the ruler encourages the ruled will carry out. Again, Lord Kou Chien of the state of Yüeh (about 480 B.C.) liked the warrior's courage, and trained his subjects accordingly. He had his palace boat set on fire. To test his soldiers he proclaimed that all the treasures of the state were contained therein. And he beat the drum himself to urge them on. Hearing the drum the soldiers rushed on in disorder. More than a hundred strong perished in the flames. Thereupon the Lord beat the gong to let them retreat.

Therefore MOTSE SAID: Now, things like scantily dyed coarse clothing and the achievement of a name at the cost of death are those in which people find difficulty. Yet when the ruler encourages them the multitude can stand them. Besides, universal love and mutual aid are different from these. Whoever loves others is loved by others; whoever benefits others is benefited by others; whoever hates others is hated by others; whoever injures others is injured by others. Then what difficulty is there with it (universal love)? Only, the ruler fails to embody it in his government and the ordinary man in his conduct.

Nevertheless, the gentlemen in the empire think that, though it would be an excellent thing if love can be universalized, it is something quite impracticable. It is like carrying Mt. T'ai and leaping over the Chi River.

MOTSE SAID: The illustration is a faulty one. Of course to be able to carry Mt. T'ai and leap over the Chi River would be an extreme feat of strength. Such has never been performed from antiquity to the present time.

But universal love and mutual aid are quite different from this. And the ancient sage-kings did practise it. How do we know they did? When Yü was working to bring the Deluge under control, he dug the West River and the Yu Tou River in the west in order to let off the water from the Ch'ü, Sun, and Huang Rivers. In the north he built a dam across the Yuan and Ku Rivers in order to fill the Hou Chih Ti (a basin) and the Hu Ch'ih River. Mt. Ti Chu was made use of as a water divide, and a tunnel was dug through Mt. Lung Men. All these were done to benefit the peoples west of the (Yellow) River and various barbarian tribes, Yen, Tai, Hu, Ho, of the north. In the east he drained the great Plain and built dykes along the Meng Chu River. The watercourse was divided into nine canals in order to regulate the water in the east and in order to benefit the people of the District of Chi. In th south he completed the Yangtze, Han, Huai, and Ju Rivers. These ran eastward and emptied themselves into the Five Lakes. This was done in order to benefit the peoples of Ching, Ch'u, Kan, Yüeh, and the barbarians of the south. All these are the deeds of Yü. We can, then, universalize love in conduct.

When King Wen was ruling the Western land, he shone forth like the sun and the moon all over the four quarters as well as in the Western land. He did not allow the big state to oppress the small state, he did not allow the multitude to oppress the single-handed, he did not allow the influential and strong to take away the grain and live stock from the farmers. Heaven visited him with blessing. And, therefore, the old and childless had the wherewithal to spend their old age, the solitary and brotherless had the opportunity to join in the social life of men, and the orphans had the support for their growth. This was what King Wen had accomplished. We can, then, universalize love in conduct.

When King Wu was about to do service to Mt. T'ai it was recorded thus: "Blessed is Mt. T'ai. Duke of Chou by a long descent is about to perform his duty. As I have obtained the approval of Heaven, the magnanimous arise to save the people of Shang Hsia as well as the barbarians (from the tyranny of Emperor Chow). Though (Emperor Chow) has many near relatives, they cannot compare with the magnanimous. If there is sin anywhere, I am solely responsible." This relates the deeds of King Wu. We can, then, universalize love in conduct.

Therefore Motse said: If the rulers sincerely desire the empire to be wealthy and dislike to have it poor, desire to have it orderly and dislike to have it chaotic, they should bring about universal love and mutual aid. This is the way of the sage-kings and the way to order for the world, and it should not be neglected.

THE CLASSIC OF FILIAL PIETY

The Classic of Filial Piety has been an important textbook in Chinese elementary education for 2000 years. It presents filial piety as the foundation of the moral life, the most natural and essential of virtues, and the source of almost all that is best in human relationships. The book illustrates the enormous emphasis Chinese culture has placed upon filiality and as one of the "Thirteen Classics" has played an important part in transmitting and reinforcing that emphasis.

The Classic of Filial Piety purports to be a conversation between Confucius (called "Kung-ni" in the first sentence) and a famous disciple, Tseng Tzu. Its author and date of composition are unknown, but it probably was written during the Fourth or Third Century B.C. It has the simplest language of any of the Chinese classics, employing less than 400 different characters and a simple syntax, thus rendering it suitable for study by young students. It is here reprinted in its entirety in the translation by Legge.

THE SCOPE AND MEANING OF THE TREATISE

(Once), when Kung-nî was unoccupied, and his disciple Tseng was sitting by in attendance on him the Master said, 'Shăn, the ancient kings had a perfect virtue and all-embracing rule of conduct, through which they were in accord with all under heaven. By the practice of it the people were brought to live in peace and harmony, and there was no ill-will between superiors and inferiors. Do you know what it was?' Tseng rose from his mat, and said, 'How should I, Shăn, who am so devoid of intelligence, be able to know this?' The Master said, '(It was filial piety). Now filial piety is the root of (all) virtue, and (the stem) out of which grows (all moral) teaching. Sit down again, and I will explain the subject to you. Our bodies—to every hair and bit of skin— are received by us from our parents, and we must not presume to injure or

The Hsiâo King, Chs. I-XVIII, James Legge, trans. (Oxford, England: Clarendon Press, 1899) pp. 465–488. Reprinted from *The Sacred Books of the East,* vol. III, ed. by F. Max-Müller.

wound them:—this is the beginning of filial piety. When we have established our character by the practice of the (filial) course, so as to make our name famous in future ages, and thereby glorify our parents:—this is the end of filial piety. It commences with the service of parents; it proceeds to the service of the ruler; it is completed by the establishment of the character.

'It is said in the Major Odes of the Kingdom,

> "Ever think of your ancestor,
> Cultivating your virtue." '

FILIAL PIETY IN THE SON OF HEAVEN

He who loves his parents will not dare (to incur the risk of) being hated by any man, and he who reveres his parents will not dare (to incur the risk of) being contemned by any man. When the love and reverence (of the Son of Heaven) are thus carried to the utmost in the service of his parents, the lessons of his virtue affect all the people, and he becomes a pattern to (all within) the four seas:—this is the filial piety of the Son of Heaven.

It is said in (the Marquis of) Fù on Punishments,

'The One man will have felicity, and the millions of the people will depend on (what ensures his happiness).'

FILIAL PIETY IN THE PRINCES OF STATES

Above others, and yet free from pride, they dwell on high, without peril; adhering to economy, and carefully observant of the rules and laws, they are full, without overflowing. To dwell on high without peril is the way long to preserve nobility; to be full without overflowing is the way long to preserve riches. When their riches and nobility do not leave their persons, then they are able to preserve the altars of their land and grain, and to secure the harmony of their people and men in office:—this is the filial piety of the prince of states.

It is said in the Book of Poetry,

> 'Be apprehensive, be cautious,
> As if on the brink of a deep abyss,
> As if treading on thin ice.'

FILIAL PIETY IN HIGH MINISTERS AND GREAT OFFICERS

They do not presume to wear robes other than those appointed by the laws of the ancient kings; nor to speak words other than those sanctioned by their speech; nor to exhibit conduct other than that exemplified by their virtuous ways. Thus none of their words being contrary to those sanctions, and none of their actions contrary to the (right) way, from their mouths there comes no exceptionable speech, and in their conduct there are found no exceptionable actions. Their words may fill all under heaven, and no error of speech will be found in them. Their actions may fill all under heaven, and no dissatisfaction or dislike will be awakened by them. When these three things—(their robes, their words, and their conduct)—are all complete as they should be, they can then preserve their ancestral temples:—this is the filial piety of high ministers and great officers.

It is said in the Book of Poetry,

'He is never idle, day or night,
In the service of the One man.

FILIAL PIETY IN INFERIOR OFFICERS

As they serve their fathers, so they serve their mothers, and they love them equally. As they serve their fathers, so they serve their rulers, and they reverence them equally. Hence love is what is chiefly rendered to the mother, and reverence is what is chiefly rendered to the ruler, while both of these things are given to the father. Therefore when they serve their ruler with filial piety they are loyal; when they serve their superiors with reverence they are obedient. Not failing in this loyalty and obedience in serving those above them, they are then able to preserve their emoluments and positions, and to maintain their sacrifices:—this is the filial piety of inferior officers.

It is said in the Book of Poetry,

'Rising early and going to sleep late,
Do not disgrace those who gave you birth.'

FILIAL PIETY IN THE COMMON PEOPLE

They follow the course of heaven (in the revolving seasons); they distinguish the advantages afforded by (different) soils; they are careful of their conduct and economical in their expenditure;—in order to nourish their parents.—this is the filial piety of the common people.

Therefore from the Son of Heaven down to the common people, there never has been one whose filial piety was without its beginning and end on whom calamity did not come.

FILIAL PIETY IN RELATION TO THE THREE POWERS

The disciple Tsăng said, 'Immense indeed is the greatness of filial piety!' The Master replied, 'Yes, filial piety is the constant (method) of Heaven, the righteousness of Earth, and the practical duty of Man. Heaven and earth invariably pursue the course (that may be thus described), and the people take it as their pattern. (The ancient kings) imitated the brilliant luminaries of heaven, and acted in accordance with the (varying) advantages afforded by earth, so that they were in accord with all under heaven; and in consequence their teachings, without being severe, were successful, and their government, without being rigorous, secured perfect order.

'The ancient kings, seeing how their teachings could transform the people, set before them therefore an example of the most extended love, and none of the people neglected their parents; they set forth to them (the nature of) virtue and righteousness, and the people roused themselves to the practice of them; they went before them with reverence and yielding courtesy, and the people had no contentions; they led them on by the rules of propriety and by music, and the people were harmonious and benignant; they showed them what they loved and what they disliked, and the people understood their prohibitions.

'It is said in the Book of Poetry,

> "Awe-inspiring are you, O Grand-Master Yin,
> And the people all look up to you." '

FILIAL PIETY IN GOVERNMENT

The Master said, 'Anciently, when the intelligent kings by means of filial piety ruled all under heaven, they did not dare to receive with disrespect the ministers of small estates;—how much less would they do so to the dukes, marquises, counts, and barons!' Thus it was that they got (the princes of) the myriad states with joyful hearts (to assist them) in the (sacrificial) services to their royal predecessors.

'The rulers of states did not dare to slight wifeless men and widows;— how much less would they slight their officers and the people! Thus it was that they got all their people with joyful hearts (to assist them) in serving the rulers, their predecessors.

'The heads of clans did not dare to slight their servants and concubines; —how much less would they slight their wives and sons! Thus it was that they got their men with joyful hearts (to assist them) in the service of their parents.

'In such a state of things, while alive, parents reposed in (the glory of) their sons; and, when sacrificed to, their disembodied spirits enjoyed their offerings. Therefore all under heaven peace and harmony prevailed; disasters and calamities did not occur; misfortunes and rebellions did not arise.

'It is said in the Book of Poetry,

> "To an upright, virtuous conduct
> All in the four quarters of the state render obedient
>   homage." '

THE GOVERNMENT OF THE SAGES

The disciple Tsăng said, 'I venture to ask whether in the virtue of the sages there was not something greater than filial piety.' The Master replied, 'Of all (creatures with their different) natures produced by Heaven and Earth, man is the noblest. Of all the actions of man there is none greater than filial piety. In filial piety there is nothing greater than the reverential awe of one's father. In the reverential awe shown to one's father there is nothing greater than the making him the correlate of Heaven. The duke of Kâu was the man who (first) did this.

'Formerly the duke of Kâu at the border altar sacrificed to Hâu-kî as the correlate of Heaven, and in the Brilliant Hall he honoured king Wǎn, and sacrificed to him as the correlate of God. The consequence was that from (all the states) within the four seas, every (prince) came in the discharge of his duty to (assist in those) sacrifices. In the virtue of the sages what besides was there greater than filial piety?

'Now the feeling of affection grows up at the parents' knees, and as (the duty of) nourishing those parents is exercised, the affection daily merges in awe. The sages proceeded from the (feeling of) awe to teach (the duties of) reverence, and from (that of) affection to teach (those of) love. The teachings of the sages, without being severe, were successful, and their government, without being rigorous, was effective. What they proceeded from was the root (of filial piety implanted by Heaven).

'The relation and duties between father and son, (thus belonging to) the Heaven-conferred nature, (contain in them the principle of) righteousness between ruler and subject. The son derives his life from his parents, and no greater gift could possibly be transmitted; his ruler and parent (in one), his father deals with him accordingly, and no generosity could be greater than this. Hence, he who does not love his parents, but loves other men, is called a rebel against virtue; and he who does not revere his parents, but reveres other men, is called a rebel against propriety. When (the ruler) himself thus acts contrary to (the principles) which should place him in accord (with all men), he presents nothing for the people to imitate. He has nothing to do with what is good, but entirely and only with what is injurious to virtue. Though he may get (his will, and be above others), the superior man does not give him his approval.

'It is not so with the superior man. He speaks, having thought whether the words should be spoken; he acts, having thought whether his actions are sure to give pleasure. His virtue and righteousness are such as will be honoured; what he initiates and does is fit to be imitated; his deportment is worthy of contemplation; his movements in advancing or retiring are all according to the proper rule. In this way does he present himself to the people, who both revere and love him, imitate and become like him. Thus he is able to make his teaching of virtue successful, and his government and orders to be carried into effect.

'It is said in the Book of Poetry,

> "The virtuous man, the princely one,
> Has nothing wrong in his deportment." '

AN ORDERLY DESCRIPTION OF THE ACTS OF FILIAL PIETY

The Master said, 'The service which a filial son does to his parents is as follows:—In his general conduct to them, he manifests the utmost reverence;

in his nourishing of them, his endeavour is to give them the utmost pleasure; when they are ill, he feels the greatest anxiety; in mourning for them (dead), he exhibits every demonstration of grief; in sacrificing to them, he displays the utmost solemnity. When a son is complete in these five things (he may be pronounced) able to serve his parents.

'He who (thus) serves his parents, in a high situation, will be free from pride; in a low situation, will be free from insubordination; and among his equals, will not be quarrelsome. In a high situation pride leads to ruin; in a low situation insubordination leads to punishment; among equals quarrelsomeness leads to the wielding of weapons.

'If those three things be not put away, though a son every day contribute beef, mutton, and pork to nourish his parents, he is not filial.'

FILIAL PIETY IN RELATION TO THE FIVE PUNISHMENTS

The Master said, 'There are three thousand offences against which the five punishments are directed, and there is not one of them greater than being unfilial.

'When constraint is put upon a ruler, that is the disowning of his superiority; when the authority of the sages is disallowed, that is the disowning of (all) law; when filial piety is put aside, that is the disowning of the principle of affection. These (three things) pave the way to anarchy.'

AMPLIFICATION OF 'THE ALL-EMBRACING RULE OF CONDUCT' IN CHAPTER I

The Master said, 'For teaching the people to be affectionate and loving there is nothing better than Filial Piety; for teaching them (the observance of) propriety and submissiveness there is nothing better than Fraternal Duty; for changing their manners and altering their customs there is nothing better than Music; for securing the repose of superiors and the good order of the people there is nothing better than the Rules of Propriety.

'The Rules of Propriety are simply (the development of) the principle of Reverence. Therefore the reverence paid to a father makes (all) sons pleased; the reverence paid to an elder brother makes (all) younger brothers pleased; the reverence paid to a ruler makes (all) subjects pleased. The reverence paid to one man makes thousands and myriads of men pleased. The reverence is paid to a few, and the pleasure extends to many;—this is what is meant by an "All-embracing Rule of Conduct."'

AMPLIFICATION OF 'THE PERFECT VIRTUE' IN CHAPTER I

The Master said, 'The teaching of filial piety by the superior man does not require that he should go to family after family, and daily see the members of each. His teaching of filial piety is a tribute of reverence to all the fathers under heaven; his teaching of fraternal submission is a tribute of reverence to all the elder brothers under heaven; his teaching of the duty of a subject is a tribute of reverence to all the rulers under heaven.

'It is said in the Book of Poetry,

> "The happy and courteous sovereign
> Is the parent of the people."

'If it were not a perfect virtue, how could it be recognised as in accordance with their nature by the people so extensively as this?'

AMPLIFICATION OF 'MAKING OUR NAME FAMOUS' IN CHAPTER I

The Master said, 'The filial piety with which the superior man serves his parents may be transferred as loyalty to the ruler; the fraternal duty with which he serves his elder brother may be transferred as submissive deference to elders; his regulation of his family may be transferred as good government in any official position. Therefore, when his conduct is thus successful in his inner (private) circle, his name will be established (and transmitted) to future generations.'

FILIAL PIETY IN RELATION TO REPROOF AND REMONSTRANCE

The disciple Tsăng said, 'I have heard your instructions on the affection of love, on respect and reverence, on giving repose to (the minds of) our parents, and on making our names famous;—I would venture to ask if (simple) obedience to the orders of one's father can be pronounced filial piety.' The Master replied, 'What words are these! what words ar.. these! Anciently, if the Son of Heaven had seven ministers who would remonstrate with him, although he had not right methods of government, he would not lose his possession of the kingdom; if the prince of a state had five such ministers, though his measures might be equally wrong, he would not lose his state; if a great officer had three, he would not, in a similar case, lose (the headship of) his clan; if an inferior officer had a friend who would remonstrate with him, a good name would not cease to be connected with his character; and the father who had a son that would remonstrate with him would not sink into the gulf of unrighteous deeds. Therefore when a case of unrighteous conduct is concerned, a son must by no means keep from remonstrating with his father, nor a minister from remonstrating with his ruler. Hence, since remonstrance is required in the case of unrighteous conduct, how can (simple) obedience to the orders of a father be accounted filial piety?'

THE INFLUENCE OF FILIAL PIETY AND THE RESPONSE TO IT

The Master said, 'Anciently, the intelligent kings served their fathers with filial piety, and therefore they served Heaven with intelligence; they served their mothers with filial piety, and therefore they served Earth with discrimination. They pursued the right course with reference to their (own) seniors and juniors, and therefore they secured the regulation of the relations between superiors and inferiors (throughout the kingdom).

'When Heaven and Earth were served with intelligence and discrimination, the spiritual intelligences displayed (their retributive power).

'Therefore even the Son of Heaven must have some whom he honours; that is, he has his uncles of his surname. He must have some to whom he concedes the precedence; that is, he has his cousins, who bear the same surname, and are older than himself. In the ancestral temple he manifests the utmost reverence, showing that he does not forget his parents; he cultivates his person and is careful of his conduct, fearing lest he should disgrace his predecessors.

'When in the ancestral temple he exhibits the utmost reverence, the spirits of the departed manifest themselves. Perfect filial piety and fraternal duty reach to (and move) the spiritual intelligences, and diffuse their light on all within the four seas;—they penetrate everywhere.

'It is said in the Book of Poetry,

> "From the west to the east,
> From the south to the north,
> There was not a thought but did him homage." '

THE SERVICE OF THE RULER

The Master said, 'The superior man serves his ruler in such a way, that when at court in his presence his thought is how to discharge his loyal duty to the utmost; and when he retires from it, his thought is how to amend his errors. He carries out with deference the measures springing from his excellent qualities, and rectifies him (only) to save him from what are evil. Hence, as the superior and inferior, they are able to have an affection for each other.

'It is said in the Book of Poetry,

> "In my heart I love him;
> And why should I not say so?
> In the core of my heart I keep him,
> And never will forget him." '

FILIAL PIETY IN MOURNING FOR PARENTS

The Master said, 'When a filial son is mourning for a parent, he wails, but not with a prolonged sobbing; in the movements of ceremony he pays no attention to his appearance; his words are without elegance of phrase; he cannot bear to wear fine clothes; when he hears music, he feels no delight; when he eats a delicacy, he is not conscious of its flavour:—such is the nature of grief and sorrow.

'After three days he may partake of food; for thus the people are taught that the living should not be injured on account of the dead, and that emaciation must not be carried to the extinction of life:—such is the rule of the sages. The period of mourning does not go beyond three years, to show the people that it must have an end.

'An inner and outer coffin are made; the graveclothes also are put on, and the shroud; and (the body) is lifted (into the coffin). The sacrificial vessels, round and square, are (regularly) set forth, and (the sight of them) fills (the mourners) with (fresh) distress. The women beat their breasts, and the men stamp with their feet, wailing and weeping, while they sorrowfully escort the coffin to the grave. They consult the tortoise-shell to determine the grave and the ground about it, and there they lay the body in peace. They prepare the ancestral temple (to receive the tablet of the departed), and there present offerings to the disembodied spirit. In spring and autumn they offer sacrifices, thinking of the deceased as the seasons come round.

'The services of love and reverence to parents when alive, and those of grief and sorrow to them when dead:—these completely discharge the fundamental duty of living men. The righteous claims of life and death are all satisfied, and the filial son's service of his parents is completed.'

28

A TREATISE ON JEN
Chu Hsi

Chu Hsi (A.D. 1130–1200) was China's greatest philosophical system-builder and after Confucius and Mencius the most influential Confucian teacher. An able administrator, he held several important offices, but his integrity caused repeated dismissals with consequent opportunities to devote himself to his preferred occupation as a scholar and philosopher. Chu Hsi's judgment that the most important texts of Confucianism were the Analects, *the* Mencius, *the* Great Learning, *and the* Doctrine of the Mean *was*

Chu Hsi, A Treatise on Jen, Wing-tsit Chan, trans. (Princeton, New Jersey: Princeton University Press, 1963), pp. 593–596. Reprinted from A Source Book in Chinese Philosophy, ed. by Wing-tsit Chan, by permission.

instrumental in establishing them as the "Four Confucian Classics," the core of Chinese higher education for 700 years and the basis of the civil service examinations that until the Twentieth Century were the entrance route into government service. His interpretation and integration of the teachings of these books in his commentaries became the orthodox view, familiar to every educated person in the Chinese culture-sphere.

Drawing upon the philosophical legacy of Taoism and Buddhism as well as Confucianism, he synthesized a speculative ontology and cosmology that has been the dominant metaphysical view in China during most of the last seven centuries. His discussions of principle, matter and energy, and the Great Ultimate deal with problems similar to those found in the works of Plato and Aristotle and his proposed solutions are not too unlike some advanced by the Greek thinkers. Despite his metaphysical interests, however, his central concerns were ethical and social and his influence on Chinese culture has been largely of a kind that in the West would be described as religious.

Chu Hsi's commentaries on the Great Learning *and the* Doctrine of the Mean *were printed with those texts. Here, in Professor Chan's translation, is the complete text of* A Treatise on Jen, *Chu Hsi's explication of the central Confucian term which has been variously rendered in English as "humanity," "goodness," "benevolence," and "human-heartedness."*

"The mind of Heaven and Earth is to produce things." In the production of man and things, they receive the mind of Heaven and Earth as their mind. Therefore, with reference to the character of the mind, although it embraces and penetrates all and leaves nothing to be desired, nevertheless, one word will cover all of it, namely, *jen* (humanity). Let me try to explain fully.

The moral qualities of the mind of Heaven and Earth are four: origination, flourish, advantages, and firmness. And the principle of origination unites and controls them all. In their operation they constitute the course of the four seasons, and the vital force of spring permeates all. Therefore in the mind of man there are also four moral qualities—namely, *jen,* righteousness, propriety, and wisdom—and *jen* embraces them all. In their emanation and function, they constitute the feeling of love, respect, being right, and discrimination between right and wrong—and the feeling of commiseration pervades them all. Therefore in discussing the mind of Heaven and Earth, it is said, "Great is *ch'ien* (Heaven), the originator!" and "Great is *k'un* (Earth), the originator." Both substance and function of the four moral qualities are thus fully implied without enumerating them. In discussing the excellence of man's mind, it is said, "*Jen* is man's mind." Both substance and function of the four moral qualities are thus fully presented without mentioning them. For *jen* as constituting the Way (Tao) consists of the fact that the mind of Heaven and Earth to produce things is present in everything. Before feelings are aroused this substance is already existent in its completeness. After feelings are aroused, its function is infinite. If we can truly practice love and preserve it, then we have in it the spring of all virtues and the root of all good deeds. This is why in the teachings of the Confucian school, the student is always urged to exert anxious and unceasing effort in the pursuit of *jen*. In the teachings (of Confucius, it is said), "Master oneself and return to propriety." This means that if we can overcome and eliminate selfishness and return to the Principle of Nature, (*T'ien-li*, Principle of Heaven), then the substance of this mind (that is, *jen*) will be present everywhere and its function will always be operative. It is also said, "Be respectful in private life, be serious in handling affairs, and be loyal in dealing with others." These are also ways to preserve this mind. Again, it is said, "Be filial in serving parents," "Be respectful in serving elder brothers," and "Be loving in dealing with all things." These are ways to put this mind into practice. It is again said, "They sought *jen* and found it," for (Po-i) declined a kingdom and left the country (in favor of his younger brother, Shu-ch'i) and they both remonstrated their superior against a punitive expedition and chose retirement and hunger, and in doing so, they prevented losing this mind. Again it is said, "Sacrifice life in order to realize *jen*." This means that we desire something more than life and hate something more than death, so as not to injure this mind. What mind is this? In Heaven and Earth it is the mind to produce things infinitely. In man it is the mind to love people gently and to benefit things. It includes the four virtues (of humanity, righteousness, propriety, and wisdom) and penetrates the Four Beginnings (of the sense of commiseration, the sense of shame, the sense of deference and compliance, and the sense of right and wrong).

SOMEONE SAID: According to our explanation, is it not wrong for Master Ch'eng to say that love is feeling while *jen* is nature and that love should not be regarded as *jen*?

ANSWER: Not so. What Master Ch'eng criticized was the application of the term to the expression of love. What I maintain is that the term should be applied to the principle of love. For although the spheres of man's nature and feelings are different, their mutual penetration is like the blood system in which each part has its own relationship. When have they become sharply separated and been made to have nothing to do with each other? I was just now worrying about students' reciting Master Ch'eng's words without inquiring into their meaning, and thereby coming to talk about *jen* as clearly apart from love. I have therefore purposely talked about this to reveal the hidden meaning of Master Ch'eng's words, and you regard my ideas as different from his. Are you not mistaken?

SOMEONE SAID: The followers of Master Ch'eng have given many explanations of *jen*. Some say that love is not *jen*, and regard the unity of all things and the self as the substance of *jen*. Others maintain that love is not *jen* but explain *jen* in terms of the possession of consciousness of the mind. If what you say is correct, are they all wrong?

ANSWER: From what they call the unity of all things and the self, it can be seen that *jen* involves love for all, but unity is not the reality which makes *jen* a substance. From what they call the mind's possession of conscious-ness, it can be seen that *jen* includes wisdom, but that is not the real reason why *jen* is so called. If you look up Confucius' answer to (his pupil) Tzu-kung's question whether conferring extensive benefit on the people and bring-ing salvation to all (will constitute *jen*) and also Master Ch'eng's statement that *jen* is not to be explained in terms of consciousness, you will see the point. How can you still explain *jen* in these terms?

Furthermore, to talk about *jen* in general terms of the unity of things and the self will lead people to be vague, confused, neglectful, and make no effort to be alert. The bad effect—and there has been—may be to consider other things as oneself. To talk about love in specific terms of consciousness will lead people to be nervous, irascible, and devoid of any quality of depth. The bad effect—and there has been—may be to consider desire as principle. In one case, (the mind) forgets (its objective). In the other (there is artificial effort to) help (it grow). Both are wrong. Furthermore, the explanation in terms of consciousness does not in any way approach the manner of (a man of *jen* who) "delights in mountains" (while a man of wisdom delights in water) or the idea that (*jen* alone) "can preserve" (what knowledge has at-tained), as taught his pupil by Confucius. How then can you still explain love in those terms? I hereby record what they said and write this treatise on *jen*.

29

INQUIRY ON THE GREAT LEARNING
Wang Yang-Ming

Wang Yang-ming (A.D. 1472–1529) was a Confucian scholar who became a successful military commander, an enlight-ened viceroy of Southern China, an influential spiritual teacher, and the dominant philosopher of the Ming dynasty (1368–1644).

Wang Yang-Ming, *Inquiry on the Great Learning*, Wing-tsit Chan, trans. (New York: Columbia University Press, 1963), pp. 272–280. Reprinted from *Instructions for Practical Living and Other Neo-Confucian Writings,* by Wang Yang-Ming, by permission of Columbia University Press.

Originally an adherent of Chu Hsi's doctrine that a man can be-
come a sage by investigating the principles of things, Wang fell
ill after spending seven days in a fruitless effort to discover the
principle of a bamboo. Years later, living in exile and hardship, he
had an illumination in which he realized that one becomes a sage
not by investigating external things but by rectifying one's mind
or will. In its original nature the mind has an innate knowledge
of the good, according to Wang, and when it is unobscured by
selfishness it will naturally extend this knowledge into action. He
went so far as to declare that knowledge and action are essentially
one for only in right action is knowledge completed. In his meta-
physical views Wang followed Lu Hsiang-shan (A.D. 1139–1193)
who had taught that one's own mind is one with the totality of all
things. Wang's advocacy of intuitive knowledge, unwavering ac-
tion, and a mystical unity with all things show affinities with Zen
Buddhism, but he criticized the Zen monks as escapists who
failed to face the world's problems.

Wang Yang-ming's Inquiry on the Great Learning, written
the year before his death, provides a summary of his principal
teachings. It is here presented in its entirety in Professor Chan's
translation.

QUESTION: The *Great Learning* was considered by a former scholar as
the learning of the great man. I venture to ask why the learning of the great
man should consist in "manifesting the clear character."

MASTER WANG SAID: The great man regards Heaven, Earth, and the
myriad things as one body. He regards the world as one family and the country as one person. As to those who make a cleavage between objects and distinguish between the self and others, they are small men. That the great man
can regard Heaven, Earth, and the myriad things as one body is not because
he deliberately wants to do so, but because it is natural to the humane nature
of his mind that he do so. Forming one body with Heaven, Earth, and the
myriad things is not only true of the great man. Even the mind of the small
man is no different. Only he himself makes it small. Therefore when he sees
a child about to fall into a well, he cannot help a feeling of alarm and commiseration. This shows that his humanity forms one body with the child. It
may be objected that the child belongs to the same species. Again, when he
observes the pitiful cries and frightened appearance of birds and animals about
to be slaughtered, he cannot help feeling an "inability to bear" their suffering.
This shows that his humanity forms one body with birds and animals. It may
be objected that birds and animals are sentient beings as he is. But when he
sees plants broken and destroyed, he cannot help a feeling of pity. This shows
that his humanity forms one body with plants. It may be said that plants are
living things as he is. Yet, even when he sees tiles and stones shattered and
crushed, he cannot help a feeling of regret. This shows that his humanity

forms one body with tiles and stones. This means that even the mind of the small man necessarily has the humanity that forms one body with all. Such a mind is rooted in his Heaven-endowed nature, and is naturally intelligent, clear, and not beclouded. For this reason it is called the "clear character." Although the mind of the small man is divided and narrow, yet his humanity that forms one body can remain free from darkness to this degree. This is due to the fact that his mind has not yet been aroused by desires and obscured by selfishness. When it is aroused by desires and obscured by selfishness, compelled by greed for gain and fear of harm, and stirred by anger, he will destroy things, kill members of his own species, and will do everything. In extreme cases he will even slaughter his own brothers, and the humanity that forms one body will disappear completely. Hence, if it is not obscured by selfish desires, even the mind of the small man has the humanity that forms one body with all as does the mind of the great man. As soon as it is obscured by selfish desires, even the mind of the great man will be divided and narrow like that of the small man. Thus the learning of the great man consists entirely in getting rid of the obscuration of selfish desires in order by his own efforts to make manifest his clear character, so as to restore the condition of forming one body with Heaven, Earth, and the myriad things, a condition that is originally so, that is all. It is not that outside of the original substance something can be added.

QUESTION: Why, then, does the learning of the great man consist in loving the people?

ANSWER: To manifest the clear character is to bring about the substance of the state of forming one body with Heaven, Earth, and the myriad things, whereas loving the people is to put into universal operation the function of the state of forming one body. Hence manifesting the clear character consists in loving the people, and loving the people is the way to manifest the clear character. Therefore, only when I love my father, the fathers of others, and the fathers of all men can my humanity really form one body with my father, the fathers of others, and the fathers of all men. When it truly forms one body with them, then the clear character of filial piety will be manifested. Only when I love my brother, the brothers of others, and the brothers of all men can my humanity really form one body with my brother, the brother of others, and the brothers of all men. When it truly forms one body with them, then the clear character of brotherly respect will be manifested. Everything from ruler, minister, husband, wife, and friends to mountains, rivers, spiritual beings, birds, animals, and plants should be truly loved in order to realize my humanity that forms one body with them, and then my clear character will be completely manifested, and I will really form one body with Heaven, Earth, and the myriad things. This is what is meant by "manifesting the clear character throughout the world." This is what is meant by "regulation of the family," "ordering the state," and "bringing peace to the world." This is what is meant by "full development of one's nature."

QUESTION: Then why does the learning of the great man consist in "abiding in the highest good"?

ANSWER: The highest good is the ultimate principle of manifesting character and loving people. The nature endowed in us by Heaven is pure and perfect. The fact that it is intelligent, clear, and not beclouded is evidence of the emanation and revelation of the highest good. It is the original substance of the clear character which is called innate knowledge of the good. As the highest good emanates and reveals itself, we will consider right as right and wrong as wrong. Things of greater or less importance and situations of grave or light character will be responded to as they act upon us. In all our changes and movements, we will stick to no particular point, but possess in ourselves the mean that is perfectly natural. This is the ultimate of the normal nature of man and the principle of things. There can be no consideration of adding or subtracting anything to or from it. Such a suggestion reveals selfish ideas and shallow cunning, and cannot be said to be the highest good. Naturally, how can anyone who does not watch over himself carefully when alone, and who has no refinement and singleness of mind, attain to such a state of perfection? Later generations fail to realize that the highest good is inherent in their own minds, but exercise their selfish ideas and cunning and grope for it outside their minds, believing that every event and every object has its own peculiar definite principle. For this reason the law of right and wrong is obscured; the mind becomes concerned with fragmentary and isolated details and broken pieces; the selfish desires of man become rampant and the Principle of Nature is at an end. And thus the learning of manifesting character and loving people is everywhere thrown into confusion. In the past there have, of course, been people who wanted to manifest their clear character. But simply because they did not know how to abide in the highest good, but instead drove their own minds toward something too lofty, they thereby lost them in illusions, emptiness, and quietness, having nothing to do with the work of the family, the state, and the world. Such are the followers of Buddhism and Taoism. There have, of course, been those who wanted to love their people. Yet simply because they did not know how to abide in the highest good, but instead sank their own minds in base and trifling things, they thereby lost them in scheming strategy and cunning techniques, having neither the sincerity of humanity nor that of commiseration. Such are the followers of the Five Despots and the pursuers of success and profit. All of these defects are due to a failure to know how to abide in the highest good. Therefore abiding in the highest good is to manifesting character and loving people as the carpenter's square and compass are to the square and the circle, or rule and measure to length, or balances and scales to weight. If the square and the circle do not abide by the compass and the carpenter's square, their standard will be wrong; if length does not abide by the rule and measure, its adjustment will be lost; if weight does not abide by the balances, its exactness will be gone; and if manifesting clear character and loving people do not abide by the highest good, their foundation will disappear. Therefore, abiding in the highest good so as to love people and manifest the clear character is what is meant by the learning of the great man.

QUESTION: "Only after knowing what to abide in can one be calm. Only after having been calm can one be tranquil. Only after having achieved tranquillity can one have peaceful repose. Only after having peaceful repose can one begin to deliberate. Only after deliberation can the end be attained." How do you explain this?

ANSWER: People fail to realize that the highest good is in their minds and seek it outside. As they believe that everything or every event has its own definite principle, they search for the highest good in individual things. Consequently, the mind becomes fragmentary, isolated, broken into pieces; mixed and confused, it has no definite direction. Once it is realized that the highest good is in the mind and does not depend on any search outside, then the mind will have definite direction and there will be no danger of its becoming fragmentary, isolated, broken into pieces, mixed, or confused. When there is no such danger, the mind will not be erroneously perturbed but will be tranquil. Not being erroneously perturbed but being tranquil, it will be leisurely and at ease in its daily functioning and will attain peaceful repose. Being in peaceful repose, whenever a thought arises or an event acts upon it, the mind with its innate knowledge will thoroughly sift and carefully examine whether or not the thought or event is in accord with the highest good, and thus the mind can deliberate. With deliberation, every decision will be excellent and every act will be proper, and in this way the highest good will be attained.

QUESTION: "Things have their roots and their branches." A former scholar considered manifesting the clear character as the root (or fundamental) and renovating the people as the branch (or secondary), and thought that they are two things opposing each other as internal and external. "Affairs have their beginnings and their ends." The former scholar considered knowing what to abide in as the beginning and the attainment of the highest good as the end, both being one thing in harmonious continuity. According to you, "renovating the people" (hsin-min) should be read as "loving the people" (ch'in-min). If so, isn't the theory of root and branches in some respect incorrect?

ANSWER: The theory of beginnings and ends is in general right. Even if we read "renovating the people" as "loving the people" and say that manifesting the character is the root and loving the people is the branches, it is not incorrect. The main thing is that root and branches should not be distinguished as two different things. The trunk of the tree is called the root, and the twigs are called the branches. It is precisely because the tree is one that its parts can be called root and branches. If they are said to be two different things, then since they are two distinct objects, how can we speak of them as root and branches of the same thing? Since the idea of renovating the people is different from that of loving the people, obviously the task of manifesting the character and that of loving the people are two different things. If it is realized that manifesting the clear character is to love the people and loving the people is to manifest the clear character, how can they be split in two? What the former scholar said is due to his failure to realize that manifesting the character and loving the people are basically one thing. Instead, he believed them to be two different things and consequently, although he knew that root and branches should be one, yet he could not help splitting them in two.

QUESTION: The passage from the phrase, "The ancients who wished to manifest their clear character throughout the world" to the clause, "first [order their state . . . regulate their families . . .] cultivate their personal lives," can be understood by your theory of manifesting the character and loving the people. May I ask what task, what procedure, and what effort are involved in the passage from "Those who wished to cultivate their personal lives would [first rectify their minds . . . make their will sincere . . . extend their knowledge]" to the clause, "the extension of knowledge consists in the investigation of things"?

ANSWER: This passage fully explains the task of manifesting the character, loving the people, and abiding in the highest good. The person, the mind, the will, knowledge, and things constitute the order followed in the task. While each of them has its own place, they are really one thing. Investigating, extending, being sincere, rectifying, and cultivating are the task performed in the procedure. Although each has its own name, they are really one affair. What is it that is called the person? It is the physical functioning of the mind. What is it that is called the mind? It is the clear and intelligent master of the person. What is meant by cultivating the personal life? It means to do good and get rid of evil. Can the body by itself do good and get rid of evil? The clear and intelligent master must desire to do good and get rid of evil before the body that functions physically can do so. Therefore he who wishes to cultivate his personal life must first rectify his mind.

Now the original substance of the mind is man's nature. Human nature being universally good, the original substance of the mind is correct. How is it that any effort is required to rectify the mind? The reason is that, while the original substance of the mind is originally correct, incorrectness enters when one's thoughts and will are in operation. Therefore he who wishes to rectify his mind must rectify it in connection with the operation of his thoughts and will. If, whenever a good thought arises, he really loves it as he loves beautiful colors, and whenever an evil thought arises, he really hates it as he hates bad odors, then his will will always be sincere and his mind can be rectified.

However, what arises from the will may be good or evil, and unless there is a way to make clear the distinction between good and evil, there will be a confusion of truth and untruth. In that case, even if one wants to make his will sincere, he cannot do so. Therefore he who wishes to make his will sincere must extend his knowledge. By extension is meant to reach the limit.

The word "extension" is the same as that used in the saying, "Mourning is to be carried to the utmost degree of grief." In the *Book of Changes* it is said: "Knowing the utmost, one should reach it." "Knowing the utmost" means knowledge and "reaching it" means extension. The extension of knowledge is not what later scholars understand as enriching and widening knowledge. It is simply extending one's innate knowledge of the good to the utmost. This innate knowledge of the good is what Mencius meant when he said, "The sense of right and wrong is common to all men." The sense of right and wrong requires no deliberation to know, nor does it depend on learning to function. This is why it is called innate knowledge. It is my nature endowed by Heaven, the original substance of my mind, naturally intelligent, shining, clear, and understanding.

Whenever a thought or a wish arises, my mind's faculty of innate knowledge itself is always conscious of it. Whether it is good or evil, my mind's innate knowing faculty itself also knows it. It has nothing to do with others. Therefore, although an inferior man may have done all manner of evil, when he sees a superior man he will surely try to disguise this fact, concealing what is evil and displaying what is good in himself. This shows that innate knowledge of the good does not permit any self-deception. Now the only way to distinguish good and evil in order to make the will sincere is to extend to the utmost the knowledge of the innate faculty. Why is this? When [a good] thought or wish arises, the innate faculty of my mind already knows it to be good. Suppose I do not sincerely love it but instead turn away from it. I would then be regarding good as evil and obscuring my innate faculty which knows the good. When [an evil] thought or wish arises, the innate faculty of my mind already knows it to be evil. If I did not sincerely hate it but instead carried it out, I would be regarding evil as good and obscuring my innate faculty which knows evil. In such cases what is supposed to be knowledge is really ignorance. How then can the will be made sincere? If what the innate faculty knows to be good or evil is sincerely loved or hated, one's innate knowing faculty is not deceived and the will can be made sincere.

Now, when one sets out to extend his innate knowledge to the utmost, does this mean something illusory, hazy, in a vacuum, and unreal? No, it means something real. Therefore, the extension of knowledge must consist in the investigation of things. A thing is an event. For every emanation of the will there must be an event corresponding to it. The event to which the will is directed is a thing. To investigate is to rectify. It is to rectify that which is incorrect so it can return to its original correctness. To rectify that which is not correct is to get rid of evil, and to return to correctness is to do good. This is what is meant by investigation. The *Book of History* says, "He [Emperor Yao] investigated (*ko*) heaven above and earth below"; "[Emperor Shun] investigated (*ko*) in the temple of illustrious ancestors"; and "[The ruler] rectifies (*ko*) the evil of his heart." The word "investigation" (*ko*) in the phrase "the investigation of things" combines the two meanings.

If one sincerely loves the good known by the innate faculty but does not in reality do the good as he comes into contact with the thing to which the will is directed, it means that the thing has not been investigated and that the will to love the good is not yet sincere. If one sincerely hates the evil known by the innate faculty but does not in reality get rid of the evil as he comes into contact with the thing to which the will is directed, it means that the thing has not been investigated and that the will to hate evil is not sincere. If as we come into contact with the thing to which the will is directed, we really do the good and get rid of the evil to the utmost which is known by the innate faculty, then everything will be investigated and what is known by our innate faculty will not be deficient or obscured but will be extended to the utmost. Then the mind will be joyous in itself, happy and without regret, the functioning of the will will carry with it no self-deception, and sincerity may be said to have been attained. Therefore it is said, "When things are investigated, knowledge is extended; when knowledge is extended, the will becomes sincere; when the will is sincere, the mind is rectified; and when the mind is rectified, the personal life is cultivated." While the order of the tasks involves a sequence of first and last, in substance they are one and cannot be so separated. At the same time, while the order and the tasks cannot be separated into first and last, their function must be so refined as not to be wanting in the slightest degree. This is why the doctrine of investigation, extension, being sincere, and rectification is a correct exposition of the true heritage of Sage-Emperors Yao and Shun and why it coincides with Confucius' own ideas.

30

THE SPIRIT OF CHINESE PHILOSOPHY
Fung Yu-Lan

Fung Yu-lan (1895–) is the author of an outstanding history of Chinese philosophy as well as books developing his own philosophical system. A graduate of Peking University with a Ph.D. from Columbia University, he has taught in several Chi-

Reprinted with permission of the Macmillan Company from *A Short History of Chinese Philosophy* by Fung Yu-lan, edited by Derk Bodde, pp. 1–10. Copyright 1948, the Macmillan Company.

nese universities and held visiting appointments in both England and the United States. In recent years he has been a professor at Peking University. In 1950 he repudiated his pre-revolutionary system as a mere twilight stage of traditional Chinese philosophy, but in 1957 he was publicly criticized by a colleague for continuing to place too little emphasis upon the concrete social situations out of which philosophies have arisen and too much emphasis upon their abstract content. Fung's pre-revolutionary philosophy employed the terminology of Chu Hsi's school of Neo-Confucianism, but it did not claim to yield information about matters of fact. Philosophy is the "empty branch of knowledge," he said, lacking practical use but capable of helping its students to become sages. This view, he pointed out, is in harmony with the implicit positions of Zen Buddhism and Wang Yang-ming. Lacking "superstitions, dogmas, rituals, and institutions," Confucianism, Philosophical Taoism, and Philosophical Buddhism should not be classified as "religious" according to Fung, but still their aim and function in his eyes is to produce "sageliness within and kingliness without."

"The Spirit of Chinese Philosophy" is about two thirds of the first chapter in Professor Fung's A Short History of Chinese Philosophy.

The place which philosophy has occupied in Chinese civilization has been comparable to that of religion in other civilizations. In China, philosophy has been every educated person's concern. In the old days, if a man were educated at all, the first education he received was in philosophy. When children went to school, the *Four Books,* which consist of the *Confucian Analects,* the *Book of Mencius,* the *Great Learning,* and the *Doctrine of the Mean,* were the first ones they were taught to read. The *Four Books* were the most important texts of Neo-Confucianist philosophy. Sometimes when the children were just begining to learn the characters, they were given a sort of textbook to read. This was known as the *Three Characters Classic,* and was so called because each sentence in the book consisted of three characters arranged so that when recited they produced a rhythmic effect, and thus helped the children to memorize them more easily. This book was in reality a primer, and the very first statement in it is that "the nature of man is originally good." This is one of the fundamental ideas of Mencius' philosophy.

PLACE OF PHILOSOPHY IN CHINESE CIVILIZATION

To the Westerner, who sees that the life of the Chinese people is permeated with Confucianism, it appears that Confucianism is a religion. As a matter of fact, however, Confucianism is no more a religion than, say, Platonism or Aristotelianism. It is true that the *Four Books* have been the Bible of the Chinese people, but in the *Four Books* there is no story of creation, and no mention of a heaven or hell.

Of course, the terms philosophy and religion are both ambiguous. Philosophy and religion may have entirely different meanings for different people. When men talk about philosophy or religion, they may have quite different ideas in their minds concerning them. For my part, what I call philosophy is systematic, reflective thinking on life. Every man, who has not yet died, is in life. But there are not many who think reflectively on life, and still fewer whose reflective thinking is systematic. A philosopher *must* philosophize; that is to say, he must think reflectively on life, and then express his thoughts systematically.

This kind of thinking is called reflective because it takes life as its object. The theory of life, the theory of the universe, and the theory of knowledge all emerge from this type of thinking. The theory of the universe arises because the universe is the background of life—the stage on which the drama of life takes place. The theory of knowledge emerges because thinking is itself knowledge. According to some philosophers of the West, in order to think, we must first find out what we can think; that is to say, before we start to think about life, we must first "think our thinking."

Such theories are all the products of reflective thinking. The very concept of life, the very concept of the universe, and the very concept of knowledge are also the products of reflective thinking. No matter whether we think about life or whether we talk about it, we are all in the midst of it. And no matter whether we think or speak about the universe, we are all a part of it. Now, what the philosophers call the universe is not the same as what the physicists have in mind when they refer to it. What the philosophers call the universe is *the totality of all that is*. It is equivalent to what the ancient Chinese philosopher, Hui Shih, called "The Great One," which is defined as "that which has nothing beyond." So everyone and everything must be considered part of the universe. When one thinks about the universe, one is thinking reflectively.

When we think about knowledge or speak about knowledge, this thinking and speaking are themselves knowledge. To use an expression of Aristotle, it is "thinking on thinking"; and this is reflective thinking. Here is the vicious circle which those philosophers follow who insist that before we think we must first think about our thinking; just as if we had another faculty with which we could think about thinking! As a matter of fact, the faculty with which we think about thinking is the very same faculty with which we think. If we are skeptical about the capacity of our thinking in regard to life and the universe, we have the same reason to be skeptical about the capacity of our thinking in regard to thinking.

Religion also has something to do with life. In the heart of every great religion there is a philosophy. In fact, every great religion *is* a philosophy with a certain amount of superstructure, which consists of superstitions, dogmas, rituals, and institutions. This is what I call religion.

If one understands the term religion in this sense, which does not really differ very much from common usage, one sees that Confucianism cannot be considered a religion. People have been accustomed to say that there were three religions in China: Confucianism, Taoism, and Buddhism. But Confucianism, as we have seen, is not a religion. As to Taoism, there is a distinction between Taoism as a philosophy, which is called *Tao chia* (the Taoist school), and the Taoist religion (*Tao chiao*). Their teachings are not only different; they are even contradictory. Taoism as a philosophy teaches the doctrine of following nature, while Taoism as a religion teaches the doctrine of working *against* nature. For instance, according to Lao Tzu and Chuang Tzu, life followed by death is the course of nature, and man should follow this natural course calmly. But the main teaching of the Taoist religion is the principle and technique of how to avoid death, which is expressly working *against* nature. The Taoist religion has the spirit of science, which is the conquering of nature. If one is interested in the history of Chinese science, the writings of the religious Taoists will supply much information.

As to Buddhism, there is also the distinction between Buddhism as a philosophy, which is called *Fo hsüeh* (the Buddhist learning), and Buddhism as a religion, which is called *Fo chiao* (the Buddhist religion). To the educated Chinese, Buddhist philosophy is much more interesting than the Buddhist religion. It is quite common to see both Buddhist monks and Taoist monks simultaneously participating in Chinese funeral services. The Chinese people take even their religion philosophically.

At present it is known to many Westerners that the Chinese people have been less concerned with religion than other people are. For instance, in one of his articles, "Dominant Ideas in the Formation of Chinese Culture," Professor Derk Bodde says: "They [the Chinese] are not a people for whom religious ideas and activities constitute an all important and absorbing part of life. . . . It is ethics (especially Confucian ethics), and not religion (at least not religion of a formal, organized type), that provided the spiritual basis in Chinese civilization. . . . All of which, of course, marks a difference of fundamental importance between China and most other major civilizations, in which a church and a priesthood have played a dominant role."

In one sense this is quite true. But one may ask: Why is this so? If the craving for what is beyond the present actual world is not one of the innate desires of mankind, why is it a fact that for most people religious ideas and activities constitute an all-important and absorbing part of life? If that craving is one of the fundamental desires of mankind, why should the Chinese people be an exception? When one says that it is ethics, not religion, that has provided the spiritual basis of Chinese civilization, does it imply that the Chinese are not conscious of those values which are higher than moral ones?

The values that are higher than the moral ones may be called super-moral values. The love of man is a moral value, while the love of God is a super-moral value. Some people may be inclined to call this kind of value a religious value. But in my opinion, this value is not confined to religion, unless what is meant here by religion differs from its meaning as described above. For instance, the love of God in Christianity is a religious value, while the love of God in the philosophy of Spinoza is not, because what Spinoza called God is really the universe. Strictly speaking, the love of God in Christianity is not really super-moral. This is because God, in Christianity, is a personality, and consequently the love of God by man is comparable to the love of a father by his son, which is a moral value. Therefore, the love of God in Christianity is open to question as a super-moral value. It is a quasi super-moral value, while the love of God in the philosophy of Spinoza is a real super-moral value.

To answer the above questions, I would say that the craving for something beyond the present actual world is one of the innate desires of mankind, and the Chinese people are no exception to this rule. They have not had much concern with religion because they have had so much concern with philosophy. They are not religious because they are philosophical. In philosophy they satisfy their craving for what is beyond the present actual world. In philosophy also they have the super-moral values expressed and appreciated, and in living according to philosophy these super-moral values are experienced.

According to the tradition of Chinese philosophy, its function is not the increase of positive knowledge (by positive knowledge I mean information regarding matters of fact), but the elevation of the mind—a reaching out for what is beyond the present actual world, and for the values that are higher than the moral ones. It was said by the *Lao-tzu*: "To work on learning is to increase day by day; to work on *Tao* (the Way, the Truth) is to decrease day by day." (See ch. 48.) I am not concerned with the difference between increasing and decreasing, nor do I quite agree with this saying of *Lao-tzu*. I quote it only to show that in the tradition of Chinese philosophy there is a distinction between working on learning and working on *Tao* (the Way). The purpose of the former is what I call the increase of positive knowledge, that of the latter is the elevation of the mind. Philosophy belongs in the latter category.

The view that the function of philosophy, especially metaphysics, is not the increase of positive knowledge, is expounded by the Viennese school in contemporary Western philosophy, though from a different angle and for a different purpose. I do not agree with this school that the function of philosophy is only the clarification of ideas, and that the nature of metaphysics is only a lyric of concepts. Nevertheless, in their arguments one can see quite clearly that philosophy, especially metaphysics, would become nonsense if it did attempt to give information regarding matters of fact.

Religion does give information in regard to matters of fact. But the information given by religion is not in harmony with that given by science. So in the West there has been the conflict between religion and science. Where science advances, religion retreats; and the authority of religion recedes before the advancement of science. The traditionalists regretted this fact and pitied the people who had become irreligious, considering them as having degenerated. They ought indeed to be pitied, if, besides religion, they had no other access to the higher values. When people get rid of religion and have no substitute, they also lose the higher values. They have to confine themselves to mundane affairs and have nothing to do with the spiritual ones. Fortunately, however, besides religion there is philosophy, which provides man with an access to the higher values—an access which is more direct than that provided by religion, because in philosophy, in order to be acquainted with the higher values, man need not take the roundabout way provided by prayers and rituals. The higher values with which man has become acquainted through philosophy are even purer than those acquired through religion, because they are not mixed with imagination and superstition. In the world of the future, man will have philosophy in the place of religion. This is consistent with Chinese tradition. It is not necessary that man should be religious, but it *is* necessary that he should be philosophical. When he is philosophical, he has the very best of the blessings of religion.

PROBLEM AND SPIRIT OF CHINESE PHILOSOPHY

The above is a general discussion of the nature and function of philosophy. In the following remarks I shall speak more specifically about Chinese philosophy. There is a main current in the history of Chinese philosophy, which may be called the spirit of Chinese philosophy. In order to understand this spirit, we must first make clear the problem that most Chinese philosophers have tried to solve.

There are all kinds and conditions of men. With regard to any one of these kinds, there is the highest form of achievement of which any one kind of man is capable. For instance, there are the men engaged in practical politics. The highest form of achievement in that class of men is that of the great statesman. So also in the field of art, the highest form of achievement of which artists are capable is that of the great artist. Although there are these different classes of men, yet all of them are men. What is the highest form of achievement of which a man *as a man* is capable? According to the Chinese philosophers, it is nothing less than being a sage, and the highest achievement of a sage is the identification of the individual with the universe. The problem is, if men want to achieve this identification, do they necessarily have to abandon society or even to negate life?

According to some philosophers, this is necessary. The Buddha said that life itself is the root and fountainhead of the misery of life. Likewise, Plato said that the body is the prison of the soul. And some of the Taoists said that life is an excrescence, a tumor, and death is to be taken as the breaking of the tumor. All these ideas represent a view which entails separation from what may be called the entangling net of the matter-corrupted world; and therefore, if the highest achievement of a sage is to be realized, the sage has to abandon society and even life itself. Only thus can the final liberation be attained. This kind of philosophy is what is generally known as "other-worldly philosophy."

There is another kind of philosophy which emphasizes what is in society, such as human relations and human affairs. This kind of philosophy speaks only about moral values, and is unable to or does not wish to speak of the super-moral ones. This kind of philosophy is generally described as "this-worldly." From the point of view of a this-worldly philosophy, an other-world philosophy is too idealistic, is of no practical use and is negative. From the point of view of an other-worldly philosophy, a this-world philosophy is too realistic, too superficial. It may be positive, but it is like the quick walking of a man who has taken the wrong road: the more quickly he walks the further he goes astray.

There are many people who say that Chinese philosophy is a this-world philosophy. It is difficult to state that these people are entirely right or entirely wrong. Taking a merely superficial view, people who hold this opinion cannot be said to be wrong, because according to their view, Chinese philosophy, regardless of its different schools of thought, is directly or indirectly concerned with government and ethics. On the surface, therefore, it is concerned chiefly with society, and not with the universe; with the daily functions of human relations, not hell and heaven; with man's present life, but not his life in a world to come. When he was once asked by a disciple about the meaning of death, Confucius replied: "Not yet understanding life, how can you understand death?" (*Analects*, XI, 11.) And Mencius said: "The sage is the acme of human relations" (*Mencius*, IVa, 2), which, taken literally, means that the sage is the morally perfect man in society. From a surface point of view, with the ideal man being of this world, it seems that what Chinese philosophy calls a sage is a person of a very different order from the Buddha of Buddhism and the saints of the Christian religion. Superficially, this would seem to be especially true of the Confucian sage. That is why, in ancient times, Confucius and the Confucianists were so greatly ridiculed by the Taoists.

This, however, is only a surface view of the matter. Chinese philosophy cannot be understood by oversimplification of this kind. So far as the main tenet of its tradition is concerned, if we understand it aright, it cannot be said to be wholly this-worldly, just as, of course, it cannot be said to be wholly other-worldly. It is both of this world *and* of the other world. Speaking about the Neo-Confucianism of the Sung Dynasty, one philosopher described it this way: "It is not divorced from daily ordinary activities, yet it goes straight to what antedated Heaven." This is what Chinese philosophy has striven for. Having this kind of spirit, it is at one and the same time both extremely idealistic and extremely realistic, and very practical, though not in a superficial way.

This-worldliness and other-worldliness stand in contrast to each other as do realism and idealism. The task of Chinese philosophy is to accomplish a synthesis out of these antitheses. That does not mean that they are to be abolished. They are still there, but they have been made into a synthetic whole. How can this be done? This is the problem which Chinese philosophy attempts to solve.

According to Chinese philosophy, the man who accomplishes this synthesis, not only in theory but also in deed, is the sage. He is both this-worldly and other-worldly. The spiritual achievement of the Chinese sage corresponds to the saint's achievement in Buddhism, and in Western religion. But the Chinese sage is not one who does not concern himself with the business of the world. His character is described as one of "sageliness within and kingliness without." That is to say, in his inner sageliness, he accomplishes spiritual cultivation; in his kingliness without, he functions in society. It is not necessary that the sage should be the actual head of the government in his society. From the standpoint of practical politics, for the most part, the sage certainly has no chance of being the head of the state. The saying "sageliness within and kingliness without" means only that he who has the noblest spirit should, theoretically, be king. As to whether he actually has or has not the chance of being king, that is immaterial.

Since the character of the sage is, according to Chinese tradition, one of sageliness within and kingliness without, the task of philosophy is to enable man to develop this kind of character. Therefore, what philosophy discusses is what the Chinese philosophers describe as the *Tao* (Way, or basic principles) of sageliness within and kingliness without.

This sounds like the Platonic theory of the philosopher-king. According to Plato, in an ideal state, the philosopher should be the king or the king should be a philosopher; and in order to become a philosopher, a man must undergo a long period of philosophical training before his mind can be "converted" from the world of changing things to the world of eternal ideas. Thus according to Plato, as according to the Chinese philosophers, the task of philosophy is to enable man to have the character of sageliness within and kingliness without. But according to Plato, when a philosopher becomes a king, he does so against his will—in other words, it is something forced on him, and entails a great sacrifice on his part. This is what was also held by the ancient Taoists. There is the story of a sage who, being asked by the people of a certain state to become their king, escaped and hid himself in a mountain cave. But the people found the cave, smoked him out and compelled him to assume the difficult task. (*Lüshih Ch'un-ch-iu*, I, 2.) This is one similarity between Plato and the ancient Taoists, and it also shows the character of other-worldliness in Taoist philosophy. Following the main tradition of Chinese philosophy, the Neo-Taoist, Kuo Hsiang of the third century A.D., revised this point.

According to Confucianism, the daily task of dealing with social affairs in human relations is not something alien to the sage. Carrying on this task is the very essence of the development of the perfection of his personality. He performs it not only as a citizen of society, but also as a "citizen of the universe," *t'ien min,* as Mencius called it. He must be conscious of his being a citizen of the universe, otherwise his deeds would not have super-moral value. If he had the chance to become a king he would gladly serve the people, thus performing his duty both as a citizen of society, and as a citizen of the universe.

Since what is discussed in philosophy is the *Tao* (Way) of sageliness within and kingliness without, it follows that philosophy must be inseparable from political thought. Regardless of the differences between the schools of Chinese philosophy, the philosophy of every school represents, at the same time, its political thought. This does not mean that in the various schools of philosophy there are no metaphysics, no ethics, no logic. It means only that all these factors are connected with political thought in one way or another, just as Plato's *Republic* represents his whole philosophy and at the same time is his political thought.

For instance, the School of Names was known to indulge in such arguments as "a white horse is not a horse," which seems to have very little connection with politics. Yet the leader of this school, Kung-sun Lung, "wished to extend this kind of argument to rectify the relationship between names and facts in order to transform the world." We have seen in our world today how every statesman says his country wants only peace, but in fact, when he is talking about peace, he is often preparing for war. Here, then, there is a wrong relationship between names and facts. According to Kung-sun Lung, this kind of wrong relationship should be rectified. This is really the first step towards the transformation of the world.

Since the subject matter of philosophy is the *Tao* of sageliness within and kingliness without, the study of philosophy is not simply an attempt to acquire this kind of knowledge, but is also an attempt to develop this kind of character. Philosophy is not simply something to be *known*, but is also something to be *experienced*. It is not simply a sort of intellectual game, but something far more serious. As my colleague, Professor Y. L. Chin, has pointed out in an unpublished manuscript: "Chinese philosophers were all of them different grades of Socrates. This was so because ethics, politics, reflective thinking, and knowledge were unified in the philosopher; in him, knowledge and virtue were one and inseparable. His philosophy required that he live it; he was himself its vehicle. To live in accordance with his philosophical convictions was part of his philosophy. It was his business to school himself continually and persistently to that pure experience in which selfishness and egocentricity were transcended, so that he would be one with the universe. Obviously this process of schooling could not be stopped, for stopping it would mean the emergence of his ego and the loss of his universe. Hence cognitively he was eternally groping, and conatively he was eternally behaving or trying to behave. Since these could not be separated, in him there was the synthesis of the philosopher in the original sense of that term. Like Socrates, he did not keep office hours with his philosophy. Neither was he a dusty, musty philosopher, closeted in his study, sitting in a chair on the periphery of life. With him, philosophy was hardly ever merely a pattern of ideas exhibited for human understanding, but was a system of precepts internal to the conduct of the philosopher; and in extreme cases his philosophy might even be said to be his biography."

JUDAISM

PART IV

In its early beginnings, the religion of the Hebrews must not have been significantly different from any other of the host of Near Eastern religions. It seems fairly clear, from a comparison of the creation myths, the flood myth, and other fragments of myth and legend contained within the biblical literature with similar accounts in Babylonian, Sumerian, Hittite, and Egyptian literature, that all the Near Eastern peoples possess several similar elements in their religious traditions. The cosmological structures envisaged within each of these cultures share many common features, such as the three-storied structure of the universe (the underworld, earth, the heavens) with its attendant categorization of the operations and delimitations of the various natural and supernatural beings and forces. All presuppose the same natural framework, the seasonal pattern readily observed in the agricultural and astronomical cycles, upon which the many rituals with their accompanying mythical explanations are imposed in order to secure the continuance of cosmic order and the maintenance of divine favor. Many of the currently observed religious holidays of Judaism are based upon the distinctive phases of the seasonal pattern, although the modern-day worshipper may be quite ignorant of this ancient genesis.

Nevertheless, Judaism has survived into modern times as an important religion even though it continues to be highly nationalistic, while other neighboring religions have ceased to exist save for the vestigial embodiment of some of their characteristics in local folklore and custom, often so heavily overlaid with subsequent religious indoctrination as to be recognizable only by experts. Several features indigenous to this religion have been instrumental in producing this state of affairs; three of these are exceptionally important. Perhaps the most commonly recognized of these features is Judaism's characteristic monotheism. In the earliest phase of its development, the religion of the Hebrews was probably polytheistic, although with some hierarchical ordering among its deities, with a principal deity ruling over the others, not unlike the divine polities of many neighboring religions. This developed into the henotheism (worship of only one God by an ethnic group, while acknowledging that other groups may have other gods) characteristic of the early biblical literature, and typified by such expressions as "the God of Abraham, Isaac, and Jacob," and "Thou shalt have no other gods before me." The exclusive worship of one God was gradually transformed into the view that there is only one God, to whom all nations are alike subservient. This latter development occurred rather late, around the Eighth Century B.C., and apparently was due to the work of the great Hebrew prophets, especially Amos and Isaiah; but over the next few centuries it became the accepted doctrine. Monotheism tended to preserve Judaism both from within and from without. Internally, it produced an intolerance for other deities among the adherents of the religion, reinforcing their sense of exclusiveness, which they attributed to their being especially chosen by God, as portrayed in the stories of the covenants with Abraham and with Moses. Externally, Judaism was surrounded by a largely polytheistic environment, making its uniqueness all the more obvious, thereby attracting some proselytes as well as affording it recognition by others as a distinctive social entity (even though that recognition was often grudgingly given by conquering nations, for whom the Jews' differences constituted a major nuisance). The sense of exclusiveness continues to characterize a large segment of contemporary Judaism even though the surrounding environment may no longer be so different. The Zionist movement, various nationalistic organizations, as well as the existence of the State of Israel, give Judaism a special distinctiveness based upon ancient geographical and ethnic criteria which first distinguished Yahweh from other gods as a god of a chosen people and a promised land.

A second major feature characteristic of Judaism, both past and present, is its emphasis upon law. The institution of the Mosaic law is generally regarded as the defining characterization of the religion, so that Judaism cannot properly be said to have existed prior to that development. Although there were analogous precedents to the Mosaic law, such as the Code of Hammurabi, the function of the law within Judaism became unique. Its value extended far beyond mere civil utility to being the major token of God's presence and concern. The "will of God" was the underlying basis of the law and obedience to the law was the initial condition for God's continuing favor. The prophets later modified this requirement to emphasize that obedience should be conscientious, not perfunctory, a matter of the heart, not of statute, although the considerable effort of many rabbis was subsequently devoted to clarifying the letter of the law in that massive commentary known as the *Talmud*. Moral emphasis continues to be an important aspect of contemporary Judaism, even to the point that in some quarters it is held to constitute the totality of religious obligation. Both the concept of the moral law and of the one God who is its author have undergone modification over the ages, an improvement in one being automatically an improvement in the other. As the concept of God prevalent in modern Judaism is no longer primarily that of the "lord of hosts," an all-powerful warrior king, so the moral code has advanced far beyond the Mosaic "eye for an eye" formulation.

Judaism is also notable for having evolved historical consciousness at an early stage of its development. In fact, it may reasonably be maintained that the Judeo-Christian tradition is largely responsible for the primarily historical orientation of contemporary western consciousness, since this emphasis was not a feature of Greek philosophical thought. In ancient Judaism, the development of this awareness is shown in the institution of religious festivals, which are as much remembrances of important events as celebrations of seasonal renewal (Passover, for example), and in the development of a strong prophetic tradition emphasizing criticism of contemporary persons and social conditions and holding forth the promise of future rewards and penalties (among the hoped-for rewards was the establishment of a Messianic kingdom). This historical awareness, in conjunction with the moral emphasis, helped to give Judaism an unique appreciation of the importance of individual men and nations as instruments of divine providence.

Judaism has been shaped by other characteristic developments although none so pervasive as the preceding. There have been mystical tendencies, both of a Gnostic type, such as appear in the Caballistic literature, and of the non-intellectual type, exemplified in Hasidism. It has also produced reflective analyses of human experience, ranging from the penetrating reflections upon man and God found in the Old Testament "wisdom" literature to full-blown philosophical explanations in the light of the prevalent philosophical methods, ranging over the centuries from Philo Judaeus to contemporary thinkers such as Martin Buber.

Needless to say, both Christian and Islamic culture possess elements of Judaic origin as essential components of their religious heritage. There has also been a feedback into Judaism from other cultures, especially from the science and philosophy of the West. Judaism, nearly as much as Christianity, has been concerned with the relevance of science to religion, and its theologians have struggled to reconcile the problems generated by this relationship. Perhaps even more than Christian thinkers, Jewish theologians have been concerned with the sciences of man. This is probably due to the centuries-old emphasis upon the importance of the community, its relation to God, and its moral obligation to the rest of mankind. This emphasis has yielded a type of faith which is unique among the world's religions in its accentuation of the presence of the community in the actions and the character of the individual, and the presence of the community and the individual within the will of God.

SUGGESTIONS FOR FURTHER READING

The Apocrypha of the Old Testament, Revised Standard Version, New York, Oxford, 1965.
Blau, Joseph L., *Modern Varieties of Judaism,* New York, Columbia University Press, 1966.
Epstein, Isidore, ed., *The Babylonian Talmud,* 35 vols., London, The Soncino Press, 1948.

Gordis, Robert, *Judaism for the Modern Age,* New York, Farrar, Straus, & Cudahy, 1955.

Glazer, Nathan, *American Judaism,* Chicago, University of Chicago Press, 1957.

Oesterley, W. O. E. and Robinson, Theodore H., *Hebrew Religion, Its Origin and Development,* New York, Macmillan, 1947.

Roth, Cecil, ed., *The Standard Jewish Encyclopedia,* Garden City, New York, Doubleday, 1959.

Schwarz, Leo Walter, ed., *Great Ages and Ideas of the Jewish People,* New York, Random House, 1956.

BIBLE READING GUIDE FOR JUDAISM

The following outline affords a helpful organization of the Old Testament literature for those who would like to acquaint themselves with its principal themes and emphases. Should the reader wish to familiarize himself with the traditional interpretations of the Torah within Judaism, it is further recommended that he consult the commentary upon the appropriate passages contained in the Talmud, of which one edition is listed in the bibliography.

I. Early Myth and Ritual
   1. The Creation Stories: *Genesis 1–4*
   2. The Flood Epic: *Genesis 6–9*
   3. The Abraham Story: *Genesis 11–25*
   4. The Jacob (Israel) Story: *Genesis 26–50*
   5. The Moses Story: *Exodus (including details of ritual and legislation, Exodus 20–34:28)*
II. The Hebrew Kingdom
   1. Conquest of Canaan: *Joshua 1–11*
   2. The Kings: Saul, *I Samuel 8–15*
                David, *I Samuel 16–24*
                Solomon, *I Kings 1–11*
III. The Hebrew Prophets
   1. The Conscience of a King—Elijah: *I Kings 17–22*
   2. A Moral Reformer: *Amos*
   3. The Vision of a Universal God and a Restored Israel: *Isaiah 1–9:7*
   4. Return from Captivity and the Hope of Future Glory: *Isaiah 46–66*
IV. Poetry and Praise
   1. Glorification of God: various psalms, *e.g., Psalms 8, 18, 19, 23, 24, 46, 91, 93, 96, 98, 100, 117, 150*
   2. Repentance and Supplication: various psalms, *e.g., Psalms 27, 51, 61, 62, 71, 90, 119*
   3. Faith and Scepticism: *Job (through 42:6), Ecclesiastes*
   4. In Praise of Wisdom: *Proverbs*

31

THE MANUAL OF DISCIPLINE

In the spring of 1947 a Bedouin boy, Muhammad adh-Dhib, stumbled upon what was to become one of the most exciting discoveries in recent biblical archeology. He discovered a cave near the ancient ruins of Qumran on the northwest shore of the Dead Sea, containing several clay jars filled with scrolls, many in advanced stages of decay. Through a series of events which read much like a detective story, these scrolls finally fell into the hands of competent scholars who recognized their singular importance. Subsequently, many other scrolls were unearthed in the vicinity of Qumran, although The Manual of Discipline *was among the first group of eleven scrolls. Evidently these manuscripts, dated variously from before the First Century B.C. to A.D. 70, had been the property of a community of religious men, probably to be identified as Essenes, who had inhabited a monastery whose remains constitute the Qumran ruins. Whereas many of the scrolls are copies of, or commentaries upon, the Hebrew scriptures, others contain information about the organization of the religious community which had owned these writings.* The Manual of Discipline *is perhaps the most interesting of the latter kind of document. It appears to be a compilation of the rules governing an Essene community, and furnishes invaluable insight into the beliefs and practices of the sect. The Essenes represent the extremely pious element in First-Century Judaism, following in a direct line of influence from the Hasidim of the Maccabean era. In this document, one sees Judaism in the form it took when, in a time of stress, oppression, and corruption, some of its most devout souls withdrew into the solitude of the desert in order that they might give one another mutual aid in the pursuit of purity and holiness.*

The translator, Theodor H. Gaster, Professor of Ancient Cultures at Fairleigh Dickinson University, is one of the most competent scholars in Hebraic and Near Eastern history, mythology, and religion.

OF THE COMMITMENT

(i, 1–15)

Everyone who wishes to join the community must pledge himself to respect God and man; to live according to the communal rule; to seek God [   ]; to do what is good and upright in His sight, in accordance with what He has commanded through Moses and through His servants the prophets; to love all that He has chosen and hate all that He has rejected; to keep far from all evil and to cling to all good works; to act truthfully and righteously and justly on earth and to walk no more in the stubbornness of a guilty heart and of lustful eyes, doing all manner of evil; to bring into a bond of mutual love all who have declared their willingness to carry out the statutes of God; to join the formal community of God; to walk blamelessly before Him in conformity with His various laws and dispositions; to love all the children of light, each according to his stake in the formal community of God; and to hate all the children of darkness, each according to the measure of his guilt, which God will ultimately requite.

All who declare their willingness to serve God's truth must bring all of their mind, all of their strength, and all of their wealth into the community of God, so that their minds may be purified by the truth of His precepts, their strength controlled by His perfect ways, and their wealth disposed in accordance with His just design. They must not deviate by a single step from carrying out the orders of God at the times appointed for them; they must neither advance the statutory times nor postpone the prescribed seasons. They must not turn aside from the ordinances of God's truth either to the right or to the left.

OF INITIATION

(i, 16–ii, 18)

Moreover, all who would join the ranks of the community must enter into a covenant in the presence of God to do according to all that He has commanded and not to turn away from Him through any fear or terror or through any trial to which they may be subjected through the domination of Belial.

When they enter into that covenant, the priests and the levites are to pronounce a blessing upon the God of salvation and upon all that He does to make known His truth; and all that enter the covenant are to say after them, Amen, amen.

Then the priests are to rehearse the bounteous acts of God as revealed in all His deeds of power, and they are to recite all His tender mercies towards Israel; while the levites are to rehearse the iniquities of the children of Israel and all the guilty transgressions and sins that they have committed through the domination of Belial. And all who enter the covenant are to make confession after them, saying, We have acted perversely, we have transgressed, we have sinned, we have done wickedly, ourselves and our fathers before us, in that we have gone counter to the truth. God has been right to bring His judgment upon us and upon our fathers. Howbeit, always from ancient times He has also bestowed His mercies upon us, and so will He do for all time to come.

Then the priests are to invoke a blessing on all that have cast their lot with God, that walk blamelessly in all their ways; and they are to say: MAY HE BLESS THEE with all good and KEEP THEE from all evil, and ILLUMINE thy heart with insight into the things of life, and GRACE THEE with knowledge of things eternal, and LIFT UP HIS gracious COUNTENANCE TOWARDS THEE to grant thee peace everlasting.

The levites, on the other hand, are to invoke a curse on all that have cast their lot with Belial, and to say in response: Cursed art thou for all thy wicked guilty works. May God make thee a thing of abhorrence at the hands of all who would wreak vengeance, and visit thine offspring with destruction at the hands of all who would mete out retribution. Cursed art thou, beyond hope of mercy. Even as thy works are wrought in darkness, so mayest thou be damned in the gloom of the fire eternal. May God show thee no favor when thou callest, neither pardon to forgive thine iniquities. May He lift up an angry countenance towards thee, to wreak vengeance upon thee. May no man wish thee peace of all that truly claim their patrimony.

And all that enter the covenant shall say alike after them that bless and after them that curse, Amen, amen.

Thereupon the priests and the levites shall continue and say: Cursed be every one that hath come to enter this covenant with the taint of idolatry in his heart and who hath set his iniquity as a stumblingblock before him so that thereby he may defect, and who, when he hears the terms of this covenant, blesses himself in his heart, saying, May it go well with me, for I shall go on walking in the stubbornness of my heart! Whether he satisfy his passions or whether he still thirst for their fulfillment, his spirit shall be swept away and receive no pardon. The anger of God and the fury of His judgments shall consume him as by fire unto his eternal extinction, and there shall cleave unto him all the curses threatened in this covenant. God shall set him apart for misfortune, and he shall be cut off from the midst of all the children of light in that through the taint of his idolatry and through the stumblingblock of his iniquity he has defected from God. God will set his lot among those that are accursed for ever! And all who have been admitted to the covenant shall say after them in response, Amen, amen.

OF THE ANNUAL REVIEW
(ii, 19–25)

The following procedure is to be followed year by year so long as Belial continues to hold sway.

The priests are first to be reviewed in due order, one after another, in respect to the state of their spirits. After them, the levites shall be similarly reviewed, and in the third place all the laity one after another, in their thousands, hundreds, fifties, and tens. The object is that every man in Israel may be made aware of his status in the community of God in the sense of the ideal, eternal society, and that none may be abased below his status nor exalted above his allotted place. All of them will thus be members of a community founded at once upon true values and upon a becoming sense of humility, upon charity and mutual fairness—members of a society truly hallowed, partners in an everlasting communion.

OF THOSE WHO ARE TO BE EXCLUDED
(ii, 25–iii, 12)

Anyone who refuses to enter the (ideal) society of God and persists in walking in the stubbornness of his heart shall not be admitted to this community of God's truth. For inasmuch as his soul has revolted at the discipline entailed in a knowledge of God's righteous judgments, he has shown no real strength in amending his way of life, and therefore cannot be reckoned with the upright. The mental, physical, and material resources of such a man are not to be introduced into the stock of the community, for such a man 'plows in the slime of wickedness' and 'these are stains on his repentance.' He is not honest in resolving the stubbornness of his heart. On paths of light he sees but darkness. Such a man cannot be reckoned as among those essentially blameless. He cannot be cleared by mere ceremonies of atonement, nor cleansed by any waters of ablution, nor sanctified by immersion in lakes or rivers, nor purified by any bath. Unclean, unclean he remains so long as he rejects the government of God and refuses the discipline of communion with Him. For it is only through the spiritual apprehension of God's truth that man's ways can be properly directed. Only thus can all his iniquities be shriven so that he can gaze upon the true light of life. Only through the holy spirit can he achieve union with God's truth and be purged of all his iniquities. Only by a spirit of uprightness and humility can his sin be atoned. Only by the submission of his soul to all the ordinances of God can his flesh be made clean. Only thus can it really be sprinkled with waters of ablution. Only thus can it really be sanctified by waters of purification. And only thus can he really direct his steps to walk blamelessly through all the vicissitudes of his destiny in all the ways of God in the manner which He has commanded, without turning either to the right or to the left and without overstepping any of God's words. Then indeed will he be acceptable before God like an atonement-offering which meets with His pleasure, and then indeed will he be admitted to the covenant of the community for ever.

OF THE TWO SPIRITS IN MAN

(iii, 13–iv, 26)

This is for the man who would bring others to the inner vision, so that he may understand and teach to all the children of light the real nature of men, touching the different varieties of their temperaments with the distinguishing traits thereof, touching their actions throughout their generations, and touching the reason why they are now visited with afflictions and now enjoy periods of well-being.

All that is and ever was comes from a God of knowledge. Before things came into existence He determined the plan of them; and when they fill their appointed roles, it is in accordance with His glorious design that they discharge their functions. Nothing can be changed. In His hand lies the government of all things. God it is that sustains them in their needs.

Now, this God created man to rule the world, and appointed for him two spirits after whose direction he was to walk until the final Inquisition. They are the spirits of truth and of perversity.

The origin of truth lies in the Fountain of Light, and that of perversity in the Wellspring of Darkness. All who practice righteousness are under the domination of the Prince of Lights, and walk in ways of light; whereas all who practice perversity are under the domination of the Angel of Darkness and walk in ways of darkness. Through the Angel of Darkness, however, even those who practice righteousness are made liable to error. All their sin and their iniquities, all their guilt and their deeds of transgression are the result of his domination; and this, by God's inscrutable design, will continue until the time appointed by Him. Moreover, all men's afflictions and all their moments of tribulation are due to this being's malevolent sway. All of the spirits that attend upon him are bent on causing the sons of light to stumble. Howbeit, the God of Israel and the Angel of His truth are always there to help the sons of light. It is God that created these spirits of light and darkness and made them the basis of every act, the [instigators] of every deed and the directors of every thought. The one He loves to all eternity, and is ever pleased with its deeds; but any association with the other He abhors, and He hates all its ways to the end of time.

This is the way those spirits operate in the world. The enlightenment of man's heart, the making straight before him all the ways of righteousness and truth, the implanting in his heart of fear for the judgments of God, of a spirit of humility, of patience, of abundant compassion, of perpetual goodness, of insight, of perception, of that sense of the Divine Power that is based at once on an apprehension of God's works and a reliance on His plenteous mercy, of a spirit of knowledge informing every plan of action, of a zeal for righteous government, of a hallowed mind in a controlled nature, of abounding love for all who follow the truth, of a self-respecting purity which abhors all the taint of filth, of a modesty of behavior coupled with a general prudence and an ability to hide within oneself the secrets of what one knows—these are the things that come to men in this world through communion with the spirit of truth. And the guerdon of all that walk in its ways is health and abundant well-being, with long life and fruition of seed along with eternal blessings and everlasting joy in the life everlasting, and a crown of glory and a robe of honor, amid light perpetual.

But to the spirit of perversity belong greed, remissness in right-doing, wickedness and falsehood, pride and presumption, deception and guile, cruelty and abundant insolence, shortness of temper and profusion of folly, arrogant passion, abominable acts in a spirit of lewdness, filthy ways in the thralldom of unchastity, a blasphemous tongue, blindness of eyes, dullness of ears, stiffness of neck and hardness of heart, to the end that a man walks entirely in ways of darkness and of evil cunning. The guerdon of all who walk in such ways is multitude of afflictions at the hands of all the angels of destruction, everlasting perdition through the angry wrath of an avenging God, eternal horror and perpetual reproach, the disgrace of final annihilation in the Fire, darkness throughout the vicissitudes of life in every generation, doleful sorrow, bitter misfortune and darkling ruin—ending in extinction without remnant or survival.

It is to these things that all men are born, and it is to these that all the host of them are heirs throughout their generations. It is in these ways that men needs must walk and it is in these two divisions, according as a man inherits something of each, that all human acts are divided throughout all the ages of eternity. For God has appointed these two things to obtain in equal measure until the final age.

Between the two categories He has set an eternal enmity. Deeds of perversity are an abomination to Truth, while all the ways of Truth are an abomination to perversity; and there is a constant jealous rivalry between their two regimes, for they do not march in accord. Howbeit, God in His inscrutable wisdom has appointed a term for the existence of perversity, and when the time of Inquisition comes, He will destroy it for ever. Then truth will emerge triumphant for the world, albeit now and until the time of the final judgment it go sullying itself in the ways of wickedness owing to the domination of perversity. Then, too, God will purge all the acts of man in the crucible of His truth, and refine for Himself all the fabric of man, destroying every spirit of perversity from within his flesh and cleansing him by the holy spirit from all the effects of wickedness. Like waters of purification He will sprinkle upon him the spirit of truth, to cleanse him of all the abominations of falsehood and of all pollution through the spirit of filth; to the end that, being made upright, men may have understanding of transcendental knowledge and of the lore of the sons of heaven, and that, being made blameless in their ways, they may be endowed with inner vision. For them has God chosen to be the partners of His eternal covenant, and theirs shall be all mortal glory. Perversity shall be no more, and all works of deceit shall be put to shame.

Thus far, the spirits of truth and perversity have been struggling in the heart of man. Men have walked both in wisdom and in folly. If a man casts his portion with truth, he does righteously and hates perversity; if he casts it with perversity, he does wickedly and abominates truth. For God has apportioned them in equal measure until the final age, until 'He makes all things new'. He foreknows the effect of their works in every epoch of the world, and He has made men heirs to them that they might know good and evil. But [when the time] of Inquisition [comes], He will determine the fate of every living being in accordance with which of the [two spirits he has chosen to follow].

OF SOCIAL RELATIONS

(v, 1-7)

This is the rule for all the members of the community—that is, for such as have declared their readiness to turn away from all evil and to adhere to all that God in His good pleasure has commanded.

They are to keep apart from the company of the froward.

They are to belong to the community in both a doctrinal and an economic sense.

They are to abide by the decisions of the sons of Zadok, the same being priests that still keep the Covenant, and of the majority of the community that stand firm in it. It is by the vote of such that all matters doctrinal, economic, and judicial are to be determined.

They are concertedly and in all their pursuits to practise truth, humility, righteousness, justice, charity and decency, with no one walking in the stubbornness of his own heart or going astray after his heart or his eyes or his fallible human mind.

Furthermore, they are concertedly to remove the impurity of their human mold, and likewise all stiffneckedness.

They are to establish in Israel a solid basis of truth.

They are to unite in a bond indissoluble for ever.

They are to extend forgiveness to all among the priesthood that have freely enlisted in the cause of holiness, and to all among the laity that have done so in the cause of truth, and likewise to all that have associated themselves with them.

They are to make common cause both in the struggle and in the upshot of it.

They are to regard as felons all that transgress the law.

OF THE OBLIGATION OF HOLINESS

(v, 7–20)

And this is the way in which all those ordinances are to be applied on a collective basis.

Everyone who is admitted to the formal organization* of the community is to enter into a covenant in the presence of all fellow-volunteers in the cause and to commit himself by a binding oath to abide with all his heart and soul by the commandments of the Law of Moses, as that Law is revealed to the sons of Zadok—that is, to the priests who still keep the Covenant and seek God's will—and to a majority of their co-covenanters who have volunteered together to adhere to the truth of God and to walk according to His pleasure.

He that so commits himself is to keep apart from all froward men that walk in the path of wickedness; for such men are not to be reckoned in the Covenant inasmuch as they have never sought nor studied God's ordinances in order to find out on what more arcane points they may guiltily have gone astray, while in regard to the things which stand patently revealed they have acted high-handedly. They have thus incurred God's angry judgment and caused Him to take vengeance upon them with all the curses threatened in the Covenant and to wreak great judgments upon them that they be finally destroyed without remnant.

No one is to go into water in order to attain the purity of holy men. For men cannot be purified except they repent their evil. God regards as impure all that transgress His word. No one is to have any association with such a man either in work or in goods, lest he incur the penalty of prosecution. Rather is he to keep away from such a man in every respect, for the Scripture says: 'Keep away from every false thing' [Exodus 23.7]. No member of the community is to abide by the decision of such men in any matter of doctrine or law. He is not to eat or drink of anything that belongs to them nor to receive anything from them except for cash, even as it is written: 'Desist from man whose breath is in his nostrils, for as what is he reckoned?' [Isaiah 2.22]. All that are not reckoned in the Covenant must be put aside, and likewise all that they possess. A holy man must not rely on works of vanity, and vanity is what all of them are that have not recognized God's Covenant. All that spurn His word will God blast out of the world. All their actions are as filth before Him, and He regards all their possessions as unclean.

* Heb. 'council'.

OF THE EXAMINATION OF INITIANTS

(v, 20–24)

When a man enters the covenant, minded to act in accordance with all the foregoing ordinances and formally to ally himself to the holy congregation, inquiry is to be made concerning his temper in human relations and his understanding and performance in matters of doctrine. This inquiry is to be conducted jointly by the priests who have undertaken concertedly to uphold God's Covenant and to supervise the execution of all the ordinances which He has commanded, and by a majority of the laity who have likewise undertaken concertedly to return to that Covenant. Every man is then to be registered in a particular rank, one after the other, by the standard of his understanding and performance. The object is that each person will be rendered subject to his superior. Their spiritual attitudes and their performance are to be reviewed, however, year by year, some being then promoted by virtue of their [improved] understanding and the integrity of their conduct, and others demoted for their waywardness.

OF ACCUSATIONS AND GRUDGES

(v, 24–vi, 1)

When anyone has a charge against his neighbor, he is to prosecute it truthfully, humbly, and humanely. He is not to speak to him angrily or querulously or arrogantly or in any wicked mood. He is not to bear hatred [towards him in the inner recesses] of his heart. When he has a charge against him, he is to proffer it then and there* and not to render himself liable to penalty by nursing a grudge. Furthermore, no man is to bring a charge publicly against his neighbor except he prove it by witnesses.

OF COMMUNAL DUTIES

(vi, 1–8)

This is the procedure which all members of the community are to follow in all dealings with one another, wherever they dwell.

Everyone is to obey his superior in rank in all matters of work or money. But all are to dine together, worship together, and take counsel together.

Wherever there be ten men who have been formally enrolled in the community, one who is a priest is not to depart from them. When they sit in

* Heb. 'on the selfsame day'.

his presence, they are to take their places according to their respective ranks; and the same order is to obtain when they meet for common counsel.

When they set the table for a meal or prepare wine to drink, the priest is first to put forth his hand to invoke a blessing on the first portion of the bread or wine.

Similarly, wherever there be ten men who have been formally enrolled in the community, there is not to be absent from them one who can interpret the Law to them at any time of day or night, for the harmonious adjustment of their human relations.

The general members of the community are to keep awake for a third of all the nights of the year reading book(s),* studying the Law and worshiping together.

OF THE GENERAL COUNCIL

(vi, 8–13)

This is the rule covering public sessions.

The priests are to occupy the first place. The elders are to come second; and the rest of the people are to take their places according to their respective ranks. This order is to obtain alike when they seek a judicial ruling, when they meet for common counsel, or when any matter arises of general concern.

Everyone is to have an opportunity of rendering his opinion in the common council. No one, however, is to interrupt while his neighbor is speaking, or to speak until the latter has finished. Furthermore, no one is to speak in advance of his prescribed rank. Everyone is to speak in turn, as he is called upon.

In public sessions, no one is to speak on any subject that is not of concern to† the company as a whole. If the superintendent of the general membership or anyone who is not of the same rank as the person who happens to be raising a question for the consideration of the community, has something to say to the company, he is to stand up and declare: I have something to say to the company; and only if they so bid him, is he to speak.

OF POSTULANTS AND NOVICES

(vi, 13–23)

If any man in Israel wish to be affiliated to the formal congregation of the community, the superintendent of the general membership is to examine him as to his intelligence and his actions and, if he then embark on a course of training, he is to have him enter into a covenant to return to the truth and turn away from all perversity. Then he is to apprise him of all the rules of the community.

* Or, 'the Book (of the Law)'.
† Or, 'to the liking of'.

Subsequently, when that man comes to present himself to the general membership, everyone is to be asked his opinion about him, and his admission to or rejection from the formal congregation of the community is to be determined by general vote.

No candidate, however, is to be admitted to the formal state of purity enjoyed by the general membership of the community until, at the completion of a full year, his spiritual attitude and his performance have been duly reviewed. Meanwhile he is to have no stake in the common funds.

After he has spent a full year in the midst of the community, the members are jointly to review his case, as to his understanding and performance in matters of doctrine. If it then be voted by the opinion of the priests and of a majority of their co-covenanters to admit him to the sodality, they are to have him bring with him all his property and the tools of his profession. These are to be committed to the custody of the community's 'minister of works'. They are to be entered by that officer into an account, but he is not to disburse them for the general benefit.

Not until the completion of a second year among the members of the community is the candidate to be admitted to the common board.* When, however, that second year has been completed, he is to be subjected to a further review by the general membership, and if then it be voted to admit him to the community, he is to be registered in the due order of rank which he is to occupy among his brethren in all matters pertaining to doctrine, judicial procedure, degree of purity, and share in the common funds. Thenceforth his counsel and his judgment are to be at the disposal of the community.

OF FALSE, IMPUDENT AND BLASPHEMOUS SPEECH

(vi, 23–vii, 5)

And these are the rules to be followed in the interpretation of the law regarding forms of speech.

If there be found in the community a man who consciously lies in the matter of (his) wealth, he is to be regarded as outside the state of purity entailed by membership, and he is to be mulcted of one fourth of his food ration.

If a man answer his neighbor defiantly or speak brusquely so as to undermine the composure† of his fellow, and in so doing flout the orders of one who is registered as his superior [   ],§ he is to be mulcted for one year.

If a man, in speaking about anything, mention that Name which is honored above all [names],‖ or if, in a moment of sudden stress or for some other personal reason, he curse the   (i.e., the man who reads the Book

---

* Heb. 'drink'.

† Heb. 'shake (or, disturb) the foundation'.

§ An imperfectly preserved phrase follows in the text. Possibly, it means, 'And if his hand act wickedly against him', i.e., if he bodily assaults him.

‖ I.e., the name of God.

of the Law or leads worship),* he is to be put out and never to return to formal membership in the community.

If a man speak in anger against one of the registered priests, he is to be mulcted for one year, placed in isolation, and regarded as outside the state of purity entailed in membership of the community. If, however, he spoke unintentionally, he is to be mulcted only for six months.

If a man dissemble about what he really knows, he is to be mulcted for six months.

If a man defames his neighbor unjustly, and does so deliberately, he is to be mulcted for one year and regarded as 'outside'.

OF FRAUD

(vii, 5–8)

If a man speak with his neighbor in guile or consciously practice deceit upon him, he is to be mulcted for six months. If, however, he practices the deceit [unintentionally],† he is to be mulcted only for three months.

If a man defraud the community, causing a deficit in its funds, he is to make good that deficit. If he lack means to do so, he is to be mulcted for sixty days.

OF VINDICTIVENESS

(vii, 8–9)

If he harbor a grudge against his neighbor without legitimate cause, he is to be mulcted for six months [supralinear correction: 'one year']. The same is to apply also to anyone who takes personal revenge on his neighbor in any respect.

OF IMPROPER SPEECH

(vii, 9)

Anyone who indulges in indecent talk is to be mulcted for three months.

* This, gap and all, is how the text reads in the original. It is apparent that the scribe found in the archetype (or heard from dictation?) a rare word which he did not understand fully. He therefore left a blank, but added a gloss giving the approximate sense. The word must have been a technical term for something like 'precentor' or 'deacon'.

† There is again a blank in the original. The scribe evidently could not decipher the word in his archetype, but the sense is clear.

OF MISCONDUCT AT PUBLIC SESSIONS

(vii, 9–12)

Anyone who interrupts his neighbor in a public session is to be mulcted for ten days.

Anyone who lies down and goes to sleep at a public session is to be mulcted for thirty days.

Anyone who leaves a public session gratuitously and without reason for as many as three times during one sitting is to be mulcted for ten days. If he be ordered to stay (?)* and he still leave, he is to be mulcted for thirty days.

OF INDECOROUS ACTS

(vii, 12–15)

If, except he be under duress (?)†, a man walk naked before his neighbor, he shall be mulcted for six months.

If a man spit into the midst of a public session, he shall be mulcted for thirty days.

If a man bring out his hand from under his cloak, and so expose himself that his private parts become visible, he be mulcted for thirty days.

If a man indulge in raucous, inane laughter, he shall be mulcted for thirty days.

If a man put forth his left hand to gesticulate with it in conversation, he shall be mulcted for ten days.

OF SLANDER AND INCRIMINATION

(vii, 15–18)

If a man slander his neighbor, he shall be regarded as outside the communal state of purity for one year, and he shall also be mulcted. But if he slander the entire group, he is to be expelled and never to return.

If a man complain against the whole basis of the community, he is to be expelled irrevocably.

If he complain against his neighbor without legitimate cause, he is to be mulcted for six months.

* This word is partly obliterated. The sense is therefore obscure.
† Heb. uncertain.

OF DEFECTION

(vii, 18–25)

If a man's spirit waver so far from the basis of the community that he betray the truth and walk in the stubbornness of his own heart, but if he subsequently repent, he shall be mulcted for two years. During the first, he shall be regarded as outside the communal state of purity altogether. During the second, he shall be excluded only from the communal board* and occupy a place behind all the other members. At the completion of the two years, the membership in general shall hold an enquiry about him. If it then be decided to readmit him, he shall again be registered with duly assigned rank and thereafter he too shall be called upon to render his opinion in deliberations concerning the rules.

If a man has been a formal member of the community for a full ten years, but then, through a spiritual relapse, betray the principles of the community and quit the general body in order to walk in the stubbornness of his own heart, he is never to return to formal membership in the community. No member of the community is to associate with him either by recognizing him as of the same state of purity or by sharing property with him. Any of the members who does so shall be liable to the same sentence: he too shall be expelled.

OF THE APPOINTMENT OF 'PRESBYTERS'

(viii, 1–19)

In the formal congregation of the community there shall be twelve laymen and three priests schooled to perfection in all that has been revealed of the entire Law. Their duty shall be to set the standard for the practice of truth, righteousness and justice, and for the exercise of charity and humility in human relations; and to show how, by control of impulse and contrition of spirit, faithfulness may be maintained on earth; how, by active performance of justice and passive submission to the trials of chastisement, iniquity may be cleared, and how one can walk with all men with the quality of truth and in conduct appropriate to every occasion.

So long as these men exist in Israel, the formal congregation of the community will rest securely on a basis of truth. It will become a plant evergreen. Insofar as the laymen are concerned, it will be indeed a sanctuary; and insofar as the priesthood is concerned, it will indeed constitute the basis for a true 'holy of holies'. The members of the community will be in all justice the witnesses of God's truth and the elect of His favor, effecting atonement for the earth and ensuring the requital of the wicked. They will be, indeed, a 'tested

* Heb. 'drink'.

bulwark' and 'a precious cornerstone' [cf. Isa. 28.16], which shall never be shaken or moved from their place. As for the priesthood, they shall be a seat for the holy of holies, inasmuch as all of them will then have knowledge of the Covenant of justice and all of them be qualified to offer what will be indeed 'a pleasant savor' to the Lord. And as for the laity, they will constitute a household of integrity and truth, qualified to maintain the Covenant as an everlasting pact. They shall prove acceptable to God, so that He will shrive the earth of its guilt, bring final judgment upon wickedness, and perversity shall be no more.

When these men have undergone, with blamelessness of conduct, a two-year preparation in the fundamentals of the community, they shall be segregated as especially sacred among the formal members of the community. Any knowledge which the expositor of the law may possess but which may have to remain arcane to the ordinary layman, he shall not keep hidden from them; for in their case there need be no fear that it might induce apostasy.

When these men exist in Israel, these are the provisions whereby they are to be kept apart from any consort with froward men, to the end that they may indeed 'go into the wilderness to prepare the way', i.e., do what Scripture enjoins when it says, 'Prepare in the wilderness the way . . . make straight in the desert a highway for our God' [Isa. 40.3]. (The reference is to the study of the Law which God commanded through Moses to the end that, as occasion arises, all things may be done in accordance with what is revealed therein and with what the prophets also have revealed through God's holy spirit.)

No member of the community—that is, no duly covenanted members— who blatantly deviates in any particular from the total body of commandments is to be permitted to come into contact with the purity enjoyed by these specially holy men or to benefit by* their counsel until his actions be free of all perversity and he has been readmitted to the common council by decision of the general membership and thereupon reinstated in his rank.

The same rule is to apply also to novices.

OF THE CONDUCT OF 'PRESBYTERS'

(viii, 20–ix, 6)

These are the rules of conduct for the 'men of perfect holiness' in their dealings with one another.

If any of those that have been admitted to the degree of special sanctity —that is, to the degree of 'those that walk blamelessly in the way as God has commanded'—transgress a single word of the Law of Moses either blatantly or deviously, he is to be excommunicated and never to return. No other person in the degree of the specially holy is to have anything to do with him in the sharing either of property or of counsel.

* Heb. 'know'.

If, however, he erred unintentionally, he is to be debarred only from that particular degree of purity and from participation in the common council. This is to be interpreted to mean that he is not to render any judgment nor is his counsel to be invited in any matter for a full two years. This holds good, however, only if, after the expiration of the full two years, his conduct be considered, in the judgment of the general membership, to be perfect alike in attendance at general assemblies, in study and in frame of mind, and if he has not meanwhile committed any further act of inadvertence. In other words, this two-year penalty is to apply only in the case of a single inadvertent error, whereas if a man acts blatantly, he is nevermore to be readmitted. In sum, it is only the man who acts by inadvertence that is to be placed on probation for two years to see whether, in the opinion of the general membership, his conduct and frame of mind have meanwhile again become blameless. If so, he may be reinstated in the body of the especially holy.

When these things obtain in Israel, as defined by these provisions, the Holy Spirit will indeed rest on a sound foundation; truth will be evinced perpetually; the guilt of transgression and the perfidy of sin will be shriven; and atonement will be made for the earth more effectively than by any flesh of burnt-offerings or fat of sacrifices. The 'oblation of the lips' will be in all justice like the erstwhile 'pleasant savor' on the altar; righteousness and integrity like that free-will offering which God deigns to accept. At that time, the men of the community will constitute a true and distinctive temple—a veritable holy of holies—wherein the priesthood may fitly foregather, and a true and distinctive synagogue made up of laymen who walk in integrity.

OF THE AUTHORITY OF THE PRIESTS

(ix, 7)

The priests alone are to have authority in all judicial and economic matters, and it is by their vote that the ranks of the various members of the community are to be determined.

OF THE PROPERTY OF 'PRESBYTERS'

(ix, 8–11)

The property of the 'specially holy men'—that is, of 'the men that walk blamelessly'—is not to be put into a common pool with that of men who may still be addicted to deceit* and may not yet have achieved that purity of conduct which leads them to keep apart from perversity and to walk in integrity.

Until the coming of the Prophet† and of both the priestly and the lay

---

* Heb. simply, 'men of deceit'.
† That is, the prophet foretold in Deuteronomy 18:18, 'I will raise them up a prophet from among their brethren, like unto thee [Moses]; and I will put My words in his mouth, and he shall speak unto them all that I shall command him.'

Messiah, these men are not to depart from the clear intent of the Law to walk in any way in the stubbornness of their own hearts. They shall judge by the original laws in which the members of the community were schooled from the beginning.

OF THE DAILY CONDUCT OF THE FAITHFUL

(ix, 12–16)

These are the ordinances for the conduct of any man that seeks after inner vision, in regard alike to human relations, the regulation of affairs on specific occasions, and the appraisal of his fellow men.

He is to perform at all times the will of God, as it has been revealed.

He is to make a point of studying all extant wisdom pertinent to different circumstances and the particular ordinance that applies to the particular occasion.

He is to respect the distinctive rank accorded to the sons of Zadok and to the elect of any specific epoch by virtue of their spiritual attitudes, and to appraise them by that criterion, thus adhering to the will of God, as He has commanded.

Everyone is to be judged by the standard of his spirituality. Intercourse with him is to be determined by the purity of his deeds,* and consort with him by the degree of his intelligence. This alone is to determine the degree to which a man is to be loved or hated.

OF RELIGIOUS DISCUSSION

(ix, 16–21)

No one is to engage in discussion or disputation with men of ill repute; and in the company of froward men everyone is to abstain from talk about† the meaning of the Law [Torah].

With those, however, that have chosen the right path everyone is indeed to discuss matters pertaining to the apprehension§ of God's truth and of His righteous judgments. The purpose of such discussions is to guide the minds of the members of the community, to give them insight into God's inscrutable wonders and truth, and to bring them to walk blamelessly each with his neighbor in harmony with all that has been revealed to them. For this is the time when 'the way is being prepared in the wilderness', and it behooves them to understand all that is happening. It is also the time when they must needs keep apart from all other men and not turn aside from the way through any form of perversity.

* Heb. 'hands' (palms).
† Heb. 'keep hidden'.
§ Heb. 'knowledge'.

OF LOVING AND HATING FELLOWMEN; AND OF DUTY TO GOD

(ix, 21–26)

And these are the regulations of conduct for every man that would seek the inner vision in these times, touching what he is to love and what he is to hate.

He is to bear unremitting hatred towards all men of ill repute, and to be minded to keep in seclusion from them. He is to leave it to them to pursue wealth and mercenary gain, like servants at the mercy of their masters or wretches truckling to a despot.

He is to be zealous to carry out every ordinance punctiliously, against the Day of Requital.

In all his emprises and in all things over which he has control he is to act in a manner acceptable to God, in accordance with what God has commanded.

He is to accept willingly whatever befalls him and to take pleasure in nothing but the will of God.

He is to make [all] the words of his mouth acceptable, and not to lust after anything that God has not commanded.

He is to watch ever for the judgment of God, and [in every vicissitude of his existence] he is to bless his Maker. Whatever befalls, he is to [recount God's glory] and to bless him [with 'the oblation of] the lips'.

32

CREATION AS A MORAL ALLEGORY
Philo Judaeus

Philo Judaeus (c. 20 B.C.–A.D. 40) lived in Alexandria, Egypt, one of the great centers of Hellenistic culture. On the one hand, he was reared in the wisdom of the Torah and was quite knowledgeable in the doctrines and moral precepts of Judaism. On

Reprinted by permission of the publishers from Loeb Classical Library. Philo Judaeus, *Allegorical Interpretation of Genesis I, II*, pp. 167–177, 183–190. Cambridge, Mass.: Harvard University Press, 1949.

the other hand, he had received the normal education of the Greek-speaking civilization to which he belonged and had absorbed much of the prevalent philosophical opinion. The philosophical positions which had the greatest influence upon him were Platonism and Stoicism, although there are also traces of Pythagorean and Aristotelian influence. Philo's philosophical eclecticism was not primarily of the creative sort issuing in a novel system of explanation; his major utilization of his philosophical expertise was devoted instead to the extra-philosophical purpose of justifying the veracity of the implicit and explicit theology of the Old Testament revelation. A variety of features in his writing implement this basically apologetic purpose. He attributes much of what he considers to be true in Greek philosophy to a Hebrew origin, usually from Moses, whom he considers to be the true father of philosophy. He also thinks that whatever knowledge the Greeks had of the divine nature could have only been achieved with God's aid. Indeed, Philo proposes a general account of the relationship of God to his creatures, through the means of the Logos (the Divine "Word" or "Reason"). Most important, however, is his initiation of the use of the allegorical method in the interpretation of scripture, whereby he is enabled to claim that the Torah contains in non-literal form the same truths discovered by the philosophers. Although Philo had no important effect upon Judaism immediately succeeding him, he affords an unique example of Hebrew revelation in an early confrontation with Hellenistic culture. His most immediate influence was felt within Christianity, since the Alexandrine theologians adopted several features of his thought, including the allegorical method; but his long-range effects have penetrated Judaism also. The following selection is an example of Philonic reasoning, in this case in the interpretation of part of the creation story in Genesis.

XII. "And God formed the man by taking clay from the earth, and breathed into his face a breath of life, and the man became a living soul" (Gen. ii. 7). There are two types of men; the one a heavenly man, the other an earthly. The heavenly man, being made after the image of God, is altogether without part or lot in corruptible and terrestrial substance; but the earthly one was compacted out of the matter scattered here and there, which Moses calls "clay." For this reason he says that the heavenly man was not moulded, but was stamped with the image of God; while the earthly is a moulded work of the Artificer, but not His offspring. We must account the man made out of the earth to be mind mingling with, but not yet blended with, body. But this earthlike mind is in reality also corruptible, were not God to breathe into it a power of real life; when He does so, it does not any more undergo moulding, but becomes a soul, not an inefficient and imperfectly formed soul, but one endowed with mind and actually alive; for he says, "man became a living soul."

XIII. The question might be asked, why God deemed the earthly and body-loving mind worthy of divine breath at all, but not the mind which had been created after the original, and after His own image; in the second place, what "breathed in" means; thirdly, why the breathing is "into the face"; fourthly, why, though he shows his knowledge of the word "spirit" when he says "and the Spirit of God was borne above the water" (Gen. i. 2), he now says "breath" not "spirit." In answer to the first query, one thing to be said is that God loves to give, and so bestows good things on all, even those who are not perfect, at the same time encouraging them to a zeal for virtue and a participation in it, by displaying His own overflowing wealth, and how there is abundance even for those who will derive no great benefit from it. This characteristic He shows very clearly in other instances also. For when He rains upon the sea, and causes springs to gush forth in the depths of the desert, and waters the poor and rough and barren soil, pouring on it rivers with their overflowings, what else does He prove save the exceeding greatness of His own wealth and goodness? This is the reason for which He created no soul barren of virtue, even if the exercise of it be to some impossible.

A second thing to be said is this. It is His will to make compliance with positive ordinances part of duty. One, then, into whom real life had not been breathed, but who was without experience of virtue, when punished for his transgressions would have said that he is unjustly punished, for that it was through inexperience of good that he failed in respect of it, and that the blame lay with Him who had failed to breathe into him any conception of it. Nay, he will perhaps say that he does not sin at all, if (as some say) involuntary acts and acts done in ignorance do not count as wrong deeds.

"Breathed into," we note, is equivalent to "inspired" or "be-souled" the soulless; for God forbid that we should be infected with such monstrous folly as to think that God employs for inbreathing organs such as mouth or nostrils; for God is not only not in the form of man, but belongs to no class or kind. Yet the expression clearly brings out something that accords with nature. For it implies of necessity three things, that which inbreathes, that which receives, that which is inbreathed: that which inbreathes is God, that which receives is the mind, that which is inbreathed is the spirit or breath. What, then, do we infer from these premises? A union of the three comes about, as God projects the power that proceeds from Himself through the mediant breath till it reaches the subject. And for what purpose save that we may obtain a conception of Him? For how could the soul have conceived of God, had He not breathed into it and mightily laid hold of it? For the mind of man would never have ventured to soar so high as to grasp the nature of God, had not God Himself drawn it up to Himself, so far as it was possible that the mind of man should be drawn up, and stamped it with the impress of the powers that are within the scope of its understanding.

The breathing "into the face" is to be understood both physically and ethically: physically, because it is in the face that He set the senses; for this part of the body is beyond other parts endowed with soul: but ethically, on this wise. As the face is the dominant element in the body, so is the mind the dominant element of the soul: into this only does God breathe, whereas He does not see fit to do so with the other parts, whether senses or organs of utterance and of reproduction; for these are secondary in capacity. By what, then, were these also inspired? By the mind, evidently. For the mind imparts to the portion of the soul that is devoid of reason a share of that which it has received from God, so that the mind was be-souled by God, but the unreasoning part by the mind. For the mind is, so to speak, God of the unreasoning part. In like manner he does not hesitate to speak of Moses as "a God to Pharaoh" (Exod. vii. 1). For of the things which come into being some come into being both by God's power and through God's agency, while others come into being by God's power but not by His agency. The most excellent things were made both by God and through God. For example, he will presently say, "God planted a pleasaunce" (Gen. ii. 8): to these the mind belongs; but the part devoid of reason was made by God's power but not by God's agency, but by that of the reasonable power which rules and holds dominion in the soul.

He uses the word "breath" not "spirit," implying a difference between them; for "spirit" is conceived of as connoting strength and vigour and power, while a "breath" is like an air or a peaceful and gentle vapour. The mind that was made after the image and original might be said to partake of spirit, for its reasoning faculty possesses robustness; but the mind that was made out of matter must be said to partake of the light and less substantial air, as of some exhalation, such as those that rise from spices: for if they are kept and not burned for incense there is still a sweet perfume from them.

XIV. "And God planted a pleasaunce in Eden toward the sun-rising, and placed there the man whom He had formed" (Gen. ii. 8). By using many words for it Moses has already made it manifest that the sublime and heavenly wisdom is of many names; for he calls it "beginning" and "image" and "vision of God"; and now by the planting of the pleasaunce he brings out the fact that earthly wisdom is a copy of this as of an archetype. Far be it from man's reasoning to be the victim of so great impiety as to suppose that God tills the soil and plants pleasaunces. We should at once be at a loss to tell from what motive He could do so. Not to provide Himself with pleasant refreshment and comfort. Let not such fables even enter our mind. For not even the whole world would be a place fit for God to make His abode, since God is His own place, and He is filled by Himself, and sufficient for Himself, filling and containing all other things in their destitution and barrenness and emptiness, but Himself contained by nothing else, seeing that He is Himself One and the Whole.

Well then, God sows and plants earthly excellence for the race of mortals as a copy and reproduction of the heavenly. For pitying our race and noting that it is compact of a rich abundance of ills, He caused earthly excellence to strike root, to bring succour and aid to the diseases of the soul. It is, as I said before, a copy of the heavenly and archetypal excellence, to which Moses gives many names. Virtue is figuratively called "pleasaunce," and the locality specially suited to the pleasaunce "Eden," which means "luxury"; excellence to be sure has for its fit adjuncts peace and welfare and joy, in which true luxury consists. Again the planting of the pleasaunce is "towards the sunrising," for right reason does not set nor is quenched, but its nature is ever to rise, and, I take it, just as the sun when it has risen fills the gloom of the atmosphere with light, so virtue also, when it has risen in the soul, illumines its mist and disperses its deep darkness.

"And He placed there" it says, "the man whom He had formed." For God, being good and training our race to virtue as the operation most proper to it, places the mind amid virtue, evidently to the end that as a good gardener it may spend its care on nothing else but this.

XVII. "And God caused to spring out of the ground every tree fair to behold and good for food, and the tree of life in the midst of the garden, and the tree of knowledge of good and evil" (Gen. ii. 9). Moses now indicates what trees of virtue God plants in the soul. These are the several particular virtues, and the corresponding activities, and the complete moral victories, and what philosophers call καθήκοντα or common duties. These are the plants of the garden. These very plants he characterizes, showing that what is good is also most fair to be seen and enjoyed. For some of the arts and sciences are theoretical indeed but not practical, such as geometry and astronomy, and some are practical, but not theoretical, as the arts of the carpenter and coppersmith, and all that are called mechanical; but virtue is both theoretical and practical; for clearly it involves theory, since philosophy, the road that leads to it, involves it through its three parts, logic, ethics, physics; and it involves conduct, for virtue is the art of the whole of life, and life includes all kinds of conduct. But while virtue involves theory and practice, it is furthermore of surpassing excellence in each respect; for indeed the theory of virtue is perfect in beauty, and the practice and exercise of it a prize to be striven for. Wherefore he says that it is both "beautiful to look upon," an expression signifying its aspect as theory, and "good to eat," words which point to its excellence in exercise and practice.

XVIII. Now the tree of life is virtue in the most comprehensive sense, which some term goodness. From it the particular virtues derive their existence. That is why it is also set in the midst of the garden, occupying the central all-embracing position, that it may, like a king, be attended by those on either side as by body-guards. But some say that it is the heart that is called the tree of life, since it is the cause of life and has been allotted the central place in the body, as it naturally would, being in their view the dominating principle. But these people should remember that they are setting forth a view worthy of the physician rather than of the philosopher, while we, as we have said, maintain that virtue in its most generic aspect is called the tree of life. Of this he expressly says that it is in the midst of the garden, but as to the other tree, that of knowing good and evil, he has not made it clear whether it is within or without the garden, but immediately after the words, "and the tree of the knowledge of good and evil," he comes to a stop without making it clear where it was. His silence is due to his desire to prevent the man unversed in natural philosophy from regarding with wonder the spot where that knowledge dwells. What then must we say? That this tree is both in the garden and outside it, in literal fact in it, virtually outside it. How so? Our dominant part is all-receptive and resembles wax that receives all impressions fair and ugly; accordingly the supplanter Jacob makes acknowledgement saying, "Upon me came all these things" (Gen. xlii. 36); for upon the soul, one as it is, the countless impressions of all things in the universe are borne. Whenever, then, it shall have received the stamp of perfect virtue, it straightway becomes the tree of life, but when it receives that of wickedness, it straightway becomes the tree of knowledge of good and evil. But wickedness has been exiled from the divine choir. The ruling part in us therefore that has received it is actually in the garden, for it has in it likewise the stamp of virtue, properly belonging to the garden; but on the other hand it is virtually not in it, because the impress of wickedness is alien to a place of divine sunrising. You may grasp what I mean in this way. At this moment my ruling part is in literal fact in my body, but virtually in Italy or Sicily, when it is pondering on these countries, and in heaven, when it is considering heaven. Accordingly it often happens that people who are actually in unconsecrated spots are really in most sacred ones, when they are forming images of all that pertains to virtue. Others, on the other hand, who are in consecrated spots are in mind profane, owing to their mind admitting bad impressions and inclinations to what is unworthy. Thus wickedness neither *is* in the garden, nor is it *not* in it, for it can be there actually, but virtually it cannot.

XIX. "A river goes forth from Eden to water the garden: thence it is separated into four heads; the name of the one is Pheison; this is that which encircles all the land of Evilat, there where the gold is; and the gold of that land is good; and there is the ruby and the emerald. And the name of the second river is Geon; this encompasses all the land of Aethiopia. And the third river is Tigris; this is that whose course is in front of Assyria. And the fourth river is Euphrates" (Gen. ii. 10–14). By these rivers his purpose is to indicate the particular virtues. These are four in number, prudence, self-mastery, courage, justice. The largest river, of which the four are effluxes, is generic virtue, which we have called "goodness." The four effluxes are the virtues of the same number. Generic virtue takes its start from Eden, the wisdom of God, which is full of joy, and brightness, and exultation, glorying and priding itself only upon God its Father; but the specific virtues, four in number, are derived from generic virtue, which like a river waters the perfect achievements of each of them with an abundant flow of noble doings.

Let us look too at the particular words used. "A river," it says "issues forth from Eden to water the garden." "River" is generic virtue, goodness. This issues forth out of Eden, the wisdom of God, and this is the Reason of God; for after that has generic virtue been made. And generic virtue waters the garden, that is, it waters the particular virtues. "Heads" he takes not in the sense of locality but of sovereignty. For each of the virtues is in very deed a sovereign and a queen. "Is separated" is equivalent to "has boundaries to define it." Prudence, concerned with things to be done, sets boundaries round them; courage round things to be endured; self-mastery round things to be chosen; justice round things to be awarded.

33

THF ATTRIBUTES OF GOD
Joseph Albo

The Sefer ha-'Ikkarim (Book of Principles) of Joseph Albo (1380–1444), a disciple of Crescas (1340–1410), is one of the best known Jewish philosophical treatises. Both Crescas and Albo were natives of Spain, in a century in which that country was the major center of Jewish religious philosophy. Both were indebted to the works of Moses Maimonides (1134–1204), the most famous medieval Jewish philosopher, whose Aristotelianism they in some measure adopted and in some measure rejected in favor of certain religious ideals which it seemed to threaten. Since Maimonides had attempted to formulate a Jewish creed, these subsequent thinkers found it necessary to comment upon that creed. Their commentary generally took the form of simplification and classification. Whereas Maimonides had proposed thirteen articles in his creed, Crescas distinguished between "principles" essential to Judaism and "beliefs" which are important but not essential and placed many of Maimonides' articles in the latter category. Albo carried this process even further, maintaining that there were only three "principles" of Judaism: God's existence, revelation, and retribution. Of course, there are corollaries to each of these princi-

Joseph Albo, *Sefer ha-'Ikkarim* (*Book of Principles*), Isaac Husik, trans. (Philadelphia: The Jewish Publication Society Press, 1929), vol. II, pp. 81–90, 165–172. Reprinted with permission of the copyright owner, The Jewish Publication Society of America, Philadelphia, Pa.

*ples; and in the selection reprinted here Albo discusses some of the
intellectual commitments involved in believing in the existence of
God.*

Chapter 27. "True" is a term used to indicate that that which is expressed is in agreement with that which is in the mind and with that which
exists in reality outside of the mind. But if the expression is in disagreement
with the thing as it exists in reality outside of the mind, though it agrees with
the thing as it is in the mind, we call it untrue. Take an instance. Reuben saw
Levi commit a homicide. Thinking that Levi was Simeon, he testified that
Simeon committed homicide. His testimony is untrue, though there is no difference between his expression and his thought, the two being in agreement.
On the other hand, if he were to testify that Levi committed homicide, thinking
that Simeon was the guilty party, he would not be saying an untruth, since the
fact is as he stated it, nevertheless he would be guilty of lying, since his expression and his thought are not in agreement and his words belie his thoughts. In
short, a lie (*kazab*) is an expression used in relation to the speaker. A lie exists
when the expression and the thought are not in agreement. Untruth (*sheker*)
is an expression used in relation to the thing itself. An untruth exists when the
expression is in disagreement with the thing as it is in reality outside of the mind.
If the expression is in disagreement alike with the thought and with the thing
as it is in reality outside of the mind, we call it a lie and an untruth. And when
all the three agree, we call it true.

It is clear therefore that the word "existent" (*nimza*) can not truly be predicated of any existing thing except God. For existing things other than God
can not have the term existent truly applicable to them at all times, but only at
the time when they exist, not after and not before. But God, being in existence
all the time in the same way, has a true existence, and the meaning of the
word existent in the mind, as applied to Him, is in agreement with the reality
outside the mind and with the expression. Therefore the word existent applies
to Him more truly than to any other existing thing.

Also the word existent applies truly to one whose existence is not dependent upon any other, but upon his own essence. For since his existence
depends upon his own essence only, he has no potentiality in him. If we say,
for example, that the heavens are in continuous motion, the statement is true
as long as the mover is in existence who causes them to move. But when the
mover ceases to exist, the statement is no longer true. In the same way, if we say
the Separate Intelligences are existent, the statement is true as long as the
author of their existence, who maintains them in being, is there. *Per se* their
existence is not absolute, since they are dependent upon another, and their
existence is determined for them by their cause. Hence there is none among
existing things to which the word existent applies truly except God, whose
existence depends upon His own essence and not upon another, hence His
existence is true.

This is what the Rabbis meant when they said, "The seal of the Holy One, blessed be He, is truth." The meaning is that there is none among existing things to whom the term existent applies at all times and from all aspects, i.e., whether we view it with reference to itself or with reference to another, except God.

This is the conception that was conveyed to Moses at the burning bush in answer to his question, "And they shall say to me: What is His name? what shall I say unto them?" Moses thought that the being who appeared to him might perhaps be one of the Separate Intelligences, whose existence depends upon another. He was therefore afraid that he might not obtain his request. For since the existence and the power of this being are dependent upon another, if this other chose to nullify the will of the former, it would no doubt become null and void, and the object of his desire would not be realized. Therefore God answered that His name is "I am that I am," i.e., the Existent whose existence depends upon His own essence and not upon another. Moses might therefore feel assured that he can realize whatever he desires. The expression "that I am" is in the first person, as if to say I am because I am, and not because another than I is. My existence and power are not dependent upon another at all, as is the case in the other existents. None of the other existents could say of himself "I am that (because) I am." They would have to say, "I am that (because) He is," the expression "He is," referring not to the first person, but to a third person, who is the cause of the first. He would say then, "I am that (because) He is," i.e., I am in existence because another than I is in existence, namely the First Cause, upon whose existence that of all other beings depends. But God's existence depends upon Himself and not upon another cause. Therefore to Him alone of all existing things is applicable the name "I am that I am," i.e., I am in existence because I am in existence, and not because another is in existence. And therefore His existence is true because He has no need of another. And the word true applies to Him more than to any other existing thing.

We can say therefore that among all attributes there is none which is applicable to Him in all respects except the attribute true, because it adds nothing to the essence, and is merely an explanation of the expression necessary existence. Just as in the proposition, man is rational animal, animal and rational are explanatory of man and not something other than man, so "true" is the explanation of necessary existence and nothing else. The expression necessary existent means nothing else except a being whose existence is absolutely true, in whom there is neither potentiality nor dependence upon another. For this reason this attribute is preferable to all the other attributes and names.

And the prophet, too, characterizes God as true in a manner different from his characterization of Him by means of other names and attributes. He says, "But the Lord God is the true God, He is the living God, and the everlasting King." In this expression he indicates the difference between describing God as true and describing Him as living or King or by any other attribute.

It is explained in the fourth book of the Metaphysics[1] that whenever we say, "the same who," there may be imagined a kind of plurality or otherness, as in the expressions, "This is Ahasuerus who reigned from India even unto Ethiopia"; "These are the same Dathan and Abiram, the elect of the congregation, who strove . . .", "These are the same Aaron and Moses . . . These are the same that spoke to Pharaoh king of Egypt." In all these cases one might suppose (but for the description) that the persons named are other than those which are described later. The same thing is true of the expression, "He is the Lord our God; His judgments are in all the earth." For one might possibly suppose that the God of Israel has a specific kingdom like the other celestial rulers, who are assigned to rule the various nations. For this reason the Bible explains that it is not so, but that the judgments of the Lord who is our God extend over all the earth, *i.e.* His rule is universal over the whole earth. So in all cases where the word "same" is used, it is for the purpose of making clear that the reference is not to another, as one might have supposed. In the word "true," however, no other reference is possible, therefore the prophet is careful in his mode of expression. When he describes God as true he does not use the word "same," but says simply, "But the Lord God is truth." But when he ascribes to Him the attributes life and royalty, he uses the expression, "The same is the living God, and the everlasting King." The meaning is that while one might suppose a distinction between God and the attributes life and royalty (though, as we said before, this supposition is not true), no such thing is possible in connection with the word truth. Hence he does not say, "But the Lord God, the same is truth." And by reason of the otherness which might be supposed in connection with the other attributes, we said above that all the attributes must be understood in a negative sense, so as not to necessitate any multiplicity in God's essence.

And because the understanding of this attribute is a more profound matter than the understanding of any of the others, Daniel said in his prayer, "Yet have we not entreated the favour of the Lord our God, that we might turn from our iniquities, and have discernment in Thy truth." Discernment in God's truth is nothing else than the understanding of His necessary existence. And inasmuch as the word "truth" points more clearly to a necessary existent than any other attribute, one of the ancient lawgivers said that truth is God.[2]

Moreover it is fitting that the word truth should be specially applicable to God as distinct from other beings, because it contains the first and last letter of the alphabet, and the *mem* too, which is the middle, indicating that

[1] The reference is no doubt to Met. IV, ch. 9, in which Aristotle defines the various uses of the word ταὐτά, same, and in particular to the statement in that chapter, p. 1018a 7: ωστε φανερὸν ὅτι ἡ ταὐτότης ἑνότης τις ἐστιν . . . πλειόνων, i.e. that the word same denotes the unity of what in other respects is more than one.

[2] An Arabic proverb, the word حق meaning truth and God.

God is first, last and middle, continually bearing all things by His power. The reason that we did not mention truth as a derivative dogma coming from the principle of the existence of God, as we mentioned unity, is because, as we have shown, truth is nothing more than an explanation of the expression necessary existent. To count it as a dogma would therefore be tautology. For to say God is true is the same thing as saying that God's is a true existence, and this is nothing else than an explanation of the term necessary existent.

Chapter 14. It has already been proved demonstratively that God is neither body nor a force residing in body. It follows that we must deny God all bodily accidents and corporeal affections. It is necessary therefore to give a reason for the expressions found in all the Prophets that God is jealous, wrathful, vengeful and bearing grudge. Thus Nahum says, "The Lord is a jealous and avenging God. The Lord avengeth and is full of wrath, The Lord taketh vengeance on His adversaries, and He reserveth wrath for His enemies." All these descriptions denote corporeal affections. Moreover, they are ignoble qualities which should not be attributed to any excellent person, not to speak of God. The Bible also attributes to Him pride, "The Lord reigneth; He is clothed in majesty"; also the emotion of pity, "My compassions are kindled together"; as well as sorrow, "And it grieved Him at His heart"; and grief, "And His soul was grieved for the misery of Israel."

The explanation is this. The purpose of the prophets is to lead all mankind to worship God and to love Him. But the masses of the people can not be made to humble themselves for service except from fear of punishment. Therefore it was necessary for the prophets to speak in a language understood by the generality of the people. Now since, in human phraseology, when a king punishes those who have rebelled against him and given his kingdom to another, he is said to be jealous and revengeful and full of wrath, so the prophets say of God when He punishes those who violate His will that He is a jealous and avenging God and is full of wrath, because the act which emanates from Him against those who transgress His will is the act of a revengeful, grudging and jealous person.

The attribution of sorrow to God must be explained in the same way. Just as human beings feel sorrow when necessity compels their works to be destroyed, so the Bible says, "And it grieved Him at His heart," and in the immediate sequel we read, "And the Lord said, 'I will blot out man whom I have created . . . for it repenteth Me that I have made them.'" God is said to repent because He does the act of a person who repents of what he has made and desires to destroy it. And just as when a human being finds himself compelled by the requirements of justice to destroy what he has made, he looks about for a way which will enable him to save some of it from destruction, so God sought a way to prevent the destruction of all things. Therefore the narrative concludes, "But Noah found grace in the eyes of the Lord."

The meaning is that God brought it about that the world should be continued through Noah and his sons.

The expression, "And His soul was grieved for the misery of Israel," is to be explained in the same way. God did the act of a person who is in sorrow, whose soul grieves for the misery of his neighbor, and who puts himself to inconvenience in order to help him. So here, though Israel had sinned and were not deserving at that time of such great deliverance, nevertheless God saved them of His own accord as if He was affected by their trouble and misery, as we read, "I have surely seen the affliction of My people that are in Egypt . . . and I am come down to deliver them out of the hand of the Egyptians." Similarly is to be explained the expression, "My compassions are kindled together."

The other expressions of corporeal affections must be understood in the same way, as a mode of bringing to the human understanding the nature of the act which emanates from Him, in a manner consonant with human habits of perception. Thus the Bible says expressly, "Take ye therefore good heed unto yourselves, for ye saw no manner of form," and yet it attributes corporeal members to God, speaking of the Tables of Stone, as "written with the finger of God"; and in the following expressions, "When I behold Thy heavens, the work of Thy fingers"; "Thy right hand, O Lord, glorious in power"; "Thy hands have made me and fashioned me"; and many others of the same kind. The explanation is that as a human person writes with the finger, finger is attributed to God; as strength in man comes from the right hand, right hand is ascribed to Him; as human acts are done with hands and fingers, hands and fingers are attributed to God; and as the acceptation of words in man is attributed to the hearing of the ears, the Bible says, "Let thine ears be attentive."

In the same way must be explained the saying of God in relation to the Temple, "And Mine eyes and Mine heart shall be there perpetually." The meaning is, My providence and My good will, indicating that God desires its permanent existence. Similarly when the prophets picture God as a king sitting on a throne, as in Isaiah, "And I saw the Lord sitting on a throne"; "For mine eyes have seen the King, the Lord of hosts"; or when they describe Him as a strong man, "The Lord will go forth as a mighty man"; "The Lord mighty in a battle";—all this is done in order to bring before human understanding a picture of His mighty glory and majesty. Thus David says, "They shall speak of the glory of Thy kingdom . . . To make known to the sons of men His mighty acts, and the glory of the majesty of His kingdom." The meaning is that the only reason why they speak of Thee thus is in order to make known to the sons of men, but not in order to compare Thy kingdom with a human kingdom, for Thy kingdom is eternal, "a kingdom for all ages." It is done merely to bring the matter before the human understanding and for no other reason.

When the Bible attributes to Him pride, which is an ignoble quality in man, as is said, "Every one that is proud in heart is an abomination to the Lord," the meaning is that man should not boast of any excellence or good quality, for all comes from God, and a man should not boast of that which does not belong to him. As regards wisdom, the Bible says, "For the Lord giveth wisdom"; also, "That turneth wise men backward, and maketh their knowledge foolish." This explains that human wisdom is worth nothing, and that wisdom comes from God and from no one else. Nor should a man boast of wealth, for that is not his either, as David says, "For all things come of Thee, and of Thine own have we given Thee."

Similarly kingdom and all exalted station and excellence come from God, as the Bible says, "Thine is the kingdom, O Lord, and Thou are exalted as head above all." And the Rabbis say, "Even the overseer of wells is appointed from heaven." The blessing concludes, "Both riches and honour come of Thee, and Thou rulest over all." That is, since everything comes from God, and man alone has nothing, which is not due to the will of God, for in His "hand it is to make great, and to give strength unto all," he should not boast of that which does not belong to him and is not in his power. Therefore pride is becoming only to God from whom everything comes. Hence the Bible attributes pride to God when it says, "The Lord reigneth; He is clothed in majesty," and in the words of Moses, "I will sing unto the Lord, for He is highly exalted"; which Onkelos translates, "Because He is exalted above the proud, and pride is His."

Therefore if a person boasts of some quality which is not his, it is proper that the quality should be taken away from him, as an indication that the honor and the excellence which he enjoys do not come to him from himself, but from God and by the divine will. Thus we find in the case of Nebuchadnezzar who boasted of glory and royal status, that the Bible expresses itself as follows: "But when his heart was lifted up, and his spirit was hardened that he dealt proudly, he was deposed from his kingly throne and his glory was taken from him . . . till thou know that the Most High ruleth in the kingdom of men, and giveth it to whomsoever He will . . . and setteth up over it the lowest of men."

The same is true of the prince of Tyre, who boasted of being a god. The Bible says about him, "Because thy heart is lifted up, and thou hast said: I am a god . . . Wilt thou yet say before him that slayeth thee: I am God? But thou art man and not God, In the hand of them that defile thee." This shows that God punishes all those who boast of that which is not theirs. If one boasts of royalty God takes his kingdom away from him and gives it to the lowest of men, so that all may know that royalty does not belong to man and is not in his power. Similarly if one boasts of divine power and makes himself a god, God punishes him and delivers him up to be killed. This is an appropriate punishment for one who boasts of being a god, as it exposes him to shame, since he can not save himself. For it is the way of God to revive the dead, "To deliver them that are drawn unto death and to rescue those that are ready to be slain." God is also eternal. But here it is the opposite. God hands him over into the hand of a slayer to show that he is no god since man can prevail over him to kill him and he has no power to save himself from death. But as to God, in whose hand is the soul of every living thing—He puts to death and brings back to life, He gives perfection to every existing thing, but He does not get any perfection from any one else, like kings, whose perfection comes from some one else. For the royalty of kings is exalted because of the honor which is shown them by others. If not for the honor shown him no one would know that he is a king and that he is superior to others. It is therefore as if honor ruled over them. But not so God, He rules over honor, therefore He is called, "King of glory."

The majesty of the king is dependent upon the multitude of the people, the more people the greater the glory. But God, being king over glory, is not exalted because of any one else nor does His kingship change or diminish as those subject to Him are diminished or changed. Thus the Psalmist says, "The voice of the Lord maketh the hinds to calve, and strippeth the forests bare, and in His temple all say: 'Glory.'" The meaning is that even when God executes judgment and destroys the forests and the animals, His royalty and His glory are not diminished thereby, for in His palace, i.e. in His degree of existence, all is glory. And the proof of this is that "The Lord sat enthroned at the flood; Yea, the Lord sitteth as King forever." That is, God existed in the time of the flood, and though of the world before the flood, which was full of men and animals, all things were destroyed, Noah alone and those with him in the ark remaining, nevertheless God's kingdom did not change in extent, hence "the Lord sitteth as King forever." The reason it says "sitteth" and not "is," is because sitting better expresses the idea of permanence, as Maimonides says where he discusses the scriptural homonym *yashab* (= to sit). For this reason the prophet, too, ascribes to God the attribute of sitting more frequently than other attributes. Thus he says, "I saw the Lord sitting upon a throne high and lifted up," and not simply: "I saw the Lord upon a throne high and lifted up." The explanation is that since sitting implies permanence, without change, it is attributed to God, though neither standing nor sitting applies to Him, as the Rabbis say in the treatise Hagigah, that up above there is neither sitting nor standing, etc. A similar interpretation must be given to all the expressions of corporeal affections ascribed to God in the Bible. They are used in order to bring the matter before human understanding, but not to indicate that it is so in reality. The Rabbis have a general maxim in this connection, "The Torah uses human expressions."

34

THE HASIDIM ON GOD AND MAN

The first Hasidim (Pious Ones) were a group of individuals during the Maccabean Era whose attention was entirely devoted to religious concerns rather than to the contemporary political turmoil. However, in more recent times the name has been applied to the members of a sect organized two centuries ago, whose locale was primarily the countries of eastern Europe. The key emphases of Hasidism were on the immanence of all things in God and on the simple, unsophisticated approach to religious matters. The founder of the sect, Israel Baal Shem Tov (c.1700–1760), taught that religious worship was a personal affair which could be practiced at practically any time and place, the true temple of God being the pure and contrite heart. The Hasidim also emphasized the religious significance of the lighter side of life, maintaining that worship through joyful song and dance was much more acceptable to God than the traditional attitudes of solemnity and mournfulness. Accompanying the emphasis upon the religious availability of God to every person honestly seeking him was an emphasis upon the social responsibilities of the truly religious individual. Piety was not conceived to be entirely a matter of prayer and thanksgiving, but also included acts of kindness toward, and respect for, one's fellowmen. Hasidism constituted a major counterbalance to the emphasis upon the scholarly and legalistic aspects of religion which had been traditional in Judaism since the time of the scribes. The major legacy of the movement consists in the variety of sayings and stories which illustrate a basically optimistic view of life based upon simple piety.

The translator of these sayings is the renowned scholar and philosopher, Martin Buber.

Reprinted by permission of Schocken Books Inc. from *Ten Rungs* by Martin Buber, pp. 13–24, Copyright © 1947 by Schocken Books Inc., New York.

THE RUNG OF GOD AND MAN

Two Kinds of Faith

Why do we say: "Our God and the God of our fathers"?

There are two kinds of people who believe in God. One believes because he has taken over the faith of his fathers, and his faith is strong. The other has arrived at faith through thinking and studying. The difference between them is this: The advantage of the first is that, no matter what arguments may be brought against it, his faith cannot be shaken; his faith is firm because it was taken over from his fathers. But there is one flaw in it: he has faith only in response to the command of man, and he has acquired it without studying and thinking for himself. The advantage of the second is that, because he found God through much thinking, he has arrived at a faith of his own. But here too there is a flaw: it is easy to shake his faith by refuting it through evidence. But he who unites both kinds of faith is invincible. And so we say, "Our God" with reference to our studies, and "God of our fathers" with an eye to tradition.

The same interpretation has been given to our saying, "God of Abraham, God of Isaac, and God of Jacob," and not "God of Abraham, Isaac, and Jacob," for this indicates that Isaac and Jacob did not merely take over the tradition of Abraham; they themselves searched for God.

Seeing and Believing

QUESTION: It is written: "And Israel saw the great hand," and further on it is written: ". . . and they believed in the Lord, and in His servant Moses." Why is this said? The question as to whether or not one believes can only be put while one does not as yet "see."

ANSWER: You are mistaken. It is only then that the true question can be put. Seeing the great hand does not mean that faith can be dispensed with. It is only after "seeing" that one realizes what the lack of faith means, and feels how very much one needs faith. The seeing of the great hand is the beginning of faith in that which one cannot "see."

The Beginning of Teaching

Rabbi Bunam began teaching with these words: "We thank You, who are blessed and who are the source of blessing, that you are manifest and hidden." Then he continued: "A fearless man must feel God as he feels the place on which he stands. And just as he cannot imagine himself without a place to stand on, so he must in all simplicity grow aware of God who is the Place of the world, and comprises it. But at the same time he must know that He is the hidden life which fills the world."

Everywhere

God says to man as he said to Moses: "Put off thy shoes from off thy feet"—put off the habitual which encloses your foot and you will recognize that the place on which you happen to be standing at this moment is holy ground. For there is no rung of being on which we cannot find the holiness of God everywhere and at all times.

The Way in Which God Hides

God hides in two ways. One way is that God hides so that it is very difficult to find him and yet he who knows that God is hiding from him can advance toward him and find him. The other way is that God hides from a man the fact that he is hiding and, since the seeker knows so little about God, he cannot find him. It is this that is referred to in the words: "I shall hide, hide." God hides the fact that he is hiding, and then those from whom he is hiding do not know him—the hidden one.

The Shepherd is There

It is written: "I saw all Israel scattered upon the mountains, as sheep that have no shepherd." This does not mean that the shepherd is not there. The shepherd is always there. But sometimes he hides, and then he is indeed not there to the sheep, because they do not see him.

Beyond Time

The understanding of man is not great enough to grasp the fact that God is beyond time. But you must understand that time exists only because we do not grasp it, only because our understanding is small. For the greater our understanding, the more time is on the wane. In a dream we live seventy years and discover, on awakening, that it was a quarter of an hour. In our life, which passes like a dream, we live seventy years and then we waken to a greater understanding which shows us that it was a quarter of an hour. With our small understanding we can never grasp what we will know with the greater. Perfect understanding is beyond time.

When the Messiah had learned what he learned since the creation of the world, and suffered what he suffered, God said to him: "Thou art My son, this day I have begotten thee."

Who Knows One?

This is what Rabbi Moshe of Kobryn said concerning the first question in the game of riddles, sung at the end of the Passover Haggadah, "Who knows one? I know one":

"Who knows one?" said he. "Who can know the One? For even the seraphim ask: 'Where is the place of His glory?' And yet—'I know one.' For, as the sage says: 'Where shall I find you? . . . And where shall I not find you!' And the seraphim too reply: 'The whole earth is full of His glory.' By his works within me, I know the One."

The Strong Thief

Every lock has its key which fits into and opens it. But there are strong thieves who know how to open locks without keys. They break the lock. So every mystery in the world can be unriddled by the particular kind of meditation fitted to it. But God loves the thief who breaks the lock open: I mean, the man who breaks his heart for God.

Two Kinds of Fear

QUESTION: When they stood at Mount Sinai, the people said to Moses: "Speak thou with us, and we will hear; but let not God speak with us, lest we die." And Moses answered: "Fear not." He went on to say that God had come "that His fear may be before you, that ye sin not." Is not that a contradiction?

ANSWER: "Fear not"—this means: this fear of yours, the fear of death, is not the fear God wants of you. He wants you to fear him, he wants you to fear his remoteness, and not to fall into sin which removes you from him.

Our Disgrace

Our disgrace is that we fear another besides God. This is what was said of Jacob in the words: "Then Jacob was greatly afraid and he was distressed." We must be distressed because of our fear of Esau.

The Solitary Tree

When I look at the world, it sometimes seems to me as if every man were a tree in the wilderness, and God had no one in his world save him alone, and he had none he could turn to, save God alone.

A Man on Earth

QUESTION: Why is it written: "In the day that God created a man on earth," and not "in the day that God created man on earth"?

ANSWER: You shall serve your Creator as if there were only one man in the world, only you yourself.

The Dividing Wall

In the Scriptures we read: "I stood between the Lord and you." The "I" stands between God and us. When a man says "I" and presumes to use his Maker's word, he is shutting himself off from him. But there is no dividing wall before him who sacrifices his "I." For of him it is written: "I am my beloved's, and his desire is toward me." When my "I" comes to belong to my beloved, then his desire is toward me.

Who May Be Called Man?

In the Scriptures we read: "When any man of you bringeth an offering unto the Lord . . ." Only he who brings himself to God as an offering may be called man.

The Pupil

Rabbi Pinhas said: "Ever since I began giving true service to my Maker, I have not tried to gain anything, but only taken what God gave me. It is because the pupil is dark that it absorbs every ray of light."

Holy Despair

In the psalm we read: "How long shall I take counsel in my soul, having sorrow in my heart by day?"

As long as I take counsel in my soul, there must be sorrow in my heart all day. Only when I know of no further counsel that can help me, and I give up taking counsel, and know of no other help but God, will help be vouchsafed me.

It Is I

QUESTION: It is written: "I am JHWH, thy God, who brought thee out of the land of Egypt." Why does it not say: "I am JHWH, thy God, who created heaven and earth"?

ANSWER: "Heaven and earth!" Then man might have said, "Heaven —that's too much for me!" So God said to man: "I am the one who fished you out of the mud. Now you come here and listen to me!"

The Shadow

Man himself is the source of all his troubles, for the light of God pours over him eternally. But through his all-too-bodily existence man comes to cast a shadow, so that the light cannot reach him.

Two Kinds of Love for God

There are two kinds of love: the love of a man for his wife, which should manifest itself in secret and not where there are spectators, for this love can be consummated only in a place apart from other beings; and there is the love for one's brothers and sisters and children, a love which does not require secrecy.

And there are two kinds of love for God: the love spent in learning and praying and fulfilling the commandments, which should be shown in silence and not in the presence of others, lest it tempt to glory and pride; and the love shown in the company of other human beings, when one hears and speaks, gives and takes, and, in one's secret heart, clings to God and never ceases dwelling upon him. And this love is on a higher rung than the other, and concerning it, we read: "Oh that thou wert as my brother, that sucked the breasts of my mother! When I should find thee without, I would kiss thee; yea and none would despise me."

Two Kinds of God's Love

There are two kinds of love: one man loves whatever his clever son does and says, and boasts about his doing clever things and speaking clever words; the other loves his son for himself, no matter what he may say or do.

It is the same with the love of God for man. When a tried and proven man keeps the commandments and does good works wisely and well, God loves what he does and is present in all that he does, and thus the outer being of the universe is bound to God. But when the tried and proven man clings to God with his own being, then God loves him even when he does not work wisely and well, but goes his way with a simple mind and clings to God. God loves him just for that reason. And so the inner being of the universe is lifted to God.

Molten Gods

It is written: "Thou shalt make thee no molten gods."

When you think of God, you should really think of him, and not of a molten god which you have made in your own image.

We Shape a Human Form for God

Our sages said: "Know what is above you . . ." The rabbi of Apt expounded this saying as follows:

" 'Know what is above you.' And what is this that is above you? The prophet Ezekiel said: 'And upon the likeness of the throne was a likeness as the appearance of a man upon it above.' How can this be said of God? For is it not written: 'To whom then will ye liken Me, that I should be his equal?' But the truth of the matter is that the 'likeness as the appearance of a man' is wrought by us. It is the form we shape when we serve with true and fervent hearts. Such service shapes a human form for our Creator, to whom no one is like or equal; it shapes him, blessed be he and blessed be his name, in the semblance of man. When a man is charitable and gives a service of love, he contributes to the form of God's right hand. And when a man fights in the ranks of God and drives evil away, he contributes to the form of his left hand. He who is above you on the throne—his shape is your work."

With God

You must know that every movement you make is bound up with the will of the Creator. That is why it is written: "Noah walked with God." For every movement is made through the impulse given by God. Noah clung to God with such very great devotion that it seemed to him that, whenever he walked, God was moving his feet. At every step it seemed to him that God was facing him and guiding him as a father teaches his little son to walk, and when the father moves further away from him, the child knows it is for his own good.

Signs

This whole world is a cloak for the lowest rung of holiness, for its feet, as it were. As it is written: "And the earth is my footstool." God limits the godliness he has in infinity, and narrows it down to the focus of the material world in which man exists. And there he assigns every man his thought and word and deed according to the day, the place, and the person, and hides therein the signs to lead men to his service.

And so a man should immerse himself in the task of understanding the signs which are cloaked in thought and word and deed and so given to him in particular, in his work and his affairs, and in everything God appoints for him day by day.

Concerning Secrecy

Sometimes a man lies in bed, and the household thinks he is asleep, but he is spending this hour in solitude with his Maker, blessed be he. If the eyes of his understanding can always behold his Maker as if he were another human being—that is a very high rung. And take this to heart: if at all times you dwell in pure thoughts, then the Maker too will look at you as though he were a human being.

Faith

Faith is a very strong thing, and if a man has faith and a simplicity that does not rationalize, he will be found worthy of reaching the rung of grace which is even higher than that of holy wisdom. He will be vouchsafed great and overwhelming grace in God in very blissful silence, until he will be able to bear the greatness of this silence no longer, and will cry aloud out of the fullness of his soul.

35

ON THE FOUNDING OF A JEWISH NATION

Theodore Herzl

Zionism is the movement within Judaism which believes
that one fundamental necessity for the good of Jews and of the
world at large is the fulfillment of the Messianic hopes through
the establishment and maintenance of a genuine Jewish nation.
The establishment of the State of Israel in 1948 was, insofar as it
gave existence to such a nation, the culmination of a major portion
of this cherished ideal. The initial impetus leading to the foundation of Israel was largely derived from the work of Theodore
Herzl (1860–1903), the founder of Zionism and the first to publicly maintain that the "Jewish problem" was a problem of international scope and to propose specific political measures whereby
it could be solved. His ideas are developed in a small volume,
Judenstaat (The Jewish State), published in 1895. This volume
outlines a scheme for the establishment of a Jewish nation. It
would be too much to expect that all details of that scheme were
those subsequently carried out in history, for Herzl's suggestion
was rather quickly put together and, of course, the entire proposal
was colored by the contemporary political situation. Nevertheless,
the book aroused great interest and was instrumental in the founding, soon thereafter (1897), of a Zionist Congress and in the establishment of world-wide interest in, and discussion of, its major
proposal. Herzl was also active politically in attempting to realize
his ambitions for a Jewish nation, and although his efforts were
never directly successful, it was his negotiations with the British
in the person of Joseph Chamberlain which began the eventually
successful concentration upon England for aid in achieving the
Zionist goal.

Theodor Herzl, The Jewish State, Ch. II (New York, American Zionist Council, 1946), pp. 85–97. Reprinted by courtesy of the American Zionist Council.

THE JEWISH QUESTION

No one can deny the gravity of the situation of the Jews. Wherever they live in perceptible numbers, they are more or less persecuted. Their equality before the law, granted by statute, has become practically a dead letter. They are debarred from filling even moderately high positions, either in the army, or in any public or private capacity. And attempts are made to thrust them out of business also: "Don't buy from Jews!"

Attacks in Parliaments, in assemblies, in the press, in the pulpit, in the street, on journeys—for example, their exclusion from certain hotels—even in places of recreation, become daily more numerous. The forms of persecutions vary according to the countries and social circles in which they occur. In Russia, imposts are levied on Jewish villages; in Rumania, a few persons are put to death; in Germany, they get a good beating occasionally; in Austria, Anti-Semites exercise terrorism over all public life; in Algeria, there are travelling agitators; in Paris, the Jews are shut out of the so-called best social circles and excluded from clubs. Shades of anti-Jewish feeling are innumerable. But this is not to be an attempt to make out a doleful category of Jewish hardships.

I do not intend to arouse sympathetic emotions on our behalf. That would be a foolish, futile, and undignified proceeding. I shall content myself with putting the following questions to the Jews: Is it not true that, in countries where we live in perceptible numbers, the position of Jewish lawyers, doctors, technicians, teachers, and employees of all descriptions becomes daily more intolerable? Is it not true, that the Jewish middle classes are seriously threatened? Is it not true, that the passions of the mob are incited against our wealthy people? Is it not true, that our poor endure greater sufferings than any other proletariat? I think that this external pressure makes itself felt everywhere. In our economically upper classes it causes discomfort, in our middle classes continual and grave anxieties, in our lower classes absolute despair.

Everything tends, in fact, to one and the same conclusion, which is clearly enunciated in that classic Berlin phrase: *"Juden Raus!"* (Out with the Jews!)

I shall now put the Question in the briefest possible form: Are we to "get out" now and where to?

Or, may we yet remain? And, how long?

Let us first settle the point of staying where we are. Can we hope for better days, can we possess our souls in patience, can we wait in pious resignation till the princes and peoples of this earth are more mercifully disposed towards us? I say that we cannot hope for a change in the current of feeling. And why not? Even if we were as near to the hearts of princes as are their other subjects, they could not protect us. They would only feel popular hatred by showing us too much favor. By "too much," I really mean less than is claimed as a right by every ordinary citizen, or by every race. The nations in whose midst Jews live are all either covertly or openly Anti-Semitic.

The common people have not, and indeed cannot have, any historic comprehension. They do not know that the sins of the Middle Ages are now being visited on the nations of Europe. We are what the Ghetto made us. We have attained pre-eminence in finance, because mediæval conditions drove us to it. The same process is now being repeated. We are again being forced into finance, now it is the stock exchange, by being kept out of other branches of economic activity. Being on the stock exchange, we are consequently exposed afresh to contempt. At the same time we continue to produce an abundance of mediocre intellects who find no outlet, and this endangers our social position as much as does our increasing wealth. Educated Jews without means are now rapidly becoming Socialists. Hence we are certain to suffer very severely in the struggle between classes, because we stand in the most exposed position in the camps of both Socialists and capitalists.

Previous Attempts at a Solution

The artificial means heretofore employed to overcome the troubles of Jews have been either too petty—such as attempts at colonization—or attempts to convert the Jews into peasants in their present homes.

What is achieved by transporting a few thousand Jews to another country? Either they come to grief at once, or prosper, and then their prosperity creates Anti-Semitism. We have already discussed these attempts to divert poor Jews to fresh districts. This diversion is clearly inadequate and futile, if it does not actually defeat its own ends; for it merely protracts and postpones a solution, and perhaps even aggravates difficulties.

Whoever would attempt to convert the Jew into a husbandman would be making an extraordinary mistake. For a peasant is in a historical category, as proved by his costume which in some countries he has worn for centuries; and by his tools, which are identical with those used by his earliest forefathers. His plough is unchanged; he carries the seed in his apron; mows with the historical scythe, and threshes with the time-honored flail. But we know that all this can be done by machinery. The agrarian question is only a question of machinery. America must conquer Europe, in the same way as large landed possessions absorb small ones. The peasant is consequently a type which is in course of extinction. Whenever he is artificially preserved, it is done on account of the political interests which he is intended to serve. It is absurd, and indeed impossible, to make modern peasants on the old pattern. No one is wealthy or powerful enough to make civilization take a single retrograde step. The mere preservation of obsolete institutions is a task severe enough to require the enforcement of all the despotic measures of an autocratically governed State.

Are we, therefore, to credit Jews who are intelligent with a desire to become peasants of the old type? One might just as well say to them: "Here is a cross-bow: now go to war!" What? With a cross-bow, while the others have rifles and long range guns? Under these circumstances the Jews are perfectly justified in refusing to stir when people try to make peasants of them. A cross-bow is a beautiful weapon, which inspires me with mournful feelings when I have time to devote to them. But it belongs by rights to a museum.

Now, there certainly are districts to which desperate Jews go out, or at any rate, are willing to go out and till the soil. And a little observation shows that these districts—such as the enclave of Hesse in Germany, and some provinces in Russia—these very districts are the principal seats of Anti-Semitism.

For the world's reformers, who send the Jews to the plough, forget a very important person, who has a great deal to say on the matter. This person is the agriculturist, and the agriculturist is also perfectly justified. For the tax on land, the risks attached to crops, the pressure of large proprietors who cheapen labor, and American competition in particular, combine to make his life hard enough. Besides, the duties on corn cannot go on increasing indefinitely. Nor can the manufacturer be allowed to starve, his political influence is, in fact, in the ascendant, and he must therefore be treated with additional consideration.

All these difficulties are well known, therefore I refer to them only cursorily. I merely wanted to indicate clearly how futile had been past attempts —most of them well intentioned—to solve the Jewish Question. Neither a diversion of the stream, nor an artificial depression of the intellectual level of our proletariat, will overcome the difficulty. The supposed infallible expedient of assimilation has already been dealt with.

We cannot get the better of Anti-Semitism by any of these methods. It cannot die out so long as its causes are not removed. Are they removable?

Causes of Anti-Semitism

We shall not again touch on those causes which are a result of temperament, prejudice and narrow views, but shall here restrict ourselves to political and economical causes alone. Modern Anti-Semitism is not to be confounded with the religious persecution of the Jews of former times. It does occasionally take a religious bias in some countries, but the main current of the aggressive movement has now changed. In the principal countries where Anti-Semitism prevails, it does so as a result of the emancipation of the Jews. When civilized nations awoke to the inhumanity of discriminatory legislation and enfranchised us, our enfranchisement came too late. It was no longer possible to remove our disabilities in our old homes. For we had, curiously enough, developed while in the Ghetto into a bourgeois people, and we stepped out of it only to enter into fierce competition with the middle classes. Hence, our emancipation set us suddenly within this middle-class circle, where we have a double pressure to sustain, from within and from without. The Christian bourgeoisie would not be unwilling to cast us as a sacrifice to Socialism, though that would not greatly improve matters.

At the same time, the equal rights of Jews before the law cannot be withdrawn where they have once been conceded. Not only because their withdrawal would be opposed to the spirit of our age, but also because it would immediately drive all Jews, rich and poor alike, into the ranks of subversive parties. Nothing effectual can really be done to our injury. In olden days our jewels were seized. How is our movable property to be got hold of now? It consists of printed papers which are locked up somewhere or other in the world, perhaps in the coffers of Christians. It is, of course, possible to get at shares and debentures in railways, banks and industrial undertakings of all descriptions by taxation, and where the progressive income-tax is in force all our movable property can eventually be laid hold of. But all these efforts cannot be directed against Jews alone, and wherever they might nevertheless be made, severe economic crises would be their immediate consequences, which would be by no means confined to the Jews who would be the first affected. The very impossibility of getting at the Jews nourishes and embitters hatred of them. Anti-Semitism increases day by day and hour by hour among the nations; indeed, it is bound to increase, because the causes of its growth continue to exist and cannot be removed. Its remote cause is our loss of the power of assimilation during the Middle Ages; its immediate cause is our excessive production of mediocre intellects, who cannot find an outlet downwards or upwards—that is to say, no wholesome outlet in either direction. When we sink, we become a revolutionary proletariat, the subordinate officers of all revolutionary parties; and at the same time, when we rise, there rises also our terrible power of the purse.

Effects of Anti-Semitism

The oppression we endure does not improve us, for we are not a whit better than ordinary people. It is true that we do not love our enemies; but he alone who can conquer himself dare reproach us with that fault. Oppression naturally creates hostility against oppressors, and our hostility aggravates the pressure. It is impossible to escape from this eternal circle.

"No!" Some soft-hearted visionaries will say: "No, it is possible! Possible by means of the ultimate perfection of humanity."

Is it necessary to point to the sentimental folly of this view? He who would found his hope for improved conditions on the ultimate perfection of humanity would indeed be relying upon a Utopia!

I referred previously to our "assimilation." I do not for a moment wish to imply that I desire such an end. Our national character is too historically famous, and, in spite of every degradation, too fine to make its annihilation desirable. We might perhaps be able to merge ourselves entirely into surrounding races, if these were to leave us in peace for a period of two generations. But they will not leave us in peace. For a little period they manage to tolerate us, and then their hostility breaks out again and again. The world is provoked somehow by our prosperity, because it has for many centuries been accustomed to consider us as the most contemptible among the poverty-stricken. In its ignorance and narrowness of heart, it fails to observe that prosperity weakens our Judaism and extinguishes our peculiarities. It is only pressure that forces us back to the parent stem; it is only hatred encompassing us that makes us strangers once more.

Thus, whether we like it or not, we are now, and shall henceforth remain, a historic group with unmistakable characteristics common to us all.

We are one people—our enemies have made us one without our consent, as repeatedly happens in history. Distress binds us together, and, thus united, we suddenly discover our strength. Yes, we are strong enough to form a State, and, indeed, a model State. We possess all human and material resources necessary for the purpose.

This is therefore the appropriate place to give an account of what has been somewhat roughly termed our "human material." But it would not be appreciated till the broad lines of the plan, on which everything depends, has first been marked out.

The Plan

The whole plan is in its essence perfectly simple, as it must necessarily be if it is to come within the comprehension of all.

Let the sovereignty be granted us over a portion of the globe large enough to satisfy the rightful requirements of a nation; the rest we shall manage for ourselves.

The creation of a new State is neither ridiculous nor impossible. We have in our day witnessed the process in connection with nations which were not largely members of the middle class, but poorer, less educated, and consequently weaker than ourselves. The Governments of all countries scourged by Anti-Semitism will be keenly interested in assisting us to obtain the sovereignty we want.

The plan, simple in design, but complicated in execution, will be carried out by two agencies: The Society of Jews and the Jewish Company.

The Society of Jews will do the preparatory work in the domains of science and politics, which the Jewish Company will afterwards apply practically.

The Jewish Company will be the liquidating agent of the business interests of departing Jews, and will organize commerce and trade in the new country.

We must not imagine the departure of the Jews to be a sudden one. It will be gradual, continuous, and will cover many decades. The poorest will go first to cultivate the soil. In accordance with a preconceived plan, they will construct roads, bridges, railways and telegraph installations; regulate rivers; and build their own dwellings; their labor will create trade, trade will create markets and markets will attract new settlers, for every man will go voluntarily, at his own expense and his own risk. The labor expended on the land will enhance its value, and the Jews will soon perceive that a new and permanent sphere of operation is opening here for that spirit of enterprise which has heretofore met only with hatred and obloquy.

If we wish to found a State today, we shall not do it in the way which would have been the only possible one a thousand years ago. It is foolish to revert to old stages of civilization, as many Zionists would like to do. Supposing, for example, we were obliged to clear a country of wild beasts, we should not set about the task in the fashion of Europeans of the fifth century. We should not take spear and lance and go out singly in pursuit of bears; we would organize a large and active hunting party, drive the animals together, and throw a melinite bomb into their midst.

If we wish to conduct building operations, we shall not plant a mass of stakes and piles on the shore of a lake, but we shall build as men build now. Indeed, we shall build in a bolder and more stately style than was ever adopted before, for we now possess means which men never yet possessed.

The emigrants standing lowest in the economic scale will be slowly followed by those of a higher grade. Those who at this moment are living in despair will go first. They will be led by the mediocre intellects which we produce so superabundantly and which are persecuted everywhere.

This pamphlet will open a general discussion on the Jewish Question, but that does not mean that there will be any voting on it. Such a result would ruin the cause from the outset, and dissidents must remember that allegiance or opposition is entirely voluntary. He who will not come with us should remain behind.

Let all who are willing to join us, fall in behind our banner and fight for our cause with voice and pen and deed.

Those Jews who agree with our idea of a State will attach themselves to the Society, which will thereby be authorized to confer and treat with Governments in the name of our people. The Society will thus be acknowledged in its relations with Governments as a State-creating power. This acknowledgment will practically create the State.

Should the powers declare themselves willing to admit our sovereignty over a neutral piece of land, then the Society will enter into negotiations for the possession of this land. Here two territories come under consideration, Palestine and Argentine. In both countries important experiments in colonization have been made, though on the mistaken principle of a gradual infiltration of Jews. An infiltration is bound to end badly. It continues till the inevitable moment when the native population feels itself threatened, and forces the Government to stop a further influx of Jews. Immigration is consequently futile unless we have the sovereign right to continue such immigration.

The Society of Jews will treat with the present masters of the land, putting itself under the protectorate of the European Powers, if they prove friendly to the plan. We could offer the present possessors of the land enormous advantages, assume part of the public debt, build new roads for traffic, which our presence in the country would render necessary, and do many other things. The creation of our State would be beneficial to adjacent countries, because the cultivation of a strip of land increases the value of its surrounding districts in innumerable ways.

Palestine or Argentine?

Shall we choose Palestine or Argentine? We shall take what is given us, and what is selected by Jewish public opinion. The Society will determine both these points.

Argentine is one of the most fertile countries in the world, extends over a vast area, has a sparse population and a mild climate. The Argentine Republic would derive considerable profit from the cession of a portion of its territory to us. The present infiltration of Jews has certainly produced some discontent, and it would be necessary to enlighten the Republic on the intrinsic difference of our new movement.

Palestine is our ever-memorable historic home. The very name of Palestine would attract our people with a force of marvellous potency. If His Majesty the Sultan were to give us Palestine, we could in return undertake to regulate the whole finances of Turkey. We should there form a portion of a rampart of Europe against Asia, an outpost of civilization as opposed to barbarism. We should as a neutral State remain in contact with all Europe, which would have to guarantee our existence. The sanctuaries of Christendom would be safeguarded by assigning to them an extra-territorial status such as is well-known to the law of nations. We should form a guard of honor about these sanctuaries, answering for the fulfilment of this duty with our existence. This guard of honor would be the great symbol of the solution of the Jewish Question after eighteen centuries of Jewish suffering.

Demand, Medium, Trade

I said in the last chapter, "The Jewish Company will organize trade and commerce in the new country." I shall here insert a few remarks on that point.

A scheme such as mine is gravely imperilled if it is opposed by "practical" people. Now "practical" people are as a rule nothing more than men sunk into the groove of daily routine, unable to emerge from a narrow circle of antiquated ideas. At the same time, their adverse opinion carries great weight, and can do considerable harm to a new project, at any rate until this new thing is sufficiently strong to throw the "practical" people and their mouldy notions to the winds.

In the earliest period of European railway construction some "practical" people were of the opinion that it was foolish to build certain lines "because there were not even sufficient passengers to fill the mail-coaches." They did not realize the truth—which now seems obvious to us—that travellers do not produce railways, but, conversely, railways produce travellers, the latent demand, of course, is taken for granted.

The impossibility of comprehending how trade and commerce are to be created in a new country which has yet to be acquired and cultivated, may be classed with those doubts of "practical" persons concerning the need of railways. A "practical" person would express himself somewhat in this fashion:

"Granted that the present situation of the Jews is in many places unendurable, and aggravated day by day; granted that there exists a desire to emigrate; granted even that the Jews do emigrate to the new country; how will they earn their living there, and what will they earn? What are they to live on when there? The business of many people cannot be artificially organized in a day."

To this I should reply: We have not the slightest intention of organizing trade artificially, and we should certainly not attempt to do it in a day. But, though the organization of it may be impossible, the promotion of it is not. And how is commerce to be encouraged? Through the medium of a demand. The demand recognized, the medium created, it will establish itself.

If there is a real earnest demand among Jews for an improvement of their status; if the medium to be created—the Jewish Company—is sufficiently powerful, then commerce will extend itself freely in the new country.

36

I AND THOU
Martin Buber

Martin Buber (1878–1965) was undoubtedly the most original and influential Jewish philosopher of the Twentieth Century. He received his education at the Universities of Leipzig, Berlin, and Zurich; and after the publication of his major work, Ich und Du (I and Thou, 1923), he was the recipient of several honorary degrees from universities throughout the world. Buber was not merely a philosopher and theologian, but was also passionately interested in the actual destiny of the Jewish people and was instrumental in achieving the establishment of the State of Israel. He was the founder of two Zionist organizations in Leipzig in 1898 and a co-founder of the Jewish National Committee in Germany in 1914. In his career as an educator, he taught at several

Reprinted with the permission of T. & T. Clark and Charles Scribner's Sons from *I and Thou*, pp. 3–34, by Martin Buber (1937).

universities and was from time to time a visiting professor at many others. His last position was as Professor of Social Philosophy at the Hebrew University in Jerusalem, a position the acceptance of which coincided with his settlement in Palestine in 1938. He became Professor Emeritus of the Hebrew University in 1951. Buber was the editor of several papers and journals, the author of a great many books, and the translator and editor of many more. His writings are so voluminous that any selection must be arbitrary, but among the more important are Deutung des Chassidismus *(1935),* Dialogisches Leben *(1947)* Two Types of Faith *(1951), and* Eclipse of God *(1953). The selection reprinted here is from the first portion of his* I and Thou, *in which he explains the major features of the concept of personal relationship, to man and to God. The* I-Thou *terminology is not unique with Buber, having been used by Hegel and quite extensively by Feuerbach, but Buber's development of the concept is sufficiently novel to mark it as a classic of philosophical theology.*

To man the world is twofold, in accordance with his twofold attitude.

The attitude of man is twofold, in accordance with the twofold nature of the primary words which he speaks.

The primary words are not isolated words, but combined words.

The one primary word is the combination *I-Thou.*

The other primary word is the combination *I-It;* wherein, without a change in the primary word, one of the words *He* and *She* can replace *It.*

Hence the *I* of man is also twofold.

For the *I* of the primary word *I-Thou* is a different *I* from that of the primary word *I-It.*

Primary words do not signify things, but they intimate relations.

Primary words do not describe something that might exist independently of them, but being spoken they bring about existence.

Primary words are spoken from the being.

If *Thou* is said, the *I* of the combination *I-Thou* is said along with it.

If *It* is said, the *I* of the combination *I-It* is said along with it.

The primary word *I-Thou* can only be spoken with the whole being.

The primary word *I-It* can never be spoken with the whole being.

There is no *I* taken in itself, but only the *I* of the primary word *I-Thou* and the *I* of the primary word *I-It.*

When a man says *I* he refers to one or other of these. The *I* to which he refers is present when he says *I.* Further, when he says *Thou* or *It,* the *I* of one of the two primary words is present.

The existence of *I* and the speaking of *I* are one and the same thing.

When a primary word is spoken the speaker enters the word and takes his stand in it.

The life of human beings is not passed in the sphere of transitive verbs alone. It does not exist in virtue of activities alone which have some *thing* for their object.

I perceive something. I am sensible of something. I imagine something. I will something. I feel something. I think something. The life of human beings does not consist of all this and the like alone.

This and the like together establish the realm of *It*.

But the realm of *Thou* has a different basis.

When *Thou* is spoken, the speaker has no thing for his object. For where there is a thing there is another thing. Every *It* is bounded by others; *It* exists only through being bounded by others. But when *Thou* is spoken, there is no thing. *Thou* has no bounds.

When *Thou* is spoken, the speaker has no *thing*; he has indeed nothing. But he takes his stand in relation.

It is said that man experiences his world. What does that mean?

Man travels over the surface of things and experiences them. He extracts knowledge about their constitution from them: he wins an experience from them. He experiences what belongs to the things.

But the world is not presented to man by experiences alone. These present him only with a world composed of *It* and *He* and *She* and *It* again.

I experience something.—If we add "inner" to "outer" experiences, nothing in the situation is changed. We are merely following the uneternal division that springs from the lust of the human race to whittle away the secret of death. Inner things or outer things, what are they but things and things!

I experience something.—If we add "secret" to "open" experiences, nothing in the situation is changed. How self-confident is that wisdom which perceives a closed compartment in things, reserved for the initiate and manipulated only with the key. O secrecy without a secret! O accumulation of information! It, always It!

The man who experiences has no part in the world. For it is "in him" and not between him and the world that the experience arises.

The world has no part in the experience. It permits itself to be experienced, but has no concern in the matter. For it does nothing to the experience, and the experience does nothing to it.

As experience, the world belongs to the primary word *I-It*.

The primary word *I-Thou* establishes the world of relation.

The spheres in which the world of relation arises are three.

First, our life with nature. There the relation sways in gloom, beneath the level of speech. Creatures live and move over against us, but cannot come to us, and when we address them as *Thou*, our words cling to the threshold of speech.

Second, our life with men. There the relation is open and in the form of speech. We can give and accept the *Thou*.

Third, our life with intelligible forms. There the relation is clouded, yet it discloses itself; it does not use speech, yet begets it. We perceive no *Thou*, but none the less we feel we are addressed and we answer—forming, thinking, acting. We speak the primary word with our being, though we cannot utter *Thou* with our lips.

But with what right do we draw what lies outside speech into relation with the world of the primary word?

In every sphere in its own way, through each process of becoming that is present to us we look out toward the fringe of the eternal *Thou*; in each we are aware of a breath from the eternal *Thou*; in each *Thou* we address the eternal *Thou*.

I consider a tree.

I can look on it as a picture: stiff column in a shock of light, or splash of green shot with the delicate blue and silver of the background.

I can perceive it as movement: flowing veins on clinging, pressing pith, suck of the roots, breathing of the leaves, ceaseless commerce with earth and air—and the obscure growth itself.

I can classify it in a species and study it as a type in its structure and mode of life.

I can subdue its actual presence and form so sternly that I recognize it only as an expression of law—of the laws in accordance with which a constant opposition of forces is continually adjusted, or of those in accordance with which the component substances mingle and separate.

I can dissipate it and perpetuate it in number, in pure numerical relation.

In all this the tree remains my object, occupies space and time, and has its nature and constitution.

It can, however, also come about, if I have both will and grace, that in considering the tree I become bound up in relation to it. The tree is now no longer *It*. I have been seized by the power of exclusiveness.

To effect this it is not necessary for me to give up any of the ways in which I consider the tree. There is nothing from which I would have to turn my eyes away in order to see, and no knowledge that I would have to forget. Rather is everything, picture and movement, species and type, law and number, indivisibly united in this event.

Everything belonging to the tree is in this: its form and structure, its colours and chemical composition, its intercourse with the elements and with the stars, are all present in a single whole.

The tree is no impression, no play of my imagination, no value depending on my mood; but it is bodied over against me and has to do with me, as I with it—only in a different way.

Let no attempt be made to sap the strength from the meaning of the relation: relation is mutual.

The tree will have a consciousness, then, similar to our own? Of that I have no experience. But do you wish, through seeming to succeed in it with yourself, once again to disintegrate that which cannot be disintegrated? I encounter no soul or dryad of the tree, but the tree itself.

If I face a human being as my *Thou*, and say the primary word *I-Thou* to him, he is not a thing among things, and does not consist of things.

This human being is not *He* or *She*, bounded from every other *He* and *She*, a specific point in space and time within the net of the world; nor is he a nature able to be experienced and described, a loose bundle of named qualities. But with no neighbour, and whole in himself, he is *Thou* and fills the heavens. This does not mean that nothing exists except himself. But all else lives in *his* light.

Just as the melody is not made up of notes nor the verse of words nor the statue of lines, but they must be tugged and dragged till their unity has been scattered into these many pieces, so with the man to whom I say *Thou*. I can take out from him the colour of his hair, or of his speech, or of his goodness. I must continually do this. But each time I do it he ceases to be *Thou*.

And just as prayer is not in time but time in prayer, sacrifice not in space but space in sacrifice, and to reverse the relation is to abolish the reality, so with the man to whom I say *Thou*. I do not meet with him at some time and place or other. I can set him in a particular time and place; I must continually do it: but I set only a *He* or a *She*, that is an *It*, no longer my *Thou*.

So long as the heaven of *Thou* is spread out over me the winds of causality cower at my heels, and the whirlpool of fate stays its course.

I do not experience the man to whom I say *Thou*. But I take my stand in relation to him, in the sanctity of the primary word. Only when I step out of it do I experience him once more. In the act of experience *Thou* is far away.

Even if the man to whom I say *Thou* is not aware of it in the midst of his experience, yet relation may exist. For *Thou* is more than *It* realises. No deception penetrates here; here is the cradle of the Real Life.

This is the eternal source of art: a man is faced by a form which desires to be made through him into a work. This form is no offspring of his soul, but is an appearance which steps up to it and demands of it the effective power. The man is concerned with an act of his being. If he carries it through, if he speaks the primary word out of his being to the form which appears, then the effective power streams out, and the work arises.

The act includes a sacrifice and a risk. This is the sacrifice: the endless possibility that is offered up on the altar of the form. For everything which just this moment in play ran through the perspective must be obliterated;

nothing of that may penetrate the work. The exclusiveness of what is facing it demands that it be so. This is the risk: the primary word can only be spoken with the whole being. He who gives himself to it may withhold nothing of himself. The work does not suffer me, as do the tree and the man, to turn aside and relax in the world of *It*; but it commands. If I do not serve it aright it is broken, or it breaks me.

I can neither experience nor describe the form which meets me, but only body it forth. And yet I behold it, splendid in the radiance of what confronts me, clearer than all the clearness of the world which is experienced. I do not behold it as a thing among the "inner" things nor as an image of my "fancy," but as that which exists in the present. If test is made of its objectivity the form is certainly not "there." Yet what is actually so much present as it is? And the relation in which I stand to it is real, for it affects me, as I affect it.

To produce is to draw forth, to invent is to find, to shape is to discover. In bodying forth I disclose. I lead the form across—into the world of *It*. The work produced is a thing among things, able to be experienced and described as a sum of qualities. But from time to time it can face the receptive beholder in its whole embodied form.

—What, then, do we experience of *Thou*?
—Just nothing. For we do not experience it.
—What, then, do we know of *Thou*?
—Just everything. For we know nothing isolated about it any more.

The *Thou* meets me through grace—it is not found by seeking. But my speaking of the primary word to it is an act of my being, is indeed *the* act of my being.

The *Thou* meets me. But I step into direct relation with it. Hence the relation means being chosen and choosing, suffering and action in one; just as any action of the whole being, which means the suspension of all partial actions and consequently of all sensations of actions grounded only in their particular limitation, is bound to resemble suffering.

The primary word I-*Thou* can be spoken only with the whole being. Concentration and fusion into the whole being can never take place through my agency, nor can it ever take place without me. I become through my relation to the *Thou*; as I become *I*, I say *Thou*.

All real living is meeting.

The relation to the *Thou* is direct. No system of ideas, no foreknowledge, and no fancy intervene between *I* and *Thou*. The memory itself is transformed, as it plunges out of its isolation into the unity of the whole. No aim, no lust, and no anticipation intervene between *I* and *Thou*. Desire itself is transformed as it plunges out of its dream into the appearance. Every means

is an obstacle. Only when every means has collapsed does the meeting come
about.

In face of the directness of the relation everything indirect becomes irrelevant. It is also irrelevant if my *Thou* is already the *It* for other *I*'s ("an
object of general experience"), or can become so through the very accomplishment of this act of my being. For the real, though certainly swaying and
swinging, boundary runs neither between experience and non-experience, nor
between what is given and what is not given, nor yet between the world of
being and the world of value; but cutting indifferently across all these provinces it lies between *Thou* and *It*, between the present and the object.

The present, and by that is meant not the point which indicates from
time to time in our thought merely the conclusion of "finished" time, the
mere appearance of a termination which is fixed and held, but the real, filled
present, exists only in so far as actual presentness, meeting, and relation exist.
The present arises only in virtue of the fact that the *Thou* becomes present.
    The *I* of the primary word *I-It*, that is, the *I* faced by no *Thou*, but
surrounded by a multitude of "contents," has no present, only the past. Put in
another way, in so far as man rests satisfied with the things that he experiences and uses, he lives in the past, and his moment has no present content.
He has nothing but objects. But objects subsist in time that has been.
    The present is not fugitive and transient, but continually present and
enduring. The object is not duration, but cessation, suspension, a breaking
off and cutting clear and hardening, absence of relation and of present being.
    True beings are lived in the present, the life of objects is in the past.

Appeal to a "world of ideas" as a third factor above this opposition will
not do away with its essential twofold nature. For I speak of nothing else but
the real man, of you and of me, of our life and of our world—not of an *I*, or a
state of being, in itself alone. The real boundary for the actual man cuts right
across the world of ideas as well.
    To be sure, many a man who is satisfied with the experience and use of
the world of things has raised over or about himself a structure of ideas, in
which he finds refuge and repose from the oncome of nothingness. On the
threshold he lays aside his inauspicious everyday dress, wraps himself in pure
linen, and regales himself with the spectacle of primal being, or of necessary
being; but his life has no part in it. To proclaim his ways may even fill him
with well-being.
    But the mankind of mere *It* that is imagined, postulated, and propa-
gated by such a man has nothing in common with a living mankind where
Thou may truly be spoken. The noblest fiction is a fetish, the loftiest fictitious
sentiment is depraved. Ideas are no more enthroned above our heads than
resident in them; they wander amongst us and accost us. The man who leaves

the primary word unspoken is to be pitied; but the man who addresses instead
these ideas with an abstraction or a password, as if it were their name, is contemptible.

    In one of the three examples it is obvious that the direct relation in-
cludes an effect on what confronts me. In art the act of the being determines
the situation in which the form becomes the work. Through the meeting that
which confronts me is fulfilled, and enters the world of things, there to be
endlessly active, endlessly to become *It,* but also endlessly to become *Thou*
again, inspiring and blessing. It is "embodied"; its body emerges from the
flow of the spaceless, timeless present on the shore of existence.
    The significance of the effect is not so obvious in the relation with the
Thou spoken to men. The act of the being which provides directness in this
case is usually understood wrongly as being one of feeling. Feelings accompany the metaphysical and metapsychical fact of love, but they do not constitute it. The accompanying feelings can be of greatly differing kinds. The
feeling of Jesus for the demoniac differs from his feeling for the beloved
disciple; but the love is the one love. Feelings are "entertained": love comes
to pass. Feelings dwell in man; but man dwells in his love. That is no metaphor, but the actual truth. Love does not cling to the *I* in such a way as to
have the *Thou* only for its "content," its object; but love is *between I* and
Thou. The man who does not know this, with his very being know this, does
not know love; even though he ascribes to it the feelings he lives through,
experiences, enjoys, and expresses. Love ranges in its effect through the whole
world. In the eyes of him who takes his stand in love, and gazes out of it,
men are cut free from their entanglement in bustling activity. Good people
and evil, wise and foolish, beautiful and ugly, become successively real to him;
that is, set free they step forth in their singleness, and confront him as *Thou.*
In a wonderful way, from time to time, exclusiveness arises—and so he can be
effective, helping, healing, educating, raising up, saving. Love is responsibility
of an *I* for a *Thou.* In this lies the likeness—impossible in any feeling whatsoever—of all who love, from the smallest to the greatest and from the blessedly
protected man, whose life is rounded in that of a loved being, to him who is
all his life nailed to the cross of the world, and who ventures to bring himself
to the dreadful point—to love *all men.*
    Let the significance of the effect in the third example, that of the crea-
ture and our contemplation of it, remain sunk in mystery. Believe in the simple magic of life, in service in the universe, and the meaning of that waiting,
that alertness, that "craning of the neck" in creatures will dawn upon you.
Every word would falsify; but look! round about you beings live their life,
and to whatever point you turn you come upon being.

    Relation is mutual. My *Thou* affects me, as I affect it. We are moulded
by our pupils and built up by our works. The "bad" man, lightly touched by

the holy primary word, becomes one who reveals. How we are educated by children and by animals! We live our lives inscrutably included within the streaming mutual life of the universe.

—You speak of love as though it were the only relation between men. But properly speaking, can you take it even only as an example, since there is such a thing as hate?

—So long as love is "blind," that is, so long as it does not see a *whole* being, it is not truly under the sway of the primary word of relation. Hate is by nature blind. Only a part of a being can be hated. He who sees a whole being and is compelled to reject it is no longer in the kingdom of hate, but is in that of human restriction of the power to say *Thou*. He finds himself unable to say the primary word to the other human being confronting him. This word consistently involves an affirmation of the being addressed. He is therefore compelled to reject either the other or himself. At this barrier the entering on a relation recognises its relativity, and only simultaneously with this will the barrier be raised.

Yet the man who straightforwardly hates is nearer to relation than the man without hate and love.

But this is the exalted melancholy of our fate, that every *Thou* in our world must become an *It*. It does not matter how exclusively present the *Thou* was in the direct relation. As soon as the relation has been worked out or has been permeated with a means, the *Thou* becomes an object among objects—perhaps the chief, but still one of them, fixed in its size and its limits. In the work of art realisation in one sense means loss of reality in another. Genuine contemplation is over in a short time; now the life in nature, that first unlocked itself to me in the mystery of mutual action, can again be described, taken to pieces, and classified—the meeting-point of manifold systems of laws. And love itself cannot persist in direct relation. It endures, but in interchange of actual and potential being. The human being who was even now single and unconditioned, not something lying to hand, only present, not able to be experienced, only able to be fulfilled, has now become again a *He* or a *She,* a sum of qualities, a given quantity with a certain shape. Now I may take out from him again the colour of his hair or of his speech or of his goodness. But so long as I can do this he is no more my *Thou* and cannot yet be my *Thou* again.

Every *Thou* in the world is by its nature fated to become a thing, or continually to re-enter into the condition of things. In objective speech it would be said that every thing in the world, either before or after becoming a thing, is able to appear to an *I* as its *Thou*. But objective speech snatches only at a fringe of real life.

The *It* is the eternal chrysalis, the *Thou* the eternal butterfly—except that situations do not always follow one another in clear succession, but often there is a happening profoundly twofold, confusedly entangled.

In the beginning is relation.

Consider the speech of "primitive" peoples, that is, of those that have a meagre stock of objects, and whose life is built up within a narrow circle of acts highly charged with presentness. The nuclei of this speech, words in the form of sentences and original pre-grammatical structures (which later, splitting asunder, give rise to the many various kinds of words), mostly indicate the wholeness of a relation. We say "far away"; the Zulu has for that a word which means, in our sentence form, "There where someone cries out: 'O mother, I am lost.'" The Fuegian soars above our analytic wisdom with a seven-syllabled word whose precise meaning is, "They stare at one another, each waiting for the other to volunteer to do what both wish, but are not able to do." In this total situation the persons, as expressed both in nouns and pronouns, are embedded, still only in relief and without finished independence. The chief concern is not with these products of analysis and reflection but with the true original unity, the lived relation.

We greet the man we meet, wishing him well or assuring him of our devotion or commending him to God. But how indirect these worn-out formulas are! What do we discern even dimly in "Hail!" of the original conferring of power? Compare these with the ever fresh Kaffir greeting, with its direct bodily relation, "I see you!" or with its ridiculous and sublime American variant, "Smell me!"

It may be supposed that characterisations and ideas, but also representations of persons and things, have been taken out from representations of incidents and situations that are specifically relational. The elementary impressions and emotional stirrings that waken the spirit of the "natural man" proceed from incidents—experience of a being confronting him—and from situations —life with a being confronting him—that are relational in character. He is not disquieted by the moon that he sees every night, till it comes bodily to him, sleeping or waking, draws near and charms him with silent movements, or fascinates him with the evil or sweetness of its touch. He does not retain from this the visual representation, say, of the wandering orb of light, or of a demonic being that somehow belongs to it, but at first he has in him only the dynamic, stirring image of the moon's effect, streaming through his body. Out of this the image of the moon personally achieving the effect only gradually emerges. Only now, that is to say, does the memory of the unknown that is nightly taken into his being begin to kindle and take shape as the doer and bringer of the effect. Thus it makes possible the transformation of the unknown into an object, a *He* or a *She* out of a *Thou* that could not originally be experienced, but simply suffered.

This initial and long-continuing relational character of every essential phenomenon makes it also easier to understand a certain spiritual element of primitive life that is much discussed and observed, but not yet properly grasped, in present-day study. I mean that mysterious power the idea of which has been traced, through many variations, in the form of the beliefs or in the knowledge (both being still one) of many nature peoples. Known as Mana or Orenda, it opens a way to the Brahman in its primal meaning, and further to the Dynamis and Charis of the Magical Papyri and of the Apostolic Epistles. It has been characterised as a supersensuous or supernatural power—descriptions which depend on our categories and do not correspond to those of the primitive man. The limits of his world are set by his bodily experience, to which visits from the dead, say, quite "naturally" belong. To accept what has no sensuous qualities at all as actually existing must strike him as absurd. The appearances to which he ascribes the "mystical power" are all elementary incidents that are relational in character, that is, all incidents that disturb him by stirring his body and leaving behind in him a stirring image. The moon and the dead, visiting him by night with pain or pleasure, have that power. But so, too, have the burning sun and the howling beast and the chief whose glance constrains him and the sorcerer whose singing loads him with power for the hunt. Mana is simply the effective force, that which has made the person of the moon, up there in the heavens, into a blood-stirring *Thou*. The memory of it left its track when the image of the object was separated out from the total stirring image; although it itself, indeed, never appears other than in the doer and bringer of an effect. It is that with which man himself, if he possesses it—perhaps in a wonderful stone—can be effective in this way. The "world-image" of primitive man is magical not because human magical power is set in the midst of it but because this human power is only a particular variety of the general magic power from which all effective action is derived. Causality in his world-image is no unbroken sequence but an ever new flashing forth of power and moving out towards its production; it is a volcanic movement without continuity. Mana is a primitive abstraction, probably more primitive than, say, number, but not any more supernatural than it. The memory as it is being trained ranges the grand relational events, the elemental emotional shocks. The most important for the instinct of preservation and the most noteworthy for the instinct to understand—that is, "that which effects," stands out most forcibly of all, and becomes independent. The less important, the non-communal, the changing *Thou* of experiences, retires and remains isolated in the memory, and is gradually transformed into an object and very slowly drawn into groups and classes. As third in the arrangement, terrible when thus separated, at times more ghostly than the dead and the moon, but always more and more irrefutably clear, there arises up the other, "unchanging" partner, "I."

Consciousness of the "I" is not connected with the primitive sway of the instinct for self-preservation any more than with that of the other instincts. It is not the "I" that wishes to propagate itself, but the body, that knows as yet of no "I." It is not the "I" but the body that wishes to make things, a tool or a toy, that wishes to be a "creator." Further, a *cognosco ergo sum*, in however naïve a form and however childlike a conception of an experiencing subject, cannot be found in the primitive function of knowledge. The "I" emerges as a single element out of the primal experiences, out of the vital primal words *I-affecting-Thou* and *Thou-affecting-I*, only after they have been split asunder and the participle has been given eminence as an object.

The fundamental difference between the two primary words comes to light in the spiritual history of primitive man. Already in the original relational event he speaks the primary word *I-Thou* in a natural way that precedes what may be termed visualisation of forms—that is, before he has recognised himself as *I*. The primary word *I-It*, on the other hand, is made possible at all only by means of this recognition—by means, that is, of the separation of the *I*.

The first primary word can be resolved, certainly, into *I* and *Thou*, but it did not arise from their being set together; by its nature it precedes *I*. The second word arose from the setting together of *I* and *It*; by nature it comes after *I*.

In the primitive relational event, in virtue of its exclusiveness, the *I* is included. While, that is to say, there are in it, in accordance with its being, only the two partners, the man and that which confronts him, in their full actuality, and while the world becomes in it a dual system, the man, without yet perceiving the *I* itself, is already aware of that cosmic pathos of the *I*.

On the other hand the *I* is not yet included in the natural, actual event which is to pass over into the primary word *I-It*, into the experience with its relation to *I*. This actual event is the separation of the human body, as the bearer of its perceptions, from the world round about it. The body comes to know and to differentiate itself in its peculiarities; the differentiation, however, remains one of pure juxtaposition, and hence cannot have the character of the state in which *I* is implied.

But when the *I* of the relation has stepped forth and taken on separate existence, it also moves, strangely tenuous and reduced to merely functional activity, into the natural, actual event of the separation of the body from the world round about it, and awakens there the state in which *I* is properly active. Only now can the conscious act of the *I* take place. This act is the first form of the primary word *I-It*, of the experience in its relation to *I*. The *I* which stepped forth declares itself to be the bearer, and the world round about to be the object, of the perceptions. Of course, this happens in a "primitive" form and not in the form of a "theory of knowledge." But whenever the sentence "I see the tree" is so uttered that it no longer tells of a relation between the man—*I*—and the tree—*Thou*—, but establishes the perception of the tree as object by the human consciousness, the barrier between subject and object has been set up. The primary word *I-It*, the word of separation, has been spoken.

—That melancholy of our fate, then, arose in earliest history?

—Indeed, yes—in so far as the conscious life of man arose in earliest history. But conscious life means the return of cosmic being as human becoming. Spirit appears in time as a product—even as a by-product of nature, yet it is in spirit that nature is timelessly enveloped.

The opposition of the two primary words has many names at different times and in different worlds; but in its nameless truth it is inherent in creation.

—But you believe then in the existence of a paradise in the earliest days of mankind?

—Even if it was a hell—and certainly that time to which I can go back in historical thought was full of fury and anguish and torment and cruelty—at any rate it was not unreal.

The relational experiences of man in earliest days were certainly not tame and pleasant. But rather force exercised on being that is really lived than shadowy solicitude for faceless numbers! From the former a way leads to God, from the latter only one to nothingness.

Only brief glimpses into the context in time of the two primary words are given us by primitive man, whose life, even if it could be made fully accessible, can represent only as it were allegorically that of the real early man. We receive fuller knowledge from the child.

Here it becomes crystal clear to us that the spiritual reality of the primary words arises out of a natural reality, that of the primary word *I-Thou* out of natural combination, and that of the primary word *I-It* out of natural separation.

The ante-natal life of the child is one of purely natural combination, bodily interaction and flowing from the one to the other. Its life's horizon, as it comes into being, seems in a unique way to be, and yet again not to be, traced in that of the life that bears it. For it does not rest only in the womb of the human mother. Yet this connexion has such a cosmic quality that the mythical saying of the Jews, "in the mother's body man knows the universe, in birth he forgets it," reads like the imperfect decipherment of an inscription from earliest times. And it remains indeed in man as a secret image of desire. Not as though his yearning meant a longing to return, as those suppose who see in the spirit—confusing it with their intellect—a parasite of nature, when it is rather (though exposed to diverse illnesses) nature's best flower. But the yearning is for the cosmic connexion, with its true *Thou*, of this life that has burst forth into spirit.

Every child that is coming into being rests, like all life that is coming into being, in the womb of the great mother, the undivided primal world that precedes form. From her, too, we are separated, and enter into personal life, slipping free only in the dark hours to be close to her again; night by night this happens to the healthy man. But this separation does not occur suddenly and catastrophically like the separation from the bodily mother; time is granted to the child to exchange a spiritual connexion, that is, *relation,* for the natural connexion with the world that he gradually loses. He has stepped out of the glowing darkness of chaos into the cool light of creation. But he does not possess it yet; he must first draw it truly out, he must make it into a reality for himself, he must find for himself his own world by seeing and hearing and touching and shaping it. Creation reveals, in meeting, its essential nature as form. It does not spill itself into expectant senses, but rises up to meet the grasping senses. That which will eventually play as an accustomed object around the man who is fully developed, must be wooed and won by the developing man in strenuous action. For no *thing* is a ready-made part of an experience; only in the strength, acting and being acted upon, of what is over against men, is anything made accessible. Like primitive man the child lives between sleep and sleep (a great part of his waking hours is also sleep) in the flash and counter-flash of meeting.

The primal nature of the effort to establish relation is already to be seen in the earliest and most confined stage. Before anything isolated can be perceived, timid glances move out into indistinct space, towards something indefinite; and in times when there seems to be no desire for nourishment, hands sketch delicately and dimly in the empty air, apparently aimlessly seeking and reaching out to meet something indefinite. You may, if you wish, call this an animal action, but it is not thereby comprehended. For these very glances will after protracted attempts settle on the red carpet-pattern and not be moved till the soul of the red has opened itself to them; and this very movement of the hands will win from a woolly Teddy-bear its precise form, apparent to the senses, and become lovingly and unforgettably aware of a complete body. Neither of these acts is experience of an object, but is the correspondence of the child—to be sure only "fanciful"—with what is alive and effective over against him. (This "fancy" does not in the least involve, however, a "giving of life to the universe": it is the instinct to make everything into *Thou,* to give relation to the universe, the instinct which completes out of its own richness the living effective action when a mere copy or symbol of it is given in what is over against him.) Little, disjointed, meaningless sounds still go out persistently into the void. But one day, unforeseen, they will have become conversation—does it matter that it is perhaps with the simmering kettle? It is conversation. Many a movement termed reflex is a firm trowel in the building up of the person in the world. It is simply not the case that the child first perceives an object, then, as it were, puts himself in relation with it. But the effort to establish relation comes first—the hand of the child arched out so that what is over against him may nestle under it; second is the actual relation, a saying of *Thou* without words, in the state preceding the word-form; the thing, like the *I,* is produced late, arising after the original experiences have been split asunder and the connected partners separated. In the beginning is relation—as category of being, readiness, grasping form, mould for the soul; it is the *a priori* of relation, *the inborn Thou.*

The inborn *Thou* is realised in the lived relations with that which meets it. The fact that this *Thou* can be known as what is over against the child, can be taken up in exclusiveness, and finally can be addressed with the primary word, is based on the *a priori* of relation.

In the instinct to make contact (first by touch and then by visual "touch" of another being) the inborn *Thou* is very soon brought to its full powers, so that the instinct ever more clearly turns out to mean mutual relation, "tenderness." But the instinct to "creation," which is established later (that is, the instinct to set up things in a synthetic, or, if that is impossible, in an analytic way—through pulling to pieces or tearing up), is also determined by this inborn *Thou,* so that a "personification" of what is made, and a "conversation," take place. The development of the soul in the child is inextricably bound up with that of the longing for the *Thou,* with the satisfaction and the disappointment of this longing, with the game of his experiments and the tragic seriousness of his perplexity. Genuine understanding of this phenomenon, which is injured by every attempt to lead it back into more confined spheres, can only be promoted if, during its observation and discussion, its cosmic and metacosmic origin is kept in mind. For it reaches out from the undivided primal world which precedes form, out of which the bodily individual who is born into the world, but not yet the personal, actualised being, has fully emerged. For only gradually, by entering into relations, is the latter to develop out of this primal world.

Through the *Thou* a man becomes *I*. That which confronts him comes and disappears, relational events condense, then are scattered, and in the change consciousness of the unchanging partner, of the *I*, grows clear, and each time stronger. To be sure, it is still seen caught in the web of the relation with the *Thou*, as the increasingly distinguishable feature of that which reaches out to and yet is not the *Thou*. But it continually breaks through with more power, till a time comes when it bursts its bonds, and the *I* confronts itself for a moment, separated as though it were a *Thou*; as quickly to take possession of itself and from then on to enter into relations in consciousness of itself.

Only now can the other primary word be assembled. Hitherto the *Thou* of relation was continually fading away, but it did not thereby become an *It* for some *I*, an object of perception and experience without real connexion—as it will henceforth become. It became rather an *It*, so to speak, for itself, an *It* disregarded at first, yet waiting to rise up in a new relational event. Further, the body maturing into a person was hitherto distinguished, as bearer of its perceptions and executor of its impulses, from the world round about. But this distinction was simply a juxtaposition brought about by its seeing its way in the situation, and not an absolute severance of *I* and its object. But now the separated *I* emerges, transformed. Shrunk from substance and fulness to a functional point, to a subject which experiences and uses, *I* approaches and takes possession of all *It* existing "in and for itself," and forms in conjunction with it the other primary word. The man who has become conscious of *I*, that is, the man who says *I-It*, stands before things, but not over against them in the flow of mutual action. Now with the magnifying glass of peering observation he bends over particulars and objectifies them, or with the field-glass of remote inspection he objectifies them and arranges them as scenery, he isolates them in observation without any feeling of their exclusiveness, or he knits them into a scheme of observation without any feeling of universality. The feeling of exclusiveness he would be able to find only in relation, the feeling of universality only through it. Now for the first time he experiences things as sums of qualities. From each relational experience qualities belonging to the remembered *Thou* had certainly remained sunk in his memory; but now for the first time things are for him actually composed of their qualities. From the simple memory of the relation the man, dreaming or fashioning or thinking, according to his nature, enlarges the nucleus, the substance that showed itself in the *Thou* with power and gathered up in itself all qualities. But now also for the first time he sets things in space and time, in causal connexion, each with its own place and appointed course, its measurability and conditioned nature.

The *Thou* appears, to be sure, in space, but in the exclusive situation of what is over against it, where everything else can be only the background out of which it emerges, not its boundary and measured limit. It appears, too, in time, but in that of the event which is fulfilled in itself: it is not lived as part of a continuous and organised sequence, but is lived in a "duration" whose purely intensive dimension is definable only in terms of itself. It appears, lastly, simultaneously as acting and as being acted upon—not, however, linked to a chain of causes, but, in its relation of mutual action with the *I*, as the beginning and the end of the event. This is part of the basic truth of the human world, that only *It* can be arranged in order. Only when things, from being our *Thou*, become our *It*, can they be co-ordinated. The *Thou* knows no system of co-ordination.

But now that we have come so far, it is necessary to set down the other part of the basic truth, without which this would be a useless fragment— namely, a world that is ordered is not the world-order. There are moments of silent depth in which you look on the world-order fully present. Then in its very flight the note will be heard; but the ordered world is its indistinguishable score. These moments are immortal, and most transitory of all; no content may be secured from them, but their power invades creation and the knowledge of man, beams of their power stream into the ordered world and dissolve it again and again. This happens in the history both of the individual and of the race.

To man the world is twofold, in accordance with his twofold attitude.

He perceives what exists round about him—simply things, and beings as things; and what happens round about him—simply events, and actions as events; things consisting of qualities, events of moments; things entered in the graph of place, events in that of time; things and events bounded by other things and events, measured by them, comparable with them: he perceives an ordered and detached world. It is to some extent a reliable world, having density and duration. Its organisation can be surveyed and brought out again and again; gone over with closed eyes, and verified with open eyes. It is always there, next to your skin, if you look on it that way, cowering in your soul, if you prefer it so. It is your object, remains it as long as you wish, and remains a total stranger, within you and without. You perceive it, take it to yourself as the "truth," and it lets itself be taken; but it does not give itself to you. Only concerning it may you make yourself "understood" with others; it is ready, though attached to everyone in a different way, to be an object common to you all. But you cannot meet others in it. You cannot hold on to life without it, its reliability sustains you; but should you die in it, your grave would be in nothingness.

Or on the other hand, man meets what exists 'and becomes as what is over against him, always simply a *single* being and each thing simply as being. What exists is opened to him in happenings, and what happens affects him as what is. Nothing is present for him except this one being, but it implicates the whole world. Measure and comparison have disappeared; it lies with yourself how much of the immeasurable becomes reality for you. These meetings are not organised to make the world, but each is a sign of the world-order. They are not linked up with one another, but each assures you of your solidarity with the world. The world which appears to you in this way is unreliable, for it takes on a continually new appearance; you cannot hold it to its word. It has no density, for everything in it penetrates everything else; no duration, for it comes even when it is not summoned, and vanishes even when it is tightly held. It cannot be surveyed, and if you wish to make it capable of survey you lose it. It comes, and comes to bring *you* out; if it does not reach you, meet you, then it vanishes; but it comes back in another form. It is not outside you, it stirs in the depth of you; if you say "Soul of my soul" you have not said too much. But guard against wishing to remove it into your soul—for then you annihiliate it. It is your present; only while you have it do you have the present. You can make it into an object for yourself, to experience and to use; you must continually do this—and as you do it you have no more present. Between you and it there is mutual giving: you say *Thou* to it and give yourself to it, it says *Thou* to you and gives itself to you. You cannot make yourself understood with others concerning it, you are alone with it. But it teaches you to meet others, and to hold your ground when you meet them. Through the graciousness of its comings and the solemn sadness of its goings it leads you away to the *Thou* in which the parallel lines of relations meet. It does not help to sustain you in life, it only helps you to glimpse eternity.

The world of *It* is set in context of space and time.

The world of *Thou* is not set in the context of either of these.

The particular *Thou*, after the relational event has run its course, *is bound* to become an *It*.

The particular *It*, by entering the relational event, *may* become a *Thou*.

These are the two basic privileges of the world of *It*. They move man to look on the world of *It* as the world in which he has to live, and in which it is comfortable to live, as the world, indeed, which offers him all manner of incitements and excitements, activity and knowledge. In this chronicle of solid benefits the moments of the *Thou* appear as strange lyric and dramatic episodes, seductive and magical, but tearing us away to dangerous extremes, loosening the well-tried context, leaving more questions than satisfaction behind them, shattering security—in short, uncanny moments we can well dispense with. For since we are bound to leave them and go back into the "world," why not remain in it? Why not call to order what is over against us, and send it packing into the realm of objects? Why, if we find ourselves on occasion with no choice but to say *Thou* to father, wife, or comrade, not say *Thou* and mean *It*? To utter the sound *Thou* with the vocal organs is by no means the same as saying the uncanny primary word; more, it is harmless to whisper with the soul an amorous *Thou*, so long as nothing else in a serious way is meant but *experience* and *make use of*.

It is not possible to live in the bare present. Life would be quite consumed if precautions were not taken to subdue the present speedily and thoroughly. But it is possible to live in the bare past, indeed only in it may a life be organised. We only need to fill each moment with experiencing and using, and it ceases to burn.

And in all the seriousness of truth, hear this: without *It* man cannot live. But he who lives with *It* alone is not a man.

THE UNIVERSAL ASPECT OF
JEWISH RELIGION
Mordecai M. Kaplan

Mordecai M. Kaplan (1881–   ) is the founder of the Re-
constructionist Movement. Born in Lithuania, he migrated to the
United States in 1889. He has been involved in education for the
majority of his career, and retired from the faculty of the Jewish
Theological Seminary in 1963, where he had been Professor of
Philosophies of Religion since 1947. The Reconstructionist Move-
ment, founded in 1935, is dedicated to the proposition that Juda-
ism is not merely a religion, but a civilization within which reli-
gion plays one, but not the only, role. (Judaism is the expression
of the peculiar goals and functions of the Jewish people, not
merely in relation to themselves but also relative to other peoples
and nations.) God is not conceived as a supernatural personality,
but as that aspect of the nature of things which leads to the de-
velopment of greater values both for the individual and for his
society. In this selection, from Judaism without Supernaturalism
(1958), Professor Kaplan outlines his conception of the relation-
ship existing between Judaism and the democratic ideals of the
contemporary world. Among his other works are Judaism as a
Civilization *(1934),* The Meaning of God in Modern Jewish Religion *(1937),* The Future of the American Jew *(1948), and* The
Meaning and Purpose of Jewish Existence *(1963).*

Only by dissociating Jewish religion from supernaturalism can the universal significance of its ideals and values be made apparent and the Jewish
contribution to world order take effect. The universal aspect of Jewish religion finds expression in its two main strands: Prophetism and Torah. In traditional Judaism these two strands were always interwoven into a single pattern.
The prophetic strand consists of the aims or goals expressed in the form of

Mordecai Kaplan, *Judaism Without Supernaturalism* (New York, The Reconstructionist Press, 1958), pp. 77–92. Reprinted with permission of the Reconstructionist
Press.

general truths about God, man, and the world, and of general principles concerning their mutual relations. The Torah strand consists of specific methods, or rules of action, whereby those aims are to be achieved and those goals attained. It is a mistake to assume that the universal message of Judaism is to be found only in the prophetic writings, and that only there can social justice, as a universal principle of human society, find adequate support. While it is true that the Prophets illumine the *meaning* of social justice, it is the Torah which points the way to what is necessary to make social justice *work*. In what follows the term "democratic process" will be used to convey fully how Jewish religion conceives social justice.

PROPHETISM AND THE DEMOCRATIC PROCESS

There are two aspects to the prophetic element in Judaism: a negative and a positive. The negative aspect is the principle of inner or spiritual freedom; the positive aspect is summed up in the Rabbinic saying that the stability of the world depends upon three things: truth, justice, and peace (*Mishnah, Abot* I, 18). Each one of these principles is the target of those persons and governments that attack the democratic process, and must therefore not only be written into the covenants of the nation but also re-established in the hearts of men, if the democratic process is to survive.

In order to emphasize the primacy of inner or spiritual freedom, Jewish religion associates every sacred occasion in its calendar and every important ethical or legal precept with the Exodus from Egypt, which marks the beginning of Israel's career as a nation. The significance of that association may be inferred from the declaration which stands at the head of the Ten Commandments. There God makes Himself known as the Redeemer and Liberator of Israel from bondage. This means that man owes to God the freedom he needs in order to fulfill his own nature as a human being. As Redeemer, God redeems not only the oppressed from the hand of the oppressor, but also the inner man from a bondage which is more crushing than that which any outward tyranny can impose. That inner freedom is the soul of whatever freedom man aspires to.

What is inner freedom? It may be defined as that character trait which expresses itself in unyielding refusal to recognize, or submit to, the authority of brute force as legitimate. The free man defies brute force, in whatever form it manifests itself, whether as ruthless nature, or as human tyranny, with its cruel violence and diabolic cunning. The man who is inwardly free possesses what has been termed "the unreconciled heart." That is the heart which refuses to make peace with sheer force, or to accept it as justified.

When man lacks inner freedom, there is no telling to what extent he is prone to dehumanize himself. We often wonder why man has not yet learned to master the machine, but is mastered by it, although it is his own creation. One reason is that it releases more power than he knows what to do with. But an additional reason is that he allows the machine to master his spirit and transfer to him its automatic, unfeeling essence. Some years ago Eugene O'Neill, in his play, *The Dynamo,* dramatized this self-effacement of man in the presence of the machine. Man is so fascinated by the machine that he tends to assimilate himself to it. The consequent robotization of man is to be dreaded no less than his occasional relapses into savagery.

Far more overpowering, however, than the fascination exercised by the mechanical energy of the machine is the hypnosis exercised by the psychic energy of crowds. The vast improvements in transportation and communication are making it progressively difficult for a person to be in possession of his own soul. It is hard to withstand the pressure of the multitude, which nowadays intrudes on one's privacy. Quite irresistible is the temptation to escape personal responsibility, by merging oneself with the multitude and sharing its manifest power. As a prerequisite to fulfilling the law of love, we have to give heed to the behest, "Thou shalt not follow a multitude to do evil, neither shalt thou bear witness in a cause to turn aside after a multitude to pervert justice." Before a man can come to respect, to say nothing of loving, the individuality in others, he must himself retain enough individuality not to surrender his soul to the multitude.

Inner freedom is only the *nay,* of which the *yea* spells truth, justice, and peace. Truth in Hebrew is expressed by the word *emet,* which connotes reliability. Truth, in Judaism, is not a philosophical concept. It is a social and ethical imperative. It calls upon a person to be honest with others and with himself. To be honest with others means to live up to expressed and tacit agreements. The earliest glimmerings of Israel's self-awareness are associated with the making of covenants that had to be kept at all costs and that could not be violated with impunity. Out of its own experience, Israel has evolved a fervid faith in the sacredness of covenants. With the bitter lesson that mankind is now learning as a result of national policies in which treaties are considered mere scraps of paper, and promises are made to be broken, the recognition of the sanctity of agreements as the foundation of civilized society might well be given primacy among the essential requirements of a civilized world order.

Honesty with ourselves is willingness to recognize and reckon with all the facts in the contexts of our lives. This inner honesty which enables us to get the better of our prejudices and wishful thinking is virtually the call of reason. Whenever our horizons widen and open up new worlds of facts and values, we fare best if we heed that call. Such was the case during the eighteenth century which brought to mankind great release and enlightenment. Much of that great gain has unfortunately been forfeited, but enough survives to make us grateful. We owe to that age of reason, or inner honesty, our Declaration of Independence and the Constitution with its Bill of Rights. Yet it has become the fashion in certain quarters to decry that passion for truth which brought within the scope of political possibility the prospect of world unity and peace. Romanticism, which sets a premium upon the un-tamed impulses and the unharnessed will, at the expense of reason, and which sees in all considered thought nothing but the sin of pride and idolatry, has reached its climax in the deification of soil and blood. When a nation decries reason, it has fallen under the spell of the demonic. How to reclaim large portions of mankind from their present fit of madness, and have them recover the sanity necessary for that truth which spells honesty with ourselves, is a problem in moral and spiritual re-education.

In the matter of justice we have a more difficult task than with truth, when we try to differentiate it from its antithesis—aggression. For we must remember that while the aggressor frankly denies the reality of truth, he is cunning enough to know that he cannot afford to belittle the worth of justice. He therefore prefers to invoke its name for his very deeds of aggression and violence. That is an old trick with evildoers, against which Isaiah seems to have found himself helpless, as when he cried out: "Woe unto them that call evil good and good evil; that change darkness into light and light into dark-ness; that change bitter into sweet, and sweet into bitter." Plato knew this when in the opening of the dialogue in the *Republic* he had Thrasymachus brutally insult Socrates as the latter struggled to articulate the true meaning of justice. "I proclaim," Thrasymachus blurted out, "that justice is nothing else than the interest of the stronger." During the late twenties Elie Faure, the French Nietzsche, proclaimed: "It is necessary to convince oneself that only force is moral."[1] Nor can one hope to expose the aggressor's world-jug-glery by asking him whether what he calls "justice" makes for peace. "Cer-tainly," he would reply.

The justice in behalf of which prophet, lawgiver, and sage in ancient Israel contended was the inalienable right of every human being and of every people to make the most of themselves, to use to the utmost their capacities, their interests, and their opportunities. This is essentially what men mean by salvation, which they conceive variously in accordance with their particular culture and world outlook. However differently endowed or circumstanced, all human beings are nevertheless equal from the standpoint of the divine and inalienable right to achieve what they regard as salvation, provided, of course, it is free from the taint of intolerance or bigotry. The only kind of state that can implement this conception of justice is the one that is based on the three principles of political democracy, (1) majority rule, (2) provision for full expression of political opposition, and (3) the Bill of Rights.

When, therefore, the aggressor constructs a philosophy of aggression and misnames it justice, the main force of his argument is directed against the principle of equality and social democracy. Salvation is, according to him, the monopoly of those who, like himself, can use other human beings as chattels, tools, or beasts of burden. In the face of this deeply rooted tendency to deny human beings the capacity for salvation because they belong to a different

[1] *The Dance over Fire and Water*, Harper and Brothers.

race or creed, the world must be so organized and administered politically, economically, and socially that every religious and cultural group shall be unhampered in its efforts to enable its members to achieve what they regard as salvation. *As the oldest living and most cruelly tormented victim of the denial of equality in salvation, the Jewish People should remind the world that there can be no peace in the world unless and until the principle of equality in salvation for all races, churches, and states is formally professed and actively practiced by all races, churches, and states.*

THE TORAH AND THE DEMOCRATIC PROCESS

The foregoing is a description of the prophetic element in Judaism, from the standpoint of its relation to the democratic process. Judaism, however, does not confine itself to dreaming beautiful dreams about the world as it might be. Its main concern is to bring the ideal from heaven down to earth. That concern has given rise to Torah. Torah, as it has been lived by the Jews during the past twenty-five centuries, is a unique synthesis of education and law.

Torah has lifted education to the level of religion. It declares the transmission of the knowledge and experience necessary for the achievement of salvation to be the most important duty which God has placed upon both parents and nations. The Church places mainly upon the parents the chief responsibility for the transmission of the means of salvation. The modern nation places that responsibility upon the State. Judaism would have both parents and nation share that responsibility, and reckon with each other in the manner of meeting it.

Apart from the fact that professing democracy does not always mean practicing it, there is the inherent difficulty of translating it into an educational policy and program. It is easier to be, and to teach others to be, aggressive than to be, and to teach others to be, just. The fact is that progressive education, or education for democracy, has so far made little progress. But it does not follow that the medieval type of education was a moral or spiritual success. The only cure for the failures of democracy is more democracy and for the failures of progressive education is more progress in education.

The free nations of the world are badly in need of reeducating themselves in the meaning and function of education. The Renaissance gave the Western peoples the ideal of education in the humanities. The result was the dehumanization which led to the devastating religious wars of the late Middle Ages. The scientific discoveries and technical inventions have given them the ideal of education in science and technology. The result is the growing barbarization of man. Unless education utilizes the humanities, the sciences and the technics as a means of humanizing man, by cultivating in him the habits of moral responsibility and good will, which are indispensable to the democratic process, it will only hasten the day of universal cataclysm.

In the remaking of human nature, both in the individual and in society, first place will have to be given to education and reeducation. In that process mankind will ultimately have to arrive at that approach to the problem of human living which was adumbrated in the humanist implications of Torah. *Training for earning a livelihood will have to be combined with training in the art of living a life based on the prophetic ideals of inner freedom, truth, justice, and peace. Education for citizenship will have to be supplemented by education for international friendship and co-operation.*

The second means by which the Torah seeks to have the prophetic ideals translated into action is law. Torah, as law, is synonymous with constitutionalism, government by law in contrast with government by men. If the purpose of education is to create in the heart of the individual a keen yearning for justice, it should be the purpose of law to give effect to that yearning through collective action. The individual human being, however well intentioned, requires the support of his fellows to live up to his own better self. That support he and his fellows fashion, when they merge their wills into one collective will which is articulated into law. The law, to be sure, cannot compel anyone to do his best, but it can prevent one from doing his worst. The Torah, though not subscribing to the doctrine of original sin as professed in non-Jewish theology, recognizes the proneness of man to evil. Against that proneness man needs a stronger safeguard than abstract moral ideals. That safeguard can only be law. To get the full significance of this Torah conception of law, one has to contrast that conception with the one propounded by Paul in his Epistle to the Romans.

The nemesis of nineteenth-century liberalism has been the principle of *laissez faire,* with its abhorrence of "too much law." Herbert Spencer shuddered at the thought that a state should prescribe sanitation laws and housing laws. Indeed, the greater the complexity of social life, the greater the need for law to insure the functioning of truth and justice. There was no need for traffic lights in a horse-and-buggy age, but how necessary they are today is evident from the snarl into which traffic is thrown the moment they fail to work. Men and nations will have to become used to the idea that laws and legal sanctions are indispensable to the safeguarding of rights. The troublesome question as to what kind of economy is best calculated to raise national income and standards of living and to bring about universal employment, whether it shall be individual, collective, or mixed enterprise, is a matter for economic strategists and experts to decide. But no economy can escape either anarchy or dictatorship, unless it is safeguarded by laws demanding publicity, accountability, and the prevalence of the merit system.

The futility of good will which is not enforced by law is eloquently demonstrated in a recent little book by Emery Reeves, called *A Democratic Manifesto.* Pointing out the dangerous fallacy that force is merely an instrument of war and should be repudiated as an instrument of peace, he adds, "If there is one law which can be deduced from the history of mankind, it is that whenever and wherever force was not used in the service of law, it was used against the law." The utter collapse of the League of Nations upon which the hopes of mankind were for a time centered is irrefutable proof of the truth implied in the method of Torah, that good intentions which are not backed by enforceable law are bound to be frustrated.

The same method of Torah will have to be extended to the two other freedoms, the freedom of worship and the freedom of expression, which properly come within the complete jurisdiction of each state. There, too, good will is not enough. Unless these freedoms are safeguarded by effective laws, they can all too easily be nullified. Under the aegis of those freedoms the most vicious and subversive propaganda of hatred and lies has been carried on with the evident purpose to destroy them. It will henceforth be necessary to enact laws to safeguard the freedom of worship and freedom of expression.

Freedom of worship will have to be interpreted not only as a right to continue one's own form of worship, but also as a duty, to be enforced by law, to refrain from interfering with all other forms of worship and to eliminate from educational texts all offensive or insulting reference to religions and peoples other than one's own.

Freedom of speech and assembly should not merely be interpreted as the right to promulgate one's own views, but should also be safeguarded by laws against all propaganda subversive of such freedom and against the incitement to violence and the spreading of class and race hatred. No doubt the formulation of such law is not easy, but more difficult problems have been solved, and this one is far from being insoluble.

The right to hold minority opinions and beliefs and to foster minority cultures should be safeguarded by laws which, on the one hand, protect the minority against the force of the majority, and, on the other hand, prevent the minority from carrying on activities looking to the suppression of freedom of speech or religion, or to discrimination against any race or creed.

THE CONDITION OF MANKIND REFLECTED IN THE FATE OF JEWRY

If the *faith* of Jewry may be said to define the democratic process, the *fate* of Jewry is a most reliable index of its functioning. It is no easy matter to determine what is really happening to the democratic process, whether it is making headway or being retarded. If the Jews as a group are destined merely to stand and wait, they can nevertheless serve mankind by functioning as the barometer of its civilization.

One of the main factors which have brought on the present world-crisis has been the failure to realize to what extent it is due to the rise of modern nationalism. H. G. Wells's remark that war is the result of bad history teaching is not as exaggerated as it sounds. We only weaken our case, for example, by interpreting what happened among the aggressor nations as the recrudescence of barbarism, paganism, or mediævalism. To be sure, the outward aspect of what has happened among them wears the face of ancient savageries and fanaticisms. But inwardly and essentially what has happened is the explosion of the most inflammatory substance of human nature—national egotism. Unfortunately for the Jews, history has placed them at the very point of the explosion. No wonder it has shattered the Jewish People into fragments. To appreciate these facts we have to take a glance at the history of modern times.

When, as a consequence of what is known as the commercial revolution in the sixteenth and seventeenth centuries, feudalism began to be undermined and, as a consequence of the industrial revolution in the eighteenth century, collapsed altogether, democracy of the free-enterprise or individualistic type came into being. The effect of that economic and political reorganization of society in western Europe on the status of the Jews is well known. The Jews, who until that time were an alien people exiled from their land and scattered among the nations, ceased to be regarded as aliens. They were given civil rights which required them to become politically and culturally integrated into the rest of the population.

But free enterprise or individualistic democracy no sooner arose than it began to be outdated. It came at a time when the agricultural economy was still strong and machine economy only at the beginning of its evolution. The machine economy, however, developed at a pace with which man could not catch up in the ordering of his affairs. Human beings grew to be so interdependent that they had to learn to act in mass in order to survive. A form of action which until then had been confined to the battlefield had to be introduced into the shops and factories. The machine was rapidly gaining momentum. The industrial revolution was soon to be left far behind by the technological revolution. That necessitated further consolidation of human beings into masses. So precarious and helpless did the machine economy render the individual that he left off yearning for opportunity and was seized with a craving for protection from exploitation and for security against unemployment and starvation. This has given rise to the bitter conflict between free-enterprise democracy and mass democracy. Out of this conflict has emerged modern nationalism which, unless tamed by education in international understanding and by machinery of international government, will destroy the human race.

The truth is that the common man, Johnnie Appleseed-American, for example, is in danger of becoming an outdated myth. He no longer is representative of the present-day social pattern. The new reality is the mass-man, who can think only in collective categories, and who is afraid to trust his individual feelings. No menace to civilization can compare in frightfulness with the menace of mass psychosis which reaches its climax in national isolationism and megalomania. Rugged individualism has brought on rugged collectivism, and rugged collectivism in turn is bringing on Armageddon. To quote Charles A. Beard: "We have an immense amount of collectivism now even in normal times, and are fated to have more of it. If I know anything, I know that."

THE FATE OF JEWRY AS BAROMETER OF THE DEMOCRATIC PROCESS

What has all this to do with the fate of Jewry? The Jews were the one group in the Western world that was the most conspicuous beneficiary of the humaneness, the reasonableness, the sweetness and light which at first characterized free-enterprise democracy. From a harassed and hunted pariah folk they became almost overnight completely westernized freemen, holding their own in the keen competitive struggle let loose by the policy of *laissez faire*. They therefore presented a shining mark for attack by the sullen masses who began to gather for battle against free-enterprise democracy. Its economic sins and failures could easily be imputed to the Jews, since they flourished under it. They were a most opportune scapegoat for those who needed to divert from themselves the masses infuriated by fear, hunger, and frustration. When, therefore, all the pent-up discontents of the central European nations broke out in the madness of Fascism, the first and most helpless victims were the Jews.

The fate of Jewry has been an infallible barometer of the fate of democracy. As long as feudalism was in power and the democratic process was unknown, the Jews were a pariah people wandering from land to land. Under the reign of free-enterprise democracy, while geographic frontiers were still open, the Jews enjoyed political equality. As for economic equality, that has remained more or less limited. The result is that Jews are crowded into areas where their very numbers are an offense, and the sins of a few become the sins of all. As for social equality, that scarcely exists. These facts reflect very accurately the ambiguous character of free-enterprise democracy, from the standpoint of general human welfare. Nevertheless, in comparison with the conditions under which Jews had lived in pre-Emancipation days, even the qualified freedom they are permitted to enjoy is keenly appreciated by them. But now, with the advent of mass democracy, the Jews have been caught in the cross fire between the contending forces of the world. Mass democracy, turned into mass tyranny, likewise envisages a world that is *Judenrein*. It is thus the destiny of the Jews to warn the world that, unless the forces which have given rise to mass democracy be reckoned with in a spirit of understanding, and channeled within the embankments of inner freedom, reason, justice, and peace, they will bring on a deluge that will sweep away the human race.

It would be quixotic for the democratic nations to attempt the task of individuating the mass-man. Much of the talk about the dignity of the human person is intended to urge just that. The fact is that the only way in which that dignity will be restored to the human person will be by redeeming his gregariousness from the tendency to mob passion and mob hysteria. To bring that about, the first item on the program of genuine democracy has to be the creation of such security against want and unemployment as to make it unnecessary for any belligerent crowds to come into being for purposes of war, whether civil or international.

The nature and sincerity of such a program will be tested by the extent to which it will provide that the Jewish people, which, in proportion to its numbers and in terms of the unspeakable horrors to which it has been subjected, has been the most martyred people on earth, shall henceforth be allowed to live in peace and share all joys and sorrows, on an equal footing with the rest of the world. Every organized manifestation of anti-Semitism is part of the struggle of mass democracy which is led by the forces of aggression and violence. To fail to suppress anti-Semitism as soon as it is noted, is to fail to stamp out flames which are bound to break into a world conflagration.

At present, however, Jews are in a position to do more than merely reaffirm the truths of ancient prophecy and Torah, or merely serve as the barometer of democracy. To limit them to a passive role is neither good for them nor likely to redound to the benefit of mankind. A group, like an individual, to function normally must have an outlet for being active and exerting initiative, otherwise it is likely to deteriorate. It is significant, therefore, that one of the most remarkable by-products of the first attempt to organize world peace on a democratic foundation was the international act of handing over to Britain the mandate for Palestine, commissioning Britain to facilitate the establishment of a Jewish national home there. Despite the fact that Britain failed to live up to the provisions and the spirit of that mandate, the Jews who benefited from it succeeded in establishing the first bridgehead of genuine democracy in the Near East. The Jews of Israel have been building a welfare state and a new society which is seeking to avoid the mistakes of free-enterprise democracy as well as those of doctrinaire socialism. Once the Arab nations outgrow their intransigent hatred of Israel, they are likely to discover in her social democracy the solution to their own problems, both inner and outer. The State of Israel offers the Jewish People the unprecedented opportunity to be the vanguard of democracy where democracy is most needed for the peace of the world: at the crossroads of the three continents of the Eastern Hemisphere.

The position of Jews in the world is such that the nature of the Jewish contribution depends more upon what the non-Jews will let them be and do than upon the initiative of the Jews themselves. This is not intended to minimize the responsibility which devolves upon the Jews themselves. Despite all that they have undergone, they should be more than merely aware of the significance of their tradition of prophecy and Torah for the democratic world order. They should translate that tradition into living institutions in their own corporate life, and seek to demonstrate the beneficent influence of that tradition by the example of what they can achieve. The opportunity of translating that tradition into example is best afforded them in the State of Israel.

CHRISTIANITY

PART V

An adequate understanding of the Christian religion requires some acquaintance with several preceding cultural orientations which it absorbed and transformed into a novel synthesis within the first centuries of its existence. Although it is undoubtedly an oversimplification of the complex historical situation, scholars have ordinarily divided this cultural indebtedness into two major traditions—the Judaic and the Hellenistic. The former of these traditions has been much emphasized by Christian theologians, and even most lay Christians are aware of the continuity of Christianity with the Judaism from which it arose. The elements of the Judaic contribution to Christianity are exceedingly numerous, but the most important can be included under two headings: the Bible and Jesus. The Bible served the early Christians both as an official guide to divine revelation and as the major source of a private culture, morality, and tradition within a world which was first indifferent and subsequently hostile. The historical Jesus, however vague the details of his life may be, seems clearly to have been a teacher who derived most of the elements of his teaching from the Hebrew scriptures and from the practices of certain contemporary Judaic sects, especially the Essenes. His knowledge of Greek culture seems to have been negligible, and his concerns were primarily moral, in the tradition of the great Hebrew prophets.

However, the first Christians rather quickly transformed the historical Jesus into "Jesus Christ, God's Son, Our Saviour," in the words of a very early Christian formula. This transformation betrays the full importance of the Hellenistic contribution to early Christianity, which has been noted by many scholars but which has not yet received sufficient emphasis to warrant popular recognition. The language of Christianity was Greek, and Christian thought necessarily conformed to the Greek idiom and conceptual structure; a trivial instance of this conformity is present in the preceding formula, since in Greek the first letters of each word together spell "fish," a Christian symbol which antedates the cross. The concept of divine sonship is familiar in Greek mythology, as is the concept of the "Saviour-God," which had been popularized all over the Hellenistic world by a variety of mystery religions and cults. Indeed, the very concept of a "theology," a reasoned approach to religion dependent upon intelligent discussion rather than tradition, which played such

399

a large role in the formation of Christian thought, is thoroughly Greek in origin, being the legacy of the ancient Greek philosophers, especially Plato, and of the contemporary Stoic moral philosophy with which Christian doctrine was forced to compete. Even the moral teaching of Jesus was modified by doctrines derived from Stoic and neo-Platonic sources, whose presence is evident before the close of the New Testament period.

The new religion found its first strength among the slaves and the poorer classes of the Greco-Roman world, partially due to its otherworldly and millennial emphases. However, by A.D. 312 it had gained legal status in the Roman Empire through Constantine's Edict of Milan; and thereafter its influence grew still more rapidly. A thorough interpenetration of civil and religious authority developed as the original otherworldliness of Christian thought gradually was modified in accommodation to the new role of power and privilege. For example, it was as much for political and economic reasons as for theological ones that the Eastern Orthodox and Roman Churches grew further apart until they finally separated officially in 1054. A similar duality of motivating forces was at work in the events which brought about the separation of the various Protestant groups from the Roman Church during the Sixteenth Century and in the wars between those factions which followed thereafter.

The involvement of Christianity with social, political, and other secular concerns has continued, and its conscientious attention to those concerns has steadily increased, especially since the extensive criticism of the significance of theological and institutional dogmas which began in the Eighteenth Century and flourished in the first half of the nineteenth. Although the secularization of Christianity has been primarily a Protestant movement, it has not failed to have influence upon the Orthodox and Roman communions; and it may fairly be said to be the most characteristic tendency of recent Christian history. On the one hand, this transformation has taken the form of a "warfare between science and theology" which science obviously has been winning. Christianity has been the first major religion to feel the full impact of the challenge of modern science to traditional mythology and belief; as a consequence, its philosophical theology has become more and more occupied with the attempt to achieve a reasoned reconciliation of the claims of religion and of science, and its dogmatic theology has become progressively more apologetic. On the other hand, Christianity has also been moving in the direction of practice, taking religion out of the churches into an increasing involvement in social action, as is exemplified by the activities of religious groups in various forms of welfare programs, in civil rights movements, and in the search for world peace. This process has brought about a greater conformity between religion and the rest of contemporary society and a mutual adaptation of moral practices and ideals. Despite these tendencies, however, most of Christendom remains fairly conservative in its attitude toward science and society, so that its complete integration into modern life is undoubtedly a struggle which will not soon be completed. Theological movements opposed to the process of secularization, such as "neo-orthodoxy," continue to be highly influential.

Another major characteristic of recent Christianity is the growth of the ecumenical movement, which seeks to reverse the process of division and schism which has characterized the major portion of Christian history. In recent years, considerable unanimity has been realized among various Protestant denominations, and still more recently, signs of conciliation with the Orthodox and Roman Churches have multiplied. Nevertheless, the missionary spirit which has always characterized Christianity has continued to foster internal competition between diverse ecclesiastical organizations as well as with other major religions.

The foregoing factors make it rather difficult to characterize contemporary Christianity, for although the majority of Christians continue to place high value upon the traditional creedal affirmations and upon the ceremonies and rites of the Church, greater and greater numbers of them are either recasting these into drastically different forms or are abandoning the Church altogether to emphasize concerns which are more vital to them. The form which the final stage of this metamorphosis will take is not now apparent, but the readings in this section have been selected to illustrate the many complexities of the Christian heritage and thereby to throw some light upon its present predicament.

SUGGESTIONS FOR FURTHER READING

Danielou, Jean, *God and the Ways of Knowing*, Walter Roberts, trans., New York, Meridian Books, 1952.

Feuerbach, Ludwig, *The Essence of Christianity*, George Eliot, trans., New York, Harper & Row, 1957.

Gilson, *The Spirit of Medieval Philosophy*, A. H. C. Downes, trans., New York, Scribner, 1936.

Halverson, Marvin, and Cohen, Arthur A., eds., *A Handbook of Christian Theology*, New York, Meridian Books, Inc., 1958.

Harnack, Adolph von, *History of Dogma*, 4 vols., Neil Buchanan, trans., New York, Dover, 1961.

Latourette, Kenneth Scott, *A History of Christianity*, New York, Harper & Row, 1953.

Lewis, C. S., *The Screwtape Letters*, New York, Macmillan, 1950.

Tillich, Paul, *Systematic Theology*, 3 vols., Chicago, University of Chicago Press, 1951–1963.

Ware, Timothy, *The Orthodox Church*, Baltimore, Penguin, 1964.

BIBLE READING GUIDE FOR CHRISTIANITY

The following outline provides a representative selection from the literature of the New Testament. It would undoubtedly enhance the reader's appreciation of this material if he were familiar both with some of the Hebrew literature produced subsequent to the Old Testament and some of the characteristic emphases of Hellenistic thought. The former could be obtained by a sampling of the Apocryphal writings, of which an edition is cited in the bibliography on Judaism. The latter might be obtained by consulting a source book of Hellenistic thought, such as Gordon H. Clark, ed., *Selections from Hellenistic Philosophy* (New York, Appleton-Century-Crofts, 1940) or by reading a good history of philosophy, such as Émile Bréhier, *The Hellenistic and Roman Age*, Vol. II of *The History of Philosophy* (Chicago, University of Chicago, 1965).

I. The Story of Jesus: *Mark*
II. The Story of Jesus Interpreted: *John*
III. Early Christianity
    1. In Jerusalem: *Acts* 1–8:3
    2. In Samaria and Syria: *Acts* 8:4–12
    3. In the Greco-Roman World: *Acts* 13–28
IV. Pauline Christianity
    1. Theology: *Romans*
    2. Morality: *Ephesians, Titus, I Timothy, Philemon*
V. Hebraic Christianity: *James*
VI. Johannine Christianity: *I John*

THE MARTYRDOM OF ST. POLY-CARP, BISHOP OF SMYRNA

This document, contemporary with the event it describes (156) is the earliest extant account of a Christian martyrdom. All the evidence, both internal to the text and external, indicates that it is genuine. As well as being an excellent example of the swift transformation of history into legend, it is valuable because it illustrates the reaction of the early Christians to martyrdom, which was quite important in the formation of the Church. It has been said that the blood of the martyrs is the nourishment of the Church, and, to some degree, that seems to have been the case. In this story a reaction characterized by firm conviction in the face of adversity is depicted, resulting in a more complete dedication to the threatened cause than would have been the case if there were no persecution. Persecutions of the Christians served to unify them by deepening their trust in the divine and in their fellow believers, because the rest of the world appeared to be against them.

The Church of God which sojourns in Smyrna, to the Church of God which sojourns in Philomelium, and to all the sojournings of the Holy Catholic Church in every place. "Mercy, peace and love" of God the Father, and our Lord Jesus Christ be multiplied.

I

1. We write to you, brethren, the story of the martyrs and of the blessed Polycarp, who put an end to the persecution by his martyrdom as though adding the seal.[1] For one might almost say that all that had gone before hap-

Reprinted by permission of the publishers from Loeb Classical Library. Trans. by Kirsopp Lake from *The Apostolic Fathers.* Cambridge, Mass.: Harvard University Press, 1913.

[1] He was the last to suffer and thus might be regarded as being the seal to the "witness" or "testimony" (μαρτύριον) of the Church. It is not clear whether μαρτυρία and μαρτύριον ought to be translated "martyrdom" or "witness"; there is an untranslateable play on the words.

[2] Or perhaps "witness."

pened in order that the Lord might show to us from above a martyrdom[2] in accordance with the Gospel. 2. For he waited to be betrayed as also the Lord had done, that we too might become his imitators, "not thinking of ourselves alone, but also of our neighbours." For it is the mark of true and steadfast love, not to wish that oneself may be saved alone, but all the brethren also.

II

1. Blessed then and noble are all the martyrdoms which took place according to the will of God, for we must be very careful to assign the power over all to God. 2. For who would not admire their nobility and patience and love of their Master? For some were torn by scourging until the mechanism of their flesh was seen even to the lower veins and arteries, and they endured so that even the bystanders pitied them and mourned. And some even reached such a pitch of nobility that none of them groaned or wailed, showing to all of us that at that hour of their torture the noble martyrs of Christ were absent from the flesh, or rather that the Lord was standing by and talking with them. 3. And paying heed to the grace of Christ they despised worldly tortures, by a single hour purchasing everlasting life. And the fire of their cruel tortures had no heat for them, for they set before their eyes an escape from the fire which is everlasting and is never quenched, and with the eyes of their heart they looked up to the good things which are preserved for those who have endured, "which neither ear hath heard nor hath eye seen, nor hath it entered into the heart of man," but it was shown by the Lord to them who were no longer men but already angels. 4. And in the same way also those who were condemned to the beasts endured terrible torment, being stretched on sharp shells and buffeted with other kinds of various torments, that if it were possible the tyrant might bring them to a denial by continuous torture. For the devil used many wiles against them.

III

1. But thanks be to God, for he had no power over any. For the most noble Germanicus encouraged their fears by the endurance which was in him, and he fought gloriously with the wild beasts. For when the Pro-Consul wished to persuade him and bade him have pity on his youth, he violently dragged the beast towards himself, wishing to be released more quickly from their unrighteous and lawless life. 2. So after this all the crowd, wondering at the nobility of the God-loving and God-fearing people of the Christians, cried out: "Away with the Atheists; let Polycarp be searched for."

IV

1. But one, named Quintus, a Phrygian lately come from Phrygia, when he saw the wild beasts played the coward. Now it was he who had forced himself and some others to come forward of their own accord. Him the Pro-Consul persuaded with many entreaties to take the oath and offer

sacrifice. For this reason, therefore, brethren, we do not commend those who give themselves up, since the Gospel does not give this teaching.

V

1. But the most wonderful Polycarp, when he first heard it, was not disturbed, but wished to remain in the city; but the majority persuaded him to go away quietly, and he went out quietly to a farm, not far distant from the city, and stayed with a few friends, doing nothing but pray night and day for all, and for the Churches throughout the world, as was his custom. 2. And while he was praying he fell into a trance three days before he was arrested, and saw the pillow under his head burning with fire, and he turned and said to those who were with him: "I must be burnt alive."

VI

1. And when the searching for him persisted he went to another farm; and those who were searching for him came up at once, and when they did not find him, they arrested young slaves, and one of them confessed under torture. 2. For it was indeed impossible for him to remain hid, since those who betrayed him were of his own house, and the police captain who had been allotted the very name, being called Herod, hastened to bring him to the arena that he might fulfil his appointed lot by becoming a partaker of Christ, while they who betrayed him should undergo the same punishment as Judas.

VII

1. Taking the slave then police and cavalry went out on Friday about supper-time, with their usual arms, as if they were advancing against a robber. And late in the evening they came up together against him and found him lying in an upper room. And he might have departed to another place, but would not, saying, "the will of God be done." 2. So when he heard that they had arrived he went down and talked with them, while those who were present wondered at his age and courage, and whether there was so much haste for the arrest of an old man of such a kind. Therefore he ordered food and drink to be set before them at that hour, whatever they should wish, and he asked them to give him an hour to pray without hindrance. 3. To this they assented, and he stood and prayed—thus filled with the grace of God—so that for two hours he could not be silent, and those who listened were astounded, and many repented that they had come against such a venerable old man.

VIII

1. Now when he had at last finished his prayer, after remembering all who had ever even come his way, both small and great, high and low, and the whole Catholic Church throughout the world, the hour came for departure, and they set him on an ass, and led him into the city, on a "great Sabbath

day."[3] 2. And the police captain Herod and his father Niketas met him and removed him into their carriage, and sat by his side trying to persuade him and saying: "But what harm is it to say, 'Lord Caesar,' and to offer sacrifice, and so forth, and to be saved?" But he at first did not answer them, but when they continued he said: "I am not going to do what you counsel me." 3. And they gave up the attempt to persuade him, and began to speak fiercely to him, and turned him out in such a hurry that in getting down from the carriage he scraped his shin; and without turning round, as though he had suffered nothing, he walked on promptly and quickly, and was taken to the arena, while the uproar in the arena was so great that no one could even be heard.

IX

1. Now when Polycarp entered into the arena there came a voice from heaven: "Be strong, Polycarp, and play the man." And no one saw the speaker, but our friends who were there heard the voice. And next he was brought forward, and there was a great uproar of those who heard that Polycarp had been arrested. 2. Therefore when he was brought forward the Pro-Consul asked him if he were Polycarp, and when he admitted it he tried to persuade him to deny, saying: "Respect your age," and so forth, as they are accustomed to say: "Swear by the genius of Caesar, repent, say: 'Away with the Atheists,'"; but Polycarp, with a stern countenance looked on all the crowd of lawless heathen in the arena, and waving his hand at them, he groaned and looked up to heaven and said: "Away with the Atheists." 3. But when the Pro-Consul pressed him and said: "Take the oath and I let you go, revile Christ," Polycarp said: "For eighty and six years have I been his servant, and he has done me no wrong, and how can I blaspheme my King who saved me?"

X

1. But when he persisted again, and said: "Swear by the genius of Caesar," he answered him: "If you vainly suppose that I will swear by the genius of Caesar, as you say, and pretend that you are ignorant who I am, listen plainly: I am a Christian. And if you wish to learn the doctrine of Christianity fix a day and listen." 2. The Pro-Consul said: "Persuade the people." And Polycarp said: "You I should have held worthy of discussion, for we have been taught to render honour, as is meet, if it hurt us not, to princes and authorities appointed by God. But as for those, I do not count them worthy that a defence should be made to them."

XI

1. And the Pro-Consul said: "I have wild beasts, I will deliver you to them, unless you repent." And he said: "Call for them, for repentance from

---

[3] This may have been the Jewish feast Purim, which, according to tradition, celebrates the triumph of the Jews in Persia over their enemies, as is related in the book of Esther, or else the Sabbath in the Passover week.

better to worse is not allowed us; but it is good to change from evil to right-eousness." 2. And he said again to him: "I will cause you to be consumed by fire, if you despise the beasts, unless you repent." But Polycarp said: "You threaten with the fire that burns for a time, and is quickly quenched, for you do not know the fire which awaits the wicked in the judgment to come and in everlasting punishment. But why are you waiting? Come, do what you will."

XII

1. And with these and many other words he was filled with courage and joy, and his face was full of grace so that it not only did not fall with trouble at the things said to him, but that the Pro-Consul, on the other hand, was astounded and sent his herald into the midst of the arena to announce three times: "Polycarp has confessed that he is a Christian." 2. When this had been said by the herald, all the multitude of heathen and Jews living in Smyrna cried out with uncontrollable wrath and a loud shout: "This is the teacher of Asia, the father of the Christians, the destroyer of our Gods, who teaches many neither to offer sacrifice nor to worship." And when they said this, they cried out and asked Philip the Asiarch to let loose a lion on Poly-carp. But he said he could not legally do this, since he had closed the Sports. 3. Then they found it good to cry out with one mind that he should burn Polycarp alive, for the vision which had appeared to him on his pillow must be fulfilled, when he saw it burning, while he was praying, and he turned and said prophetically to those of the faithful who were with him, "I must be burnt alive."

XIII

1. These things then happened with so great speed, quicker than it takes to tell, and the crowd came together immediately, and prepared wood and faggots from the work-shops and baths and the Jews were extremely zeal-ous, as is their custom, in assisting at this. 2. Now when the fire was ready he put off all his clothes, and loosened his girdle and tried also to take off his shoes, though he did not do this before, because each of the faithful was al-ways zealous, which of them might the more quickly touch his flesh. For he had been treated with all respect because of his noble life, even before his martyrdom. 3. Immediately therefore, he was fastened to the instruments which had been prepared for the fire, but when they were going to nail him as well he said: "Leave me thus, for He who gives me power to endure the fire, will grant me to remain in the flames unmoved even without the security you will give by the nails."

XIV

1. So they did not nail him, but bound him, and he put his hands be-hind him and was bound, as a noble ram out of a great flock, for an oblation,

a whole burnt offering made ready and acceptable to God; and he looked up to heaven and said: "O Lord God Almighty, Father of thy beloved and blessed Child, Jesus Christ, through Whom we have received full knowledge of thee, the God of Angels and powers, and of all creation, and of the whole family of the righteous, who live before thee! 2. I bless thee, that Thou hast granted me this day and hour, that I may share, among the number of the martyrs, in the cup of thy Christ, for the Resurrection to everlasting life, both of soul and body in the immortality of the Holy Spirit. And may I, to-day, be received among them before Thee, as a rich and acceptable sacrifice, as Thou, the God who lies not and is truth, hast prepared beforehand, and shown forth, and fulfilled. 3. For this reason I also praise Thee for all things, I bless Thee, I glorify Thee through the everlasting and heavenly high Priest, Jesus Christ, thy beloved Child, through whom be glory to Thee with him and the Holy Spirit, both now and for the ages that are to come, Amen."

XV

1. Now when he had uttered his Amen and finished his prayer, the men in charge of the fire lit it, and a great flame blazed up and we, to whom it was given to see, saw a marvel. And we have been preserved to report to others what befell. 2. For the fire made the likeness of a room, like the sail of a vessel filled with wind, and surrounded the body of the martyr as with a wall, and he was within it not as burning flesh, but as bread that is being baked, or as gold and silver being refined in a furnace. And we perceived such a fragrant smell as the scent of incense or other costly spices.

XVI

1. At length the lawless men, seeing that his body could not be consumed by the fire, commanded an executioner to go up and stab him with a dagger, and when he did this, there came out a dove, and much blood, so that the fire was quenched and all the crowd marvelled that there was such a difference between the unbelievers and the elect. 2. And of the elect was he indeed one, the wonderful martyr Polycarp, who in our days was an apostolic and prophetic teacher, bishop of the Catholic[4] Church in Smyrna. For every word which he uttered from his mouth both was fulfilled and will be fulfilled.

XVII

1. But the jealous and envious evil one who resists the family of the righteous, when he saw the greatness of his martyrdom, and his blameless career from the beginning, and that he was crowned with the crown of immortality, and had carried off the unspeakable prize, took care that not even his poor body should be taken away by us, though many desired to do so, and to have fellowship with his holy flesh. 2. Therefore he put forward Niketas, the father of Herod, and the brother of Alce, to ask the Governor not to give

---

[4] If the reading "Catholic" be right, it is the earliest clear example of this use of the word (but cf. Ignatius, *Symrn.* viii.).

his body, "Lest," he said, "they leave the crucified one and begin to worship this man." And they said this owing to the suggestions and pressure of the Jews, who also watched when we were going to take it from the fire, for they do not know that we shall not ever be able either to abandon Christ, who suffered for the salvation of those who are being saved in the whole world, the innocent for sinners, or to worship any other. 3. For him we worship as the Son of God, but the martyrs we love as disciples and imitators of the Lord; and rightly, because of their unsurpassable affection toward their own King and Teacher. God grant that we too may be their companions and fellow-disciples.

XVIII

1. When therefore the centurion saw the contentiousness caused by the Jews, he put the body in the midst, as was their custom, and burnt it. 2. Thus we, at last, took up his bones, more precious than precious stones, and finer than gold, and put them where it was meet. 3. There the Lord will permit us to come together according to our power in gladness and joy, and celebrate the birthday of his martyrdom, both in memory of those who have already contested,[5] and for the practice and training of those whose fate it shall be.

XIX

1. Such was the lot of the blessed Polycarp, who though he was, together with those from Philadelphia, the twelfth martyr in Smyrna, is alone especially remembered by all, so that he is spoken of in every place, even by the heathen. He was not only a famous teacher, but also a notable martyr, whose martyrdom all desire to imitate, for it followed the Gospel of Christ. 2. By his endurance he overcame the unrighteous ruler, and thus gained the crown of immortality, and he is glorifying God and the Almighty Father, rejoicing with the Apostles and all the righteous, and he is blessing our Lord Jesus Christ, the Saviour of our souls, and Governor of our bodies, and the Shepherd of the Catholic Church throughout the world.

XX

1. You, indeed, asked that the events should be explained to you at length, but we have for the present explained them in summary by our brother Marcion; therefore when you have heard these things, send the letter to the brethren further on, that they also may glorify the Lord, who takes his chosen ones from his own servants.

2. And to him who is able to bring us all in his grace and bounty, to his heavenly kingdom, by his only begotten Child, Jesus Christ, be glory, honour, might, and majesty for ever. Greet all the saints. Those who are with us, and Evarestus, who wrote the letter, with his whole house, greet you.

[5] This is almost a technical term for martyrdom, cf. Ignatius's epistle to Polycarp 1, 3.

XXI

1. Now the blessed Polycarp was martyred on the second day of the first half of the month of Xanthicus, the seventh day before the kalends of March, a great sabbath, at the eighth hour. And he was arrested by Herod, when Philip of Tralles was High Priest, when Statius Quadratus was Pro-Consul, but Jesus Christ was reigning for ever, to whom be glory, honour, majesty and an eternal throne, from generation to generation, Amen.

XXII

1. We bid you God-speed, brethren, who walk according to the Gospel, in the word of Jesus Christ (with whom be glory to God and the Father and the Holy Spirit), for the salvation of the Holy Elect, even as the blessed Polycarp suffered martyrdom, in whose footsteps may it be granted us to be found in the Kingdom of Jesus Christ.

2. Gaius copied this from the writing of Irenaeus, a disciple of Polycarp, and he lived with Irenaeus, and I, Socrates, wrote it out in Corinth, from the copies of Gaius. Grace be with you all. 3. And I, again, Pionius, wrote it out from the former writings, after searching for it, because the blessed Polycarp showed it me in a vision, as I will explain in what follows,[6] and I gathered it together when it was almost worn out by age, that the Lord Jesus Christ may also gather me together with his elect into his heavenly kingdom, to whom be glory with the Father and the Holy Spirit, for ever and ever, Amen.

39

ON PAGAN LITERATURE
Basil of Caesarea

St. Basil the Great (330–379) was born in Cappadocia and educated in Constantinople and at Athens, where the Greek Classics constituted the major part of the curriculum. Having become a convert to the blossoming ascetic movement within Christianity,

Reprinted by permission of the publishers from Loeb Classical Library. Trans. by Roy J. Deferrari and Martin R. P. McGuire from Saint Basil, The Letters. Cambridge, Mass.: Harvard University Press, 1934.

6 No explanation is given: probably because the "Pionian" text was part of a larger "Acts of Polycarp." Either these Acts have entirely disappeared except for this letter of the church of Smyrna, or a fragment preserved in p may perhaps belong to them.

Basil traveled to Egypt to become acquainted with monasticism at first hand. He subsequently became the great advocate for monasticism in eastern Christendom, popularizing the cenobitic variety of monasticism throughout Asia Minor. Tradition holds him to be the author of the Rule of St. Basil, which emphasizes work, spiritual devotions, and helpfulness to those outside the monasteries, and which continues to be the basic foundation of monasticism in the Eastern Church. Despite his monasticism, however, Basil was not one to sever himself from the great issues of his day, and he fought vigorously for causes which he deemed worthwhile. Moreover, after his appointment as the bishop of Caesarea in Cappadocia (370), he possessed sufficient influence and power to make his efforts felt. He, together with his Cappadocian associates, Gregory of Nazianzus (c. 329–c. 389) and Gregory of Nyssa (c. 331–c. 396), worked for the unification of the Church under the Nicene creed, including its implications as well as its explicit pronouncements. Basil was noted for his ability as an administrator and church politician, and also for his eloquent preaching and writing. In the present selection, the best known of all his many works, he displays those talents, as well as his knowledge of Greek literature, in pleading with the Christian youth for greater discernment in their reading of classical secular literature. This essay, probably composed late in his career, advocates an appraisal of the classics based upon balanced judgment employing moral criteria, rather than the more sweeping rejection espoused by some of his contemporaries.

BASIL THE GREAT'S TO YOUNG MEN, ON HOW THEY MIGHT DERIVE PROFIT FROM PAGAN LITERATURE

I. There are many considerations which urge me to counsel you, my children, on what things I judge to be best, and on those which I am confident, if you accept them, will be to your advantage. For the fact that I have reached this age, and have already been trained through many experiences, and indeed also have shared sufficiently in the all-teaching vicissitude of both good and evil fortune, has made me conversant with human affairs, so that I can indicate the safest road, as it were, to those who are just entering upon life. Moreover, I come immediately after your parents in natural relationship to you, so that I myself entertain for you no less good-will than do your fathers; and I am sure, unless I am somewhat wrong in my judgment of you, that you do not long for your parents when your eyes rest upon me. If, then, you should receive my words with eagerness, you will belong to the second class of those praised by Hesiod;[1] but should you not do so, I indeed should

[1] "That man is altogether best who considers all things himself and marks what will be better afterwards and at the end; and he, again, is good who listens to a good adviser; but whoever neither thinks for himself nor keeps in mind what another tells him, he is an unprofitable man." Trans. by H. G. Evelyn-White in L.C.L.

not like to say anything unpleasant, but do you of yourselves remember the verses in which he says: "Best is the man who sees of himself at once what must be done, and excellent is he too who follows what is well indicated by others, but he who is suited for neither is useless in all respects."

Do not think it strange, then, if I say to you, who each day resort to teachers and hold converse with the famous men of the ancients through the words which they have left behind them, that I myself have discovered something of especial advantage to you. This it is, and naught else, that I have come to offer you as my counsel—that you should not surrender to these men once for all the rudders of your mind, as if of a ship, and follow them whithersoever they lead; rather, accepting from them only that which is useful, you should know that which ought to be overlooked. What, therefore, these things are, and how we shall distinguish between them, is the lesson which I shall teach you from this point on.

II. We, my children, in no wise conceive this human life of ours to be an object of value in any respect, nor do we consider anything good at all, or so designate it, which makes its contribution to this life of ours only. Therefore neither renown of ancestry, nor strength of body, nor beauty, nor stature, nor honours bestowed by all mankind, nor kingship itself, nor other human attribute that one might mention, do we judge great, nay, we do not even consider them worth praying for, nor do we look with admiration upon those who possess them, but our hopes lead us forward to a more distant time, and everything we do is by way of preparation for the other life. Whatever, therefore, contributes to that life, we say must be loved and pursued with all our strength; but what does not conduce to that must be passed over as of no account. Now just what this life is, and how and in what manner we shall live it, would take too long to discuss in view of our present purpose, and would be for the more mature to hear than for hearers of your age. After saying this much at least, I may perhaps be able to show you that if one sums up all the happiness together from the time men have first existed and collects it into one whole, he will find that it is equivalent not even to a trivial part of those other goods, but that the total of the goods of the present life is more removed in value from the least among the former goods of the other life than shadows and dreams fall short of reality. Nay, rather—that I may use a more suitable illustration—to the degree that the soul is more precious than the body in all respects, so great is the difference between the two lives. Now to that other life the Holy Scriptures lead the way, teaching us through mysteries. Yet so long as, by reason of your age, it is impossible for you to understand the depth of the meaning of these, in the meantime, by means of other analogies which are not entirely different, we give, as it were in shadows and reflections, a preliminary training to the eye of the soul, imitating those who perform their drills in military tactics, who, after they have gained experience by means of gymnastic exercises for the arms and dance-steps for the feet, enjoy when it comes to the combat the profit derived from what was done in sport. So we also must consider that a contest, the greatest of all contests, lies before us, for which we must do all things, and, in preparation for it, must strive to the best of our power, and must associate with poets and writers of prose and orators and with all men from whom there is any prospect of benefit with reference to the care of our soul. Therefore, just as dyers first prepare by certain treatments whatever material is to receive the dye, and then apply the colour, whether it be purple or some other hue, so we also in the same manner must first, if the glory of the good is to abide with us indelible for all time, be instructed by these outside means, and then shall understand the sacred and mystical teachings; and like those who have become accustomed to seeing the reflection of the sun in water, so we shall then direct our eyes to the light itself.

III. Now if there is some affinity between the two bodies of teachings, knowledge of them should be useful to us; but if not, at least the fact that by setting them side by side we can discover the difference between them, is of no small importance for strengthening the position of the better. And yet with what can you compare the two systems of education and hit upon the true similitude? Perhaps, just as it is the proper virtue of a tree to be laden with beautiful fruit, although it also wears like a fair raiment leaves that wave about its branches, so likewise the fruit of the soul, the truth is primarily its fruitage, yet it is clad in the certainly not unlovely raiment even of the wisdom drawn from the outside, which we may liken to foliage that furnishes both protection to the fruit and an aspect not devoid of beauty. Now it is said that even Moses, that illustrious man whose name for wisdom is greatest among all mankind, first trained his mind in the learning of the Egyptians, and then proceeded to the contemplation of Him who is. And like him, although in later times, they say that the wise Daniel at Babylon first learned the wisdom of the Chaldaeans and then applied himself to the divine teachings.

IV. But that this pagan learning is not without usefulness for the soul has been sufficiently affirmed; yet just how you should participate in it would be the next topic to be discussed.

First, then, as to the learning to be derived from the poets, that I may begin with them, inasmuch as the subjects they deal with are of every kind, you ought not to give your attention to all they write without exception; but whenever they recount for you the deeds or words of good men, you ought to cherish and emulate these and try to be as far as possible like them; but when they treat of wicked men, you ought to avoid such imitation, stopping your ears no less than Odysseus did, according to what those same poets say, when he avoided the songs of the Sirens. For familiarity with evil words is, as it were, a road leading to evil deeds. On this account, then, the soul must be watched over with all vigilance, lest through the pleasure the poets' words give we may unwittingly accept something of the more evil sort, like those who take poisons along with honey. We shall not, therefore, praise the poets when they revile or mock, or when they depict men engaged in amours or drunken, or when they define happiness in terms of an over-abundant table or dissolute

songs. But least of all shall we give attention to them when they narrate anything about the gods, and especially when they speak of them as being many,
and these too not even in accord with one another. For in their poems brother
is at feud with brother, and father with children, and the latter in turn are
engaged in truceless war with their parents. But the adulteries of gods and
their amours and their sexual acts in public, and especially those of Zeus, the
chief and highest of all, as they themselves describe him, actions which one
would blush to mention of even brute beasts—all these we shall leave to the
stage-folk.

These same observations I must make concerning the writers of prose
also, and especially when they fabricate tales for the entertainment of their
hearers. And we shall certainly not imitate the orators in their art of lying.
For neither in courts of law nor in other affairs is lying befitting to us, who
have chosen the right and true way of life, and to whom refraining from liti-
gation has been ordained in commandment. But we shall take rather those
passages of theirs in which they have praised virtue or condemned vice. For just
as in the case of other beings enjoyment of flowers is limited to their fragrance
and colour, but the bees, as we see, possess the power to get honey from them
as well, so it is possible here also for those who are pursuing not merely what
is sweet and pleasant in such writings to store away from them some benefit
also for their souls. It is, therefore, in accordance with the whole similitude of
the bees, that we should participate in the pagan literature. For these neither
approach all flowers equally, nor in truth do they attempt to carry off entire
those upon which they alight, but taking only so much of them as is suitable
for their work, they suffer the rest to go untouched. We ourselves too, if we are
wise, having appropriated from this literature what is suitable to us and akin
to the truth, will pass over the remainder. And just as in plucking the blooms
from a rose-bed we avoid the thorns, so also in garnering from such writings
whatever is useful, let us guard ourselves against what is harmful. At the very
outset, therefore, we should examine each of the branches of knowledge and
adapt it to our end, according to the Doric proverb, "bringing the stone to the
line."

VIII. But let us return again to the same subject of which we were
speaking at the beginning: we ought not to take everything without exception,
but only such matter as is useful. For it is disgraceful to reject foods that are
harmful, yet for the teachings which nourish our souls to have no concern, but
to charge onward like a mountain torrent, carrying along everything it chances
upon. And further, what sense or reason is there that a pilot does not heed-
lessly give over his ship to the winds, but steers it to harbour, or that a bowman
shoots at a mark, or indeed, that any bronzesmith or worker in wood strives for
the end proper to his craft, but that we should fall behind even such artisans,
in respect at least to the ability to perceive our own interests? For can it be that
handicraftsmen have some end in view in their work, but that there is no goal
for the life of man, keeping his eye upon which that man at least, who does

not intend to be wholly similar to the brute beasts, ought to do and say whatever he does or says? In that case we should really be like ships without ballast, if we had no intellect sitting at the steering-oars of the soul, being tossed up and down aimlessly through life. On the contrary, it is just as in the athletic contests, or, if you prefer, the competitions in music: there are practice exercises in preparation for those contests in which the prize offered is a crown, and no one who is training for the wrestling-match or the pancratium takes to practising on the lyre or flute. Certainly Polydamas did no such thing, but before the contest at Olympia he practised bringing speeding chariots to a stop, and by this means was wont to enhance his strength. And Milo could not be pushed away from his greased shield, but held out against the pushing no less firmly than those statues hold which are fastened to their bases with lead. And, in a word, their exercises were a preparation for the games. But if they had wasted their time on the airs of Marsyas or Olympus the Phrygians, abandoning the rust and the exercise of the gymnasia, would they soon have obtained crowns or glory, or would they have escaped incurring ridicule for their physical condition? Neither, on the other hand, did Timotheus neglect his composition of chorals and spend his time in the wrestling-schools. For had he done so it would not have been possible for him so far to excel all men in the musical art that he could arouse the passions through his vehement and severe harmony and yet, on the other hand, through his relaxed and sensuous strains, mollify and allay them again, whenever he willed. It was by such art that once, when he was playing the Phrygian mode to Alexander on his flute, he caused the prince, as it is said, to leap up and rush to his arms in the midst of a banquet, and then, by relaxing the harmony, brought him back again to his boon companions. So great is the power, in both music and the athletic contests, produced by practice directed towards the attainment of the end in view.

And since I have made mention of crowns and athletes, let me add that these men, after enduring toils by the thousand, and after increasing their strength by every possible means, after shedding much sweat in the labours of the gymnasium, and taking many blows at the school of the physical trainer, and choosing, not the pleasantest fare, but that which the gymnastic masters had prescribed, and in all other ways (that I may not waste time by enumerating them) so passing their days that their life before the contest might be a preparation for the contest, then, when the moment comes, they strip for the race, undergo all hardships and run all risks, so as to receive a crown of wild olive or of parsley or of some such thing, all that they may win the victory and have their name proclaimed by the herald. But as for us, before whom are set for the life we lead prizes so marvellous in multitude and in grandeur that they cannot be described in words, if we sleep on both ears and live lives of abundant licence, will it be possible for us to reach out and seize them with one hand? In that event slothfulness would be of great value for living, and the Sardanapalus would carry off the highest prizes of all as regards happiness, or even Margites, who was neither a ploughman nor a digger nor anything else useful in life, as Homer said—if indeed this work is really Homer's. Yet is not rather the saying of Pittacus true, that "it is hard to be good"? For though we pass through many toils that are really toils, we can scarcely succeed in obtaining those goods of which, as we have already said above, no human goods can serve as an example. Therefore we ought not to idle away our time, nor for an ease that can last but a short while give up in exchange glorious hopes—that is, if we are not to be reproached and to incur retributions; I do not mean any that are inflicted here among men, although even that is no slight matter to a man of sense, but in the places of punishment, whether these are under the earth or wheresoever in the universe they may happen to be. Since, in the case of one who fails involuntarily in his duty, some degree of pardon may perhaps be granted by God; but for him who has deliberately chosen the worse course in life there is no excuse that will save him from suffering the punishment many times over.

IX. What, then, shall we do? someone may ask. What else, indeed, than devote ourselves to the care of our souls, keeping all our leisure free from other things. Accordingly, we should not be slaves of the body, except so far as is strictly necessary; but our souls we should supply with all things that are best, through philosophy freeing them, as from a prison, from association with the passions of the body, and at the same time making the body likewise master of the passions, supplying the belly with what it cannot do without, but not with sweet dainties as those do who look everywhere for table-dressers and cooks and scour every land and sea, bringing tribute, as it were, to a stern master, pitiable objects because of their ceaseless activity, and suffering not a whit more tolerable pains than those who are chastised in Hades by being forced actually to card wool into a fire, fetch water in a sieve, or to pour it into a perforated jar, having labour which never ends. And to spend one's time, beyond what is necessary, on the care of the hair or on dress, is, according to the saying of Diogenes, the mark of men who are either unfortunate or doing wrong. Hence, to be a dandy and get the name of being one ought, I maintain, to be considered by persons so inclined just as disgraceful as to keep company with harlots or to seduce other men's wives. For what difference should it make, at least to a man of sense, whether he is clothed in a costly robe or wears a cheap workman's cloak, so long as what he has on gives adequate protection against the cold of winter and the heat of summer? And in all other matters likewise, one ought not to be furnished out more elaborately than need requires, nor to be more solicitous for the body than is good for the soul. For it is no less a reproach to a man, who is truly worthy of that appellation, to be a dandy and a pamperer of the body than to be ignoble in his attitude towards any other vice. For to take all manner of pains that his body may be as beautiful as possible is not the mark of a man who either knows himself or understands that wise precept: "That which is seen is not the man, but there is need of a certain higher wisdom which will enable each of us, whoever he is, to recognize himself." But unless we have purified our minds this is more impossible for us than for a blear-eyed man to gaze at the sun.

Now purification of the soul—that I may speak in general terms and in a manner sufficient for your understanding—consists in scorning the pleasures that arise through the senses, in not feasting the eyes on the silly exhibitions of jugglers or on the sight of bodies which gives the spur to sensual pleasure, in not permitting licentious songs to enter through the ears and drench your souls. For passions sprung of lack of breeding and baseness are naturally engendered by this kind of music. But we should cultivate that other kind, which is better and leads to the better, through his use of which, as they say, David, the poet of the Sacred Songs, freed the king from his madness. And it is related that Pythagoras too, chancing upon some drunken revellers, commanded the flute-player who led the revel to change his harmony and play to them the Doric mode; and that thus the company came back to its senses under the influence of the strain, so that, tearing off their garlands, they went home ashamed. Yet others at the sound of the flute act like Corybantes and are excited to Bacchic frenzy. Such is the difference between giving full ear to wholesome and to licentious music. Hence, since this latter is now in vogue, you should participate in it less than in the very basest of things. Furthermore, the mixing with the air of all manner of vapours that bring pleasure to the sense of smell, or the smearing of the body with perfumes, I am ashamed even to forbid. And what can one say about the importance of not cultivating the pleasures associated with the senses of touch and taste than that these compel those who are devoted to their pursuit to live, like animals, with all their attention centred upon the belly and the members below it?

But, in a single word, the body in every part should be despised by everyone who does not care to be buried in its pleasures, as it were in slime; or we ought to cleave to it only in so far as we obtain from it service for the pursuit of wisdom, as Plato advises, speaking in a manner somewhat similar to Paul's when he admonishes us to make no provision for the body unto the arousing of concupiscences. Or in what way do those differ, who are solicitous how the body may be as well off as possible, but overlook the soul, which is to make use of it, as utterly worthless, from those who are much concerned about their implements but neglect the art which uses them for its work? Hence we must do quite the opposite—chastise the body and hold it in check, as we do the violent chargings of a wild beast, and by smiting with reason, as with a whip, the disturbances engendered by it in the soul, calm them to sleep; instead of relaxing every curb upon pleasure and suffering the mind to be swept headlong, like a charioteer by unmanageable horses riotously running at large. And we ought to recall Pythagoras, who, on perceiving that one of his followers was putting on superfluous flesh by exercises and heavy eating, said to him, "Pray cease making your prison-house more wretched for you to live in!" It was for this reason, in fact, that Plato also, as we are told, providing against the harmful influence of the body, deliberately occupied the pestilential region in Attica, the Academy, in order that he might prune away, as one prunes the vine of its excessive growth, the too great well-being of his body. And I myself have heard physicians say that extreme good health is even dangerous.

Since, then, such excessive concern for the body is not only unprofitable to the body itself but also a hindrance to the soul, that it should be subject to the body and be its servant is sheer madness. Yet surely, if we should make it a practice to despise the body, we should be slow, methinks, to feel admiration for any other thing that man may possess. For to what end shall we go on employing wealth if we scorn the pleasures arising through the body? As for me, I do not see, except that it might furnish us with a sort of pleasure to keep awake at night guarding, like the dragons of mythology, buried treasures! Assuredly, however, that man who has been trained to regard such goods as a freeman should would be quite unlikely ever to choose anything base or shameful in word or deed. For that which is in excess of any need, even if it be the gold-dust of Lydia or the wealth of the gold-gathering ants, he will despise all the more the less he needs it; and "need" itself he will, of course, define in terms of the requirements of nature and not in terms of pleasure. For those who go beyond the bounds of necessity are like men who rush headlong down a slope and, being unable to bring up against any firm object, find it impossible to halt at any point their onward impetus; nay, the more they gather in to themselves the more they require that much, or even a greater amount, for the fulfilment of their desires, according to Solon son of Execestides, who declares: "Of wealth no limit lies revealed to men." And we ought to use Theognis as a teacher in these matters, when he says: "I am not eager to be rich, nor do I pray for this, but may it be mine to live on little, suffering no evil."

And I admire also the scorn of Diogenes for all human goods without exception, who declared himself richer than the Great King by reason of the fact that he needed less for living than the King. But for us of to-day, it would seem, nothing will suffice except all the talents of Pythias the Mysian, and so-and-so many acres of land, and herds of cattle past numbering. But, in my opinion, we ought not to long for wealth if it be lacking, and, if we have it, we should not pride ourselves so much on its possession as on the knowledge that it is being put to good uses. For the saying of Socrates is well put. He, when a wealthy man was manifesting great pride in his riches, said that he would not admire him before he had found out by trial that he also knew how to use them. Would not Pheidias and Polycleitus, one of whom made the Zeus for the Elians and the other the Hera for the Argives, if they had prided themselves greatly on the gold and the ivory in them, have been objects of derision for glorying in a wealth not their own, passing over the art which enabled them to render the gold both more pleasing and more precious; but if we suppose that human virtue is not sufficient to itself for an adornment, do we imagine that what we are doing merits a lesser shame than would have been theirs?

But, forsooth, are we to despise wealth and have contempt for the pleasures of the senses, and yet go seeking for flattery and adulation, and imitate the shiftiness and cunning of the fox of Archilochus? On the contrary, there is nothing which a prudent man must shun more carefully than living with a view to popularity and giving serious thought to the things esteemed by the multitude, instead of making sound reason his guide of life, so that, even if he must gainsay all men and fall into disrepute and incur danger for the sake of what is honourable, he will in no wise choose to swerve from what has been recognized as right. Or in what respect shall we say that a person of so unstable a character differs from the Egyptian mountebank who, whenever he wished, became a plant, or a wild beast, or fire or water or anything else, if in sooth he himself is at one time to praise justice when in the presence of those who esteem that, but will at another time take quite the opposite position whenever he perceives that injustice is held in honour—as is the way of flatterers? And just as the polyp, they say, changes its colour to match the ground on which it lies, so will he change his mind according to the opinions of those about him.

X. But although we Christians shall doubtless learn all these things more thoroughly in our own literature, yet for the present, at least, let us trace out a kind of rough sketch, as it were, of what virtue is according to the teaching of the pagans. For by those who make it their business to gather the benefit to be derived from each source many accretions from many sides are wont to be received, as happens to mighty rivers. Indeed we are entitled to consider that the poet's saying about "adding little to little" holds good no more for increment of money than it does for increment in respect of knowledge of any kind whatever. Bias, for instance, when he was asked by his son, who was about to depart for Egypt, what he could do that would gratify him most, replied: "By acquiring travel-supplies for your old age," meaning by "travel-supplies" virtue, no doubt, though the terms in which he defined it were too narrow, seeing that he limited to human life the benefit to be derived from virtue. But as for me, if anyone should mention the old age of Tithonus, or that of Arganthonius, or of Mathusala, whose life was the longest of any man's (for he is said to have lived a thousand years lacking thirty), or if anyone reckons up all the time which has elapsed since men have existed, I shall laugh thereat as at a childish idea when I gaze towards that long and ageless eternity whose limit the mind can in no wise grasp any more than it can conceive an end for the immortal soul. It is for this eternity that I would exhort you to acquire travel-supplies, leaving no stone unturned, as the proverb has it, wherever any benefit towards that end is likely to accrue to you. And because this is difficult and calls for toil, let us not on this account draw back, but recalling the words of him who urged that every man should choose the life which is in itself best, in the expectation that through habit it will prove agreeable, we should attempt the best things. For it would be disgraceful that we, having thrown away the present opportunity, should at some later time attempt to summon back the past when all our vexation will gain us nothing.

Accordingly, of the things which in my judgment are best, some I have told you at this time, while others I shall continue to recommend to you throughout my whole life: but as for you, remembering that there are three infirmities, pray do not seem to resemble the one which is incurable, nor to exhibit the disease of the mind, which resembles that which those endure who are afflicted in body. For whereas those who suffer from slight ailments go of themselves to physicians, and those who are attacked by more serious diseases summon to their homes those who will treat them; yet those who have reached the stage of melancholy that is absolutely beyond remedy do not even admit physicians when they call. Pray do you not become afflicted in this last-named manner, characteristic of the men of the present time, by avoiding those whose reasoning faculties are sound.

40

ON THE TRINITY
Gregory of Nyssa

One of the greatest and most prolonged controversies in early Christendom was that over the nature of the Godhead—whether there was a Trinity, and, if so, how the three persons were related to each other. The Council of Nicea (325) had decided that the Son was of the "same essence" (homoousion), not merely of a "similar essence" (homoiousion) with the Father. The final triumph of the Nicene creed was in large measure due to writings by the Cappadocian fathers, Basil of Caesarea (330–379), Gregory of Nazianzus (c. 329–c. 389), and Gregory of Nyssa, the younger brother of Basil (c. 331–c. 396). The formulation of the doctrine of the Trinity by these thinkers, especially the two Gregories, resulted in the interpretation which has continued to be accepted by orthodox theology. Gregory of Nyssa did not possess the oratorical skill nor the organizing abilities of his two compatriots, but he was one of the best thinkers, as well as one of the clearest writers, in Christian history. He was influenced by the theology of Alexandrian Christianity as contained in the writings of Origen (c. 185–c. 254). However, although he accepted a basic orientation towards Christian doctrine derivative from the philosophical viewpoint of Origen, Gregory's independence and

From *Christology of the Later Fathers*, ed. Edward R. Hardy. Published 1954, The Westminster Press, Vol. III, pp. 256–267. Used by permission.

originality were shown by his rejection of Origen's doctrines of the pre-existence of souls and of the world as a prison for fallen souls. In his writing on the Trinity, he not only emphasizes the unity of the divine persons in one nature but also the unity of mankind—a teaching which is the foundation of the Eastern Church's emphasis upon communality.

AN ANSWER TO ABLABIUS: THAT WE SHOULD NOT THINK OF SAYING THERE ARE THREE GODS [1]

The Text

By rights it is you, who are in the prime of all your inner powers, who ought to continue the war against the enemies of truth and not to shrink from the task. Thus we fathers may be gladdened by the noble efforts of our children. For this is what the law of nature presupposes. But since you have turned your ranks and direct toward us the assaults of those darts which are hurled by the opponents of truth, and bid us old men to quench with the shield of faith their "hot, burning coals" and their missiles sharpened by knowledge (as they falsely call it), we accept the challenge. We make ourselves a pattern of ready obedience so that you, yourself, Ablabius, Christ's noble soldier, may give us an equal response to a similar challenge, should we ever summon you to such a contest.

It is no small matter which you have broached with us; nor is it such as to involve little damage if it is not properly examined. For the force of the question, on the surface, compels us to accept one of two totally incongruous views. Either we must say there are three gods, which is blasphemy; or else we must deny divinity to the Son and the Holy Spirit, which is irreligious and absurd.

The argument you state runs like this: Peter, James, and John are called three men, despite the fact they share in a single humanity. And there is nothing absurd in using the word for their nature in the plural, if those who are thus united in nature be many. If, then, general usage grants this, and no one forbids us to speak of two as two, or of more than two as three, how is it that we in some way compromise our confession, by saying on the one hand that the Father, the Son, and the Holy Spirit have a single Godhead, and by denying on the other that we can speak of three gods? For in speaking of the mysteries [of the faith], we acknowledge three Persons and recognize there is no difference in nature between them.

As I have already said, it is very difficult to deal with the question. If, indeed, we could find something to support the mind in its uncertainty, so that it no longer doubted and wavered in the face of this extraordinary dilemma, it would be well. But if our rather feeble powers of reason prove unequal to the

[1] Ablabius: a younger bishop to whom two of Gregory's letters are addressed, Epistles 6 and 21.

problem, we must guard the tradition we have received from the Fathers, as ever sure and immovable, and seek from the Lord a means of defending our faith. If this should be discovered by anyone endowed with grace, we shall give thanks to Him who granted the grace. If not, we shall nonetheless hold on to our unchangeable faith in those points which have been established.

Why is it, then, that we are accustomed to use the plural when we make a count of those who are shown to have the same nature? We say there are "so many men," and we do not call them all "one." And yet, when we refer to the divine nature, why does our dogma exclude a multitude of gods, and while enumerating the Persons, not admit their plural significance? Were one speaking superficially to simple folk, one might seem to give an answer by this, viz., that our doctrine refused to enumerate a number of gods in order to avoid similarity with Greek polytheism. Were we to speak of the Deity not in the singular, but in the plural, as they are accustomed to do, there might be thought to be some kinship between their doctrine and ours. Such an answer, given to rather naïve people, might seem satisfactory. To others, however, who demand that one or other of the alternatives must stand—either that we should not acknowledge the divinity of the three Persons, or that we should, without hesitation, count as three those who share the same divinity—such an answer as we have just given would not suffice to resolve the problem. We must, therefore, make our reply at greater length, tracking down the truth as best we can, for the question is no ordinary one.

Our first point is this: To use in the plural the word for the nature of those who do not differ in nature, and to speak of "many men," is a customary misuse of language. It is like saying that there are many human natures. That this is so is clear from the following instance. When we address someone, we do not call him by the name of his nature. Since he would have that name in common with others, confusion would result; and everyone within hearing would think that he was being addressed. For the summons was not by an individual name, but by the name of a common nature. Rather do we distinguish him from the multitude by using his proper name, that name, I mean, which signifies a particular subject. There are many who have shared in the same nature—disciples, apostles, martyrs, for instance—but the "man" in them all is one. Hence, as we have said, the term "man" does not refer to the particularity of each, but to their common nature. For Luke is a man, as is Stephen. But that does not mean that if anyone is a man he is therefore Luke or Stephen. Rather does the distinction of persons arise from the individual differences we observe in each. When we see them together, we can count them. Yet the nature is one, united in itself, a unit completely indivisible, which is neither increased by addition nor diminished by subtraction, being and remaining essentially one, inseparable even when appearing in plurality, continuous and entire, and not divided by the individuals who share in it.

Just as we speak of a people, a mob, an army, and an assembly always in the singular, and yet each of them entails plurality, so even the term "man" should properly and most accurately be used in the singular, even if those we observe to share in the same nature constitute a plurality. Thus it would be much better to correct our misguided habit and no longer use the word for a nature in the plural than by bondage to it to transfer the same error to our teaching about God. Yet it is impracticable to correct the habit, for how could you persuade anyone not to call those he observes having the same nature "many men"? Habit, indeed, is always hard to change. Hence, in not resisting the prevailing habit in the case of a lower nature, we should not go very far wrong. No damage arises from such a misguided use of words. In the case, however, of our teaching about God the indiscriminate use of words entails no similar freedom from danger. For trifles here are far from trifling. Therefore we must confess one God, as Scripture bears witness, "Hear, O Israel, the Lord thy God is one Lord," even though the term "Godhead" embraces the holy Trinity. This I say in accordance with the principle which we have given in reference to human nature and by which we have learned that we must not use the word for this nature in the plural. We must now make a more careful examination of the word "Godhead," in order that from the meaning attaching to the word we may get some help in clarifying the matter in hand.

Most people think that the word "Godhead" refers to God's nature in a special way. Just as the heaven, the sun, or any other of the world's elements is denoted by a proper name which signifies its subject, so they say that, in reference to the transcendent and divine nature, the word "Godhead" is fitly applied, like some proper name, to what it represents. We, however, following the suggestions of Holy Scripture, have learned that His nature cannot be named and is ineffable. We say that every name, whether invented by human custom or handed down by the Scriptures, is indicative of our conceptions of the divine nature, but does not signify what that nature is in itself. It is not very difficult to prove that this is the case. For, even without going into their origins, you will find that all terms that refer to the created world are accidentally applied to their subjects. We are content, in whatever way, to signify things by their names so as to avoid confusion in our knowledge of the things we refer to. But whatever terms there are to lead us to the knowledge of God, each of them contains a particular idea of its own; and you will not find any word among the terms especially applied to God which is without some meaning. From this it is clear that the divine nature in itself is not signified by any of these terms. Rather is some attribute declared by what is said. For we say, perhaps, that the divine is incorruptible or powerful or whatever else we are in the habit of saying. But in each of these terms we find a particular idea which by thought and expression we rightly attribute to the divine nature, but which does not express what that nature essentially is. For the subject, whatever it may be, is incorruptible, but our idea of incorruptibility is this: that that which is, is not resolved into decay. In saying, then, that He is incorruptible, we tell what his nature does not suffer. But what that is which does not suffer corruption we have not defined. Or again, even if we say he is the creator of life, while we indicate by the expression what it is he creates, we do not reveal by the word what creates it. By the same principle, we find in all other cases that the significance attaching to divine names lies either in their forbidding wrong conceptions of the divine nature or in their teaching right ones. But they do not contain an explanation of the nature in itself.

We perceive, then, the varied operations of the transcendent power, and fit our way of speaking of him to each of the operations known to us. Now one of these is the power of viewing and seeing, or, one might say, of beholding. By it God surveys all things and oversees them all. He discerns our thoughts, and by his power of beholding penetrates even what is invisible. From this we suppose that "Godhead" (*theotēs*) is derived from "beholding" (*thea*), and that by general custom and the teaching of the Scriptures, he who is our beholder (*theatēs*) is called God (*theos*). Now if anyone admits that to behold and see are the same thing, and that the God who oversees all things both is and is called the overseer of the universe, let him consider whether this operation belongs to one of the Persons we believe to constitute the holy Trinity, or whether the power extends to the three Persons. For if our interpretation of "Godhead" is the right one, and the things which are seen are said to be beheld (*theata*), and that which beholds them is called God (*theos*), no one of the Persons of the Trinity could properly be excluded from this form of address on the ground of the meaning of the word. For Scripture attributes sight equally to Father, Son, and Holy Spirit. David says, "See, O God our defender." From this we learn that the power of sight is proper to the idea of God so far as he is conceived. For David said, "See, O Lord." But Jesus, too, sees the thoughts of those who condemn him because he forgives men's sins on his own authority. For it says, "Jesus, seeing their thoughts." And in reference to the Holy Spirit, Peter says to Ananias, "Why has Satan filled your heart to lie to the Holy Spirit?" Thus he shows that the Holy Spirit, by whom the secret was disclosed to Peter, was a faithful witness and privy to what Ananias dared to do in secret. For Ananias became a thief of his own property, imagining he was escaping everyone's notice and hiding his sin. But at the same moment the Holy Spirit was in Peter and discerned his degraded and avaricious intention and Himself gave Peter the power to penetrate the secret; which He clearly could not have done had He been unable to discern what is hidden.

But someone will say that our manner of argument does not yet touch the question raised. For even granted that the term "Godhead" has reference to the common nature, that is no proof we should not speak of "gods." On the contrary, it rather forces us to do so. For we find that people are not accustomed to use the singular when referring to many—not only when these share a common nature, but even when they are in the same business. Thus we speak of "many orators," or "surveyors," or "farmers," or "shoemakers," and so on. If, indeed, "Godhead" were a way of talking about God's nature, it would be more proper, following the line of reasoning given, to include the three

Persons in the singular, and to speak about one God, since the nature is indivisible and inseparable. But since we have proved by the foregoing that the word "Godhead" signifies an operation and not a nature, our argument seems to be driven to the contrary conclusion. Hence we must rather speak of three gods who are beheld in the same operation, just as they do who speak of "three philosophers" or "three orators," or any other name derived from a profession, when there are many who share it.

I have taken pains to go into this matter fully by adducing our adversaries' objections, so that our teaching may be the more firmly fixed, being strengthened by the forcefulness of their contradictions. Let us now resume our argument.

We have fairly well proved by our argument that the word "Godhead" does not refer to a nature, but to an operation. Perhaps, then, someone might with good cause adduce the following reason why men who share the same profession with one another can be counted and referred to in the plural, while the Diety is spoken of in the singular as one God and one Godhead, despite the fact that the three Persons are not excluded from the significance attaching to "Godhead." He might argue that in the case of men, even if many share the same operation, each one separately and by himself undertakes the matter at hand. By his individual action each contributes nothing to the others engaged in the same task. For if there are many orators, their pursuit, being identical, bears the same name despite their plurality. Yet each one who follows this pursuit goes about it on his own. This one pleads in his special way, that one in his. In the case of men, therefore, since we can differentiate the action of each while they are engaged in the same task, they are rightly referred to in the plural. Each is distinguished from the others by his special environment and his particular way of handling the task.

With regard to the divine nature, on the other hand, it is otherwise. We do not learn that the Father does something on his own, in which the Son does not co-operate. Or again, that the Son acts on his own without the Spirit. Rather does every operation which extends from God to creation and is designated according to our differing conceptions of it have its origin in the Father, proceed through the Son, and reach its completion by the Holy Spirit. It is for this reason that the word for the operation is not divided among the persons involved. For the action of each in any matter is not separate and individualized. But whatever occurs, whether in reference to God's providence for us or to the government and constitution of the universe, occurs through the three Persons, and is not three separate things.

We can grasp this by reference to a single instance. From Him, I say, who is the source of gifts, all things that share in this grace have obtained life. When, then, we inquire whence this good gift came to us, we find through the guidance of the Scriptures that it was through the Father, the Son, and the Holy Spirit. But though we take it for granted that there are three Persons and names, we do not imagine that three different lives are granted us—one from each of them. Rather is it the same life which is produced by the Father, prepared by the Son, and depends on the will of the Holy Spirit.

Thus the holy Trinity brings to effect every operation in a similar way. It is not by seperate action according to the number of the Persons; but there is one motion and disposition of the good will which proceeds from the Father, through the Son, to the Spirit. For we do not call those who produce a single life three life-givers; nor do we say they are three good beings who are seen to share the same goodness; nor do we speak of them in the plural in reference to all their other attributes. In the same way we cannot enumerate as three gods those who jointly, inseparably, and mutually exercise their divine power and activity of overseeing us and the whole creation.

When we learn from Scripture that it is the God of the universe who judges all the earth, we say he is the judge of all things through the Son. And again, when we hear that the Father judges no one, we do not think that Scripture is at variance with itself. For he who judges all the earth does this through the Son to whom he has given all judgment. And everything done by the Only-begotten has reference to the Father, so that he both is the judge of all and yet judges no one. For, as was said, he has committed all judgment to the Son; and all the judgment of the Son is not something alien to the Father's will. Hence no one can properly say either that there are two judges or that one of them is excluded from the authority and power of judgment.

In the same way, with reference to the word "Godhead," Christ is the power of God and wisdom of God. And the Father exercises his power of overseeing or beholding (theatikēn), which we call "Godhead" (theotēta), through the Only-begotten, who by the Holy Spirit makes all power perfect, and who judges, as Isaiah says, by the spirit of judgment and the spirit of fire. Thus he acts in accordance with the gospel saying made to the Jews. For he says, "If I by the Spirit of God cast out demons." By the unity of the action, he embraces every form of doing good in this instance. For the word for the operation cannot be divided among many when they mutually bring to effect a single action.

As we have already said, the principle of the overseeing and beholding (theatikēs) power is a unity in Father, Son, and Holy Spirit. It issues from the Father, as from a spring. It is actualized by the Son; and its grace is perfected by the power of the Holy Spirit. No activity is distinguished among the Persons, as if it were brought to completion individually by each of them or separately apart from their joint supervision. Rather is all providence, care and direction of everything, whether in the sensible creation or of heavenly nature, one and not three. The preservation of what exists, the rectifying of what is amiss, the instruction of what is set right, is directed by the holy Trinity. But it is not divided into three parts according to the number of the Persons acknowledged by the faith, so that each operation, viewed by itself, should be the work of the Father alone, or of the Only-begotten by himself, or of the Holy Spirit separately. But while, as the apostle says, the one and the same Spirit distributes his benefits to each one severally, this beneficent movement of the Spirit is not without beginning. Rather do we find that the power we conceive as preceding it, namely, the only-begotten God, effects everything. Apart from him nothing comes into being; and again, this source of goodness issues from the Father's will.

Every good thing and everything we name as good depends on the power and purpose which is without beginning. And it is brought to completion by the power of the Holy Spirit and through the only-begotten God, immediately and independent of time. No delay exists or is to be conceived in the movement of the divine will from the Father through the Son and to the Holy Spirit. Now the Godhead is one of these good names and concepts; and hence the word cannot be rightly used in the plural, since the unity of operation forbids the plural number.

The Saviour of all men, especially of believers, is spoken of by the apostle as one. Yet no one argues from this expression that the Son does not save believers, or that those who share in salvation receive it apart from the Spirit. But God who is over all is the Saviour of all, while the Son brings salvation to effect by the grace of the Spirit. Yet on this account Scripture does not call them three Saviours, although salvation is recognized to come from the holy Trinity. In the same way they are not three gods according to the meaning we have given to the term "Godhead," although this expression attaches to the holy Trinity.

It does not seem to me entirely necessary for the proof of my present argument to refute opponents who claim that "Godhead" should not be conceived in terms of operation. For we believe that the divine nature is unlimited and incomprehensible, and hence we do not conceive of its being comprehended. But we declare that the nature is in every way to be thought of as infinite. What is altogether infinite is not limited in one respect and not in another, but infinity entirely transcends limitation. Therefore that which is without limit is certainly not limited by the word we use for it. In order, then, that our conception of the divine nature should remain unlimited, we say that the divine transcends every name for it. And one of these names is "Godhead." The same thing, then, cannot on the one hand be identical with the name, and yet on the other be conceived as transcending every name.

If, however, our opponents want to claim that "Godhead" refers to nature and not to operation, we shall revert to our former argument. [We shall say] that the habit of giving a plural significance to the word for a nature is mistaken. When a nature is observed in a larger or in a smaller number, neither increase nor diminution properly attaches to it. Only those things are enumerated by addition which are seen to be individually circumscribed. This circumscription is noted by bodily appearance, by size, by place, and by distinction of form and color. What is observed to transcend these things is beyond circumscription by means of these categories. What is not circumscribed cannot be numbered; and what is not numbered cannot be observed in quantities.

We say of gold, when it is made into small coins, that it is one and that it is spoken of as such. While we speak of many coins or many staters, we find no multiplication of the nature of gold by reason of the numbers of staters. That is why we speak of "much gold" in view of a large quantity of plate or coins. But we do not say "many golds" on account of the quantity of the material, unless one speaks this way of "many gold [pieces]," such as darics or staters. In which case it is not the material but the coins which admit of the plural signification. For properly speaking we should not say "many gold [pieces]," but "many golden ones."

As, then, there may be many golden staters, but gold is one, so we may be confronted with many who individually share in human nature, such as Peter, James, and John, yet the "man" [the human nature] in them is one. Even if the Scripture extends the word to a plural significance by saying, "Men swear by the greater," or, "sons of men," and so on, we must realize that it here uses the prevailing mode of speech. It does not lay down rules how words ought to be used in one way or another. It does not record these phrases by way of giving technical instruction in the use of words. But it uses the word according to prevailing custom, having only this in view, that the word may be helpful to those who receive it. It does not use language with precision in matters where no harm arises in the understanding of the phrases. Indeed, it would be a lengthy task to list the inaccurate expressions from Scripture to prove my point. But where there is danger of a point of truth being perverted, we no longer find this careless and indifferent use of words in Scripture.

It is for this reason that Scripture allows "men" to be used in the plural because, by such an expression, no one would be misled to suppose there is a multitude of "humanities," or to think that, by the plural use of the word for that nature, many human natures are signified. But the word "God" it carefully uses in the singular, guarding against introducing different natures in the divine essence by the plural significance of "gods." Wherefore it says, "The Lord God is one Lord." By the word "Godhead" it proclaims, too, the only-begotten God, and does not divide the unity into a duality so as to call the Father and the Son two gods, although each is called God by holy writers. The Father is God and the Son is God; and yet by the same affirmation God is one, because no distinction of nature or of operation is to be observed in the Godhead.

For if, as those who are misled suppose, there are differences of nature in the holy Trinity, it would follow that their number would be extended to a plurality of gods and divided by the divinity of essence in their subjects. But since the divine, single, and unchanging nature eschews all diversity of essence, in order to guard its unity, it admits of itself no plural significance. But as it is said to be one nature, so all the other attributes are numbered in the singular—God, good, holy, saviour, righteous, judge, and any other conceivable attribute of God, whether one says these refer to his nature or to his operation—a point we shall not dispute.

Should anyone cavil at our argument that, by refusing to acknowledge distinctions in the nature, it makes for an admixture and confusion of the Persons, we will give the following answer to such a charge. Although we acknowledge the nature is undifferentiated, we do not deny a distinction with respect to causality. That is the only way by which we distinguish one Person from the other, by believing, that is, that one is the cause and the other depends on the cause. Again, we recognize another distinction with regard to that which depends on the cause. There is that which depends on the first cause and that which is derived from what immediately depends on the first cause. Thus the attribute of being only-begotten without doubt remains with the Son, and we do not question that the Spirit is derived from the Father. For the mediation of the Son, while it guards his prerogative of being only-begotten, does not exclude the relation which the Spirit has by nature to the Father.

When we speak of a cause and that which depends on it, we do not, by these words, refer to nature. For no one would hold that cause and nature are identical. Rather do we indicate a difference in manner of existence. For in saying the one is caused and the other uncaused, we do not divide the nature by the principle of causality, but only explain that the Son does not exist without generation, nor the Father by generation. It is necessary for us first to believe that something exists, and then to examine in what way the object of our belief exists. The question of what exists is one thing: the manner of its existence is another. To say that something exists without generation explains the mode of its existence. But what it is is not made evident by the expression. If you asked a gardener about some tree, whether it was planted or grew wild, and he replied either that it had or had not been planted, would his answer tell you what sort of tree it was? By no means. In telling you how it grew, he would leave the question of its nature obscure and unexplained. In the same way here, when we learn that he is unbegotten, we are taught the mode of his existence and how we must think of it. But we do not learn from the expression what he is.

When, then, we acknowledge such a distinction in the holy Trinity that we believe that one is the cause and the other depends on it, we can no longer be charged with dissolving the distinction of the Persons in the common nature. The principle of causality distinguishes, then, the Persons of the holy Trinity. It affirms that the one is uncaused, while the other depends on the cause. But the divine nature is in every way understood to be without distinction or difference. For this reason we rightly say there is one Godhead and one God, and express all the other attributes that befit the divine in the singular.

41

ON HIS CONVERSION
St. Augustine

> St. Augustine (354–430), who was the bishop of Hippo, in
> Algeria, is undoubtedly the most famous of the Latin Church
> Fathers. He was greatly responsible for forming the characteristic
> spirit of western Christianity, both in its medieval and in its
> reformation expression. Augustine's theology gives emphasis to
> the doctrines of the equality of persons in the Trinity, the impor-
> tance of the humanity of Jesus, freedom of the will, original sin,
> salvation through grace, predestination, and the conception of the
> sacraments as including all the rites of the Church. Subsequent
> theologians, both Catholic and Protestant, have selectively ap-
> pealed to these Augustinian emphases as traditional justification
> for their most cherished beliefs. Indeed, Augustine was already
> well known as a teacher in his own time, primarily due to a famous
> controversy which he carried on with Pelagius, a British monk,
> whose extreme emphasis upon human freedom led him to a denial
> of original sin. Pelagianism was eventually condemned, largely be-
> cause of Augustine's efforts. In all probability, Augustine's great
> influence upon Christianity is as much a function of his personal
> character and piety as of his philosophical or theological abilities.
> Among his many writings, which include such treatises as On the
> Freedom of the Will, On the Trinity, and The City of God, prob-
> ably his best known work is the Confessions (c. 400). The Con-
> fessions is the only spiritual autobiography produced by the early
> church, and it remains a classic account of an individual's religious
> experience. The following selection from the Confessions is Au-
> gustine's account of his conversion to Christianity.

But now, the more ardently I loved those, whose healthful affections I
heard of, that they had resigned themselves wholly to Thee to be cured, the
more did I abhor myself, when compared with them. For many of my years
(some twelve) had now run out with me since my nineteenth, when, upon

Augustine, *Confessions of St. Augustine*, E. B. Pusey, trans. (London: J. M. Dent
& Sons, and New York: E. P. Dutton & Co., 1907), pp. 162–172.

the reading of Cicero's *Hortensius,* I was stirred to an earnest love of wisdom; and still I was deferring to reject mere earthly felicity, and give myself to search out that, whereof not the finding only, but the very search, was to be preferred to the treasures and kingdoms of the world, though already found, and to the pleasures of the body, though spread around me at my will. But I wretched, most wretched, in the very commencement of my early youth, had begged chastity of Thee, and said, "Give me chastity and continency, only not yet." For I feared lest Thou shouldest hear me soon, and soon cure me of the disease of concupiscence, which I wished to have satisfied, rather than extinguished. And I had wandered through crooked ways in a sacrilegious superstition, not indeed assured thereof, but as preferring it to the others which I did not seek religiously, but opposed maliciously.

18. And I had thought, that I therefore deferred from day to day to reject the hopes of this world, and follow Thee only, because there did not appear aught certain, whither to direct my course. And now was the day come wherein I was to be laid bare to myself, and my conscience was to upbraid me. "Where art thou now, my tongue? Thou saidst, that for an uncertain truth thou likedst not to cast off the baggage of vanity; now, it is certain, and yet that burthen still oppresseth thee, while they who neither have so worn themselves out with seeking it, nor for ten years and more have been thinking thereon, have had their shoulders lightened, and received wings to fly away." Thus was I gnawed within, and exceedingly confounded with an horrible shame, while Pontitianus was so speaking. And he having brought to a close his tale and the business he came for, went his way; and I into myself. What said I not against myself? with what scourges of condemnation lashed I not my soul, that it might follow me, striving to go after Thee! Yet it drew back; refused, but excused not itself. All arguments were spent and confuted; there remained a mute shrinking; and she feared, as she would death, to be restrained from the flux of that custom, whereby she was wasting to death.

[VIII.] 19. Then in this great contention of my inward dwelling, which I had strongly raised against my soul, in *the chamber* of my heart, troubled in mind and countenance, I turned upon Alypius. "What ails us?" I exclaim: "what it is? what heardest thou? The unlearned start up and *take heaven by force,* and we with our learning, and without heart, lo, where we wallow in flesh and blood! Are we ashamed to follow, because others are gone before, and not ashamed not even to follow?" Some such words I uttered, and my fever of mind tore me away from him, while he, gazing on me in astonishment, kept silence. For it was not my wonted tone; and my forehead, cheeks, eyes, colour, tone of voice, spake my mind more than the words I uttered. A little garden there was to our lodging, which we had the use of, as of the whole house; for the master of the house, our host, was not living there. Thither had the tumult of my breast hurried me, where no man might hinder the hot contention wherein I had engaged with myself, until it should end as Thou knewest, I knew not. Only I was healthfully distracted and dying, to live; knowing what evil thing I was, and not knowing what good thing I was shortly to become. I retired then into the garden, and Alypius, on my steps. For his presence did not lessen my privacy; or how could he forsake me so disturbed? We sat down as far removed as might be from the house. I was troubled in spirit, most vehemently indignant that I entered not into Thy will and covenant, O my God, which *all my bones cried* out unto me to enter, and praised it to the skies. And therein we enter not by ships, or chariots, or feet, no, move not so far as I had come from the house to that place where we were sitting. For, not to go only, but to go in thither was nothing else but to will to go, but to will resolutely and thoroughly; not to turn and toss, this way and that, a maimed and half-divided will, struggling, with one part sinking as another rose.

20. Lastly, in the very fever of my irresoluteness, I made with my body many such motions as men sometimes would, but cannot, if either they have not the limbs, or these be bound with bands, weakened with infirmity, or any other way hindered. Thus, if I tore my hair, beat my forehead, if locking my fingers I clasped my knee; I willed, I did it. But I might have willed, and not done it, if the power of motion in my limbs had not obeyed. So many things then I did, when "to will" was not in itself "to be able;" and I did not what both I longed incomparably more to do, and which soon after, when I should will, I should be able to do; because soon after, when I should will, I should will thoroughly. For in these things the ability was one with the will, and to will was to do; and yet was it not done: and more easily did my body obey the weakest willing of my soul, in moving its limbs at its nod, than the soul obeyed itself to accomplish in the will alone this its momentous will.

[IX] 21. Whence is this monstrousness? and to what end? Let Thy mercy gleam that I may ask, if so be the secret penalties of men, and those darkest pangs of the sons of Adam, may perhaps answer me. Whence is this monstrousness? and to what end? The mind commands the body, and it obeys instantly; the mind commands itself, and is resisted. The mind commands the hand to be moved; and such readiness is there, that command is scarce distinct from obedience. Yet the mind is mind, the hand is body. The mind commands the mind, its own self, to will, and yet it doth not. Whence this monstrousness? and to what end? It commands itself, I say, to will, and would not command, unless it willed, and what it commands is not done. But it willeth not entirely: therefore doth it not command entirely. For so far forth it commandeth, as it willeth: and, so far forth is the thing commanded, not done, as it willeth not. For the will commandeth that there be a will; not another, but itself. But it doth not command entirely, therefore what it commandeth, is not. For were the will entire, it would not even command it to be, because it would already be. It is therefore no monstrousness partly to will, partly to nill, but a disease of the mind, that it doth not wholly rise, by truth up-borne, borne down by custom. And therefore are there two wills, for that one of them is not entire: and what the one lacketh, the other hath.

[X.] 22. *Let them perish from Thy presence*, O God, as perish *vain talkers, and seducers* of the soul: who observing that in deliberating there were two wills, affirm, that there are two minds in us of two kinds, one good, the other evil. Themselves are truly evil, when they hold these evil things; and themselves shall become good, when they hold the truth, and assent unto the truth, that Thy Apostle may say to them, *Ye were sometimes darkness, but now light in the Lord*. But they, wishing to be light, not *in the Lord*, but in themselves, imagining the nature of the soul to be that which God is, are made more gross darkness thought a dreadful arrogancy; for that they *went back farther from Thee, the true Light that enlighteneth every man that cometh into the world*. Take heed what you say, and blush for shame: *draw near unto Him and be enlightened, and your faces shall not be ashamed*. Myself when I was deliberating upon serving the Lord my God now, as I had long purposed, it was I who willed, I who nilled, I, I myself. I neither willed entirely, nor nilled entirely. Therefore was I at strife with myself, and rent asunder by myself. And this rent befel me against my will, and yet indicated, not the presence of another mind, but the punishment of my own. *Therefore it was no more I that wrought it, but sin that dwelt in me*; the punishment of a sin more freely committed, in that I was a son of Adam.

23. For if there be so many contrary natures, as there be conflicting wills; there shall now be not two only, but many. If a man deliberate, whether he should go to their conventicle, or to the theatre; these Manichees cry out, Behold, here are two natures: one good, draws this way; another bad, draws back that way. For whence else is this hesitation between conflicting wills? But I say, that both be bad: that which draws to them, as that which draws back to the theatre. But they believe not that will to be other than good, which draws to them. What then if one of us should deliberate, and amid the strife of his two wills be in a strait, whether he should go to the theatre, or to our church? Would not these Manichees also be in a strait what to answer? For either they must confess, (which they fain would not,) that the will which leads to our church is good, as well as theirs, who have received and are held by the mysteries of theirs: or they must suppose two evil natures, and two evil souls conflicting in one man, and it will not be true, which they say, that there is one good and another bad; or they must be converted to the truth, and no more deny, that where one deliberates, one soul fluctuates between contrary wills.

24. Let them no more say then, when they perceive two conflicting wills in one man, that the conflict is between two contrary souls, of two contrary substances, from two contrary principles, one good, and the other bad. For Thou, O true God, dost disprove, check, and convict them; as when, both wills being bad, one deliberates, whether he should kill a man by poison, or by the sword; whether he should seize this or that estate of another's, when he cannot both; whether he should purchase pleasure by luxury, or keep his money by covetousness; whether he go to the circus, or the theatre, if both be open on one day; or, thirdly, to rob another's house, if he have the opportunity; or,

fourthly, to commit adultery, if at the same time he have the means thereof also; all these meeting together in the same juncture of time, and all being equally desired, which cannot at one time be acted: for they rend the mind amid four, or even (amid the vast variety of things desired) more, conflicting wills, nor do they yet allege that there are so many divers substances. So also in wills which are good. For I ask them, is it good to take pleasure in reading the Apostle?[1] or good to take pleasure in a sober Psalm? or good to discourse on the Gospel? They will answer to each, "It is good." What then if all give equal pleasure, and all at once? Do not divers wills distract the mind, while he deliberates, which he should rather choose? yet are they all good, and are at variance till one be chosen, whither the one entire will may be borne, which before was divided into many. Thus also, when, above, eternity delights us, and the pleasure of temporal good holds us down below, it is the same soul which willeth not this or that with an entire will; and therefore is rent asunder with grievous perplexities, while out of truth it sets this first, but out of habit sets not that aside.

[XI.] 25. Thus soul-sick was I, and tormented, accusing myself much more severely than my wont, rolling and turning me in my chain, till that were wholly broken, whereby I now was but just, but still was, held. And Thou, O Lord, pressedst upon me in my inward parts by a severe mercy, redoubling the lashes of fear and shame, lest I should again give way, and not bursting the same slight remaining tie, it should recover strength, and bind me the faster. For I said within myself, "Be it done now, be it done now." And as I spake, I all but enacted it. I all but did it, and did it not: yet sunk not back to my former state, but kept my stand hard by, and took breath. And I essayed again, and wanted somewhat less of it, and somewhat less, and all but touched and laid hold of it; and yet came not at it, nor touched, nor laid hold of it: hesitating to die to death and to live to life: and the worse whereto I was inured, prevailed more with me than the better, whereto I was unused: and the very moment wherein I was to become other than I was, the nearer it approached me, the greater horror did it strike into me; yet did it not strike me back, nor turned me away, but held me in suspense.

26. The very toys of toys, and vanities of vanities, my ancient mistresses, still held me; they plucked my fleshly garment, and whispered softly, "Dost thou cast us off? and from that moment shall we no more be with thee for ever? and from that moment shall not this or that be lawful for thee for ever?" And what was it which they suggested in that I said, "this or that," what did they suggest, O my God? Let Thy mercy turn it away from the soul of Thy servant. What defilements did they suggest! what shame! And now I much less than half heard them, and not openly shewing themselves and contradicting me, but muttering as it were behind my back, and privily plucking me, as I was departing, but to look back on them. Yet they did retard me, so that I hesitated to burst and shake myself free from them, and to spring over

[1] St. Paul.

whither I was called; a violent habit saying to me, "Thinkest thou, thou canst live without them?"

27. But now it spake very faintly. For on that side whither I had set my face, and whither I trembled to go, there appeared unto me the chaste dignity of Continency, serene, yet not relaxedly gay, honestly alluring me to come, and doubt not; and stretching forth to receive and embrace me, her holy hands full of multitudes of good examples. There were so many young men and maidens here, a multitude of youth and every age, grave widows and aged virgins; and Continence herself in all, not barren, but a *fruitful mother of children* of joys, by Thee her Husband, O Lord. And she smiled on me with a persuasive mockery, as would she say, "Canst not thou what these youths, what these maidens can? or can they either in themselves, and not rather in the Lord their God? The Lord their God gave me unto them. Why standest thou in thyself, and so standest not? Cast thyself upon Him, fear not He will not withdraw Himself that thou shouldest fall; cast thyself fearlessly upon Him, He will receive, and will heal thee." And I blushed exceedingly, for that I yet heard the muttering of those toys, and hung in suspense. And she again seemed to say, "Stop thine ears against *those* thy unclean *members on the earth, that they may be mortified. They tell thee of delights, but not as doth the law of the Lord thy God.*" This controversy in my heart was self against self only. But Alypius sitting close by my side, in silence waited the issue of my unwonted emotion.

[XII.] 28. But when a deep consideration had from the secret bottom of my soul drawn together and heaped up all my misery in the sight of my heart; there arose a mighty storm, bringing a mighty shower of tears. Which that I might pour forth wholly, in its natural expressions, I rose from Alypius: solitude was suggested to me as fitter for the business of weeping; so I retired so far that even his presence could not be a burthen to me. Thus was it then with me, and he perceived something of it; for something I suppose I had spoken, wherein the tones of my voice appeared choked with weeping, and so had risen up. He then remained where we were sitting, most extremely astonished. I cast myself down I know not how, under a certain fig-tree, giving full vent to my tears; and the floods of mine eyes gushed out, an *acceptable sacrifice to Thee.* And, not indeed in these words, yet to this purpose, spake I much unto Thee: *And Thou, O Lord, how long? how long, Lord, wilt Thou be angry, for ever? Remember not our former iniquities,* for I felt that I was held by them. I sent up these sorowful words; How long? how long, "to-morrow, and to-morrow?" Why not now? why not is there this hour an end to my uncleanness?

29. So was I speaking, and weeping in the most bitter contrition of my heart, when, lo! I heard from a neighbouring house a voice, as of boy or girl, I know not, chanting, and oft repeating, "Take up and read; Take up and read." Instantly, my countenance altered, I began to think most intently, whether children were wont in any kind of play to sing such words: nor could

I remember ever to have heard the like. So checking the torrent of my tears, I arose; interpreting it to be no other than a command from God, to open the book, and read the first chapter I should find. For I had heard of Antony, that coming in during the reading of the Gospel, he received the admonition, as if what was being read, was spoken to him; *Go, sell all that thou hast, and give to the poor, and thou shalt have treasure in heaven, and come and follow me.* And by such oracle he was forthwith converted unto Thee. Eagerly then I returned to the place where Alypius was sitting; for there had I laid the volume of the Apostle, when I arose thence. I seized, opened, and in silence read that section, on which my eyes first fell: *Not in rioting and drunkenness, not in chambering and wantonness, not in strife and envying: but put ye on the Lord Jesus Christ, and make not provision for the flesh,* in concupiscence. No further would I read; nor needed I: for instantly at the end of this sentence, by a light as it were of serenity infused into my heart, all the darkness of doubt vanished away.

30. Then putting my finger between, or some other mark, I shut the volume, and with a calmed countenance made it known to Alypius. And what was wrought in him, which I knew not, he thus shewed me. He asked to see what I had read: I shewed him; and he looked even further than I had read, and I knew not what followed. This followed, *him that is weak in the faith, receive;* which he applied to himself, and disclosed to me. And by this admonition was he strengthened; and by a good resolution and purpose, and most corresponding to his character, wherein he did always very far differ from me, for the better, without any turbulent delay he joined me. Thence we go into my mother; we tell her; she rejoiceth: we relate in order how it took place; she leaps for joy, and triumpheth, and blesseth Thee, *Who art able to do above that which we ask or think;* for she perceived that Thou hadst given her more for me, than she was wont to beg by her pitiful and most sorrowful groanings. For Thou convertedst me unto Thyself, so that I sought neither wife, nor any hope of this world, standing in that rule of faith, where Thou hadst shewed me unto her in a vision, so many years before. And Thou didst *convert her mourning into joy,* much more plentiful than she had desired, and in a much more precious and purer way than she erst required, by having grandchildren of my body.

42

MAN'S ULTIMATE HAPPINESS
Thomas Aquinas

> *St. Thomas Aquinas (1225–1274) was the greatest theologian and philosopher of medieval western Christianity; and in recognition of this fact, he has been given the title of Doctor angelicus. Thomas, despite the opposition of his family, joined the Dominican order in 1244 and left his native Italy for Paris, where he became a student of St. Albert the Great. The combination of his own native ability and interest with the stimulation afforded by close contact with a scholar of the caliber of Albert resulted in Thomas's pursuing a life devoted to research and teaching. His earliest written work, a commentary on the Sentences of Peter Lombard (c.1100–1160) was composed between 1254 and 1256. (The Sentences is a compendium of the principal utterances of the Church Fathers on various theological topics, and it was highly regarded during the medieval era.) His magnum opus, the Summa Theologica, was written during the period 1265–1273. As its title indicates, this work is a critical summation of the doctrines of Christianity, which masterfully organizes the teachings of the Fathers into a relatively coherent system whose character was greatly influenced by Thomas's investigations of Aristotelian philosophy. Nearly as famous is Thomas's Summa contra Gentiles (c.1260), a book intended to be a manual for missionaries, which presents Thomas's interpretation of Christian teaching in a much more readable fashion than the Summa Theologica, since it does not possess the elaborate documentation and scholarly commentary of that work. The following selection from the Summa contra Gentiles offers what Thomas considers to be the Christian answer to the question posed by the ancient Greek philosophers: "What is the greatest good for man?"*

CHAPTER XXXVII: THAT MAN'S ULTIMATE HAPPINESS CONSISTS IN CONTEMPLATING GOD

Accordingly, if man's ultimate happiness does not consist in external things, which are called goods of fortune; nor in goods of the body; nor in goods of the soul, as regards the sensitive part; nor as regards the intellectual part, in terms of the life of moral virtue; nor in terms of the intellectual virtues which are concerned with action, namely, art and prudence:—it remains for us to conclude that man's ultimate happiness consists in the contemplation of truth.

For this operation alone is proper to man, and it is in it that none of the other animals communicates.

Again. This is not directed to anything further as to its end, since the contemplation of the truth is sought for its own sake.

Again. By this operation man is united to beings above him, by becoming like them; because of all human actions this alone is both in God and in the separate substances. Also, by this operation man comes into contact with those higher beings, through knowing them in any way whatever.

Besides, man is more self-sufficing for this operation, seeing that he stands in little need of the help of external things in order to perform it.

Further. All other human operations seem to be ordered to this as to their end. For perfect contemplation requires that the body should be disencumbered, and to this effect are directed all the products of art that are necessary for life. Moreover, it requires freedom from the disturbance caused by the passions, which is achieved by means of the moral virtues and of prudence; and freedom from external disturbance, to which the whole governance of the civil life is directed. So that, if we consider the matter rightly, we shall see that all human occupations appear to serve those who contemplate the truth.

Now, it is not possible that man's ultimate happiness consist in contemplation based on the understanding of first principles; for this is most imperfect, as being most universal, containing potentially the knowledge of things. Moreover, it is the beginning and not the end of human inquiry, and comes to us from nature, and not through the pursuit of the truth. Nor does it consist in contemplation based on the sciences that have the lowest things for their object, since happiness must consist in an operation of the intellect in relation to the most noble intelligible objects. It follows then that man's ultimate happiness consists in wisdom, based on the consideration of divine things.

It is therefore evident also by way of induction that man's ultimate happiness consists solely in the contemplation of God, which conclusion was proved above by arguments.

CHAPTER XXXVIII: THAT HUMAN HAPPINESS DOES NOT CONSIST IN THE KNOWLEDGE OF GOD WHICH IS POSSESSED GENERALLY BY THE MAJORITY

It remains for us to inquire in what kind of knowledge of God the ultimate happiness of an intellectual substance consists. For there is a certain general and confused knowledge of God, which is in almost all men, whether from the fact that, as some think, the existence of God, like other principles of demonstration, is self-evident, as we have stated in the First Book, or, as seems nearer to the truth, because by his natural reason man is able at once to arrive at some knowledge of God. For seeing that natural things run their course according to a fixed order, and since there cannot be order without a cause of order, men, for the most part, perceive that there is one who orders the things that we see. But who or of what kind this cause of order may be, or whether there be but one, cannot be gathered from this general consideration; just as, when we see a man in motion, and performing other works, we perceive that in him there is some cause of the operations which is not in other things, and we give this cause the name of *soul*, but without knowing yet what the soul is, whether it be a body, or how it brings about operations in question.

Now, this knowledge of God cannot possibly suffice for happiness.

For the activity of the happy man must be without any defect; but this knowledge of God is subject to an admixture of many errors. Thus, some believed that there was no other governor of mundane things than the heavenly bodies; and so they said that the heavenly bodies were gods.—Some ascribed this order to the elements and to the things generated from them; as though they thought that their movements and natural operations were not introduced into them by an external governor, but that the order in other things was caused by them.—And some, deeming human acts not to be subject to any but a human rule, declared that men who cause order in other men were gods.— Evidently *this* knowledge of God is not sufficient for happiness.

Moreover. Happiness is the end of human acts. But human acts are not directed to the aforesaid knowledge as to their end; indeed, it is in everyone almost right from the very beginning. Therefore happiness does not consist in this kind of knowledge of God.

Again. No one appears to be blamed for lacking happiness; nay, those who lack it and seek it are praised. But he who lacks the aforesaid knowledge of God is seemingly very much to be blamed, since it is a very clear sign of a man's dullness of perception if he fail to perceive such evident signs of God; even as a man would be deemed dull who, seeing man, understood not that he has a soul. Hence it is said in the Psalm (xiii. 1: lii. 1): *The fool hath said in his heart: There is no God.* Therefore it is not this knowledge of God which suffices for happiness.

Further. Knowledge of a thing in general only, and not in terms of what is proper to it, is most imperfect. Such is the knowledge which is had of man from the fact that he is moved; for this is a knowledge whereby a thing is known only potentially, because the proper is only potentially contained in the common. Now happiness is a perfect operation: and man's highest good must needs be in terms of what exists actually, and not in terms of what exists only potentially; since potentiality perfected by act has the character of a good. Therefore the aforesaid knowledge of God is not sufficient for our happiness.

CHAPTER XXXIX: THAT MAN'S HAPPINESS DOES NOT CONSIST
IN THE KNOWLEDGE OF GOD ACQUIRED BY DEMONSTRATION

There is also another knowledge of God, higher than the one just mentioned, which is acquired by means of a demonstration, and which approaches
nearer to a proper knowledge of Him; for by means of a demonstration many
things are removed from Him, so that in consequence we understand Him as
something apart from other things. For demonstration proves that God is immovable, eternal, incorporeal, utterly simple, one, and the like, as we have
shown in the First Book. Now we arrive at the proper knowledge of a thing
not only by affirmations, but also by negations. For just as it is proper to man
to be a rational animal, so is it proper to him not to be inanimate or irrational.
Yet there is this difference between these two modes of proper knowledge,
that when we have proper knowledge of a thing by affirmations we know what
that thing is, and how it is distinguished from others; whereas when we have
proper knowledge of a thing by negations, we know that it is distinct from
others, but remain ignorant of what it is. Such is the proper knowledge of God
that can be obtained by demonstrations. But neither does this suffice for man's
ultimate happiness.

For things belonging to one species for the most part attain to the end
of that species, because nature achieves its purpose always or nearly always,
and fails in a few instances because of some corruption. Now happiness is the
end of the human species, since all men naturally desire it. Therefore happiness is a common good that can be attained by all men, unless some obstacle
occur to some whereby they be deprived of it. Few, however, attain to the possession of the aforesaid knowledge of God by way of demonstration, because
of the obstacles to this knowledge mentioned at the beginning of this work.
Therefore this knowledge is not essentially man's happiness.

Again. To be actual is the end of that which exists potentially, as was
made clear above. Therefore happiness, which is the last end, is an act free of
any potentiality to a further act. Now this knowledge of God that is acquired
by way of demonstration is still in potentiality to a further knowledge of God,
or to the same knowledge, but by a better way: because those who came afterwards endeavored to add something to the knowledge of God besides that
which they found handed down to them by those who preceded them. Therefore such knowledge is not man's ultimate happiness.

Further. Happiness excludes all unhappiness, for no man can be at the
same time happy and unhappy. Now deception and error have a large place
in unhappiness, since all naturally avoid them. But the aforesaid knowledge
of God is subject to the admixture of many errors, as evidenced by many who
knew some truths about God through demonstration, yet, following their own
opinions, when they lacked proof, fell into many errors. And if there were
some who by the way of demonstration discovered the truth about divine

things, without any admixture of error in their opinions, it is evident that they were very few. This fact is not in keeping with happiness, which is the common end. Therefore man's ultimate happiness is not seated in such knowledge as this.

Moreover. Happiness consists in a perfect operation. Now perfect knowledge requires certitude, and that is why we cannot be said to know unless we know what cannot be otherwise, as is stated in *Post. Anal.* 1. But the aforesaid knowledge is beset with uncertainty, as is clear from the diversity among sciences about divine things elaborated by those who endeavored to discover something about God by the way of demonstration. Therefore ultimate happiness does not consist in such knowledge.

Besides. When the will has obtained its last end, its desire is at rest. Now the ultimate end of all human knowledge is happiness. Therefore happiness is essentially that knowledge of God the possession of which leaves no knowledge to be desired of anything knowable. Such, however, is not the knowledge which the philosophers were able to have about God by the way of demonstration; because even when we have this knowledge, we still desire to know other things—things that we do not yet know by means of this knowledge. Therefore happiness does not consist in such a knowledge of God.

Furthermore. The end of everything that exists in potentiality is that it be brought to actuality; for to this does it tend by means of the movement with which it is moved to its end. Now every potential being tends to becoming actualized as far as possible. For there are things in potentiality whose whole potentiality is reducible to act: the end of such things is that they be wholly actualized. Thus, a heavy body that is outside its medium is in potentiality to its proper place. There are also things whose potentiality cannot be actualized all at once,—for instance primary matter: so that by its movement it seeks actualization by various forms in succession, which cannot be in the matter at the same time because of their diversity. Furthermore, our intellect is in potentiality to all intelligibles, as was stated in the Second Book. Now it is possible for two intelligible objects to be in the possible intellect at the same time according to the first act which is *science*, although perhaps not in respect of the second act which is *consideration*. Accordingly, it is clear that the whole potentiality of the possible intellect can be actualized at one time; and consequently this is required for its ultimate end, which is happiness. But the aforesaid knowledge, which can be acquired about God by the way of demonstration, does not accomplish this, since when we have it we still are ignorant of many things. Therefore such a knowledge of God does not suffice for ultimate happiness.

CHAPTER XL: THAT MAN'S HAPPINESS DOES NOT CONSIST IN THE KNOWLEDGE OF GOD BY FAITH

There is yet another knowledge of God, in one respect superior to the knowledge we have been discussing, namely, that whereby God is known by men through faith. Now this knowledge surpasses the knowledge of God through demonstration in this respect, namely, that by faith we know certain things about God which are so sublime that reason cannot reach them by means of demonstration, as we have stated at the beginning of this work. But not even in this knowledge of God can man's ultimate happiness consist.

For happiness is the intellect's perfect operation, as was already declared. But in knowledge by faith, the operation of the intellect is found to be most imperfect as regards the contribution of the intellect, although it is most perfect on the part of the object; for the intellect in believing does not grasp the object of its assent. Therefore neither does man's happiness consist in this knowledge of God.

Again. It has been shown that ultimate happiness does not consist chiefly in an act of the will. Now in knowledge by faith, the will has the leading place; for the intellect assents by faith to things proposed to it, because it so wills, and not through being constrained by the evidence of their truth. Therefore man's final happiness does not consist in this knowledge.

Besides. A believer assents to things proposed to him by another, but not seen by himself; so that the knowledge of faith resembles hearing rather than seeing. Now a man would not believe in what is unseen by him, and proposed to him by another, unless he thought this other to have a more perfect knowledge of the things proposed than he himself has who sees not. Either therefore the judgment of the believer is wrong, or the proposer must have more perfect knowledge of the things proposed. And if the latter also knows these things only through hearing them from another, we cannot proceed thus indefinitely, for then the assent of faith would be without foundation or certitude, since we should not come to some first principle certain in itself, to give certitude to the faith of believers. Now, in reality, it is not possible that the assent of faith be false and without foundation, as is clear from what we have said at the beginning of this work; and yet if it were false and baseless, happiness could not consist in such knowledge. There is therefore some knowledge of God that is higher than the knowledge of faith, whether he who proposes faith sees the truth immediately, as when we believe Christ, or whether he receives the truth from him who sees it immediately, as when we believe the Apostles and Prophets. Since, then, man's happiness consists in the highest knowledge of God, it cannot consist in the knowledge of faith.

Moreover. Since happiness is the last end, the natural desire is set at rest thereby. But the knowledge of faith does not set the desire at rest, but inflames it; for everyone desires to see what he believes. Therefore man's ultimate happiness does not consist in the knowledge of faith.

Further. The knowledge of God has been declared to be the end inasmuch as it unites us to the last end of all, namely, God. Now the knowledge of faith does not make the thing believed to be perfectly present to the intellect, since faith is of absent, and not present, things. Hence the Apostle says (2 Cor. v. 6, 7) that *so long as we walk by faith, we are pilgrims from the*

Lord. Yet faith makes God to be present to love, since the believer assents to God voluntarily, according to the saying of *Ephes.* iii. 17: *That Christ may dwell by faith in our hearts.* Therefore the knowledge of faith cannot be man's ultimate happiness.

CHAPTER XLVIII: THAT MAN'S ULTIMATE HAPPINESS IS NOT IN THIS LIFE

Seeing, then, that man's ultimate happiness does not consist in that knowledge of God whereby He is known by all or many in a vague kind of opinion, nor again in that knowledge of God whereby He is known in the speculative sciences through demonstration, nor in that knowledge whereby He is known through faith, as we have proved above; and seeing that it is not possible in this life to arrive at a higher knowledge of God in His essence, or at least so that we understand other separate substances, and thus know God through that which is nearest to Him, so to say, as we have proved; and since we must place our ultimate happiness in some kind of knowledge of God, as we have shown:—it is impossible for man's happiness to be in this life.

Again. Man's last end is the term of his natural appetite, so that when he has obtained it, he desires nothing more; because if he still has a movement towards something, he has not yet reached an end wherein to be at rest. Now this cannot happen in this life, since the more man understands, the more is the desire to understand increased in him (for this is natural to man), unless perhaps there be someone who understands all things. Now in this life this never did nor can happen to anyone that was a mere man, seeing that in this life we are unable to know separate substances which in themselves are most intelligible, as we have proved. Therefore man's ultimate happiness cannot possibly be in this life.

Besides. Whatever is in motion towards an end has a natural desire to be established and at rest therein. Hence a body does not move away from the place towards which it has a natural movement, except by a violent movement which is contrary to that appetite. Now happiness is the last end which man naturally desires. Therefore it is his natural desire to be established in happiness. Consequently, unless together with happiness he acquires a state of immobility, he is not yet happy, since his natural desire is not yet at rest. When, therefore, a man acquires happiness, he also acquires stability and rest; so that all agree in conceiving stability as a necessary condition of happiness. Hence the Philosopher says: *We do not look upon the happy man as a kind of chameleon.* Now in this life there is no sure stability, since, however happy a man may be, sickness and misfortune may come upon him, so that he is hindered in the operation, whatever it be, in which happiness consists. Therefore man's ultimate happiness cannot be in this life.

Moreover. It would seem unfitting and unreasonable for a thing to take a long time in becoming, and to have but a short time in being; for it would follow that for a longer duration of time nature would be deprived of its end. Hence we see that animals which live but a short time are perfected in a short time. But if happiness consists in a perfect operation according to perfect virtue, whether intellectual or moral, it cannot possibly come to man except after a long time. This is most evident in speculative matters, wherein man's ultimate happiness consists, as we have proved; for hardly is man able to arrive at perfection in the speculations of science, even though he reach the last stage of life, and then, in the majority of cases, but a short space of life remains to him. Therefore man's ultimate happiness cannot be in this life.

Further. All admit that happiness is a perfect good, or else it would not bring rest to the appetite. Now perfect good is that which is wholly free from any admixture of evil; just as that which is perfectly white is that which is entirely free from any admixture of black. But man cannot be wholly free from evils in this state of life, and not only from evils of the body, such as hunger, thirst, heat, cold and the like, but also from evils of the soul. For there is no one who at times is not disturbed by inordinate passions; who sometimes does not go beyond the mean, wherein virtue consists, either in excess or in deficiency; who is not deceived in some thing or another; or who at least is not ignorant of what he would wish to know, or does not feel doubtful about an opinion of which he would like to be certain. Therefore no man is happy in this life.

Again. Man naturally shuns death, and is sad about it, not only shunning it at the moment when he feels its presence, but also when he thinks about it. But man, in this life, cannot obtain not to die. Therefore it is not possible for man to be happy in this life.

Besides. Ultimate happiness consists, not in a habit, but in an operation, since habits are for the sake of actions. But in this life it is impossible to perform any action continuously. Therefore man cannot be entirely happy in this life.

Further. The more a thing is desired and loved, the more does its loss bring sorrow and pain. Now happiness is most desired and loved. Therefore its loss brings the greatest sorrow. But if there be ultimate happiness in this life, it will certainly be lost, at least by death. Nor is it certain that it will last till death, since it is possible for every man in this life to encounter sickness, whereby he is wholly hindered from the operation of virtue, e.g., madness and the like, which hinder the use of reason. Such happiness therefore always has sorrow naturally connected with it, and consequently it will not be perfect happiness.

But someone might say that, since happiness is a good of the intellectual nature, perfect and true happiness is for those in whom the intellectual nature is perfect, namely, in separate substances, and that in man it is imperfect, and by a kind of participation. For man can arrive at a full understanding of the truth only by a sort of movement of inquiry; and he fails entirely to understand things that are by nature most intelligible, as we have proved. Therefore neither is happiness, in its perfect nature, possible to man; but he has a certain participation of it, even in this life. This seems to have been Aristotle's opinion about happiness. Hence, inquiring whether misfortunes destroy happiness, he shows that happiness seems especially to consist in deeds of virtue, which seem to be most stable in this life, and concludes that those who in this life attain to this perfection are happy *as men*, as though not attaining to happiness absolutely, but in a human way.

We must now show that this explanation does not remove the foregoing arguments. For although man is below the separate substances according to the order of nature, he is above irrational creatures, and so he attains his ultimate end in a more perfect way than they. Now these attain their last end so perfectly that they seek nothing further. Thus a heavy body rests when it is in its own proper place, and when an animal enjoys sensible pleasure, its natural desire is at rest. Much more, therefore, when man has obtained his last end, must his natural desire be at rest. But this cannot happen in this life. Therefore in this life man does not obtain happiness considered as his proper end, as we have proved. Therefore he must obtain it after this life.

Again. Natural desire cannot be empty, since *nature does nothing in vain*. But nature's desire would be empty if it could never be fulfilled. Therefore man's natural desire can be fulfilled. But not in this life, as we have shown. Therefore it must be fulfilled after this life. Therefore man's ultimate happiness is after this life.

Besides. As long as a thing is in motion towards perfection, it has not reached its last end. Now in the knowledge of truth all men are always in motion and tending towards perfection; because those who follow make discoveries in addition to those made by their predecessors, as is also stated in *Metaph.* ii. Therefore in the knowledge of truth man is not situated as though he had arrived at this last end. Since, then, as Aristotle himself shows, man's ultimate happiness in this life consists apparently in speculation, whereby he seeks the knowledge of truth, we cannot possibly allow that man obtains his last end in this life.

Moreover. Whatever is in potentiality tends to become actual, so that as long as it is not wholly actual, it has not reached its last end. Now our intellect is in potentiality to the knowledge of all the forms of things, and it becomes actual when it knows any one of them. Consequently, it will not be wholly actual, nor in possession of its last end, except when it knows all things, at least all these material things. But man cannot obtain this through the speculative sciences, by which we know truth in this life. Therefore man's ultimate happiness cannot be in this life.

For these and like reasons, Alexander and Averroes held that man's ultimate happiness does not consist in that human knowledge obtained through the speculative sciences, but in that which results from a union with a separate substance, which union they deemed possible to man in this life. But as Aristotle realized that man has no knowledge in this life other than that which he obtains through the speculative sciences, he maintained that man attains to a happiness which is not perfect, but a human one.

Hence it becomes sufficiently clear how these great minds suffered from being so straitened on every side. We, however, shall be freed from these straits if we hold, in accordance with the foregoing arguments, that man is able to reach perfect happiness after this life, since man has an immortal soul; and that in that state his soul will understand in the same way as separate substances understand, as we proved in the Second Book.

Therefore man's ultimate happiness will consist in that knowledge of God which the human mind possesses after this life, a knowledge similar to that by which separate substances know him. Hence our Lord promises us a *reward . . . in heaven* (*Matt.* v. 12) and states (*Matt.* xxii. 30) that the saints *shall be as the angels*, who always see God in heaven (*Matt.* xviii. 10).

CHAPTER LI: HOW GOD MAY BE SEEN IN HIS ESSENCE

Since, then, it is impossible for a natural desire to be empty (and it would be, were it impossible to arrive at understanding the divine substance, for all minds desire this naturally), we must conclude that it is possible for the divine substances to be seen through the intellect, both by separate intellectual substances, and by our souls.

It is sufficiently clear, from what has been said, what manner of vision this is. For we have proved that the divine substance cannot be seen by the intellect by means of any created species. Therefore, if God's essence is to be seen at all, it must be that the intellect sees it through the divine essence itself; so that in that vision the divine essence is both the object and the medium of vision.

Since, however, the intellect is unable to understand any particular substance unless it be actualized by a species informing it, which is the likeness of the thing understood, someone might deem it impossible for a created intellect to see the very substance of God through the divine essence as an intelligible species. For the divine essence is self-subsistent, and we have proved in the First Book that God cannot be the form of anything.

In order to understand this truth, we must note that a self-subsisting substance is either a form alone, or a composite of matter and form. Accordingly, that which is composed of matter and form cannot be the form of something else, because the form therein is already confined to that matter, so that it cannot be the form of another thing. But that which so subsists that it is yet a form alone, can be the form of something else, provided its being be such that some other thing can participate in it, as we have proved concerning the human soul in the Second Book. If, however, its being cannot be participated in by another, it cannot be the form of anything, because by its very being it is determined in itself, just as material things are determined by their matter. Now we must consider this as being the case not only with regard to substantial or natural being, but also as regards intelligible being. For, since truth is the perfection of the intellect, that intelligible which is truth itself will be a pure form in the genus of intelligible things. This applies solely to God, for, since truth is consequent upon being, that alone is its own truth, which is its own being; and this belongs to God alone, as we have proved in the Second Book. Consequently, other subsistent intelligibles are not pure forms in the genus of intelligible things, but have a form in a subject; for each of them is a true thing, but not the truth, even as it is a being, but not being itself. It is therefore clear that the divine essence can be compared to the created intellect as an intelligible species by which it understands; which cannot be said of the essence of any separate substance. And yet it cannot be the form of another thing through its natural being. For it would follow that, once united to another being, it would constitute one nature; which is impossible, since the divine essence is in itself perfect in its own nature. But an intelligible species, in its union with the intellect, does not constitute a nature, but perfects the intellect for understanding; and this is not inconsistent with the perfection of the divine essence.

This immediate vision of God is promised to us in Holy Scripture (1 Cor. xiii. 12): *We see now through a glass in a dark manner; but then face to face*. It would be impious to understand this in a material way, and imagine a material face in the Godhead; for we have proved that God is not a body. Nor is it possible for us to see God with a bodily face, since the eyes of the body, which are situated in the face, can see only bodily things. Thus then shall we see God face to face, because we shall see Him immediately, even as a man whom we see face to face.

It is through this vision that we become most like God, and participators of His blessedness, since God understands His substance through His essence, and this is His blessedness. Therefore it is said (1 John iii. 2): *When He shall appear, we shall be like to Him; because we shall see Him as He is*. Again, our Lord said (Luke xxii. 29, 30): *I dispose to you, as My Father hath disposed to Me, a banquet, that you may eat and drink at My table in My kingdom*. Now these words cannot be understood as referring to bodily food and drink, but to that which is taken from the table of Wisdom, of which Wisdom says (Prov. ix. 5): *Eat my bread and drink the wine which I have mingled for you*. Accordingly, to eat and drink at God's table is to enjoy the same blessedness as that which makes God happy, and to see God as He sees Himself.

THE FREEDOM OF A CHRISTIAN
Martin Luther

The first, and in Germany the foremost, of the major Reformation figures was Martin Luther (1483–1546). The son of a peasant family, Luther, following his father's wishes, was pursuing a university curriculum leading to a career in law when, in 1505, the sudden death of a friend and his own near death by lightning prompted a state of concern with his spiritual welfare, which resulted in his joining the Augustinian order. He was ordained as a priest two years later and received his doctorate in theology in 1512. In the course of preparing his lectures on the Bible, especially the lectures on Romans (1515), Luther, considerably influenced by Augustine, came to conceive salvation as a personal gift from God to man. Since this conviction contradicted the basic principles upon which the selling of indulgences rested, Luther protested against some features of this practice by posting the famous Ninety-five Theses on the door of the church in Wittenberg on October 31, 1517. This document created considerable consternation in the church, and the following years Luther spent attempting to justify his position to others, until on April 17, 1521, at Worms, the final break with the Church and Empire came when Luther refused to recant. Luther's greatest work during those four years was done in 1520, which saw the publication of his essays On Good Works, To the Christian Nobility of the German Nation, The Babylonian Captivity of the Church, and The Freedom of a Christian. This final essay, an analysis of the Christian religious experience, is perhaps the clearest statement of the major features of Luther's position.

Reformation Writings of Martin Luther, translated by Bertram Lee Woolf, Vol. I, pp. 357–379. Lutterworth Press, 1957.

TEXT AND NOTES

To the sagacious and learned gentleman, Jerome Mühlpfordt, Mayor of Zwickau, a very kind friend and patron, I, Martin Luther, Augustinian, present my compliments and best wishes.

Wise and learned sir, and my dear friend, your excellent civic chaplain, the reverend John Egran,[1] has spoken in very warm terms of the love and delight with which you regard Holy Scripture, and, indeed, how you readily avow and heartily commend it before men. That is why he wished to introduce me personally to you, and I am indeed very eager and happy that it should be so, for it gives me special pleasure to hear of any one who holds the divine truth so dear. Unfortunately there are very many others, especially those who are proud of some title, who use pressure and cunning of all kinds in striving against that truth. Indeed, it is ordained that many must come into collision with Christ, and fall, but rise again to renewed attacks, because He is set as a stumbling block and a sign that must be spoken against.

Wherefore, in order to initiate our acquaintance and friendship, I would dedicate the German form of this tractate and homily to you. I have already dedicated the Latin version to the pope, in order to explain the grounds of my teachings and writings about the papacy; and I hope to have made them unexceptionable to all. I present to you herewith my respects and pray all God's blessing upon you. Amen.

Wittenberg, 1520.

Jesus

1. In order that we may have a true and proper understanding of what it is to be a Christian, or what is the freedom which Christ has won for us and given to us, and of which St. Paul often writes, I propose to begin with two propositions.

A Christian is free and independent in every respect, a bondservant to none.

A Christian is a dutiful servant in every respect, owing a duty to everyone.

These two axioms are clearly found in 1 Corinthians 9, where St. Paul says: "Though I am free from all men, I have made myself a servant to all." Again, Romans 13: "Owe no one anything, except to love one another. But love owes a duty, and is a bondservant of what she loves"; in the same way also in regard to Christ, Galatians 4: "God sent forth His Son, born of a woman, and made Him a bondservant of the law."

---

[1] Johannes Egranus was one of the earliest adherents of Luther in Zwickau, where he was an influential preacher. He visited Luther in Nov., 1520, in Wittenberg, and this seems to have been the occasion when the mayor's name was mentioned.

2. In order to understand these two antithetic assertions concerning freedom and bondage, we ought to remember that in every Christian there are two natures, a spiritual and a bodily. In as far as he possesses a soul, a Christian is a spiritual person, an inward, regenerate self; and in as far as he possesses flesh and blood, he is a sensual person, an outward, unregenerate self. Because of this difference, the Scriptures, in passages which directly contradict each other, speak of his freedom and bondage in the way I have just said.

3. When we consider the inner, spiritual man and see what belongs to him if he is to be a free and devout Christian, in fact and in name, it is evident that, whatever the name, no outer thing can make him either free or religious. For his religion and freedom, and, moreover, his sinfulness and servitude, are neither bodily nor outward. What avail is it to the soul if the body is free, active, and healthy; or eats, drinks, and lives as it likes? Again, what harm does it do to the soul if the body is imprisoned, ill and weakly; or is hungry, thirsty, and in pain, even if one does not bear it gladly? This sort of thing never touches the soul a little bit, nor makes it free or captive, religious or sinful.

4. Thus it does not help the soul if the body puts on sacred vestments as the priests and clergy do. It does not help even when the body is in church or in holy places, or when busy with sacred affairs; nor when the body is offering prayers, keeping fasts, or making pilgrimages, and doing other good works, which are performed only in and through the body. It must surely be something quite different which brings religion and freedom to the soul. For even a sinful man, or a hypocrite and pretender, may have all the afore-named things, do these works, and follow these ways. Also, this is the way to make men nothing but sheer hypocrites. Further it does no harm to the soul if the body wears worldly clothes, tarries in worldly places, eats, drinks, does not go on pilgrimages, nor keep the appointed hours of prayer; and if it neglects all the works that hypocrites perform, as already said.

5. The only means, whether in heaven or on earth, whereby the soul can live, and be religious, free, and Christian, is the holy Gospel, the word of God preached by Christ. He Himself says in John 11, "I am the resurrection and the life. He that believeth in Me shall live eternally"; and John 14, "I am the way, the truth and the life"; and Matthew 4, "Man does not live by bread alone, but by every word that proceeds out of the mouth of God." Therefore, we can be certain that the soul can do without anything but the word of God; and apart from the word of God it has no means of help. When it has the word, however, it has no need of anything else. In short, it possesses food, joy, peace, light, ability, righteousness, truth, wisdom, freedom, and sufficient to overflowing of everything good. Thus we read in the Psalms, especially in Psalm 119, that the prophet cries only for the word of God. And in the Scriptures, the worst calamity, the worst sign of God's wrath, is when He withdraws His word from man. On the other hand, it is held the greatest grace when He sends forth His word, as it is written in Psalm 107: "He sent His

word and helped them thereby." Christ came for no other object than to preach the word of God. Moreover all apostles, bishops, priests, and the whole clergy, were called and instituted only for the sake of the word; although, unfortunately, things happen differently nowadays.

6. You may ask, however: "What then is that word which gives such signal grace, and how shall I use it?" The answer is: It is nothing else than the message proclaimed by Jesus, as contained in the gospel; and this should be, and, in fact, is, so presented that you hear your God speak to you. It shows how all your life and labour are as nothing in God's sight, and how you and all that is in you, must eternally perish. If you truly believe this, and that you are indeed guilty, you necessarily despair of yourself; you believe that Hosea was right when he said: "O Israel, there is nought in you except your corruption, but in Me is your help." In order that you may come out of yourself and flee from yourself, i.e., escape your corruption, He sets you face to face with His beloved Son, Jesus Christ, and says to you by means of His living and comforting word: "You should surrender yourself to Him with firm faith, and trust Him gladly." Then, for your faith's sake, all your sins shall be forgiven and all your wickedness overcome. You yourself will be righteous, upright, serene, and devout. You will fulfil all commands, and be free from all things, as St. Paul says in Romans 1: "A justified Christian lives only by his faith"; and in Romans 10: "Christ is the end and the fulfilment of all commandments for them that believe in him."

7. Therefore it is reasonable to say that the only purpose for which all Christians should labour, is that they should build up both the divine word and Christ in themselves, by exercising and strengthening their faith continually. No other works can make a man a Christian. Thus Christ answered the Jews (John 6), when they asked Him what they should do in order to do works of a godly and Christian kind. He said: "That is the only divine work, that you believe in Him whom God has sent," whom God the Father has alone ordained to that end.

Therefore a right faith in Christ is, truly, superabundant wealth, for He brings with Himself all felicity, and takes away all infelicity. Thus Mark says, in the last chapter: "Therefore he who believes and is baptized is saved, and he who does not believe is condemned." The prophet Isaiah (Chapter 10) surveyed the wealth of the same faith, and said: "God will make a small remnant on earth, and into the remnant righteousness will flow like a flood," namely the faith, in which the fulfilling of all commands is quite briefly contained, will abundantly justify all who have it, till they need nothing more to become righteous and religious. Thus St. Paul says in Romans 10: "That which a man believes in his heart, makes him righteous and devout."

8. But how does it come about that faith alone can make one religious, and give such exceeding wealth apart from any works, seeing that so many laws, commandments, works, and other means are prescribed in the Scriptures? In this connection we must be sure to note and carefully remember

that, as we shall see later, faith alone, apart from any act of ours, makes us religious, sets us free, and saves us. We should understand that the entire Holy Scriptures can be divided under two heads: Commandment or God's Law, and Promise or Covenant. The commandments teach and prescribe many good works, but this does not mean that they are fulfilled by us. They give good instructions, but no assistance. They teach what man should do, but give no power to do it. Hence they are only fitted to show a man his own incapacity for goodness, and to make him learn to doubt himself. For this reason they are called the Old Testament, and all belong to the Old Testament. The commandment: "Thou shalt not have sinful appetites," shows that all of us are sinners, and there can be no man without sinful appetites, let him do what he may. Thereby a man learns not to depend on himself, but to seek help elsewhere in order that he may be without sinful appetites. Thus he may fulfil the commandment through another, although he could not do so of himself. In the same way, all other commandments are impossible to us.

9. Now when a man has learned from the commandments, and perceived his own incapacity, then he will be anxious to know how to keep the commandment, for unless he fulfils the commandment he will be damned. This will take away all his pride, and he will become as nothing in his own eyes; he will find nothing in himself to make him acceptable to God. Then comes the other word, the divine promise, the covenant which says: If you would fulfil all the commandments, and escape from your evil passions and sins, as the commandments urge and require, lo! believe on Christ. In Him I promise that you will find all the needful grace, righteousness, peace, and freedom. If you believe, you will possess; if you do not believe, you will not possess. What is impossible to you in attempting all the works of the commandments, which are necessarily many and yet of no avail, will come to you quickly and easily through faith. I have summed everything up in faith alone, so that whoever has faith shall have all, and be saved; without faith, no one shall have anything. Thus God's covenants give what the commandments require, and bring about that for which the commandments are intended; all this is in order that everything, both commandment and fulfilment, might be God's own. He alone commands and alone fulfils. Therefore the covenants of God are the words of the New Testament, and their proper place is the New Testament.

10. Now these, and all God's words, are holy, true, right, peace-giving, free, and entirely good. The soul of the man who cleaves to them with a true faith will be so completely united with God that all the virtues of the word will become the qualities of his soul. Through faith and by God's word, the soul will become holy, righteous, true, peaceful, free, and entirely good, and he will become a true child of God. Thus it says in John 1: "He gave power to all them that believe in His name to become children of God."

From this standpoint it is easy to see why faith can do so much, and why good works can never be equivalent to it. For works of merit are not such as to depend on the divine word as in the case of faith, nor can they live in

the soul. Only the word and faith exercise sway in the soul. Just as iron becomes red like fire through its union with the fire, so does the soul become like
the word through its union with the word. Thus we see that a Christian has
sufficient in his faith. Works are not needed to make him become acceptable
to God. And if such works are no longer a prerequisite, then assuredly all
commandments and laws are like broken chains; and if his chains are broken,
he is assuredly free. That is Christian freedom, gained by faith alone. It is
wrong to think this means that we can either be idle or do evil; rather it means
that we have no need to perform works of merit in order to attain godliness
and salvation. But we shall deal further with this matter later on.

11. Again it is to be noticed in regard to faith, that when one man believes in another, he does so because he holds him to be duteous and trustworthy, which is the greatest honour that one man can pay another. On the
other hand, it is the greatest insult if he holds him to be loose, untruthful, or
shallow. Thus also, if the soul firmly believes in God's word, she holds Him
trustworthy, good, and righteous; and thereby she pays Him the greatest honour in her power. For then she acknowledges Him to be in the right, obeys
His law, and honours His name, and lets Him do with her what He will,
because the soul has no doubt that He is good and trustworthy in all His
words. Further, no one can show God greater disrespect than not to trust Him.
By lack of reverence and faith, the soul holds Him to be incompetent, deceptive, and shallow, and, as far as she is concerned, she disclaims Him by such
unbelief. She sets up in her heart a false god of her own imagination, as if she
understood better than He. But when God sees that the soul acknowledges
Him to be true, and honours Him by her faith, He honours her in return and
holds her to be devout and trustworthy on account of such faith. For to hold
God to be good and true, is itself good and true, and makes a man good and
true; this is not done by those who have no faith, even though they are busily
concerned doing many meritorious works.

12. Faith not only gives the soul enough for her to become, like the
divine word, gracious, free, and blessed. It also unites the soul with Christ, like
a bride with the bridegroom, and, from this marriage, Christ and the soul become one body, as St. Paul says. Then the possessions of both are in common,
whether fortune, misfortune, or anything else; so that what Christ has, also
belongs to the believing soul, and what the soul has, will belong to Christ. If
Christ has all good things, including blessedness, these will also belong to the
soul. If the soul is full of trespasses and sins, these will belong to Christ. At
this point a contest of happy exchanges takes place. Because Christ is God and
man, and has never sinned, and because His sanctity is unconquerable, eternal,
and almighty, He takes possession of the sins of the believing soul by virtue
of her wedding-ring, namely faith, and acts just as if He had committed those
sins Himself. They are, of course, swallowed up and drowned in Him, for
His unconquerable righteousness is stronger than any sin whatever. Thus the
soul is cleansed from all her sins by virtue of her dowry, i.e., for the sake of her

faith. She is made free and unfettered, and endowed with the eternal righteousness of Christ, her bridegroom. Is that not a happy household, when
Christ, the rich, noble, and good bridegroom, takes the poor, despised, wicked
little harlot in marriage, sets her free from all evil, and decks her with all good
things? It is not possible for her sins to damn her, for now they rest on Christ,
and are swallowed up in Him. In this way she has such a rich righteousness in
her bridegroom that she can always withstand sins, although they indeed lie in
wait for her. Paul speaks of this in 1 Corinthians 15: "Praise and thanks be
to God, who has given us that victory in Christ Jesus, in which death is swallowed up together with sin."

13. From this you will understand on what ground it is rightly attributed to faith, that it fulfils all laws, and makes us godly without the help of
anything else. You will see that, of itself, it fulfils the first commandment,
which decrees: "Thou shalt honour thy God." If you were constituted entirely
of meritorious works from top to toe, you would still not be a godly man, nor
do God honour; nor would you have fulfilled the very first commandment. For
God is not honoured unless truth and good and all are ascribed to Him, their
true source. Meritorious works do not make that ascription, but only genuine
faith. Therefore faith alone is the means of man's righteousness, and the fulfilment of all commandments; for he who fulfils the first and chief commandment, will also fulfil all other commandments with certainty and without
strain. Works, however, are lifeless things. They can neither honour nor praise
God, although they may be done, and admit of being done, to God's honour
and glory. But we are not discussing works just now, for they are mere consequences; rather our subject is the initiator, the shipwright, himself. The active
agent is the one who discharges his duty to God and who does the works.
That active agent is none other than faith, and it resides in our hearts. Faith
is the beginning and the end of religion. It is therefore a dangerous and dubi-
ous proceeding to teach that God's commandments can be met by performing
works of merit. They are met by faith, and this before any works have been
done. Works follow, once the commandments have been met, as we shall see.

14. The next point to consider is the treasure we possess in Christ, and
how valuable is the right kind of faith. Let us be clear that, before Old Testament times, as well as during them, God chose and reserved for Himself all
the first-born, whether human or animal. Moreover, the eldest son was of
special dignity, and had two great privileges as distinct from all the younger
children: he was given authority, and he was a priest. The kingship and the
priesthood were his. Thus, in practice, the eldest son was the master of all
the other brothers; he was also a priest, or pope, of God. This is a figure sym-
bolizing Jesus Christ, who is that self-same, human Son of God the Father by
the Virgin Mary. He is therefore a king and a priest—but in the spiritual sense.
His kingdom is not earthly, nor does it consist in earthly things, but in those
of the spirit, such as truth, wisdom, peace, joy, salvation, and the like. Temporal goods are not excluded, however, for all things in heaven, earth, or hell

are subject to Him, although He is unseen owing to the fact that He rules spiritually and invisibly.

Thus even His priesthood does not consist in rites and vestments such as we see among men. Rather it consists in the spirit, and is invisible, in order that He may stand continually before God's face, and offer Himself on behalf of those who are His, and do all that a devout priest should do. He prays for us, as St. Paul says in Romans 8; and also teaches us inwardly in our hearts. These two offices are right and proper for a priest; and therefore ordinary, human, and temporal priests pray and teach in the same manner.

15. Since Christ has the primogeniture with all appropriate honour and worth, He shares it with all Christians who are His, that, through faith, all may be kings and priests with Christ, as St. Peter says in 1 Peter 2: "You are a priestly kingdom and a royal priesthood." The result is that a Christian is lifted up by faith so high above all things that he becomes the spiritual lord of all, for nothing can hinder his salvation. Rather, everything is subject to him, and helps him to reach salvation. Thus St. Paul teaches in Romans 8: "Everything must help to secure the good of the elect," whether life, death, sin, piety, good or evil, or whatever it may be. So also, 1 Corinthians 3: "All things are yours, whether life or death, present or future," etc. It is not to be understood that we exercise material authority over all things, so that we possess or use them like ordinary men. Indeed as far as the body is concerned, we must die, for no one can avoid death. In the same way, we are necessarily subject to many other things, as we see exemplified also in Christ and His saints. For ours is a spiritual rulership, exercised even to the extent of repressing the body. Thus I can gain benefit in my soul quite apart from material things, and I can make even death and suffering of service to my salvation. That is surely a high and noble dignity, a proper and all-powerful lordship, a spiritual royalty. Nothing is so good or so evil but that it must serve me for good, if I have faith. Indeed, I need none of these things. My faith is sufficient for me. How precious then is the freedom and potency which Christians possess!

16. In addition, we are priests, and thus greater than mere kings, the reason being that priesthood makes us worthy to stand before God, and to pray for others. For to stand and pray before God's face is the prerogative of none except priests. Christ redeemed us that we might be able spiritually to act and pray on behalf of one another just as, in fact, a priest acts and prays on behalf of the people. But nothing avails to the benefit of a person who does not believe in Christ. He is nought but a slave; he is always worried; it is hard for him to pray, and his prayers do not come under God's eye. By contrast, who can fully conceive the honour and the elevation of a Christian? By virtue of his kingship he exercises authority over all things, and by virtue of his priesthood he exercises power with God, for God does what he asks and desires. Thus it is written in the book of Psalms: "God does the will of those that fear Him, and hears their prayers." This is an honour to which Christians attain through faith alone and not through any works. Thereby it becomes clear that

a Christian always enjoys freedom, and is always master. He requires no good works to make him godly or to save him; faith brings everything in abundance to him. If he were so foolish as to think that by good works he would become godly, free, blessed, or a Christian, he would lose both faith and all else. He would be like the dog which, while carrying a piece of meat in its mouth, snapped at its reflection in the water, and thereby lost the meat and spoiled the reflection.

17. Should you ask: "What is the difference between the priests and the laity in Christian standing, if all are priests?" the answer is that spiritual mischief and other wrongs have been done to the little words "priest" or "pastor." These words have been taken away from the community in general and handed over to those little communities which we now call "the clergy." The Holy Scriptures make no distinction beyond calling the instructed or the consecrated, *ministros, servos, œconomos,* i.e., helpers, servants, stewards, whose duty is to preach Christ, and faith, and Christian freedom to others. For although we are all equally priests, still not all of us can serve and minister and preach. Thus St. Paul says in 1 Corinthians 4: "We do not desire to be held by the people to be other than servants of Christ and stewards of the gospel." But there has now grown out of the stewardship such a worldly, outer, gorgeous and awe-inspiring lordship and authority that the worldly powers proper cannot compare with them. Indeed, it is as if the laity were something other than Christian people. The whole meaning of Christian grace and liberty and faith is taken away, together with everything we have in Christ, and, indeed, we are robbed of Christ Himself. Instead, we have received much man-made law and many man-made works, and we have become altogether the servants of the most unsuitable people on earth.

18. From all this we understand that it is not enough just to take the life and work of Christ, and, in preaching, merely tell the story and the chronicle of events. It is even worse to pass over these altogether, and preach about ecclesiastical law or other man-made rules and doctrines. There are also many who preach and understand Christ as if they rather pitied Him, and were angry with the Jews; they carry on in some other childish manner. But He should and must be preached in such a way that, in both you and me, faith grows out of, and is received from, the preaching. And that faith is received and grows when I am told why Christ came, how men can use and enjoy Him, and what He has brought and given me. This takes place whenever a proper explanation is given of that Christian freedom which we have from Him: how we are kings and priests with power over all things; and how everything we do is well-pleasing to and granted by God, as I have already said. For when our heart hears about Christ in this way, it must rejoice through and through. It yearns for Christ, receives consolation, and loves Him in return. Neither regulations nor good deeds can effect as much as that. For who can do hurt to such a soul, or terrify it? If sin or death fall upon it, it has faith that the spiritual worth of Christ is its own, and that its sins are no longer its own,

but Christ's. Thus sin must vanish away through the goodness of Christ in faith, as I said above. The heart learns with the apostle to defy death and sin, and say: "Where is thy victory, O death? Where, death, is now thy sting? Thy sting is sin. But praise and thanks be to God who has given us the victory through Jesus Christ our Lord. Death is swallowed up in His victory," etc.

19. We have now probably said sufficient about the inner man, about his liberty and the principal features of his righteousness which requires neither laws nor "good works." Indeed, it is harmful to that righteousness when any one pretends to have been made righteous on that basis.

We now come to the second part, namely, to the outer man. Here we must deal with all those who take offence at the foregoing arguments, and are wont to say: "Oh! then if faith is the whole thing and sufficient in itself to make one religious, why are good works demanded? We shall be in good case without doing anything at all." No, my dear man, not so. That would perhaps be true if you were nothing but your inner self, and had become pure soul and pure spirit, a thing which will never happen before the last day. There will never be anything else on earth than a beginning and a growth; these will only be completed in the next world. That is why the apostle called it *primitias spiritus*, or the first-fruits of the spirit. From this fact we can understand what was said above: *"A Christian man is a dutiful menial, a bondservant to everyone,"* which is as much as to say: "In as far as he is free, he requires to do nothing. In as far as he is a servant, he must do everything." How that happens we shall now see.

20. Inwardly, and as regards his soul, a man is sufficiently justified by faith. He possesses all he ought to have, except that his very faith and sufficiency must always increase until his entry into the next life; nevertheless he still remains on earth during his bodily life. Therefore he must rule his own body, and he must mix with other people. That is where the need for good works enters. He must not be idle. Yes, the body must be disciplined and exercised with fasting, watching, labouring, and all due training, in order that it may be obedient to, and in harmony with, both the inner man and with faith; and not hinder nor oppose, as is its nature when it is not restrained. For the inner man is one with God. He is joyful and glad on account of Christ who has done so much for him. All his pleasure consists in serving God in return, without reward, and out of unconstrained love. It is true that a man finds in his body a refractory will which wants to seek and serve the world, and which finds pleasure in doing so. Faith cannot tolerate that. She eagerly lays hold of it by the throat to subdue it and keep it in order. Thus St. Paul says in Romans 7: "In the inward man I have a desire for God's will, but I find another will in my flesh, which would make me prisoner together with sin"; and again: "I discipline my body and bring it to obedience lest I myself become culpable, who should teach others"; and again, in Galatians 5: "All who belong to Christ crucify their body with its evil desires."

21. But none of these works must be done under the impression that a

man becomes devout in God's sight thereby. Faith cannot tolerate this false view; for faith alone is, and cannot be anything else than, godliness in God's sight. Works must be understood only in the sense that doing them makes the body obedient and keeps it clean from its evil desires; and the eye may only look on evil desires in order to drive them out. Through faith, the soul is made pure, and caused to love God; yet she wishes that all things were pure, especially her own body, and that every one loved and praised God along with her. Thus, for his own body's sake, a man may not be idle. He must do many good deeds in order to constrain it. Nevertheless the deeds are not the real essence of being good, and it is not true that they make a man dutiful and righteous before God. Rather he does them voluntarily and freely, out of love, in order to please God. His only object is to seek to do what pleases God, whose will he gladly does as well as ever he can. As a consequence, such a man can form his own rule and judge for himself about mortifying his body; for he will fast, watch, and labour as much as he sees his body needs, in order to neutralize its wantonness. The rest, however, who believe they will become religious by virtue of what they do, pay no attention to the self-discipline, but only to the actions. They believe that, if they only do many impressive works, all is well, and they will be godly. They sometimes go to great trouble, and even harm their bodies in the attempt. But it is undoubtedly very foolish, and a complete misunderstanding of the Christian life, to think that they can become religious and saved by what they do apart from faith.

22. To give a few illustrations of the matter, we should consider what a Christian does, who is justified and saved by faith, and by the free grace of God. These acts must be regarded as exactly like those which were done by Adam and Eve in the garden of Eden. It is written in Genesis 2 that God took the man whom He had created and put him in the garden to till and guard it. Now God created Adam duteous and acceptable, and without sin. He had no need to become godly or to be justified by working or guarding. But lest he be idle, God gave him something to do. He gave him work to do: plant the garden, cultivate and look after it. These labours were performed for themselves alone, and for no other reason than to please God. They were not for the purpose of attaining godliness, since Adam had that already, like all of us, naturally and inherently. Thus is to be understood also the life of a believing man who, by his faith, is planted once more in the Garden of Eden and created anew. He has no need to do certain things to make himself devout; but only that he be not idle, and that he discipline and care for his body. That is the only reason why such self-imposed duties are good for him; and thereby he pleases God.

Further, when a consecrated bishop consecrates churches, confirms, or discharges other duties of his office, these duties do not make him a bishop. Indeed, were he not already consecrated a bishop, these same duties would be useless and foolish. In the same way, a Christian who is consecrated by faith, and who also does good, is not made a better or more consecrated Christian by his works, for only an increase of faith effects that. Indeed, if he had no faith and were no Christian beforehand, all his works would be valueless; they would be merely foolish, culpable, and damnable sins.

23. Hence both expressions are true: "Good and devout works never make a man good and duteous; but a good and religious man does good and religious works." Nor do sinful works make a man sinful. Rather it is a sinful man who does sinful works. Thus every argument proves that the person must first be good and godly; after that come all the works that are good. Good works proceed logically from a godly and good person. It is as Christ said: "An evil tree bears no good fruit, a good tree bears no evil fruit." It is evident that the fruits do not bear the tree, nor do the trees grow on the fruits, but rather the trees bear the fruits, and the fruits grow on the trees. Since the trees must precede the fruits, and since the fruits do not make the trees good or evil, for the trees make the fruits, so also must a man be personally godly or sinful in himself, before what works he does can be good or sinful, as the case may be. It is not his works that make him either good or sinful, but he himself that makes them good or evil. We see the same thing in all kinds of handicrafts. A good or bad house does not make a carpenter good or bad, but a good or bad carpenter makes a good or bad house. No work makes a workman of the same quality as the work, but as the workman is, so is his work. Thus also are a man's (religious) works to be understood: his actions are good or sinful just according as it stands with him in faith or unbelief. The reverse is not true: it is not true that he is good or believing according to his kind of works. Just as works do not make a man a believer, so also they do not make him godly. But just as faith makes one godly, so also does it produce good works. Therefore, it is not what one does that makes one religious. A man must be religious before he can do the works of religion. And it is evident that only faith, coming from pure grace through Christ and His word, is sufficient to make a person religious and save him; neither works nor commandments are necessary to a Christian before he can be saved. He is free from all commandments. He does all that he does quite voluntarily without recompense, and apart from seeking his own advantage or salvation. He already has sufficient, and he is already saved through his faith and the grace of God. What he does is done just to please God.

24. Further, no meritorious works are of any avail to the godliness or salvation of one who is without faith; neither do sinful actions make him sinful or damn him; but the unbelief which makes the person and the tree sinful, is what does the sinful and damnable things. Therefore, when a man becomes either devout or sinful, the process does not begin with his actions, but with his faith. Thus Solomon says: "The beginning of sin is in departing from God, and in not trusting Him." So also Christ teaches that one must not begin with conduct. He says: "Either make the tree good, and its fruits good, or make the tree evil and its fruits evil"; which is much as if He said: "Whoever wishes to have good fruits must first begin with the tree and make that right." Similarly, whoever wants to do what is good must not begin with the actions, but

with the person who does them. But nothing makes that person good except his faith, and nothing makes that person evil except his unbelief. It is true, of course, that his conduct makes a man appear either good or evil in other men's eyes, i.e., it shows who is outwardly devout or sinful. Thus Christ said, in Matthew 7: "By their fruits you shall know them." But all that is a matter of appearance and outward show. This outward show leads many people astray. They write and teach that we must do meritorious works and so become godly, but they never give a thought to faith. They go on in that way, and one blind man leads another. They load themselves with many duties, and yet never reach the real religion of which Paul speaks in 2 Timothy 3: "They have an appearance of godliness, but the foundation is not there. They go away, and learn more and more, and yet never come to knowledge of true godliness." He who does not wish to go astray with those blind people must look beyond the works, the commandments, and the doctrines concerning what a man must do. A man must look into his own heart before everything else, and see how it may become godly. But the heart becomes devout and is saved, not by commandments or works, but by the word of God, that is, by His promise of grace, and by faith. In this way, His divine honour will stand firm, and He will save us, not by what we do, but by His gracious word. He will do it freely and out of pure mercy.

25. From all this it is easy to understand how meritorious works are to be condemned, and how they are not to be condemned; and also how one must understand all doctrines enjoining meritorious work. For, wherever are found the false addition and the perverse opinion that we become devout and are saved by means of our conduct, this is already far from good, and quite to be condemned; for a life of that kind is not free, and it contemns the grace of God. This grace alone makes men religious and saves them through faith. Works cannot do this; nevertheless they propose to do it, and in this way attack grace in its work and in its honour. Thus we condemn works of merit, not for their own sakes, but because of the evils they bring in, and their false perverse tendency to appear good in a way in which they are not good. Thus these people deceive themselves and everyone else at the same time, like ravening wolves in sheep's clothing. But that evil addition and that false tendency on the part of meritorious works are insuperable unless faith be present. This is of necessity the experiences of those people who are "sanctified" by works, until faith comes and destroys the edifice. Nature by herself can neither cure nor even recognize the evil. She holds the appearance of good as precious and blessed, and thereby many are led astray. On that account, although it is good to write and preach about repentance, confessions, and restitution, yet, if one does not go on to deal with faith, they are simply impious and seductive doctrines. We must preach neither one nor the other alone, but both together. We must preach the word of God and the commandments of God, to alarm sinners, and make their sins plain so that they repent and are converted. But we must not stop there. We must also preach the second word, the promise of

grace, and teach the faith without which commandments, repentance, and everything else are useless. There are some preachers, of course, who preach repentance from sin and proclaim grace; but they do not emphasize the commandments and promise of God for us to learn either whence or how repentance and grace do come. For repentance flows from the commandments of God, and faith flows from His promises. Thus a man who is cast down by fear of the commandments of God, and so has reached knowledge of Him, is justified and exalted by faith in the divine word.

26. All this concerns meritorious works in general and those which a Christian may perform as far as his own self is concerned. But now we would speak of other actions, those which he does in relation to other men. For a man does not live alone, in his own body, but among other men, in the world. Therefore, he cannot remain without works in his contacts with others; he must speak to and co-operate with them, although none of these actions is necessary for his own godliness or salvation. In all such works his will should be subject to no constraint, and should only be directed to the way in which he may serve other people, and be helpful to them. He should have no other thought than of what is needful to others. That would mean living a true Christian life; and that is the way in which faith proceeds to work with joy and love, as St. Paul teaches the Galatians. Also, in Philippians, after he has taught how they had all grace and sufficiency through their faith in Christ, he teaches them further, and says: "I exhort you by all the comfort which you have in Christ, and by all the comfort which you have by our love towards you, and by all the fellowship which you have with all spiritual and devout Christians, that you would cause my heart altogether to rejoice, by henceforth willing to be all of one mind, and showing love towards each other. Let each serve the other, and each have care, not for himself and his own concerns, but for others and what they need." Consider how clearly Paul thereby depicted the Christian life. All that we do must be designed for the benefit of our neighbour, because each one has sufficient for himself in his faith. Other deeds or another kind of life are unnecessary to himself, and so he may serve his neighbour out of unconstrained love. In addition, St. Paul cites the example of Christ and says: "Have the same mind as you see in Christ who, although He was filled with the divine form and had sufficient for Himself, and His life and works and suffering were not necessary to Him in order that He might become devout and be saved, nevertheless, He emptied Himself of all these things, and assumed the form of a servant. He did and suffered everything with no other object than our advantage. Thus, although He was free, for our sakes He became a servant."

27. It follows that, like Christ his head, a Christian must let himself be completely and sufficiently content with his faith, always increasing in this which is his life, his religion, and his salvation. It gives him everything that Christ and God possess, as is said above, and also as St. Paul says in Galatians 2: "The life which I now live in the body, I live in the faith of Christ

the Son of God." And although he is now quite free, yet a Christian ought voluntarily to make himself a servant and help his neighbour. He should associate and deal with him as God has done with himself through Christ, everything being free, and nothing being sought except to please God. He should therefore think within himself: "Unworthy and guilty man that I am, and without any desert, yet my God, quite freely and out of pure mercy, has given me, in and through Christ, the full wealth of all religion and salvation, so that henceforth I need nothing except faith. So let it be. Yes, for the sake of such a Father, who has heaped upon me His superabundant good things, will I freely, gladly, and without reward, do what pleases Him. To my neighbour, I will be, as a Christian, what Christ has become to me, and do just what I see is needful, helpful, or acceptable to him, for I have enough of all things in Christ through my faith." Lo, that is how love and joy in God flow out of faith, and how love gives rise to a free, eager, and glad life of serving one's neighbour without reward. For just as our neighbour is needy, and requires our excess, so we were needy in God's eyes, and required His grace. Therefore, just as God helped us without payment through Christ, so ought we, through our body and its works, always to help our neighbour. Thus we see that the Christian life is a truly noble life. Unhappily it is now not merely held in poor esteem everywhere, but is neither known nor preached any longer.

28. Accordingly, we read in Luke 2 that the Virgin Mary went to church, after six weeks, for her purification according to the law, like all other women, although she was not unclean like them, nor under the same obligation of purification; nor did she need it. But she did it voluntarily, out of love, that she might not look down upon other women, but remain on the level of the rest. Similarly also, St. Paul had St. Timothy circumcized not because it was necessary, but lest he gave cause to Jews weak in faith to think evil thoughts. On the other hand, he refused to allow Titus to be circumcized because some urged that he must needs be circumcized, and that it was necessary for salvation. And when toll was required of His disciples (Matthew 17), Christ discussed with St. Peter whether the children of the king were not free from paying toll. Yet when St. Peter agreed, He told him to go to the sea, and said: "Lest we vex them, go and take the first fish you catch, and you will find a penny in its mouth; pay it for me and you." That is a notable example of the case in point, for Christ called Himself and His disciples free children of the king, under no compulsion; and yet He voluntarily submitted. He acted as a subject and paid toll. Now just to the extent that that act was necessary to Christ, and of use to His own godliness or salvation, so all His other deeds, and the deeds of His Christian followers, are necessary for their salvation. But this means that everything will be done freely, and only to please and benefit others. Therefore all that is done by the priests, monasteries, and religious foundations should be done in a similar manner. Let each one discharge the duties of his rank or order, only to assist others, to discipline his own body, or to give an example to others in mastering their own bodies as they find it

necessary. But all the time we must beware lest we suppose ourselves to become devout or attain salvation by doing so, for that is within the power of faith alone. St. Paul also teaches in Romans 13 and Titus 3 that we should be subject and well-disposed to the secular power, not for the sake of becoming godly by these means, but that we may freely serve our neighbours and the authorities, and do their will in love and freedom. Those who have this understanding of things can easily find their right attitude to the numberless rules and regulations of the pope, of bishops, of monasteries, of religious houses, of princes and lords, regulations which certain foolish prelates press on us as if they were needful to salvation. These are called laws of the church, although unjustifiably. But a free Christian says: "I will fast and pray, I will do this or that as is commanded, not because I need to do so, or would thereby become devout or attain salvation; but I will comply with the will of the pope, the bishop, the ordinary priest, or my fellow man, as if he were my master. I will set an example, and do a service, just because Christ did and suffered much greater things for my sake, although it was far less needful for Him to do so. And, although the tyrants do injustice in requiring such a thing, nevertheless it does not hurt me so long as it is not against God's will."

29. On this basis, each man may form a sure judgment, and make a clear distinction in regard to all works and laws. He can also tell which prelates are blind and foolish, and which are wise and right-minded. For unless the enjoined works tend to serve another man or to comply with his will, even if they do not compel us to act against God, they are not sound Christian works. Therefore it comes about, I fear, that few religious houses, churches, monasteries, altars, masses, or endowments are Christian; and, in particular, the observance of fasts, or the offering of prayers to certain saints. For I fear that, as a rule, each seeks only his own interest, yet believes he is atoning for his sins and being saved. But all this springs from ignorance of the nature of faith and Christian freedom. Certain blind prelates lead the people astray, and praise such doings, pile on indulgences, but never once teach faith. But I advise you if you wish to pray, or fast, or make an endowment, let it not be with the idea that you will benefit yourself. Rather do it freely in order that others may benefit; do it for their advantage—then you will be a real Christian. What is the value of your property or your merits if they are more than you require to enable you to master and provide for your body? You have a sufficiency in the faith through which God has given you all things. Remember that all the good things of God should flow from one man to another, and become common to all, so that each one may be as concerned for his neighbour as for his own self. All good things come to us from Christ, who has received us into His own life as if He had been what we are. From us they should flow to those who are in need of them. This should be so completely true that I must offer even my faith and righteousness before God on behalf of my neighbour, to blot out his sins, and take them upon myself. I must act as if they were my own, just as Christ has done for us all. Indeed, that is the nature of love if it

is real. And it is real if faith is real. Therefore, in 1 Corinthians 13, the holy Apostle says that love is of such a kind that it does not seek its own advantage, but its neighbour's.

30. From all the foregoing, the conclusion follows that a Christian lives not in himself, but in Christ and his neighbour; in Christ by faith and in his neighbour by love. By faith he rises above himself unto God; from God he stoops below himself by love, and yet he remains always in God and in divine love, just as Christ says in John 1: "You will see the heavens open and the angels ascending and descending upon the Son of Man." Yes, that is the true, spiritual, and Christian freedom. It liberates our hearts from all sins, laws, and commandments. It exceeds all other freedom as much as heaven the earth. God grant that we rightly understand and retain this freedom. Amen.

44

ON THE CHRISTIAN LIFE
John Calvin

What Martin Luther was to Germany, John Calvin (1509–1564) was to French-speaking Switzerland, and his influence throughout the subsequent history of religion and theology has been even more pronounced than that of his German counterpart. Calvin began his university studies in theology but afterwards transferred to the study of law and published his first book in that field. However, he had a profound religious experience—evidently from reading the scriptures—in 1532, which turned him from his humanist interests towards religion. Finding the Catholic community in France too conservative for his opinions, Calvin united with the Protestants and soon had to flee to Basel. It was in an attempt to defend French Protestants from what he regarded as slanderous characterizations of them by the king, Francis I, that he composed the first edition of his now-famous Institutes of the Christian Religion *(1536). Soon afterwards, he went to Geneva where he attempted to set up a theocratic society and as a conse-*

From Calvin: Institutes of the Christian Religion, ed. John T. McNeill. Tr. Ford Lewis Battles. Vol. XX, LCC, pp. 689–701. Copyright © 1960, W. L. Jenkins. The Westminster Press. Used by permission.

quence was expelled by the citizens of that city in 1538, only to be invited back following a change in local government in 1541. Thereafter Calvin retained great power in Geneva, although he once kept control only by cowing his opposition by burning the noted heretic, Servetus. In 1559, the final, much enlarged, edition of the Institutes *was published. Calvin's doctrine is characterized by his emphasis upon divine power, holding that man is totally corrupt and totally unable to save himself and that his salvation is a matter of divine choice or predestination. He also emphasized obedience to divine law as taught in the scriptures, and reduced the sacraments to two. The following selection from the* Institutes *contains Calvin's sketch of the major features of the Christian way of life.*

CHAPTER VII: THE SUM OF THE CHRISTIAN LIFE: THE DENIAL OF OURSELVES

(The Christian philosophy of unworldliness and self-denial; we are not our own, we are God's, 1-3)

1. We are not our own masters, but belong to God

Even though the law of the Lord provides the finest and best-disposed method of ordering a man's life, it seemed good to the Heavenly Teacher to shape his people by an even more explicit plan to that rule which he had set forth in the law. Here, then, is the beginning of this plan: the duty of believers is "to present their bodies to God as a living sacrifice, holy and acceptable to him," and in this consists the lawful worship of him [Rom. 12:1]. From this is derived the basis of the exhortation that "they be not conformed to the fashion of this world, but be transformed by the renewal of their minds, so that they may prove what is the will of God" [Rom. 12:2]. Now the great thing is this: we are consecrated and dedicated to God in order that we may thereafter think, speak, meditate, and do, nothing except to his glory. For a sacred thing may not be applied to profane uses without marked injury to him.

If we, then, are not our own [cf. I Cor. 6:19] but the Lord's, it is clear what error we must flee, and whither we must direct all the acts of our life.

We are not our own: let not our reason nor our will, therefore, sway our plans and deeds. We are not our own: let us therefore not set it as our goal to seek what is expedient for us according to the flesh. We are not our own: in so far as we can, let us therefore forget ourselves and all that is ours.

Conversely, we are God's: let us therefore live for him and die for him. We are God's: let his wisdom and will therefore rule all our actions. We are God's: let all the parts of our life accordingly strive toward him as our only lawful goal [Rom. 14:8; cf. I Cor. 6:19]. O, how much has that man profited who, having been taught that he is not his own, has taken away dominion and rule from his own reason that he may yield it to God! For, as consulting our self-interest is the pestilence that most effectively leads to our destruction, so the sole haven of salvation is to be wise in nothing and to will nothing through ourselves but to follow the leading of the Lord alone.

Let this therefore be the first step, that a man depart from himself in order that he may apply the whole force of his ability in the service of the Lord. I call "service" not only what lies in obedience to God's Word but what turns the mind of man, empty of its own carnal sense, wholly to the bidding of God's Spirit. While it is the first entrance to life, all philosophers were ignorant of this transformation, which Paul calls "renewal of the mind" [Eph. 4:23]. For they set up reason alone as the ruling principle in man, and think that it alone should be listened to; to it alone, in short, they entrust the conduct of life. But the Christian philosophy bids reason give way to, submit and subject itself to, the Holy Spirit so that the man himself may no longer live but hear Christ living and reigning within him [Gal. 2:20].

2. Self-denial through devotion to God

From this also follows this second point: that we seek not the things that are ours but those which are of the Lord's will and will serve to advance his glory. This is also evidence of great progress: that, almost forgetful of ourselves, surely subordinating our self-concern, we try faithfully to devote our zeal to God and his commandments. For when Scripture bids us leave off self-concern, it not only erases from our minds the yearning to possess, the desire for power, and the favor of men, but it also uproots ambition and all craving for human glory and other more secret plagues. Accordingly, the Christian must surely be so disposed and minded that he feels within himself it is with God he has to deal throughout his life. In this way, as he will refer all he has to God's decision and judgment, so will he refer his whole intention of mind scrupulously to Him. For he who has learned to look to God in all things that he must do, at the same time avoids all vain thoughts. This, then, is that denial of self which Christ enjoins with such great earnestness upon his disciples at the outset of their service [cf. Matt. 16:24]. When it has once taken possession of their hearts, it leaves no place at all first either to pride, or arrogance, or ostentation; then either to avarice, or desire, or lasciviousness, or effeminacy, or to other evils that our self-love spawns [cf. II Tim. 3:2–5]. On the other hand, wherever denial of ourselves does not reign, there either the foulest vices rage without shame or if there is any semblance of virtue, it is vitiated by depraved lusting after glory. Show me a man, if you can, who, unless he has according to the commandment of the Lord renounced himself, would freely exercise goodness among men. For all who have not been possessed with this feeling have at least followed virtue for the sake of praise. Now those of the philosophers who at any time most strongly contended that virtue should be pursued for its own sake were puffed up with such great arrogance as to show they sought after virtue for no other reason than to have occasion for pride. Yet God is so displeased, both with those who court the popular breeze and with such swollen souls, as to declare that they have received their reward in this world [Matt. 6:2,5,16], and to make harlots and publicans nearer to the Kingdom of Heaven than are they [Matt. 21:31]. Yet we have still not clearly explained how many and how great are the obstacles that hinder man from a right course so long as he has not denied himself. For it was once truly said: "A world of vices is hidden in the soul of man." And you can find no other remedy than in denying yourself and giving up concern for yourself, and in turning your mind wholly to seek after those things which the Lord requires of you, and to seek them only because they are pleasing to him.

3. Self-renunciation according to Titus, ch. 2

In another place, Paul more clearly, although briefly, delineates the individual parts of a well-ordered life. "The grace of God has appeared, bringing salvation to all men, training us to renounce irreligion and worldly passions and to live sober, upright, and godly lives, in the present age; awaiting our blessed hope, and the appearing of the glory of our great God and of our Savior Jesus Christ, who gave himself for us to redeem us from all iniquity and to purify for himself a people of his own who are zealous for good deeds." [Titus 2:11–14.] For, after he proffered the grace of God to hearten us, in order to pave the way for us to worship God truly he removed the two obstacles that chiefly hinder us: namely, ungodliness, to which by nature we are too much inclined; and second, worldly desires, which extend more widely. And by ungodliness, indeed, he not only means superstition but includes also whatever contends against the earnest fear of God. Worldly lusts are also equivalent to the passions of the flesh [cf. I John 2:16; Eph. 2:3; II Peter 2:18; Gal. 5:16; etc.]. Thus, with reference to both Tables of the Law, he commands us to put off our own nature and to deny whatever our reason and will dictate. Now he limits all actions of life to three parts: soberness, righteousness, and godliness. Of these, soberness doubtless denotes chastity and temperance as well as a pure and frugal use of temporal goods, and patience in poverty. Now righteousness embraces all the duties of equity in order that to each one be rendered what is his own [cf. Rom. 13:7]. There follows godliness, which joins us in true holiness with God when we are separated from the iniquities of the world. When these things are joined together by an inseparable bond, they bring about complete perfection. But, nothing is more difficult than, having bidden farewell to the reason of the flesh and having bridled our desires—nay, having put them away—to devote ourselves to God and our brethren, and to meditate, amid earth's filth, upon the life of the angels. Consequently, Paul, in order to extricate our minds from all snares, recalls us to the hope of blessed immortality, reminding us that we strive not in vain [cf. I Thess. 3:5]. For, as Christ our Redeemer once appeared, so in his final coming he will show the fruit of the salvation brought forth by him. In this way he scatters all the allurements that becloud us and prevent us from aspiring as we ought to heavenly glory. Nay, he teaches us to travel as pilgrims in this world that our celestial heritage may not perish or pass away.

(The principle of self-denial in our relations with our fellow men, 4-7)

4. Self-denial gives us the right attitude toward our fellow men

Now in these words we perceive that denial of self has regard partly to men, partly, and chiefly, to God.

For when Scripture bids us act toward men so as to esteem them above ourselves [Phil. 2:3], and in good faith to apply ourselves wholly to doing them good [cf. Rom. 12:10], it gives us commandments of which our mind is quite incapable unless our mind be previously emptied of its natural feeling. For, such is the blindness with which we all rush into self-love that each one of us seems to himself to have just cause to be proud of himself and to despise all others in comparison. If God has conferred upon us anything of which we need not repent, relying upon it we immediately lift up our minds, and are not only puffed up but almost burst with pride. The very vices that infest us we take pains to hide from others, while we flatter ourselves with the pretense that they are slight and insignificant, and even sometimes embrace them as virtues. If others manifest the same endowments we admire in ourselves, or even superior ones, we spitefully belittle and revile these gifts in order to avoid yielding place to such persons. If there are any faults in others, not content with noting them with severe and sharp reproach, we hatefully exaggerate them. Hence arises such insolence that each one of us, as if exempt from the common lot, wishes to tower above the rest, and loftily and savagely abuses every mortal man, or at least looks down upon him as an inferior. The poor yield to the rich; the common folk, to the nobles; the servants, to their masters; the unlearned, to the educated. But there is no one who does not cherish within himself some opinion of his own pre-eminence.

Thus, each individual, by flattering himself, bears a kind of kingdom in his breast. For claiming as his own what pleases him, he censures the character and morals of others. But if this comes to the point of conflict, his venom bursts forth. For many obviously display some gentleness so long as they find everything sweet and pleasant. But just how many are there who will preserve this even tenor of modesty when they are pricked and irritated? There is no other remedy than to tear out from our inward parts this most deadly pestilence of love of strife and love of self, even as it is plucked out by Scriptural teaching. For thus we are instructed to remember that those talents which God has bestowed upon us are not our own goods but the free gifts of God; and any persons who become proud of them show their ungratefulness. "Who causes you to excel?" Paul asks. "If you have received all things, why do you boast as if they were not given to you?" [I Cor. 4:7].

Let us, then, unremittingly examining our faults, call ourselves back to humility. Thus nothing will remain in us to puff us up; but there will be much occasion to be cast down. On the other hand, we are bidden so to esteem and regard whatever gifts of God we see in other men that we may honor those men in whom they reside. For it would be great depravity on our part to deprive them of that honor which the Lord has bestowed upon them. But we are taught to overlook their faults, certainly not flatteringly to cherish them; but not on account of such faults to revile men whom we ought to cherish with good will and honor. Thus it will come about that, whatever man we deal with, we shall treat him not only moderately and modestly but also cordially and as a friend. You will never attain true gentleness except by one path: a heart imbued with lowliness and with reverence for others.

5. Self-renunciation leads to proper helpfulness toward our neighbors

Now, in seeking to benefit one's neighbor, how difficult it is to do one's duty! Unless you give up all thought of self and, so to speak, get out of yourself, you will accomplish nothing here. For how can you perform those works which Paul teaches to be the works of love, unless you renounce yourself, and give yourself wholly to others? "Love," he says, "is patient and kind, not jealous or boastful, is not envious or puffed up, does not seek its own, is not irritable," etc. [I Cor. 13: 4–5 p.] If this is the one thing required—that we seek not what is our own—still we shall do no little violence to nature, which so inclines us to love of ourselves alone that it does not easily allow us to neglect ourselves and our possessions in order to look after another's good, nay, to yield willingly what is ours by right and resign it to another. But Scripture, to lead us by the hand to this, warns that whatever benefits we obtain from the Lord have been entrusted to us on this condition: that they be applied to the common good of the church. And therefore the lawful use of all benefits consists in a liberal and kindly sharing of them with others. No surer rule and no more valid exhortation to keep it could be devised than when we are taught that all the gifts we possess have been bestowed by God and entrusted to us on condition that they be distributed for our neighbors' benefit [cf. 1 Peter 4:10].

But Scripture goes even farther by comparing them to the powers with which the members of the human body are endowed [I Cor. 12:12 ff.]. No member has this power for itself nor applies it to its own private use; but each pours it out to the fellow members. Nor does it take any profit from its power except what proceeds from the common advantage of the whole body. So, too, whatever a godly man can do he ought to be able to do for his brothers, providing for himself in no way other than to have his mind intent upon the common upbuilding of the church. Let this, therefore, be our rule for generosity and beneficence: We are the stewards of everything God has conferred on us by which we are able to help our neighbor, and are required to render account of our stewardship. Moreover, the only right stewardship is that which is tested by the rule of love. Thus it will come about that we shall not only join zeal for another's benefit with care for our own advantage, but shall subordinate the latter to the former.

And lest perhaps we should not realize that this is the rule for the proper management of all gifts we have received from God, he also in early times applied it to the least gifts of his generosity. For he commanded that the first fruits be brought to him by which the people were to testify that it was unlawful to accept for themselves any enjoyment of benefits not previously consecrated to him [Ex. 23:19; cf. ch. 22:29, Vg.]. But if the gifts of God are only thus sanctified to us when we have dedicated them by our hand to the Author himself, that which does not savor of such dedication is clearly a corrupt abuse. Yet you wish to strive in vain to enrich the Lord by sharing your possessions; since, then, your generosity cannot extend to him, you must, as the prophet says, practice it toward the saints on earth [Ps. 16:2-3]. And alms are compared to holy sacrifices so as to correspond now to those requirements of the law [Heb. 13:16].

6. Love of neighbor is not dependent upon manner of men but looks to God

Furthermore, not to grow weary in well-doing [Gal. 6:9], which otherwise must happen immediately, we ought to add that other idea which the apostle mentions: "Love is patient . . . and is not irritable" [I Cor. 13:4-5]. The Lord commands all men without exception "to do good" [Heb. 13:16]. Yet the great part of them are most unworthy if they be judged by their own merit. But here Scripture helps in the best way when it teaches that we are not to consider that men merit of themselves but to look upon the image of God in all men, to which we owe all honor and love. However, it is among members of the household of faith that this same image is more carefully to be noted [Gal. 6:10], in so far as it has been renewed and restored through the Spirit of Christ. Therefore, whatever man you meet who needs your aid, you have no reason to refuse to help him. Say, "He is a stranger"; but the Lord has given him a mark that ought to be familiar to you, by virtue of the fact that he forbids you to despise your own flesh [Isa. 58:7 Vg.]. Say, "He is contemptible and worthless"; but the Lord shows him to be one to whom he has deigned to give the beauty of his image. Say that you owe nothing for any service of his; but God, as it were, has put him in his own place in order that you may recognize toward him the many and great benefits with which God has bound you to himself. Say that he does not deserve even your least effort for his sake; but the image of God, which recommends him to you, is worthy of your giving yourself and all your possessions. Now if he has not only deserved no good at your hand, but has also provoked you by unjust acts and curses, not even this is just reason why you should cease to embrace him in love and to perform the duties of love on his behalf [Matt. 6:14; 18:35; Luke 17:3]. You will say, "He has deserved something far different of me." Yet what has the Lord deserved? While he bids you forgive this man for all sins he has committed against you, he would truly have them charged against himself. Assuredly there is but one way in which to achieve what is not merely difficult but utterly against human nature: to love those who hate us, to repay their evil deeds with benefits, to return blessings for reproaches [Matt. 5:44]. It is that we remember not to consider men's evil intention but to look upon the image of God in them, which cancels and effaces their transgressions, and with its beauty and dignity allures us to love and embrace them.

7. The outward work of love is not sufficient, but it is intention that counts

This mortification, then, will take place in us only if we fulfill the duties of love. Now he who merely performs all the duties of love does not fulfill them, even though he overlooks none; but he, rather, fulfills them who does this from a sincere feeling of love. For it can happen that one who indeed discharges to the full all his obligations as far as outward duties are concerned is still all the while far away from the true way of discharging them. For you may see some who wish to seem very liberal and yet bestow nothing that they do not make reprehensible with a proud countenance or even insolent words. And in this tragic and unhappy age it has come to this pass, that most men give their alms contemptuously. Such depravity ought not to have been tolerable even among the pagans; of Christians something even more is required than to show a cheerful countenance and to render their duties pleasing with friendly words. First, they must put themselves in the place of him whom they see in need of their assistance, and pity his ill fortune as if they themselves experienced and bore it, so that they may be impelled by a feeling of mercy and humaneness to go to his aid just as to their own.

He who, thus disposed, proceeds to give help to his brethren will not corrupt his own duties by either arrogance or upbraiding. Furthermore, in giving benefits he will not despise his needy brother or enslave him as one indebted to himself. This would no more be reasonable than that we should either chide a sick member that the rest of the body labors to revive or consider it especially obligated to the remaining members because it has drawn more help to itself than it can repay. Now the sharing of tasks among members is believed to have nothing gratuitous about it but, rather, to be a payment of that which, due by the law of nature, it would be monstrous to refuse. Also, in this way it will come about that he who has discharged one kind of task will not think himself free, as commonly happens when a rich man, after he has given up something of his own, delegates to other men other burdens as having nothing at all to do with him. Rather, each man will so consider with himself that in all his greatness he is a debtor to his neighbors, and that he ought in exercising kindness toward them to set no other limit than the end of his resources; these, as widely as they are extended, ought to have their limits set according to the rule of love.

(The principle of self-denial in our relation to God, 8–10)

8. Self-denial toward God: devotion to his will!

Let us reiterate in fuller form the chief part of self-denial, which, as we have said, looks to God. And indeed, many things have been said about this already that it would be superfluous to repeat. It will be enough to show how it forms us to fair-mindedness and tolerance.

To begin with, then, in seeking either the convenience or the tranquillity of the present life, Scripture calls us to resign ourselves and all our possessions to the Lord's will, and to yield to him the desires of our hearts to be tamed and subjugated. To covet wealth and honors, to strive for authority, to heap up riches, to gather together all those follies which seem to make for magnificence and pomp, our lust is mad, our desire boundless. On the other hand, wonderful is our fear, wonderful our hatred, of poverty, lowly birth, and humble condition! And we are spurred to rid ourselves of them by every means. Hence we can see how uneasy in mind all those persons are who order their lives according to their own plan. We can see how artfully they strive—to the point of weariness—to obtain the goal of their ambition or avarice, while, on the other hand, avoiding poverty and a lowly condition.

In order not to be caught in such snares, godly men must hold to this path. First of all, let them neither desire nor hope for, nor contemplate, any other way of prospering than by the Lord's blessing. Upon this, then, let them safely and confidently throw themselves and rest. For however beautifully the flesh may seem to suffice unto itself, while it either strives by its own effort for honors and riches or relies upon its diligence, or is aided by the favor of men, yet it is certain that all these things are nothing; nor will we benefit at all, either by skill or by labor, except in so far as the Lord prospers them both. On the contrary, however, his blessing alone finds a way, even through all hindrances, to bring all things to a happy and favorable outcome for us; again, though entirely without it, to enable us to obtain some glory and opulence for ourselves (as we daily see impious men amassing great honors and riches), yet, inasmuch as those upon whom the curse of God rests taste not even the least particle of happiness, without this blessing we shall obtain nothing but what turns to our misfortune. For we ought by no means to desire what makes men more miserable.

9. Trust in God's blessing only

Therefore, suppose we believe that every means toward a prosperous and desirable outcome rests upon the blessing of God alone; and that, when this is absent, all sorts of misery and calamity dog us. It remains for us not greedily to strive after riches and honors—whether relying upon our own dexterity of wit or our own diligence, or depending upon the favor of men, or having confidence in vainly imagined fortune—but for us always to look to the Lord so that by his guidance we may be led to whatever lot he has provided for us. Thus it will first come to pass that we shall not dash out to seize upon riches and usurp honors through wickedness and by stratagems and evil arts, or greed, to the injury of our neighbors; but pursue only those enterprises which do not lead us away from innocence.

Who can hope for the help of a divine blessing amidst frauds, robberies, and other wicked arts? For as that blessing follows only him who thinks purely and acts rightly, thus it calls back from crooked thoughts and wicked actions all those who seek it. Then will a bridle be put on us that we may not burn with an immoderate desire to grow rich or ambitiously pant after honors. For with what shamelessness does a man trust that he will be helped by God to obtain those things which he desires contrary to God's Word? Away with the thought that God would abet with his blessing what he curses with his mouth! Lastly, if things do not go according to our wish and hope, we will still be restrained from impatience and loathing of our condition, whatever it may be. For we shall know that this is to murmur against God, by whose will riches and poverty, contempt and honor, are dispensed. To sum up, he who rests solely upon the blessing of God, as it has been here expressed, will neither strive with evil arts after those things which men customarily madly seek after, which he realizes will not profit him, nor will he, if things go well, give credit to himself or even to his diligence, or industry, or fortune. Rather, he will give God the credit as its Author. But if, while other men's affairs flourish, he makes but slight advancement, or even slips back, he will still bear his low estate with greater equanimity and moderation of mind than some profane person would bear a moderate success which merely does not correspond with his wish. For he indeed possesses a solace in which he may repose more peace-fully than in the highest degree of wealth or power. Since this leads to his salvation, he considers that his affairs are ordained by the Lord. We see that David was so minded; while he follows God and gives himself over to his leading, he attests that he is like a child weaned from his mother's breast, and that he does not occupy himself with things too deep and wonderful for him [Ps. 131:1–2].

10. Self-denial helps us bear adversity

And for godly minds the peace and forbearance we have spoken of ought not to rest solely in this point; but it must also be extended to every occurrence to which the present life is subject. Therefore, he alone has duly denied himself who has so totally resigned himself to the Lord that he permits every part of his life to be governed by God's will. He who will be thus composed in mind, whatever happens, will not consider himself miserable nor complain of his lot with ill will toward God. How necessary this disposition is will appear if you weigh the many chance happenings to which we are subject. Various diseases repeatedly trouble us: now plague rages; now we are cruelly beset by the calamities of war; now ice and hail, consuming the year's expecta-tion, lead to barrenness, which reduces us to poverty; wife, parents, children, neighbors, are snatched away by death; our house is burned by fire. It is on account of these occurrences that men curse their life, loathe the day of their birth, abominate heaven and the light of day, rail against God, and as they are eloquent in blasphemy, accuse him of injustice and cruelty. But in these matters the believer must also look to God's kindness and truly fatherly in-dulgence. Accordingly, if he sees his house reduced to solitude by the removal of his kinsfolk, he will not indeed even then cease to bless the Lord, but rather will turn his attention to this thought: nevertheless, the grace of the Lord, which dwells in my house, will not leave it desolate. Or, if his crops are blasted by frost, or destroyed by ice, or beaten down with hail, and he sees famine threatening, yet he will not despair or bear a grudge against God, but will remain firm in this trust [cf. Ps. 78:47]: "Nevertheless we are in the Lord's protection, sheep brought up in his pastures" [Ps. 79:13]. The Lord will therefore supply food to us even in extreme barrenness. If he shall be afflicted by disease, he will not even then be so unmanned by the harshness of pain as to break forth into impatience and expostulate with God; but, by considering the righteousness and gentleness of God's chastening, he will recall himself to forbearance. In short, whatever happens, because he will know it ordained of God, he will undergo it with a peaceful and grateful mind so as not obstinately to resist the command of him into whose power he once for all surrendered himself and his every possession.

Especially let that foolish and most miserable consolation of the pagans be far away from the breast of the Christian man; to strengthen their minds against adversities, they charged these to fortune. Against fortune they considered it foolish to be angry because she was blind and unthinking, with unseeing eyes wounding the deserving and the undeserving at the same time. On the contrary, the rule of piety is that God's hand alone is the judge and governor of fortune, good or bad, and that it does not rush about with heedless force, but with most orderly justice deals out good as well as ill to us.

45

SOCIAL CHRISTIANITY AND PERSONAL RELIGION
Walter Rauschenbusch

One of the more prominent movements in American religious thought, which also achieved world-wide interest, was the Social Gospel movement of the first part of this century. The most influential and widely known leader in that movement was Walter

Reprinted with permission of The Macmillan Company from *Christianizing the Social Order* by Walter Rauschenbusch, pp. 103–122. Copyright 1912 by The Macmillan Company.

Rauschenbusch (1861–1918). Rauschenbusch was the son of a German emigrant who came to the United States in 1845 to do religious work and who was for a long time a teacher at Rochester Theological Seminary. The young Rauschenbusch received his secondary education in Germany, but took his B.A. at the University of Rochester and his B.D. at Rochester Theological Seminary, receiving the latter degree in 1886. Afterwards, he was successively pastor of the Second German Baptist Church in New York, Professor of New Testament, and Professor of Church History, the last two posts both being at Rochester Theological Seminary. In his early career he wrote several books in German, designed primarily for the German Baptist readership. However, his Christianity and the Social Crisis *(1907) is both his first English work and his best known treatise. He subsequently published several other volumes on the theme of Christian social consciousness, including* Christianizing the Social Order *(1912) and* A Theology for the Social Gospel *(1917). The Social Gospel movement was characterized by the attempt to remove Christianity from the isolation of the churches to a significant and humane role in the areas of social welfare and enlightened government. In the following selection, Rauschenbusch argues for a rapprochement between the social and the personal aspects of religious experience.*

We who know personal religion by experience know that there is nothing on earth to compare with the moral force exerted by it. It has demonstrated its social efficiency in our own lives. It was personal religion which first set us our tasks of service in youth, and which now holds us to them when our body droops and our spirit flags. Religion can turn diffident, humble men like Shaftesbury into invincible champions of the poor. All social movements would gain immensely in enthusiasm, persuasiveness, and wisdom, if the hearts of their advocates were cleansed and warmed by religious faith. Even those who know religious power only by observation of others will concede that.

But will the reënforcement work the other way, also? Religion strengthens the social spirit; will the social spirit strengthen personal religion? When a minister gets hot about child labor and wage slavery, is he not apt to get cold about prayer meetings and evangelistic efforts? When young women become interested in social work, do they not often lose their taste for the culture of the spiritual life and the peace of religious meditation? A hot breakfast is an event devoutly to be desired, but is it wise to chop up your precious old set of colonial furniture to cook the breakfast? Would the reënforcement of the social spirit be worth while if we lost our personal religion in the process?

If this is indeed the alternative, we are in a tragic situation, compelled to choose between social righteousness and communion with God.

Personal religion has a supreme value for its own sake, not merely as a feeder of social morality, but as the highest unfolding of life itself, as the blossoming of our spiritual nature. Spiritual regeneration is the most important fact in any life history. A living experience of God is the crowning knowledge attainable to a human mind. Each one of us needs the redemptive power of religion for his own sake, for on the tiny stage of the human soul all the vast world tragedy of good and evil is reënacted. In the best social order that is conceivable men will still smolder with lust and ambition, and be lashed by hate and jealousy as with the whip of a slave driver. No material comfort and plenty can satisfy the restless soul in us and give us peace with ourselves. All who have made test of it agree that religion alone holds the key to the ultimate meaning of life, and each of us must find his way into the inner mysteries alone. The day will come when all life on this planet will be extinct, and what meaning will our social evolution have had if that is all? Religion is eternal life in the midst of time and transcending time. The explanations of religion have often been the worst possible, God knows, but the fact of religion is the biggest thing there is.

If, therefore, our personal religious life is likely to be sapped by our devotion to social work, it would be a calamity second to none. But is it really likely that this will happen? The great aim underlying the whole social movement is the creation of a free, just, and brotherly social order. This is the greatest moral task conceivable. Its accomplishment is the manifest will of God for this generation. Every Christian motive is calling us to it. If it is left undone, millions of lives will be condemned to a deepening moral degradation and to spiritual starvation. Does it look probable that we shall lose our contact with God if we plunge too deeply into this work? Does it stand to reason that we shall go astray from Jesus Christ if we engage in the unequal conflict with organized wrong? What kind of "spirituality" is it which is likely to get hurt by being put to work for justice and our fellow-men?

Some of the anxiety about personal religion is due to a subtle lack of faith in religion. Men think it is a fragile thing that will break up and vanish when the customs and formulas which have hitherto incased and protected it are broken and cast aside. Most of us have known religion under one form, and we suppose it can have no other. But religion is the life of God in the soul of man, and is God really so fragile? Will the tongue of fire sputter and go out unless we shelter it under a bushel? Let the winds of God roar through it, and watch it! Religion unites a great variability of form with an amazing constancy of power. The Protestant Reformation changed the entire outward complexion of religion in the nations of northern Europe. All the most characteristic forms in which Christianity had expressed itself and by which its strength had hitherto been gauged were swept away. No pope, no priest, no monk, no mass, no confessional, no rosary, no saints, no images, no processions, no pilgrimages, no indulgences! It was a clean sweep. What was left of religion? Religion itself! At least your Puritans and Huguenots seemed to think they had personal religion; more, in fact, than ever before. Catholics thought it was the destruction of personal religion; really it was the rise of a new type of religion. In the same way the social Christianity of to-day is not a dilution of personal religion, but a new form of experimental Christianity, and its religious testimony will have to be heard henceforth when "the varieties of religious experience" are described.[1]

Nevertheless, conservative Christian men are not frightened by their own imaginings when they fear that the progress of the social interest will mean a receding of personal religion. They usually have definite cases in mind in which that seemed to be the effect, and it is well worth while to examine these more closely.

In the first place, personal religion collapses with some individuals, because in their case it had long been growing hollow and thin. Not all who begin the study of music or poetry in youth remain lovers of art and literature to the end, and not all who begin a religious life in the ardor of youth keep up its emotional intimacy as life goes on. Take any group of one hundred religious people, laymen or ministers, and it is a safe guess that in a considerable fraction of them the fire of vital religion is merely flickering in the ashes. As long as their life goes on in the accustomed way, they maintain their religious connections and expressions, and do so sincerely, but if they move to another part of the country, or if a new interest turns their minds forcibly in some other direction, the frayed bond parts and they turn from their Church and religion. If it is the social interest which attracts them, it may seem to them and others that this has extinguished their devotional life. In reality there was little personal religion to lose, and that little would probably have been lost in some other way. This would cover the inner history of some ministers as well as of church members.

In other cases we must recognize that men become apathetic about church activities in which they have been interested, because they have found something better. The Hebrew prophets turned in anger from the sacrificial doings of their people; Jesus turned away from the long prayers of the Pharisees, who were the most pious people of his day; the Reformers repudiated many of the most devout activities of medieval Catholicism. Wherever there is a new awakening of spiritual life, there is a discarding of old religious forms, and it is to the interest of personal religion that there should be. Is there nothing petty, useless, and insipid in the Catholic or Protestant church life of our day from which a soul awakened to larger purposes ought really to turn away? Is it reprehensible if some drop out of a dress parade when they hear the sound of actual fighting just across the hills?

It is also true that in this tremendous awakening and unsettlement some turn away in haste from things which have lasting value. Few men and few movements have such poise that they never overshoot the mark. When the Reformation turned its back on medieval superstition, it also smashed the

[1] My friend Elie Gounelle has a fine discussion on this in his book, "Pourquoi sommes-nous chrétiens sociaux?" p. 29 (Librairie Fischbacher, Paris). A remarkable little book.

painted windows of the cathedrals and almost banished art and music from its services. When mystics feel the compelling power of the inner word of God, they are apt to slight the written word. So when religious souls who have been shut away from social ideals and interests and pent up within a fine but contracted religious habitation get the new outlook of the social awakening, it sweeps them away with new enthusiasms. Their life rushes in to fill the empty spaces. Their mind is busy with a religious comprehension of a hundred new facts and problems, and the old questions of personal religion drop out of sight. In such cases we can safely trust to experience to restore the equilibrium. In a number of my younger friends the balancing is now going on. As they work their way in life and realize the real needs of men and the real values of life, they get a new comprehension of the power and preciousness of personal and intimate religion, and they turn back to the old truths of Christianity with a fresh relish and a firmer accent of conviction. We shall see that rediscovery in thousands within a few years. No doubt they are to blame for their temporary one-sidedness, but their blame will have to be shared by generations of religious individualists whose own persistent one-sidedness had distorted the rounded perfection of Christianity and caused the present excessive reaction.

The question takes a wider meaning when we turn to the alienation of entire classes from religion. There is no doubt that in all the industrialized nations of Europe, and in our own country, the working classes are dropping out of connection with their churches and synagogues, and to a large extent are transferring their devotion to social movements, so that it looks as if the social interest displaced religion. But here, too, we must remember that solid masses of the population of continental Europe have never had much vital religion to lose. Their religion was taught by rote and performed by rote. It was gregarious and not personal. Detailed investigations have been made of the religious thought world of the peasantry or industrial population of limited districts, and the result always is that the centuries of indoctrination by the Church have left only a very thin crust of fertile religious conviction and experience behind. This is not strange, for whenever any spontaneous and democratic religion has arisen among the people, the established churches have done their best to wet-blanket and suppress it, and they have succeeded finely. When these people cut loose from their churches, they may not be getting much farther away from God. Usually these unchurched people still have a strong native instinct for religion, and when the vital issues and convictions of their own life are lifted into the purer light of Jesus Christ and set on fire by religious faith, they respond.

A new factor enters the situation when we encounter the influence of "scientific socialism." It is true, the party platform declares that "religion is a private affair." The saving of souls is the only industry that socialism distinctly relegates to private enterprise. If that meant simply separation of Church and State, Americans could heartily assent. If it meant that the Socialist Party proposes to be the political organization of the working class for the attainment of economic ends and to be neutral in all other questions, it would be prudent tactics. But in practice it means more. The socialism of continental Europe, taking it by and large, is actively hostile, not only to bad forms of organized religion, but to religion itself. Churchmen feel that a man is lost to religion when he joins the Socialist Party, and socialist leaders feel that a socialist who is still an active Christian is only half baked. When French and German socialists learn that men trained in the democracy and vitality of the free churches of England and America combine genuine piety and ardent devotion to the Socialist Party, it comes to them as a shock of surprise. In May, 1910, about 260 delegates of the English "Brotherhoods" visited Lille in France and were received by the French trades-unionists and socialists with parades and public meetings. The crowds on the streets did not know what to make of it when they saw the Englishmen marching under the red flag of socialism and yet bearing banners with the inscriptions: "We represent 500,000 English workmen;" "We proclaim the Fatherhood of God and the Brotherhood of Man;" "Jesus Christ leads and inspires us." What were these men, Christians or socialists? They could not be both. The Frenchmen lost all their bearings when they heard Keir Hardie, the veteran English labor leader and socialist, repudiating clericalism, but glorifying the Gospel and the spirit of Christ, and declaring that it was Christianity which had made a socialist of him.

The antireligious attitude of continental socialism is comprehensible enough if we study its historical causes dispassionately. Its most active ingredient is anticlericalism. I surmise that if some of us Americans had been in the shoes of these foreign workingmen and had seen the priest from their angle of vision, we should be anticlerical too. But in the old churches religion, the Church, and the priest mean the same thing; you must accept all or reject all. Men do not discriminate when they are hot with ancient wrongs.

Another ingredient in socialist unbelief is modern science and skepticism. Socialists share their irreligion with other radicals. They are unbelievers, not simply because they are socialists, but because they are children of their time. Great masses of upper-class and middle-class people in Europe are just as skeptical and materialistic, though they show no touch of red. Socialists have no monopoly of unbelief.

But in addition to this, materialistic philosophy does come to socialists embodied in their own literature as part of socialist "science." The socialist faith was formulated by its intellectual leaders at a time when naturalism and materialism was the popular philosophy of the intellectuals, and these elements were woven into the dogma of the new movement. Great movements always perpetuate the ideas current at the time when they are in their fluid and formative stage. For instance, some of the dogmas of the Christian Church are still formulated in the terminology of a philosophy that was current in the third and fourth centuries. Calvin worked out a system of thought that is stamped with his powerful personality and with the peculiarities of his age.

But after it had once become the dogmatic fighting faith of great organized bodies, it was all handed on as God's own truth. Socialism is the most solid and militant organization since Calvinism, and it is just as dogmatic. Thus we have the tragic fact that the most idealistic mass movement of modern times was committed at the outset to a materialistic philosophy with which it had no essential connection, and every individual who comes under its influence and control is liable to be assimilated to its type of thought in religion as well as in economics.[2]

Those who fear the influence of the social interest on personal religion are not, therefore, wholly wrong. In any powerful spiritual movement, even the best, there are yeasty, unsettling forces which may do good in the long run, but harm in the short run. Atheistic socialism may influence the religious life of great classes as deforestation affects a mountain side.

On the other hand, where the new social spirit combines harmoniously with the inherited Christian life, a new type of personal religion is produced which has at least as good a right to existence as any other type. Jesus was not a theological Christian, nor a churchman, nor an emotionalist, nor an ascetic, nor a contemplative mystic. A mature social Christian comes closer to the likeness of Jesus Christ than any other type.

In religious individualism, even in its sweetest forms, there was a subtle twist of self-seeking which vitiated its Christlikeness. Thomas a Kempis' "Imitation of Christ" and Bunyan's "Pilgrim's Progress" are classical expressions of personal religion, the one Roman Catholic and monastic, the other Protestant and Puritan. In both piety is self-centered. In both we are taught to seek the highest good of the soul by turning away from the world of men. Doubtless the religion of the monastery and of the Puritan community was far more social and human than the theory might indicate. Bunyan seems to have felt by instinct that it was not quite right to have Christian leave his wife and children and neighbors behind to get rid of his burden and reach the heavenly city. So he wrote a sequel to his immortal story in which the rest of the family with several friends set out on the same pilgrimage. This second part is

---

[2] While I was writing these pages I received a letter from a socialist who had read "Christianity and the Social Crisis." "Speaking for the proletarian class, I shall say that we all, who have gone far enough in the study of socialism to become revolutionary, regard the so-called Christian churches as our bitterest enemies. It is an axiom among us that any man who comes into our party must drop his religion (by that, of course, I mean churchianity) before he can become a valuable member of the socialist party. And he always does. I did. It is a fact that most of us are atheists, not because we want to be, but because the churches are always on the side of our enemies. They preach against us. As a consequence, the hardest person to wake up is the workingman who has been chloroformed by the church in the interest of the master class. . . . Personally I do not want to see the churches take your advice. Keep them out of our movement. We have built it so far with blood and tears without their help. I believe in God. I do not know whether I believe in immortality. I would like to, and so would all my comrades. I am by nature religious. Worship is a necessity of the human heart and I am lost without something to cling to." This letter in its mixture of anger and longing doubtless expresses the attitude of a great number.

less thrilling, but more wholesomely Christian. There is family life, love-making, and marriage on the way. A social group coöperate in salvation. Bunyan was feeling his way toward social Christianity.

Evangelicalism prides itself on its emphasis on sin and the need of conversion, yet some of the men trained in its teachings do not seem to know the devil when they meet him on the street. The most devastating sins of our age do not look like sins to them. They may have been converted from the world, but they contentedly make their money in the common ways of the world. Social Christianity involves a more trenchant kind of conversion and more effective means of grace. It may teach a more lenient theory of sin, but it gives a far keener eye for the lurking places of concrete and profitable sins. A man who gets the spiritual ideals of social Christianity is really set at odds with "the world" and enlisted in a lifelong fight with organized evil. But no man who casts out devils is against Christ. To fight evil involves a constant affirmation of holiness and hardens the muscles of Christian character better than any religious gymnasium work. To very many Christians of the old type the cross of Christ meant only an expedient in the scheme of redemption, not a law of life for themselves. A man can be an exponent of "the higher life" and never suffer any persecution whatever from the powers that control our sin-ridden social life. On the other hand, if any man takes social Christianity at all seriously, he will certainly encounter opposition and be bruised somehow. Such an experience will throw him back on the comforts of God and make his prayers more than words. When he bears on his own body and soul the marks of the Lord Jesus, the cross will be more than a doctrine to him. It will be a bond uniting him with Christ in a fellowship of redemptive love.

The personal religion created by social Christianity will stand one practical test of true religion which exceeds in value most of the proofs offered by theology: it creates a larger life and the power of growth. Dead religion narrows our freedom, contracts our horizon, limits our sympathies, and dwarfs our stature. Live religion brings a sense of emancipation, the exhilaration of spiritual health, a tenderer affection for all living things, widening thoughts and aims, and a sure conviction of the reality and righteousness of God. Devotion to the Reign of God on earth will do that for a man, and will do it continuously. A self-centered religion reaches the dead line soon. Men get to know the whole scheme of salvation, and henceforth they march up the hill only to march down again. On the contrary, when a man's prime object is not his soul, but the Kingdom of God, he has set his hands to a task that will never end and will always expand. It will make ever larger demands on his intellect, his sympathy, and his practical efficiency. It will work him to the last ounce of his strength. But it will keep him growing.

It is charged that those who become interested in "social work" lose interest in "personal work." Doubtless there is truth in that, and it is a regrettable one-sidedness. It is only fair to remember, however, that they share this loss of interest with the entire American Church. Evangelism itself had long become so one-sided, mechanical, and superficial in its gospel and methods that the present apathy can be explained only as a reaction from it. Precisely those who have themselves gone through its experiences are now reluctant to submit young people to it. The social gospel will gradually develop its own evangelistic methods and its own personal appeals. What was called "personal work" was often not personal at all, but a wholesale regimentation of souls. It offered the same prescription, the same formula of doctrine, the same spiritual exercises and emotions for all. Those who add the new social intelligence to the old religious love of man's soul will take every man in his own social place and his own human connections, will try to understand his peculiar sin and failure from his own point of view, and see by what means salvation can effectively be brought to him. Such an evangelism would be more truly personal than the old; it would have more sense of the individuality of each man. As Robert A. Woods finely says, "It calls each man by his name."

Christianity must offer every man a full salvation. The individualistic gospel never did this. Its evangelism never recognized more than a fractional part of the saving forces at work in God's world. Salvation was often whittled down to a mere doctrinal proposition; assent to that, and you were saved. Social Christianity holds to all the real values in the old methods, but rounds them out to meet all the needs of human life.

Salvation is always a social process. It comes by human contact. The word must become flesh if it is to save. Some man or woman, or some group of people, in whom the saving love of Jesus Christ has found a new incarnation, lays hold of an enfeebled, blinded human atom and infuses new hope and courage and insight, new warmth of love and strength of will, and there is a new breathing of the soul and an opening of the inner eye. Salvation has begun. That man or group of men was a fragment of the Kingdom of God in humanity; God dwelt in them and therefore power could go out from them. When a lost soul is infolded in a new society, a true humanity, then there is a chance of salvation. No matter what set of opinions they hold, such men and women have been one of the most precious assets of our American life, and a social theorist who scoffs at them is blind with dogmatic prejudice.

When the Church insisted that it is the indispensable organ of salvation, it insisted on the social factor in redemption. The Church stands for the assimilating power exerted by the social group over its members. The same influence which a semicriminal gang exerts over a boy for evil is exerted by the Church for good. The advice in the Gospel to win an offending brother back by pleading with him first alone, then drawing two or three others into it, and finally bringing the matter before the Church, shows a keen insight into the powers of the social group over its members. More and more units of power are switched on until the current is overpowering.

In a small and simple country or village community the Church could follow a man in all his relations. In our modern society the social contact of the Church covers only a small part of life, and the question is whether the influence it exerts on the saved man is strong and continuous enough to keep him saved. Suppose a poor "bum" leaves the Salvation Army barracks with a new light of hope in his eyes. He passes out on the streets among saloons and gambling dens, among sights and sounds and smells that call to his passions, among men and women who are not part of the saving Kingdom of God, but of the carnivorous kingdom of the devil. So the poor fellow backslides. Suppose a millionaire has been at a meeting where he has caught a vision of a new order of business, in which men are not boozy with profits, but in which such as he might be brothers to all. Next morning stocks are tumbling on 'Change, and profit is calling to him. So the poor fellow backslides. The churches do save men, but so many of them do not stay saved. Even in very active churches an enormous percentage of members are in the long run swept back so that all can see the failure, and if love of money and the hardness of social pride were properly reckoned as a religious collapse, the percentage of waste would be still greater. The social organism of the Church becomes increasingly unable in modern life to supply the social forces of salvation single-handed. It may save, but its salvation is neither complete nor durable.

Sin is a social force. It runs from man to man along the lines of social contact. Its impact on the individual becomes most overwhelming when sin is most completely socialized. Salvation, too, is a social force. It is exerted by groups that are charged with divine will and love. It becomes durable and complete in the measure in which the individual is built into a social organism that is ruled by justice, cleanness, and love. A full salvation demands a Christian social order which will serve as the spiritual environment of the individual. In the little catechism which Luther wrote for the common people he has a charmingly true reply to the question: "What is 'our daily bread'?" He says: "All that belongs to the nourishment and need of our body, meat and drink, clothes and shoes, house and home, field and cattle, money and property, a good wife and good children, good servants and good rulers, good government, good weather, peace, health, education, honor, good friends, trusty neighbors, and such like." Yes, especially "such like." In the same way "salvation" involves a saved environment. For a baby it means the breast and heart and love of a mother, and a father who can keep the mother in proper condition. For a workingman salvation includes a happy home, clean neighbors, a steady job, eight hours a day, a boss that treats him as a man, a labor union that is well led, the sense of doing his own best work and not being used up to give others money to burn, faith in God and in the final triumph and present power of the right, a sense of being part of a movement that is lifting his class and all mankind, "and such like." Therefore the conception of salvation which is contained in the word "the Kingdom of God" is a truer and completer conception than that which is contained in the word "justification by faith," as surely as the whole is better than a part.

I set out with the proposition that social Christianity, which makes the

Reign of God on earth its object, is a distinct type of personal religion, and that in its best manifestations it involves the possibility of a purer spirituality, a keener recognition of sin, more durable powers of growth, a more personal evangelism, and a more all-around salvation than the individualistic type of religion which makes the salvation of the soul its object. I want to add that this new type of religion is especially adapted to win and inspire modern men.[3]

It must be plain to any thoughtful observer that immense numbers of men are turning away from traditional religion, not because they have lapsed into sin, but because they have become modernized in their knowledge and points of view. Religion itself is an eternal need of humanity, but any given form of religion may become antiquated and inadequate, leaving the youngest and livest minds unsatisfied, or even repelling where it ought to attract. The real religious leaders of this generation must face the problem how they can give to modern men the inestimable boon of experiencing God as a joy and a power, and of living in him as their fathers did. I claim that social Christianity is by all tokens the great highway by which this present generation can come to God.

For one thing, it puts an end to most of the old conflicts between religion and science. The building of the Kingdom of God on earth requires surprisingly little dogma and speculative theology, and a tremendous quantity of holy will and scientific good sense. It does not set up a series of propositions which need constant modernizing and which repel the most active intellects, but it summons all to help in transforming the world into a reign of righteousness, and men of good will are not very far apart on that. That kind of religion has no quarrel with science. It needs science to interpret the universe which Christianity wants to transform. Social Christianity sets up fewer obstacles for the intellect and puts far heavier tasks on the will, and all that is sound in modern life will accept that change with profound relief.

Social Christianity would also remove one other obstacle which bars even more men out of religion than the scientific difficulties of belief. The most effective argument against religion to-day is that religion has been "against the people." The people are coming to their own at last. For a century and a half at least they have been on the upgrade, climbing with inexpressible toil and suffering toward freedom, equality, and brotherhood. The spirit of Christ has been their most powerful ally, but the official Church, taking Christendom as a whole, has thrown the bulk of its great resources to the side of those who are in possession, and against those who were in such deadly need of its aid. This is the great scandal which will not down. Scientific doubt may alienate thousands, but the resentment against the Church for going over

---

[3] In the following pages I am deeply indebted to the inaugural address of Leonhard Ragaz, "Zur gegenwärtigen Umgestaltung des Christentums," published in *Neue Wege*, Basel, October, 1909. Professor Ragaz is one of the most brilliant preachers of Switzerland, professor of systematic theology in the University of Zurich, together with Kutter one of the most eminent leaders of Christian Socialism in Switzerland, and all together one of the finest examples of the new type of Social Christianity that I have met.

to the enemy has alienated entire nations. Nothing would so expiate that guilt and win back the lost respect for religion, as determined coöperation on the part of the Church in creating a social order in which the just aspirations of the working class will be satisfied. Those Christian men who are the outstanding and bold friends of the people's cause are to-day the most effective apologists of Christianity.

The Christian demand for the Kingdom of God on earth responds to the passionate desire for liberty which pervades and inspires the modern world. That desire is really a longing for redemption. Just as an individual may long to be free from vicious habits that enslave him and rob him of his manhood and self-respect, so great social classes now want freedom from the social unfreedom and degradation which denies their human worth and submerges their higher nature in coarseness, ignorance, and animal brutality. The theological word "redemption" originally meant the ransoming of slaves and prisoners. Christ is the great emancipator. Every advance in true Christianity has meant a broadening path for liberty. The highest Christian quality is love; but love is supreme freedom, a state in which even moral compulsion ceases because goodness has become spontaneous. This world-wide desire for freedom is the breath of God in the soul of humanity. Men instinctively know it as such, and they hate a Church that would rob them of it. Social Christianity would rally that desire in the name of the Kingdom of God, and help the people to a consciousness that they are really moved by religion when they love freedom. On the other hand, by its strong emphasis on social solidarity and the law of service, it will counteract that exaggerated assertion of individual rights and that selfish soul-culture which dog the steps of Freedom.

Every individual reconstructs his comprehension of life and duty, of the world and of God, as he passes from one period of his development to the next. If he fails to do so, his religion will lose its grasp and control. In the same way humanity must reconstruct its moral and religious synthesis whenever it passes from one era to another. When all other departments of life and thought are silently changing, it is impossible for religion to remain unaffected. Otherworldly religion was the full expression of the highest aspirations of ancient and medieval life. Contemporary philosophy supported it. The Ptolemaic astronomy made it easy to conceive of a heaven localized above the starry firmament, which was only a few miles up. But to-day the whole *Weltanschauung* which supported those religious conceptions has melted away irretrievably. Copernican astronomy, the conviction of the universal and majestic reign of law, the evolutionary conception of the history of this earth and of the race, have made the religious ideas that were the natural denizens of the old world of thought seem like antique survivals to-day, as if a company of Athenians should walk down Broadway in their ancient dress. When Christianity invaded the ancient world, it was a modernist religion contemptuously elbowing aside the worn-out superstitions of heathenism, and the live intellects seized it as an adequate expression of their religious consciousness. To-day the livest intellects have the greatest difficulty in maintaining their connection with it. Many of its defenders are querulously lamenting the growth of unbelief. They stand on a narrowing island amid a growing flood, saving what they can of the wreckage of faith. Is religion dying? Is the giant faith of Christianity tottering to its grave?

Religion is not dying. It is only molting its feathers, as every winged thing must at times. A new springtide is coming. Even now the air is full of mating calls and love songs. Soon there will be a nest in every tree.

As the modern world is finding itself, religion is returning to it in new ways. Philosophy in its most modern forms is tending toward an idealistic conception of the universe, even when it calls itself materialistic. It realizes spirit behind all reality. The new psychology is full of the powers and mysteries of the soul. It is no slight achievement of faith to think of God immanent in the whole vast universe, but those who accomplish that act of faith feel him very near and mysteriously present, pulsating in their own souls in every yearning for truth and love and right. Life once more becomes miraculous; for every event in which we realize God and our soul is a miracle. All history becomes the unfolding of the purpose of the immanent God who is working in the race toward the commonwealth of spiritual liberty and righteousness. History is the sacred workshop of God. There is a presentiment abroad in modern thought that humanity is on the verge of a profound change, and that feeling heralds the fact. We feel that all this wonderful liberation of redemptive energy is working out a true and divine order in which our race will rise to a new level of existence. But such a higher order can rise out of the present only if superior spiritual forces build and weave it. Thousands of young minds who thought a few years ago that they had turned their back on religion forever are full of awe and a sense of mystery as they watch the actualities of life in this process of upbuilding.[4] By coöperating with God in his work they are realizing God. Religion is insuppressible.

It is true that the social enthusiasm is an unsettling force which may unbalance for a time, break old religious habits and connections, and establish new contacts that are a permanent danger to personal religion. But the way to meet this danger is not to fence out the new social spirit, but to let it fuse with the old religious faith and create a new total that will be completer and more Christian than the old religious individualism at its best. Such a combination brings a triumphant enlargement of life which proves its own value and which none would give up again who has once experienced it. There is so much religion even in nonreligious social work that some who had lost their conscious religion irretrievably have found it again by this new avenue. God has met them while they were at work with him in social redemption, and they have a religion again and a call to a divine ministry. Faith in a new social

---

[4] This line of thought was worked out more fully by me in a sermon preached before the National Conference of Charities and Corrections, 1912, and in a little book, "Unto Me," published by the Pilgrim Press, Boston, 1912.

order is so powerful a breeder of religion that great bodies of men who in theory scorn and repudiate the name of religion, in practice show evidence of possessing some of the most powerful instincts and motives of religion.[5] One of the most valuable achievements in the domain of personal religion which is now open to any man is to build up a rounded and harmonious Christian personality in which all the sweetness and intensity of the old religious life shall combine with the breadth, intelligence, and fighting vigor of the social spirit. Every such individuality will reproduce itself in others who are less mature, and so multiply this new species of the genus "Christian."

46

THE COURAGE TO BE
Paul Tillich

Paul Tillich (1886–1965) was one of the most original and influential Christian theologians of the Twentieth Century. He was not a dogmatic theologian, but a philosophical theologian whose major concern was the relating of religious symbols and experiences to the problems of contemporary man. This "method of correlation," accompanied by a strong emphasis upon man's freedom and duty to make his own destiny, which he termed "the Protestant Principle," was a fundamental presupposition of his thought. Tillich, born in eastern Germany, was greatly influenced by his reading of Kant, Hegel, Fichte, Schleiermacher, and especially Schelling, whose philosophy of religion was the subject-matter of his thesis for the degree of Licentiat of Theology. He was subsequently influenced by Kierkegaard and existentialism, and after his emigration to the United States in 1933, by American thought and practice. His writings range from relatively popularized forms such as sermons to quite technical treatises in philosophy

Reprinted by permission of Yale University Press from *The Courage To Be*, by Paul Tillich, pp. 163–190. Copyright 1952 by Yale University Press.

[5] This is the message of the brilliant book of Kutter of Zurich, "Sie müssen," which has been edited in English by Rufus W. Weeks, and published by the Coöperative Printing Company, Chicago. Richard Heath has summed up all the teachings of Kutter in "Social Democracy: Does it Mean Darkness or Light?" Letchworth, England, 1910.

and theology. His most important work is the three-volume Sys-
tematic Theology, published between 1951 and 1963. The selec-
tion reprinted here is an excerpt from a smaller work, The Courage
To Be *(1952), which is the published version of his Terry Lectures*
at Yale University. Tillich believed that the concept of courage
furnished a common terminus for many problems of theology, phi-
losophy, and sociology; and his treatment of this concept should
afford the reader significant insight into some of the unique features
of his theology.

GUILT AND THE COURAGE TO ACCEPT ACCEPTANCE

In the center of the Protestant courage of confidence stands the courage to accept acceptance in spite of the consciousness of guilt. Luther, and in fact the whole period, experienced the anxiety of guilt and condemnation as the main form of their anxiety. The courage to affirm oneself in spite of this anxiety is the courage which we have called the courage of confidence. It is rooted in the personal, total, and immediate certainty of divine forgiveness. There is belief in forgiveness in all forms of man's courage to be, even in neocollectiv-ism. But there is no interpretation of human existence in which it is so pre-dominant as in genuine Protestantism. And there is no movement in history in which it is equally profound and equally paradoxical. In the Lutheran for-mula that "he who is unjust is just" (in the view of the divine forgiveness) or in the more modern phrasing that "he who is unacceptable is accepted" the victory over the anxiety of guilt and condemnation is sharply expressed. One could say that the courage to be is the courage to accept oneself as accepted in spite of being unacceptable. One does not need to remind the theo-logians of the fact that this is the genuine meaning of the Pauline-Lutheran doctrine of "justification by faith" (a doctrine which in its original phrasing has become incomprehensible even for students of theology). But one must remind theologians and ministers that in the fight against the anxiety of guilt by psychotherapy the idea of acceptance has received the attention and gained the significance which in the Reformation period was to be seen in phrases like "forgiveness of sins" or "justification through faith." Accepting acceptance though being unacceptable is the basis for the courage of confidence.

Decisive for this self-affirmation is its being independent of any moral, intellectual, or religious precondition: it is not the good or the wise or the pious who are entitled to the courage to accept acceptance but those who are lacking in all these qualities and are aware of being unacceptable. This, however, does not mean acceptance by oneself as oneself. It is not a justification of one's accidental individuality. It is not the Existentialist courage to be as oneself. It is the paradoxical act in which one is accepted by that which infinitely tran-scends one's individual self. It is in the experience of the Reformers the ac-ceptance of the unacceptable sinner into judging and transforming commun-ion with God.

The courage to be in this respect is the courage to accept the forgiveness of sins, not as an abstract assertion but as the fundamental experience in the encounter with God. Self-affirmation in spite of the anxiety of guilt and condemnation presupposes participation in something which transcends the self. In the communion of healing, for example the psychoanalytic situation, the patient participates in the healing power of the helper by whom he is accepted although he feels himself unacceptable. The healer, in this relationship, does not stand for himself as an individual but represents the objective power of acceptance and self-affirmation. This objective power works through the healer in the patient. Of course, it must be embodied in a person who can realize guilt, who can judge, and who can accept in spite of the judgment. Acceptance by something which is less than personal could never overcome personal self-rejection. A wall to which I confess cannot forgive me. No self-acceptance is possible if one is not accepted in a person-to-person relation. But even if one is personally accepted it needs a self-transcending courage to accept this acceptance, it needs the courage of confidence. For being accepted does not mean that guilt is denied. The healing helper who tried to convince his patient that he was not really guilty would do him a great disservice. He would prevent him from taking his guilt into his self-affirmation. He may help him to transform displaced, neurotic guilt feelings into genuine ones which are, so to speak, put on the right place, but he cannot tell him that there is no guilt in him. He accepts the patient into his communion without condemning anything and without covering up anything.

Here, however, is the point where the religious "acceptance as being accepted" transcends medical healing. Religion asks for the ultimate source of the power which heals by accepting the unacceptable, it asks for God. The acceptance by God, his forgiving or justifying act, is the only and ultimate source of a courage to be which is able to take the anxiety of guilt and condemnation into itself. For the ultimate power of self-affirmation can only be the power of being-itself. Everything less than this, one's own or anybody else's finite power of being, cannot overcome the radical, infinite threat of nonbeing which is experienced in the despair of self-condemnation. This is why the courage of confidence, as it is expressed in a man like Luther, emphasizes unceasingly exclusive trust in God and rejects any other foundation for his courage to be, not only as insufficient but as driving him into more guilt and deeper anxiety. The immense liberation brought to the people of the 16th century by the message of the Reformers and the creation of their indomitable courage to accept acceptance was due to the *sola fide* doctrine, namely to the message that the courage of confidence is conditioned not by anything finite but solely by that which is unconditional itself and which we experience as unconditional in a person-to-person encounter.

FATE AND THE COURAGE TO ACCEPT ACCEPTANCE

As the symbolic figures of death and the devil show, the anxiety of this period was not restricted to the anxiety of guilt. It was also an anxiety of death and fate. The astrological ideas of the later ancient world had been revived by the Renaissance and had influenced even those humanists who joined the Reformation. We have already referred to the Neo-Stoic courage, expressed in some Renaissance pictures, where man directs the vessel of his life although it is driven by the winds of fate. Luther faced the anxiety of fate on another level. He experienced the connection between the anxiety of guilt and the anxiety of fate. It is the uneasy conscience which produces innumerable irrational fears in daily life. The rustling of a dry leaf horrifies him who is plagued by guilt. Therefore conquest of the anxiety of guilt is also conquest of the anxiety of fate. The courage of confidence takes the anxiety of fate as well as the anxiety of guilt into itself. It says "in spite of" to both of them. This is the genuine meaning of the doctrine of providence. Providence is not a theory about some activities of God; it is the religious symbol of the courage of confidence with respect to fate and death. For the courage of confidence says "in spite of" even to death.

Like Paul, Luther was well aware of the connection of the anxiety of guilt with the anxiety of death. In Stoicism and Neo-Stoicism the essential self is not threatened by death, because it belongs to being-itself and transcends nonbeing. Socrates, who in the power of his essential self conquered the anxiety of death, has become the symbol for the courage to take death upon oneself. This is the true meaning of Plato's so-called doctrine of immortality of the soul. In discussing this doctrine we should neglect the arguments for immortality, even those in Plato's *Phaedon,* and concentrate on the image of the dying Socrates. All the arguments, skeptically treated by Plato himself, are attempts to interpret the courage of Socrates, the courage to take one's death into one's self-affirmation. Socrates is certain that the self which the executioners will destroy is not the self which affirms itself in his courage to be. He does not say much about the relation of the two selves, and he could not because they are not numerically two, but one in two aspects. But he makes it clear that the courage to die is the test of the courage to be. A self-affirmation which omits taking the affirmation of one's death into itself tries to escape the test of courage, the facing of nonbeing in the most radical way.

The popular belief in immortality which in the Western world has largely replaced the Christian symbol of resurrection is a mixture of courage and escape. It tries to maintain one's self-affirmation even in the face of one's having to die. But it does this by continuing one's finitude, that is one's having to die, infinitely, so that the actual death never will occur. This, however, is an illusion and, logically speaking, a contradiction in terms. It makes endless what, by definition, must come to an end. The "immortality of the soul" is a poor symbol for the courage to be in the face of one's having to die.

The courage of Socrates (in Plato's picture) was based not on a doctrine of the immortality of the soul but on the affirmation of himself in his essential, indestructible being. He knows that he belongs to two orders of reality and that the one order is transtemporal. It was the courage of Socrates which more than any philosophical reflection revealed to the ancient world that everyone belongs to two orders.

But there was one presupposition in the Socratic (Stoic and Neo-Stoic) courage to take death upon oneself, namely the ability of every individual to participate in both orders, the temporal and the eternal. This presupposition is not accepted by Christianity. According to Christianity we are estranged from our essential being. We are not free to realize our essential being, we are bound to contradict it. Therefore death can be accepted only through a state of confidence in which death has ceased to be the "wages of sin." This, however, is the state of being accepted in spite of being unacceptable. Here is the point in which the ancient world was transformed by Christianity and in which Luther's courage to face death was rooted. It is the being accepted into communion with God that underlies this courage, not a questionable theory of immortality. The encounter with God in Luther is not merely the basis for the courage to take upon oneself sin and condemnation, it is also the basis for taking upon oneself fate and death. For encountering God means encountering transcendent security and transcendent eternity. He who participates in God participates in eternity. But in order to participate in him you must be accepted by him and you must have accepted his acceptance of you.

Luther had experiences which he describes as attacks of utter despair (*Anfechtung*), as the frightful threat of a complete meaninglessness. He felt these moments as satanic attacks in which everything was menaced: his Christian faith, the confidence in his work, the Reformation, the forgiveness of sins. Everything broke down in the extreme moments of this despair, nothing was left of the courage to be. Luther in these moments, and in the descriptions he gives of them, anticipated the descriptions of them by modern Existentialism. But for him this was not the last word. The last word was the first commandment, the statement that God is God. It reminded him of the unconditional element in human experience of which one can be aware even in the abyss of meaninglessness. And this awareness saved him.

It should not be forgotten that the great adversary of Luther, Thomas Münzer, the Anabaptist and religious socialist, describes similar experiences. He speaks of the ultimate situation in which everything finite reveals its finitude, in which the finite has come to its end, in which anxiety grips the heart and all previous meanings fall apart, and in which just for this reason the Divine Spirit can make itself felt and can turn the whole situation into a courage to be whose expression is revolutionary action. While Luther represents ecclesiastical Protestantism, Münzer represents evangelical radicalism. Both men have shaped history, and actually Münzer's views had even more influence in America than Luther's. Both men experienced the anxiety of meaninglessness and described it in terms which had been created by Christian mystics. But in doing so they transcended the courage of confidence which is based on a personal encounter with God. They had to receive elements from the courage to be which is based on mystical union. This leads to a last question: whether the two types of the courage to accept acceptance can be united in view of the all-pervasive presence of the anxiety of doubt and meaninglessness in our own period.

ABSOLUTE FAITH AND THE COURAGE TO BE

We have avoided the concept of faith in our description of the courage to be which is based on mystical union with the ground of being as well as in our description of the courage to be which is based on the personal encounter with God. This is partly because the concept of faith has lost its genuine meaning and has received the connotation of "belief in something unbelievable." But this is not the only reason for the use of terms other than faith. The decisive reason is that I do not think either mystical union or personal encounter fulfills the idea of faith. Certainly there is faith in the elevation of the soul above the finite to the infinite, leading to its union with the ground of being. But more than this is included in the concept of faith. And there is faith in the personal encounter with the personal God. But more than this is included in the concept of faith. Faith is the state of being grasped by the power of being-itself. The courage to be is an expression of faith and what "faith" means must be understood through the courage to be. We have defined courage as the self-affirmation of being in spite of nonbeing. The power of this self-affirmation is the power of being which is effective in every act of courage. Faith is the experience of this power.

But it is an experience which has a paradoxical character, the character of accepting acceptance. Being-itself transcends every finite being infinitely; God in the divine-human encounter transcends man unconditionally. Faith bridges this infinite gap by accepting the fact that in spite of it the power of being is present, that he who is separated is accepted. Faith accepts "in spite of"; and out of the "in spite of" of faith the "in spite of" of courage is born. Faith is not a theoretical affirmation of something uncertain, it is the existential acceptance of something transcending ordinary experience. Faith is not an opinion but a state. It is the state of being grasped by the power of being which transcends everything that is and in which everything that is participates. He who is grasped by this power is able to affirm himself because he knows that he is affirmed by the power of being-itself. In this point mystical experience and personal encounter are identical. In both of them faith is the basis of the courage to be.

This is decisive for a period in which, as in our own, the anxiety of doubt and meaninglessness is dominant. Certainly the anxiety of fate and death is not lacking in our time. The anxiety of fate has increased with the degree to which the schizophrenic split of our world has removed the last remnants of former security. And the anxiety of guilt and condemnation is not lacking either. It is surprising how much anxiety of guilt comes to the surface in psychoanalysis and personal counseling. The centuries of puritan and bourgeois repression of vital strivings have produced almost as many guilt feelings as the preaching of hell and purgatory in the Middle Ages.

But in spite of these restricting considerations one must say that the anxiety which determines our period is the anxiety of doubt and meaninglessness. One is afraid of having lost or of having to lose the meaning of one's existence. The expression of this situation is the Existentialism of today.

Which courage is able to take nonbeing into itself in the form of doubt and meaninglessness? This is the most important and most disturbing question in the quest for the courage to be. For the anxiety of meaninglessness undermines what is still unshaken in the anxiety of fate and death and of guilt and condemnation. In the anxiety of guilt and condemnation doubt has not yet undermined the certainty of an ultimate responsibility. We are threatened but we are not destroyed. If, however, doubt and meaninglessness prevail one experiences an abyss in which the meaning of life and the truth of ultimate responsibility disappear. Both the Stoic who conquers the anxiety of fate with the Socratic courage of wisdom and the Christian who conquers the anxiety of guilt with the Protestant courage of accepting forgiveness are in a different situation. Even in the despair of having to die and the despair of self-condemnation meaning is affirmed and certitude preserved. But in the despair of doubt and meaninglessness both are swallowed by nonbeing.

The question then is this: Is there a courage which can conquer the anxiety of meaninglessness and doubt? Or in other words, can the faith which accepts acceptance resist the power of nonbeing in its most radical form? Can faith resist meaninglessness? Is there a kind of faith which can exist together with doubt and meaninglessness? These questions lead to the last aspect of the problem discussed in these lectures and the one most relevant to our time: How is the courage to be possible if all the ways to create it are barred by the experience of their ultimate insufficiency? If life is as meaningless as death, if guilt is as questionable as perfection, if being is no more meaningful than nonbeing, on what can one base the courage to be?

There is an inclination in some Existentialists to answer these questions by a leap from doubt to dogmatic certitude, from meaninglessness to a set of symbols in which the meaning of a special ecclesiastical or political group is embodied. This leap can be interpreted in different ways. It may be the expression of a desire for safety; it may be as arbitrary as, according to Existentialist principles, every decision is; it may be the feeling that the Christian message is the answer to the questions raised by an analysis of human existence; it may be a genuine conversion, independent of the theoretical situation. In any case it is not a solution of the problem of radical doubt. It gives the courage to be to those who are converted but it does not answer the question as to how such a courage is possible in itself. The answer must accept, as its precondition, the state of meaninglessness. It is not an answer if it demands the removal of this state; for that is just what cannot be done. He who is in the grip of doubt and meaninglessness cannot liberate himself from this grip; but he asks for an answer which is valid within and not outside the situation of his despair. He asks for the ultimate foundation of what we have called the "courage of despair." There is only one possible answer, if one does not try to escape the question: namely that the acceptance of despair is in itself faith and on the boundary line of the courage to be. In this situation the meaning of life is reduced to despair about the meaning of life. But as long as this despair is an act of life it is positive in its negativity. Cynically speaking, one could say that it is true to life to be cynical about it. Religiously speaking, one would say that one accepts oneself as accepted in spite of one's despair about the meaning of this acceptance. The paradox of every radical negativity, as long as it is an active negativity, is that it must affirm itself in order to be able to negate itself. No actual negation can be without an implicit affirmation. The hidden pleasure produced by despair witnesses to the paradoxical character of self-negation. The negative lives from the positive it negates.

The faith which makes the courage of despair possible is the acceptance of the power of being, even in the grip of nonbeing. Even in the despair about meaning being affirms itself through us. The act of accepting meaninglessness is in itself a meaningful act. It is an act of faith. We have seen that he who has the courage to affirm his being in spite of fate and guilt has not removed them. He remains threatened and hit by them. But he accepts his acceptance by the power of being-itself in which he participates and which gives him the courage to take the anxieties of fate and guilt upon himself. The same is true of doubt and meaninglessness. The faith which creates the courage to take them into itself has no special content. It is simply faith, undirected, absolute. It is undefinable, since everything defined is dissolved by doubt and meaninglessness. Nevertheless, even absolute faith is not an eruption of subjective emotions or a mood without objective foundation.

An analysis of the nature of absolute faith reveals the following elements in it. The first is the experience of the power of being which is present even in face of the most radical manifestation of nonbeing. If one says that in this experience vitality resists despair one must add that vitality in man is proportional to intentionality. The vitality that can stand the abyss of meaninglessness is aware of a hidden meaning within the destruction of meaning. The second element in absolute faith is the dependence of the experience of nonbeing on the experience of being and the dependence of the experience of meaninglessness on the experience of meaning. Even in the state of despair one has enough being to make despair possible. There is a third element in absolute faith, the acceptance of being accepted. Of course, in the state of despair there is nobody and nothing that accepts. But there is the power of acceptance itself which is experienced. Meaninglessness, as long as it is experienced, includes an experience of the "power of acceptance." To accept this power of acceptance consciously is the religious answer of absolute faith, of a faith which has been deprived by doubt of any concrete content, which nevertheless is faith and the source of the most paradoxical manifestation of the courage to be.

This faith transcends both the mystical experience and the divine-human encounter. The mystical experience seems to be nearer to absolute faith but it is not. Absolute faith includes an element of skepticism which one cannot find in the mystical experience. Certainly mysticism also transcends all specific contents, but not because it doubts them or has found them meaningless; rather it deems them to be preliminary. Mysticism uses the specific contents as grades, stepping on them after having used them. The experience of meaninglessness, however, denies them (and everything that goes with them) without having used them. The experience of meaninglessness is more radical than mysticism. Therefore it transcends the mystical experience.

Absolute faith also transcends the divine-human encounter. In this encounter the subject-object scheme is valid: a definite subject (man) meets a definite object (God). One can reverse this statement and say that a definite subject (God) meets a definite object (man). But in both cases the attack of doubt undercuts the subject-object structure. The theologians who speak so strongly and with such self-certainty about the divine-human encounter should be aware of a situation in which this encounter is prevented by radical doubt and nothing is left but absolute faith. The acceptance of such a situation as religiously valid has, however, the consequence that the concrete contents of ordinary faith must be subjected to criticism and transformation. The courage to be in its radical form is a key to an idea of God which transcends both mysticism and the person-to-person encounter.

THE COURAGE TO BE AS THE KEY TO BEING-ITSELF

Nonbeing Opening Up Being

The courage to be in all its forms has, by itself, revelatory character. It shows the nature of being, it shows that the self-affirmation of being is an affirmation that overcomes negation. In a metaphorical statement (and every assertion about being-itself is either metaphorical or symbolic) one could say that being includes nonbeing but nonbeing does not prevail against it. "Including" is a spatial metaphor which indicates that being embraces itself and that which is opposed to it, nonbeing. Nonbeing belongs to being, it cannot be separated from it. We could not even think "being" without a double negation: being must be thought as the negation of the negation of being. This is why we describe being best by the metaphor "power of being." Power is the possibility a being has to actualize itself against the resistance of other beings. If we speak of the power of being-itself we indicate that being affirms itself against nonbeing. In our discussion of courage and life we have mentioned the dynamic understanding of reality by the philosophers of life. Such an understanding is possible only if one accepts the view that nonbeing belongs to being, that being could not be the ground of life without nonbeing. The self-affirmation of being without nonbeing would not even be self-affirmation but an immovable self-identity. Nothing would be manifest, nothing expressed, nothing revealed. But nonbeing drives being out of its seclusion, it forces it to affirm itself dynamically. Philosophy has dealt with the dynamic self-affirmation of being-itself wherever it spoke dialectically, notably in Neo-platonism, Hegel, and the philosophers of life and process. Theology has done the same whenever it took the idea of the living God seriously, most obviously in the trinitarian symbolization of the inner life of God. Spinoza, in spite of his static definition of substance (which is his name for the ultimate power of being), unites philosophical and mystical tendencies when he speaks of the love and knowledge with which God loves and knows himself through the love and knowledge of finite beings. Nonbeing (that in God which makes his self-affirmation dynamic) opens up the divine self-seclusion and reveals him as power and love. Nonbeing makes God a living God. Without the No he has to overcome in himself and in his creature, the divine Yes to himself would be lifeless. There would be no revelation of the ground of being, there would be no life.

But where there is nonbeing there is finitude and anxiety. If we say that nonbeing belongs to being-itself, we say that finitude and anxiety belong to being-itself. Wherever philosophers or theologians have spoken of the divine blessedness they have implicitly (and sometimes explicitly) spoken of the anxiety of finitude which is eternally taken into the blessedness of the divine infinity. The infinite embraces itself and the finite, the Yes includes itself and the No which it takes into itself, blessedness comprises itself and the anxiety of which it is the conquest. All this is implied if one says that being includes nonbeing and that through nonbeing it reveals itself. It is a highly symbolic language which must be used at this point. But its symbolic character does not diminish its truth; on the contrary, it is a condition of its truth. To speak unsymbolically about being-itself is untrue.

The divine self-affirmation is the power that makes the self-affirmation of the finite being, the courage to be, possible. Only because being-itself has the character of self-affirmation in spite of nonbeing is courage possible. Courage participates in the self-affirmation of being-itself, it participates in the power of being which prevails against nonbeing. He who receives this power in an act of mystical or personal or absolute faith is aware of the source of his courage to be.

Man is not necessarily aware of this source. In situations of cynicism and indifference he is not aware of it. But it works in him as long as he maintains the courage to take his anxiety upon himself. In the act of the courage to be the power of being is effective in us, whether we recognize it or not. Every act of courage is a manifestation of the ground of being, however questionable the content of the act may be. The content may hide or distort true being, the courage in it reveals true being. Not arguments but the courage to be reveals the true nature of being-itself. By affirming our being we participate in the self-affirmation of being-itself. There are no valid arguments for the "existence" of God, but there are acts of courage in which we affirm the power of being, whether we know it or not. If we know it, we accept acceptance consciously.

If we do not know it, we nevertheless accept it and participate in it. And in our acceptance of that which we do not know the power of being is manifest to us. Courage has revealing power, the courage to be is the key to being-itself.

Theism Transcended

The courage to take meaninglessness into itself presupposes a relation to the ground of being which we have called "absolute faith." It is without a *special* content, yet it is not without content. The content of absolute faith is the "God above God." Absolute faith and its consequence, the courage that takes the radical doubt, the doubt about God, into itself, transcends the theistic idea of God.

Theism can mean the unspecified affirmation of God. Theism in this sense does not say what it means if it uses the name of God. Because of the traditional and psychological connotations of the word God such an empty theism can produce a reverent mood if it speaks of God. Politicians, dictators, and other people who wish to use rhetoric to make an impression on their audience like to use the word God in this sense. It produces the feeling in their listeners that the speaker is serious and morally trustworthy. This is especially successful if they can brand their foes as atheistic. On a higher level people without a definite religious commitment like to call themselves theistic, not for special purposes but because they cannot stand a world without God, whatever this God may be. They need some of the connotations of the word God and they are afraid of what they call atheism. On the highest level of this kind of theism the name of God is used as a poetic or practical symbol, expressing a profound emotional state or the highest ethical idea. It is a theism which stands on the boundary line between the second type of theism and what we call "theism transcended." But it is still too indefinite to cross this boundary line. The atheistic negation of this whole type of theism is as vague as the theism itself. It may produce an irreverent mood and angry reaction of those who take their theistic affirmation seriously. It may even be felt as justified against the rhetorical-political abuse of the name God, but it is ultimately as irrelevant as the theism which it negates. It cannot reach the state of despair any more than the theism against which it fights can reach the state of faith.

Theism can have another meaning, quite contrary to the first one: it can be the name of what we have called the divine-human encounter. In this case it points to those elements in the Jewish-Christian tradition which emphasize the person-to-person relationship with God. Theism in this sense emphasizes the personalistic passages in the Bible and the Protestant creeds, the personalistic image of God, the word as the tool of creation and revelation, the ethical and social character of the kingdom of God, the personal nature of human faith and divine forgiveness, the historical vision of the universe, the idea of a divine purpose, the infinite distance between creator and creature, the absolute separation between God and the world, the conflict between holy God and sinful man, the person-to-person character of prayer and practical devotion. Theism in this sense is the nonmystical side of biblical religion and historical Christianity. Atheism from the point of view of this theism is the human attempt to escape the divine-human encounter. It is an existential—not a theoretical—problem.

Theism has a third meaning, a strictly theological one. Theological theism is, like every theology, dependent on the religious substance which it conceptualizes. It is dependent on theism in the first sense insofar as it tries to prove the necessity of affirming God in some way; it usually develops the so-called arguments for the "existence" of God. But it is more dependent on theism in the second sense insofar as it tries to establish a doctrine of God which transforms the person-to-person encounter with God into a doctrine about two persons who may or may not meet but who have a reality independent of each other.

Now theism in the first sense must be transcended because it is irrelevant, and theism in the second sense must be transcended because it is one-sided. But theism in the third sense must be transcended because it is wrong. It is bad theology. This can be shown by a more penetrating analysis. The God of theological theism is a being beside others and as such a part of the whole of reality. He certainly is considered its most important part, but as a part and therefore as subjected to the structure of the whole. He is supposed to be beyond the ontological elements and categories which constitute reality. But every statement subjects him to them. He is seen as a self which has a world, as an ego which is related to a thou, as a cause which is separated from its effect, as having a definite space and an endless time. He is a being, not being-itself. As such he is bound to the subject-object structure of reality, he is an object for us as subjects. At the same time we are objects for him as a subject. And this is decisive for the necessity of transcending theological theism. For God as a subject makes me into an object which is nothing more than an object. He deprives me of my subjectivity because he is all-powerful and all-knowing. I revolt and try to make *him* into an object, but the revolt fails and becomes desperate. God appears as the invincible tyrant, the being in contrast with whom all other beings are without freedom and subjectivity. He is equated with the recent tyrants who with the help of terror try to transform everything into a mere object, a thing among things, a cog in the machine they control. He becomes the model of everything against which Existentialism revolted. This is the God Nietzsche said had to be killed because nobody can tolerate being made into a mere object of absolute knowledge and absolute control. This is the deepest root of atheism. It is an atheism which is justified as the reaction against theological theism and its disturbing implications. It is also the deepest root of the Existentialist despair and the widespread anxiety of meaninglessness in our period.

Theism in all its forms is transcended in the experience we have called absolute faith. It is the accepting of the acceptance without somebody or something that accepts. It is the power of being-itself that accepts and gives the courage to be. This is the highest point to which our analysis has brought us. It cannot be described in the way the God of all forms of theism can be described. It cannot be described in mystical terms either. It transcends both mysticism and personal encounter, as it transcends both the courage to be as a part and the courage to be as oneself.

The God Above God and the Courage To Be

The ultimate source of the courage to be is the "God above God"; this is the result of our demand to transcend theism. Only if the God of theism is transcended can the anxiety of doubt and meaninglessness be taken into the courage to be. The God above God is the object of all mystical longing, but mysticism also must be transcended in order to reach him. Mysticism does not take seriously the concrete and the doubt concerning the concrete. It plunges directly into the ground of being and meaning, and leaves the concrete, the world of finite values and meanings, behind. Therefore it does not solve the problem of meaninglessness. In terms of the present religious situation this means that Eastern mysticism is not the solution of the problems of Western Existentialism, although many people attempt this solution. The God above the God of theism is not the devaluation of the meanings which doubt has thrown into the abyss of meaninglessness; he is their potential restitution. Nevertheless absolute faith agrees with the faith implied in mysticism in that both transcend the theistic objectivation of a God who is a being. For mysticism such a God is not more real than any finite being, for the courage to be such a God has disappeared in the abyss of meaninglessness with every other value and meaning.

The God above the God of theism is present, although hidden, in every divine-human encounter. Biblical religion as well as Protestant theology are aware of the paradoxical character of this encounter. They are aware that if God encounters man God is neither object nor subject and is therefore above the scheme into which theism has forced him. They are aware that personalism with respect to God is balanced by a transpersonal presence of the divine. They are aware that forgiveness can be accepted only if the power of acceptance is effective in man—biblically speaking, if the power of grace is effective in man. They are aware of the paradoxical character of every prayer, of speaking to somebody to whom you cannot speak because he is not "somebody," of asking somebody of whom you cannot ask anything because he gives or gives not before you ask, of saying "thou" to somebody who is nearer to the I than the I is to itself. Each of these paradoxes drives the religious consciousness toward a God above the God of theism.

The courage to be which is rooted in the experience of the God above the God of theism unites and transcends the courage to be as a part and the courage to be as oneself. It avoids both the loss of oneself by participation and the loss of one's world by individualization. The acceptance of the God above the God of theism makes us a part of that which is not also a part but is the ground of the whole. Therefore our self is not lost in a larger whole, which submerges it in the life of a limited group. If the self participates in the power of being-itself it receives itself back. For the power of being acts through the power of the individual selves. It does not swallow them as every limited whole, every collectivism, and every conformism does. This is why the Church, which stands for the power of being-itself or for the God who transcends the God of the religions, claims to be the mediator of the courage to be. A church which is based on the authority of the God of theism cannot make such a claim. It inescapably develops into a collectivist or semicollectivist system itself.

But a church which raises itself in its message and its devotion to the God above the God of theism without sacrificing its concrete symbols can mediate a courage which takes doubt and meaninglessness into itself. It is the Church under the Cross which alone can do this, the Church which preaches the Crucified who cried to God who remained his God after the God of confidence had left him in the darkness of doubt and meaninglessness. To be as a part in such a church is to receive a courage to be in which one cannot lose one's self and in which one receives one's world.

Absolute faith, or the state of being grasped by the God beyond God, is not a state which appears beside other states of the mind. It never is something separated and definite, an event which could be isolated and described. It is always a movement in, with, and under other states of the mind. It is the situation on the boundary of man's possibilities. It *is* this boundary. Therefore it is both the courage of despair and the courage in and above every courage. It is not a place where one can live, it is without the safety of words and concepts, it is without a name, a church, a cult, a theology. But it is moving in the depth of all of them. It is the power of being, in which they participate and of which they are fragmentary expressions.

One can become aware of it in the anxiety of fate and death when the traditional symbols, which enable men to stand the vicissitudes of fate and the horror of death have lost their power. When "providence" has become a superstition and "immortality" something imaginary that which once was the power in these symbols can still be present and create the courage to be in spite of the experience of a chaotic world and a finite existence. The Stoic courage returns but not as the faith in universal reason. It returns as the absolute faith which says Yes to being without seeing anything concrete which could conquer the nonbeing in fate and death.

And one can become aware of the God above the God of theism in the anxiety of guilt and condemnation when the traditional symbols that enable men to withstand the anxiety of guilt and condemnation have lost their power. When "divine judgment" is interpreted as a psychological complex and forgiveness as a remnant of the "father-image," what once was the power in those symbols can still be present and create the courage to be in spite of the experience of an infinite gap between what we are and what we ought to be. The Lutheran courage returns but not supported by the faith in a judging and forgiving God. It returns in terms of the absolute faith which says Yes although there is no special power that conquers guilt. The courage to take the anxiety of meaninglessness upon oneself is the boundary line up to which the courage to be can go. Beyond it is mere non-being. Within it all forms of courage are re-established in the power of the God above the God of theism. *The courage to be is rooted in the God who appears when God has disappeared in the anxiety of doubt.*

ISLAM

Islam is the youngest of the major religions, and two of the older ones were to some extent instrumental in its formation. Its founder, Mohammed, was obviously influenced in his religious teaching by those forms of Christianity (Monophysitism and Nestorianism) and Judaism which were present in the Arabian peninsula. Nevertheless, there are distinctive traits in Islam which are not merely borrowings from previously established faiths, which differentiate it from its predecessors, and which have enabled it to achieve and maintain a position of dominance among a large segment of the world population.

Two of the most characteristic of these traits find expression in the *shahāda*, "The only god is Allah, and Mohammed is Allah's apostle," which is the universally accepted confession of faith in Islam. Although the ancient Arabian religious background is quite similar to that of the early Hebrews, the fact that Islam is a relatively modern religion exempted it from passing through polytheistic and henotheistic stages of development. It comes upon the historical scene as a rigorous monotheism; and Mohammed himself thought that this distinction was highly important and that it signalled a return to the pre-Christian and pre-Judaic religion of Abraham, whereas both of these subsequent traditions had compromised the monotheistic ideal to varying degrees. The Arabic "Allah" merely means "the God," that is, the one and only supreme being. Because of this monotheistic commitment, Islamic theologians have tended to emphasize the topic of unity, including both the divine unity and the unity of the faith. In addition, God is ordinarily conceived as being eternal, transcendent, the creator, and the judge and avenger of wrong; and the constantly recurring adjectives assigned to him by the Koran are "the Compassionate, the Merciful." These predicates are manifest within the interior life of Islam, which tends to be exceptionally tolerant of divergent opinions and heresies, provided only that the foregoing two basic articles of faith are affirmed. This tolerance has not always extended to those outside the faith, for during its early years the exceptionally rapid expansion of Islam was as much a history of military conquest as of religious persuasion.

The second part of the *shahāda* does not mean that Mohammed is the only source of revelation concerning God. On the contrary, Islam accepts many prophets prior to Mohammed, including Moses and Jesus. The affirmation means that Mohammed is the last of the apostles, whose message sums up God's revelation to mankind. None of these apostles, including Jesus and Mohammed, are given divine status, as has been bestowed upon Jesus within orthodox Christianity. Mohammed is fully human, mortal, and fallible, although his life is regarded as exemplary and his pronouncements upon religious questions as authoritative.

The *shahāda* is the first of Five Pillars of the Faith, or obligatory religious duties, recognized within Islam. The others are prayer, almsgiving, pilgrimage, and fasting. Normally, the devout Muslim prays five times each day at traditionally set times, facing towards the sacred mosque at Mecca. Preferably, these prayers are said in a mosque, the Islamic counterpart of synagogue or church, whose very name, meaning place of prostration, indicates the importance of prayer to the Muslim. Almsgiving is usually on a voluntary basis, as seems to have been the case in early Islam. However, there has also traditionally been a required offering or tithe, amounting to one-fortieth of one's annual income. Pilgrimage is a religious requirement which apparently goes back to ancient Arabian practice prior to the rise of Islam and which was continued by the new religion. Every Muslim, unless hindered by reason of physical condition or poverty, is obliged to travel to Mecca at least once in his life (preferably the trip should also include a visit to Mohammed's tomb in Medina). Certain traditional rites must be performed by the pilgrims at Mecca, preceded by changes of dress to insure ritual purity. The practice of fasting was originally based upon Judeo-Christian practice, but was made much more severe in Islam. The Muslim fasts for one entire lunar month, Ramadān, the month in which the Koran was revealed to the Prophet. The fasting consists of abstaining from all food and drink between sunrise and sunset; and the practice is binding upon all save the sick and the traveler, who must make up the fast days they miss at some subsequent time. Furthermore, in agreement with the dietary taboos which are found in practically all religions, some foods are permanently proscribed, namely wine and pork.

Islam is perhaps even more a religion of law than Judaism, and in general Muslim countries utilize religious law as civil law also, although there are exceptions, such as Turkey, which has a non-religious civil code. The primary source of Islamic law is the Koran. The orthodox view holds that every word of the Koran is eternal and that Mohammed contributed none of his human fallibility to it, being only a means through which the revelation was accomplished. This extreme literalistic interpretation of revelation has meant that even the most liberal reform movements have continued to emphasize the importance of the Koran as a source of religious authority. Among the injunctions of the Koran are the Five Pillars of the Faith, regulations concerning diet, marriage and divorce, slavery, and a variety of crimes, such as theft, murder, fraud, and slander.

However, in addition to the Koran, many of the orthodox Islamic rules and practices derive from an oral tradition, known as the *sunna*, the practice or "custom" of the Prophet not contained in the Koran. The vehicle for *sunna* is *hadīth,* a traditional story or account, ultimately derived from one of Mohammed's companions. Much of Islamic legal criticism has been directed to authenticating the *hadīth.* An example of ritual sanctioned by *sunna* can be found in the Five Pillars themselves, for although the Koran enjoins prayer, the requirement that it be practiced five times each day is not in the Koran. Still another source of religious authority is *ijimā',* the "consent of the community," which is the ultimate appeal in determining the correctness of various possible interpretations of *hadīth.* Islamic orthodoxy accepts all these standards, and the orthodox are known as the *Sunnis,* because they follow the tradition.

The major dissenting sect within Islam, the *Shī'ite* sect, which traces its beginnings back to Ali, Mohammed's son-in-law and the fourth Caliph, rejects the authority of *ijimā'.* Instead, authoritative interpretations are derived from an *Imām* ("leader"), an infallible interpreter of the Koran who is heir to the authority originally invested in Ali. The *Shī'īs* recognize a series of these *Imāms,* although various schools disagree about their precise number, personal identification, and degree of superhuman status. *Shī'ism* is the recognized religion in Iran and counts additional followers in other Muslim countries, including India, Iraq, Syria, and Egypt. *Shī'ite* practice is in most respects similar to *Sunni* practice, although there are some differences, such as the recognition of temporary marriages and certain practices deriving from their belief that non-Muslims are ritually unclean.

Islam also has its mystical side, and those who stand in that tradition are known as *Sūfīs.* The mystical goal in Islam, as elsewhere, is union with the divine; but a great diversity of practices designed to achieve this end and as great a variety of descriptions of the mystic state have developed within Islam. Consequently there are many *Sūfī* orders, whose members are known as *faquirs* (Arabic) or *darwīshes* (Persian), "poor men," because they tend to devote themselves to the religious discipline necessary for attaining mystical union rather than to practical affairs. *Sūfiism* has, and still continues, to wield considerable influence upon Islamic faith and practice.

As is the case with other religions confronted with modern science and technology, Islam is currently undergoing a period of reevaluation. Much of this is directed at modifying traditional moral practices, such as the permission of slavery and polygamy. Other efforts are aimed at finding good psychological and sociological bases for traditional practices, and towards the interpretation of Islam as a civilization or culture rather than as a religion. The ultimate outcome of these tendencies cannot now be foreseen.

SUGGESTIONS FOR FURTHER READING

Daniel, Norman, *Islam and the West,* Edinburgh, The University Press, 1960.
De Vaux, Baron Carra, *Les Penseurs de L'Islam,* 5 vols., Paris, Librairie Paul Geuthner, 1921–1926.

Donaldson, Dwight M., *The Shī'ite Religion*, London, Luzac, 1933.

Gibb, H. A. R., *Mohammedanism*, New York, Oxford, 1962.

Levy, Reuben, *The Social Structure of Islam*, Cambridge, England, Cambridge University Press, 1957.

Padwick, Constance E., *Muslim Devotions*, London, S. P. C. K., 1961.

Schroeder, Eric, trans., *Muhammad's People*, Portland, Maine, The Bond Wheelwright Company, 1954.

Smith, Wilfred Cantwell, *Islam in Modern History*, Princeton, New Jersey, Princeton University Press, 1957.

Watt, William Montgomery, *Islamic Philosophy and Theology*, Edinburgh, The University Press, 1962.

47

THE KORAN

The Koran is the major authority within Islam upon all matters of belief and practice. Islamic orthodoxy accepts it as the product of divine revelation, the literal word of God delivered to his prophet Mohammed by the angel Gabriel. Mohammed himself seems to have regarded the several portions of the Koran, mystically conveyed to him in Arabic, as such a gift from God. Thus the Koran is sharply distinguished from the sunna, or traditions, which record the practice and belief of the prophet, by being a divine gift rather than Mohammed's own creation. A widespread Islamic doctrine maintains that the Koran is uncreated and that it eternally exists with God, and that it was conveyed part by part to the prophet as required to meet needs occasioned by particular events and circumstances. Although the orthodox view clearly rules out the possibility of any historical antecedents, critical scholars have regarded the Koran as being based largely upon a mixture of Jewish and Christian sources, with an especially great debt to Syriac Christianity. The separate parts of the Koran had not been assembled into one volume at the time of Mohammed's death (632); but the book was compiled shortly thereafter by Mohammed's close companions, who had memorized the revelation. The book is composed of 114 Suras, arranged, for the most part, in order of decreasing size. The two Suras reprinted here typify the content and spirit of this important document. The translation is that of the noted Arabic scholar, Arthur J. Arberry, whose English rendition of the sacred book is notable for its literary excellence.

WOMEN

In the Name of God, the Merciful, the Compassionate

Mankind, fear your Lord, who created you
of a single soul, and from it created
its mate, and from the pair of them scattered
abroad many men and women; and fear God

The Koran Interpreted, Arthur J. Arberry, trans. (London: Allen & Unwin, 1955), pp. 100–126, 316–329. Reprinted by permission of George Allen & Unwin, Ltd.

by whom you demand one of another,
and the wombs; surely God ever
         watches over you.

Give the orphans their property, and do not
exchange the corrupt for the good; and devour
not their property with your property; surely
         that is a great crime.
If you fear that you will not act justly
towards the orphans, marry such women
as seem good to you, two, three, four;
but if you fear you will not be equitable,
then only one, or what your right hands own;
so it is likelier you will not be partial.
And give the women their dowries as a gift
spontaneous; but if they are pleased
to offer you any of it, consume it
         with wholesome appetite.
But do not give to fools their property
that God has assigned to you to manage;
provide for them and clothe them out of it,
and speak to them honourable words.
Test well the orphans, until they reach
the age of marrying; then, if you perceive
in them right judgment, deliver to them
their property; consume it not wastefully
         and hastily
ere they are grown. If any man is rich,
let him be abstinent; if poor, let him
         consume in reason.
And when you deliver to them their property,
take witnesses over them; God suffices
         for a reckoner.

To the men a share of what parents and kinsmen
leave, and to the women a share of what
parents and kinsmen leave, whether it be
little or much, a share apportioned;
and when the division is attended by
kinsmen and orphans and the poor,
make provision for them out of it,
and speak to them honourable words.
And let those fear who, if they left
behind them weak seed, would be afraid

on their account, and let them fear
God, and speak words hitting the mark.
Those who devour the property of orphans
unjustly, devour Fire in their bellies,
and shall assuredly roast in a Blaze.

God charges you, concerning your children:
to the male the like of the portion
of two females, and if they be women
above two, then for them two-thirds
of what he leaves, but if she be one
then to her a half; and to his parents
to each one of the two the sixth
of what he leaves, if he has children;
but if he has no children, and his
heirs are his parents, a third to his
mother, or, if he has brothers, to his
mother a sixth, after any bequest
he may bequeath, or any debt.
Your fathers and your sons—you know not
which out of them is nearer in profit
to you. So God apportions; surely God is
    All-knowing, All-wise.
And for you a half of what your wives
leave, if they have no children; but
if they have children, then for you of what
they leave a fourth, after any bequest
they may bequeath, or any debt.
And for them a fourth of what you leave,
if you have no children; but if you
have children, then for them of what
you leave an eighth, after any bequest
you may bequeath, or any debt.
If a man or a woman have no heir
direct, but have a brother or a sister,
to each of the two a sixth; but if they
are more numerous than that, they share
equally a third, after any bequest
he may bequeath, or any debt not
prejudicial; a charge from God. God is
    All-knowing, All-clement.

Those are God's bounds. Whoso obeys God
and His Messenger, He will admit him

to gardens underneath which rivers flow,
therein dwelling forever; that is
        the mighty triumph.
But whoso disobeys God, and His Messenger,
and trangresses His bounds, him He will
admit to a Fire, therein dwelling
forever, and for him there awaits
        a humbling chastisement.

Such of your women as commit indecency,
call four of you to witness against them;
and if they witness, then detain them
in their houses until death takes them
or God appoints for them a way.
And when two of you commit indecency,
punish them both; but if they repent
and make amends, then suffer them to be;
God turns, and is All-compassionate.
God shall turn only towards those who do
evil in ignorance, then shortly repent;
God will return towards those; God is
        All-knowing, All-wise.
But God shall not turn towards those
who do evil deeds until, when one of them
is visited by death, he says, 'Indeed
now I repent,' neither to those who die
disbelieving; for them We have prepared
        a painful chastisement.

O believers, it is not lawful for you
to inherit women against their will;
neither debar them, that you may go off
with part of what you have given them,
except when they commit a flagrant indecency.
Consort with them honourably; or if
you are averse to them, it is possible
you may be averse to a thing, and God set
        in it much good.
And if you desire to exchange a wife
in place of another, and you have given
to one a hundredweight, take of it nothing.
What, will you take it by way of calumny
        and manifest sin?
How shall you take it, when each of you has been

privily with the other, and they have taken from you
    a solemn compact?
And do not marry women that your fathers
married, unless it be a thing of the past;
surely that is indecent and hateful,
    an evil way.

Forbidden to you are your mothers and daughters,
your sisters, your aunts paternal and maternal,
your brother's daughters, your sister's daughters,
your mothers who have given suck to you,
your suckling sisters, your wives' mothers,
your stepdaughters who are in your care
being born of your wives you have been in to—
but if you have not yet been in to them
it is no fault in you—and the spouses
of your sons who are of your loins,
and that you should take to you two sisters
together, unless it be a thing of the past;
God is All-forgiving, All-compassionate;
and wedded women, save what your right hands own.
So God prescribes for you. Lawful for you,
beyond all that, is that you may seek,
using your wealth, in wedlock and not
in licence. Such wives as you enjoy thereby,
give them their wages apportionate; it is no
fault in you in your agreeing together,
after the due apportionate. God is
    All-knowing, All-wise.

Any one of you who has not the affluence
to be able to marry believing freewomen
in wedlock, let him take believing handmaids
that your right hands own; God knows very well
your faith; the one of you is as the other.
So marry them, with their people's leave,
and give them their wages honourably
as women in wedlock, not as in licence
    or taking lovers.
But when they are in wedlock, if they
commit indecency, they shall be liable
to half the chastisement of freewomen.
That provision is for those of you who fear
fornication; yet it is better for you

to be patient. God is All-forgiving
    All-compassionate.
God desires to make clear to you, and to
guide you in the institutions of those
before you, and to turn towards you; God is
    All-knowing, All-wise;
and God desires to turn towards you, but
those who follow their lusts desire you
to swerve away mightily. God desires
to lighten things for you, for man was
    created a weakling.

O believers, consume not your goods
between you in vanity, except there be
trading, by your agreeing together.
And kill not one another. Surely God is
    compassionate to you.
But whosoever does that in transgression
and wrongfully, him We shall certainly
roast at a Fire; and that for God is
    an easy matter.
If you avoid the heinous sins that
are forbidden you, We will acquit you
of your evil deeds, and admit you by
    the gate of honour.

Do not covet that whereby God in bounty
has preferred one of you above another.
To the men a share from what they have earned,
and to the women a share from what they
have earned. And ask God of His bounty;
    God knows everything.

To everyone We have appointed heirs
of that which parents and kinsmen leave,
and those with whom you have sworn compact.
So give to them their share; God is witness
    over everything.

Men are the managers of the affairs of women
for that God has preferred in bounty
one of them over another, and for that
they have expended of their property.
Righteous women are therefore obedient,
guarding the secret for God's guarding.

And those you fear may be rebellious
admonish; banish them to their couches,
and beat them. If they then obey you,
look not for any way against them; God is
     All-high, All-great.
And if you fear a breach between the two,
bring forth an arbiter from his people
and from her people an arbiter, if they
desire to set things right; God will
compose their differences; surely God is
     All-knowing, All-aware.

     Serve God,
and associate naught with Him.

Be kind to parents, and the near kinsman,
and to orphans, and to the needy,
and to the neighbour who is of kin,
and to the neighbour who is a stranger,
and to the companion at your side,
and to the traveller, and to that your
right hands own. Surely God loves not
     the proud and boastful
such as are niggardly, and bid other men
to be niggardly, and themselves conceal
the bounty that God has given them.
We have prepared for the unbelievers
     a humbling chastisement,
and such as expend of their substance
to show off to men, and believe not
in God and the Last Day. Whosoever
has Satan for a comrade, an evil
     comrade is he.
Why, what would it harm them, if they
believed in God and the Last Day, and
expended of that God has provided them?
     God knows them.
Surely God shall not wrong so much as the
weight of an ant; and if it be a good deed
He will double it, and give from Himself
     a mighty wage.

How then shall it be, when We bring forward from every
nation a witness, and bring thee to witness against those?

Upon that day the unbelievers, those who have disobeyed
the Messenger, will wish that the earth might be levelled
with them; and they will not conceal from God one tiding.

O believers, draw not near to prayer
when you are drunken until you know
what you are saying, or defiled—unless
you are traversing a way—until you
have washed yourselves; but if you are
sick, or on a journey, or if any of you
comes from the privy, or you have touched
women, and you can find no water,
then have recourse to wholesome dust
and wipe your faces and your hands; God is
        All-pardoning, All-forgiving.

Hast thou not regarded those who were given
a share of the Book purchasing error,
and desiring that you should also err
from the way? God knows well your enemies;
God suffices as a protector, God suffices
        as a helper.
Some of the Jews pervert words from their meanings
saying, 'We have heard and we disobey'
and 'Hear, and be thou not given to hear'
and 'Observe us,' twisting with their tongues and
        traducing religion.
If they had said, 'We have heard and obey'
and 'Hear' and 'Regard us,' it would have been
better for them, and more upright; but God has
cursed them for their unbelief, so they believe not
        except a few.
You who have been given the Book, believe
in what We have sent down, confirming
what is with you, before We obliterate
faces, and turn them upon their backs, or
curse them as We cursed the Sabbath-men, and
        God's command is done.
God forgives not that aught should be with Him
associated; less than that He forgives
to whomsoever He will. Whoso associates
with God anything, has indeed forged
        a mighty sin.

Hast thou not regarded those who purify
themselves? Nay; only God purifies
whom He will; and they shall not be wronged
  a single date-thread.
Consider how they forge falsehood
against God; and that suffices for
  a manifest sin.

Hast thou not regarded those who were given
a share of the Book believing in demons
and idols, and saying to the unbelievers,
'These are more rightly guided on the way
  than the believers'?
Those are they whom God has cursed; he whom God
has cursed, thou wilt not find for him
  any helper.
Or have they a share in the Kingdom?
If that is so, they do not give the people
  a single date-spot.
Or are they jealous of the people
for the bounty that God has given them?
Yet We gave the people of Abraham
the Book and the Wisdom, and We gave them
  a mighty kingdom.
And some of them there are that believe, and
some of them that bar from it; Gehenna suffices
  for a Blaze!
Surely those who disbelieve in Our Signs—We
shall certainly roast them at a Fire; as often
as their skins are wholly burned, We shall
give them in exchange other skins, that they
may taste the chastisement. Surely God is
  All-mighty, All-wise.
And those that believe, and do deeds of righteousness,
them We shall admit to gardens underneath
which rivers flow, therein dwelling forever and ever;
therein for them shall be spouses purified,
and We shall admit them to a shelter
  of plenteous shade.

God commands you to deliver trusts
back to their owners; and when you judge
between the people, that you judge with justice.

Good is the admonition God gives you; God is
    All-hearing, All-seeing.

O believers, obey God, and obey the Messenger
and those in authority among you. If you
should quarrel on anything, refer it to God
and the Messenger, if you believe in God
and the Last Day; that is better, and fairer
    in the issue.
Hast thou not regarded those who assert
that they believe in what has been sent down
to thee, and what was sent down before thee,
desiring to take their disputes to idols,
yet they have been commanded to disbelieve
in them? But Satan desires to lead them astray
    into far error.
And when it is said to them, 'Come now to
what God has sent down, and the Messenger,'
then thou sees the hypocrites barring
    the way to thee.
How shall it be, when they are visited
by an affliction for what their own hands
have forwarded, then they come to thee
swearing by God, 'We sought only kindness and
    conciliation'?
Those—God knows what is in their hearts;
so turn away from them, and admonish them,
and say to them penetrating words
    about themselves.
We sent not ever any Messenger, but
that he should be obeyed, by the leave of God.
If, when they wronged themselves, they had
come to thee, and prayed forgiveness of God,
and the Messenger had prayed forgiveness
for them, they would have found God turns,
    All-compassionate.
But no, by thy Lord! they will not believe
till they make thee the judge regarding
the disagreement between them, then they
shall find in themselves no impediment
touching thy verdict, but shall surrender
    in full submission.
But had We prescribed for them, saying,
'Slay yourselves' or 'Leave your habitations,'

they would not have done it, save a few of them;
yet if they had done as they were admonished
it would have been better for them, and stronger
    confirming them,
and then We surely would have given them
from Us a mighty wage, and guided them
    on a straight path.
Whosoever obeys God, and the Messenger—
they are with those whom God has blessed,
Prophets, just men, martyrs, the righteous;
    good companions they!
That is the bounty from God; God suffices
    as One who knows.

O believers, take your precautions; then
move forward in companies, or move forward
    all together.
Some of you there are that are dilatory;
then, if an affliction visits you, he says,
'God has blessed me, in that I was not
    a martyr with them.'
But if a bounty from God visits you, he
will surely say, as if there had never been
any affection between you and him,
'Would that I had been with them, to attain
    a mighty triumph!'
So let them fight in the way of God who
sell the present life for the world to come;
and whosoever fights in the way of God
and is slain, or conquers, We shall bring him
    a mighty wage.
How is it with you, that you do not fight
in the way of God, and for the men,
women, and children who, being abased,
say, 'Our Lord, bring us forth from this city
whose people are evildoers, and appoint to us
a protector from Thee, and appoint to us
    from Thee a helper'?
The believers fight in the way of God,
and the unbelievers fight in the idols' way.
Fight you therefore against the friends
of Satan; surely the guile of Satan
    is ever feeble.
Hast thou not regarded those to whom it was said,

'Restrain your hands, and perform the prayer,
and pay the alms'? Then, as soon as fighting
is prescribed for them, there is a party
of them fearing the people as they would
fear God, or with a greater fear, and they say,
'Our Lord, why hast thou prescribed fighting for us?
Why not defer us to a near term?'
Say: 'The enjoyment of this world is little;
the world to come is better for him
who fears God; you shall not be wronged
        a single date-thread.'
Wherever you may be, death will overtake you,
though you should be in raised-up towers.
And if a good thing visits them, they say,
'This is from God'; but if an evil thing
visits them, they say, 'This is from thee.'
Say: 'Everything is from God.' How is it
with this people? They scarcely understand
        any tiding.
Whatever good visits thee, it is of God;
whatever evil visits thee is of thyself.
And We have sent thee to men a Messenger; God
        suffices for a witness.

Whosoever obeys the Messenger, thereby
obeys God; and whosoever turns his
back—We have not sent thee to be a
        watcher over them.
They say, 'Obedience'; but when they sally
forth from thee, a party of them meditate
all night on other than what thou sayest. God
writes down their meditations; so turn away from
them, and put thy trust in God; God suffices
        for a guardian.
What, do they not ponder the Koran?
If it had been from other than God
surely they would have found in it much
        inconsistency.
When there comes to them a matter, be it
of security or fear, they broadcast it;
if they had referred it to the Messenger
and to those in authority among them, those
of them whose task it is to investigate
would have known the matter. And but for

the bounty of God to you, and His mercy,
you would surely have followed Satan,
    except a few.

So do thou fight in the way of God;
thou art charged only with thyself.
And urge on the believers; haply God
will restrain the unbelievers' might;
God is stronger in might, more terrible
    in punishing.

Whoso intercedes with a good intercession
shall receive a share of it; whosoever
intercedes with a bad intercession, he
shall receive the like of it; God has power
    over everything.

And when you are greeted with a greeting
greet with a fairer than it, or return it;
surely God keeps a watchful count
    over everything.

    God—
there is no god but He.
He will surely gather you
    to the Resurrection Day,
    no doubt of it.
And who is truer in tidings than God?

How is it with you, that you are two parties
touching the hypocrites, and God has overthrown
them for what they earned? What, do you desire
to guide him whom God has led astray?
Whom God leads astray, thou wilt not find
    for him a way.
They wish that you should disbelieve as
they disbelieve, and then you would be
equal; therefore take not to yourselves
friends of them, until they emigrate in
the way of God; then, if they turn their backs,
take them, and slay them wherever you find them;
take not to yourselves any one of them
    as friend or helper
except those that betake themselves to a people

who are joined with you by a compact,
or come to you with breasts constricted
from fighting with you or fighting their people.
Had God willed, He would have given them
authority over you, and then certainly
they would have fought you. If they withdraw
from you, and do not fight you, and offer you
peace, then God assigns not any way
            to you against them.
You will find others desiring to be secure
from you, and secure from their people, yet
whenever they are returned to temptation, they
are overthrown in it. If they withdraw not
from you, and offer you peace, and restrain
their hands, take them, and slay them wherever
you come on them; against them We have given you
            a clear authority.

It belongs not to a believer to slay
a believer, except it be by error.
If any slays a believer by error, then
let him set free a believing slave,
and bloodwit is to be paid to his family
unless they forgo it as a freewill offering.
If he belong to a people at enmity
with you and is a believer, let the slayer
set free a believing slave. If he belong
to a people joined with you by a compact,
then bloodwit is to be paid to his family
and the slayer shall set free a believing slave.
But if he finds not the means, let him fast
two successive months—God's turning; God is
            All-knowing, All-wise.
And whoso slays a believer wilfully,
his recompense is Gehenna, therein
dwelling forever, and God will be wroth with him
and will curse him, and prepare for him
            a mighty chastisement.

O believers, when you are journeying
in the path of God, be discriminating,
and do not say to him who offers you
a greeting, 'Thou art not a believer,'

seeking the chance goods of the present life.
With God are spoils abundant. So you were
aforetime; but God has been gracious to you.
So be discriminating; surely God is aware of
  the things you do.

Such believers as sit at home—unless
they have an injury—are not the equals
of those who struggle in the path of God
with their possessions and their selves.
God has preferred in rank those who struggle
with their possessions and their selves
over the ones who sit at home; yet to each
God has promised the reward most fair;
and God has preferred those who struggle
over the ones who sit at home for the bounty
  of a mighty wage,
in ranks standing before Him, forgiveness
and mercy; surely God is All-forgiving,
  All-compassionate.

And those the angels take, while still they
are wronging themselves—the angels will say,
'In what circumstances were you?' They will say,
'We were abased in the earth.' The angels
will say, 'But was not God's earth wide,
so that you might have emigrated in it?'
Such men, their refuge shall be Gehenna—
  an evil homecoming!—
except the men, women, and children
who, being abased, can devise nothing
and are not guided to a way; haply
them God will yet pardon, for God is
  All-pardoning, All-forgiving.
Whoso emigrates in the way of God
will find in the earth many refuges
and plenty; whoso goes forth from his house
an emigrant to God and His Messenger,
and then death overtakes him, his wage
shall have fallen on God; surely
God is All-forgiving, All-compassionate.
And when you are journeying in the land
there is no fault in you that you shorten

the prayer, if you fear the unbelievers
may afflict you; the unbelievers are for you
     a manifest foe.
When thou art amongst them, and performest
for them the prayer, let a party of them
stand with thee, and let them take their weapons.
When they bow themselves, let them be behind you;
and let another party who have not prayed
come and pray with thee, taking their precautions
and their weapons. The unbelievers wish
that you should be heedless of your weapons
and your baggage, then they would wheel on you
all at once. There is no fault in you,
if rain molests you, or you are sick, to
lay aside your weapons; but take your precautions.
God has prepared for the unbelievers
     a humbling chastisement.
When you have performed the prayer, remember
God, standing and sitting and on your sides.
Then, when you are secure, perform the prayer;
surely the prayer is a timed prescription
     for the believers.

Faint not in seeking the heathen; if you
are suffering, they are also suffering as
you are suffering, and you are hoping from God
for that for which they cannot hope; God is
     All-knowing, All-wise.

Surely We have sent down to thee the Book
with the truth, so that thou mayest judge
between the people by that God has shown thee.
So be not an advocate for the traitors;
and pray forgiveness of God; surely
God is All-forgiving, All-compassionate.
And do not dispute on behalf of those
who betray themselves; surely God loves not
     the guilty traitor.
They hide themselves from men, but hide not
themselves from God; for He is with them
while they meditate at night discourse
unpleasing to Him; God encompasses
     the things they do.

Ha, there you are; you have disputed
on their behalf in the present life; but
who will dispute with God on their behalf
on the Resurrection Day, or who will be
     a guardian for them?

Whosoever does evil, or wrongs himself,
and then prays God's forgiveness, he shall find
God is All-forgiving, All-compassionate.
And whosoever earns a sin, earns it
against himself only; and God is ever
     All-knowing, All-wise.
And whosoever earns a fault or a sin
and then casts it upon the innocent,
thereby has laid upon himself calumny
     and manifest sin.

But for God's bounty to thee and His mercy
a party of them purposed to lead thee
astray; but they lead only themselves astray;
they do not hurt thee in anything.
God has sent down on thee the Book and
the Wisdom, and He has taught thee that
thou knowest not; God's bounty to thee
     is ever great.
No good is there in much of their conspiring,
except for him who bids to freewill
offering, or honour, or setting things right
between the people. Whoso does that, seeking
God's good pleasure, We shall surely give him
     a mighty wage.
But whoso makes a breach with the Messenger
after the guidance has become clear to him,
and follows a way other than the believers',
him We shall turn over to what he has turned to
and We shall roast him in Gehenna—
     an evil homecoming!

God forgives not that aught should be with Him
associated; less than that He forgives
to whomsoever He will. Whoso associates
with God anything, has gone astray
     into far error.

In stead of Him, they pray not except to
female beings; they pray not except to
        a rebel Satan
accursed by God. He said, 'Assuredly
I will take unto myself a portion
appointed of Thy servants, and I will
lead them astray, and fill them with fancies,
and I will command them and they will cut off
the cattle's ears; I will command them
and they will alter God's creation.'
Whoso takes Satan to him for a friend,
instead of God, has surely suffered
        a manifest loss.
He promises them and fills them with fancies,
but there is nothing Satan promises them
        except delusion.
Such men—their refuge shall be Gehenna,
and they shall find no asylum from it.
But those that believe, and do deeds of righteousness,
them We shall admit to gardens underneath
which rivers flow, therein dwelling for ever and ever;
God's promise in truth; and who is truer
        in speech than God?
It is not your fancies, nor the fancies
of the People of the Book. Whosoever
does evil shall be recompensed for it,
and will not find for him, apart from God,
        a friend or helper.
And whosoever does deeds of righteousness,
be it male or female, believing—
they shall enter Paradise, and not be wronged
        a single date-spot.
And who is there that has a fairer religion
than he who submits his will to God
being a good-doer, and who follows
the creed of Abraham, a man of pure faith?
And God took Abraham for a friend.

To God belongs all that is in the heavens
and in the earth, and God encompasses
        everything.

They will ask thee for a pronouncement
concerning women. Say: 'God pronounces

to you concerning them, and what is recited
to you in the Book concerning the orphan
women to whom you give not what is prescribed
for them, and yet desire to marry them,
and the oppressed children, and that you secure
justice for orphans. Whatever good you do,
  God knows of it.'

If a woman fear rebelliousness or aversion
in her husband, there is no fault in them
if the couple set things right between them;
right settlement is better; and souls are very
prone to avarice. If you do good
and are godfearing, surely God is aware of
  the things you do.
You will not be able to be equitable
between your wives, be you ever so eager;
yet do not be altogether partial
so that you leave her as it were suspended.
If you set things right, and are godfearing,
God is All-forgiving, All-compassionate.
But if they separate, God will enrich
each of them of His plenty; God is
  All-embracing, All-wise.

To God belongs all that is in the heavens
and in the earth. We have charged those
who were given the Book before you,
and you, 'Fear God.' If you disbelieve,
to God belongs all that is in the heavens
and in the earth; God is All-sufficient,
  All-laudable.
To God belongs all that is in the heavens
and in the earth; God suffices
  for a guardian.
If He will, He can put you away, O men,
and bring others; surely God is powerful
  over that.
Whoso desires the reward of this world,
with God is the reward of this world
and of the world to come; God is
  All-hearing, All-seeing.

O believers, be you securers of
justice, witnesses for God, even though

it be against yourselves, or your parents
and kinsmen, whether the man be rich
or poor; God stands closest to either.
Then follow not caprice, so as to swerve;
for if you twist or turn, God is aware of
  the things you do.

O believers, believe in God and His Messenger
and the Book He has sent down on His Messenger
and the Book which He sent down before.
Whoso disbelieves in God and His angels
and His Books, and His Messengers,
and the Last Day, has surely gone astray
  into far error.
Those who believe, and then disbelieve,
and then believe, and then disbelieve,
and then increase in unbelief—God is not
likely to forgive them, neither to guide them
  on any way.

Give thou good tidings to the hypocrites that
for them awaits a painful chastisement.
Those who take unbelievers for their friends
instead of believers—do they seek glory
in them? But glory altogether
  belongs to God.
He has sent down upon you in the Book:
'When you hear God's signs being disbelieved
and made mock of, do not sit with them
until they plunge into some other talk, or
else you will surely be like to them.' God
will gather the hypocrites and the unbelievers
  all in Gehenna.
Those who wait upon you and, if a victory comes
to you from God, say, 'Were we not with you?'
but if the unbelievers get a share, they say,
'Did we not gain the mastery over you, and
did we not defend you from the believers?' God
will judge between you on the Resurrection Day,
and God will not grant the unbelievers any way
  over the believers.
The hypocrites seek to trick God, but God
is tricking them. When they stand up to pray
they stand up lazily, showing off to the people

and not remembering God save a little; wavering
all the time—not to these, not to those;
and whom God leads astray, thou wilt not find
  for him a way.
O believers, take not the unbelievers
as friends instead of the believers; or
do you desire to give God over you
  a clear authority?
Surely the hypocrites will be in the lowest
reach of the Fire; thou wilt not find for them
  any helper;
save such as repent, and make amends, and
hold fast to God, and make their religion
sincerely God's; those are with the believers,
and God will certainly give the believers
  a mighty wage.
What would God do with chastising you
if you are thankful, and believe? God is
  All-thankful, All-knowing.

God likes not the shouting of evil words
unless a man has been wronged; God is
  All-hearing, All-knowing.

If you do good openly or in secret
or pardon an evil, surely God is
  All-pardoning, All-powerful.

Those who disbelieve in God and His Messengers
and desire to make division between God
and His Messengers, and say, 'We believe
in part, and disbelieve in part,' desiring
to take between this and that a way—
those in truth are the unbelievers;
and We have prepared for the unbelievers
  a humbling chastisement.
And those who believe in God and His Messengers
and make no division between any of them,
those—We shall surely give them their wages;
God is All-forgiving, All-compassionate.

The People of the Book will ask thee to bring down
upon them a Book from heaven; and they asked
Moses for greater than that, for they said,

'Show us God openly.' And the thunderbolt
took them for their evildoing. Then they took
to themselves the Calf, after the clear signs
had come to them; yet We pardoned them
that, and We bestowed upon Moses
        a clear authority.
And We raised above them the Mount, taking
compact with them; and We said to them, 'Enter in
at the gate, prostrating'; and We said to them,
'Transgress not the Sabbath'; and We took from them
        a solemn compact.
So, for their breaking the compact, and disbelieving
in the signs of God, and slaying the Prophets
without right, and for their saying, 'Our hearts
are uncircumcised'—nay, but God sealed them
for their unbelief, so they believe not,
        except a few—
and for their unbelief, and their uttering
against Mary a mighty calumny,
and for their saying, 'We slew the Messiah,
Jesus son of Mary, the Messenger of God'—
yet they did not slay him, neither crucified him,
only a likeness of that was shown to them.
Those who are at variance concerning him surely
are in doubt regarding him; they have no knowledge
of him, except the following of surmise;
and they slew him not of a certainty—
no indeed; God raised him up to Him; God is
        All-mighty, All-wise.
There is not one of the People of the Book
but will assuredly believe in him before his
death, and on the Resurrection Day he will be
        a witness against them.
And for the evildoing of those of Jewry, We
have forbidden them certain good things that
were permitted to them, and for their barring
        from God's way many,
and for their taking usury, that they were
prohibited, and consuming the wealth
of the people in vanity; and We have
prepared for the unbelievers among them
        a painful chastisement.
But those of them that are firmly rooted in
knowledge, and the believers believing in

what has been sent down to thee, and what was
sent down before thee, that perform the prayer
and pay the alms, and those who believe in God
and the Last Day—them We shall surely give
    a mighty wage.

We have revealed to thee as We revealed
to Noah, and the Prophets after him,
and We revealed to Abraham, Ishmael,
Isaac, Jacob, and the Tribes,
Jesus and Job, Jonah and Aaron
and Solomon, and We gave to David
    Psalms,
and Messengers We have already told thee of
before, and Messengers We have not told thee of;
and unto Moses God spoke directly—
Messengers bearing good tidings, and warning,
so that mankind might have no argument
against God, after the Messengers; God is
    All-mighty, All-wise.
But God bears witness to that He has sent down
to thee; He has sent it down with His knowledge;
and the angels also bear witness; and God suffices
    for a witness.

Surely those who disbelieve, and bar
from the way of God, have gone astray
    into far error.
Surely the unbelievers, who have done evil,
God would not forgive them, neither guide them
    on any road
but the road to Gehenna, therein dwelling
forever and ever; and that for God is
    an easy matter.

O men, the Messenger has now come to you
with the truth from your Lord; so believe;
better is it for you. And if you disbelieve,
to God belongs all that is in the heavens
and in the earth; and God is
    All-knowing, All-wise.

People of the Book, go not beyond the bounds
in your religion, and say not as to God

but the truth. The Messiah, Jesus son of Mary,
was only the Messenger of God, and His Word
that He committed to Mary, and a Spirit from
Him. So believe in God and His Messengers,
and say not, 'Three.' Refrain; better is it
for you. God is only One God. Glory be
to Him—that He should have a son!
To Him belongs all that is in the heavens
and in the earth; God suffices
          for a guardian.
The Messiah will not disdain to be a servant
of God, neither the angels who are near
          stationed to Him.
Whosoever disdains to serve Him, and waxes
proud, He will assuredly muster them to
          Him, all of them.
As for the believers, who do deeds of righteousness,
He will pay them in full their wages,
and He will give them more, of His bounty;
and as for them who disdain, and wax proud,
them He will chastise with a painful chastisement,
and they shall not find for them, apart from God,
          a friend or helper.

O men, a proof has now come to you from your Lord;
We have sent down to you a manifest light.
As for those who believe in God, and hold fast
to Him, He will surely admit them to mercy
from Him, and bounty, and will guide them to Him
          on a straight path.

They will ask thee for a pronouncement.
Say: 'God pronounces to you concerning
the indirect heirs. If a man perishes
having no children, but he has a sister,
she shall receive a half of what he leaves,
and he is her heir if she has no children.

If there be two sisters, they shall receive
two-thirds of what he leaves; if there be
brothers and sisters, the male shall receive
the portion of two females. God makes clear
to you, lest you go astray; God has knowledge
          of everything.

THE CAVE

In the Name of God, the Merciful, the Compassionate

Praise belongs to God
who has sent down upon His servant the Book
        and has not assigned unto it any
                crookedness;
        right, to warn of great violence
        from Him, and to give good tidings
unto the believers, who do righteous deeds,
        that theirs shall be a goodly wage
                therein to abide for
                ever,
and to warn those who say, 'God has taken to Himself
                a son;
        they have no knowledge of it, they
        nor their fathers; a monstrous word
        it is, issuing out of their mouths;
                they say nothing but a lie.
        Yet perchance, if they believe not
        in this tiding, thou wilt consume
        thyself, following after them, of
                grief.
We have appointed all that is on the earth
for an adornment for it, and that We may
        try which of them is fairest in
                works;
and We shall surely make all that is on it
                barren dust.

Or dost thou think the Men of the Cave
and Er-Rakeem were among Our signs a
                wonder?
When the youths took refuge in the Cave
saying, 'Our Lord, give us mercy from Thee,
and furnish us with rectitude in our
                affair.'
Then We smote their ears many years in
                the Cave.
Afterwards We raised them up again, that
We might know which of the two parties
would better calculate the while they had
                tarried.

We will relate to thee their tidings
truly. They were youths who believed
in their Lord, and We increased them in
        guidance.
And We strengthened their hearts, when
they stood up and said, 'Our Lord is
the Lord of the heavens and earth;
we will not call upon any god, apart
from Him, or then we had spoken
        outrage.
These our people have taken to them
other gods, apart from Him. Ah, if only
they would bring some clear authority
regarding them! But who does greater
evil than he who forges against God
        a lie?
So, when you have gone apart from them
and that they serve, excepting God,
take refuge in the Cave, and your Lord
will unfold to you of His mercy, and will
furnish you with a gentle issue of your
        affair.'
And thou mightest have seen the sun,
when it rose, inclining from their Cave
towards the right, and, when it set,
passing them by on the left, while they
were in a broad fissure of the Cave.
That was one of God's signs; whomsoever
God guides, he is rightly guided,
and whomsoever He leads astray, thou
wilt not find for him a protector to
        direct.
Thou wouldst have thought them awake,
as they lay sleeping, while We turned them
now to the right, now to the left,
and their dog stretching its paws on
the threshold. Hadst thou observed them
surely thou wouldst have turned thy back on
them in flight, and been filled with terror
        of them.
And even so We raised them up again
that they might question one another.
One of them said, 'How long have you
tarried? They said, 'We have tarried

a day, or part of a day.' They said,
'Your Lord knows very well how long
you have tarried. Now send one of you
forth with this silver to the city,
and let him look for which of them has
purest food, and bring you provision thereof;
let him be courteous, and apprise no man
                of you.
If they should get knowledge of you
they will stone you, or restore you to
their creed, then you will not prosper
                ever.'
And even so We made them stumble upon
them, that they might know that God's
promise is true, and that the Hour—
there is no doubt of it. When they were
contending among themselves of their affair
then they said, 'Build over them a
building; their Lord knows of them very well.'
Said those who prevailed over their affair,
'We will raise over them a place of
                worship.'
(They will say, 'Three; and their dog
was the fourth of them.' They will say,
'Five; and their dog was the sixth of them.'
guessing at the Unseen. They will say,
'Seven; and their dog was the eighth of them.'
Say: 'My Lord knows very well their
number, and none knows them, except
                a few.'
So do not dispute with them, except
in outward disputation, and ask not
any of them for a pronouncement
                on them.
And do not say, regarding anything,
'I am going to do that tomorrow,'
but only, 'If God will'; and mention
thy Lord, when thou forgettest, and say,
'It may be that my Lord will guide me
unto something nearer to rectitude
                than this.')
And they tarried in the Cave three
hundred years, and to that they added
                nine more.

Say: 'God knows very well how long
they tarried. To Him belongs the Unseen
in the heavens and in the earth.
How well He sees! How well He hears!
They have no protector, apart from Him,
and He associates in His government
                no one.'

Recite what has been revealed to thee of the Book of thy Lord;
no man can change His words. Apart from Him, thou wilt find
                no refuge.
And restrain thyself with those who call upon their Lord
at morning and evening, desiring His countenance,
and let not thine eyes turn away from them, desiring
the adornment of the present life; and obey not him
whose heart We have made neglectful of Our remembrance
so that he follows his own lust, and his affair has become
                all excess.
Say: 'The truth is from your Lord; so let whosoever will
believe, and let whosoever will disbelieve.' Surely We
have prepared for the evildoers a fire, whose pavilion
encompasses them; if they call for succour, they will be
succoured with water like molten copper, that shall
scald their faces—how evil a potion, and how evil a
                resting-place!
Surely those who believe, and do deeds of righteousness—
surely We leave not to waste the wage of him who does
                good works:
those—theirs shall be Gardens of Eden, underneath which
rivers flow; therein they shall be adorned with bracelets
of gold, and they shall be robed in green garments
of silk and brocade, therein reclining upon couches—
O, how excellent a reward! And O, how fair a
                resting-place!

And strike for them a similitude:
                two men.
To one of them We assigned two gardens of
vines, and surrounded them with palm-trees,
and between them We set a sown field;
each of the two gardens yielded its produce
and failed naught in any wise; and We
caused to gush amidst them a river.
                So he
had fruit; and he said to his fellow,

as he was conversing with him, 'I have
more abundance of wealth than thou
and am mightier in respect of men.'
And he entered his garden, wronging
himself; he said, 'I do not think that
this will ever perish; I do not think
that the Hour is coming; and if I
am indeed returned to my Lord, I shall
surely find a better resort than this.'
   Said his fellow,
as he was conversing with him, 'What,
disbelievest thou in Him who created
thee of dust, then of a sperm-drop,
then shaped thee as a man? But lo,
   He is God, my Lord,
and I will not associate with my Lord
   any one.
Why, when thou wentest into thy garden,
didst thou not say, "As God will;
there is no power except in God"?
If thou seest me, that I am less
than thou in wealth and children, yet
it may be that my Lord will give me
better than thy garden, and loose on it
a thunderbolt out of heaven, so that
in the morning it will be a slope
   of dust,
or in the morning the water of it will
be sunk into the earth, so that thou
wilt not be able to seek it out.'
And his fruit was all encompassed,
and in the morning he was wringing
his hands for that he had expended
upon it, and it was fallen down upon
its trellises, and he was saying,
'Would I had not associated with my Lord
   any one!'
But there was no host to help him,
apart from God, and he was helpless.
Thereover protection belongs only to God
the True; He is best rewarding, best in
   the issue.

And strike for them the similitude of
   the present life:

it is as water that We send down
out of heaven, and the plants of
the earth mingle with it; and in
the morning it is straw the winds
scatter; and God is omnipotent over
        everything.

Wealth and sons are the adornment of the present world;
but the abiding things, the deeds of righteousness,
are better with God in reward, and better in hope.
And on the day We shall set the mountains in motion,
and thou seest the earth coming forth, and We muster them
so that We leave not so much as one of them behind;
and they shall be presented before their Lord in ranks—
'You have come to Us, as We created you upon the first time;
nay, you asserted We should not appoint for you a tryst.'
And the Book shall be set in place; and thou wilt see
the sinners fearful at what is in it, and saying,
'Alas for us! How is it with this Book, that it leaves
nothing behind, small or great, but it has numbered it?'
And they shall find all they wrought present, and thy Lord
        shall not wrong anyone.

And when We said to the angels, 'Bow
yourselves to Adam'; so they bowed
themselves, save Iblis; he was one of
the jinn, and committed ungodliness
against his Lord's command. What,
and do you take him and his seed
to be your friends, apart from Me,
and they an enemy to you? How evil
is that exchange for the evildoers!
I made them not witnesses of the
creation of the heavens and earth,
neither of the creation of themselves;
I would not ever take those who lead
others astray to be My supporters.

And on the day He shall say, 'Call on My associates whom
you asserted'; and then they shall call on them, but they
will not answer them, and We shall set a gulf between them.
Then the evildoers will see the Fire, and think that they
are about to fall into it, and will find no escape from it.

We have indeed turned about for men
in this Koran every manner of
similitude; man is the most disputatious
   of things.
And naught prevented men from believing
when the guidance came unto them,
and seeking their Lord's forgiveness,
but that the wont of the ancients
should come upon them, or that the
chastisement should come upon them
   face to face.
And We send not the Envoys, but
good tidings to bear, and warning.
Yet do the unbelievers dispute
with falsehood, that they may rebut
thereby the truth. They have taken
My signs, and what they are warned of,
   in mockery.
And who does greater evil than he
who, being reminded of the signs
of his Lord, turns away from them and
forgets what his hands have forwarded?
Surely We have laid veils on their hearts
lest they understand it, and in their ears
   heaviness;
and though thou callest them to the
guidance, yet they will not be guided
   ever.
But thy Lord is the All-forgiving,
full of mercy. If He should take them
to task for that they have earned, He would
hasten for them the chastisement; but they
have a tryst, from which they will find no
   escape.
And those cities, We destroyed them when they
did evil, and appointed for their destruction
   a tryst.

 And when Moses said to his page,
'I will not give up until I reach
the meeting of the two seas,
though I go on for many years.'
Then, when they reached their meeting,
they forgot their fish, and it took

its way into the sea, burrowing.
When they had passed over, he said
to his page, 'Bring us our breakfast;
indeed, we have encountered
weariness from this our journey.'
He said, 'What thinkest thou? When we
took refuge in the rock, then I
forgot the fish—and it was Satan
himself that made me forget it
so that I should not remember it—
and so it took its way into
the sea in a manner marvellous.'
Said he, 'This is what we were
seeking!' And so they returned
upon their tracks, retracing them.
Then they found one of Our servants
unto whom We had given mercy
from Us, and We had taught him
knowledge proceeding from Us.
Moses said to him, 'Shall I follow thee
so that thou teachest me, of what
thou hast been taught, right judgment?'
Said he, 'Assuredly thou wilt not
be able to bear with me patiently.
And how shouldst thou bear patiently
that thou hast never encompassed
in thy knowledge?' He said,
'Yet thou shalt find me, if God
will, patient; and I shall not
rebel against thee in anything.'
Said he, 'Then if thou followest
me, question me not on anything
until I myself introduce
the mention of it to thee.'
So they departed; until, when
they embarked upon the ship,
he made a hole in it. He said,
'What, hast thou made a hole in it
so as to drown its passengers? Thou
hast indeed done a grievous thing.'
Said he, 'Did I not say that thou
couldst never bear with me patiently?'
He said, 'Do not take me to task
that I forgot, neither constrain me

to do a thing too difficult.'
So they departed; until, when
they met a lad, he slew him.
He said, 'What, hast thou slain
a soul innocent, and that not to
retaliate for a soul slain? Thou
hast indeed done a horrible thing.'
Said he, 'Did I not say that thou
couldst never bear with me patiently?'
He said, 'If I question thee
on anything after this,
then keep me company no more;
thou hast already experienced
excuse sufficient on my part.'
So they departed; until, when
they reached the people of a city,
they asked the people for food,
but they refused to receive them
hospitably. There they found
a wall about to tumble down,
and so he set it up. He said,
'If thou hadst wished, thou couldst
have taken a wage for that.'
Said he, 'This is the parting between
me and thee. Now I will tell thee
the interpretation of that
thou couldst not bear patiently.
As for the ship, it belonged
to certain poor men, who toiled
upon the sea; and I desired
to damage it, for behind them
there was a king who was seizing
every ship by brutal force.
As for the lad, his parents were
believers; and we were afraid
he would impose on them insolence
and unbelief; so we desired
that their Lord should give to them
in exchange one better than he in
purity, and nearer in tenderness.
As for the wall, it belonged
to two orphan lads in the city,
and under it was a treasure
belonging to them. Their father

was a righteous man; and thy Lord
desired that they should come of age
and then bring forth their treasure
as a mercy from thy Lord. I
did it not of my own bidding.
This is the interpretation of that
thou couldst not bear patiently.'

They will question thee concerning
Dhool Karnain. Say: 'I will
recite to you a mention of him.'
We established him in the land,
and We gave him a way to everything;
    and he followed a way
until, when he reached the setting
of the sun, he found it setting
in a muddy spring, and he found
      nearby a people.
We said, 'O Dhool Karnain,
either thou shalt chastise them,
or thou shalt take towards them a
    way of kindness.'
He said, 'As for the evildoer,
him we shall chastise, then he
shall be returned to his Lord
and He shall chastise him with a
    horrible chastisement.
But as for him who believes, and
does righteousness, he shall receive
as recompense the reward most fair,
and we shall speak to him, of our
    command, easiness.'
    Then he followed a way
until, when he reached the rising
of the sun, he found it rising
upon a people for whom We had
not appointed any veil to shade
    them from it.
So; and We encompassed in knowledge what
    was with him.
    Then he followed a way
until, when he reached between the
two barriers, he found this side
of them a people scarcely able to

understand speech.
They said, 'O Dhool Karnain, behold,
Gog and Magog are doing corruption
in the earth; so shall we assign
to thee a tribute, against thy setting
up a barrier between us and
      between them?'
He said, 'That wherein my Lord has
established me is better; so aid me
forcefully, and I will set up
a rampart between you and
      between them.
Bring me ingots of iron!' Until,
when he had made all level between
the two cliffs, he said, 'Blow!' Until,
when he had made it a fire, he said,
'Bring me, that I may pour molten
      brass on it.'
So they were unable either to scale it
      or pierce it.
He said, 'This is a mercy
      from my Lord.
But when the promise of my Lord
comes to pass, He will make it into
powder; and my Lord's promise
      is ever true.'

Upon that day We shall leave them surging on one another,
and the Trumpet shall be blown, and We shall gather them together,
and upon that day We shall present Gehenna to the unbelievers
whose eyes were covered against My remembrance, and they
were not able to hear. What, do the unbelievers reckon
that they may take My servants as friends, apart from Me?
We have prepared Gehenna for the unbelievers' hospitality.

Say: 'Shall We tell you who will be
the greatest losers in their works?
Those whose striving goes astray
in the present life, while they think
that they are working good deeds.
Those are they that disbelieve in the
signs of their Lord and the encounter
with Him; their works have failed,
and on the Day of Resurrection We

shall not assign to them any weight.
That is their recompense—Gehenna
for that they were unbelievers and took
My signs and My messengers in mockery.
But those who believe, and do deeds
of righteousness—the Gardens of
Paradise shall be their hospitality,
therein to dwell forever,
desiring no removal out of them.'

Say: 'If the sea were ink
for the Words of my Lord,
the sea would be spent before the Words of my Lord are spent,
though We brought replenishment the like of it.'

Say: 'I am only a mortal
the like of you; it is revealed to me
that your God
is One God.
So let him, who hopes for
the encounter with his Lord,
work righteousness, and not associate with his Lord's service
anyone.'

48

ON PRAYER
Avicenna

Avicenna, or Ibn Sīnā (980–1037), was one of the best and most original Islamic thinkers, being the creator of a complete system of philosophy. Born in Persia, he spent his adult life moving from one province to another because of changing political situations, which also caused him to experience changes of status rang-

Avicenna, *Avicenna on Theology*, Arthur J. Arberry, trans. (London: John Murray, Ltd., 1951), pp. 50–63. Reprinted by permission of the publisher.

ing from prison inmate to vizier. His philosophical system, although largely based on Aristotle, also possesses many original features which betray the workings of a brilliant and creative mind. However, philosophy was not his only interest, for he seems to have been a truly universal genius, mastering the Koran, Arabic literature, law, physics, and mathematics, as well as being a practicing physician. The influence upon medieval Europe produced by the translation of Avicenna's two chief works into Latin in the Twelfth Century was tremendous. The Qānūn, a medical treatise, became the principal text in the medieval universities; and his Aš-Šifā, containing his system of philosophy, exerted considerable influence upon the Scholastics, not excluding the greatest of them—Thomas Aquinas and Duns Scotus. Avicenna also attempted to establish a system of theology, largely based upon philosophical grounds. However, after his death he was accused of heresy and even of atheism (which was untrue). The publication of a comprehensive attack against his position, the Tahāfut al-Falāsifa (The Incoherence of the Philosophers) by another Persian thinker, Ghazālī, or Algazel (1058–1111), undermined Avicenna's influence upon Islamic theology. Nevertheless, his emphasis upon the reasonableness of religion and the importance of the intellectual function within religion represents a significant development in Islamic thought.

ON THE NATURE OF PRAYER

When God had created the animals, after the plants, the minerals and the elements, and after the spheres, the stars, the unsubstantial spirits and the intelligences perfect in themselves; when He had completed His work of origination and creation, He desired to finish His creation with the most perfect species, even as He had begun it with the most perfect genus. He therefore distinguished Man from out of all His creatures, so that as the beginning had been with Intelligence, so too the conclusion should be. He began with the noblest of substances, Intelligence, and He concluded with the noblest of beings, the Intelligent. The high purpose of creation was Man, and nothing else.

Having realized all this, thou must know that Man is the Microcosm; and as all other beings are graded in their world, so too man is graded according to his deeds and his nobility. Some men there are whose deeds accord with those of angels; some whose acts accord with those of devils, so that they perish. For Man has not been produced out of one thing only, that he should be subject to a single set of conditions: God has compounded him of many things of various sorts, and temperaments of divers kinds. God divided Man's substantiality into body and soul, the former containing his grosser and the latter his subtler elements. He bestowed upon him sense and reason, both secret and manifest; then He adorned his outward and manifest part, his body, with the five senses in the amplest degree and fullest order. Next out of his inward and secret parts He chose those which were strongest and noblest. The physical element He implanted in his liver, to regulate his digestion and evacuation (or attraction and repulsion), to balance the members and replace by means of nourishment the parts lost through dissolution. The animal element He associated with his heart, connected with the faculties of appetite and anger, to accord with the congenial and oppose the uncongenial: this He made the fountainhead of the five senses, and the source of the imagination and of movement. Lastly He fashioned the human, rational soul in the brain, which He lodged in the highest situation and most appropriate station. He adorned it with thought, memory and recollection, and gave the intellectual substance power over it, that it might be as it were a commander with the faculties for soldiers; the "common-sense" served as a courier, to act as an intermediary between the brain and the senses. The senses were to be the spies of the brain, each stationed at its appropriate gate, to sally forth from time to time into their own world and pick up all that was let fall by their fellows, which they should convey to the particular messenger; the latter would then deliver it, sealed and enveloped, to the faculty of the intelligence, to discriminate and choose what accorded with it, and to reject that which was not genuine.

Man was thus equipped with these souls out of all the world, through each faculty sharing with one class or other of living beings. By virtue of the animal soul he shares with the animals; his physical soul links him with the plants; his human soul is a bond between him and the angels. Moreover each of these faculties has a special sphere, and a particular function to perform: according as one of the three prevails over the other two, the individual is defined by that prevalent sphere, and related after his perception to his own genus. Similarly each function has its own sphere, its own reward, and its own purpose.

The function of the physical soul is to eat and drink, to maintain the parts of the body, and to cleanse the body of superfluities: that is all: it has no business to compete or dispute with the function of any other. The purpose of its function is to keep the body in order and the limbs in proper balance, while supplying strength to the physique. The proper order of the body is proved by a well-oiled flesh, sturdy limbs and a strong physique; and these are acquired from eating and drinking. The reward of the physical souls' function is not to be expected in the spiritual world, and does not wait upon the resurrection, for this soul will not be raised up after death: it resembles a plant, in that when it dies it is dispersed and obliterated, never to be recalled to life.

The function of the animal soul is movement, imagination, and the defence of all the body by good management. Its necessary sphere and particular function is confined to appetite and anger; anger is a branch of appetite, since it seeks to repress, to overcome, to dominate and to tyrannize; these are the various sorts of leadership, and leadership is the fruit of appetite. The special function of the animal soul is fundamentally appetite, and incidentally anger. Its purpose is to preserve the body through the faculty of anger, and to perpetuate the species through the faculty of appetite; for the species is perpetuated always by means of generation, and generation is regulated by the faculty of appetite; while the body remains guarded from injuries by virtue of its being defended, which means to dominate the enemy, to bar the gate of harm, and to prevent the harmful effects of tyranny, and all these ideas are contained and confined within the faculty of anger. Its reward is the realization of its hopes in this lower world; it is not to be expected after death, for the animal soul dies with the body, and will not be raised up at the resurrection. It resembles all the animals, in that it is not qualified to receive the Divine Allocution, and may not therefore expect any reward. When the emanation of a thing is annihilated, it cannot be raised up after death; upon death its entire existence dies, and its happiness is past.

The function of the human, rational soul is the noblest function of all, for it is itself the noblest of spirits. Its function consists of reflecting upon things of art and meditating upon things of beauty: its gaze being turned towards the higher world, it loves not this lower abode and meaner station. Belonging as it does to the higher side of life and to the primal substances, it is not its business to eat and drink, neither does it require luxury and coition; rather its function is to wait for the revelation of truths, and to reflect with perfect intuition and unclouded wit upon the perception of subtle ideas, reading with the eye of inner vision the tablet of Divine Mystery and opposing with strenuous devices the causes of vain fancy. It is distinguished from other spirits by the possession of perfect reason and far-reaching, all-embracing thought; its ambition and striving all through life is to purify the sensual impressions and to perceive the world of intelligible truths. God has singled it out above all other spirits for the gift of the faculty of reason. Reasoning is the tongue of the angels, who have no speech or utterance; reasoning belongs to them especially, which is perception without sensing and communication without words. Man's relation to the world of Spirit is established by reasoning; speech follows after it. If a man possesses no knowledge of reasoning; he is incapable of expressing truth.

The function of the soul is therefore as we have summarized it here, in the fewest possible words. The subject can be greatly amplified, but we have abbreviated its discussion here, since our purpose in this treatise is not to give an account of the human faculties and their functions. We have therefore brought forward and established merely what we required by way of preface.

The function peculiar to the human soul is knowledge and perception: its use is manifold. To it belong remembrance, humble petition, and worship. When a man knows his Lord by the medium of his thoughts, and apprehends His Essence through his reason acting upon his knowledge, and perceives His Goodness with his intellect acting upon his reason, he considers attentively the inward nature of creation, and perceives creation as most perfectly

displayed in the heavenly bodies and supernal substances: these are the most
perfect of created beings because they are the furthest removed from corruption, impurities and diverse compounds. Then he sees within his rational soul
a semblance of that immortality and rationality which subsist in those bodies.
Reflecting upon the Creator, he realizes that Command is indeed associated
with Creation, as God Himself declares: *To Him belong the Creation and
the Command* (Koran vii. 52). Knowing thus that the Divine Emanation
descends into creation out of the world of Command (which is to say, those
spiritual substances), he desires ardently to comprehend their several ranks,
and is eager to establish relations with them and to resemble their elevation.
So he is ever humbling himself and meditating passionately, with prayers and
fasting; and he attains to a great reward. For the human soul has indeed a
reward: it survives after the body has perished, and decays not with the lapse
of time; it is raised up after death. Death is the separation of the soul from
the body; resurrection is its union with those spiritual substances; the soul's
reward and felicity come after these events. A man is rewarded according to
his acts; if he is perfect in works, he obtains an ample reward; but if his acts
are imperfect and fall short, in like measure is his felicity imperfect and his
reward falls short, so that he remains forever sorrowful and downcast, nay,
forsaken and damned. If his animal and physical faculties prevail over his
rational faculty, he is bewildered after death and wretched after resurrection;
but if his blameworthy faculties are deficient, and his soul is divorced from
evil thoughts and mean passions, if his self is adorned with the ornament of
reason and the necklace of knowledge, if he has trained himself to acquire all
praiseworthy qualities, he will remain forever pure, refined and happy; having
attained his heavenly reward, he will abide eternally with his own dear kith
and kin.

Now that we have finished this preamble, we would remark that it is
prayer which causes the human, rational soul to resemble the heavenly bodies,
eternally worshipping Absolute Truth, and seeking the imperishable reward.
The Prophet of God declared, "Prayer is the foundation-stone of religion";
and religion is the purifying of the human soul of all devilish impurities and
carnal suggestions, turned away from mean worldly interests. Prayer is the
worship of the First Cause, the One Supreme and Mightiest Worshipful;
adoration is to know Him Whose Being is Necessary. It needs not that we
should interpret the text *And jinns and men were not created save to worship
Me* (Koran li. 56) as meaning "to know Me", for worship is knowledge, and
to be aware of the existence of One Whose Being is necessary and absolute,
being seized of His Being with a pure heart, a spirit undefiled, and a soul
wholly devoted to Him. The real nature of prayer is therefore to know Almighty God in His Uniqueness, as a Being wholly Necessary, Whose Essence is infinitely exalted and Whose Qualities are infinitely holy, with habits
of sincerity in prayer; by which sincerity I mean, that one should know the
Qualities of God in such a manner that there remains no opening to a multi-

plicity of gods, no intent to join others to His worship. Whoso acts thus may be said to be truly sincere in prayer, not erring or straying from the path; but he who acts not thus is a forger, a liar and a rebel against God, Who is Supreme and Omnipotent beyond all such confoundings.

OF THE OUTWARD FORM AND INWARD TRUTH OF PRAYER

When thou hast understood all that we have already stated in this discourse regarding the nature of prayer, it now becomes necessary for thee to realize that prayer is divided into two parts, one being outward (the part of discipline, that appertains to the body) and one inward (the real prayer, that concerns the soul). The outward part of prayer is that prescribed by the religious law and recognized as a fundamental duty of religion: our Lawgiver imposed it as an obligation for every man, calling it ṣalāt and making it the foundation of faith, saying, "There is no faith in him who has no ṣalāt, and there is no faith in him who is not faithful."

The numbers of prayer are recognized, and its times precisely laid down: the Prophet counted it as the noblest of devotions, and assigned it the highest rank among all acts of worship. This outward or disciplinary part is connected with the body, because it is composed of certain postures and elements such as recitation, genuflection and prostration: while the body is likewise compounded of certain principles and elements, such as water, earth, air, fire and similar temperaments. The body is the physical envelope of man; and that which is composed is itself connected with its like. These postures of prayer, composed of recitation, genuflection and prostration and occurring in regular and definite numbers, are visible evidence of that real prayer which is connected with and adherent to the rational soul. They act as controlling the body, to bring it into tune with the general harmony of the universe. The numbers of prayer are part of the scheme of discipline prescribed by the religious law; the Lawgiver imposed them upon every adult man of sound mind. In this manner the body is made to imitate that attitude, proper to the soul, of submission to the Higher Self, so that through this act man may be distinguished from the beasts. The beasts are not favoured by the Divine Allocution; they are exempt from Judgment; they do not look for Divine chastisement and reward. Man however has received the Word of God, and shall be chastised or rewarded according as he obeys the commandments and prohibitions of religion and reason. The Law follows in the wake of Reason. The Lawgiver, having observed that Reason imposes upon the rational soul the duty of prayer true and unadulterated—the knowledge and apprehension of God—therefore prescribed prayer for the body as an outward symbol of that other prayer; he compounded it of numbers, and arranged it precisely in the most beautiful forms and most perfect postures, so that the body might follow after the spirit in worship, even though it does not accord with it in rank. The Lawgiver realized that all men are not capable of mounting the steps of reason; they therefore required some regular bodily training and discipline to oppose their natural inclinations. He pioneered a road and fashioned a rule consisting of these numbers of prayer, which men could generally follow and understand with the senses; they would be connected with the outer parts of man, and would prevent him from imitating the beasts and other animals. He ordained this as a supreme commandment, saying, "Pray in the manner that ye have seen me pray." There is much advantage in this, and a general benefit which will not escape the notice of any intelligent man, even though the ignorant may not acknowledge the fact.

As for the second or inward part or truth of prayer: this is to contemplate God with a pure heart, and a spirit abstracted and cleansed of all desires. This part does not follow the way of bodily numbers and sensual elements, but rather the path of pure thoughts and eternal spirits. The Prophet himself was often preoccupied with the true apprehension of God, and was thereby prevented from following the numerical order of formal prayer, which he sometimes shortened and sometimes prolonged. This is the kind of prayer that is exclusively the concern of the intellect; reason confirms this statement, bearing in mind the Prophet's words, "The man at prayer is in secret converse with his Lord." It is obvious to the intelligent man that such converse is not effected through the physical parts and the audible and visible tongue, because conversation and converse of that kind can only take place with somebody contained in space and determined by time. As for the One Supreme Being, Who is circumscribed not by space nor touched by time, to Whom reference cannot be made through any direction, Whose Predicament varies not in respect of any particular Attribute, and Whose Essence changes not at any time: how should He be perceived by man, who is limited by form and body, is subject to physical dimensions and empowered only to the extent of his senses, faculties and physical frame? How should mortals have converse with Him, the confines of Whose Directions they know not, neither perceive the environs of the paths of His Tendings? The True and Absolute Being is absent from the sensible world, and is neither seen nor contained in space; while it is the wont of corporeal beings only to have converse and concourse with such beings as they can see and point to, reckoning as absent and far off any that they cannot so behold; and converse with one absent is plainly impossible. It is axiomatic that He Whose Being is Necessary must be absent and far off from these physical bodies, since they are subject to accidental change and corporeal accident, require space and preservation, and by virtue of their weight and grossness dwell upon the face of this dark earth. Even those simple, sublime substances which are not touched by time, nor set in any measured space, flee away from these bodies as animated by the hostility of contrariety; and the Necessary Being is loftier than all simple substances, far more exalted and sublime than they—how then should He be associated with by sensual, corporeal beings?

Since it is established that it is impossible and absurd to assert and specify God in relation to any direction, it is obviously still more absurd to suppose or conjecture that converse with Him may be established through the external senses. The Prophet's words, "The man at prayer is in secret converse with his Lord," are therefore only to be predicated of that inward knowledge which belongs solely to pure souls that are abstracted and free from events in time and directions in space: they contemplate God intellectually, and behold Him with spiritual, not corporeal vision. It is thus evident that true prayer is spiritual contemplation, and that pure worship is spiritual Divine love.

All the foregoing argument proves conclusively that prayer is of two kinds. And now we would observe that the outward, disciplinary part of prayer, which is connected with personal motions according to certain numbered postures and confined elements, is an act of abasement, and of passionate yearning on the part of this lower, partial, compound and limited body towards the lunary sphere; which latter, operating through the Active Intellect, controls this world of generation and decay. Praying after this fashion is converse with that Intellect by means of the human tongue; for it sustains and controls all created beings. Outward prayer is a humble petition that the Active Intellect may preserve and maintain the integrity of the person so abasing himself in worship and emulation, that he shall thereby continue guarded and protected against the misfortunes of time, so long as he remains in this world. The true, inward part of prayer, which is unassociated with postures and divorced from all changes, is an abasement unto God through the rational soul, which knows and is aware of the Unicity of the True God: this kind of prayer has no reference to any direction, and is not in any way confounded with any physical element. It is an imploring of Absolute Being to perfect the soul through contemplation of Him, and to complete the worshipper's felicity through the inner knowledge and apprehension of Him. The Intellectual Command and Holy Emanation descends from the Heavenly Void into the confines of the rational soul as a result of this prayer; this form of worship is imposed without corporeal weariness or human imposition. Whoso prays after this fashion is delivered out of his physical faculties and natural vestiges, and climbs the intellectual steps until he beholds the mysteries of Eternity. It is to this that God refers in the words, *Prayer prohibits abomination and all blameworthy acts; the remembrance of God is greater than all other deeds; and God knoweth what things ye do* (Koran xxix. 44).

WHAT PART OF PRAYER IS INCUMBENT UPON WHOM

Now that we have set forth the nature of prayer, and shown that it is divided into two parts each of which we have explained, it remains for us to remark to which class of people each part belongs and is appropriate.

It is clear that man has in him something of the lower world and something of the upper world also: these two portions of human nature we have briefly expounded above. It has emerged from the discussion that prayer is divided into the disciplinary-physical and the real-spiritual; I have accorded each part sufficient treatment as befits the scope of the present treatise. I will now add that men vary one from the other according to the influence of the powers of the spirits compounded in each. If the physical and animal element prevails, he will be passionately attached to the body, loving to keep it in good order, nurtured and healthy, fond of feeding it, giving it to drink and clothing it, attentive to securing its advantage and to ward off mischief from it. A man so intending is to be numbered among the animals, nay, he is to be counted as belonging to the order of the brute beasts; his days are wholly absorbed in caring for his bodily welfare; his every moment is dedicated to his personal interests; he is heedless of the Creator and ignorant of the True God. It is therefore not permissible for him to neglect the commandment of the religious law, which is absolutely binding and incumbent upon him. If he is not accustomed to perform this duty, he must be disciplined and compelled to such a point that he will not omit to discharge his obligation, to be reverent and yearningly to betake himself to the Active Intellect and the Revolving Sphere, that it may emanate in its bounty over him and deliver him from the chastisement inherent in his existence, freeing him from bodily desires and bringing him safely to the true goal of his hopes. And truly, if but a little portion of the emanation of that grace were denied to him, swiftly would he hasten into great evil, and become the lowest of the animals and ravening beasts.

As for the man in whom the spiritual faculties prevail, so that his rational faculty dominates his passion, and his soul is abstracted from terrestrial preoccupations and the attachments of this lower world: such a man has attained true security and spiritual worship; and that pure prayer which we have described is incumbent upon him most urgently and is his most strong obligation. Being ready in the cleanliness of his soul to receive the emanation of God's grace, if he but turns towards God in love and is earnest to worship Him, supernal blessings and heavenly felicity will swiftly flow over him; when the time comes for him to be separated from the body and to depart out of this life, he will immediately contemplate his God, dwelling in His Presence and enjoying the company of those his true kin, the dwellers in the Divine Kingdom, the bodies of the celestial worlds.

This is the type of prayer which was incumbent upon our Lord and Founder of our Faith, Muhammad the Elect of God, on the night when he was separated from his body and divested of all worldly desire, so that there remained with him no trace of animal passion or the pull of natural wants. He enjoyed converse with God in his soul and intellect, saying, "O Lord, I have discovered a strange joy this night: grant me the means to perpetuate it, and provide for me a way that will always bring me unto it." It was then that God commanded the Prophet to pray, saying, "O Muhammad, the man at prayer is in secret converse with his Lord."

Those who practice only the outer part of prayer experience but a defective portion of that joy; but those who pray in the spirit know that joy in full and abundant measure; and the fuller that measure is, the ampler is their reward.

This is as much as I desired to say briefly in the present treatise, and only then after hesitating long to embark at all upon the interpretation of prayer, the dissecting of its real nature and the setting forth of its two parts. But when I saw intelligent men disregarding its external forms, without considering its inward meanings, I felt that it was my duty to explain the subject, and my obligation to state these facts. The intelligent man will thus be able to reflect upon what I have said, and the learned and fully qualified man proceed to examine the matter further; he will then come to realize who is called upon to discharge the disciplinary part of prayer only, and to whom the spiritual side is appropriate and attainable. He will find it easy to proceed along the path of worship, and to persist in his prayers; enjoying converse with God, not indeed as in person, by word of mouth, by ocular vision and the senses, but in the spirit and reason, with the inward vision and speculative insight; for it is a delusion to suppose that one can ever approach God in person, and a vain fancy to desire to see Him, and to worship and converse with Him through the senses.

All the other ordinances of religion are explicable along the lines which have been sketched in the present treatise. We would have desired to expound each particular act of worship separately; but it was impossible for us to enter upon matters which may not fitly be communicated to every man. We have accordingly established this clear and straightforward division, knowing that a mere hint is sufficient for the liberal mind. And I forbid that this treatise be presented to any man whom passion has led astray, or whose heart has been stamped with its brand. The impotent man can have no conception of the pleasures of intercourse, any more than the blind man can believe the joys of sight.

I wrote this treatise, thanks be to God's assistance and abundant grace, in a period of less than half an hour, and that despite numerous hindrances and little leisure. I therefore ask the indulgence of those who read it; and I request that all who are blessed with the emanation of reason, and the light of justice, will not disclose my secret, even though they may be secure from any mischief that I may be the cause of. The matter rests with my Creator; and my Creator knows all my affair, and none other beside Him.

49

ON THE INCOHERENCE OF THE INCOHERENCE

Averroes

The last of the great medieval Islamic philosophers was Averroes, or Ibn Rušd (1126–1198). He was referred to as "The Commentator," by the Scholastics, because of his series of commentaries on the philosophy of Aristotle, which Averroes viewed with the highest regard. This regard for Aristotelian thought led him to defend it against criticism, in addition to undertaking the exposition of it. Since the most devastating attack upon Aristotle, in the form of a criticism of his disciples, Alfarabi and Avicenna, who had written in Arabic, had been put forth by the great Sūfī mystic and philosopher, Ghazālī (Algazel), it was against Ghazālī's book that Averroes launched his counterattack. Since that work had been entitled Tahāfut al-Falāsifa (The Incoherence of the Philosophers), Averroes bestowed upon his attempted refutation the striking name of Tahāfut al-Tahāfut (The Incoherence of the Incoherence). This book is written in the manner of a commentary, quoting selections from Ghazālī which are then subjected to criticism and rebuttal. The tenor of the discussion tends to be rather technically philosophical, but this is to be expected in a thinker whose major contribution consists in the subordination of theology to philosophy. This view, like the milder rationalism of Avicenna, never achieved the sanction of orthodoxy, but nevertheless remains an interesting chapter in the history of Islamic theology.

THE FOURTH DISCUSSION

Showing That They are Unable to Prove the Existence of A Creator of the World

GHAZALI SAYS:

WE SAY: Mankind is divided into two categories; one, the men of truth who have acknowledged that the world has become and know by necessity

Averroes, *Averroes' Tahafut Al-Tahafut* (*The Incoherence of the Incoherence*), Simon van den Bergh, trans. (London: Luzac & Company, Ltd., 1954), vol. I, pp. 156–170. Reprinted by permission of the translator and publisher.

that what has become does not become by itself but needs a creator, and the reasonableness of their view lies in their affirmation of a creator; the other, the materialists, believe the world, in the state in which it exists, to be eternal and do not attribute a creator to it, and their doctrine is intelligible, although their proof shows its inanity. But as to the philosophers, they believe the world to be eternal and still attribute a creator to it. This theory is self-contradictory and needs no refutation.

I SAY:

The theory of the philosophers is, because of the factual evidence, more intelligible than both the other theories together. There are two kinds of agents: (1) the agent to which the object which proceeds from it is only attached during the process of its becoming; once this process is finished, the object is not any more in need of it—for instance, the coming into existence of a house through the builder; (2) the agent from which nothing proceeds but an act which has no other existence than its dependence on it. The distinctive mark of this act is that it is convertible with the existence of its object, i.e. when the act does not exist the object does not exist, and when the act exists the object exists—they are inseparable. This kind of agent is superior to the former and is more truly an agent, for this agent brings its object to being and conserves it, whereas the other agent only brings its objects to being, but requires another agent for its further conservation. The mover is such a superior agent in relation to the moved and to the things whose existence consists only in their movement. The philosophers, believing that movement is the act of a mover and that the existence of the world is only perfected through motion, say that the agent of motion is the agent of the world, and if the agent refrained for only one moment from its action, the world would be annihilated. They use the following syllogism: The world is an act, or a thing whose existence is consequent upon this act. Each act by its existence implies the existence of an agent. Therefore the world has an agent existing by reason of its existence. The man who regards it as necessary that the act which proceeds from the agent of the world should have begun in time says: This world is temporal through an eternal agent. But the man for whom the act of the Eternal is eternal says: The world has come into being from an eternal agent having an eternal act, i.e. an act without beginning or end; which does, however, not mean that the world is eternal by itself, as people who call the world eternal imagine it to be.

Ghazali says, on behalf of the philosophers:

The philosophers might answer: When we affirm that the world has a creator, we do not understand thereby a voluntary agent who acts after not having acted, as we observe in the various kinds of agents, like tailors, weavers, and builders, but we mean the cause of the world, and we call it the First Principle, understanding by this that there is no cause for its existence, but that it is a cause of the existence of other things; and if we call this principle the Creator, it is in this sense. It is easy to establish by a strict proof an existent for the existence of which there is no cause. For we say that the world and its existents either have a cause or have not. If it has a cause, this cause itself either has or has not a cause, and the same can be said about the latter cause, and either we go on *ad infinitum* in this way, and this is absurd, or we arrive at a last term, and this end is the First Cause, which has no cause for its existence and which we call First Principle. And if the world existed by itself without cause, then it would be clear what the First Principle is, for we only mean by it an existent without a cause and which is necessarily eternal. However, it is not possible that the First Principle should be the heavens, for there are many of these and the proof of unity contradicts this, and its impossibility is shown on examination of the attribute of the principle. Nor can it be said that one single heaven, or one single body, the sun or any other body, can be the First Principle; for all these are bodies, and body is composed of matter and form, and the First Principle cannot be composite, as is clear on a second examination. Our intention is to show that an existent which has no cause is external by necessity and by universal consent, and only about its qualities is there a divergence of opinion. And this is what we mean by a first principle.

I SAY:

This argument carries a certain conviction, but still it is not true. For the term 'cause' is attributed equivocally to the four causes—agent, form, matter, and end. Therefore if this were the answer of the philosophers, it would be defective. For if they were asked which cause they mean by their statement that the world has a first cause, and if they answered, 'That agent whose act is uncreated and everlasting, and whose object is identical with its act', their answer would be true according to their doctrine; for against this conception, in the way we expounded it, there is no objection. But if they answered 'The formal cause', the objection would be raised whether they suppose the form of the world to subsist by itself in the world, and if they answered, 'We mean a form separate from matter', their statement would be in harmony with their theory; but if they answered, 'We mean a form in matter', this would imply that the First Principle was not something incorporeal; and this does not accord with philosophical doctrine. Further, if they said, 'It is a cause which acts for an end', this again would agree with the philosophical doctrine. As you see, this statement is capable of many interpretations, and how can it be represented there as an answer of the philosophers?

And as to Ghazali's words:

We call it the First Principle, understanding by this that there is no cause for its existence, but that it is a cause for the existence of other things.

This again is a defective statement, for this might be said also of the first sphere, or of heaven in its entirety, or generally of any kind of existents which could be supposed to exist without a cause; and between this and the materialistic theory there is no difference.

And as to Ghazali's words:

It is easy to establish by a strict proof an existent for the existence of which there is no cause.

This again is a defective statement, for the causes must be specified, and it must be shown that each kind has an initial term without cause—that is, that the agents lead upwards to a first agent, the formal causes to a first form, the material causes to a first matter, and the final causes to a first end. And then it must still be shown that these four ultimate causes lead to a first cause. This is not clear from the statement as he expresses it here.

And in the same way the statement in which he brings a proof for the existence of a first cause is defective, i.e. his statement:

> For we say that the world and its existents either have a cause or have not. . . .

For the term 'cause' is used in an equivocal way. And similarly the infinite regress of causes is according to philosophical doctrine in one way impossible, in another way necessary; impossible when this regress is essential and in a straight line and the prior cause is a condition of the existence of the posterior, not impossible when this regress is accidental and circular, when the prior is not a condition for the posterior and when there exists an essential first cause —for instance, the origin of rain from a cloud, the origin of a cloud from vapour, the origin of vapour from rain. And this is according to the philosophers an eternal circular process, which of necessity, however, presupposes a first cause. And similarly the coming into existence of one man from another is an eternal process, for in such cases the existence of the prior is not a condition for the existence of the posterior; indeed, the destruction of some of them is often a necessary condition. This kind of cause leads upwards to an eternal first cause which acts in each individual member of the series of causes at the moment of the becoming of its final effect; for instance, when Socrates engenders Plato, the ultimate mover, according to the philosophers, is the highest sphere, or the soul, or the intellect, or all together, or God the Creator. And therefore Aristotle says that a man and the sun together engender a man, and it is clear that the sun leads upwards to its mover and its mover to the First Principle. Therefore the past man is not a condition for the existence of the future man. Similarly, when an artisan produces successively a series of products of craftsmanship with different instruments, and produces these instruments through instruments and the latter again through other instruments, the becoming of these instruments one from another is something accidental, and none of these instruments is a condition for the existence of the product of craftsmanship except the first instrument which is in immediate contact with the work produced. Now the father is necessary for the coming into existence of the son in the same way as the instrument which comes into immediate contact with the product of craftsmanship is necessary for its coming into existence. And the instrument with which this instrument is produced will be necessary for the production of this instrument, but will not be necessary for the production of the product of craftsmanship unless accidentally. Therefore sometimes, when the posterior instrument is produced from the matter of the anterior, the destruction of the anterior is a condition for the existence of the posterior, for instance, when a man comes into being from a man who has perished, through the latter becoming first a plant, then sperm or menstrual blood. And we have already discussed this problem. Those, however, who regard an infinite series of essential causes as possible are materialists, and he who concedes this does not understand the efficient cause. And about the efficient cause there is no divergence of opinion among philosophers.

And as to Ghazali's words:

And if the world existed by itself without cause, then it would be clear what the First Principle is.

he means that the materialists as well as others acknowledge a first cause which has no cause, and their difference of opinion concerns only this principle, for the materialists say that it is the highest sphere and the others that it is a principle beyond the sphere and that the sphere is an effect; but these others are divided into two parties, those who say that the sphere is an act that has a beginning and those who say that it is an eternal act. And having declared that the acknowledgement of a first cause is common to the materialists as well as to others, GHAZALI SAYS:

However, it is not possible that the First Principle should be the heavens, for there are many of these and the proof of unity contradicts this;

meaning that from the order of the universe it is evident that its directing principle is one, just as it appears from the order in an army that its leader is one, namely, the commander of the army. And all this is true.

And as to Ghazali's words:

Nor can it be said that one single heaven or one single body, the sun or any other body, can be the First Principle; for all these are bodies, and body is composed of matter and form, and the first body cannot be composite.

I SAY:

The statement that each body is composed of matter and form does not accord with the theory of the philosophers (with the exception of Avicenna) about the heavenly body, unless one uses 'matter' here equivocally. For according to the philosophers everything composed of matter and form has a beginning, like the coming into existence of a house and a cupboard; and the heavens, according to them, have not come into existence in this sense, and so they called them eternal, because their existence is coeternal with the First Principle. For since according to them the cause of corruption is matter, that which is incorruptible could not possess matter, but must be a simple entity. If generation and corruption were not found in sublunary bodies, we should not draw the conclusion that they were composed of matter and form, for the fundamental principle is that body is a single essence not less in its existence than in perception, and if there were no corruption of sublunary bodies, we should judge that they were simple and that matter was body. But the fact that the body of the heavens does not suffer corruption shows that its matter is actual corporeality. And the soul which exists in this body does not exist in it because this body requires, as the bodies of animals do, the soul for its continuance, nor because it is necessary for the existence of this body to be animated, but only because the superior must of necessity exist in the condition of the superior and the animate is superior to the inanimate. According to the philosophers there is no change in the heavenly bodies, for they do not possess a potency in their substance. They therefore need not have matter in the way the generable bodies need this, but they are either, as Themistius affirms, forms, or possess matter in an equivocal sense of the word. And I say that either the matters of the heavenly bodies are identical with their souls, or these matters are essentially alive, not alive through a life bestowed on them.

GHAZALI SAYS:

To this there are two answers. The first is that it can be said: Since it follows from the tenets of your school that the bodies of the world are eternal, it must follow too that they have no cause, and your statement that on a second examination such a conclusion must be rejected will itself be rejected when we discuss God's unity and afterwards the denial of attributes to God.

I SAY:

Ghazali means that since they cannot prove the unity of the First Principle, and since they cannot prove either that the One cannot be body—for since they cannot deny the attributes, the First Principle must, according to them, be an essence endowed with attributes, and such an essence must be a body or a potency in a body—it follows that the First Principle which has no cause is the celestial bodies. And this conclusion is valid against those who might argue in the way he says the philosophers argue. The philosophers, however, do not argue thus, and do not say that they are unable to prove the unity and incorporeality of the First Principle. But this question will be discussed later.

GHAZALI SAYS:

The second answer, and it is the answer proper to this question, is to say: it is established as a possibility that these existents can have a cause, but perhaps for this cause there is another cause, and so on *ad infinitum*. And you have no right to assert that to admit an infinite series of causes is impossible, for we ask you, 'Do you know this by immediate necessary intuition or through a middle term?' Any claim to intuition is excluded, and any method of deductive proof is forbidden to you, since you admit celestial revolutions without an initial term; and if you permit a coming into existence for what is without end, it is not impossible that the series should consist of causal relations and have as a final term an effect which has no further effect, although in the other direction the series does not end in a cause which has no anterior cause, just as the past has a final term, namely the ever-changing present, but no first term. If you protest that the past occurrences do not exist together at one moment or at certain moments, and that what does not exist cannot be described as finite or infinite, you are forced to admit this simultaneous existence for human souls in abstraction from their bodies; for they do not perish, according to you, and the number of souls in abstraction from their bodies is infinite, since the series of becoming from sperma to man and from man to sperma is infinite, and every man dies, but his soul remains and is numerically different from the soul of any man who dies before, simultaneously, or afterwards, although all these souls are one in species. Therefore at any moment there is an infinite number of souls in existence.

If you object that souls are not joined to each other, and that they have no order, either by nature or by position, and that you regard only those infinite existents as impossible which have order in space, like bodies which have a spatial order of higher and lower, or have a natural order like cause and effect, and that this is not the case with souls; we answer: 'This theory about position does not follow any more than its contrary; you cannot regard one of the two cases as impossible without involving the other, for where is your proof for the distinction? And you cannot deny that this infinite number of souls must have an order, as some are prior to others and the past days and nights are infinite. If we suppose the birth of only one soul every day and night, the sum of souls, born in sequence one after the other, amounts at the present moment to infinity.

The utmost you can say about the cause is that its priority to the effect exists by nature, in the way that its superiority to the effect is a matter of essence and not of space. But if you do not regard an infinite sequence as impossible for real temporal priority, it cannot be impossible for natural essential priority either. But what can the philosophers mean when they deny the possibility of an infinite spatial superposition of bodies, but affirm the possibility of an infinite temporal sequence? Is this theory not really an inept theory without any foundation?

I say: As to Ghazali's words:

But perhaps for this cause there is another cause and so on *ad infinitum* . . . and any method of deductive proof is forbidden to you, since you admit celestial revolutions without an initial term:

To this difficulty an answer was given above, when we said that the philosophers do not allow an infinite causal series, because this would lead to an effect without a cause, but assert that there is such a series accidentally from an eternal cause—not, however, in a straight line, nor simultaneously, nor in infinite matters, but only as a circular process.

What he says here about Avicenna, that he regarded an infinite number of souls as possible and that infinity is only impossible in what has a position, is not true and no philosopher has said it; indeed, its impossibility is apparent from their general proof which we mentioned, and no conclusion can be drawn against them from this assumption of an actual infinity of souls. Indeed, those who believed that the souls are of a certain number through the number of bodies and that they are individually immortal profess to avoid this assumption through the doctrine of the transmigration of souls.

And as to Ghazali's words:

But what can the philosophers mean when they deny the possibility of an infinite spatial superposition of bodies, but affirm the possibility of an infinite temporal sequence?

I say:

The difference between these two cases is very clear to the philosophers, for from the assumption of infinite bodies existing simultaneously there follows an infinite totality and an actual infinite, and this is impossible. But time has no position, and from the existence of an infinite temporal series of bodies no actual infinite follows.

Ghazali says on behalf of the philosophers:

The philosophers might say: The strict proof of the impossibility of an infinite causal series is as follows: each single cause of a series is either possible in itself or necessary; if it is necessary, it needs no cause, and if it is possible, then the whole series needs a cause additional to its essence, a cause standing outside the series.

I say:

The first man to bring into philosophy the proof which Ghazali gives here as a philosophical one, was Avicenna, who regarded this proof as superior to those given by the ancients, since he claimed it to be based on the essence of the existent, whereas the older proofs are based on accidents consequent on the First Principle. This proof Avicenna took from the theologians, who regarded the dichotomy of existence into possible and necessary as self-evident, and assumed that the possible needs an agent and that the world in its totality, as being possible, needs an agent of a necessary existence. This was a theory of the Mu'tazilites before the Ash'arites, and it is excellent, and the only flaw in it is their assumption that the world in its totality is possible, for this is not self-evident. Avicenna wanted to give a general sense to this statement, and he gave to the 'possible' the meaning of 'what has a cause', as Ghazali relates. And even if this designation can be conceded, it does not effect the division which he had in view. For a primary division of existence into what has a cause and what has no cause is by no means self-evident. Further, what has a cause can be divided into what is possible and what is necessary. If we understand by 'possible' the truly possible we arrive at the necessary-possible and not at the necessary which has no cause; and if we understand by 'possible' that which has a cause and is also necessary, there only follows from this that what has a cause has a cause and we may assume that this cause has a cause and so *ad infinitum*. We do not therefore arrive at an existent without cause—for this is the meaning of the expression 'entity of a necessary existence'—unless by the possible which Avicenna assumes as the opposite of what has no cause we understand the truly possible, for in these possibles there cannot exist an infinite series of causes. But if by 'possible' is meant those necessary things which have a cause, it has not yet been proved that their infinite number is impossible, in the way it is evident of the truly possible existents, and it is not yet proved that there is a necessary existent which needs a cause, so that from this assumption one can arrive at a necessary entity existing without a cause. Indeed, one has to prove that what applies to the total causal series of possible entities applies also to the total causal series of necessary existents.

GHAZALI SAYS:

The terms 'possible' and 'necessary' are obscure, unless one understands by 'necessary' that which has no cause for its existence and by 'possible' that which has a cause for its existence, then, by applying the terms as defined to the statement, we say: Each member of a causal series is possible in this sense of 'possible', namely, that it has a cause additional to its essence, but the series as a whole is not possible in this sense of 'possible'. And if anything else is meant by 'possible', it is obscure. If it is objected that this makes the necessary existent consist of possible existents and this is impossible, we answer: By defining 'necessary' and 'possible' as we have done, you have all that is needed and we do not concede that it is impossible. To say that it is impossible would be like saying that it is impossible that what is eternal should be made up of what is temporal, for time according to you philosophers is eternal, but the individual circular movements are temporal and have initial terms, though collectively they have no initial term; therefore, that which has no initial term consists of entities having initial terms, and it is true of the single units that they have a beginning, but not true of them collectively. In the same way it can be said of each term of the causal series that it has a cause, but not of the series as a whole. And so not everything that is true of single units is true of their collectivity, for it is true of each single unit that it is one and a portion and a part, but not true of their collectivity; and any place on the earth which we choose is illuminated by the sun by day and is dark by night, and according to the philosophers each unit has begun, but not the whole. Through this it is proved that the man who admits temporal entities without a beginning, namely, the forms of the four elements, cannot at the same time deny an infinity of causes, and we conclude from this that because of this difficulty there is no way in which they can prove the First Principle, and their dichotomy is purely arbitrary.

I SAY:

The assumption of infinite possible causes implies the assumption of a possible without an agent, but the assumption of infinite necessary entities having causes implies only that what was assumed to have a cause has none, and this argument is true with the restriction that the impossibility of infinite entities which are of a possible nature does not involve the impossibility of infinite necessary entities. If one wanted to give a demonstrative form to the argument used by Avicenna one should say: Possible existents must of necessity have causes which precede them, and if these causes again are possible it follows that they have causes and that there is an infinite regress; and if there is an infinite regress there is no cause, and the possible will exist without a cause, and this is impossible. Therefore the series must end in a necessary cause, and in this case this necessary cause must be necessary through a cause or without a cause, and if through a cause, this cause must have a cause and so on infinitely; and if we have an infinite regress here, it follows that what was assumed to have a cause has no cause, and this is impossible. Therefore the series must end in a cause necessary without a cause, i.e., necessary by itself, and this necessarily is the necessary existent. And when these distinctions are indicated, the proof becomes valid. But if this argument is given in the form in which Avicenna gives it, it is invalid for many reasons, one of which is that the term 'possible' used in it is an equivocal one and that in this argument the primary dichotomy of all existents into what is possible and what is not possible, i.e. this division comprising the existent *qua* existent, is not true.

And as to Ghazali's words in his refutation of the philosophers:

WE SAY: Each member of a causal series is possible in this sense of 'possible', namely, that it has a cause additional to its essence, but the whole series is not possible in this sense of 'possible'.

I SAY:

Ghazali means that when the philosophers concede that they understand by 'possible existent' that which has a cause and by 'necessary existent' that which has no cause, it can be said to them: 'According to your own principles the existence of an infinite causal series is not impossible, and the series in its totality will be a necessary existent,' for according to their own principles the philosophers admit that different judgements apply to the part and to the whole collectively. This statement is erroneous for many reasons, one of which is that the philosophers, as was mentioned before, do not allow an infinite series of essential causes, whether causes and effects of a possible or of a necessary nature, as we have shown. The objection which can be directed against Avicenna is that when you divide existence into possible and necessary and identify the possible existent with that which has a cause and the necessary existent with that which has none, you can no longer prove the impossibility of the existence of an infinite causal series, for from its infinite character it follows that it is to be classed with existents which have no cause and it must therefore be of the nature of the necessary existent, especially as, according to him and his school, eternity can consist of an infinite series of causes each of which is temporal. The fault in Avicenna's argument arises only from his division of the existent into that which has a cause and that which has none. If he had made his division in the way we have done, none of these objections could be directed against him. And Ghazali's statement that the ancients, since they admit an infinite number of circular movements, make the eternal consist of an infinite number of entities, is false. For the term 'eternal', when it is attributed both to this infinite series and to the one eternal being, is used equivocally.

And as to the words of Ghazali:

If it is objected that this makes the necessary existent consist of possible existents, and this is impossible, we answer: By defining 'necessary' and 'possible' as we have done you have all that is needed, and we do not concede that it is impossible.

I SAY:

Ghazali means that the philosophers understand by 'necessary' that which has no cause and by 'possible' that which has a cause, and that he, Ghazali, does not regard it as impossible that what has no cause should consist of an infinite number of causes, because, if he conceded that this was impossible, he would be denying the possibility of an infinity of causes, whereas he only wants to show that the philosophers' deduction of a necessary being is a *petitio principii*.

Then Ghazali says:

To say that it is impossible would be like saying that it is impossible that what is eternal should be made up of what is temporal, for time, according to you philosophers, is eternal, but the individual circular movements are temporal and have initial terms; therefore that which has no initial term consists of entities having initial terms, and it is true of the single units that they have a beginning, but not true of them collectively. In the same way it can be said of each term of the causal series that it has a cause, but not of the series as a whole. And so not everything that is true of single units is true of their collectivity, for it is true of each single unit that it is one and a portion and a part, but not true of their collectivity.

I SAY:

Ghazali means that it is not impossible that what has no cause should consist of infinite effects in the way the eternal, according to the philosophers, consists of temporal entities, which are infinite in number. For time, according to the philosophers, is eternal, and consists of limited temporal parts, and likewise the movement of heaven is eternal according to the philosophers, and the circular movements of which it consists are infinite. And the answer is that the existence of an eternal consisting of temporal parts, in so far as they are infinite in number, is not a philosophical principle; on the contrary they deny it most strongly, and only the materialists affirm it. For the sum must consist either of a finite number of transitory members or of an infinite number. If the former is the case, it is generally admitted that the members must also be generically transitory. For the latter case there are two theories. The materialists believe that the totality is of a possible nature and that the collectivity must be eternal and without a cause. The philosophers admit this infinity and believe that such genera, because they consist of possible transitory constituents, must necessarily have an external cause, lasting and eternal, from which they acquire their eternity. It is not true either, as Ghazali seems to imply, that the philosophers believe that the impossibility of an infinite series of causes depends on the impossibility that the eternal should consist of an infinity of constituents. They affirm that the eternity of these generically different movements must lead to one single movement, and that the reason why there exist genera which are transitory in their individuals, but eternal as a whole, is that there is an existent, eternal partly and totally, and this is the body of the heavens. The infinite movements are generically infinite only because of the one single continuous eternal movement of the body of the heavens. And only for the mind does the movement of heaven seem composed of many circular movements. And the movement of the body of the heavens acquires its eternity—even if its particular movements are transitory—through a mover which must always move and through a body which also must always be moved and cannot stop in its motion, as happens with things which are moved in the sublunary world.

About genera there are three theories, that of those who say that all genera are transitory, because the individuals in them are finite, and that of those who say that there are genera which are eternal and have no first or last term, because they appear by their nature to have infinite individuals; the latter are divided into two groups: those, namely the philosophers, who say that such genera can only be truly said to be everlasting, because of one and the same necessary cause, without which they would perish on innumerable occasions in infinite time; and those, namely the materialists, who believe that the existence of the individuals of these genera is sufficient to make them eternal. It is important to take note of these three theories, for the whole controversy about the eternity or non-eternity of the world, and whether the world has an agent or not, is based on these fundamental propositions. The theologians and those who believe in a temporal creation of the world are at one extreme, the materialists at the other, while the philosophers hold an intermediate position.

If all this is once established, you will see that the proposition that the man who allows the existence of an infinite series of causes cannot admit a first cause is false, and that on the contrary the opposite is evident, namely, that the man who does not acknowledge infinite causes cannot prove the existence of an eternal first cause, since it is the existence of infinite effects which demands the necessity of an eternal cause from which the infinite causes acquire their existence; for if not, the genera, all of whose individuals are temporal, would be necessarily finite. And in this and no other way can the eternal become the cause of temporal existents, and the existence of infinite temporal existents renders the existence of a single eternal first principle necessary, and there is no God but He.

Ghazali, answering this objection in the name of the philosophers, says:

The philosophers might say: The circular movements and the forms of the elements do not exist at the present moment; there actually exists only one single form of them, and what does not exist can be called neither finite nor infinite, unless one supposes them to exist in the imagination, and things which are only suppositions in the mind cannot be regarded as impossible, even if certain of these suppositions are supposed to be causes of other suppositions, for man assumes this only in his imagination, and the discussion refers only to things in reality, not to things in the mind. The only difficulty concerns the souls of the dead and, indeed, some philosophers have arrived at the theory that there is only one eternal soul before it is united with bodies, and that after its separation from the bodies it becomes one again, so that it has no numerical quantity and can certainly not be called infinite. Other philosophers have thought that the soul follows from the constitution of the body, that death is nothing but the annihilation of the soul, and that the soul cannot subsist by itself without the body. In that case souls have no existence except in respect of the living, and the living are beings limited in number, and their finitude is not denied, and those that have ceased to exist cannot be qualified at all, either by finitude or by infinity, except when they are supposed to exist in imagination.

Then Ghazali says:

We answer: This difficulty about the souls has come to us from Avicenna and Farabi and the most acknowledged philosophers, since they concluded that the soul was a substance subsistent by itself; and this is also the view taken by Aristotle and by the commentators on the ancient philosophers. And to those philosophers who turn aside from this doctrine we say: Can you imagine that at each moment something comes into being which will last for ever? A negative answer is impossible, and if they admit this possibility, we say: If you imagine that every day some new thing comes into being and continues to exist, then up to the present moment there will have been an infinite collection of existents and, even if the circular movement itself comes to an end, the lasting and endless existence of what has come into being during its revolution is not impossible. In this way this difficulty is firmly established, and it is quite irrelevant whether this survival concerns the soul of a man or a Jinni, the soul of a devil or an angel, or of any being whatever. And this is a necessary consequence of every philosophical theory which admits an infinity of circular movements.

I SAY:

The answer which he gives in the name of the philosophers, that the past revolutions and the past forms of the elements which have come from each other are non-existent, and that the non-existent can be called neither finite nor infinite, is not a true one. And as to the difficulty he raises against them as to their theory about souls, no such theory is held by any philosophers, and the transference of one problem to another is a sophistical artifice.

ON LOVE AND LIVING
Jalāl Al-Dīn Rūmī

  Jalāl al-Dīn Rūmī (1207–1273) is undoubtedly Islam's su-preme mystical poet; and in the opinion of Dr. Arberry, the trans-lator of the discourses reprinted here, he is the "greatest mystical poet in the history of mankind." Jalāl was the son of a noted Sūfī mystic and scholar, Bahā'al-Dīn, whose life and writings, composed in the anti-philosophical tradition of Ghazālī, exerted considerable influence upon his son. After the death of his father, Jalāl al-Dīn spent some sixteen years in religious studies, the first portion of which was under the direction of another noted Sūfī and friend of his father, Burhān al-Dīn. Following this period of education, he entered upon a career as a religious scholar, teaching and writ-ing commentaries and sermons. However, this quiet career was interrupted in 1244, when he underwent a profound spiritual ex-perience precipitated by his acquaintance with an evidently over-powering personality, one Shams al-Dīn, a dervish. Under the influence of this relationship Jalāl al-Dīn was metamorphosed into an ecstatic poet; moreover, he invented the famous whirling dance of the dervishes supposedly to symbolize his search for Shams, who, after about three years, had vanished as suddenly as he had appeared. He became the leader of his own dervish order, the Mevlevis. Subsequently, he achieved the reputation of being an oracle and was consulted by many prominent personages. His Dis-courses recount some of the discussions of that period of his life, during which he also composed the Masnavi, his collection of mystical poems. The following three discourses typify this mysti-cal approach to the mysteries of life.

16

  THE MASTER SAID: Whoever is loved is beautiful, but this statement is not reversible; it does not necessarily follow that whoever is beautiful is loved. Beauty is a part of lovableness, and lovableness is the root principle. If a thing

  Jalāl al-Dīn Rūmī, *Discourses of Rumi,* A. J. Arberry, trans. (London: John Murray, Ltd., 1961), pp. 83–88, 227–35. Reprinted by permission of the publisher.

is loved it is of course a beautiful thing; a part of a thing cannot exist apart from its whole, and is inherent in that whole.

In Majnūn's time there were many girls more beautiful than Lailā, but they were not loved of Majnūn.

'There are girls more beautiful then Lailā,' they used to tell Majnūn. 'Let us bring some to you.'

'Well,' Majnūn would reply, 'I do not love Lailā after form. Lailā is not form. Lailā in my hand is like a cup; I drink wine out of that cup. So I am in love with the wine which I drink out of it. You have eyes only for the beaker, and are unaware of the wine. If I had a golden beaker studded with precious stones, and in the beaker there were vinegar or something else other than wine, of what use would that be to me? An old broken gourd in which there is wine is better in my eyes than such a goblet and a hundred like it.'

A man requires to be moved with passion and yearning, for him to tell the wine apart from the beaker. So it is with the man who is hungry, not having eaten anything for ten days, and the other man who is full and has eaten five times a day. Both see a loaf of bread. The full man sees the form of the bread, whereas the hungry man sees the form of the living soul. For this bread is like the goblet, and the pleasure it imparts is as the wine in the goblet. That wine cannot be perceived save by the regard of appetite and yearning. Therefore acquire appetite and yearning, so that you may not be merely a viewer of form, but in all being and space you may see the Beloved.

These creatures are as cups, and these sciences and arts and branches of knowledge are inscriptions upon the cup. Do you not see that when the cup is broken those inscriptions no more remain? The wine therefore is the thing, which is in the cup of the physical moulds, and he who drinks the wine sees that.

The abiding things, the deeds of righteousness . . .

The man who asks must first conceive two premisses. First, he must be certain that he is erring in what he says, and that something different is the case. Secondly he must reflect that over and above this, and better than this, there is a statement and a wisdom of what he knows nothing. Hence we realise the meaning of the saying, 'Asking is the half of knowing.'

Everyone has his face turned to somebody, and the ultimate object of all is God. In this hope all men expend their lives. But as between these two there must be one who discriminates and who knows, as between the two, which of them is hitting the mark; who is scarred with the blow of the polostick of the King, so that he declares and believes that there is One God.

A man is said to be absorbed when the water has absolute control of him and he has no control of the water. The man absorbed and the swimmer are both in the water; but the former is carried along and borne by the water, whereas the swimmer carries his own strength and moves at his own free will.

So every movement made by the man absorbed, and every act and word that issues from him, all that proceeds from the water and not from him: he is present there as the pretext. In the same way when you hear words coming from a wall, you know that they do not proceed from the wall but that there is someone who has brought the wall into speech.

The saints are like that. They have died before physical death and have taken on the status of door and wall. Not so much as a hair's tip of separate existence has remained in them. In the hands of Omnipotence they are as a shield: the movement of the shield proceeds not from the shield. This is the meaning of the statement, 'I am the Truth': the shield says, 'I am not there at all, the movement proceeds from the Hand of God.' Regard such a shield as God, and do not use violence against God; for those who rain blows against such a shield have declared war against God and ranged themselves against God.

From the time of Adam down to the present day you hear what things have befallen such as have used violence against God—Pharaoh, Shaddad, Nimrod, the peoples of 'Ad and Lot and Thamud, and so on and so on. And that shield stands firm till the resurrection, age after age; now in the form of prophets, now in the form of saints; to the end that the godfearing may be distinguished from the ungodly, God's enemies from His friends.

Therefore every saint is God's proof against men, whose rank and station are determined by the degree of their attachment to him. If they act hostilely against him, they act hostilely against God; if they befriend him, they have made friendship with God. 'Whosoever sees him has seen Me; whosoever repairs to him has repaired to Me.'

God's servants are confidants of the sanctuary of God. Just as God most High has cut away from His servitors every vein of separate existence and lust, every root of perfidy, inevitably they have become masters of a whole world and intimate with the Divine mysteries, which *none but the purified shall touch.*

The Master said: If that man has turned his back on the tombs of the great saints, he has done so not out of disavowal and neglect: he has turned his face towards their souls. For these words which proceed from my mouth are their soul. It does no harm to turn the back on the body and the face towards the soul.

It is a habit with me, that I do not desire that any heart should be distressed through me. During the séance a great multitude thrust themselves upon me, and some of my friends fend them off. That is not pleasing to me, and I have said a hundred times, 'Say nothing to any man on my account; I am well content with that.' I am affectionate to such a degree that when these friends come to me, for fear that they may be wearied I speak poetry so that they may be occupied with that. Otherwise, what have I to do with poetry? By Allah, I care nothing for poetry, and there is nothing worse in my eyes than that. It has become incumbent upon me; as when a man plunges his hands into tripe and washes it out for the sake of a guest's appetite, because the guest's appetite is for tripe.

After all, a man considers what wares are needed in such and such a city and what wares its inhabitants want to buy; those wares he buys, and those he sells, even though the articles be somewhat inferior. I have studied many sciences and taken much pains, so that I may be able to offer fine and rare and precious things to the scholars and researchers, the clever ones and the deep thinkers who come to me. God most High Himself willed this. He gathered here all those sciences, and assembled here all those pains, so that I might be occupied with this work. What can I do? In my own country and amongst my own people there is no occupation more shameful than poetry. If I had remained in my own country, I would have lived in harmony with their temperament and would have practised what they desired, such as lecturing and composing books, preaching and admonishing, observing abstinence and doing all the outward acts.

The Amir Parvāna said to me, 'The root of the matter is acts.' I replied, 'Where are the people of action and the seekers of action, so that I may show them action? Now you seek after words, and have cocked your ears to hear something. If I do not speak, you become upset. Become a seeker of action, so that I may show you action! I am looking all over the world for action, so that I may show you action! I am looking all over the world for a man to whom I may show action. Since I find no purchaser of action but only of words, I occupy myself with words. What do you know of action, seeing that you are not a man of action? Action can only be known through action, science can only be understood through science; form through form, meaning through meaning. Since there is not one traveller upon this road and it is empty, how will they see if we are on the road and in action?'

After all, this action is not prayer and fasting. These are the forms of action; action is an inward meaning. After all, from the time of Adam to the time of Muhammad, God bless him and give him peace, prayer and fasting were not in the form we know, but action was. So this is the form of action; action is a meaning within a man. Similarly you say, 'The medicine acted'; but that is no form of action, it is its meaning. Again they say, 'That man is agent in such and such a city'; they see nothing of mere form but call him agent in respect of the works which appertain to him.

Hence action is not what men have generally supposed. Men suppose that action is this outward show; but if a hypocrite performs that form of action it does not profit him, since the meaning of sincerity and faith is not in him.

The root principle of all things is speech and words. You have no true knowledge of speech and words, and consider them of little account. Speech is the fruit of the tree of action, for words are born of action. God most High created the world by a word.

His command, when He desires a thing, is to say to it
'Be,' and it is.

You may have faith in your heart, but unless you speak it in words it is nothing worth. Prayer too, which is an act, is not perfect unless you recite the Koran. When you say, 'In this present age words are of no account,' you negate this assertion also by means of words. If words are of no account, how is it that we hear you say that words are of no account? After all, you say that also by means of words.

SOMEONE ASKED: When we do a good deed and perform a righteous act, if we entertain hopes and expectations of a good recompense from God, does that harm us?

THE MASTER ANSWERED: By Allah, one must always entertain hope. Faith itself consists of fear and hope. Someone once asked me, 'Hope itself is goodly, so what is this fear?' I replied, 'Show me a fear that is without hope, or a hope without fear. Since the twain are never apart, how can you ask such a question?' For example, a man has sown wheat; he naturally hopes that wheat will come up, whilst at the same time he is afraid lest some impediment or blight may intervene. Hence it is realised that there is no such thing as hope without fear, nor can one ever conceive of fear without hope or hope without fear. Now if a man is hopeful and expectant of recompense and benefit, he will assuredly apply himself with greater diligence to that action. Expectation is a wing, and the stronger the wing the longer the flight. If on the other hand he is without hope he becomes slothful, and no more good and service proceeds from him. Similarly a sick man will drink a bitter medicine and will give up ten sweet pleasures, but if he has no hope of being restored to health how will he be able to endure this?

'Man is a rational animal.' Man is a compound of animal and speech; just as the animal is constant in him and inseparable from him, so too speech is constant in him. If he does not speak outwardly, yet he speaks inwardly; he is constantly speaking. He is like a torrent in which clay is mixed up; the pure water is his speech, whilst the clay is his animality; but the clay in him is accidental. Do you not see how those pieces of clay and material moulds have departed and rotted away, whilst their speech and narration and their sciences, bad and good, have remained?

The 'man of heart' is a plenum; when you have seen him, you have seen all. 'All game is in the belly of the wild ass.' All creatures in the world are parts of him, and he is the whole.

> All, good and evil, parts of the dervish be,
> And whoso is not so, no dervish is he.

Now when you have seen him who is the whole, assuredly you will have seen the whole world, and whomsoever you see after him is a mere repetition.

Their speech is contained in the words of the whole; when you have heard their words, every word you may hear thereafter is a mere repetition.

> Whoso beholds him, in whatever place,
> Has seen all men and viewed the whole of space.

THE POET SAYS:

> Thyself a true transcription art
>   Of the archetype Divine,
> Or else a glass, wherein the King's
>   Own loveliness doth shine.
>
> Whatever then in all the world
>   Without thyself doth lie,
> Whatso thou cravest, in thyself
>   Seek, and declare, "Tis I!"

62

Some have said that love is the cause of service. This is not so. Rather it is the inclination of the beloved that is the requisite of service. If the beloved desires that the lover should be occupied with service, then service proceeds from the lover; if the beloved does not desire it, then the lover abandons service. The abandonment of service is not contrary to love; after all, even if the lover does no service, love does service in him. No; on the contrary, the root of the matter is love, and service is the branch of love.

If the sleeve moves, that happens because the hand moves. On the other hand it does not necessarily follow that if the hand moves the sleeve also moves. For instance, a man has a large gown, so that he rolls about in his gown and the gown does not move. That can happen; but what is not possible is that the gown should move without the person himself moving.

Some people have deemed the gown itself a person, have considered the sleeve a hand and imagined the boot and breeches a foot. This hand and foot are the sleeve and boot of another hand and foot. They say, 'So-and-so is under the hand of So-and-so,' and 'So-and-so has a hand in so many things,' and 'You have to hand it to So-and-so when he speaks.' Certainly what is meant by that hand and foot is not this hand and foot.

That prince came and assembled us, and himself departed. In the same way the bee united the wax with the honey and itself departed and flew away. Because his existence was a condition, after all his continuance is not a condition. Our mothers and fathers are like bees, uniting the seeker with the sought and assembling together the lover and the beloved. They then suddenly fly away. God most High has made them a means for uniting the wax and the honey, and then they fly away; but the wax and honey remain, and the garden. They themselves do not go out of the garden; this is not such a garden that it is possible to go out of it; but they depart from one corner of the garden to another corner of the garden.

Our body is like a beehive in which are the wax and honey of the love of God. Though the bees, our mothers and fathers, are the means, yet they too are tended by the gardener; the gardener also makes the beehive. God most High gave those bees another form; at the time when they were doing this work they had another garment appropriate to that work, but when they departed into the other world they changed garment, for there another work proceeds from them. Yet the person is the same as he was in the first place. Thus for example: a man went into battle, and put on battledress, girded on armour and placed a helmet on his head, because it was the time of combat. But when he comes to the feast he puts off those garments, for he will be occupied with another business. Yet he is the same person. But since you have seen him in that garment, whenever you bring him to mind you will picture him in that shape and that garment, even though he may have changed garments a hundred times.

A man has lost a ring in a certain place. Though the ring has been transported from that place, nevertheless he circles around that place, implying, 'It was here that I lost it.' So a bereaved person circles around the grave and ignorantly circumambulates about the earth and kisses it, implying, 'I lost that ring here'; yet how should it be left there?

God most High has performed so many wonderful works to display His omnipotence. It was here for the sake of Divine wisdom that He composed for a day or two spirit with body. If a man should sit with a corpse in a tomb even for a moment, there is fear that he may go mad. How then, when he escapes from the trap of form and the ditch of the bodily mould, how should he remain there? God most High has appointed that to strike fear into men's hearts and as a token to renew that striking of fear again and again, so that a terror may be manifest in the hearts of men because of the desolation of the tomb and the dark earth. In the same way, when a caravan has been ambushed in a certain place on the road, two or three stones are placed together there to act as a waysign, as much as to say, 'Here is a place of danger.' These graves too are a visible waysign indicating a place of danger.

Fear makes its mark on men; though it does not necessarily follow that it should be realised. For instance if people say to you, 'So-and-so is afraid of you,' without any act issuing from him, an affection manifests in you in regard to him without doubt. If on the contrary they say, 'So-and-so is not in the least afraid of you,' and 'There is no terror of you in his heart,' by the mere fact of this being said an anger towards him appears in your heart.

This running about is the effect of fear. All the world is running; but the running of each one is appropriate to his state. The running of a man is of one kind, the running of a plant is of another kind, the running of a spirit is of another kind. The running of the spirit is without step and visible sign. After all, consider the unripe grape, how much it runs until it attains the blackness of the ripe grape; the moment it has become sweet, at once it reaches that station. Yet that running is invisible and imperceptible; but when it reaches that stage, it becomes realised that it has run very much until it arrived there. Similarly a man enters the water, and nobody has seen him go; when suddenly he brings his head out of the water, then it is realised that he entered the water, for he has reached this point.

63

Lovers have heartaches which no cure can mend, neither sleeping nor faring abroad nor eating, only the sight of the beloved. 'Meet the friend and your sickness will end': this is true to such an extent, that if a hypocrite sits in the company of believers, under their influence he becomes a believer that very instant. So God most High declares:

> *When they meet those who believe, they say, 'We believe.'*

How then, when a believer sits with a believer? Since that has such an effect on a hypocrite, consider what benefits it confers on the believer! Consider how wool, through being in the vicinity of an intelligent man, has become a figured carpet; and this earth, through the vicinity of an intelligent man, has become such a fine palace! The society of an intelligent man has had such an effect on inanimate things; consider then what effect the society of a believer has on the believer!

Through the society of a partial soul and a miniature intellect inanimate things have attained this rank, and these are all the shadow of a partial intellect. One can deduce a person from his shadow. Now deduce from this what manner of intellect and reason is required for yonder heavens, and the moon and sun, and the seven layers of the earth to become manifest through it, and all that lies between earth and heaven. All these existing things are the shadow of the Universal Intellect. The shadow of the partial intellect is proportionate to the shadow of its person; the shadow of the Universal Intellect, which is the whole of existing things, is proportionate to That.

The saints of God have beheld other heavens besides these heavens; for these heavens are disregarded by them and appear lowly before them; they have set their foot upon them and transcended them.

> Heavens there are in the province of the soul
> That hold our worldly heaven in their control.

What is there so wonderful in the fact that a certain man out of the whole of mankind should discover this particular quality, that he can set his foot upon the head of the seventh heaven? Were we not all congeners of the earth? Yet God most High implanted in us a faculty whereby we became distinguished from our genus, we in control of that and that under our control. We control that in whatever manner we desire, now lifting it up and now setting it down;

now we fashion it into a palace, now we make it a cup and a goblet; now we stretch it out, now we shorten it. If in the first place we were this very earth and its congener, God most High distinguished us by means of that faculty. In like manner, what is there so wonderful in the fact that out of the midst of us, who are all congeners, God most High should distinguish a certain one, in relation to whom we are as some inanimate thing, he controlling us, we being unaware of him whilst he is aware of us?

When I say 'unaware,' I do not mean utterly unaware. On the contrary, everyone who is aware of one thing is unaware of another thing. Even earth, inanimate as it is, is aware of what God has given it. For if it were unaware, how would it have been receptive to water, and how would it have nursed and nourished every seed accordingly? When a person applies himself earnestly and attentively to a particular task, his attentiveness to that task means that he is unaware of any other. But by this inattention we do not mean total inattention. Some people wanted to catch a cat, but found it impossible to do so. One day that cat was preoccupied with hunting a bird, and became inattentive through hunting the bird; so they caught it.

So it is not necessary to become wholly preoccupied with worldly affairs. One must take them easily, and not be in bondage to them, lest this should fret and that should fret. The treasure must not fret; for if these things should fret, that will transform them; whereas if that frets (we seek refuge with God!) who then will transform that? If for instance you have many kinds of cloth of every sort, when you are absorbed, why, which of them will you clutch? Though all are indispensable, yet it is certain that in the bundle you will lay hands on something precious and to be treasured; for with one pearl and a single ruby one can make a thousand decorations.

From a certain tree sweet fruit materialises; though that fruit is a part of it, yet God most High has chosen and distinguished that part above the whole, for in it He deposited a sweetness that He did not deposit in the rest; and by virtue of that, that part became superior to that whole, and proved the pith and purpose of the tree. So God most High declares:

> Nay, but they marvel that a warner has come to
> them from among them.

A certain man said, 'I have a certain state in which neither Muhammad nor the angel near the Throne is contained.' The shaikh replied 'Is it so amazing that a man should have a state in which Muhammad is not contained? Muhammad does not have a state in which a stinking creature like you is not contained!'

A certain jester desired to restore the king to his humour. Every one engaged with him for a certain sum, for the king was greatly vexed. The king was walking angrily along the bank of a river. The jester was walking on the other side level with the king. The king paid not the slightest attention to the jester; he kept staring in the water. The jester, becoming desperate, said, 'O king, what do you see in the water, that you are staring so?' The king replied, 'I see a cuckold.' The jester said, 'Your slave is also not blind.'

So now, since you have a time when Muhammad is not contained, why, Muhammad does not have a state in which such a stinking creature is not contained! After all, this degree of spiritual state which you have discovered is due to his blessing and influence. For in the first place all gifts are showered on him, then they are distributed from him to other men. Such is the rule. God most High said, 'O Prophet, peace be upon thee, and God's mercy and blessings!' 'We have scattered all gifts upon thee.' Said Muhammad, 'And upon God's righteous servants!'

God's way is exceeding fearful, blocked and full of snow. He was the first to risk his life, driving his horse and pioneering the road. Whoever goes on this road, does so by his guidance and guarding. He discovered the road in the first place and set up waymarks everywhere, posting pieces of wood to say, 'Do not go in this direction, and do not go in that direction. If you go in that direction you will perish, even as the people of 'Ad and Thamud; and if you go in this direction you will be saved, like the believers. All of the Koran expounds this, for *therein are clear signs*—that is to say, upon these ways We have given waymarks. If any man attempts to break any of these pieces of wood, all attack him, saying, 'Why do you destroy the road for us, and why do you labour to accomplish our destruction? Perchance you are a highwayman.'

Know now that Muhammad is the guide. Until a man first comes to Muhammad he cannot reach unto Us. Similarly, when you wish to go to a certain place, first reason leads the way, saying, 'You must go to a certain place, that is in your best interests.' After that the eyes act as a guide, and then the limbs begin to move, all in that order; though the limbs have no knowledge of the eye, neither the eye of the reason.

Though a man is inadvertent, others are not unaware of him. If you labour strenuously in pursuit of the world, you become unaware of your real concern. It is necessary to seek God's approval, not the approval of men; for approval and love and affection are only on loan in men, being placed there by God. If God so wishes, He gives no composure or enjoyment; with all the means of ease and bread and luxury provided, everything becomes pain and affliction. Therefore all secondary means are as it were a pen in the hand of God's omnipotence; God is the mover and the writer. Until He wishes, the pen does not move. You fix your eye on the pen; you say, 'There must be a hand to this pen.' You see the pen, but you do not see the hand. You see the pen and remember the hand; where is that which you see, and that which you say? They however always see the hand, and they say, 'There must also be a pen'; but beholding the beauty of the hand, they do not care to behold the pen. They simply say, 'Such a hand cannot be without a pen'; whilst you are so delighted with beholding the pen that you do not care for the hand, they are so delighted with beholding the hand, how could they care for the pen? Whilst you find such pleasure in barley bread that you do not remember wheaten bread, since they have wheaten bread how could they remember barley bread? Since He has bestowed upon you such joy upon earth that you have no desire for heaven, which is the true place of joy, and since earth derives its life from heaven, how should the inhabitants of heaven remember earth?

So do not regard happiness and pleasure as coming from secondary causes, for those realities are merely on loan to the secondary causes. It is He who hurts and profits, for all hurt and profit come from Him. Why do you cling so to secondary causes?

'The best words are those which are few and telling.' The best words are those which convey a lesson, not those which are many. Though the Sura *Say, He is One* is little in form, yet it is superior to the Sura of the Cow though that is very long, from the standpoint of conveying a message. Noah preached for a thousand years and forty persons rallied to him; it is well known how long Muhammad preached, yet so many climes believed in him, so many saints and 'pegs' appeared because of him. Much and little therefore are no criterion; the true object is the conveying of a lesson.

With some men it may be that few words convey the lesson better than many. In the same way, when the fire of a stove is extremely fierce you cannot derive any benefit from it and are unable to go near it; whereas you derive a thousand advantages from a feeble lamp. Hence it is realised that it is benefit gained which is the true objective. With some men it is beneficial not to hear any words at all; it is enough for them to see; that is what profits such a man, and if he hears any words it actually harms him.

A certain shaikh from India was seeking to come to a great saint. When he reached Tabriz and came to the door of the saint's cell, a voice came to him from within the cell, saying, 'Return! In your case the benefit is that you have come to the door. If you see the saint, that will harm you.'

A few words which convey a lesson are like a lit lamp which kissed an unlit lamp and departed. That is enough for him, and he has attained his purpose. After all, the prophet is not that visible form; that form is the steed of the prophet. The prophet is that true love and affection, and that is immortal; just as the she-camel of Salih, his form is the she-camel. The prophet is that true love and affection, and that is eternal.

Someone asked the question, 'Why do they not praise God only upon the minaret? Why do they also mention Muhammad?' He was answered, 'Well, praising Muhammad is praising God. It may be compared with a man saying, "God give the king a long life, and him who showed me the way to the king, or told me of the king's name and attributes!" Praising the man is in reality praising the king.'

This Prophet says, 'Give me something. I am in need. Either give me your cloak, or your wealth, or clothes.' What would he do with your cloak and wealth? He desires to lighten your garment, so that the warmth of the sun may reach you.

> And lend to God a good loan.

He does not want wealth and cloak only. He has given you many things besides wealth—knowledge, and thought, and wisdom, and vision. He means, 'Expend on Me a moment's regard and thought and consideration and reason; after all, you have acquired wealth by means of these instruments which I have given.' God desires alms alike from bird and snare. If you are able to go before the sun naked, that is better; for that Sun does not burn black, it makes a man white. Or at least make your clothes lighter, that you may enjoy the feel of the Sun. You have become accustomed for a while to bitterness; at least make trial of sweetness too!

51

THE PHYSICAL, MORAL, AND SPIRITUAL STATES OF MAN
Mirza Ghulam Ahmad

> Mirza Ghulam Ahmad (1835–1908), a native of India, was widely recognized as an excellent exponent of the faith of Islam. He wrote voluminously, authoring some eighty volumes in the Urdu, Arabic, and Persian languages. He claimed to have received a special revelation from God, and regarded himself as the Messiah prophesied in the Koran. Having gathered a group of disciples, in 1889 he organized them as the Ahmadiyya Movement. The Ahmadiyya Movement emphasizes moral and spiritual perfection and is quite missionary in character, having established mosques all over the world, including the United States. The selection from the writings of Ahmad reprinted here is a portion of an address

Mirza Ghulam Ahmad, The Philosophy of the Teachings of Islam (Washington, The American Fazl Mosque, 1953), pp. 19–32. Reprinted by permission of M. M. Ahmad, Secretary, Ahmadiyya Muslim Foreign Missions.

which he delivered before the Great Religions Conference in 1896 in Lahore. His aim was to present the basic principles of Islam as he understood them to the representatives of other major religions. His means for achieving this goal was the exegesis of passages from the Koran, and he announced that his exposition would "depend solely upon the Koran for every assertion and argument, stating only that which is set forth in it in plain words, or what may be reasonably inferred from them."

The first question relates to the physical, moral and spiritual states of man. The Holy Quran observes this division by fixing three respective sources for this threefold state of man. In other words, it mentions three springs out of which these three states flow.

THE FIRST STATE:

The first of these in which the physical state of man takes its birth is termed the *Nafs i ammāra*, which signifies the uncontrollable spirit, or the spirit prone to evil. Thus it says:

$$\text{اِنَّ النَّفْسَ لَاَمَّارَةٌ' بِالسُّوَءِ}$$

It is the characteristic of the *Nafs-i-ammāra* that it inclines man towards evil, tends to lead him into iniquitous and immoral paths and stands in the way of his attainment of perfection and moral excellence.[1]

In short, man's nature is prone to evil and transgression at a certain stage in his development, and so long as he is devoid of high moral qualities, this evil nature is predominant in him. He is subject to this state so long as he does not walk in the light of true wisdom and knowledge but acts in obedience to the natural inclinations of eating, drinking, sleeping, becoming angry or excited, etc., like the lower animals.

THE SECOND STATE:

As soon, however, as he frees himself from the control of animal passions and guided by reason and knowledge, puts a check on his natural desires and governs them instead of being governed by them—in short, when a transformation is worked in his soul from grossness to virtue, he then passes out of the physical state and becomes a moral being in the strict sense of the word. The source of the moral state of man is called the *Nafs-i-lawwāma* or the self-accusing spirit (conscience), in the terminology of the Holy Quran. In the chapter entitled *Al-Qiyāmah* we have:

[1] The Holy Quran, *Sura Yūsuf*, Verse 54. (References of the Holy Quran hereafter given only by the *Sura* and number of the verse.)

$$ \text{وَلاَ أُقْسِمُ بِالنَّفْسِ اللَّوَّامَةِ} $$

And I call to witness the spirit that blames itself (on every dereliction of duty or on the slightest act of disobedience, being conscious of having offended).[2]

This is the spring from which flows a highly moral life and, on reaching this stage man is freed from bestiality. The calling to witness of the self-accusing spirit indicates the regard in which it is held. For, the change from the disobedient to the self-accusing spirit, being a sure sign of improvement and purification, makes it deserving of approbation in the sight of God. *Lawwāma* literally means one who reproves severely, and the *Nafs-i-lawwāma* or the self-accusing spirit has been so called because it upbraids a man for the doing of evil deeds and restrains unbridled passions and bestial appetites. Its tendency on the other hand is to generate noble qualities and a virtuous disposition so to transform life as to bring the whole course and conduct of it to moderation, and to restrain the carnal passions and sensual desires so as to keep them within due bounds. Although as we have said above, the self-accusing spirit upbraids itself for its faults and frailties, yet it is not complete master of its tendencies, nor is it powerful enough to practice virtue exclusively. The weakness of the flesh still gets the upper hand sometimes and then it stumbles and falls down. Its weakness then resembles that of a child who does not wish to fall but whose infirm legs are sometimes unable to support him. It does not, however, persist in its fault; every failure brings a fresh reproach. In short, at this stage the soul is anxious to attain moral excellence and revolts against disobedience which is the characteristic of the first, or the animal stage, but does, notwithstanding its yearning for virtue, sometimes deviate from the line of duty.

THE THIRD STATE:

The third or the last stage in the onward movement of the soul is reached on attaining to the source of all spiritual qualities. The soul at this stage is, in the words of the Holy Quran, the *Nafs-i-mutmainnah,* or the soul at rest. Thus it says:

$$ \text{يَا أَيَّتُهَا النَّفْسُ الْمُطْمَئِنَّةُ ارْجِعِى إِلَى رَبِّكِ رَاضِيَةً} $$

$$ \text{مَّرْضِيَّةً فَادْخُلِى فِى عِبَادِى وَادْخُلِى جَنَّتِى} $$

O thou soul that are at rest (and restest fully contented with the Lord), return to thy Lord, thou being pleased with Him and He pleased with thee; so enter among My servants and enter into My paradise.[3]

[2] *Al-Qiyāmah,* Verse 3.
[3] *Al-Fajr,* Verses 28–31.

At this stage the soul is freed from all weakness and frailty and is braced with spiritual strength. It is perfectly united with God and cannot exist in separation from Him. As water flows with great force down a slope and, on account of its great mass and the total absence of all obstacles, dashes down with irresistible force, so does the soul at this stage, casting off all trammels, flow unrestrained towards its Maker. It is to this that the verse quoted above refers. It is further clear from the words, "O soul that hast found rest in the Lord, return to Him", that it is in this life and not after death that this great transformation is worked and that it is in this world and not elsewhere that access to paradise is granted to it. Again, as the soul has been commanded to return to its Lord (*Rabb* literally, Supporter), it is clear that such a soul finds its support only in its Lord. The love of God is its sustenance and it drinks deep at this fountain of life and is therefore delivered from death. The same idea is expressed elsewhere in the Holy Quran in the following words:

$$ \text{قَدْ أَفْلَحَ مَنْ زَكَّاهَا ۞ وَقَدْ خَابَ مَنْ دَسَّاهَا ۞} $$

He who has purified his soul of the carnal passions is saved and shall not be destroyed but he who gives vent to unbridled earthly passions should surely despair of life.[4]

In short, these three states of the soul may be called the physical, the moral and the spiritual states of man. Of these, the physical state, viz., that in which man seeks to satisfy the passions of the flesh, is most dangerous when the passions run riot; for it is then that they deal a death blow to the moral and spiritual qualities of man, and hence this state has been termed the disobedient spirit in the Holy Word of God.

The next question for us to consider is, what is the effect of the teachings of the Holy Quran upon the physical state of man, how does it guide us with respect to it, and what practical limits does it set to the natural inclinations? It may be remarked at the outset that, according to the Muslim Scriptures, the physical state of man is closely connected with his moral and spiritual states, so much so that even his modes of eating and drinking play a part in the moulding of his moral and spiritual qualities. If, therefore, his natural desires are properly regulated, they assume the character of moral qualities and deeply affect his spiritual state. It is for this reason that in all forms of devotion and prayer and in all the injunctions relating to internal purity and moral rectitude the greatest stress has been laid upon external purity and cleanliness and on the proper attitudes of the body. Also the relation between the physical and spiritual natures of man would become evident on a careful consideration of the reaction induced by physical acts and *vice versa*.

[4] *Al-Shams*, Verses 10–11.

Weeping, even if artificially induced, saddens the heart while laughter, even artificially stimulated, makes it cheerful. Likewise prostration of the body as is done in Muslim prayer induces humility and inclines the soul towards adoration of the Creator; whereas strutting stimulates vanity and vain glory.

These examples will suffice to illustrate the effect of physical postures upon the spiritual state of a man. Experience also shows the effect produced by food upon the heart and mind. For instance, vegetarians ultimately lose the quality of courage. Thus the result of giving up animal food is weakness of the heart and loss of a noble quality. The operation of the same law is witnessed even among the animals, for the herbivorous animals do not possess even a hundredth part of the courage of the carnivora, and the same may be said of birds. There is not the least doubt then that food plays an important part in the formation of character. Further, as total exclusion of meat from one's diet results in certain deficiencies, excess of meat is also injurious to character, for instance, it would tend to destroy the qualities of humility and meekness. Those who adopt the middle course are heirs to both sets of qualities, viz., courage as well as meekness. It is with this great law in view that the Holy Quran says:

$$\text{كُلُوْا وَاشْرَبُوْا وَلَا تُسْرِفُوْا}$$

Eat (meat as well as other food) but do not give way to excess (in any particular form of diet so that your character and health may not suffer from it).[5]

I have spoken to the effect of the physical upon the moral nature of man but it should also be borne in mind that internal experiences also have external manifestations. Grief brings tears into the eyes and joy makes one laugh. Thus there is a natural relation between the body and the soul and all physical acts such as eating, drinking, sleeping, walking, moving, resting, etc., necessarily produce a corresponding effect upon that which pertains to the state of the soul as distinguished from external manifestations. A shock communicated to one point in the brain causes loss of memory, and to another brings about insensibility. Air containing the poisonous germs of the plague soon corrupts first the body and then the mind, and in a few hours the whole internal system in which reside the moral impulses is impaired and the unfortunate victim passes away like a madman. All this shows that there is a mysterious relation between the body and the soul of man though the solution of the mystery may lie beyond human comprehension.

THE SOUL IS AN EMANATION FROM THE BODY

Another argument bearing upon the subject in hand is that the body itself is the mother of the soul. The soul does not come from some place in

5 *Al-A'rāf*, Verse 32.

the heavens and enter the body in the womb of the mother but it is as it were a light or an essence that lies concealed in the seed and grows with the growth of the body. The Holy Word of God gives us to understand that the soul grows from the body while it is developed in the womb of the mother. Thus it says:

$$ ثُمَّ اَنْشَأْنَاهُ خَلْقًا اٰخَرَ فَتَبَارَكَ اللّٰهُ اَحْسَنُ الْخَالِقِيْنَ $$

Then we bring the body (which has been prepared in the womb) into another form and manifest another creation out of it (which is called the soul), and blessed is God the most excellent Creator who has no equal.[6]

There is a deep secret in the words, "We manifest another creation out of the body." It throws light on the nature of the soul and indicates the strong and mysterious tie between it and the body. The indication which the Word of God has here given us as to the nature of the connection between the body and the soul leads us to other important conclusions. It teaches us that the words which a man speaks and the deeds which he does, if said or done for the sake of God and to manifest His glory, and if regulated by His command- ments, are subject to the same Divine law, viz., that in all the sincere outward actions there is a soul hidden as in the seed of man, and as the body of these actions is gradually developed, the hidden soul appears in it. When the com- plete embodiment of the actions takes place, the soul flashes of a sudden in perfect brightness and glory, and shows itself so far as the spirit can be seen and there appears a plain movement of life. The full development of the body of actions is followed by a blazing of the light within just like a flash of light- ning. This stage is allegorically described in the Holy Quran in the following words:

$$ فَاِذَا سَوَّيْتُهُ وَنَفَخْتُ فِيْهِ مِنْ رُّوْحِىْ $$

$$ فَقَعُوْا لَهُ سَاجِدِيْنَ $$

When I have formed the body of it and set right all the manifestations of glory and breathed into it My soul, prostrate yourself (in obedience) before it.[7]

This verse also suggests the same idea, viz., that on the complete embodi- ment of good actions, the spirit within lights up. This Almighty God describes as His Own soul, thus indicating that it partakes of a Divine nature. For the body is fully developed only after the extinction of the physical desires and, therefore, the Divine light, which before was dim, shines out in full lustre and thus makes it incumbent upon everybody to bow down before the mani- festation of this glory. Therefore everyone is naturally attracted towards it

[6] Al-Mu'minun, Verse 16.
[7] Al-Hijr, Verse 30.

and falls down upon his face before it, except the spirit of evil which loves darkness.

To return to the subject in hand. The soul is a light which springs up from the body which is being prepared in the womb. By the springing up of the soul, I mean that at first it is hidden and imperceptible, though its essence is contained in the seed itself, and that as the body is gradually developed, the soul grows along with it and becomes manifest. There is not the least doubt that the mysterious relationship of the soul with the seed is in accordance with the design of God and His will. It is a bright essence in the seed itself. It is not a part of it in the sense in which matter is part of matter, but at the same time it would be incorrect to say that it comes from outside, or, as some wrongly imagine, falling upon the earth is mixed with the substance of the seed. It is latent in the seed as fire is latent in the flint. The Holy Word of God lends no support to the view that the soul comes from the heavens as something distinct from the body, or that it falls suddenly upon the earth and enters the womb. The idea is utterly false and totally opposed to the laws of nature. The thousands of insects which we observe daily in stinking and rotten articles of food or in unwashed wounds do not come from outside or descend from heaven. Their existence proves that the soul comes out of the body and is as surely a creation of God as anything else.

THE SECOND BIRTH OF THE SOUL

From this we conclude that Almighty God Who with His perfect wisdom and omnipotence has created the soul out of the body, has willed and intended that a second birth of the soul should also be made manifest through the body. The movement of the soul depends upon that of the body and if the body is drawn in any direction the soul must follow. The physical state of man's life being of such great importance to the soul, the Word of God could not remain silent on the point. The Holy Quran has, therefore, applied itself abundantly to the reformation of the physical state of man's life. It gives the most valuable and minute directions on all matters of importance with which man is concerned. All his movements, the manner of the satisfaction of all his needs, his family, social and general connections, health and sickness, are all regulated by laws and it is shown how external order and purity have their effect upon the spiritual state of man. Considering the limited time I have at my disposal today, I shall briefly note only a few of the guiding rules. To describe them in detail would require more time than is here available.

THREEFOLD REFORMATION OF MAN

A close study of the Word of God on this important point, viz., the injunctions and directions relating to the reformation of the external life of man and his gradual advancement from a state of barbarity to one of culture and then on until he reaches the highest stage of spiritual development reveals the following all-wise method. In the first place Almighty God has been pleased to lead him out of darkness and raise him up from a savage state by teaching him the rules relating to his ordinary daily actions and mode of social life. Thus the process starts at the lowest point of man's development and, first of all drawing a line of distinction between man and the lower animals teaches him the elementary rules of morality which may pass under the name of social behavior. Next, it seeks to improve upon this degree of morality by regulating man's conduct and actions, thus turning them into high moral qualities. Both these developments relate to only one stage of advancement, the difference being only one of degree. The Wise Author of the Universe has so arranged the system of moral evolution that a person can easily advance from a low state to a higher one.

We pass on now to the next stage of advancement when man completely loses himself in the love of God and in doing His will and his whole life is lived only for the sake of his Master. This is the stage indicated by the word "Islam." It signifies complete resignation to the will and service of God and total forgetfulness of self. Says the Holy Quran:

$$ بَلَى مَنْ اَسْلَمَ وَجْهَهُ لِلّٰهِ وَهُوَ مُحْسِنٌ فَلَهُ $$
$$ اَجْرُهُ عِنْدَ رَبِّهِ وَلَا خَوْفٌ عَلَيْهِمْ وَلَا هُمْ يَحْزَنُوْنَ $$

Verily he is saved (i.e., shall attain salvation) who sacrifices his life (or interests) for the sake of God, and submits himself to His will; who does not rest satisfied with mere lip-sincerity, but proves it by righteous conduct. Such a one will surely have his reward with his Lord, and there shall come no fear upon him, nor shall he be grieved.[8]

$$ قُلْ اِنَّ صَلَاتِيْ وَ نُسُكِيْ وَمَحْيَايَ وَمَمَاتِيْ لِلّٰهِ $$
$$ رَبِّ الْعٰلَمِيْنَ لَا شَرِيْكَ لَهُ ۚ وَبِذَٰلِكَ اُمِرْتُ $$
$$ وَاَنَا اَوَّلُ الْمُسْلِمِيْنَ $$

Say (O Prophet) my prayers and my sacrifices and my life and my death, are only for God Whose Lordship extends over the whole universe, and Who has no partner. Thus have I been commanded and I am the first Muslim, (i.e., the first to resign himself and to sacrifice his life in the way of Almighty God.)[9]

'Also:

[8] *Al-Baqara,* Verse 113.
[9] *Al-An'ām,* Verse 163.

وَأَنَّ هَذَا صِرَاطِي مُسْتَقِيمًا فَاتَّبِعُوهُ
وَلَا تَتَّبِعُوا السُّبُلَ فَتَفَرَّقَ بِكُمْ عَنْ سَبِيلِهِ

This is my path: it is the right one; therefore, follow it and follow not any other path, for if you do, it will surely lead you away from God.[10]

And again:

قُلْ إِنْ كُنْتُمْ تُحِبُّونَ اللهَ فَاتَّبِعُونِي يُحْبِبْكُمُ اللهُ
وَيَغْفِرْ لَكُمْ ذُنُوبَكُمْ ۗ وَاللهُ غَفُورٌ رَحِيمٌ

Say to them (O Prophet), if you love God, follow me; then will God love you and forgive you your sins; He is surely Forgiving, Merciful.[11]

Now I shall take up and deal with the three states of life, one after the other. But before I proceed to do so, I must repeat the caution that the physical state of man's life, the dominant factor in which is "the disobedient spirit," cannot, according to the Word of God, be treated as something distinct from the moral state. Man's natural inclinations and the desires and passions of the flesh are classified by the Holy Quran as physical conditions. These, when operating under proper regulation and co-ordination, are converted into excellent moral qualities. Similarly no hard and fast line can be drawn between the spheres of the moral and spiritual states. Man passes from one into the other through absolute surrender of self to God, complete purification of the soul, entire elimination of all lower inclinations thus achieving union with God and perfect peace in a state of absolute loyalty to, perfect love of, and complete submission to the will of God. A person does not begin to deserve the title of man so long as his physical conditions are not elevated into moral qualities, for the natural desires are common to man and the lower animals and there is nothing to mark the distinction between them except such elevation and transmutation.

Nor does the mere possession of a few seeming moral qualities foster spiritual life. For instance, meekness, peacefulness, and a disinclination towards mischief are only so many natural qualities which may be possessed even by a person who is utterly ignorant of the significance of moral and spiritual values. Not a few animals are, for instance, quite harmless and apparently free from savage tendencies. When tamed, they are not ferocious in the least and even submit to chastisement without resistance. Yet, it would be wrong to ascribe moral qualities to them. Similarly persons entertaining the darkest and most superstitious beliefs, nay, sometimes even those who

10 *Al-An'ām*, Verse 154.
11 *Al-Imrān*, Verse 32.

otherwise are guilty of the blackest deeds may possess such qualities. It is possible for a person to be so tender hearted as not to suffer the killing of the worms in his own wounds, intestines, or stomach. In some instances tenderness of heart may induce a man to give up the use of honey or musk as the procuring of the one involves the destruction and dispersion of the bees and that of the other the killing of the deer. There may even be persons so compassionate who refrain even from the use of pearls or silk, as both are obtained by the destruction of the life of worms. Soft-hearted persons have been known who have preferred to suffer severe pain rather than have leeches applied to them as the alleviation of the pain would be procured at the cost of the lives of the leeches. It is also possible to imagine that the feeling of tenderness may grow so strong in a man that he may even give up the drinking of water and thus put an end to his own life rather than destroy the animalcules contained in the water.

All this I admit, but would any reasonable person consider all such folly to be productive of any moral excellence or necessary to the state of a moral being? Is it thus that the soul of man can be purified of all internal corruptions which are obstacles in the way of the true realization of God? Such harmlessness, or inoffensiveness, which is met with to a greater extent in some animals and birds than in man, cannot be the means of attaining to the desired degree of perfection. Nay, it really amounts to a fight with nature and constitutes opposition to its laws. It is rejecting the faculties and blessings with which nature has endowed us. We cannot attain to spiritual perfection unless we put into operation our various faculties within their appropriate spheres as occasion may require and walk with perseverance in the path which Almighty God has pointed out to us submitting ourselves wholly to His will. He is like a fish, sacrificed by God's hand, a fish which lives in the waters of His Love.

To resume. As already stated, there are the three factors which give rise to the threefold nature of man, viz., the disobedient spirit, the self-accusing, and the soul at rest. Accordingly, there are three stages of reformation corresponding to these three factors. In the first stage we are concerned with mere ignorant savages whom it is our duty to raise to the status of cultured beings by teaching them the social laws regulating their mutual relations. The first step, therefore, consists in teaching the savage not to walk about naked or devour carcasses, or indulge in other barbarous practices. This is the lowest stage in the reformation of man. In humanizing people upon whom no ray of the light of culture has yet fallen, it is necessary, first of all, to take them through this stage and acquaint them with elementary rules of morality. When the savage has learned the rudiments of social conduct, he is prepared for the second stage of reformation. He is then taught the high and excellent moral qualities pertaining to humanity as well as the proper use of his faculties and of what lies hidden beneath them. Those who have acquired excellent morals are then prepared for the third stage and, after they have attained to outward perfection, they taste of union with, and the love of God. These are the three stages which the Holy Quran has prescribed for a wayfarer who desires to travel along the path that leads to God.

52

THE RELIGIOUS SPIRIT OF ISLAM
Amīr Alī

One of the major liberalizing influences in Islam has been the impact of Sayyid Amīr Alī's The Spirit of Islam, first published in 1891 and reprinted many times since then. Amīr Alī, a prominent jurist, was a native of India and a Shī'ite. The Shī'īs, as opposed to the Sunnīs, who represent the majority opinion in Islam, hold the view that the source of religious authority in addition to the sayings of the Prophet does not reside in the consensus of the community but is personally invested in the Imāms, the successors to Mohammed's chief disciple, Alī. This acceptance of additional interpretations of religious truth has made the Shī'īs somewhat more receptive to liberalizations of Islamic theology, although they are perhaps more conservative politically than the orthodox. Amīr Alī's chief aim was to interpret Islam in terms of all the available modern knowledge, which results in his not taking its superiority to other religions as dogmatically certain but as requiring substantiation by a critical survey of its historical contributions to civilization and a constant re-evaluation of its emphases in the light of current intellectual and social conditions. In this selection from his book, he defends the rightness of the basic religious duties enjoined by Mohammed, not by appealing to the infallibility of the Prophet or even of the Koran, but by trying to show how these duties are productive of genuine value and are socially desirable. Much of Amīr Alī's exposition has received general adoption within Islam as the basis for justification of the worth of Islamic culture in a world largely dominated by the values of the Christian Occident.

Ameer Ali, The Spirit of Islam (London: Chatto and Windus, Educational Ltd.), Chapter II, pp. 159–187. Reprinted by permission of the publisher and Judge Ameer Ali, Exec. Late Right Hon. Syed Ameer Ali.

مَلْ لِمَنْ مَا فِي السَّمَـــوتِ وَالْأَرْضِ

مَلْ لِلَّهِ • كَتَبَ عَلَى نَفْسِهِ الرَّحْمَةَ

قُلْ تَعَالَوْا أَتْلُ مَا حَرَّمَ رَبُّكُمْ عَلَيْكُمْ أَلَّا تُشْرِكُوا بِهِ شَيْئًا وَبِالْوَالِدَيْنِ إِحْسَانًا • وَلَا تَقْتُلُوا أَوْلَادَكُمْ مِنْ إِمْلَاقٍ • نَحْنُ نَرْزُقُكُمْ وَإِيَّاهُمْ • وَلَا تَقْرَبُوا الْفَوَاحِشَ مَا ظَهَرَ مِنْهَا وَمَا بَطَنَ • وَلَا تَقْتُلُوا النَّفْسَ الَّتِي حَرَّمَ اللَّهُ إِلَّا بِالْحَقِّ • ذَلِكُمْ وَصَّاكُمْ بِهِ لَعَلَّكُمْ تَعْقِلُونَ • لَا تَقْرَبُوا مَالَ الْيَتِيمِ إِلَّا بِالَّتِي هِيَ أَحْسَنُ حَتَّى يَبْلُغَ أَشُدَّهُ • أَوْفُوا الْكَيْلَ وَالْمِيزَانَ بِالْقِسْطِ • لَا نُكَلِّفُ نَفْسًا إِلَّا وُسْعَهَا • وَإِذَا قُلْتُمْ فَاعْدِلُوا وَلَوْ كَانَ ذَا قُرْبَى • وَبِعَهْدِ اللَّهِ أَوْفُوا • ذَلِكُمْ وَصَّاكُمْ بِهِ لَعَلَّكُمْ تَذَكَّرُونَ •

For the conservation of a true religious spirit, Mohammed attached to his precepts certain practical duties, of which the following are the principal: (1) prayer, (2) fasting, (3) alms-giving, and (4) pilgrimage.

Man's consciousness of a supreme, all-pervading Power; his helplessness in the eternal conflict of nature; his sense of benefaction,—all lead him to pour out the overflowing sentiments of his heart in words of gratitude and love, or repentance and solicitation, to One who is ever-wakeful and merciful. Prayers are only the utterance of the sentiments which fill the human heart. All these emotions, however, are the result of a superior development. The savage, if supplications do not answer his purpose, resorts to the castigation of his fetish. But every religious system possessing any organic element has recognised, in some shape, the efficacy of prayer. In most, however, the theurgic character predominates over the moral; in some, the moral idea is entirely wanting.

The early Hindu worship consisted of two sets of acts—oblations and sacrifice accompanied with invocations. In the infancy of religious thought the gods are supposed to possess the same appetites and passions as human beings; and thus whilst man needs material benefits, the gods require offerings and propitiation. This idea often finds expression in the old hymns of the *Rig Veda*. With the development of religious conceptions, it is probable that, among at least the more advanced or thoughtful minds, the significance attached to oblations and sacrifice underwent considerable modification. But as the hold of the priestly caste, which claimed the possession of a "secret virtue" transmissible only through the blood, strengthened on the minds of the masses, Brahmanism crystallised into a literally sacrificial cult. The sacrifice could be performed only by the priest according to rigid and unalterable formulæ; whilst he recited the *mantras* and went through the rites in a mechanical spirit, without religious feeling or enthusiasm, the worshipper stood by, a passive spectator of the worship which was performed on his behalf. The smallest mistake undid the efficacy of the observances. The devotional spirit, however, could not have been entirely wanting, or the *Bhagavad Gita* could not have been composed. But for the people as a whole, their worship had become a vast system of sacrifice, the value of which depended not so much upon the moral conduct of the individual worshipper as upon the qualification of the officiating priest. The former had only to believe in the efficacy of the rite and be in a state of legal purity at the time.

The Mago-Zoroastrian and the Sabæan lived in an atmosphere of prayer. The Zoroastrian prayed when he sneezed, when he cut his nails or hair, while preparing meals, day and night, at the lighting of lamps, etc. Ormuzd was first invoked, and then not only heaven, earth, the elements and stars, but trees, especially the moon-plant, and beasts. The formulæ were often to be repeated as many as twelve hundred times. The moral idea, however pure with the few, would be perfectly eliminated from the minds of the common people. But even the sort of spiritual life enjoyed by exceptional minds was monopolised by the ministers of religion. The barriers of special holiness which divided the priesthood from the laity, shut out the latter from all spiritual enjoyments of a nobler type. The Magians, like the Ophici, had two forms of worship, or rather, two modes of understanding the objects of worship: one esoteric, especially reserved for the priestly classes; the other exoteric, in which alone the vulgar could participate.

The Mosaic law contained no ordinances respecting prayers; only on the payment of tithes to the priests, and the domestic solemnity of the presentation of the firstlings, was there a prescribed formula of a prayer and acknowledgement, when the father of the house, on the strength of his having obediently performed the behests of the law, supplicated blessings from Jehovah on Israel, "even as He had sworn unto their fathers." But, with the rise of a more spiritual idea of the Deity among the people and the teachers, and the decline of an uncompromising anthropomorphism, the real nature of prayer, as the medium of intercommunication between God and man, began to be understood. Tradition and custom, in default of any express regulation by the law, made the Jews at last, as Döllinger says, a people of prayer. Three hours daily were consecrated to devotional exercises, viz. nine, twelve, and three o'clock. The necessity, however, for the service of priests, combined with the absence of any positive precedent coming down from the Lawgiver himself, tended to make prayer, in the majority of cases, merely mechanical. Phylacteries were in use in the time of Jesus, and the Koran reproaches the Jews in bitter terms for "selling the signs of God."

The teachings of Jesus, representing a later development of the religious faculty in man, recognised the true character of prayer. He consecrated the practice by his own example. The early disciples, in the spirit of their Master, laid great stress on the habit of devotion and thanksgiving to God. But the want of some definite rule for the guidance of the masses, in process of time, left them completely adrift in all that regarded the practice of devotion, and under subjection to the priests, who monopolised the office of regulating the number, length, and the terminology of prayers. Hence missals, liturgies, councils, and convocations to settle articles of faith and matters of conscience; hence also, the mechanical worship of droning monks, and the hebdomadal flocking into churches and chapels on one day in the week to make up for the deficiency of spiritual food during the other six; hence also the "presbyter," who, merely a "servant" at first, came to regard himself as "the Lord of the spiritual heritage" bequeathed by Jesus.

All these evils had culminated to a point in the seventh century, when the Prophet of Arabia began to preach a reformed religion. In instituting prayers, Mohammed recognised the yearning of the human soul to pour out its love and gratitude to God, and by making the practice of devotion periodic, he impressed that disciplinary character on the observance of prayer which keeps the thoughts from wandering into the regions of the material. The formulæ, consecrated by his example and practice, whilst sparing the Islâmic world the evils of contests regarding liturgics, leave to the individual worshipper the amplest scope for the most heartfelt outpouring of devotion and humility before the Almighty Presence.

The value of prayer as the means of moral elevation and the purification of the heart, has been clearly set forth in the Koran:

"Rehearse that which hath been revealed unto thee of the Book, and be constant at prayer, for prayer preserveth from crimes and from that which is blameable; and the remembering of God is surely a most sacred duty."

The forms of the supplicatory hymns, consecrated by the example of the Prophet, evince the beauty of the moral element in the teachings of Islâm:

"O Lord! I supplicate Thee for firmness in faith and direction towards rectitude, and to assist me in being grateful to Thee, and in adoring Thee in every good way: and I supplicate Thee for an innocent heart, which shall not incline to wickedness; and I supplicate Thee for a true tongue, and for that virtue which Thou knowest; and I pray Thee to defend me from that vice which Thou knowest, and for forgiveness of those faults which Thou knowest. O my Defender! assist me in remembering Thee and being grateful to Thee, and in worshipping Thee with the excess of my strength. O Lord! I have injured my own soul, and no one can pardon the faults of Thy servants but Thou; forgive me out of Thy loving-kindness, and have mercy on me; for verily Thou art the forgiver of offences and the bestower of blessings on Thy servants."

Another traditional prayer, called the prayer of David, runs thus; "O Lord, grant to me the love of Thee; grant that I may love those that love Thee; grant that I may do the deeds that may win Thy love; make Thy love to be dearer to me than self, family or than wealth."

The two following prayers of Ali (the Caliph) evince the highest devotional spirit.

"Thanks be to my Lord; He the Adorable, and only to be adored. My Lord, the Eternal, the Ever-existing, the Cherisher, the True Sovereign whose mercy and might overshadow the universe; the Regulator of the world, and Light of the creation. His is our worship; to Him belongs all worship; He existed before all things, and will exist after all that is living has ceased. Thou art the adored, my Lord; Thou art the Master, the Loving and Forgiving; Thou bestowest power and might on whom Thou pleasest; him whom Thou hast exalted none can lower; and him whom Thou hast lowered none can exalt. Thou, my Lord, art the Eternal, the Creator of all, All-wise Sovereign Mighty; Thy knowledge knows everything; Thy beneficence is all-pervading; Thy forgiveness and mercy are all-embracing. O my Lord, Thou art the Helper of the afflicted, the Reliever of all distress, the Consoler of the broken-hearted; Thou art present everywhere to help Thy servants. Thou knowest all secrets, all thoughts, art present in every assembly, Fulfiller of all our needs, Bestower of all blessings. Thou art the Friend of the poor and bereaved; my Lord, Thou art my Fortress; a Castle for all who seek Thy help. Thou art the Refuge of the weak; the Helper of the pure and true. O my Lord, Thou art my Supporter, my Helper, the Helper of all who seek Thy help. . . . O my Lord, Thou art the Creator, I am only created; Thou art my Sovereign, I am only Thy servant; Thou art the Helper, I am the beseecher; Thou, my Lord art my Refuge; Thou art the Forgiver, I am the sinner; Thou, my Lord, art the Merciful, All-knowing, All-loving; I am groping in the dark; I seek Thy knowledge and love. Bestow, my Lord, all Thy knowledge and love and mercy; forgive my sins, O my Lord, and let me approach Thee, my Lord."

"O my Lord, Thou the Ever-praised, the Eternal, Thou art the Ever-present, Ever-existing, the Ever-near, the All-knowing. Thou livest in every heart, in every soul, all-pervading; Thy knowledge is ingrained in every mind." "He bears no similitude, has no equal, One, the Eternal; thanks be to the Lord whose mercy extends to every sinner, who provides for even those who deny Him. To Him belong the beginning and the end, all knowledge and the most hidden secret of the heart. He never slumbers, the Ever-just, the Ever-wakeful. He forgiveth in His mercy our greatest sins,—loveth all creation. I testify to the goodness of my Lord, to the truth of His Messenger's message, blessings on him and his descendants and his companions."

"It is one of the glories of Islâm," says an English writer, "that its tem-

ples are not made with hands, and that its ceremonies can be performed anywhere upon God's earth or under His heaven." Every place in which the Almighty is faithfully worshipped is equally pure. The Moslem, whether he be
at home or abroad, when the hour of prayer arrives, pours forth his soul in a
brief but earnest supplicatory address; his attention is not wearied by the
length of his prayers, the theme of which is always self-humiliation, the glorification of the Giver of all good, and reliance on His mercy. The intensity
of the devotional spirit embalmed in the church of Mohammed has hardly
been realised by Christendom. Tradition, that faithful chronicler of the past,
with its hundred corroborative witnesses, records how the Prophet wept during his prayers with the fervour of his emotions; how his noble cousin and
son-in-law became so absorbed in his devotions that his body grew benumbed.

The Islâm of Mohammed recognises no caste of priesthood, allows no
monopoly of spiritual knowledge or special holiness to intervene between man
and his God. Each soul rises to its Creator without the intervention of priest
or hierophant. No sacrifice, no ceremonial, invented by vested interests, is
needed to bring the anxious heart nearer to its Comforter. Each human being
is his own priest; in the Islâm of Mohammed no one man is higher than the
other.

European rationalists have complained of the complex character of the
Moslem prayers, but the ritual of the Koran is astonishing in its simplicity
and soberness. It includes the necessary acts of faith, the recital of the creed,
prayer, almsgiving, fasting, and pilgrimage, but lays down scarcely any rules
as to how they are to be performed. "Observe the prayers and the mid-day
prayer, and stand ye attent before God; seek aid from patience and prayer.
Verily, God is with the patient;" but nothing is said regarding the manner in
which the prayers should be offered. "When ye journey about the earth," says
the Koran, "it is no crime to you that ye come short in prayer if ye fear that
those that disbelieve will set upon you. God pardons everything except associating aught with Him."

The practice of the Prophet has, however, attached certain rites and
ceremonies to the due observance of prayers. At the same time it is pointed
out in unmistakeable terms that it is to the devotional state of the mind the
Searcher of the spirit looks: "It is not the flesh or the blood of that which ye
sacrifice which is acceptable to God: it is your piety which is acceptable to
the Lord." "It is not righteousness," continues the Koran, "that ye turn your
faces in prayer towards the east or the west; but righteousness is of him who
believeth in God; . . . who giveth money for God's sake unto his kindred,
and unto orphans, and the needy, and the stranger, and those who ask, and
for the redemption of captives; who is constant at prayers and giveth alms;
and of those who perform their covenant, when they have covenanted; and
who behave themselves patiently in hardship and adversity, and in times of
violence; these are they who are true." . . .

It was declared that prayer without "the presence of the heart" was of no avail, and that God's words which were addressed to all mankind and not to one people, should be studied with the heart and lips in absolute accord. And the Caliph Ali held that devotion offered without understanding was useless and brought no blessing. The celebrated Imâm al-Ghazzâli has pronounced that in reading the sacred book heart and intelligence must work together; the lips only utter the words; intelligence helps in the due apprehension of their meaning; the heart, in paying obedience to the dictates of duty. "It is not a sixth nor a tenth of a man's devotion," said the Prophet, "which is acceptable to God, but only such portion thereof as he offers with understanding and true devotional spirit."

The practice of baptism in the Christian Church, even the lustrations, which the Egyptians, the Jews, or the hierophants of the heathen religions in the East and the West, required as preliminary to the performance of devotional or religious exercises, show the peculiar sanctity which was attached to external purifications. Mohammed, by his example, consecrated this ancient and beneficent custom. He required cleanliness as a necessary preliminary to the worship and adoration of God. At the same time, he especially inculcated that mere external, or rather physical, purity does not imply true devotion. He distinctly laid down that the Almighty can only be approached in purity and humility of spirit. Imâm al-Ghazzâli expressly says, as against those who are only solicitous about external purifications, and have their hearts full of pride and hypocrisy, that the Prophet of God declared the most important purification to be the cleansing of the heart from all blameable inclinations and frailties, and the mind from all vicious ideas, and from all thoughts which distract attention from God.

In order to keep alive in the Moslem world the memory of the birthplace of Islâm, Mohammed directed that during prayers the Moslem should turn his face towards Mecca, as the glorious centre which saw the first glimmerings of the light of regenerated truth. With the true instinct of a prophet he perceived the consolidating effect of fixing a central spot around which, through all time, should gather the religious feelings of his followers; and he accordingly ordained that everywhere throughout the world the Moslem should pray looking towards the Kaaba. "Mecca is to the Moslem what Jerusalem is to the Jew. It bears with it all the influence of centuries of associations. It carries the Moslem back to the cradle of his faith, the childhood of his Prophet, it reminds him of the struggle between the old faith and the new, of the overthrow of the idols, and the establishment of the worship of the one God; and, most of all, it bids him remember that all his brother Moslems are worshipping towards the same sacred spot; that he is one of a great company of believers, united by one faith, filled with the same hopes, reverencing the same things, worshipping the same God. Mohammed showed his knowledge of the religious emotions in man when he preserved the sanctity of the temple of Islâm." But that this rule is not an essential requisite for devotion, is evident from the passage of the Koran quoted above.

The institution of fasting has existed more or less among all nations. But it may be said that throughout the ancient world the idea attached to it was, without exception, more of penitence than of abstinence. Even in Judaism the notion of fasting as an exercise of self-castigation or self-abnegation was of later growth. The Essenians (from their connection with the Pythagoreans, and, through them, with the asceticism of the further East) were the first among the Jews to grasp this moral element in the principle of fasting; and Jesus probably derived this idea, like other conceptions, from them.

The example of Jesus consecrated the custom in the Church. But the predominating idea in Christianity, with respect to fasts generally, is one of penitence or expiation; and partially, of precedent. Voluntary corporal mortifications have been as frequent in the Christian Church as in other Churches; but the tendency of such mortifications has invariably been the destruction of mental and bodily energies, and the fostering of a morbid asceticism. The institution of fasting in Islâm, on the contrary, has the legitimate object of restraining the passions, by diurnal abstinence for a limited and definite period, from all the gratifications of the senses, and directing the overflow of the animal spirits into a healthy channel. Useless and unnecessary mortification of the flesh is discountenanced, nay, condemned. Fasting is prescribed to the able-bodied and the strong, as a means of chastening the spirit by imposing a restraint on the body. For the weak, the sickly, the traveller, the student (who is engaged in the pursuit of knowledge—the *Jihâd-ul-Akbar*), the soldier doing God's battle against the assailants of the faith, and women in their ailments, it is disallowed. Those who bear in mind the gluttony of the Greeks, the Romans, the Persians, and the pre-Islâmite Arabs, their excesses in their pleasures as well as their vices, will appreciate the value of the regulation, and comprehend how wonderfully adapted it is for keeping in check the animal propensities of man, especially among semi-civilised races.

Mark the wisdom of the rule as given in the Koran: "O ye that have believed, a fast is ordained to you . . . that ye may practise piety, a fast of a computed number of days. But he among you who shall be ailing, or on a journey, (shall fast) an equal number of other days; and they that are able to keep it (and do not), shall make atonement by maintaining a poor man. . . . But if ye fast, it will be better for you if ye comprehend; . . . God willeth that which is easy for you."

This rule of abstinence is restricted to the day; in the night, in the intervals of prayer and devotion, the Moslem is allowed, perhaps indeed, is bound, to refresh the system by partaking in moderation of food and drink, and otherwise enjoying himself lawfully. In the true spirit of the Teacher, the legists invariably laid down the rule that, during the fast, abstinence of mind from all base thoughts is as incumbent as the abstinence of the body.

No religion of the world prior to Islâm had consecrated charity, the support of the widow, the orphan, and the helpless poor, by enrolling its principles among the positive enactments of the system.

The *agapæ*, or feasts of charity among the early Christians, depended on the will of individuals; their influence, therefore, could only be irregular and spasmodic. It is a matter of history that this very irregularity led to the suppression of the "feasts of charity or love-feasts" only a short time after their introduction.

By the laws of Islâm every individual is bound to contribute a certain part of his substance towards the help and assistance of his poorer neighbours. This portion is usually one part of forty, or 2½ percent on the value of all goods, chattels, emblements, on profits of trade, mercantile business, etc. But alms are due only when the property amounts to a certain value, and has been in the possession of a person for one whole year; nor are any due from cattle employed in agriculture or in the carrying of burdens. Besides, at the end of the month of Ramazân (the month of fasting), and on the day of the *Id-ul-Fitr*, the festival which celebrates the close of the Moslem Lent, each head of a family has to give away in alms, for himself and for every member of his household, and for each guest who breaks his fast and sleeps in his house during the month, a measure of wheat, barley, dates, raisins, rice, or any other grain, or the value of the same.

The rightful recipients of the alms, as pointed out by the practice of Mohammed and his disciples, are (1) the poor and the indigent; (2) those who help in the collection and distribution of the obligatory alms; (3) slaves, who wish to buy their freedom and have not the means for so doing; (4) debtors, who cannot pay their debts; (5) travellers and strangers. General charity is inculcated by the Koran in the most forcible terms. But the glory of Islâm consists in having embodied the beautiful sentiment of Jesus into definite laws.

The wisdom which incorporated into Islâm the time-honoured custom of annual pilgrimage to Mecca and to the shrine of the Kaaba, has breathed into Mohammed's religion a freemasonry and brotherhood of faith in spite of sectarian divisions. The eyes of the whole Moslem world fixed on that central spot, keep alive in the bosom of each some spark of the celestial fire which lighted up the earth in that century of darkness. Here, again, the wisdom of the inspired Lawgiver shines forth in the negative part of the enactment, in the conditions necessary to make the injunction obligatory:—(1) ripeness of intelligence and discernment; (2) perfect freedom and liberty; (3) possession of the means of transport and subsistence during the journey; (4) possession of means sufficient to support the pilgrim's family during his absence; (5) the possibility and practicability of the voyage.

Owing to the minute regulations, almost Brahminical in their strictness, in force among the heathen Arabs regarding the lawful or unlawful character of various kinds of food, the Teacher of Islâm had frequently to admonish his followers that, with certain exceptions, all food was lawful. "And eat of what God hath given you for food that which is lawful and wholesome: and fear God, in whom ye believe." "Say," says the Koran, "I find not in what hath been revealed to me aught forbidden to the eater to eat, except it be that which dieth of itself, or blood poured forth, or swine's flesh, for that is an abomination, and meat which has been slain in the name of other than God [idols]." This is amplified in the fifth sura, which is also directed against various savage and idolatrous practices of the pagan Arabs. "That which dieth of itself, and blood, and swine's flesh, and all that hath been sacrificed under the invocation of any other name than that of God, and the strangled, and the killed by a blow or by a fall, or by goring, and that which hath been eaten by beasts of prey, unless ye give the death-stroke your-selves, and that which hath been sacrificed on the blocks of stone, is forbidden to you: and to make division of the slain by consulting the arrows, is impiety in you." "Eat ye of the good things wherewith we have provided you and give thanks to God."

Intoxication and gambling, the curse of Christian communities, and the bane of all uncultured and inferior natures, and excesses of all kinds, were rigorously prohibited.

Nothing can be simpler or more in accord with the advance of the hu-man intellect than the teachings of the Arabian Prophet. The few rules for religious ceremonial which he prescribed were chiefly with the object of main-taining discipline and uniformity, so necessary in certain stages of society; but they were by no means of an inflexible character. He allowed them to be broken in cases of illness or other causes. "God wishes to make things easy for you, for," says the Koran, "man was created weak." The legal principles which he enunciated were either delivered as answers to questions put to him as the Chief Magistrate of Medina, or to remove or correct patent evils. The Prophet's Islâm recognised no ritual likely to distract the mind from the thought of the one God; no law to keep enchained the conscience of advanc-ing humanity.

The ethical code of Islâm is thus summarised in the fourth Sura: "Come, I will rehearse what your Lord hath enjoined on you—that ye assign not to Him a partner; that ye be good to your parents; and that ye slay not your children because of poverty: for them and for you will We provide; and that ye come not near to pollutions, outward or inward; and that ye slay not a soul whom God hath forbidden, unless by right . . . and draw not nigh to the wealth of the orphan, save so as to better it . . . and when ye pronounce judgment then be just, though it be the affair of a kinsman. And God's com-pact fulfil ye; that is, what He hath ordained to you. Verily, this is my right way; follow it, then." And again, "Blessed are they who believe and humbly offer their thanks-giving to their Lord . . . who are constant in their charity, and who guard their chastity, and who observe their trust and covenants . . . Verily, God bids you do justice and good, and give to kindred their due; and He forbids you to sin and to do wrong and oppress."

"Faith and charity," to use the words of the Christian historian, "are not incompatible with external rites and positive institutions, which, indeed, are necessary in this imperfect state to keep alive a sense of religion in the common mass." And, accordingly, Mohammed had attached a few rites to his teachings in order to give a more tangible conception to the generality of mankind. Jesus himself had instituted two rites, baptism and the "Holy Supper." Probably, had he lived longer, he would have added more. But one thing is certain, that had a longer career been vouchsafed to him, he would have placed his teachings on a more systematic basis. This fundamental defect in Christianity has been, in fact, the real cause of the assembling of councils and convocations for the establishment of articles and dogmas, which snap asunder at every slight tension of reason and free thought. The work of Jesus was left unfinished. It was reserved for another Teacher to systematise the laws of morality.

Our relations with our Creator are matters of conscience; our relations with our fellow-beings must be matters of positive rules; and what higher sanction—to use a legal expression—can be attached to the enforcement of the relative duties of man to man than the sanction of religion. Religion is not to be regarded merely as a subject for unctuous declamations by "select preachers," or as some strange theory for the peculiar gratification of dreamy minds. Religion ought to mean the rule of life; its chief object ought to be the elevation of humanity towards that perfection which is the end of our existence. The religion, therefore, which places on a systematic basis the fundamental principles of morality, regulating social obligations and human duties, which brings us nearer and nearer, by its compatibility with the highest development of intellect, to the All-Perfect—that religion, we say, has the greatest claim to our consideration and respect. It is the distinctive characteristic of Islâm, as taught by Mohammed, that it combines within itself the grandest and the most prominent features in all ethnic and catholic religions compatible with the reason and moral intuition of man. It is not merely a system of positive moral rules, based on a true conception of human progress, but it is also "the establishment of certain principles, the enforcement of certain dispositions, the cultivation of a certain temper of mind, which the conscience is to apply to the ever-varying exigencies of time and place." The Teacher of Islâm preached, in a thousand varied ways, universal love and brotherhood as the emblem of the love borne towards God. "How do you think God will know you when you are in His presence—by your love of your children, of your kin, of your neighbours, of your fellow-creatures?" "Do you love your Creator? love your fellow-beings first." "Do you wish to approach the Lord? love His creatures, love for them what you love yourself, reject for them what you reject for yourself, do unto them what you wish to be done unto you." He condemned in scathing language the foulness of impurity, the meanness of hypocrisy, and the ungodliness of self-deceit. He proclaimed, in unmistakable terms, the preciousness of truth, charity, and brotherly love.

The wonderful adaptability of Islâmic precepts to all ages and nations; their entire concordance with the light of reason; the absence of all mysterious doctrines to cast a shade of sentimental ignorance round the primal truths implanted in the human breast,—all prove that Islâm represents the latest development of the religious faculties of our being. Those who have ignored the historic significance of some of its precepts have deemed that their seeming harshness, or unadaptability to present modes of thought ought to exclude it from any claim to universality. But a little inquiry into the historic value of laws and precepts, a little more fairness in the examination of facts, would evince the temporary character of such rules as may appear scarcely consonant with the requirements or prejudices of modern times. The catholicity of Islâm, its expansiveness, and its charity towards all moral creeds, has been utterly mistaken, perverted, or wilfully concealed by the bigotry of rival religions.

"Verily," says the Koran, "those who believe (the Moslems), and those who are Jews, Christians, or Sabæans, whoever hath faith in God and the last day (future existence), and worketh that which is right and good,—for them shall be the reward with their Lord; there will come no fear on them; neither shall they be grieved."

The same sentiment is repeated in similar words in the fifth Sura; and a hundred other passages prove that Islâm does not confine "salvation" to the followers of Mohammed alone:—"To every one have we given a law and a way. . . . And if God had pleased, He would have made you all (all mankind) one people (people of one religion). But He hath done otherwise, that He might try you in that which He hath severally given unto you: wherefore press forward in good works. Unto God shall ye return, and He will tell you that concerning which ye disagree."

Of all the religions of the world that have ruled the conscience of mankind, the Islâm of Mohammed alone combines both the conceptions which have in different ages furnished the mainspring of human conduct,—the consciousness of human dignity, so valued in the ancient philosophies, and the sense of human sinfulness, so dear to the Christian apologist. The belief that man will be judged by his work solely, throws the Moslem on the practice of self-denial and universal charity; the belief in Divine Providence, in the mercy, love, and omnipotence of God, leads him to self-humiliation before the Almighty, and to the practice of those heroic virtues which have given rise to the charge that the virtues of Islâm are stoical, patience, resignation, and firmness in the trials of life. It leads him to interrogate his conscience with nervous anxiety, to study with scrupulous care the motives that actuate him, to distrust his own strength, and to rely upon the assistance of an Almighty and All-Loving Power in the conflict between good and evil.

In some religions the precepts which inculcated duties have been so utterly devoid of practicability, so completely wanting in a knowledge of human nature, and partaking so much of the dreamy vagueness of enthusiasts, as to become in the real battles of life simply useless. The practical character of a religion, its abiding influence on the common relations of mankind, in the affairs of everyday life, its power on the masses, are the true criteria for judging of its universality. We do not look to exceptional minds to recognise the nature of a religion. We search among the masses to understand its true character. Does it exercise deep power over them? does it elevate them? does it regulate their conception of rights and duties? does it, if carried to the South Sea islander, or preached to the Caffrarians, improve or degrade them?—are the questions we naturally ask. In Islâm is joined a lofty idealism with the most rationalistic practicality. It did not ignore human nature; it never entangled itself in the tortuous pathways which lie outside the domains of the actual and the real. Its object, like that of other systems, was the elevation of humanity towards the absolute ideal of perfection; but it attained, or tries to attain, this object by grasping the truth that the nature of man is, in his existence, imperfect. If it did not say, "If thy brother smite thee on one cheek, turn thou the other also to him"; if it allowed the punishment of the wanton wrong-doer to the extent of the injury he had done, it also taught, in fervid words and varied strains, the practice of forgiveness and benevolence, and the return of good for evil:—"Who speaketh better," says the Koran, "than he who inviteth unto God, and worketh good? . . . Good and evil shall not be held equal. Turn away evil with that which is better." And again, speaking of paradise, it says, "It is prepared for the godly, who give alms in prosperity and adversity, who bridle their anger, and forgive men; for God loveth the beneficent."

The practice of these noble precepts does not lie enshrined in the limbo of false sentimentalism. With the true follower of the Prophet they form the active principles of life. History has preserved, for the admiration of wondering posterity, many examples of patience under suffering exhibited by the followers of other creeds. But the practice of the virtue of patient forgiveness is easier in adversity, when we have no power to punish the evil-doer, than in prosperity. It is related of Husain, the noble martyr of Kerbela, that a slave having once thrown the contents of a scalding dish over him as he sat at dinner, fell on his knees and repeated the verse of the Koran, "Paradise is for those who bridle their anger." "I am not angry," answered Husain. The slave proceeded, "and for those who forgive men." "I forgive you." The slave, however, finished the verse, adding, "for God loveth the beneficent." "I give you your liberty and four hundred pieces of silver," replied Husain.

The author of the *Kashshâf* thus sums up the essence of the Islâmic teachings: "Seek again him who drives you away; give to him who takes away from you; pardon him who injures you: for God loveth that you should cast into the depth of your soul the roots of His perfections."

In the purity of its aspiration, can anything be more beautiful than the following: "The servants of the Merciful are they that walk upon the earth softly; and when the ignorant speak unto them, they reply, Peace! they that spend the night worshipping their Lord, prostrate, and standing, and resting: those that, when they spend, are neither profuse nor niggardly, but take a middle course: . . . those that invoke not with God any other God, and slay not a soul that God hath forbidden otherwise than by right; and commit not fornication: . . . they who bear not witness to that which is false; and when they pass by vain sport, they pass it by with dignity: who say, 'Oh, our Lord, grant us of our wives and children such as shall be a comfort unto us, and make us examples unto the pious,'—these shall be the rewarded, for that they persevered; and they shall be accosted in paradise with welcome and salutation:—For ever therein,—a fair abode and resting place!"

This is the Islâm of Mohammed. It is not "a mere creed; it is a life to be lived in the present"—a religion of right-doing, right-thinking, and right-speaking, founded on divine love, universal charity, and the equality of man in the sight of the Lord. However much the modern professors of Islâm may have dimmed the glory of their Prophet (and a volume might also be written on the defects of modern Mohammedanism), the religion which enshrines righteousness and "justification by work" deserves the recognition of the lovers of humanity.

مي نواني از ره آسـمان شدن بر آسـمان

راست باش و راست رو كانجا نباشد كاستي

"Wishest thou to approach God?
Live purely, and act righteously."

Jalâl un-din Rûmi says,—

از بهايم بهره داري وز ملايك نيز هم

بگذر از بهايم تا از ملايك هم بگذري

"Thou partakest of the nature of the beast as well as the angel;
Leave the nature of the beast, that thou mayest surpass the angel."

The present life was the seed-ground of the future. To work in all humility of spirit for the human good, to strive with all energy to approach the perfection of the All-Perfect, is the essential principle of Islâm. The true Moslem is a true Christian, in that he accepts the ministry of Jesus, and tries to work out the moral preached by him. Why should not the true Christian do honour to the Preacher who put the finishing stroke to the work of the earlier Masters? Did not he call back the wandering forces of the world into the channel of progress?

Excepting for the conception of the sonship of Jesus, there is no fundamental difference between Christianity and Islâm. In their essence they are one and the same; both are the outcome of the same spiritual forces working in humanity. One was a protest against the heartless materialism of the Jews and the Romans; the other a revolt against the degrading idolatry of the Arabs, their ferocious customs and usages. Christianity, preached among a more settled and civilised people subject to an organised government, had to contend with comparatively milder evils. Islâm, preached among warring tribes and clans, had to fight against all the instincts of self-interest and ancient superstition. Christianity, arrested in its progress towards the East by a man of cultured but bizarre character, who, though a Jew by birth, was by education an Alexandrian Greek, was carried to Greece and Rome, and there gathering up the pagan civilisation of centuries, gave birth to new ideas and doctrines. Christianity ceased to be Christian the moment it was transplanted from the home of its birth. It became the religion of Paul, and ceased to be that of Jesus. The pantheons of ancient paganism were tottering to their fall. Greek and Alexandrian philosophy had prepared the Roman world for the recognition of an incarnate God—a demiurgus, an Æon born in the bosom of eternity, and this conception imbedded itself in Pauline Christianity. Modern idealistic Christianity, which is more a philosophy than a positive religion, is the product of centuries of pre-Christian and post-Christian civilisation. Islâm was preached among a people, among conditions social and moral, wholly divergent. Had it broken down the barrier which was raised against it by a degraded Christianity, and made its way among the higher races of the earth, its progress and its character would have presented a totally different aspect from what it now offers to the observer among the less cultured Moslem communities. Like rivers flowing through varied tracts, both these creeds have produced results in accordance with the nature of the soil through which they have found their course. The Mexican who castigates himself with cactus leaves, the idol-worshipping South American, the lower strata of Christian nations, are hardly in any sense Christians. There exists a wide gulf between them and the leaders of modern Christian thought. Islâm, wherever it has found its way among culturable and progressive nations, has shown itself in complete accord with progressive tendencies, it has assisted civilisation, it has idealised religion.

A religion has to be eminently positive in its "commandments and prohibitions" to exercise an abiding salutary influence on the ignorant and uncultured. The higher and more spiritualised minds are often able to forge on the anvils of their own hearts, lines of duty in relation to their fellow creatures without reference to outside directions. They are in commune with God and are guided by the consciousness of right and wrong, of truth and purity which had grown up with their being. Plato and Aristotle, who had never received the light of the Semitic revelations, spoke to the world of the highest principles of morality in as distinct terms as the great prophets. They too had heard the voice of God, and were lifted up to Him by their own thoughts.

To the mass of mankind, however, sunk either in ignorance or barbarism, for the uncultured and the sodden, moral enunciations convey no meaning unless they are addressed in a positive form and formulated with the precision of enactments surrounded with definite sanctions. The ethical side of a religion does not appeal to their feelings or sentiments; and philosophical conceptions exercise no influence on their minds, their daily conduct or their lives.

They are swayed far more by authority and precedent than by sermons on abstract principles. They require definite prescriptions to regulate not only their relations towards their fellow-beings but also towards their Creator whom, in the absence of such rules, they are apt to forget.

The success of Islâm in the seventh century of the Christian era, and its rapid and marvellous diffusion over the surface of the globe, were due to the fact that it recognised this essential need of human nature. To a world of wrangling sects and creeds, to whom words were of far greater importance than practice, it spoke in terms of positive command from an Absolute Source. Amidst the moral and social wreck in which it found its birth, it aimed at the integration of the worship of a Personal Will, and thereby to recall humanity to the observance of duty which alone pointed to the path of spiritual development. And by its success in lifting up the lower races to a higher level of social morality it proved to the world the need of a positive system. It taught them sobriety, temperance, charity, justice and equality as the commandments of God. Its affirmation of the principle of equality of man and man and its almost socialistic tendency represented the same phase of thought that had found expression on the shores of Galilee. But even in his most exalted mood the great Teacher of Islâm did not forget the limitations imposed on individual capacity which occasion economic inequalities.

Alas for the latter-day professors of Islâm! The blight of patristicism has ruined the blossom of true religion and a true devotional spirit.

A Christian preacher has pointed out with great force the distinction between religion and theology, and the evils which have followed in his Church from the confusion of the two. What has happened in Christianity has happened in Islâm. Practice has given way to the mockery of profession, ceremonialism has taken the place of earnest and faithful work,—doing good to mankind for the sake of doing good, and for the love of God. Enthusiasm has died out, and devotion to God and His Prophet are meaningless words. The earnestness without which human existence is no better than that of the brute creation, earnestness in right-doing and right-thinking, is absent. The Moslems of the present day have ignored the spirit in a hopeless love for the letter. Instead of living up to the ideal preached by the Master, instead of "striving to excel in good works," "of being righteous"; instead of loving God, and for the sake of His love loving His creatures,—they have made themselves the slaves of opportunism and outward observance. It was natural that in their reverence and admiration for the Teacher his early disciples should stereotype his ordinary mode of life, crystallise the passing incidents of a chequered career, imprint on the heart orders, rules, and regulations enunciated for the common exigencies of the day in an infant society. But to suppose that the greatest Reformer the world has ever produced, the greatest upholder of the sovereignty of Reason, the man who proclaimed that the universe was governed and guided by law and order, and that the law of nature meant progressive development, ever contemplated that even those injunctions which were called forth by the passing necessities of a semi-civilised people should become immutable to the end of the world, is doing an injustice to the Prophet of Islâm.

No one had a keener perception than he of the necessities of this world of progress with its ever-changing social and moral phenomena, nor of the likelihood that the revelations vouchsafed to him might not meet all possible contingencies. When Muâz was appointed as governor of Yemen, he was asked by the Prophet by what rule he would be guided in his administration of that province. "By the law of the Koran," said Muâz. "But if you find no direction therein?" "Then I will act according to the example of the Prophet." "But if that fails?" "Then I will exercise my own judgment." The Prophet approved highly of the answer of his disciple, and commended it to the other delegates.

The great Teacher, who was fully conscious of the exigencies of his own times, and the requirements of the people with whom he had to deal,—people sunk in a slough of social and moral despond,—with his keen insight and breadth of views, perceived, and one may say foretold, that a time would come when the accidental and temporary regulations would have to be differentiated from the permanent and general. "Ye are in an age," he declared, "in which, if ye abandon one-tenth of what is ordered, ye will be ruined. After this, a time will come when he who shall observe one-tenth of what is now ordered will be redeemed."

وَعَنْ اَبِي هُرَيْرَةَ قَالَ قَلَ رَسُوْلُ اللَّهِ صَلَّى اللَّهُ عَلَيْهِ وَسَلَّمَ اِنَّكُمْ فِيْ زَمَانٍ مَنْ

تَرَكَ مِنْكُمْ عُشْرَ مَا اُمِرَبِهِ هَلَكَ ثُمَّ يَاتِيْ زَمَانٌ مَنْ عَمِلَ مِنْهُمْ عُشْرَمَا اُمِرَبِهِ نَجَا

رَوَاهُ التِّرْمِذِيُّ ۔ مِشْكُوةُ الْمَصَابِيْحِ ۔ بَابُ الْاِعْتِصَامِ بِالْكِتَابِ وَالسُّنَّةِ

As we have already observed, the blight which has fallen on Musulman nations is not due to the teachings of the Master. No religion contained greater promise of development, no faith was purer, or more in conformity with the progressive demands of humanity.

The present stagnation of the Musulman communities is principally due to the notion which has fixed itself on the minds of the generality of Moslems, that the right to the exercise of private judgment ceased with the early legists, that its exercise in modern times is sinful, and that a Moslem in order to be regarded as an orthodox follower of Mohammed should belong to one or the other of the schools established by the schoolmen of Islâm, and abandon his judgment absolutely to the interpretations of men who lived in the ninth century, and could have no conception of the necessities of the twentieth.

Among the Sunnis, it is the common belief that since the four Imâms, no doctor has arisen qualified to interpret the laws of the Prophet. No account is taken of the altered circumstances in which Moslems are now placed; the conclusions at which these learned legists arrived several centuries ago are held to be equally applicable to the present day. Among the Shiahs, the Akhbâri will not allow his judgment to travel beyond the dictates of "the expounders of the law." The Prophet had consecrated reason as the highest and noblest function of the human intellect. Our schoolmen and their servile followers have made its exercise a sin and a crime.

As among Christians, so among Moslems. The lives and conduct of a large number of Moslems at the present day are governed less by the precepts and teachings of the Master, and more by the theories and opinions of the *mujtahids* and *imâms* who have tried, each according to his light, to construe the revelations vouchsafed to the Teacher. Like men in a crowd listening to a preacher who from a lofty position addresses a large multitude and from his vantage ground overlooks a vast area, they observed only their immediate surroundings, and, without comprehending the wider meaning of his words or the nature of the audience whom he addressed, adapted his utterances to their own limited notions of human needs and human progress. Oblivious of the universality of the Master's teachings, unassisted by his spirit, devoid of his inspiration, they forgot that the Prophet, from the pinnacle of his genius, had spoken to all humanity. They mixed up the temporary with the permanent, the universal with the particular. Like many of the ecclesiastics of Christendom, not a few were the servants of sovereigns and despots whose demands were not consistent with the precepts of the Master. Canons were invented, theories started, traditions discovered, and glosses put upon his words utterly at variance with their spirit. And hence it is that most of the rules and regulations which govern now the conscience of so many professors of the faith are hardly derived from any express and positive declarations of the Koran, but for the most part from the lego-religious books with which the Islâmic world was flooded in the later centuries. "Just as the Hebrews deposed their Pentateuch in favour of the Talmud," justly observes an English writer, "so the Moslems have abolished the Koran in favour of the traditions and decisions of the learned." "We do not mean to say," he adds most pertinently, "that any Mohammedan if asked what was the text-book of his religion, would answer anything but the 'Koran'; but we do mean that practically it is not the Koran that guides his belief or practice. In the Middle Ages of Christendom it was not the New Testament, but the *Summa Theologica* of Thomas Aquinas, that decided questions of orthodoxy; and in the present day, does the orthodox churchman usually derive his creed from a personal investigation of the teaching of Christ in the Gospels? Probably, if he refers to a document at all, the Church Catechism contents him; or if he be of a peculiarly inquiring disposition, a perusal of the Thirty-nine Articles will resolve all doubts. Yet he too would say his religion was drawn from the Gospels, and would not confess to the medium through which it was filtered. In precisely the same way modern Mohammedanism is constructed, and a large part of what Moslems now believe and practise is not to be found in the Koran at all."

And yet each system, each school contains germs of improvement, and if development is now stopped, it is not even the fault of the lawyers. It is due to a want of apprehension of the spirit of the Master's enunciations, and even of those of the fathers of the Church.

In the Western world, the Reformation was ushered in by the Renaissance and the progress of Europe commenced when it threw off the shackles of Ecclesiasticism. In Islâm also, enlightenment must precede reform; and, before there can be a renovation of religious life, the mind must first escape from the bondage which centuries of literal interpretation and the doctrine of "conformity" have imposed upon it. The formalism that does not appeal to the heart of the worshipper must be abandoned; externals must be subordinated to the inner feelings; and the lessons of ethics must be impressed on the plastic mind; then alone can we hope for that enthusiasm in the principles of duty taught by the Prophet of Islâm. The reformation of Islâm will begin when once it is recognised that divine words rendered into any language retain their divine character and that devotions offered in any tongue are acceptable to God. The Prophet himself had allowed his foreign disciples to say their prayers in their own tongue. He had expressly permitted others to recite the Koran in their respective dialects; and had declared that it was revealed in seven languages.

In the earliest ages of Islâm there was a consensus of opinion that devotion without understanding was useless. Imâm Abû Hanifa considered the recitation of the namâz and also of the Khutba or sermon, lawful and valid in any language. The disciples of Abû Hanîfa, Abû Yusuf and Mohammed, have accepted the doctrine of their master with a certain variation. They hold that when a person does not know Arabic, he may validly offer his devotions in any other language.

There is, however, one great and cogent reason why the practice of reciting prayers in Arabic should be maintained wherever it is possible and practicable. Not because it was the language of the Prophet, but because it has become the language of Islâm and maintains the unity of sentiment throughout the Islâmic world. And wherein lies more strength than in unity?

53

THE SŪFĪ MESSAGE
Inayat Khan

The mystic tradition has played a major role within Islam, and those who have been adherents to that tradition have been known as Sūfīs. Many of the great figures in Islamic history have been Sūfīs, and the influence of their thought and actions upon their culture has been considerable. Nevertheless, due to its eso- teric character, one finds it quite difficult to characterize this form of religion, since it has no creed or generally accepted rules of practice. The emphasis here, as in all mysticism, is upon the indi- vidual's relationship to the divine throughout all aspects of his life; and this relationship, being personal and subjective, is usually impossible to express adequately in words. Nevertheless, mystics of all religions frequently have attempted to give verbal expression to their practices in order that the ideal they seek might be con- veyed to others. One of the best known of recent Sūfīs was Inayat Khan, an Indian musician, who became an apostle of Sūfīism in the western world in 1910 and who continued to lecture there until his death in 1927. Inayat Khan attempted to distill some basic traits from the Sūfī experience so that he might communi- cate intelligibly to audiences to whom this religious approach was foreign. He has captured some of the major features of Sūfīism in a clear and concise exposition. The organization which Hazrat Inayat Khan founded, the Sūfī Movement, is still in existence with headquarters in Geneva.

SUFI THOUGHTS

There are ten principal Sufi thoughts, which comprise all the important subjects with which the inner life of man is concerned.

i

'There is One God, the Eternal, the Only Being; none exists save He.'
The God of the Sufi is the God of every creed, and the God of all.

Hazrat Inayat Khan, *The Sufi Message of Hazrat Inayat Khan* (London: Barrie and Rockliff, 1961–63), vol. I, pp. 13–22, vol. IX, pp. 247–251, 264–266. Reprinted by permission of the Sufi Movement and its Secretary-General, Baron F. van Pallandt.

Names make no difference to him. Allah, God, Gott, Dieu, Khuda, Brahma, or Bhagwan, all these names and more are the names of his God; and yet to him God is beyond the limitation of name. He sees his God in the sun, in the fire, in the idol which diverse sects worship; and he recognizes Him in all the forms of the universe, yet knowing Him to be beyond all form: God in all, and all in God, He being the Seen and the Unseen, the Only Being. God to the Sufi is not only a religious belief, but also the highest ideal the human mind can conceive.

The Sufi, forgetting the self and aiming at the attainment of the divine ideal, walks constantly all through life in the path of love and light. In God the Sufi sees the perfection of all that is in the reach of man's perception and yet he knows Him to be above human reach. He looks to Him as the lover to his beloved, and takes all things in life as coming from Him, with perfect resignation. The sacred name of God is to him as medicine to the patient. The divine thought is the compass by which he steers the ship to the shores of immortality. The God-ideal is to a Sufi as a lift by which he raises himself to the eternal goal, the attainment of which is the only purpose of his life.

ii

'There is One Master, the Guiding Spirit of all Souls, Who constantly leads His followers towards the light.'

The Sufi understands that although God is the source of all knowledge, inspiration, and guidance, yet man is the medium through which God chooses to impart His knowledge to the world. He imparts it through one who is a man in the eyes of the world, but God in his consciousness. It is the mature soul that draws blessings from the heavens, and God speaks through that soul. Although the tongue of God is busy speaking through all things, yet in order to speak to the deaf ears of many among us, it is necessary for Him to speak through the lips of man. He has done this all through the history of man, every great teacher of the past having been this Guiding Spirit living the life of God in human guise. In other words, their human guise consists of various coats worn by the same person, who appeared to be different in each. Shiva, Buddha, Rama, Krishna on the one side, Abraham, Moses, Jesus, Mohammad on the other; and many more, known or unknown to history, always one and the same person.

Those who saw the person and knew Him recognized Him in whatever form or guise; those who could only see the coat went astray. To the Sufi therefore there is only one Teacher, however differently He may be named at different periods of history, and He comes constantly to awaken humanity from the slumber of this life of illusion, and to guide man onwards towards divine perfection. As the Sufi progresses in this view he recognizes his Master, not only in the holy ones, but in the wise, in the foolish, in the saint and in the sinner, and has never allowed the Master who is One alone, and the only One who can be and who ever will be, to disappear from his sight.

The Persian word for Master is Murshid. The Sufi recognizes the Murshid in all beings of the world, and is ready to learn from young and old, educated and uneducated, rich and poor, without questioning from whom he learns. Then he begins to see the light of *Risalat*, the torch of truth which shines before him in every being and thing in the universe. Thus he sees *Rasul*, his Divine Message Bearer, a living identity before him. Thus the Sufi sees the vision of God, the worshipped deity, in His immanence, manifest in nature, and life now becomes for him a perfect revelation both within and without.

It is often for no other reason than clinging to the personality of their particular teacher, claiming for him superiority over other teachers, and degrading a teacher held in the same esteem by others, that people have separated themselves from one another, and caused most of the wars and factions and contentions which history records among the children of God.

What the Spirit of Guidance is, can be further explained as follows: as in man there is a faculty for art, music, poetry and science, so in him is the faculty or spirit of guidance; it is better to call it spirit because it is the supreme faculty from which all the others originate. As we see that in every person there is some artistic faculty, but not everyone is an artist, as everyone can hum a tune but only one in a thousand is a musician, so every person possesses this faculty in some form and to a limited degree; but the spirit of guidance is found among few indeed of the human race.

A Sanskrit poet says, 'Jewels are stones, but cannot be found everywhere; the sandal is a tree, but does not grow in every forest; as there are many elephants, but only one king elephant, so there are human beings all over the world, but the real human being is rarely to be found.'

When we arise above faculty and consider the spirit of guidance, we shall find that it is consummated in the Bodhisatva, the spiritual teacher or divine messenger. There is a saying that the reformer is the child of civilization, but the prophet is its father. This spirit has always existed, and must always exist; and in this way from time to time the message of God has been given.

iii

'There is One Holy Book, the sacred manuscript of nature, the only scripture which can enlighten the reader.'

Most people consider as sacred scriptures only certain books or scrolls written by the hand of man, and carefully preserved as holy, to be handed down to posterity as divine revelation. Men have fought and disputed over the authenticity of these books, have refused to accept any other book of similar character, and, clinging thus to the book and losing the sense of it, have formed diverse sects. The Sufi has in all ages respected all such books, and has traced in the Vedanta, Zendavesta, Kabala, Bible, Qur'an, and all other sacred scriptures, the same truth which he reads in the incorruptible manuscript of nature, the only Holy Book, the perfect and living model that teaches the inner law of life; all scriptures before nature's manuscript are as little pools of water before the ocean.

To the eye of the seer every leaf of the tree is a page of the holy book that contains divine revelation, and he is inspired every moment of his life by constantly reading and understanding the holy script of nature.

When man writes, he inscribes characters upon rock, leaf, paper, wood or steel; when God writes, the characters He writes are living creatures.

It is when the eye of the soul is opened and the sight is keen that the Sufi can read the divine law in the manuscript of nature; and that which the teachers of humanity have taught to their followers was derived by them from the same source; they expressed what little it is possible to express in words, and so they preserved the inner truth when they themselves were no longer there to reveal it.

iv

'There is One Religion, the unswerving progress in the right direction towards the ideal, which fulfils the life's purpose of every soul.'

Religion in the Sanskrit language is termed *Dharma*, which means duty. The duty of every individual is religion. 'Every soul is born for a certain purpose, and the light of that purpose is kindled in his soul', says Sa'di. This explains why the Sufi in his tolerance allows everyone to have his own path, and does not compare the principles of others with his own, but allows freedom of thought to everyone, since he himself is a freethinker.

Religion, in the conception of a Sufi, is the path that leads man towards the attainment of his ideal, worldly as well as heavenly. Sin and virtue, right and wrong, good and bad are not the same in the case of every individual; they are according to his grade of evolution and state of life. Therefore the Sufi concerns himself little with the name of the religion or the place of worship. All places are sacred enough for his worship, and all religions convey to him the religion of his soul. 'I saw Thee in the sacred Ka'ba and in the temple of the idol also Thee I saw.'

v

'There is One Law, the law of reciprocity, which can be observed by a selfless conscience, together with a sense of awakened justice.'

Man spends his life in the pursuit of all that seems to him to be profitable for himself, and when so absorbed in self-interest in time he even loses touch with his own real interest. Man has made laws to suit himself, but they are laws by which he can get the better of another. It is this that he calls justice, and it is only that which is done to him by another that he calls injustice. A peaceful and harmonious life with his fellow-men cannot be led until the sense of justice has been awakened in him by a selfless conscience. As the judicial authorities of the world intervene between two persons who are at variance, knowing that they have a right to intervene when the two parties in dispute are blinded by personal interest, so the Almighty Power intervenes in all disputes however small or great.

It is the law of reciprocity which saves man from being exposed to the higher powers, as a considerate man has less chance of being brought before the court. The sense of justice is awakened in a perfectly sober mind; that is, one which is free from the intoxication of youth, strength, power, possession, command, birth, or rank. It seems a net profit when one does not give but takes, or when one gives less and takes more; but in either case there is really a greater loss than profit; for every such profit spreads a cover over the sense of justice within, and when many such covers have veiled the sight, man becomes blind even to his own profit. It is like standing in one's own light. 'Blind here remains blind in the hereafter.'

Although the different religions, in teaching man how to act harmoniously and peacefully with his fellow-men, have given out different laws, they all meet in this one truth: do unto others as thou wouldst they should do unto thee. The Sufi, in taking a favour from another, enhances its value, and in accepting what another does to him he makes allowance.

<h2 style="text-align:center">vi</h2>

'There is One Brotherhood, the human brotherhood which unites the children of earth indiscriminately in the Fatherhood of God.'

The Sufi understands that the one life emanating from the inner Being is manifested on the surface as the life of variety; and in this world of variety man is the finest manifestation, for he can realize in his evolution the oneness of the inner being even in the external existence of variety. But he evolves to this ideal, which is the only purpose of his coming on earth, by uniting himself with another.

Man unites with others in the family tie, which is the first step in his evolution, and yet families in the past have fought with each other, and have taken vengeance upon one another for generations, each considering his cause to be the only true and righteous one. Today man shows his evolution in uniting with his neighbours and fellow-citizens, and even developing within himself the spirit of patriotism for his nation. He is greater in this respect than those in the past; and yet men so united nationally have caused the catastrophe of the modern wars, which will be regarded by the coming generations in the same light in which we now regard the family feuds of the past.

There are racial bonds which widen the circle of unity still more, but it has always happened that one race has looked down on the other.

The religious bond shows a still higher ideal. But it has caused diverse sects, which have opposed and despised each other for thousands of years, and have caused endless splits and divisions among men. The germ of separation exists even in such a wide scope for brotherhood, and however widespread the brotherhood may be, it cannot be a perfect one as long as it separates man from man.

The Sufi, realizing this, frees himself from national, racial, and religious boundaries, uniting himself in the human brotherhood, which is devoid of the differences and distinctions of class, caste, creed, race, nation, or religion, and unites mankind in the universal brotherhood.

vii

'There is One Moral, the love which springs forth from self-denial and and blooms in deeds of beneficence.'

There are moral principles taught to mankind by various teachers, by many traditions, one differing from the other, which are like separate drops coming out of the fountain. But when we look at the stream, we find there is but one stream, although it turns into several drops on falling. There are many moral principles, just as many drops fall from one fountain; but there is one stream that is at the source of all, and that is love. It is love that gives birth to hope, patience, endurance, forgiveness, tolerance, and to all moral principles. All deeds of kindness and beneficence take root in the soil of the loving heart. Generosity, charity, adaptability, an accommodating nature, even renunciation, are the offspring of love alone. The great, rare and chosen beings, who for ages have been looked up to as ideal in the world, are the possessors of hearts kindled with love. All evil and sin come from the lack of love.

People call love blind, but love in reality is the light of the sight. The eye can only see the surface; love can see much deeper. All ignorance is the lack of love. As fire when not kindled gives only smoke, but when kindled, the illuminating flame springs forth, so it is with love; it is blind when undeveloped, but, when its fire is kindled, the flame that lights the path of the traveller from mortality to everlasting life springs forth; the secrets of earth and heaven are revealed to the possessor of the loving heart, the lover has gained mastery over himself and others, and he not only communes with God but unites with Him.

'Hail to thee, then, O love, sweet madness! Thou who healest all our infirmities! Who art the physician of our pride and self-conceit! Who art our Plato and our Galen!' says Rumi.

viii

'There is One Object of Praise, the beauty which uplifts the heart of its worshippers through all aspects from the seen to the unseen.'

It is said in the Hadith, 'God is beautiful, and He loves beauty.'

This expresses the truth that man, who inherits the Spirit of God, has beauty in him and loves beauty, although that which is beautiful to one is not beautiful to another. Man cultivates the sense of beauty as he evolves, and prefers the higher aspect of beauty to the lower. But when he has observed the highest vision of beauty in the Unseen by a gradual evolution from praising the beauty in the seen world, then the entire existence becomes to him one single vision of beauty.

Man has worshipped God, beholding the beauty of sun, moon, stars, and planets; he has worshipped God in plants, in animals; he has recognized God in the beautiful merits of man, and he has with his perfect view of beauty found the source of all beauty in the Unseen, from whence all this springs, and in Whom all is merged.

The Sufi, realizing this, worships beauty in all its aspects, and sees the face of the Beloved in all that is seen, and the Beloved's spirit in the Unseen. So wherever he looks his ideal of worship is before him. 'Everywhere I look, I see Thy winning face; everywhere I go, I arrive at Thy dwelling-place.'

ix

'There is One Truth, the true knowledge of our being, within and without, which is the essence of all wisdom.'

Hazrat Ali says, 'Know thyself, and thou shalt know God.' It is the knowledge of self which blooms into the knowledge of God. Self-knowledge answers such problems as: whence have I come? Did I exist before I became conscious of my present existence? If I existed, as what did I exist? As an individual such as I now am, or as a multitude, or as an insect, bird, animal, spirit, jinn, or angel? What happens at death, the change to which every creature is subject? Why do I tarry here awhile? What purpose have I to accomplish here? What is my duty in life? In what does my happiness consist, and what is it that makes my life miserable? Those whose hearts have been kindled by the light from above, begin to ponder such questions but those whose souls are already illumined by the knowledge of the self understand them. It is they who give to individuals or to the multitudes the benefit of their knowledge, so that even men whose hearts are not yet kindled, and whose souls are not illuminated, may be able to walk on the right path that leads to perfection.

This is why people are taught in various languages, in various forms of worship, in various tenets in different parts of the world. It is one and the same truth; it is only seen in diverse aspects appropriate to the people and the time. It is only those who do not understand this who can mock at the faith of another, condemning to hell or destruction those who do not consider their faith to be the only true faith.

The Sufi recognizes the knowledge of self as the essence of all religions; he traces it in every religion, he sees the same truth in each, and therefore he regards all as one. Hence he can realize the saying of Jesus, 'I and my Father are one.' The difference between creature and Creator remains on his lips, not in his soul. This is what is meant by union with God. It is in reality the dissolving of the false self in the knowledge of the true self, which is divine, eternal, and all-pervading. 'He who attaineth union with God, his very self must lose,' said Amir.

X

'There is One Path, the annihilation of the false ego in the real, which raises the mortal to immortality, in which resides all perfection.'

'I passed away into nothingness—I vanished; and lo! I was all living.' All who have realized the secret of life understand that life is one, but that it exists in two aspects. First as immortal, all-pervading and silent; and secondly as mortal, active, and manifest in variety. The soul being of the first aspect becomes deluded, helpless, and captive by experiencing life in contact with the mind and body, which is of the next aspect. The gratification of the desires of the body and the fancies of the mind do not suffice for the purpose of the soul, which is undoubtedly to experience its own phenomena in the seen and the unseen, though its inclination is to be itself and not anything else. When delusion makes it feel that it is helpless, mortal and captive, it finds itself out of place. This is the tragedy of life, which keeps the strong and the weak, the rich and poor, all dissatisfied, constantly looking for something they do not know. The Sufi, realizing this, takes the path of annihilation, and, by the guidance of a teacher on the path, finds at the end of this journey that the destination was himself. As Iqbal says:

'I wandered in the pursuit of my own self; I was the traveller, and I am the destination.'

THE SUFI MESSAGE

The word *Message* in itself conveys a different meaning from that of an intellectual philosophy. There are two ideas prevailing in the world: one is that man has evolved through years and centuries, and the other that, as Solomon has said, there is nothing new under the sun. And this explains to us that divine truth has always been and always will be the same. No one can improve upon it, and nobody can give a new message. It is the divine tongue which at times has spoken louder, and at times in a whisper, and it is the consciousness of the divine spirit which made Christ say 'I am Alpha and Omega.' Those who limit Christ to the historic period of the life of the Prophet of Nazareth surely limit the message, in spite of his open declaration that he is the first and the last.

According to this point of view, the message has been given each time in a form suited to the evolution of the people in that particular age. Man divides, God unites, humanity. Man takes pleasure in thinking and feeling, 'I am different from you; you are different from me' in nationality, race, creed, or religion. In animals this feeling is still more pronounced. But as man evolves, his tendency is to unite, to become one. Did Jesus Christ come to form an exclusive community called Christian, or Buddha to found a creed called Buddhism? Or was it Mohammad's ideal to form a community called Mohammadan? On the contrary, the Prophet warned his disciples that they should not attach his name to his message, but that it should be called Islam, the Message of Peace.

Not one of the masters came with the thought of forming an exclusive community, or to give a certain religion. They came with the same message from one and the same God. Whether the message was in Sanskrit, Hebrew, Zend, or Arabic, it had one and the same meaning. The difference between religions is external; their inner meaning is one.

If man had only understood this, the world would have avoided many wars, for war has mostly been caused by religion, religon which was given to the world to establish peace and harmony. What a pity that war and disaster should come from the same source!

The Sufi message is a reminder to humanity, not to any one nation but to all; not to one but to every creed. It is a reminder of the truth taught by all the great teachers of humanity: that God, truth, religion are one, and that duality is only a delusion of human nature. Think then what a great task lies before this message, at this time when nation is against nation and race against race; when the followers of one religion are constantly working against the followers of another religon, and class against class; competition, hate, and prejudice prevailing everywhere. What will be the outcome of it all? What can poison produce? Not nectar; only poison. The message is not for one nation, race, or community; it is for the whole of humanity. Its one and only object is to bring about a better understanding between the divided sections of humanity by awakening their consciousness to the fact that humanity is one family. If one person in the family is ill or unhappy, this must certainly cause unhappiness to the whole family. Yet even this is not the most appropriate simile. Humanity is one body, the whole of life being one in its source and in its goal, its beginning and its end. No scientist will deny this. And if part of the body is in pain, sooner or later the whole body is affected; if our finger aches, our body is not free from pain. Thus no nation, race, or community can be considered as a separate part of humanity.

Today in education, in politics, in all directions of life, there seems to be an individualistic view, but where will such a tendency end, where will it lead humanity? If each one thinks he must get the better of another, where will be the harmony and peace for which all are longing, no matter to what race or religion they belong?

No doubt this condition has been brought about by a long-continued materialism and commercialism, which have taught every soul the spirit of competition and rivalry, the whole life of each being absorbed in guarding his own interests, and in trying to take the best in life for himself. Life is one continual battle, and only one thing can ease this battle: consideration for others, reciprocity, unselfishness instead of selfishness.

With selfishness as the central theme, the world's progress will never lead to the soul's desire and aim. It must culminate in destruction. At one time the call was to guard self-interest; now the moment has come for mankind to be given a message of understanding and consideration for one another, since individual peace and happiness depend upon the peace and happiness of the whole of humanity.

What is missing in modern education, in art and science, in social, political, and commercial life, is the ideal, the ideal which is the secret of heaven and earth, the mystery hidden behind both man and God. With all he possesses in the objective world, man is poor in the absence of the ideal, and it is this poverty which creates irritation, conflicts, and disagreements, thereby causing wars and disasters of all kinds. Man's greatest need today is for the exploration of the human personality, in order to find there the latent inspiration and power upon which to build the whole structure of his life. For life means not only to live, but to ennoble oneself and reach that perfection which is the innate yearning of the soul. The solution to the problem of the day is the awakening of the consciousness of humanity to the divinity of man. The undertone of all religions is the realization of the one life which culminates in the thought of unity. It is towards raising humanity to this consciousness that the efforts of the Sufi Movement are directed.

Very often people divide the esoteric or inner part of life from the exoteric or outer form of religion. But although to divide them in a conception is possible, to divide them in reality is like separating the head from the body. As the head linked with the body makes the form complete, so religion together with inner life makes the spiritual ideal perfect. Nevertheless, the thoughtful and wise of all ages, with their philosophical minds, with their scientific tendencies, with their intellectual strife, often thought of separating religion from the inner life. But when they are separated, it is just like bread without butter, it is like milk without sugar, it is like food without salt. And the reason why this tendency often appears, especially among thoughtful people, is a natural one. When life leaves the body, even those who loved the one who died begin to think that they should bury the body as soon as possible; for the one whom they loved is gone from it, and what is left is only a corpse. And so when the inner life, which is just like the breath in the body of religion, departs from it, then the religion becomes like a dead body; then even its most faithful adherents begin to feel that it is a corpse.

In all ages and in all periods of history we notice that there has been a limit to the number of years that a religion has lasted. During that time the religion prospered and was of benefit to humanity. Why? Because it had breath, it had spirituality. But when that inner life departed it was left like a corpse. Still the faithful kept to it, but those with intelligence could not do so any longer.

As the rain falls year after year, and gives new life and new sustenance to the earth, so it became neecssary that the new message of spiritual upliftment should come. But whenever it has come, people have fought against it, not knowing that it is the same truth, the same breath, the same soul of religion that had come again, not understanding the secret of religion. The rainfall of last year is not different from this year's; it is the same water, the same sustenance, the same energy. As vapour it rises and as raindrops it falls. It has always been the same message, only brought in different bottles and with new labels.

The most important philosophical point in religion is that besides all the moral principles and ethics that religion teaches, there is the central theme which can be traced as the nature of life, of spirit, and that is to make the perfect Being intelligible to the limited mind of man. To do this the ideal of God is preached. The central theme of every religion the messengers have brought was the God-ideal, and every one of them has tried his best to make a picture of that ideal, in order that the people of that time could easily grasp it and benefit by it, to fulfil the purpose of spiritual perfection.

It is true that the different pictures that the great prophets of the world have drawn very often differ from one another. But one finds that in order to make one clear photograph there have to be many different processes; a plate has to be made and has to be developed, and then the picture is transferred to paper; then it is touched up, and all these different processes go to make a photograph complete.

And so it has been with those who have tried to make a picture of the Deity, a picture which cannot be made fully, because it is beyond man's power to do so. They have done their best; artists have painted that picture. When three artists paint the portrait of one person, the three pictures are different. They only differ because they are different artists; and so it is with the prophets, though all have one and the same motive: to make that picture intelligible to the limited mind of man, who only knows what he knows about himself and about his fellow-man. Thus the best picture he can make of God is that of a man. In the ancient religions of the East, God was first pictured in the form of man; then in the pictures of later days man was pictured as God. After that came a reformation by which man and God were separated in order to break with the confusion caused by these two opposite ideas, that God was man and man was God.

But the present message, which comes from the need of humanity, is that God is in man and man in God, and yet God is God and man is man.

THE IDEAL OF THE SUFI

Sufism has never in any period of history been a religion or a certain creed; it has always been considered as the essence of every religion and of all religions. Thus when it was given to the world of Islam, it was presented by the great Sufis in Muslim terminology. Whenever the Sufi ideal was presented to a certain people, it was presented in such a way as to make it intelligible to those people.

Sufism is neither a dogma nor a doctrine; it is neither a form nor a ceremony. This does not mean that a Sufi does not make use of a doctrine, a dogma, a ritual, or a ceremony. He makes use of them while at the same time remaining free from them. It is neither dogma, doctrine, ceremony, nor ritual that makes a Sufi a Sufi; it is wisdom alone which is his property, and all other things he uses for his convenience, his benefit. But a Sufi is not against any creed, doctrine, dogma, ritual, or ceremony; he is not even against the man who has no belief in God or spirit, for a Sufi has a great respect for man.

The God of the Sufi is the God of all, and He is his very being. The Christ is his ideal, and therefore no one's saviour is foreign to a Sufi, for he sees the beauty and greatness and perfection of a human being in everyone's ideal. He does not mind if that ideal is called Buddha by one person, Krishna by another, and Mohammad by yet another; names make little difference to the Sufi; his ideal does not belong to history or tradition, but to the sacred feelings of his heart. So how can he compare the ideals of the different creeds which dispute in vain about historical and traditional points of view, without making any impression upon each other? The ideal of the Lord, the Lord in the form of man, is the outcome of his heart's deepest devotion. One cannot dispute and argue about an ideal like this, nor can it be compared; so the Sufi believes that the less spoken about this subject the better, for he respects that one ideal which people call by different names.

Life, human nature, the nature around us, are all a revelation to a Sufi. This does not mean that a Sufi has no respect for the sacred scriptures revered by humanity. On the contrary, he holds them as sacred as do the followers of those scriptures; but the Sufi says that all scriptures are only different interpretations of that one scripture which is constantly before us like an open book—if we could only read and understand it.

The Sufi's object of worship is beauty. Not only beauty in form and line and colour, but beauty in all its aspects, from gross to fine.

What is the moral of the Sufi? Every religion, every creed, has certain moral teachings: that this particular principle is right, and that particular principle is wrong. No principle or action is in itself labelled by a Sufi as being either; it is its application which makes it right or wrong. The light which guides the Sufi on the path is his own conscience, and harmony is the justification which guides him onward step by step to his idealized goal. To harmonize with oneself is not sufficient; one must also harmonize with others in thought, speech, and action; that is the attitude of the Sufi.

The highest heaven of the Sufi is his own heart, and that which man generally knows as love, to a Sufi is God. Different people have thought of the Diety as the Creator, as the Judge, as the King, as the Supreme Being; but the Sufis call him the Beloved. Are there any dogmas, are there any rituals or ceremonies which may be called Sufi? There is nothing which restricts a Sufi, so that he can only be a Sufi by doing it. At the same time he is free to make use of any ritual, any ceremony that he thinks suited to his purpose.

How can the Sufi idea be made intelligible? Truth is that which can never be spoken in words, and that which can be spoken in words is not the truth. The ocean is the ocean; the ocean is not a few drops of water that one puts in a bottle. Just so truth cannot be limited by words: truth must be experienced, for it is natural that the knowledge of truth should come sooner or later. The disputes and discussions and arguments that people of different communities and creeds have with one another, do not interest the Sufi, for he sees the right in all things, and the wrong of certain things also.

There is no right that has no wrong side to it, nor is there any wrong that has not a right side to it. Very often a wrong turned inside out may appear right, and very often the right turned inside out may appear wrong. Therefore, as Christ said: judge not. The Sufi, if he judges at all, judges himself instead of others; his only concern is whether he himself is doing right. Nearly everyone judges others, but that is where people make a mistake. Few judge themselves, but the one who really does so has no time to judge others; there is too much to judge in himself, and this occupies him fully.

What the Sufi strives for is self-realization, and he arrives at this self-realization by means of his divine ideal, his God. By this he touches that truth which is the ultimate goal and the yearning of every soul. It is not only realization; it is a happiness which words cannot explain. It is that peace which is yearned for by every soul.

And how does he attain to it? By practising the presence of God; by realizing the oneness of the whole being; by continually holding, every moment of the day, consciously or subconsciously, the truth before his vision, in spite of the waves of illusion which arise incessantly, diverting the glance of man from the absolute truth. And no matter what may be the name of any sect, cult, or creed, so long as the souls are striving towards that object, to a Sufi they are all Sufis. The attitude of the Sufi to all the different religions is one of respect. His religion is the service of humanity, and his only attainment is the realization of truth.

54

IS RELIGION POSSIBLE?
Mohammad Iqbal

Mohammad Iqbal (1875–1938) was the most significant Muslim philosopher-theologian of this century. In addition, he is recognized as one of the greatest poets by those who have been able to read him in the languages of his poems, Urdu and Persian. Born at Sialkot, the son of Sheikh Noor Mohammad, Mohammad Iqbal distinguished himself quite early by his outstanding scholastic achievements. He obtained his M.A. at Lahore with specialization in Arabic and philosophy, and taught at the Oriental College there. Subsequently, he traveled to Europe to complete his education, going first to Cambridge and then to Munich, where he received his Doctorate in Philosophy. He also passed his bar examinations in London, and upon his return to India pursued a diverse career utilizing his many capabilities. He taught for some time at the Government College in Lahore, practiced law, and was elected to membership in the Punjab Legislative Assembly in 1926. As President of the All-India Muslim League, in 1929 he suggested a plan for a separate Muslim nation in India. In the light of his many accomplishments, the date of his death, April 21, is observed as a national holiday in Pakistan. While being active in education and in politics, he never ceased to write poetry and philosophy. He is best known to the world at large for his The Reconstruction of Religious Thought in Islam, *a volume composed of a series of lectures given in 1928 in English. These lectures propose a thorough reformulation of Islamic doctrine in order to make it compatible with the science and philosophy of the modern era.*

Broadly speaking religious life may be divided into three periods. These may be described as the periods of 'Faith,' 'Thought,' and 'Discovery.' In the first period religious life appears as a form of discipline which the individual

Mohammad Iqbal, *The Reconstruction of Religious Thought in Islam* (Lahore: Shaikh Muhammad Ashraf, 1944), pp. 180–198. Reprinted by permission of Dr. Javid Ibal.

or a whole people must accept as an unconditional command without any rational understanding of the ultimate meaning and purpose of that command. This attitude may be of great consequence in the social and political history of a people, but is not of much consequence in so far as the individual's inner growth and expansion are concerned. Perfect submission to discipline is followed by a rational understanding of the discipline and the ultimate source of its authority. In this period religious life seeks its foundation in a kind of metaphysics—a logically consistent view of the world with God as a part of that view. In the third period metaphysics is displaced by psychology, and religious life develops the ambition to come into direct contact with the ultimate Reality. It is here that religion becomes a matter of personal assimilation of life and power; and the individual achieves a free personality, not by releasing himself from the fetters of the law, but by discovering the ultimate source of the law within the depths of his own consciousness. As in the words of a Muslim Sufi—'no understanding of the Holy Book is possible until it is actually revealed to the believer just as it was revealed to the Prophet.' It is, then, in the sense of this last phase in the development of religious life that I use the word religion in the question that I now propose to raise. Religion in this sense is known by the unfortunate name of Mysticism, which is supposed to be a life-denying, fact-avoiding attitude of mind directly opposed to the radically empirical outlook of our times. Yet higher religion, which is only a search for a larger life, is essentially experience and recognized the necessity of experience as its foundation long before science learnt to do so. It is a genuine effort to clarify human consciousness, and is, as such, as critical of its level of experience as Naturalism is of its own level.

As we all know, it was Kant who first raised the question: 'Is metaphysics possible?' He answered this question in the negative; and his argument applies with equal force to the realities in which religion is especially interested. The manifold of sense, according to him, must fulfil certain formal conditions in order to constitute knowledge. The thing in itself is only a limiting idea. Its function is merely regulative. If there *is* some actuality corresponding to the idea it falls outside the boundaries of experience, and consequently its existence cannot be rationally demonstrated. This verdict of Kant cannot be easily accepted. It may fairly be urged that in view of the more recent developments of science, such as the nature of matter as 'bottled-up light waves,' the idea of the universe as an act of thought, finiteness of space and time and Heisenberg's principle of indeterminancy in nature, the case for a system of rational theology is not so bad as Kant was led to think. But for our present purposes it is unnecessary to consider this point in detail. As to the thing in itself, which is inaccessible to pure reason because of its falling beyond the boundaries of experience, Kant's verdict can be accepted only if we start with assumption that all experience other than the normal level of experience is impossible. The only question, therefore, is whether the normal level is the only level of knowledge-yielding experience. Kant's view of the thing in itself and the thing as it appears to us very much determined the character of his question regarding the possibility of metaphysics. But what if the position, as understood by him, is reversed? The great Muslim Sufi philosopher, Muhyuddin Ibnul Arabi of Spain, has made the acute observation that God is a precept; the world is a concept. Another Muslim Sufi thinker and poet, Iraqi, insists on the plurality of space-orders and time-orders and speaks of a Divine Time and a Divine Space. It may be that what we call the external world is only an intellectual construction, and that there are other levels of human experience capable of being systematized by other orders of space and time—levels in which concept and analysis do not play the same role as they do in the case of our normal experience. It may, however, be said that the level of experience to which concepts are inapplicable cannot yield any knowledge of a universal character; for concepts alone are capable of being socialized. The standpoint of the man who relies on religious experience for capturing Reality must always remain individual and incommunicable. This objection has some force if it is meant to insinuate that the mystic is wholly ruled by his traditional ways, attitudes, and expectations. Conservatism is as bad in religion as in any other department of human activity. It destroys the ego's creative freedom and closes up the paths of fresh spiritual enterprise. This is the main reason why our medieval mystic techniques can no longer produce original discoveries of ancient Truth. The fact, however, that religious experience is incommunicable does not mean that the religious man's pursuit is futile. Indeed, the incommunicability of religious experience gives us a clue to the ultimate nature of the ego. In our daily social intercourse we live and move in seclusion, as it were. We do not care to reach the inmost individuality of men. We treat them as mere functions, and approach them from those aspects of their identity which are capable of conceptual treatment. The climax of religious life, however, is the discovery of the ego as an individual deeper than his conceptually describable habitual self-hood. It is in contact with the Most Real that the ego discovers its uniqueness, its metaphysical status, and the possibility of improvement in that status. Strictly speaking, the experience which leads to this discovery is not a conceptually manageable intellectual fact; it is a vital fact, an attitude consequent on an inner biological transformation which cannot be captured in the net of logical categories. It can embody itself only in a world-making or world-shaking act; and in this form alone the content of this timeless experience can diffuse itself in the time-movement, and make itself effectively visible to the eye of history. It seems that the method of dealing with Reality by means of concepts is not at all a serious way of dealing with it. Science does not care whether its electron is a real entity or not. It may be a mere symbol, a mere convention. Religion, which is essentially a mode of actual living, is the only serious way of handling Reality. As a form of higher experience it is corrective of our concepts of philosophical theology or at least makes us suspicious of the purely rational process which forms these concepts. Science can afford to ignore metaphysics altogether, and may even believe it to be 'a justified form of poetry,' as Lange defined it, or 'a legitimate play of grown-ups,' as Nietzsche described it. But the religious expert who seeks to discover his personal status in the constitution of things cannot, in view of the final aim of his struggle, be satisfied with what science may regard as a vital lie, a mere 'as-if' to regulate thought and conduct. In so far as the ultimate nature of Reality is concerned nothing is at stake in the venture of science; in the religious venture the whole career of the ego as an assimilative personal centre of life and experience is at stake. Conduct, which involves a decision of the ultimate fate of the agent cannot be based on illusions. A wrong concept misleads the understanding; a wrong deed degrades the whole man, and may eventually demolish the structure of the human ego. The mere concept affects life only partially; the deed is dynamically related to reality and issues from a generally constant attitude of the whole man towards reality. No doubt the deed, i.e., the control of psychological and physiological processes with a view to tune up the ego for an immediate contact with the ultimate Reality is, and cannot but be, individual in form and content; yet the deed, too, is liable to be socialized when others begin to live through it with a view to discover for themselves its effectiveness as a method of approaching the Real. The evidence of religious experts in all ages and countries is that there are potential types of consciousness lying close to our normal consciousness. If these types of consciousness open up possibilities of life-giving and knowledge-yielding experience the question of the possibility of religion as a form of higher experience is a perfectly legitimate one and demands our serious attention.

But, apart from the legitimacy of the question, there are important reasons why it should be raised at the present moment of the history of modern culture. In the first place, the scientific interest of the question. It seems that every culture has a form of Naturalism peculiar to its own world-feeling; and it further appears that every form of Naturalism ends in some sort of Atomism. We have Indian Atomism, Greek Atomism, Muslim Atomism, and Modern Atomism. Modern Atomism is, however, unique. Its amazing mathematics which sees the universe as an elaborate differential equation; and its physics which, following its own methods, has been led to smash some of the old gods of its own temple, have already brought us to the point of asking the question whether the causality-bound aspect of nature is the whole truth about it? Is not the ultimate Reality invading our consciousness from some other direction as well? Is the purely intellectual method of overcoming nature the only method? 'We have acknowledged,' says Professor Eddington, 'that the entities of physics can from their very nature form only a partial aspect of the reality. How are we to deal with the other part? It cannot be said that that other part concerns us less than the physical entities. Feelings, purpose, values, make up our consciousness as much as sense-impressions. We follow up the sense-impressions and find that they lead into an external world dicussed by science; we follow up the other elements of our being and find that they lead—not into a world of space and time, but surely somewhere.'

In the second place we have to look to the great practical importance of the question. The modern man with his philosophies of criticism and scientific specialism finds himself in a strange predicament. His Naturalism has given him an unprecedented control over the forces of nature, but has robbed him of faith in his own future. It is strange how the same idea affects different cultures differently. The formulation of the theory of evolution in the world of Islam brought into being Rumi's tremendous enthusiasm for the biological future of man. No cultured Muslim can read such passages as the following without a thrill of joy:

> Low in the earth
> I lived in realms of ore and stone;
> And then I smiled in many-tinted flowers;
> Then roving with the wild and wandering hours,
> O'er earth and air and ocean's zone,
> In a new birth,
> I dived and flew,
> And crept and ran,
> And all the secret of my essence drew
> Within a form that brought them all to view—
> And lo, a Man!
> And then my goal,
> Beyond the clouds, beyond the sky,
> In realms where none may change or die—
> In angel form; and then away
> Beyond the bounds of night and day,
> And Life and Death, unseen or seen,
> Where all that is hath ever been,
> As One and Whole.
>
> (*Rumi*: Thadani's Translation.)

On the other hand, the formulation of the same view of evolution with far greater precision in Europe has led to the belief that 'there now appears to be no scientific basis for the idea that the present rich complexity of human endowment will ever be materially exceeded'. That is how the modern man's secret despair hides itself behind the screen of scientific terminology. Nietzsche, although he thought that the idea of evolution did not justify the belief that man was unsurpassable, cannot be regarded as an exception in this respect. His enthusiasm for the future of man ended in the doctrine of eternal recurrence—perhaps the most hopeless idea of immortality ever formed by man. This eternal repetition is not eternal 'becoming'; it is the same old idea of 'being' masquerading as 'becoming'.

Thus, wholly overshadowed by the results of his intellectual activity, the modern man has ceased to live soulfully, *i.e.*, from within. In the domain of thought he is living in open conflict with himself; and in the domain of economic and political life he is living in open conflict with others. He finds himself unable to control his ruthless egoism and his infinite gold-hunger which is gradually killing all higher striving in him and bringing him nothing but life-weariness. Absorbed in the 'fact', that is to say, the optically present source of sensation, he is entirely cut off from the unplumbed depths of his own being. In the wake of his systematic materialism has at last come that paralysis of energy which Huxley apprehended and deplored. The condition of things in the East is no better. The technique of medieval mysticism by which religious life, in its higher manifestations, developed itself both in the East and in the West has now practically failed. And in the Muslim East it has, perhaps, done far greater havoc than anywhere else. Far from reintegrating the forces of the average man's inner life, and thus preparing him for participation in the march of history, it has taught him a false renunciation and made him perfectly contented with his ignorance and spiritual thraldom. No wonder then that the modern Muslim in Turkey, Egypt, and Persia is led to seek fresh sources of energy in the creation of new loyalties, such as patriotism and nationalism which Nietzsche described as 'sickness and unreason', and 'the strongest force against culture'. Disappointed of a purely religious method of spiritual renewal which alone brings us into touch with the everlasting fountain of life and power by expanding our thought and emotion, the modern Muslim fondly hopes to unlock fresh sources of energy by narrowing down his thought and emotion. Modern atheistic socialism, which possesses all the fervour of a new religion, has a broader outlook; but having received its philosophical basis from the Hegelians of the left wing, it rises in revolt against the very source which could have given it strength and purpose. Both nationalism and atheistic socialism, at least in the present state of human adjustments, must draw upon the psychological forces of hate, suspicion, and resentment which tend to impoverish the soul of man and close up his hidden sources of spiritual energy. Neither the technique of medieval mysticism nor nationalism nor atheistic socialism can cure the ills of a despairing humanity. Surely the present moment is one of great crisis in the history of modern culture. The modern world stands in need of biological renewal. And religion, which in its higher manifestations is neither dogma, nor priesthood, nor ritual, can alone ethically prepare the modern man for the burden of the great responsibility which the advancement of modern science necessarily involves, and restore to him that attitude of faith which makes him capable of winning a personality here and retaining it hereafter. It is only by rising to a fresh vision of his origin and future, his whence and whither, that man will eventually triumph over a society motivated by an inhuman competition, and a civilization which has lost its spiritual unity by its inner conflict of religious and political values.

As I have indicated before, religion as a deliberate enterprise to seize the ultimate principle of value and thereby to reintegrate the forces of one's own personality, is a fact which cannot be denied. The whole religious literature of the world, including the records of specialists' personal experiences, though perhaps expressed in the thought-forms of an out-of-date psychology, is a standing testimony to it. These experiences are perfectly natural, like our normal experiences. The evidence is that they possess a cognitive value for the recipient, and, what is much more important, a capacity to centralize the forces of the ego and thereby to endow him with a new personality. The view that such experiences are neurotic or mystical will not finally settle the question of their meaning or value. If an outlook beyond physics is possible, we must courageously face the possibility, even though it may disturb or tend to modify our normal ways of life and thought. The interests of truth require that we must abandon our present attitude. It does not matter in the least if the religious attitude is originally determined by some kind of physiological disorder. George Fox may be a neurotic; but who can deny his purifying power in England's religious life of his day? Mohammed, we are told, was a psychopath. Well, if a psychopath has the power to give a fresh direction to the course of human history, it is a point of the highest psychological interest to search his original expedience which has turned slaves into leaders of men, and has inspired the conduct and shaped the career of whole races of mankind. Judging from the various types of activity that emanated from the movement initiated by the Prophet of Islam, his spiritual tension and the kind of behaviour which issued from it, cannot be regarded as a response to a mere fantasy inside his brain. It is impossible to understand it except as a response to an objective situation generative of new enthusiasms, new organizations, new starting-points. If we look at the matter from the standpoint of anthropology it appears that a psychopath is an important factor in the economy of humanity's social organization. His way is not to classify facts and discover causes: he thinks in terms of life and movement with a view to create new patterns of behaviour for mankind. No doubt he has his pitfalls and illusions just as the scientist who relies on sense-experience has his pitfalls and illusions. A careful study of his method, however, shows that he is not less alert than the scientist in the matter of eliminating the alloy of illusion from his experience.

The question for us outsiders is to find out an effective method of inquiry into the nature and significance of this extraordinary experience. The Arab historian Ibn Khaldun, who laid the foundations of modern scientific history, was the first to seriously approach this side of human psychology and reached what we now call the idea of the subliminal self. Later, Sir William Hamilton in England and Leibnitz in Germany interested themselves in some of the more unknown phenomena of the mind. Jung, however, is probably right in thinking that the essential nature of religion is beyond the province of analytic psychology. In his discussion of the relation of analytic psychology to poetic art he tells us that the process of artistic *form* alone can be the object of psychology. The essential nature of art, according to him, cannot be the object of a psychological method of approach. 'A similar distinction', says Jung, 'must also be made in the realm of religion; there also a psychological consideration is permissible only in respect of the emotional and symbolical phenomena of a religion, wherein the essential nature of religion is in no way involved, as indeed it cannot be. For were this possible, not religion alone, but art also could be treated as a mere sub-division of psychology.' Yet Jung has violated his own principle more than once in his writings. The result of this procedure is that instead of giving us a real insight into the essential nature of religion and its meaning for human personality, our modern psychology has given us quite a plethora of new theories which proceed on a complete misunderstanding of the nature of religion as revealed in its higher manifestations, and carry us in an entirely hopeless direction. The implication of these theories, on the whole, is that religion does not relate the human ego to any objective reality beyond himself; it is merely a kind of well-meaning biological device calculated to build barriers of ethical nature round human society in order to protect the social fabric against the otherwise unrestrainable instincts of the ego. That is why, according to this newer psychology, Christianity has already fulfilled its biological mission, and it is impossible for the modern man to understand its original significance. Jung concludes:

'Most certainly we should still understand it, had our customs even a breath of ancient brutality, for we can hardly realize in this day the whirlwinds of the unchained libido which roared through the ancient Rome of the Cæsars. The civilized man of the present day seems very far removed from that. He has become merely neurotic. So for us the necessities which brought forth Christianity have actually been lost, since we no longer understand their meaning. We do not know against what it had to protect us. For enlightened people the so-called religiousness has already approached very close to a neurosis. In the past two thousand years Christianity has done its work and has erected barriers of repression which protect us from the sight of our own sinfulness.'

This is missing the whole point of higher religious life. Sexual self-restraint is only a preliminary stage in the ego's evolution. The ultimate purpose of religious life is to make this evolution move in a direction far more important to the destiny of the ego than the moral health of the social fabric which forms his present environment. The basic perception from which religious life moves forward is the present slender unity of the ego, his liability to dissolution, his amenability to reformation and his capacity for an ampler freedom to create new situations in known and unknown environments. In view of this fundamental perception higher religious life fixes its gaze on experiences symbolic of those subtle movements of reality which seriously affect the destiny of the ego as a possibly permanent element in the constitution of reality. If we look at the matter from this point of view modern psychology has not yet touched even the outer fringe of religious life, and is still far from the richness and variety of what is called religious experience. In order to give you an idea of its richness and variety I quote here the substance of a passage from a great religious genius of the seventeenth century—Sheikh Ahmad of Sarhand—whose fearless analytical criticism of contemporary Sufiism resulted in the development of a new technique. All the various systems of Sufi technique in India came from Central Asia and Arabia; his is the only technique which crossed the Indian border and is still a living force in the Punjab, Afghanistan, and Asiatic Russia. I am afraid it is not possible for me to expound the real meaning of this passage in the language of modern psychology; for such language does not yet exist. Since, however, my object is simply to give you an idea of the infinite wealth of experience which the ego in his Divine quest has to sift and pass through, I do hope you will excuse me for the apparently outlandish terminology which possesses a real substance of meaning, but which was formed under the inspiration of a religious psychology developed in the atmosphere of a different culture. Coming now to the passage. The experience of one Abdul Momin was described to the Sheikh as follows:

'Heavens and Earth and God's throne and Hell and Paradise have all ceased to exist for me. When I look round I find them nowhere. When I stand in the presence of somebody I see nobody before me: nay even my own being is lost to me. God is infinite. Nobody can encompass Him; and this is the extreme limit of spiritual experience. No saint has been able to go beyond this.'

On this the Sheikh replied:

'The experience which is described has its origin in the ever-varying life of the *qalb;* and it appears to me that the recipient of it has not yet passed even one-fourth of the innumerable "Stations" of the "Qalb". The remaining three-fourths must be passed through in order to finish the experiences of this first "Station" of spiritual life. Beyond this "Station" there are other "Stations" known as *Ruh, Sirr-i-Khafi,* and *Sirr-i-Akhfa,* each of these "Stations" which together constitute what is technically called *Alam-i-Amr* has its own characteristic states and experiences. After having passed through these "Stations" the seeker of truth gradually receives the illuminations of "Divine Names" and "Divine Attributes" and finally the illuminations of the Divine Essence.'

Whatever may be the psychological ground of the distinctions made in this passage it gives us at least some idea of a whole universe of inner experience as seen by a great reformer of Islamic Sufiism. According to him this *Alam-i-Amr, i.e.,* 'the world of directive energy' must be passed through before one reaches that unique experience which symbolizes the purely objective. This is the reason why I say that modern psychology has not yet touched even the outer fringe of the subject. Personally, I do not at all feel hopeful of the present state of things in either biology or psychology. Mere analytical criticism with some understanding of the organic conditions of the imagery in which religious life has sometimes manifested itself is not likely to carry us to the living roots of human personality. Assuming that sex-imagery has played a role in the history of religion, or that religion has furnished imaginative means of escape from, or adjustment to, an unpleasant reality, these ways of looking at the matter cannot, in the least, affect the ultimate aim of religious life, that is to say, the reconstruction of the finite ego by bringing him into contact with an eternal life-process, and thus giving him a metaphysical status of which we can have only a partial understanding in the half-choking atmosphere of our present environment. If, therefore, the science of psychology is ever likely to possess a real significance for the life of mankind it must develop an independent method calculated to discover a new technique better suited to the temper of our times. Perhaps a psychopath endowed with a great intellect—the combination is not an impossibility—may give us a clue to such a technique. In modern Europe Nietzsche whose life and activity form, at least to us Easterns, an exceedingly interesting problem in religious psychology, was endowed with some sort of a constitutional equipment for such an undertaking. His mental history is not without a parallel in the history of Eastern Sufiism. That a really 'imperative' vision of the Divine in man did come to him cannot be denied. I call his vision 'imperative' because it appears to have given him a kind of prophetic mentality which, by some kind of technique, aims at turning its visions into permanent life forces. Yet Nietzsche was a failure; and his failure was mainly due to his intellectual progenitors such as Schopenhauer, Darwin, and Lange whose influence completely blinded him to the real significance of his vision. Instead of looking for a spiritual rule which would develop the Divine even in a plebeian and thus open up before him an infinite future, Nietzsche was driven to seek the realization of his vision in such schemes as aristocratic radicalism. As I have said of him elsewhere:

> The 'I am' which he seeketh,
> Lieth beyond philosophy, beyond knowledge.
> The plant that groweth only from the invisible soil of the heart
>   of man,
> Groweth not from a mere heap of clay!

Thus failed a genius whose vision was solely determined by his internal forces, and remained unproductive for want of expert external guidance in his spiritual life. And the irony of fate is that this man, who appeared to his friends 'as if he had come from a country where no man lived,' was fully conscious of his great spiritual need. 'I confront alone,' he says, 'an immense problem: it is as if I am lost in a forest, a primeval one. I need help. I need disciples: I need a *master*. It would be so sweet to obey.' And again: 'Why do I not find among the living, men who see higher than I do and have to look down on me? Is it only that I have made a poor search? And I have so great a longing for such.'

The truth is that the religious and the scientific processes, though involving different methods, are identical in their final aim. Both aim at reaching the most real. In fact, religion, for reasons which I have mentioned before, is far more anxious to reach the ultimately real than science. And to both the way to pure objectivity lies through what may be called the purification of experience. In order to understand this we must make a distinction between experience as a natural fact, significant of the normally observable behaviour of reality, and experience as significant of the inner nature of reality. As a natural fact it is explained in the light of its antecedents, psychological and physiological; as significant of the inner nature of reality we shall have to apply criteria of a different kind to clarify its meaning. In the domain of science we try to understand its meaning in reference to the external *behaviour* of reality; in the domain of religion we take it as representative of some kind of reality and try to discover its meanings in reference mainly to the inner *nature* of that reality. The scientific and the religious processes are in a sense parallel to each other. Both are really descriptions of the same world with this difference only that in the scientific process the ego's standpoint is necessarily exclusive whereas in the religious process the ego integrates its competing tendencies and develops a single inclusive attitude resulting in a kind of synthetic transfiguration of his experiences. A careful study of the nature and purpose of these really complementary processes shows that both of them are directed to the purification of experience in their respective spheres. An illustration will make my meaning clear. Hume's criticism of our notion of cause must be considered as a chapter in the history of science rather than that of philosophy. True to the spirit of scientific empiricism we are not entitled to work with any concepts of a subjective nature. The point of Hume's criticism is to emancipate empirical science from the concept of force which, as he urges, has no foundation in sense-experience. This was the first attempt of the modern mind to purify the scientific process.

Einstein's mathematical view of the universe completes the process of purification started by Hume, and, true to the spirit of Hume's criticism, dispenses with the concept of force altogether. The passage I have quoted from the great Indian saint shows that the practical student of religious psychology has a similar purification in view. His sense of objectivity is as keen as that of the scientist in his own sphere of objectivity. He passes from experience to experience, not as a mere spectator, but as a critical sifter of experience who by the rules of a peculiar technique, suited to his sphere of inquiry, endeavours to eliminate all subjective elements, psychological or physiological, in the content of his experience with a view finally to reach what is absolutely objective. This final experience is the revelation of a new life-process—original, essential, spontaneous. The eternal secret of the ego is that the moment he reaches this final revelation he recognizes it as the ultimate root of his being without the slightest hesitation. Yet in the experience itself there is no mystery. Nor is there anything emotional in it. Indeed with a view to secure a wholly nonemotional experience the technique of Islamic Sufiism at least takes good care to forbid the use of music in worship, and to emphasize the necessity of daily congregational prayers in order to counteract the possible anti-social effects of solitary contemplation. Thus the experience reached is a perfectly natural experience and possesses a biological significance of the highest importance to the ego. It is the human ego rising higher than mere reflection, and mending its transiency by appropriating the eternal. The only danger to which the ego is exposed in this Divine quest is the possible relaxation of his activity caused by his enjoyment of and absorption in the experiences that precede the final experience. The history of Eastern Sufiism shows that this is a real danger. This was the whole point of the reform movement initiated by the great Indian saint from whose writings I have already quoted a passage. And the reason is obvious. The ultimate aim of the ego is not to *see* something, but to *be* something. It is in the ego's effort to *be* something that he discovers his final opportunity to sharpen his objectivity and acquire a more fundamental 'I am' which finds evidence of its reality not in the Cartesian 'I think' but in the Kantian 'I can'. The end of the ego's quest is not emancipation from the limitations of individuality; it is, on the other hand, a more precise definition of it. The final act is not an intellectual act, but a vital act which deepens the whole being of the ego, and sharpens his will with the creative assurance that the world is not something to be merely seen or known through concepts, but something to be made and re-made by continuous action. It is a moment of supreme bliss and also a moment of the greatest trial for the ego:

> Art thou in the stage of 'life', 'death', or 'death-in-life'?
> Invoke the aid of three witnesses to verify thy 'Station'.
> The first witness is thine own consciousness—
> See thyself, then with thine own light.
> The second witness is the consciousness of another ego—
> See thyself, then, with the light of an ego other than thee.
> The third witness is God's consciousness—
> See thyself, then, with God's light.
> If thou standest unshaken in front of this light,
> Consider thyself as living and eternal as He!
> That man alone is real who dares—
> Dares to see God face to face!
> What is 'Ascension'? Only a search for a witness

Who may finally confirm thy reality—
A witness whose confirmation alone makes thee eternal.
No one can stand unshaken in His Presence;
And he who can, verily, he is pure gold.
Art thou a mere particle of dust?
Tighten the knot of thy ego;
And hold fast to thy tiny being!
How glorious to burnish one's ego
And to test its lustre in the presence of the Sun!
Re-chisel, then, thine ancient frame;
And build up a new being.
Such being is real being;
Or else thy ego is a mere ring of smoke!

                                                                    —*Jawid Nama.*

55

THE RELATION OF ISLAM TO CHRISTIANITY
Alfred Guillaume

Alfred Guillaume (1888–   ) is a noted scholar of Arabic and of Islamic culture. He is Professor Emeritus of Arabic in the University of London, where he taught from 1947 to 1955. Educated at Oxford, he received honors in Oriental languages and in Hebrew. After serving in Egypt in World War I on the staff of the High Commissioner, he entered upon a varied career. Rev. Guillaume has taught at several colleges and universities, specializing in Old Testament studies, Hebrew, and Arabic, has served as rector of a church, and has held various administrative posts. The honors he has received include being the Bampton lecturer for 1938 and election to the Arab Academies of Damascus and of Baghdad. He is the author of many books, among which are The Traditions of Islam *(1924),* The Influence of Judaism on Islam *(1927),* The Life of Muhammad *(1955), and* New Light on the

Alfred Guillaume, *Islam* (Harmondsworth, England: Penguin Books, Ltd., 1956), pp. 194–199. Reprinted by permission of the publisher.

Life of Muhammad (1960). *The selection reprinted here offers an unique comparison of Islam and Christianity which is notable for its conciseness and clarity.*

The brief statement which follows is not a polemic in any sense of the word, but a purely objective summary of the relation between the two religions. It is impossible to write of Islam without saying something about its predecessors, if only because the Qurān claims to confirm and to correct the earlier scriptures of Jews and Christians.

Perhaps the most direct way of indicating the relation would be to take the Apostles' Creed, as the document regarded by practically all Christians as an authoritative summary of their faith, and see how far the Qurān agrees with it (the words in italics are rejected by Islam):

I believe in God
the Father
Almighty, Maker of heaven and earth;
And in Jesus Christ
His only Son, our Lord,
Who was conceived by the Holy Ghost, Born of the Virgin Mary,
Suffered under Pontius Pilate, Was crucified
Dead? *and buried, He descended into hell; The third day*
He rose again from the dead,
He ascended into heaven,
And sitteth on the right hand of God the Father Almighty;
From thence He shall come
to judge the quick and the dead.
I believe in the Holy Ghost;
The Holy Catholic Church;
The Communion of Saints;
The Forgiveness of sins;
The Resurrection of the body, And the life everlasting.

If we went outside the Qurān for parallels with Christian doctrine we should find some, but we should enter into the field of controversy, and therefore these notes will be confined exclusively to what the Qurān itself says on the subjects which fall within the scope of the Apostles' Creed.

THE FATHER. This is a term abhorrent to Muslims in reference to God, because it is understood in the sense of physical generation, and to say that God is a father implies to them that he must have a wife: therefore on that ground they are perfectly right in rejecting the term as blasphemous. Nor do they admit the term in the metaphorical sense that God is the father of all men, who stand to him in the relation of children.

Jesus Christ is believed to be an apostle sent by God. He is a man and the slave of God.

CONCEIVED BY THE HOLY GHOST. Cf. sura 21, 'We breathed into her who was chaste of Our Spirit, and we made her and her son a sign (*āya*) to the worlds.' This inbreathing of the divine spirit is recorded also of the creation of Adam (15:29): 'And when I have made him a complete man and breathed into him of my spirit, fall you down prostrating yourselves to him.' It is clear from these two passages that the Holy Spirit is not necessarily a person, but rather an emanation. In Islam in other texts it is understood to be Gabriel, because it is he that communicated the Qurān to Muhammad in 2:291, while in 16:104 it is the Holy Spirit. Similarly 19:17 reads, 'We sent to her our spirit and he took the form of a full-grown man.' Further 4:169 says of Jesus: 'The Messiah, the Son of Mary, is only the apostle of God and His Word which He cast to Mary and a spirit from Him. So believe in God and His apostles and do not say "Three". Forbear! (it is) better for you. Allah is only One God; so transcendent is He that He cannot have a Son.' The conception of spirit in the Qurān is difficult to follow. Other passages speak of angels being sent down with the spirit to whom God wills of his creatures.

The 'Holy Spirit' is mentioned four times in the Qurān: 2:81, 'We gave Jesus the Son of Mary the plain indications and strengthened him with the Holy Spirit', and similarly 5:109. But all true believers are strengthened with the Holy Spirit, cf. 58:22 and 16:104.

The most that can be said is that it is the plain teaching of the Qurān that, as St. Paul said, Jesus is the Second Adam in that he was created by the immediate action of God through his breath, and not by human generation. It cannot be said that it teaches that the Holy Spirit is God himself: he is the breath or wind of God.

VIRGIN MARY. The virginity of Mary is taught almost in the words of Luke 1:34 in sura 19:20; and 66:12 says that 'she was chosen and purified by God.'

WAS CRUCIFIED. 4:155 ff. explicitly deny the crucifixion in the words 'They did not kill him and they did not crucify him, but one was made to resemble him' (or, perhaps, 'they thought they did').

DEAD. In spite of the denial of the crucifixion, there are some passages which speak of the death of Jesus, who is said to have said, 'The day that I die and the day that I am raised to life'. 19:34. The passage in 3:48, 'I am about to cause thee to die and lift thee up to Me', is not clear. It need not necessarily mean more than it does in 6:60, where Allah takes the souls of the sleepers to himself during their sleep and returns them when they awake years afterwards. However, in Arabic the verb normally means to die; but it is seldom safe to insist on interpreting the Qurān by later usage, as naturally it sometimes gave meanings to words which derive from the sense in which the Arabs understood them rather than from the true philological meaning. (A notable example of this is *ummī*, which unquestionably means 'gentile', but is everywhere taken to mean 'illiterate' because of the assumption that Muhammad could not write.)

HE ASCENDED INTO HEAVEN. See what has just been said.

FROM THENCE HE SHALL COME. It is impossible to say what the Qurānic doctrine is here. The passage (4:156) which denies the crucifixion continues, 'and there are none of the people of the scriptures but will believe in him before his death and on the day of resurrection he will be a witness against them.' What does this mean? Does it mean that Jesus will return to the earth and Jews and Christians will believe in him as Muhammadan tradition asserts, or does it mean that confronted with Jesus in heaven on the day of judgement they will believe when it is too late and he will be a witness against those who rejected him? The question seems unanswerable. Another passage which might have thrown light on the subject is equally obscure: 43:61 reads, 'Verily he [Jesus] is a knowledge (*'ilm*) [or a sign (*'alam*) with another reading of the consonantal text giving it different vowels as some authorities do] of the Hour.' The first rendering makes very poor sense, and the second is difficult to interpret. At any rate it would seem to be impossible that Jesus could be a 'sign' of the Hour, i.e. of the end of all things, unless he were on earth. Some Muslim commentators take the Qurān to be the subject of the sentence. This would better fit the reading 'knowledge' and could possibly apply to 'sign'. No definite conclusion can be drawn from the Qurān. All that can be said is that there is a persistent tradition that Jesus will appear on earth again before the judgement day, and very early tradition asserted that he was to be seen on earth from time to time. Still, holding the view I do about *hadīth*, it would not be honest to appeal to it to prove something that is not clear in the Qurān.

HOLY GHOST. See above.

COMMUNION OF SAINTS. The brotherhood of believers is a theme of the Qurān, but there is no suggestion of a doctrine of the communion of saints. This belongs to popular Islam. The tombs of holy men are visited, and prayers at their sepulchres are believed to be especially effective. But I know no straightforward text in support of such practices. The Wahhābīs have repressed such forms of piety with the utmost rigour.

FORGIVENESS OF SINS. This follows naturally from the doctrine of God in the Qurān.

RESURRECTION OF THE BODY. This was one of the central tenets of Muhammad's teaching.

THE LIFE EVERLASTING. Heaven and hell are described in vivid language in the Qurān. Heaven is a garden watered by rivers where grow rich fruits and flowers. There the Muslims drink the wine they have been denied on earth, wine that has no after-effects. It is brought to them by handsome youths, and dark-eyed houris wait on their every pleasure. Again and again the sensuous joys of Paradise are described in great detail. The faithful will be welcomed with the blessing of peace and see the angels round the throne of God, and join with them in declaiming the praise of God. Hell is a place of fire. It has seven gates, and a wall divides it from the heaven of the believers. The sufferings of the damned are described in horrific detail much as they were in medieval Europe.

From this rapid glance at the teaching of the Qurān as compared with Christianity it can be seen that the difference between them lies rather in what Islam denies than in what it affirms. It is agreed that God is the creator of the universe, that Jesus was miraculously born of a pure virgin, and that he ascended into heaven. It is agreed that there is a holy spirit; that God will forgive men's sins and grant them everlasting life if they obey his revealed will. With the negations we are not here concerned.

In conclusion, one cannot refrain from saying that the Muslim doctrine of God in philosophical theology is not so far removed from the Christian system until the crucial question of the Trinity comes into question. But even here the Ash'arites taught that God's attributes were additional to his essence and subsisted eternally in him, thus recognizing distinctions within the one Godhead. There are writers in Islam such as al-Ghazālī whose deep spiritual insight commands the respect of Christian readers, and there are mystics whose writings shine with the light of the illuminative life. The day may come when Muslims and Christians will realize that they have so much in common that they need no longer regard one another with suspicion and dislike. Such a rapprochement could only come about by an eclectic process.

Meanwhile all men of goodwill may take comfort from the words of the Secretary-General of the Arab League, Abdul-Rahman Azzam Pasha who, in a Christmas message a year or two ago, prayed that Christmas would remind the peoples of the world of the principles of peace and mercy that Christ taught. The Arabs, he said, would specially remember their Christian Arab brethren who stood shoulder to shoulder with them in the struggle in which they were engaged.

Date Due